ECONOMIC GEOGRAPHY

ECONOMIC GEOGRAPHY:

Resource Use, Locational Choices, and Regional Specialization in the Global Economy

BRIAN J. L. BERRY
The University of Texas at Dallas

EDGAR C. CONKLING
State University of New York at Buffalo

D. MICHAEL RAY
Carleton University

Prentice-Hall, Inc., Englewood Cliffs, New Jersey 07632

Library of Congress Cataloging-in-Publication Data

BERRY, BRIAN JOE LOBLEY, (date)
  Economic geography.

  Includes bibliographies and index.
  1. Geography, Economic. 2. Natural resources.
3. Industry—Location. 4. Commerce. I. Conkling,
Edgar C. II. Ray, D. Michael (David Michael),
(date)   . III. Title.
HC59.B52 1987   330.9   87-2250
ISBN 0-13-231440-1

Editorial/production supervision
  and interior design: Kathleen M. Lafferty
Cover design: Lundgren Graphics Ltd.
Manufacturing buyer: Barbara Kelly Kittle
Cartography: Maps and diagrams were prepared under the
  direction of Greg Theisen, Cartography Laboratory,
  Department of Geography, State University of New York
  at Buffalo; and Christine Earl, Department of
  Geography, Carleton University, Ottawa, Canada.
Cover Illustration: The early 1980s saw the focus of world
  commerce shift to the Pacific basin, ending four centuries
  of dominance by the Atlantic basin. The cover map shows
  the nations that belong to each of these blocs. Because
  Canada and the United States are members of both
  groups, Northern America plays a pivotal role in the new
  world economic order now emerging.

Portions of this volume previously appeared in
The Geography of Economic Systems.

Printed in the United States of America

10 9 8 7 6 5 4 3 2 1

ISBN 0-13-231440-1 01

PRENTICE-HALL INTERNATIONAL (UK) LIMITED, *London*
PRENTICE-HALL OF AUSTRALIA PTY. LIMITED, *Sydney*
PRENTICE-HALL CANADA INC., *Toronto*
PRENTICE-HALL HISPANOAMERICANA, S.A., *Mexico*
PRENTICE-HALL OF INDIA PRIVATE LIMITED, *New Delhi*
PRENTICE-HALL OF JAPAN, INC., *Tokyo*
PRENTICE-HALL OF SOUTHEAST ASIA PTE. LTD., *Singapore*
EDITORA PRENTICE-HALL DO BRASIL, LTDA., *Rio de Janeiro*

Contents

PART TWO
Fundamentals of Economic Geography: People and Resources

PART THREE
Fundamentals of Spatial Economics

PART FOUR
Principles of Locational Choice

PART FIVE
Exchange and Interaction

PART SIX
The Geography of Development

Preface

A number of major concerns have troubled the world throughout the contemporary period. As the end of the twentieth century approaches, we are still contending with the seemingly intractible problems of population growth in the Third World, a shrinking store of non-renewable resources, a deteriorating physical environment, and widening disparities between rich countries and poor and between prosperous people and impoverished masses within countries. Although these issues persist, they are assuming new forms in the wake of several recent world events. Wars and revolutions, the emergence of a powerful oil cartel, and the rise of dynamic new economic regions have made the world's peoples even more interdependent than before. This has complicated old problems and created new ones. Given the spatially related nature of these problems, the systems approach used in this book, *Economic Geography: Resource Use, Locational Choices, and Regional Specialization in the Global Economy,* seems an appropriate method for dealing with them.

One of these concerns, the population issue (Chapters 3 and 4), is evolving in new ways that threaten the economic and political relations among countries.

For instance, as their own populations stabilize, the older industrial countries of Europe and North America not only must address the unfamiliar problems of an aging citizenry, but they also have to consider the prospect of being overwhelmed by the continuing rapid growth of Third World populations. Meanwhile, surprising developments have been taking place within the Third World itself. Even as hope has dimmed that sub-Saharan Africa could soon bring its soaring population growth under control, the People's Republic of China, the world's most populous country, has unexpectedly—and to the great relief of everyone—joined the group of other East Asian lands that have sharply reduced their birth rates.

The resource question, too, has undergone some startling developments (Chapter 5). Famine in Africa has underscored that troubled continent's increasing inability to feed itself, as drought and desertification compound the effects of runaway population increase. Several other major parts of the Third World meanwhile have gained an unforeseen respite from food shortages thanks to the fortunate and previously underappreciated success of the Green Revolution in agriculture.

This postponing of the time of absolute global food shortage thus serves to highlight perhaps the hardest problem of all: the difficulty of ensuring an equitable distribution of resources among the world's people.

During the 1970s the Organization of Oil Exporting Countries (OPEC) was driving up energy prices, thereby causing economic dislocation throughout the world. The cartel's excesses have since backfired. Inflated oil prices not only spurred development of non-OPEC sources of oil, but they also brought on a global recession that reduced demand, and they prompted the general adoption of effective conservation measures. These events have, in turn, hastened a restructuring of the world economy, with growing emphasis on knowledge-intensive activities that use less energy and fewer industrial raw materials. Although the ultimate depletion of these nonrenewable resources still looms, that event recedes further into the future.

No doubt the current restructuring of world industry helps to reduce the pressure upon physical resources; yet new scientific evidence has confirmed that environmental pollution continues undiminished and has heightened concern that it is no longer a local problem. We now understand that acid rain, the contamination of rivers and seas, the greenhouse effect of carbon dioxide emissions into the atmosphere, and the destruction of tropical forests have impacts that know no international boundaries but threaten the health of everyone and even the future habitability of the earth itself.

To understand the effects of these events upon the global economy, and especially the shifts in locational relationships they can be expected to produce, we need to learn certain fundamental principles of spatial economics, including the processes by which land is allocated among prospective users, industrial locations are selected, trade between regions and countries is generated, and urban hierarchies emerge. Chapters 6 through 10 are devoted to supplying the economic building blocks required to understand these principles: the geography of price, the theories of urban and rural land use, and industrial location.

Chapter 11 introduces a significant new feature to the study of economic geography: the Kondratieff theory of "long waves." Many of the fundamental changes that have occurred recently in the global spatial economy can be explained in terms of this theory, which interprets the tendency of economic events to converge at certain intervals of time. Viewing economic history since the beginning of the first such cycle in the eighteenth century, long-wave theory distinguishes a series of rises and falls in the level of economic activity at approximately 50-year intervals. The recession of 1982 appears to have signaled the end of the most recent such wave,

and the swarm of innovations that have created new industries and transformed older ones foretells the beginning of a new cycle of growth. The decline of depressed regions suffering the collapse of their principal industries, together with the rise of new economic areas having concentrations of the newer industries, constitutes a spatial expression of such long-wave phenomena.

The historic shift in the focus of world trade during the past decade can likewise be interpreted in the light of long-wave theory. The deindustrialization of Western Europe and North America and the rise of vigorous new centers of industrial and commercial activity on the western margins of the Pacific have brought an end to 400 years of dominance by the North Atlantic trade routes. Chapters 12, 13, and 14 trace these events and provide the theoretical bases for understanding them. Chapter 13 also introduces another significant new subject to the field of economic geography: the theory of the multinational enterprise, which is one of the prime agents of locational change in the current world scene. Chapter 15 completes this part of the book with a presentation of the theories of local and interregional trade and urban hierarchies.

The final section, comprising a single chapter, is concerned with the geography of development, a process that has proved to be far more complex than mere economic growth. This chapter examines the global dependency relations that evolved during the nineteenth-century era of colonization: the heartland-hinterland organization of the world economy and the distinctive spatial adaptations that arose within the colonies. The book then concludes with an analysis of the sources of growth in the economic heartland, the process by which growth spreads to other areas, and the courses that are open to developing countries for overcoming the conditions that have inhibited their growth.

In preparing this work the authors have given close attention to the comments and suggestions of reviewers and other experienced teachers of economic geography. One problem often encountered in presenting such material is the difficulty some young students have in assimilating certain economic concepts. Because a firm grasp of these basic ideas is important for an understanding of the spatial processes discussed in succeeding chapters, we have made a special effort to present these concepts in simple, straightforward language and have employed numerous illustrations to make these ideas clearer.

Although we feel that students need to master these economic fundamentals in order to become fully prepared economic geographers, we recognize that in many institutions the introductory course in this subject area serves a much wider clientele. In such cases, where the aim is to provide nongeographers with the special insights into global issues that economic geography has to offer, an alternative approach would be to omit Part Three (Chapters 6 to 8) when teaching the subject. Abbreviating the course in this manner would also provide a solution for those instructors working under the time constraints imposed by the quarter system.

Whether students reading this book are using it as a first step toward further, more-specialized study or merely to enhance their knowledge of the economic environment in which they live, it is our aim to provide them with an appreciation for the interrelatedness of spatial processes in today's international economy and a better understanding of the many ways in which global events affect them as citizens of the world.

We would like to acknowledge the help of the following reviewers in the preparation of this text: Russell B. Adams, University of Minnesota; Arthur Gibb, Jr., United States Naval Academy; Peter O. Muller, University of Miami; Robert Sinclair, Wayne State University; Robert H. Stoddard, University of Nebraska; Susan Trussler, University of Scranton; and Wayne Walcott, University of North Carolina, Charlotte.

Brian J. L. Berry
Edgar C. Conkling
D. Michael Ray

ECONOMIC GEOGRAPHY

CHAPTER 1

Contemporary World Issues

Ours is an age of crises. Many people are concerned about world population growth and food supplies, potential shortages of energy and nonrenewable resources, and the effects of environmental pollution. Some fear that world population may "overshoot" global resources, producing catastrophic collapse; others speak optimistically of new high-technology growth.

Too much focus on global issues may distract us from the severity of geographical disparities in economic development and the quality of life. These disparities appear at a hierarchy of scales, from the differences between the prosperity of neighborhoods at the local level to differences between major world regions at the international level.

Attempts to deal with these problems, global or regional, cannot hope to succeed unless they take into account the principles of resource use and of exchange and interaction. No discussion of these principles is complete, however, unless it takes place within the context of current world events. Indeed, the essential facts described by economic geographers help to shape world events no less than the world events help shape the subject matter of economic geography.

Objectives:

- to place the subject of economic geography within the framework of world events
- to introduce key facts on world population, world food supplies, and other global issues, to be developed in subsequent chapters
- to illustrate the growing interdependence among regions with respect to population growth, economic development, and trade
- to outline disparities in economic development, especially at a world regional scale, as described in the call for a New International Economic Order

A CRISIS IN GLOBAL DEVELOPMENT

Ours is an age of increasing uncertainty. The technological optimism fed by the splitting of the atom and culminating in landing human beings on the moon has faded. The economic boom that followed World War II, powered by cheap energy, has ended too. In 1973, an energy crisis brought on by the organization of an oil-producer cartel (OPEC) precipitated higher inflation rates, greater unemployment, and the slower economic growth of the world's industrial nations. Recurring harvest failures—such as those of 1972 and 1973, which sliced grain reserves from more than 100 days of world consumption in previous years to a mere 39 days—have underlined the narrow safety margin in world food supplies. The rise of world fishing catches has been checked since 1970. Meanwhile, increases in food supplies brought on by the "green revolution" have failed to keep pace with rapid population growth in many less-developed countries.

The response of many writers to these problems has been pessimistic. The issues identified (for example, by the Club of Rome in its Project on the Predicament of Mankind) are always the same: population growth, food supplies, the scarcity of energy and of other resources, and environmental pollution. The mood is usually one of urgent concern. Growth is exponential or even greater: Population doubles and redoubles in ever-shorter time spans. More people, all striving for higher living standards, doubly multiply the demand for food, goods, and services. Some writers argue that world population even faces the danger of overshooting the world's physical capacity to feed us, to provide our other resource needs, and to absorb ever-rising levels of pollution. As a result, some even apply the World War I procedure of "triage" to those countries thought to be beyond help: They would look to their own interests, help those with reasonable prospects, and leave the rest to an uncertain fate. They argue that the price of sharing resources on a global basis rather than preserving them for national needs would simply be to spread the misery.

The data on which any scenario of the future must be based are incomplete and inaccurate, however. Conflicting projections can always be extrapolated and defended. It is possible to paint a future of abundance. Herman Kahn, the most optimistic of futurologists, wrote enthusiastically about human progress in *The Next Two Hundred Years.* Julian L. Simon, in *The Ultimate Resource,* insists that resources that seem to be nearing depletion generally turn out to be more plentiful than anyone anticipated, and that the fear of shortages induces people to use their imagination and talents to increase the supply or to develop alternatives. In his view, people are the "ultimate resource."

Similarly, while René Dubos believes that we may remain on the brink of disaster for two or three more decades, he argues (in *Celebrations of Life*) that global population growth is slowing more rapidly than previously thought possible, that industrialization is proceeding with technologies far less destructive of the environment than the old ones, and that nature is far more resilient than was thought only a decade ago. Above all, he says, human beings are blessed with the freedom and flexibility to engineer social evolution, which means that we can shape the future according to our values and can change course if we so desire. Trend, Dubos says, is not destiny.

One thing is certain: Whether pessimistic or optimistic, none of these global overviews adequately addresses some of the real problems needing attention. Undue focus on global trends masks regional disparities and ignores our failure to narrow the glaring disparities in the quality of life that exist between rich and poor lands and peoples. If natural resources are really in short supply, will developed countries continue to use them at a disproportionate rate, thereby aggravating the development problems of poorer countries? If resources are not in short supply, will the efforts of developed countries to reduce consumption of resources hurt the economies of those poorer countries that export those commodities? Will concern with pollution of the environment in rich countries draw attention away from the "pollution of poverty" in poorer countries and lead to standards in production technology and a banning of hazardous products that will hinder development?

Many authorities point to the unprecedented interconnectedness of things today—to the challenges of global interdependence—and believe as a result that regional disparities in economic development and quality of life will in the long run be more serious problems than the global issues of world population and world food supplies. Indeed, poorer countries are already speaking out for strategies of development that emphasize *equality* as well as *efficiency* (the greatest possible returns on investment) and *sustainability* (steady growth over the long run), and for *regional and national self-sufficiency* as well as *global interdependence*. These countries have already called for a New International Economic Order (NIEO) about which we will say more later. In turn, whereas more-developed countries have on the one hand become embroiled in the "North-South" debate about sharing the benefits of economic growth with poorer countries, they have at the same time been awakened to the "paradox of growth." The paradox is that rapid economic development and rising standards of living have made them more conscious of and more concerned about differences in economic growth rates among the developed countries themselves, and about disparities in income levels among regions within their own boundaries.

Thus, multiple concerns exist concerning growth and how its fruits are shared, with people (both their numbers and potentials), and with resources—their scarcity or abundance, their use and abuse. The overriding issues appear to be scarcity at a global scale and disparity at a regional scale, and it is these issues that will be introduced in the balance of this chapter, thus providing a context for what follows in the rest of the book.

WORLD ISSUES

Population

World population growth is the prime variable in all scenarios of the future and all projections of resource needs. The world population total passed the five billion mark in 1986. It had not reached one billion until the early nineteenth century, and it took more than 100 years to add the next billion. The third billion was added in only 30 years, the fourth billion in just 15 years, and the fifth billion in a mere 11 years. World population growth has, in fact, risen faster than simple exponential growth. A population growing exponentially has a "doubling time": It doubles its number in a given time

period. The world population has been doubling its numbers in ever-shorter time periods, however (Figure 1.1).

This trend is unlikely to continue; demographers speculate that the growth rate is slowing. World population may reach six billion by the year 2000 and stabilize at around 10 billion by the middle of the twenty-first century.

Projections of population are complicated by the interrelationships known to exist among demographic, social, and economic characteristics. For instance, some of the characteristics thought to influence birth rates are the status of women and age of marriage, infant and general mortality rates, life expectancy, income and education levels, inequalities in the distributions of national income, and levels of urbanization. The statistical relationships are not straightforward, however; even apart from the difficulty of projecting changes in all of these socioeconomic characteristics, difficulties exist in determining what kinds of effects these changes will have on birth rates. For instance, improvements in education levels can be expected to depress birth rates, but they also tend to increase income levels. In Puerto Rico, where higher income levels are associated with higher birth rates, a program to improve education levels ended up increasing birth rates in the short run because of the indirect income effect, rather than decreasing it as expected.

The science of population forecasting is relatively new and its record unimpressive. Although interest in demography developed rapidly in the 1930s and 1940s,

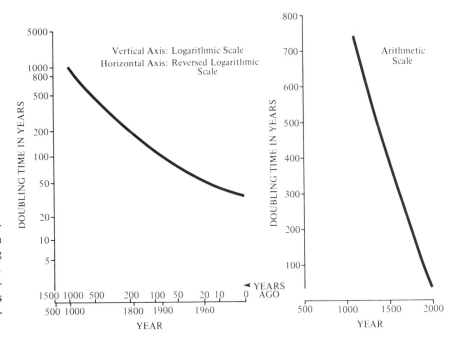

FIGURE 1.1 The accelerating doubling time of world population growth. A population that is growing exponentially has a *doubling time.* The doubling time for the world population has shortened from 500 years in the year 1500 to about 40 years today.

demographers of that period mistakenly predicted a declining population, not foreseeing the world's post–World War II population explosion. Hence, they made a qualitative error in forecasting the direction of population change, not merely a quantitative error in the amount of change. This cloudiness of the forecasters' crystal balls means that population projections should be viewed only as extrapolations of past trends rather than firm predictions of the future. (See Table 1.1.)

World trends in population growth rates mask sharp regional differences. Africa's annual growth rate, currently about 3.0 percent, is still rising, and no clear sign of when that rate may begin to ease has yet emerged. Meanwhile, the industrialized countries have already reduced their average annual growth rates to 0.7 percent; the rate for the Federal Republic of Germany averaged −0.1 percent for the period 1973–1983. The proportion of the world's population in these countries is therefore falling (see Chapter 4). The political and economic consequences of this have not passed unnoticed. Industrialized countries must depend upon less-developed countries for many essential raw materials. Their economies could be disrupted if commodity imports were seriously reduced to meet the domestic needs of the less-developed countries or if the prices of raw materials were sharply increased by OPEC-like cartels. Even more serious is the increased difficulty of meeting basic human needs in countries with rapidly rising populations.

Resources

Food Supplies

The most immediate resource problem is that of world food supplies. Can production be increased fast enough to meet the needs of some six billion people by the year 2000, and perhaps 10 billion by the middle of the next century? How widespread is inadequate nutrition today? Could famine be solved by more equitable sharing of available food supplies or would such action precipitate other problems? Opinions on these matters differ sharply, and the available information on food resources is less satisfactory than on population.

There is no agreement on minimum dietary needs. Estimates of people suffering from an inadequate supply of protein and energy have been placed by some as high as two-thirds of the population of the less-developed countries, but recent United Nations' sources put the ratio closer to one-fourth, placing half a billion people below the minimum dietary level needed to sustain health and energy. Eight countries averaged less than 80 percent of their minimum daily per capita calorie needs in the mid 1970s: Bolivia, in South America; Somalia, on the Horn of Africa; and the countries of the African Sahel: Algeria, Mauritania, Mali, Upper Volta (now Burkina Faso), Niger, and Chad. The droughts of the late 1960s and early 1970s caused many tens of thousands of deaths among the nomads of the Sahel, and drought of even greater severity returned in the late 1970s and 1980s, bringing starvation to millions of people throughout sub-Saharan Africa as far east as Ethiopia and Somalia (see Chapter 5, pages 97–98).

As Africa's population growth continues to outstrip the growth of food production, chronic food shortages have spread along the whole of East Africa, from Somalia and Ethiopia to Zambia, Mozambique, and into Zimbabwe. Drought is a major contributor to the food shortages; but political unrest, inadequate storage and distribution facilities, and bad marketing policies have also contributed to a harvest of despair that threatens the lives of millions.

Although other parts of the world have generally fared better than Africa, the continuing effort to increase per capita food supplies has made uneven progress. Some of the best data on food supplies are for commercial grain production. The world average per capita grain production increased 31 percent from 251 kilograms (kg) in 1950 to 330 kg in 1971 and 351 kg in 1978. By 1980 the figure fell back to 324 kg, however, following poor harvests, especially in the USSR. World grain reserves, measured at the rate of daily world consumption, fell from a peak of 102 days in 1960 to 40 days in 1974, to recover to a barely satisfactory 62 days in 1978, and to slip again to 40 days in 1980. By the mid-1980s, grain harvests in the main growing areas had recovered substantially, and even the USSR, the People's Republic of China, and India were producing surpluses. Given our past experience with the variability of harvests, however, such periods of simultaneously good crops worldwide have to be viewed as occasional aberrations of nature.

The "green revolution" contributed much of the increase in food output that has occurred since the late 1960s. Dr. Norman Borlaug won the 1970 Nobel Peace Prize for his role in pioneering high-yield strains of

TABLE 1.1

Changes in world population: 1950–1985 (millions)

	1950	1960	1970	1985 (estimated)
Population	2,501	2,986	3,675	4,842
Births	90	102	120	130
Deaths	50	46	48	51
Natural Increase	40	56	72	79

Source: Data adjusted from *United Nations Demographic Yearbook* (United Nations, New York).

dwarf wheat and maize. Similar achievements for rice were made by the International Rice Research Institute in the Philippines. Adoption of these new strains was rapid. India more than doubled its wheat production and became a net exporter in some years. The Philippines was able to become self-sufficient in rice after half a century of dependence on imports. This research continues, but its benefits are continually threatened by the pressures of population growth. The green revolution—its successes, limitations, and promise—is discussed at greater length in Chapter 5.

The "Tragedy of the Commons"

Future prospects for increasing our food output may be limited by the "tragedy of the commons." This metaphor was used by Garrett Hardin to describe the breakdown in the management of resources that are common property. Imagine an area of common land open to herders who may keep as many cattle as they choose. If the commons is overgrazed, because each chooses a maximum, it would be in the collective interest of all to reduce the number of cattle to maintain the productivity of the land. But isolated action by a single herder in the absence of similar actions by all would serve only to reduce that individual's own income without substantial benefit to the general community. Because independent action would fail, and collective action is not manageable, the commons deteriorates to an irreducibly low carrying capacity and everyone loses.

Hardin argues that we all live in a global commons. The air, the sea, rivers, and lakes are obvious examples. The world fish catch, after an average increase of 5 percent a year between 1950 and 1970, has fluctuated at or below its 1970 level. The haddock catch peaked in 1965; that of cod, halibut, and herring in 1968; and that of anchovies off Peru, the world's leading fishing nation, in 1970. Many species of whales are now endangered. Other examples of the tragedy of the commons include: deforestation, especially of delicate tropical ecosystems, to meet the needs for pulp and paper, lumber, and firewood; overgrazing in semiarid lands; and pollution from polychlorinated biphenyls (PCBs), mercury, acid rain, and the products of the nuclear industry.

Which herders will be the first to reduce their flocks? Which industrialist will voluntarily reduce air or water pollution? Which nation will willingly agree to reduce its quota of whales, or fish? And, if the answer is none, should we be surprised that the Sahara Desert encroaches southwards into the Sahel, that the acid rain continues unabated, or that world fishing catches drop?

Hardin carries the lesson to its extreme. To the extent that we are prepared to share the world's resources with all people, we treat the world as a global commons and must face the inevitable consequences. Even foreign aid becomes counterproductive according to Hardin. We manage the world's resources best, Hardin argues, when each nation manages its own resources and each nation depends on its own capacities.

Nonrenewable Resources

What are the future world prospects for nonrenewable resources? This question is particularly difficult to answer because of both measurement and conceptual problems. Total population and total food supplies can be physically measured; total nonrenewable resources cannot. The definitions of population and of food supplies are straightforward; the definition of nonrenewable resources is complex. The concepts of what exactly constitutes a resource, and measurements of how much of any given resource exists, differ widely. One group of experts, such as Hardin, holds an "environmentalist" view, another an "economist" view.

The environmentalist view of nonrenewable resources is that the world has a fixed upper carrying capacity of population that it can support and of resources that it can supply. Technology can raise current levels toward, but not beyond, the full potential of the world's productive capacity. The environmentalist focus is long-term. Its concern is with the results of the next doubling of the world's population and the impact of that doubling on environmental pollution and on demands for resources.

The alternative view offered by many economists is that resources are not fixed in amount but created, in response to needs, through market mechanisms. If a resource becomes scarce, its price rises and the quantity consumed drops. The price increase stimulates an increase in the supply of the product and the search for substitute products.

Strong arguments can be made to support both the environmentalist and the economist viewpoints. The environmentalist view appeals to common sense. The metaphor of "spaceship earth" comes naturally to mind in this space age. There must be a fixed, finite supply of oil on this, our spaceship. Every barrel we use is one less barrel that remains. But how much does remain and how long will it last? The Workshop on Alternative Energy Strategies shows that estimates of ultimately recoverable reserves of crude oil from conventional sources rose sharply from 600 billion barrels in 1942 to 2480 billion in 1965. Since then, they have hovered at the 2000-billion-barrel mark. Proven reserves are only a fraction of this—perhaps 500 billion barrels. Depending on whether we can hold consumption to present world levels, or whether it continues to grow at recent

TABLE 1.2

Estimates of total world reserves of crude oil

Year	Barrels (billions)	Year	Barrels (billions)
1942	600	1965	2480
1946	400	1967	2090
1946	555	1968	1800
1948	610	1968	2200
1949	1500	1969	1350–2100
1949	1010	1970	1800
1953	1000	1971	1200–2000
1956	1250	1971	2290
1958	1500	1975	2000
1959	2000		

Source: Quoted in Lester R. Brown, *The Twenty-Ninth Day* (New York: W. W. Norton & Co., Inc., 1978), p. 105. Copyright © 1978 by Worldwatch Institute. After *Energy: Global Prospects 1980–2000.* Workshop on Alternative Energy Strategies (New York: McGraw-Hill, 1977).

Note: Amounts quoted are for ultimately recoverable reserves from conventional oil sources. Data are from various sources. Duplicated years indicate conflicting estimates from different sources.

rates, these proven reserves would last as much as 30 years, or as little as 20 years (Table 1.2). The reality is much more complex, and the economist view would place little value on these figures of the reserve life of oil, preferring a much more flexible approach (Figure 1.2).

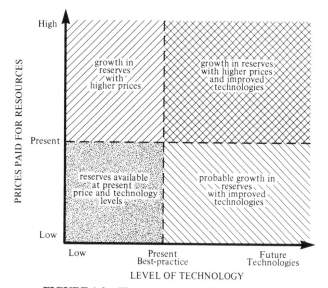

FIGURE 1.2 The economist's view of world resources. This figure is suggested by a diagram in G. Alexanderson and B. I. Klevebring, *World Resources: Energy, Metals and Minerals* (New York: W. deGruyter, 1978), p. 6. It implies that the quantity of resources available responds to prices and technology. Resource prices rise in the face of scarcity, but supplies do not run out.

SCENARIOS OF THE FUTURE

Overshoot and Collapse

Limits to Growth

The environmentalist vision of a growing population pressing against fixed upper limits of nonrenewable resources regained worldwide attention with the publication in 1972 of *Limits to Growth,* the first report for the Club of Rome's Project on The Predicament of Mankind. The Club of Rome was formed in 1968 by prominent industrialists and scientists from around the developed world who were convinced that the major problems facing humanity are so complexly interrelated that traditional institutions and policies cannot cope with them. They felt that "systems dynamics" models were needed to make wiser decisions. These mathematical tools can be made to account for the fact that population growth, for instance, depends on trends in food production, pollution, and industrial output, and each of these in turn depends on the others. The specific models that were used were developed by Professor Jay Forrester of the Massachusetts Institute of Technology, whereas the specific analysis for *Limits to Growth* was undertaken by his colleagues Dennis Meadows and Donnella Meadows, along with Jorgen Randers and William W. Behrens.

Limits to Growth projects world population, food supplies, industrial output, and pollution over a long duration, to the year 2010, with dramatic results. World population is projected to continue its exponential growth until it overshoots the world's carrying capacity, and the world's economic system collapses. This unstable pattern of overshoot and collapse is projected to occur even if the constraints on population growth are successively reduced. Doubling natural resource reserves, cutting pollution to one-fourth of its present level, increasing agricultural productivity, and introducing birth control were each added as assumptions in the model simulations, but the general results remained the same. The precise sequence of events that triggers the catastrophic fall of population numbers differs according to the specific assumptions, but the basic pattern is always the same: overshoot and collapse, as illustrated by the results for "world-model standard run" (Figure 1.3). The key policy conclusion of the study, therefore, is that an immediate slowdown in economic growth must be initiated so as to create an equilibrium between population and resources.

Meadows and his colleagues were deeply concerned with the results they obtained, and the apprehension evident throughout the book struck a responsive chord, especially in North America and Western

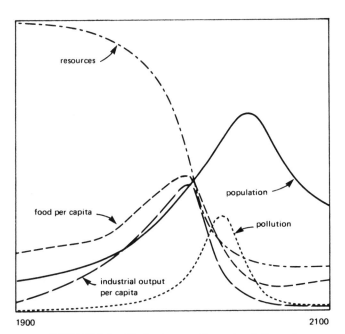

FIGURE 1.3 Limits to growth: a simulation of world collapse. Dennis Meadows and his colleagues projected overshoot and collapse of the world's population unless world economic and population growth slowed immediately. In this model, collapse occurs because of the depletion of nonrenewable resources, shown by the dramatic drop in the resources curve. This collapse triggers declines in *food per capita* and *industrial output per capita*. [*Source:* D. H. Meadows, D. L. Meadows, J. Randers, and W. W. Behrens, *The Limits to Growth* (New York: Universe Books, 1972), p. 97.]

Europe. The authors admitted that their work was in a preliminary state, but they did not believe that their broad conclusions would be substantially altered by further revisions. They believed that their conclusions had important implications for decision-makers in industry and government that went far beyond the domain of scientific inquiry. They argued that their purpose was to raise these implications for public debate. And open a massive debate they did.

Basic Questions in Systems Modeling

Limits to Growth was subjected to intensive scrutiny by scientists in every discipline dealing with population and resources. As a result, every facet of the work has been attacked by one critic or another, and some telling points have been made. Nevertheless, most subsequent scenarios of the future have made at least some reference to the concerns it raised. Interest was reawakened in the work of an earlier prophet of doom, the Rev.

Thomas R. Malthus, whose *Essay on the Principle of Population* in the late eighteenth century similarly attracted widespread debate on physical limits to growth and on the policy consequences that followed, as we shall see in Chapter 3. Indeed, one critic labeled Meadows "Malthus with a computer."

The criticisms were of four kinds and related to: (1) the relationships among population and the supply of resources, (2) the use of world averages rather than specific regional data, (3) the growth of the system components and the nature of growth itself, and (4) the stability of such models under differing assumptions.

The most general criticism of mathematical models of the kind used by Meadows and colleagues concerns the data requirements. A system is an entity that functions as a whole because of the interdependence of the parts. *Systems modeling* requires good data not only on each component of the system but also on all the interrelationships among the components. Yet, as we noted in the case of Puerto Rico's birth rates, it is sometimes difficult to predict even the direction of change (an increase or a decrease in birth rates), let alone the amount that will result from changes in socioeconomic conditions. But demography is better documented than pollution; if we find it difficult to trace interrelationships among social and economic characteristics of populations, how much confidence can we place in estimates of the impact of pollution on food production, industrial output, birth rates, and death rates?

A second and quite separate issue is whether a set of global average values should be used in a single model. Are the interdependencies between human beings and land the same in all nations of the world, or are the relationships and the policy issues fundamentally different in countries as varied as Canada, Chad, and China? And if, for example, the scenarios raised in *Limits to Growth* were basically correct, would not the overshoot begin in some regions before serious problems were felt in some others, thereby triggering policies to soften the blow in the affected areas and to reduce the risks elsewhere? To treat the earth as a homogeneous entity, ignoring geographic diversity and disparity, makes analyses and policies both academically unacceptable and politically pointless.

A third set of questions involves the growth rates of systems components. A valid distinction can be drawn between simple (arithmetic) and multiplicative (exponential) growth. In multiplicative growth, for which human population is one of the best examples, what grows is itself capable of creating growth. More people beget yet more people. In simple growth, such as the amount of land in crops, growth depends on the efforts of some external agent; cropland does not reproduce!

The question of which growth curve best describes the trajectory of population, pollution, food production, and so on is crucial. Assuming that the demands driven by population growth increase exponentially and that the supply of food and nonrenewable resources grows arithmetically, then the outcome of overshoot and collapse is a foregone conclusion; an exponential growth rate will always outstrip an incremental one. Indeed, Kenneth Boulding noted that anything growing exponentially would, in the end, outstrip the universe itself unless that too is growing exponentially. It should be no surprise, then, that doubling natural resources or cutting pollution levels to a quarter of existing levels has little effect on the systems models. These figures sound impressive but they are equivalent to a fraction of a percent per year over the 180 years of extrapolation in the model, well below a current world population growth rate of closer to 2 percent per year.

Indeed, one service of *Limits to Growth* has been to drive home to policymakers and the public alike the sheer impossibility of maintaining exponential growth and the need to move toward a conserver society. This lesson is particularly valuable for measuring reserves of resources. Until *Limits to Growth,* it was usual to calculate a *static* reserve index by dividing known global reserves of a resource by current consumption. Thus, at the current rate of consumption, Meadows and his colleagues calculate that known chromium reserves would last 420 years. Consumption rates are increasing, however, at a rate above the population growth rate. If chromium consumption rates continue to grow at the past average rate, known reserves will last only 95 years, not 420 years. If known reserves grow fivefold, this *dynamic* reserve index increases to only 154 years. The reserves run out because a fivefold increase equals less than 2 percent a year over the 154 years, and consumption is assumed to grow at 2.6 percent per year.

The fourth and perhaps most serious flaw in *Limits to Growth* is that quite different results are obtained if new assumptions reflecting the technological-optimist view are incorporated into the model. Robert Boyd, a zoologist, assumes, for example, that an additional key variable is needed in the model developed by Meadows and colleagues, namely technology. He further assumes that investment in technology would accelerate if there were a decline in quality of life and that this increased investment would, in turn, increase the growth of technology. He then assumes that a growth in technology would increase food output, decrease the consumption of natural resources, and decrease pollution. He also assumes that birth rates would fall with an increase in food supplies once these were above some minimal level. The results of incorporating these assumptions into the Meadows model are that population grows to a steady-

state level by the year 2100 and that, as population growth slows, the quality of life increases (Figure 1.4).

Limits to Growth demonstrates that systems modeling is limited by the assumptions used. It cannot resolve underlying theoretical conflicts. Meadows and his colleagues argue that the basic behavior of the world models appears to be so fundamental and general that they do not expect their broad conclusions to be substantially altered by further revisions. That is, world population overshoot and collapse appear inevitable if world population and economic growth continue their present course. This is true regardless of whether one accepts an environmentalist or economist perspective. In fact, Meadows and his associates are incorrect. Boyd demonstrates that computer simulations simply feed back the assumptions fed in. Start off with a Malthusian framework and the models make Malthusian predictions. Begin with optimistic assumptions and an optimist future unfolds. In "computerese": garbage in, garbage out (GIGO). The computer models fail to resolve the crucial difference between the two viewpoints; they merely project the consequences of the investigators' initial assumptions onto a time scale.

A Second Look at Doom

As these basic questions about systems modeling began to emerge, it became clear that the Forrester-Meadows

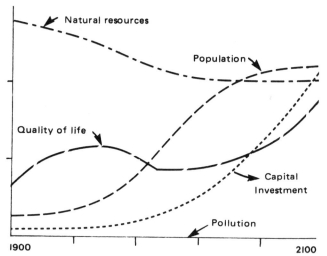

FIGURE 1.4   The greening of the globe: a technological-optimist view of the future. Robert Boyd makes changes in the Meadows model by allowing changes in technology to produce optimistic results for food production, pollution levels, and quality of life. The result is a "new age" with a stable population level and improving quality of life. [*Source:* Robert Boyd, "World Dynamics: A Note," *Science,* 177 (August 1972), 516–519.]

model needed refinement. The Club of Rome thereupon turned to Milhajlo Mesarovic and Edvard Pestel for a second study, *Mankind at the Turning Point,* published in 1974.

Mesarovic and Pestel made a number of refinements in the computer models. For instance, they divided the world into 10 regions, permitting the simulation of the effects of alternative policies for particular regions. One experiment deals with the regional economic impacts of alternative oil pricing and production strategies by Middle Eastern exporters. The result of this exercise is the apparently counterintuitive conclusion that the developed world—comprising Western Europe, North America, Japan, and Oceania—does better over the long run if oil prices increase than if they do not! Rising oil prices would stimulate the growth of alternative energy sources, reduce the risk of disruptions in supplies, and therefore prevent the most serious economic consequences.

Mesarovic and Pestel also demonstrate the foolhardiness of conflict between suppliers and consumers over nonrenewable resources. Comparing the results of alternative scenarios, including a squeeze by producers and retaliation by consumers, they show the decisive advantage of a cooperation scenario (Figure 1.5).

They also point to the long-run benefits to all people of what they term *organic growth,* according to which each region contributes to total world development in accordance with its particular resources and

technology. Growth remains balanced by increasing the economic specialization and interdependence of regions.

The Marxist Reaction

Western critics rejected the conclusions of the Club of Rome studies because of their assumptions. Marxists rejected the studies because they found the ideological framework unacceptable. They argued that research takes place in a social setting and has political implications. Indeed, social values influence the scientific methods selected, methods affect the conclusions reached, and these in turn point to particular policy needs. David Harvey, a Marxist geographer, has noted that fears of overpopulation are historically associated with the political, social, and economic repression of the poor. Harvey points to the cynical implications of the conventional argument: If population tends to outrun its physical resource base, human misery is inevitable; relieve this misery and one of the checks on population growth is eased, making the problem worse in the long run; therefore do nothing to help the poor.

If the overpopulation argument is merely a political ploy to undermine policies to help the poor, what is the "real issue" according to Marx? Marx argued that production creates its own population growth patterns and social structure. Poverty in Western societies cannot be explained away by resort to some natural law of

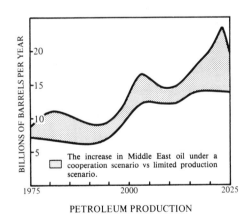

PETROLEUM PRODUCTION
IN THE MIDDLE EAST

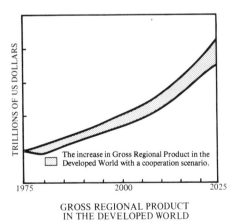

GROSS REGIONAL PRODUCT
IN THE DEVELOPED WORLD

FIGURE 1.5 Petroleum strategies and development. Unrestricted petroleum output in the Middle East is critical to output in the developed world. These graphs compare the results of two scenarios. One scenario involves reduced oil production in the Middle East and a slower rate of growth of gross regional product in the developed world. This scenario includes a Middle East ceiling of 14 billion barrels of oil per year. In the cooperation scenario, production is controlled by market forces and output of petroleum in the Middle East and gross regional product in the developed world both increase faster. [*Source:* Based upon Mihajlo Mesarovic and Edvard Pestel, *Mankind at the Turning Point* (New York: E. P. Dutton, 1974), Figures 8-2B, C, and Figures 8-3B, C.]

overpopulation. It has to be recognized as a condition endemic to the capitalist mode of production.

The overpopulation problem, according to Marx, is actually a human-exploitation problem and reflects the capitalist need for an ''industrial reserve army'' (a standby supply of unemployed workers). The argument is based on the notions of *surplus labor* and *surplus value.* Workers may produce enough to cover their subsistence in, say, six hours, but they must work 10. If the capitalist then pays a subsistence wage only, the capitalist can then convert the output from the four hours of ''free'' labor into surplus value. Surplus value pays rents, interest, and profits. If the profits are plowed back into more production, a larger labor force is needed, although labor needs can be reduced by mechanization. Marx noted that once labor creates capital equipment, it produces the means by which it becomes relatively superfluous. This superfluous labor becomes an industrial reserve army, a mass of human material always ready for exploitation. Its existence prevents wages from rising because for every worker demanding higher wages, there are substitutes willing to replace them for a subsistence wage.

Marxist arguments, in which wealth is created by labor, leave little room for a shortage of resources. Indeed, in Marx's method of dialectical materialism, resources can be defined only in relationship to a particular production process. Marxists thus reject outright the notion of any worldwide resource crisis as presented by the Club of Rome. The official Soviet view, as given in *Pravda,* is that the crisis described in the Club of Rome studies is confined to Western nations. *Pravda* states categorically that the USSR and other socialist countries have no energy crisis, have resolved their shortages of raw materials, and do not show any signs of a food crisis. The results of research by Soviet experts, *Pravda* says, lend no support to the pessimistic conclusions drawn in the reports of the Club of Rome. The Club of Rome studies are seen as an attempt by multinational corporations and Western governments to increase their profits from trade in raw materials, to doom the less-developed countries to earning minimal subsistence wages, and to increase the dependency of these poorer countries on the developed world.

The developing countries have had deep concerns about the implications of the first two reports of the Club of Rome. Many of them have preferred, however, to couch these concerns in specific proposals for reshaping the world economy and their future within it rather than to become embroiled in mere ideological arguments. Reshaping their future means, in particular, changing their links with the developed world and forging a new international economic order.

GLOBAL DISPARITIES AND THE NEW INTERNATIONAL ECONOMIC ORDER

The New International Economic Order (NIEO) is a movement initiated by the developing countries to achieve greater economic, social, and political equality with the developed world. The main economic goal is to diminish existing global disparities by a more balanced distribution of future growth. The major political objective is to gain more control over the use of their own natural resources as well as over their interaction with the developed world in trade, investment, aid, and migration. The ''Declaration on the Establishment of a NIEO'' was introduced at the Sixth Special Session of the General Assembly of the United Nations in 1974 and approved as a resolution on ''Development and International Economic Cooperation'' in the Seventh Session one year later.

The NIEO is a response to the growing disenchantment of developing countries with their economic and political links with the developed world and the glaring disparities in income and wealth perpetuated by these relationships. *Limits to Growth* demonstrated the developed world's concern with the pollution of the environment. However, the developing countries are more concerned with the ''pollution of poverty.'' In issues of human rights, developed countries tend to emphasize freedom of expression, equality before the law, and protection of individual rights. Developing countries emphasize the basic human rights of adequate food, clothing, housing, and medical care. Developing countries depend in part on foreign aid to help them meet these basic human rights. They suspect that foreign aid is often tuned to the political needs of east-west relations rather than the humanitarian needs of north-south disparities.

International disparities in income and wealth are indeed extreme, as we shall see in Chapter 16. North America, with about 6 percent of the world's population, accounts for about 30 percent of the world's gross national product (GNP); the developing countries, with about 50 percent of the world's population, account for only 15 percent of the world's GNP. A statistical measure of the value of all goods and services produced by a country, the GNP may be an inadequate measure of economic performance and international disparities. However, many measures of quality of life are both very highly associated with per capita GNP and reveal similar geographies of international disparity. Measures of food consumption, life expectancy, and health care correspond in pattern and degree with the standard economic indicators (Table 1.3). Moreover, these disparities between developed and developing countries appear

TABLE 1.3

Growth of gross national product and gross national product per capita, 1960–1980

	GNP		GNP per capita	
	1960–1970	1970–1980	1960–1970	1970–1980
All developing countries	5.6	5.3	3.1	2.9
Low-income countries	4.2	4.0	1.8	1.7
Africa (sub-Saharan)	4.2	3.0	1.7	0.2
Asia	4.2	4.2	1.8	2.0
Middle-income countries	6.0	5.6	3.5	3.1
East Asia and Pacific	7.7	8.0	4.9	5.7
Latin America and the Caribbean	5.7	5.8	2.9	3.2
North Africa and Middle East	3.6	6.4	1.1	3.8
Africa (sub-Saharan)	4.8	4.5	2.3	1.6
Southern Europe	7.0	4.6	5.6	3.2
Industrialized countries[a]	5.0	3.1	3.9	2.4
Capital-surplus oil exporters[b]	10.5	8.4	7.3	5.0
Centrally planned economies	—[c]	5.2	—[c]	3.8

Source: World Bank estimates quoted in *Report*, Sept.-Oct. 1980, Washington, D.C.: World Bank, p. 3.

Note: Average annual percentage growth rates; at 1977 prices.

[a]Australia, Austria, Belgium, Canada, Denmark, Finland, France, the Federal Republic of Germany, Iceland, Ireland, Italy, Japan, Luxembourg, the Netherlands, New Zealand, Norway, Sweden, Switzerland, the United Kingdom, and the United States.

[b]Iran, Iraq, Kuwait, Libya, Qatar, Saudi Arabia, and the United Arab Emirates.

[c]Not available.

to have widened in the postwar years, notwithstanding two United Nations' Development Decades and large foreign-aid contributions by developed countries.

Perhaps the most important single factor making the New International Economic Order politically feasible was the success of OPEC (Organization of Petroleum Exporting Countries) in raising oil prices in 1973. This demonstration of the power of a resource-producer cartel was made possible in part by the Western world's fear of global resource scarcity and by its growing reliance on developing countries for raw material imports. Fred Hirsh reported that at the 1964 UNCTAD meetings (United Nations Conference on Trade and Development), the typical assessment of the poorer countries was "a demand for everything by those who have nothing." Ten years later it was clear that some of these countries did have one thing that really mattered: oil.

Oil price increases threatened economic recession and balance-of-payments problems in both developed and developing countries alike. But OPEC demonstrated that political solidarity of the resource hinterland in a new "trade union" of poorer countries could produce better export prices for raw materials.

Western experts had not expected OPEC to succeed in maintaining high prices for oil. Efforts to raise international prices of raw materials have generally ended in failure, as in the case of coffee in Brazil in earlier decades of this century, sugar cane in the years 1930–1936, and natural rubber in the period 1922–1928.

These efforts failed because increased prices brought competition from nonparticipating countries and from competing products (sugar beets and synthetic rubber, for example). OPEC succeeded because OPEC oil could not be replaced by cheaper oil from other producers or superseded by alternative energy sources in the short run. Oil is an exceptional commodity, and few other raw materials are likely to achieve similar price increases. Indeed, it took 12 years until declining consumption and new production from the North Sea and Alaska reduced OPEC's share of world output from two-thirds to one-third. But the point had been made. The developed countries had to weigh the economic costs of accommodating the demands of the less-developed countries against the economic and political consequences of resisting approval of the NIEO.

SOME PRIORITIES FOR THE 1980s AND BEYOND

The comprehensive measures called for in the NIEO, together with the problems of growth outlined in the first part of the chapter, will dominate the agenda of economic geographers in developing countries, if not throughout the world, during the remaining years of the twentieth century. The measures of the NIEO are grouped under five headings in the UN resolution—international trade, transfer of real resources, science and technology, industrialization, and food and agriculture.

International Trade

For the past 150 years, international economic policy has rested on the belief that free trade was in the best interests of all. Free trade depended on these propositions:

1. Free trade increases total wealth by enabling countries to concentrate on commodities they produce best.
2. Therefore, all countries benefit from free trade.
3. Hence, barriers to free trade should be reduced.

Today these propositions are being questioned by developing countries. The truth of proposition 1 is demonstrated in Chapters 12 and 13. It is self-evident in the case of agricultural commodities, for example, that countries are limited in the range of crops they can produce by the range of their climates. Thus, Canada exports wheat and Brazil exports coffee. But it is now being argued that the global interdependence implied by the first proposition must be balanced with a measure of national self-reliance. It is also noted that the second proposition does not necessarily follow from the first. The benefits of trade have accrued to the industrial nations at the cost of those nations specializing in raw material production. And it is noted that barriers to free trade are usually lowered selectively, making it easier for developing countries to export their raw materials than to participate in the more profitable trade in manufactured goods.

Prices for raw materials exported from developing countries have tended to be unstable in the short run, and to fall over the longer term relative to the cost of imported manufactured goods. As a result, exports of raw materials buy fewer imports of finished products, and the share of developing countries in world trade has tended to fall. This share was more than 30 percent in the early 1950s; it is now about 20 percent. The developing countries want measures to ensure stable and equitable prices for their exports, including long-term multilateral commitments and adequate international financial and storage arrangements.

Developing countries also want to diversify their exports by processing raw materials in the country of production and by developing exports of semimanufactured and manufactured goods. Barriers to the export of such goods to developed countries must be reduced to accommodate these goals. Developing countries also want a larger share in the transportation, marketing, and distribution of their products.

The stakes in reshaping international trade are large. It has been estimated that developed countries have paid $200 billion a year for commodities imported from developing countries, and for the products made from them. The share of this that went to the developing countries for producing the raw material has been only $30 billion.

Transfer of Real Resources

The NIEO does not involve any substantial redistribution of accumulated wealth from developed to developing countries. It does ask that developed countries live up to their pledge, made for the Second United Nations Development Decade, of providing 0.7 percent of their gross national product as official development assistance. Foreign aid has tended to fall since that pledge was made instead of increasing to meet it. The World Bank estimates that assistance may have fallen to about one-fourth of 1 percent of the GNP of the developed countries.

Foreign aid figures can be placed in perspective by comparing them with armaments spending. The Brandt Commission estimated that global spending on armaments reached $450 billion in 1980. Official development aid totals a mere $20 billion, about 5 percent of armaments spending. Nor do the developing countries get to keep all of this aid money. Most foreign aid is in the form of loans that must be repaid. The debts of developing countries reached $300 billion in 1979 and passed $500 billion in 1985. The burden of debt repayment from some poor countries will soon exceed new foreign aid. The anomalous situation would then exist of reverse foreign aid, with net payments from poor to rich countries. In addition, foreign aid is often "tied," that is, given for the purchase of specific goods and services from the donor country, regardless of whether these goods and services are the cheapest or most appropriate. Developing countries need a substantial increase in aid that is given under favorable terms and conditions, that is not tied, and that is assured on a long-term basis.

In addition to foreign aid, developing countries want changes in the monetary system to control inflation, to provide a more equitable method of creating and distributing reserves, and to promote the flow of nonaid capital to developing countries. In the effort to resolve the issues raised by such transfers of resources, a key task for the economic geographer is to evaluate the regional impact of aid programs, particularly in the poorest developing countries. In a recent conference, one regional expert spoke of the way that aid and development can widen gaps in living standards in developing countries. He was struck, for instance, by the construction in those countries of superhighways elevated on stilts so as to fly over the shacks of the urban poor as they carry the rich whizzing home from downtown offices to their residences in the suburbs.

Science and Technology

Developed countries will have to expand their assistance for science and technology significantly if developing countries are to accelerate their economic growth, capture a larger share of world trade in manufactured goods, and narrow disparities in income levels. No disparity is more marked than that in science and technology. Virtually the entire world budget for science and technology is accounted for by developed countries. It is now recognized that the transfer of technology poses major problems; thus, the concentration of research in developed countries tends to widen and entrench disparities in economic development and income.

Indeed, the problem goes beyond the adaptation of Western technology to the needs of developing countries. Western science and technology may not always meet the needs of developing countries. E. F. Schumacher has advocated an "intermediate technology" for developing countries. Such technology would take account of the scarcity of capital and abundance of labor in developing countries. Its objective would be to create the most jobs possible per dollar of capital investment. Michael Todaro has broadened the issue to one of

whether Western medical practice and education meet the needs of developing countries.

The difficulties of accelerating research and development in science and technology in developing countries is seriously hampered by the so-called brain drain. The extent of this loss of knowledge and skills by the less-developed countries is generally underestimated. UNCTAD found on the basis of its own calculations that aid to the developing countries from the United States, Canada, and the United Kingdom did not in fact even cover their loss of skilled technicians leaving for the United States, Canada, and the United Kingdom. The urgent need to formulate national and international policies to reduce the brain drain and minimize its adverse effects is high on the list of priorities of the NIEO, and some proposals have already been put forward to increase the financial compensation for the loss of skilled workers. (See Figure 1.6.)

Industrialization

At the crux of many questions relating to science and technology, to trade, to capital flows, and to industrialization is the role of the multinational corporations (MNCs), or transnationals as they are sometimes called. The sheer size of these corporations is not generally appreciated. They rival in importance the nation-state and stand, with the latter, as the two most important institutions of the contemporary world.

It is a sobering exercise to compare the gross annual sales of the MNCs with the gross national products of individual countries. The results will vary somewhat, year by year, but a recent ranking placed General Motors, the largest MNC, ahead of such countries as East

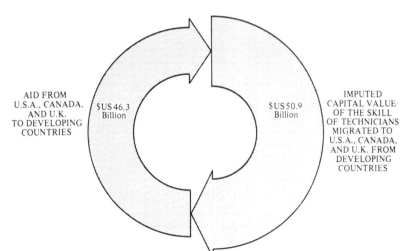

Net Loss for Developing Countries is $US 4.6 Billion

FIGURE 1.6 Foreign aid versus the brain drain. This figure highlights both the inadequacy of present foreign aid levels and the difficulties faced by developing countries in improving their economies. The recent problems created by the brain drain drew attention in developed countries earlier this century when there was heavy migration from rural areas to industrial heartlands. [*Source:* Based upon a diagram in *Reshaping the International Order,* by Jan Tinbergen, Anthony J. Dolman, and Jan van Ettinger (New York: E. P. Dutton, 1976), p. 40. Data are from UNCTAD secretariat and are for the years 1960–1972.]

AID FROM U.S.A., CANADA, AND U.K. TO DEVELOPING COUNTRIES

$US 46.3 Billion

$US 50.9 Billion

IMPUTED CAPITAL VALUE OF THE SKILL OF TECHNICIANS MIGRATED TO U.S.A., CANADA, AND U.K. FROM DEVELOPING COUNTRIES

Germany, Belgium, and Switzerland. Standard Oil, Ford Motor Co., and Royal Dutch Shell all ranked ahead of Hungary, Turkey, and Norway.

Despite awareness of the economic benefits conferred by multinationals, increasing attention is now being paid to the disadvantages. For long it was assumed that the country in which the head office of an MNC was located would have little effect on the corporation's policies. The "invisible hand" of economic law applied to all industry, it was argued, regardless of country ownership. In fact, the majority of MNCs have headquarters in the United States, Europe, or Japan, and they make visible the nationality of their main office very frequently in their decision making.

Hence, developing countries have become aware of a need for strict controls over MNCs' practices in management, budgeting for research and development, adaptation of product design to local market needs, use of local components, pricing policies, and reinvestment of profits.

Food and Agriculture

The NIEO also calls for a rapid increase in food production in the developing countries, coupled with increased aid in the form of food from developed countries. Emphasis is given to the supply of fertilizers and other production inputs from developed countries to achieve these increases. Developing countries, recognizing their responsibility to cut postharvest food losses, set a goal of a 50-percent reduction by 1985. In addition, they see the need for an international undertaking to improve world food security. World food-grain stores must be built up nationally and regionally to cover major production shortfalls.

Other Priorities

Some of the concerns raised at the global scale by the NIEO apply at a regional scale within countries in both the developing and the developed world. Thus, peripheral regions in developed countries also complain about disparities in income levels and employment opportunities. They too suffer from an overconcentration in primary industries and the problems of branch-plant economies. They too depend on science and technology developed in the metropolitan heartlands and endure the brain drain of skilled workers. Indeed, some models of the world economy we shall review in Chapter 16 articulate regional heartlands and hinterlands into the global heartland and hinterland. Thus, the concerns of economic geography in the 1980s and beyond must include

the heartland-hinterland problems at a hierarchy of scales from local to global.

INTEGRATING CONCEPTS

Problems of scarcity at a global scale and of disparity at a regional scale tend to be perceived as separate issues competing for attention. In fact, they are a single issue viewed from different perspectives. For it is the growth of the world economic system, proceeding at different rates in different regions, that creates the spatial structure of the world economy with its pattern of regional disparities. Conversely, the severity of regional disparities is fundamental to the New International Economic Order, which is attempting to achieve a more equitable distribution of growth. That is, growth patterns at one geographic scale create distributions and concomitant disparities at other geographical scales, which in turn have implications for further growth. More simply, as we shall see in Chapter 16, growth creates form, but form limits growth.

There is another less obvious link between growth and distribution that twists the promised benefits of economic growth into a cruel social irony. This is the unspoken belief that if only the poor, whether we are speaking of individuals or nations, could attain the income levels of the rich, then they could emulate their lifestyle. Fred Hirsch has pointed out that the goods of this world are often "positional," creating social limits to growth. The individual confronts a hierarchy of job levels at work that translate into corresponding ranks and status in the social world. Housing is ranked in desirability on the basis of location, spaciousness, and comfort. All other goods and services are graded and priced accordingly. The catch is that although growth creates more goods and services, it cannot produce goods of equal quality and desirability.

Economic growth by itself cannot solve the issues of distribution. On the contrary, it is an observed fact that economic growth increases concerns about the distribution of wealth rather than diminishing them. Thus, The Economic Council of Canada noted in 1969 that rapid economic growth, far from solving the country's problems, would create new problems, new wants, and perhaps accentuated competition for resources. Indeed, it has been asserted that the limits-to-growth debate was sparked by concern for the distributional problems that growth creates, rather than by fears of physical scarcity of resources, as we shall see in Chapter 5.

The twin themes of growth and distribution are interwoven in the chapters that follow. Chapters 3 to 5 focus more particularly on the problems of distribution.

The theoretical issues raised by the NIEO are examined in Chapters 6 to 15. The problems of growth and distribution are then reviewed in the concluding chapter, the Geography of Development.

The way in which economic geographers perceive these problems of growth and distribution reflects the development of the discipline over the century or more that it has been the subject of serious academic inquiry. The nature of the human relationships implied by these views has changed substantially over the years. Although a history of the subject is of interest for its own sake, it is also important if we are to understand the context in which economic geographers view the issues of current global concern.

TOPICS FOR DISCUSSION

1. Why have the developed and developing countries changed their perceptions of their interdependencies and of their development opportunities since the 1970s?

2. To what extent do current world news items on population growth, grain harvests, energy supplies, and pollution problems feed fears of limits to growth? Give specific examples.

3. What is meant by the "tragedy of the commons"? Review the arguments for and against this concept of resource ownership and management.

4. Why has the idea of limits to growth been rejected by both socialist and developing countries? How far do differences in economic priorities among the Western, socialist, and developing countries reflect differences in level of economic development, and how far do they reflect doctrinaire political differences?

5. To what extent does the movement for a New International Economic Order result from the failure of the developed countries to control their consumption of nonrenewable resources?

6. What are the causes identified by the NIEO for the persistence of disparities between developed and developing countries?

7. The persistence of regional disparities raises questions about the validity of the theories that describe economic systems. Which theories in particular are challenged by the agenda of the NIEO?

8. Growth and distribution are the same issue viewed at different geographic scales. What local issues in your community illustrate this relationship?

9. The failure of past efforts to raise the prices of raw materials through cartels provides support for the economist's view of resources. Does the success of OPEC then support the environmentalist view? Why do these different commodities support conflicting views of resources?

10. Conflicting views of future population growth, food supplies, and economic development reflect conflicts of theory rather than conflicts of fact. Discuss.

FURTHER READINGS

The literature dealing with the issues raised in this chapter is extensive. A small selection has been made of the most helpful items. For more references on specific topics, refer to the relevant chapters.

BARBOUR, IAN. "Justice, Freedom and Sustainability." In *Global Resources: Perspectives and Alternatives,* pp. 73–94. Edited by Clair N. McRostie. Nobel Conference, 14th, Gustavus Adolphus College, 1978. Baltimore: University Park Press, 1980.

A telling rebuttal of the lifeboat ethic presented by Garrett Hardin.

BENNETT, R. J., and R. J. CHORLEY. *Environmental Systems: Philosophy, Analysis and Control.* Princeton, N.J.: Princeton University Press, 1978.

See Chapter 9, pp. 504–527, for a penetrating review of the Club of Rome Studies.

BHAGWATI, JAGDISH N. (Ed.). *The New International Economic Order: The North-South Debate.* Cambridge, Mass.: MIT Press, 1977.

A comprehensive overview of the wide range of issues confronting the NIEO.

BOYD, ROBERT. "World Dynamics: A Note," *Science,* 177 (August 11, 1972), 515–519.

A technological-optimist view of the future.

BROWN, LESTER R. *The Twenty-Ninth Day: Accommodating Human Needs and Numbers to the Earth's Resources.* New York: W. W. Norton & Co., Inc., 1978.

A very readable account of the interaction of the world ecological, economic, and social systems from the environmental viewpoint.

DUBOS, RENÉ. *Celebrations of Life.* New York: McGraw-Hill, 1981.

A positive statement of the potentialities for further human evolution.

HARDIN, GARRETT. "An Ecolate View of the Human Predicament." In *Global Resources: Perspectives and Alternatives,* pp. 49–72. Edited by Clair N. McRostie. Nobel Conference, 14th, Gustavus Adolphus College, 1978. Baltimore: University Park Press, 1980.

Hardin presents and defends his lifeboat ethic.

HARVEY, DAVID. "Population, Resources and the Ideology of Science," *Economic Geography,* L (July 1974), 256–277.

The Marxist viewpoint of the political implications of the limits-to-growth debate.

HIRSCH, FRED. "Is there a New International Economic Order?," *International Organization,* XXX (1976), 521–531.

Post–World War II changes leading to a NIEO.

HIRSCH, FRED. *Social Limits to Growth.* London: Routledge & Kegan Paul, 1977.

Hirsch explains why economic growth increases concern with income distribution.

KAHN, HERMAN, WILLIAM BROWN, and LEON MARTEL. *The Next Two Hundred Years: A Scenario for America and the World.* New York: Morrow, 1976.

An optimistic view of the future by the most optimistic of the futurologists.

LASZLO, ERWIN, ROBERT BAKER, JR., ELLIOTT EISENBERG, and VENKATA RAMAN. *The Objectives of the New International Economic Order.* New York: Pergamon Press, 1978.

A detailed statement supporting the need for a NIEO.

LOZOYA, JORGE, JAIME ESTEVEZ, and ROSARIO GREEN. *Alternative Views of the New International Economic Order.* New York: Pergamon Press, 1979.

A useful table of the many organizations that have reviewed world issues and of their key findings can be found on pp. 34–38; see "Development as a Global Concept," pp. 5–38.

MEADOWS, DONNELLA H., DENNIS L. MEADOWS, JORGEN RANDERS, and WILLIAM W. BEHRENS. *The Limits to Growth: A Report for the Club of Rome's Project on the Predicament of Mankind.* New York: Universe Books, 1972.

The first report of the Club of Rome triggered a worldwide debate on the possibility of world overpopulation and collapse.

MESAROVIC, MILHAJLO, and EDVARD PESTEL. *Mankind at the Turning Point.* The Second Report of the Club of Rome. New York: E. P. Dutton and Reader's Digest, 1974.

This second report of the Club of Rome softened the stand taken by Meadows, stressed the concept of "organic growth," and divided the world into regions for the simulation of future scenarios.

MOTYLEV, V. "Forecasts of the 'Club of Rome,' Reality and Prophecy," *Problems in Economics,* XX, No. 6 (October 1977), 75–94. Translation of review that appeared in *Pravda.*

A pragmatic Marxist approach to the limits-to-growth debate.

ORGANISATION FOR ECONOMIC COOPERATION AND DEVELOPMENT. *Facing the Future: Mastering the Probable and Managing the Unpredictable.* Paris: Organisation for Economic Cooperation and Development, 1979.

A balanced view of future global issues.

SIMON, JULIAN L. *The Ultimate Resource.* Princeton, N.J.: Princeton University Press, 1981.

The "ultimate resource" is humankind. This book presents the possibility of evolution in social organizations.

TINBERGEN, JAN, ANTONY J. DOLMAN, and JAN VAN ETTINGER. *Reshaping the International Order. A Report to the Club of Rome.* New York: E. P. Dutton, 1976.

A useful summary of the objectives of the NIEO and their rationale.

TODARO, MICHAEL P. *Economics for a Developing World.* London: Longman Group Ltd., 1977. See Chapter 25, "Global Interdependence and the New International Economic Order," pp. 379–410.

Todaro provides an excellent general introduction to economics for the economic geographer.

UNITED NATIONS GENERAL ASSEMBLY, 6th Special Session. *Declaration on the Establishment of a New International Economic Order,* A/RES/3201 (S-VI), 9 May 1974.

UNITED NATIONS GENERAL ASSEMBLY, 6th Special Session. *Programme of Action of the Establishment of a New International Economic Order,* A/RES/3202 (S-VI), 16 May 1974.

UNITED NATIONS GENERAL ASSEMBLY, 7th Special Session. *Development and International Economic Cooperation,* Supplement No. 1 (A/10301), RES/3362 (S-VII), 16 September 1975.

These resolutions are summarized in Tinbergen (see above).

WORLD BANK. *World Development Report.* Washington, D.C.: World Bank.

A series of annual reports on global development issues beginning in 1979. An excellent statistical annex with over 200 characteristics for 125 countries is provided.

ZIMMERMANN, ERICH W. *World Resources and Industries.* New York: Harper and Brothers, 1951. See Part I, "Introduction to the Study of Resources," pp. 1–143.

Provides the classic statement of the economist viewpoint on resources.

CHAPTER 2

The Changing Nature of Economic Geography as a Field of Study

Economic geography is primarily concerned with the location of economic activity, the spatial organization and growth of economic systems, and people's use and abuse of the earth's resources. Economic geography traces its roots to the emergence of the highly practical field of *commercial geography.* This new subject provided prospective merchants and governments with information on products and exports of the principal regions of the world.

From 1900 until the early 1930s, an analytic, explanatory approach based on a philosophy of *environmentalism* dominated the discipline. In this approach, the dependence of people's activities upon the natural environment was emphasized.

The following 25 years saw a variety of regional and topical approaches to the study of the *areal differentiation* of economic activities, accompanied by a growing concern for conservation and the wise management of the earth's resources.

From the mid-1950s, interest grew in *locational analysis, spatial organization, and the dynamics of spatial systems,* and then in the 1970s economic geographers began to explore *behavioral approaches to individual decision making,* as well as to reintroduce *ecological concerns* for the relationships of people and nature, and to respond to the alternative ideological perspectives of adherents to Marxist philosophies.

As a result of this evolution, economic geography now is characterized by a *complex mosaic* of ideas and approaches.

Objectives:

- to help you understand contemporary thinking by following the steps by which ideas have been developed
- to describe the work of geographers who have played a leading role in shaping the subject
- to illustrate the difficulties of developing new theory, and the resulting succession of probes into theory and retreats into fact
- to indicate the concerns about the images of humanity that underlie macrotheories about the interrelationships between population and resources as well as microtheories of how the decisions are made that determine the spatial organization and growth of economic systems

FOUR PERIODS IN THE HISTORY OF ECONOMIC GEOGRAPHY

The history of economic geography may be divided into four distinct periods. Each period provided a different approach to the subject, involved a particular emphasis in content, and implied a specific image of humanity. As a result, the continuity in the field is to be found not in the way in which economic geographers have undertaken their research and written their results, but in the central problems they have sought to understand.

Perhaps the most enduring of these central concerns, throughout the history of economic geography, has been to describe and to understand the similarities and the differences from place to place in the ways people make a living, the trade flows generated by differences in regional specializations, and the associated disparities in living standards. The emphasis at first was on the facts of *commerce,* in an effort to form some reasonable forecasts of future commercial development that might serve as a guide to business interests and to governments. The search for better explanations led next to a more theoretical economic geography that focused on the study of the relationships between economic activity and the physical environment. However, *environmental determinism,* the theory that economic differences were caused by environmental factors, failed to explain the diversity of economies in similar physical environments, and ignored the freedom of individuals to make their own choices, within limits, of what they produced. A retreat from theory back to fact followed. A third economic geography emerged that concerned itself with *areal variation* in production, and the economic regions that resulted.

Beginning in the 1950s, economic geographers made new attempts at creating a theoretical approach, building on the work of economists, and relying heavily on quantitative methods to understand the *spatial organization* of economic systems. Some economic geographers are now retreating from the approaches of the 1960s, however, in part because of a rejection of the image of "economic being," the "profit maximizer," on which it is based. They seek instead a new behavioral economic geography and a more comprehensive understanding of the motivations that direct decision-makers.

The history of economic geography is a fascinating subject worthy of study in its own right. More important, it makes a fundamental contribution to understanding contemporary economic geography. You will find that tracing out the history of the subject makes it easier to understand current approaches. New approaches often take as given the lessons of the past and cannot be appreciated fully outside their historical context. Furthermore, the difficulties in establishing a theoretical approach to the subject and the traps into which economic geography has fallen need to be relearned by each new generation of students.

Kenneth Boulding once observed that "nothing fails like success." It is perhaps also true that nothing succeeds like failure. Out of the constant questioning and frequent rejection of approaches to economic geography there may yet emerge new and more powerful approaches. In tracing the history of the subject, we therefore attempt to draw out the progression of ideas that have contributed to current thinking in the field. We pinpoint some of the geographers who dominated the subject and describe their work. We underline the insights that have propelled the subject forward, and the excesses that have sidetracked it. We also direct attention to the components that we believe must be integrated into any new synthesis. We begin at the beginning with the emergence of commercial geography.

COMMERCIAL GEOGRAPHY

Modern economic geography traces its roots to commercial geography. Commercial geography had grown up as the Western European nations expanded their trading relationships and empires across the globe, creating a demand for commercial information about world regions that previously had been unknown to the Europeans. One of the first textbooks in the field was written in the middle of the seventeenth century by the geographer Bernhardus Varenius to provide practical commercial information for Amsterdam merchants. Later, other volumes were published: Patrick Gordon's *Geography Anatomized,* which had 20 editions in England between 1693 and 1728; William Guthrie's *New System of Modern Geography,* published in 1770 and revised through 1843; and Jedidiah Morse's *Geography Made Easy.* These books were the world's first financially rewarding educational publications.

George G. Chisholm

Commercial geography reached its zenith in the work of a Scottish scholar, G. G. Chisholm, who founded the school of geography at the University of Edinburgh in 1908. Chisholm's *Handbook of Commercial Geography* was first published in 1889 and reached its tenth edition in 1925 when he was 77 years old. This distinguished book, subsequently rewritten by L. Dudley Stamp and others, still occupies an important place in the literature and may well have had a more profound and lasting influence on economic geography than any other single book.

The *Handbook,* which provided a precise account

of world production and trade, was organized first by commodity, using as a basis such factors as climate and geology, which Chisholm thought helped explain the world distribution of their production, and second by country, to describe the detailed locality of production. Chisholm was a stickler for accuracy and detail, but he argued that the most important contribution of commercial geography was not the facts themselves, but the clues they provided to the likely future course of commercial development.

Production and Trade

Chisholm introduced the first edition of his book with this essential truth: "The great geographic fact on which commerce depends is that different parts of the world yield different products, or furnish the same product under unequally favorable conditions." The view that particular geographic conditions offer absolute advantages to the production of specific commodities, whose production will therefore tend to become concentrated in those regions, became more firmly entrenched in geographic thinking with each new edition of the *Handbook.*

Chisholm also elaborated the interdependence of production and trade. Regional concentration in production is not possible without the transportation facilities to distribute the goods to their markets. Trade is thus the great equalizer, increasing the variety of goods available in any location and reducing differences in price for a good between any two regions to the costs of transportation and any tariffs involved in shipment of the good. Improvements in transportation technology, he found, reduced regional price differences and increased the range of commodities traded. Chisholm noted that early Egyptian, Assyrian, and Phoenician trade was in only the most expensive and transportable luxuries—gold, silver, precious stones, ebony and fine woods, ivory and inlaid work, incense, perfumes, balsams and gums, apes, peacocks, panther skins, and slaves. By the time he wrote the first edition of the *Handbook,* these commodities had been displaced by bulk items. In Chisholm's day, one drug, opium, shipped mainly to China, held a leading place by value in world exports, but trade was otherwise dominated by raw materials and manufactured items in common use, such as wheat, wool, iron, and ironware.

Concentration and Deconcentration

Improvements in transportation technology, Chisholm observed, had led to more concentrated patterns of production and to increases in regional specialization. Distant centers, previously unable to compete in local markets because of shipping costs, found

that they could undersell local producers as transportation costs fell. More particularly, established centers with highly skilled labor and more advanced equipment benefited most from improvements in transportation technology. Along with this, these improvements tied the world's distant raw-material-producing regions into a single system, revolving around a Western European industrial "heartland." Chisholm cited the example of the refrigeration technology that was just developing as his first edition went to press in 1889 and that played such an essential role in the establishment of the commercial dairy and livestock industries in countries such as New Zealand, Australia, and Argentina. Shipment of these low-cost agricultural goods to Europe stimulated the further concentration of manufacturing activity in Europe at the same time that the animal industries concentrated in the Southern Hemisphere. Improvements in transportation and trade encouraged increasing concentration of production.

Chisholm also identified countervailing forces of decentralization, and he believed these forces would in the end outweigh the forces of concentration and would lead to a more equal worldwide distribution of industrial activity. One of the primary forces of decentralization was what he called the "Law of Diminishing Returns" (more correctly, the "Law of Vanishing Assets"). Given a choice, industrialists will mine raw materials such as coal and iron ore where they are most favorably located. Thus, the thickest, richest coal seams, those closest to existing manufacturing activity, will usually be mined first. Once these best, most conveniently located reserves are used up, the costs of production can be expected to rise, imposing an increasing cost burden on older industrial centers and forcing both raw materials and industrial production into new locations.

Chisholm did not address questions of limits to growth, however. In the years that he was working on the various editions of his *Handbook,* 1889 to 1925, he was interested in the effects that *local* depletion of resources (not shortages at the global scale) would have on the distribution of industry. Improved transportation technology, he thought, could be expected to alleviate the effects of any local resource depletion. If there were to be any problems of shortages, they would be shortages of workers, not resources. Thus, he wrote in the introduction to his fourth edition:

> Demands are constantly made for more men for our mercantile navy, for agriculture, and for various industries, while it is notoriously the case that more men are finding employment in the service of the rich and well-to-do, and in connection with amusement and education, including under one or other of these last two heads all the varied forms

of literature. When such demands are made the population returns raise the question, Do the men exist to meet them?[1]

Chisholm worked on his *Handbook* in an age of rapid technological change. The last few decades of the nineteenth century saw the coming into general use of hydroelectric power, refrigerated steamships, subways, the telephone, electric light, steel skyscrapers, and the elevator. Industrial technology was changing rapidly, with the Gilchrist-Thomas process of steelmaking in Germany in 1879. The manufacture of calcium nitrate by the fixation of atmospheric nitrogen began in Norway in 1905, providing artificial fertilizers for world agricultural output. New agricultural lands were opening up, and the Canadian prairies enjoyed a wheat boom made possible by new strains of fast-maturing wheats. A subdued optimism thus characterized Chisholm's writing. He would have been appalled at the ideas contained in *Limits to Growth,* by Meadows and his colleagues, and sympathetic to the concerns expressed by the New International Economic Order.

ENVIRONMENTAL DETERMINISM

Economic geography developed as a separately named field of study in the United States at the time when Chisholm was writing successive editions of his *Handbook,* but it followed a different path. The first article to use the term *economic geography* in the United States was published in 1888. Some years later, World War I proved a great stimulus to this field of study; economic geographers were called upon to provide knowledge about sources of food and raw materials in the world, and for understanding of the economic problems of different countries. By the early 1920s the field was well established, and a special journal, *Economic Geography,* appeared in 1925. This new economic geography was not closely related to economics, but instead was a discipline whose ideas were consistent with the philosophies of *environmentalism* that dominated the social sciences as they emerged out of natural philosophy in the latter part of the nineteenth century.

The Environmental Idea

The basic environmentalist idea was clearly expressed by the first president of the Association of American Geographers, William Morris Davis, in his 1906 presidential address: "Any statement is of geographic quality if it contains . . . some relation between an element of inorganic control and one of organic response." To Davis, human society was an organism that survived by adjustment to the physical environment; the nature of its growth was thus environmentally prescribed.

Davis was a tireless scholar who sought for many years to impose the environmentalist concept on American geographic education. This viewpoint is best illustrated in the following quotation from one of his contemporaries.

> Man is a product of the earth's surface. This means not merely that he is a child of the earth, dust of her dust; but that the earth has mothered him, fed him, set him tasks, directed his thoughts, confronted him with difficulties that have strengthened his body and sharpened his wits, given him his problems of navigation or irrigation, and at the same time whispered hints of their solution.[2]

'The Geographical Theory'

The environmentalist idea was so strong that when sociologist Pitirim A. Sorokin published his masterful review and critique, *Contemporary Sociological Theories Through the First Quarter of the Twentieth Century,* he devoted one-sixth of his study to what he termed *The Geographical Theory:* "Almost since the beginning of man's history," he wrote, "it has been known that the characteristics, behavior, social organization, social processes and historical destiny of a society depend upon the geographical environment."[3]

Among the phenomena Sorokin noted that the environmentalists tried to explain by environmental causes were: population distribution and density, housing types, road location, clothing, and the amount of wealth produced and owned by a society. A dominating belief was that all brilliant and wealthy civilizations of early times occurred in "favorable" natural environments, whereas "unfavorable" climates and inaccessible or isolated areas bred backwardness and savagery. The location and nature of industry, business cycles, and the rhythms of economic life, race, and physiological, social, and historical differences among societies all were explained on the basis of environmental determinants. So were health, energy and efficiency, suicide, insanity, crime, birth, death, and marriage rates, religion, art,

[1]G. G. Chisholm, *Handbook of Commercial Geography,* 4th ed. (London: Longmans, Green and Co., 1903), p. xxv.

[2]Ellen Semple, *The Influences of Geographic Environment* (New York: Henry Holt & Co., 1911), p. 1.

[3]P. A. Sorokin, *Contemporary Sociological Theories Through the First Quarter of the Twentieth Century* (New York: Harper & Row, 1928), p. 99.

and literature, and the social and political organization of society!

Ellsworth Huntington

The strongest hypotheses about civilization and climate were those of a geographer named Ellsworth Huntington, who argued that climate was the decisive factor in health and physical and mental efficiency; and that since a civilization is the result of the energy, efficiency, intelligence, and genius of the population, ergo, climate is the "mainspring" factor in the progress or regress of civilizations.

How does one establish a link between civilization and climate? Ellsworth Huntington began by writing to 214 well-traveled and well-read geographers, historians, diplomats, business people, and others in 27 countries to help him. They were asked to rate the level of civilization in each of a given list of regions on a scale of 1 to 10.

Huntington provided them with a definition of civilization:

> Qualities (of civilization) find expression in high ideals, respect for law, inventiveness, ability to develop philosophical systems, stability and honesty of government, a highly developed system of education, the capacity to dominate the less civilized parts of the world, and the ability to carry out far-reaching enterprises covering long periods of time and great areas of the earth's surface.[4]

How objective are the replies likely to be when individuals are asked to rate the level of civilization in all regions across the world, including their own? In one respect, Huntington considered himself lucky. He undertook the enterprise in 1913 before the hopes for international objectivity and cooperation were dashed by World War I. Nevertheless, his expert eye detected some bias in the replies he received. Thus, he noted that Americans put America, particularly its more backward parts, higher than what one would expect. To reduce this bias he grouped the replies (54 in all) by the region in which the respondent lived and produced regional averages. In this way the American replies (numbering 25) carried no more weight than that of the Teutonic Europeans (6) or Asiatics (also 6).

The disparities in the averaged ratings revealed systematic spatial patterns. The North America map, for example, showed that, in general, the lower the rating for a region, the greater the disparity in the rating suggested by different contributors (Figure 2.1). The highest rating given was for the manufacturing belt stretching from New York to Chicago (rating 95 to 100). The Canadian Prairies rated 64 points (out of 100), and Greenland a mere 50. But the range in average maximum and minimum values ranged from 1 for New York, to 30 for Manitoba, to 51 for Greenland.

An ethnocentric bias is even more obvious. Contributors tended to rate their own immediate regions higher than more distant contributors. The Austrian Alps are rated 90 by "Teutons," but 74 by Americans. Southern China is rated 84 by all Asiatics, but only 44 by the British. One exception to the tendency of ratings to drop with the distance of the contributor is Quebec Province. The lowest rating for Quebec was by the North American contributors (85), which compares with 89 by British contributors.

The major objective of the maps of civilization was to determine "much more fully than has yet been the case, how far various moral and mental qualities are influenced by physical environment, race, historical development, biological variations and other causes."[5] The method of rating civilization and the disparities in the results obtained dispel any respect for the work among those not repelled by the very idea of ranking civilization itself.

Huntington's writing on civilization has caused subsequent geographers acute embarrassment. Taken for what it pretends to be, the work is blatantly ethnocentric and ludicrously pompous. Thus, when British geographer T. W. Freeman included a chapter on Huntington in his book *The Geographer's Craft* (1967), an American reviewer was in a gloomily humorous vein and was "led to wonder if some, perhaps unconscious, anti-American bias had not motivated the writer to choose the figure whom most contemporary American geographers might most avidly choose to forget."[6]

Whereas geographers are trying to forget about the work of Huntington and the conclusions he made between climate and civilization, some contemporary economists are beginning to ponder whether in fact such a relationship might not exist. Thus, economist Michael Todaro, writing on the differences between initial conditions of the developed world before its economic take-off and those of the developing world today, notes climate as one of eight major differences:

> Almost all Third World countries are situated in tropical or subtropical climatic zones. *It is a his-*

---

[4]Ellsworth Huntington, *Civilization and Climate* (New Haven: Yale University Press, 1915), p. 150.

[5]Ibid., p. 151.

[6]Andrew H. Clarke, quoted in Geoffrey J. Martin, *Ellsworth Huntington: His Life and Thought* (Hamden, Conn.: Archon Books, 1973), p. 251.

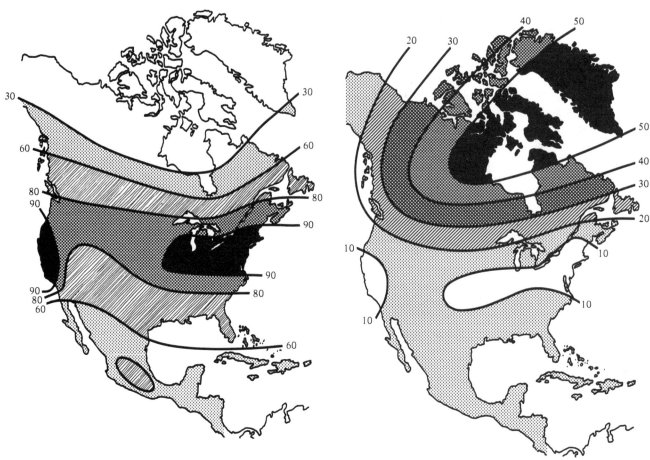

FIGURE 2.1   The level of civilization and range of civilization scores in North America: Huntington, 1915. The strongest hypotheses about civilization and climate were those of Ellsworth Huntington. The map of civilization in North America appears in *Civilization and Climate* (New Haven: Yale University Press, 1915), p. 173, and was used to argue that the northeastern United States had the ideal climate to stimulate the highest levels of "civilization."

torical fact that all successful examples of modern economic growth have occurred in temperate zone countries. Such a dichotomy cannot simply be attributed to coincidence: it must bear some relation to the special difficulties caused directly or indirectly by differing climatic conditions.

One obvious climatic factor directly affecting conditions of production is that in general the extremes of heat and humidity in most poor countries contribute to deteriorating soil qualities and the rapid depreciation of many natural goods. It also contributes to the low productivity of certain crops, the weakened regenerative growth of forests, and the poor health of animals. Finally, and perhaps most important, these extremes of heat and humidity not only cause discomfort to workers but also weaken their health, reduce their de-

sire to engage in strenuous physical work and generally lower their levels of productivity and efficiency.[7]

In his own day, Huntington's work had a much weaker impact in the United Kingdom than in North America. Chisholm was among the wide circle of academics with whom Huntington corresponded regularly. Chisholm thought highly of Huntington's work in general, but wrote in one review that "the tendency to lack due care in generalizing cannot be denied, and there are . . . too many evil consequences thereof."[8] Chisholm is not among the list of those British geographers who

[7]Michael Todaro, *Economic Development in the Third World* (New York: Longman, 1981), pp. 100–101.

[8]Quoted in Martin, *Ellsworth Huntington,* p. 133.

agreed to contribute to the map of civilization. Nor did Huntington's work have any visible impact on Chisholm's *Handbook of Commercial Geography.*

J. Russell Smith

One geographer who did agree to contribute to the map of civilization was the American J. Russell Smith. Smith, asked in 1916 to evaluate Huntington's work, could say categorically, "Huntington is doing what I regard as the most important geographical work now being carried out." Smith's view is important because he wrote the first and one of the most influential textbooks in economic geography in the United States, and because his approach to the subject was strongly influenced by Huntington's work.

J. Russell Smith began his university studies in economics at the Wharton School of Finance and Economy at the University of Pennsylvania, and he began his teaching career there in 1903 as an instructor in commerce. He later became Professor of Geography and Industry and then became Professor of Economic Geography at Columbia University in 1919. Smith claimed he was dissatisfied with Chisholm's textbook because he found it too descriptive. Notwithstanding his own early training as an economist, he felt the need for a book that would analyze the underlying relationships among the physical environment and people's economic activities and resource utilization.[9] The result was Smith's *Industrial and Commercial Geography,* published in 1913, with various editions (with M. O. Phillips and his son T. R. Smith) ending in 1961.

The first edition of Smith's *Industrial and Commercial Geography* predates Huntington's *Civilization and Climate,* but the first chapter bears the imprint of Huntington's work and refers at length to one of Huntington's earlier papers. Thus, Smith begins his book with a chapter titled "Our Changing Environment" and the words, "A group of people can only prosper, increase and grow powerful when their environment furnishes them an abundance of food and of other materials for making appliances to supply the other necessities of existence."[10] But like Huntington, he believed in a challenge-response element in development. Smith viewed civilization as a product of adversity, advancing most where nature restricted production to certain seasons, requiring people to work and to save to keep themselves during the other season. Where things were too good, "the native may sit and doze most of

the time, as for untold generations, his ancestors have done before him—enervated by plenty."[11] Civilization, he thought, had gained by moving north into the cold regions.

> Cold is a great stimulus to activity. Men and animals alike want to move more rapidly on a brisk, cold day of winter than on a sultry summer afternoon. This is as true of nations as of persons. The most energetic and powerful nations, therefore, are those living in a climate where frost forces them to activity and where the warm summer enables them to produce vast supplies of food.[12]

Like G. G. Chisholm, J. Russell Smith viewed commerce as the key to the distribution of commodities in all regions, few of which could produce the complete range needed. But the term *civilization* constantly reappears in the opening chapter of his book even when discussing commerce and transportation. Nevertheless, Smith's discussion of trade and commerce makes the same basic points as did Chisholm. Improvements in transportation were recognized to have changed the staples of trade to the cheap, bulky items, and to have evened out in time and space the supply of foods.

The very strong environmentalism evident in the opening chapter of the first edition of Smith's book was modified in later editions. Nevertheless, a reference to Huntington's *Civilization and Climate* appeared in virtually identical form after its publication in 1915 in all later editions of Smith's book.

Three world maps were presented; the first two were from Huntington: distribution of human energy on the basis of climate, and the level of civilization. The civilization map has been discussed. The climate-energy map was equally ethnocentric, with "best" physical health and energy placed at an average temperature of 64°F at night to 70°F by day, and "best" mental health at somewhat lower temperatures. Smith then added a third map that showed the percentage of the labor force in manufacturing activity. The connection among the three maps was inescapable. Smith concluded:

> By a strange coincidence these areas of high civilization in Europe and North America happen to have the best and most accessible coal in the world. Suppose that coal had been in the Amazon, Congo, and lower Mackenzie valleys![13]

[9]See Virginia M. Rowley, *J. Russell Smith* (Philadelphia: University of Pennsylvania Press, 1964), p. 50.

[10]J. Russell Smith, *Industrial and Commercial Geography* (New York: Henry Holt & Co., 1913), p. 1.

[11]Ibid., p. 7.

[12]Ibid., pp. 9–10.

[13]J. Russell Smith and M. O. Phillips, *Industrial and Commercial Geography,* 3d ed. (Henry Holt & Co., 1946), p. 15.

It is unlikely that Huntington would have approved of such extreme statements. In one letter in 1932, Huntington wrote, "I used the words *control* and *determine*. Now my tendency is very strongly to say *permit* and *favor* [Huntington's italics]. I think that what the environment does is mainly first to offer a choice of different conditions which man may utilize, and then favor one type of activity rather than another." An article written by Huntington in 1931, which reflected his thinking on "The Content of Modern Geography," was, however, rejected by the editors of the *Annals of the Association of American Geographers,* who felt that their journal should concentrate on the results of original field investigations.[14]

T. Griffith Taylor

The environmental relationships between energy resources and economic development, voiced in such a simplistic way by Smith, were stated much more astutely by the Australian T. Griffith Taylor, a determinist who also maintained an active correspondence with Ellsworth Huntington. Griffith Taylor probably was the most controversial geographer ever, and his biography makes interesting reading. He had become a world celebrity because of his participation in Robert Scott's last expedition to the Antarctic, his work in both surveying and naming Australia's new capital, Canberra, and his fierce disagreement with government officials on the settlement possibilities of Australia.

Taylor established the first university departments of geography in both Australia (at Sydney in 1920) and Canada (at Toronto in 1935). He wrote major books on both countries, with titles that left no doubt about his deterministic leanings. His *Australia* text (first published in 1941) was subtitled, "A Study of Warm Environments and Their Effect on British Settlement." His *Canada* book (first published in 1947) was subtitled, "A Study of Cool Continental Environments and Their Effects on British and French Settlement." Australia's description certainly sounds cozier than Canada's, but Taylor was very pessimistic about its settlement future, at least by the standards of the day. He castigated as irresponsible claims that Australia could support 100 million population or more. His own assessment was based on a careful appraisal of the distribution, reliability, and total amount of rainfall across the country, for he believed that rainfall would prove to be the single most important factor limiting settlement. He therefore summarized his thinking in a set of maps emphasizing environmental control (Figure 2.2). The government of Australia banned some of his books, and Griffith Tay-

lor left his post for a professorship at the University of Chicago and later at the University of Toronto.

Taylor was more optimistic about settlement possibilities in Canada. His inaugural address at Convocation Hall, Toronto, Ontario, given in 1935 and attended by the lieutenant-governor and other dignitaries of the province, as well as the president of the university, seems as prescient today as it must have appeared far-fetched at the time.

Griffith Taylor predicted in that address that Alberta would probably become the most powerful province in Canada. Calgary, he said, might one day be larger than Montreal or Toronto, although at the time Calgary's population was about one-tenth that of Montreal and Toronto. He based these predictions on Alberta's oil and coal fields, and he then accused the Canadian government of neglecting their development. The day would come, he predicted, when the capital of Canada would be moved from Ottawa to Calgary and Canada itself would become the center of the British Empire. He also had encouraging words about the Mackenzie River Valley. It might, as Smith emphasized, lack coal, but it has a warmer summer climate than the Gaspe Peninsula. Northern Canada could duplicate the Russian experience and establish a string of cities with populations of more than 20,000 each.

Taylor also made careful estimates of the total population that the world could support. The figures depended on the standard of living expected; thus, Australia's population could climb to 60 million, given European living standards, or 30 million at Australian living standards. Taylor believed in "carrying capacity" and limits to growth. Had he lived to see the publication of the Club of Rome's studies he would have been quick to point out that, whereas Meadows and colleagues based population limits on an undifferentiated world, and Mesarovic and Pestel on a world of only 10 regions, he had used 74 economic regions for his estimates as far back as 1922. All that without the help of any computer!

Taylor summarized his thinking about the relationship between population and physical environment, and the role of the geographer, in a paragraph that reappeared in many of his books. He wrote:

> The writer is a determinist. He believes that the best economic program for a country to follow has in large part been determined by Nature, and it is the geographer's duty to interpret this program. Man is able to accelerate, slow or stop the progress of a country's development. But he should not, if he is wise, depart from the directions as indicated by the natural environment—What the Possibilists fail to recognize is that Nature has laid down a

[14]Martin, *Ellsworth Huntington,* pp. 242–244.

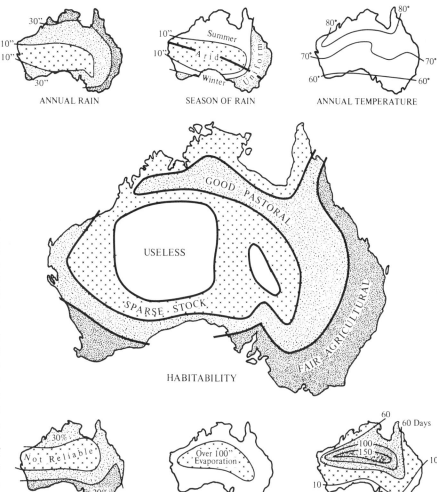

30"
10"
10"
30"
ANNUAL RAIN

10"
Summer
Arid
Uniform
Winter
10"
SEASON OF RAIN

80°
80°
70°
60°
70°
60°
ANNUAL TEMPERATURE

GOOD PASTORAL
USELESS
SPARSE STOCK
FAIR AGRICULTURAL
HABITABILITY

30%
Not Reliable
20%
%Variation
RELIABILITY OF RAIN

Over 100"
Evaporation
EVAPORATION AND DISCOMFORT

60
60 Days
100
150
10
10
Maximum=90° F
HEAT SPELLS

FIGURE 2.2 Environmental determinants of Australian settlement: Griffith Taylor, 1940. Journalists and politicians anticipated that Australia's population would grow to 100 million or more. Taylor suggested that environmental limits, as described in these maps, set a reasonable limit at 20 to 30 million. He was called unpatriotic, and some of his books were banned. His views were later vindicated, and in 1952 he returned to Australia to retire in Sydney. The university there named its geography building after him. [*Source:* Griffith Taylor, *Australia: A Study of War Environments and Their Effect on British Settlement* (London: Methuen and Co. Ltd., first pubished 1940; seventh edition reprinted 1966), frontispiece.]

"Master Plan" for the World—This pattern will never be greatly altered; though man may modify one or two percent of the desert areas, and extend the margins of settlement. It is the duty of geographers to study Nature's plan, and to see how best their national area may be developed in accord with temperature, rainfall, soil, etc., whose bounds are quite beyond our control in any general sense.[15]

The Waning of Environmentalism

Even as environmentalism reached its height, geography was developing new ideas that were to supersede it, however. Frederic Le Play, a French geographer, developed the first scientific method for the study and analysis of social phenomena, and he correlated the character of places with the type of work, forms of property, types of family organization, and other institutions and social processes, emphasizing the *mutual interdependence* of place, economy, and culture, rather than any single-factor causation of environment.

The idea of the interdependence of culture and nature was developed more fully by another French geographer, Vidal de la Blache, in his *Principles of Human Geography* (1926). According to de la Blache:

The dominant idea in all geographical progress is that of terrestrial unity. The conception of the earth as a whole, whose parts are coordinated, where phenomena follow a definite sequence and obey general laws to which particular cases are related, had early entered the field of science by way of astronomy.[16]

[15]Quoted in John K. Rose, "Griffith Taylor, 1880-1963," *Annals of the Association of American Geographers,* Vol. 54, No. 4 (December 1964), pp. 622-629.

[16]Vidal de la Blache, *Principles of Human Geography* (London: Constable, 1926), pp. 6-7.

What was emerging out of environmentalism was an early concern in geography for *ecology*. Vidal de la Blache thought that "every region is a domain where many dissimilar things, artificially brought together, have subsequently adapted themselves to a common existence" and in which "the influences of environment are seen only through masses of historical events which enshroud them." He also believed that the physical environment sets limits or margins within which humans are free to work, rather than controlling people directly.

The gradual change in thinking can be traced in the following series of quotations from successive editions of Nels August Bengtson and William Van Royen's textbook *Economic Geography*. In 1935, the authors indicated that "differences in the natural environment not only affect the physical activities of man, but generally they also lead to fundamental differences in thoughts and ideals. . . . The Norwegians of today—strong, agile, alert, and serious—are in large measure the product of the environment which has fostered them." The next edition of the text (1942) made certain adjustments. The first edition's "differences in environment lead to differences in activities" became "differences in productive activities are often results of differences in environment." Again, "the Norwegians of today—virile, agile, alert, and sincere—in large measure have been shaped as a regional group by the environment which has fostered them." The subtle change is noteworthy. Finally, in 1956 the authors indicated that "the physical environment does not determine the economic activity and the mode of life of man." Evidently some old dogs were willing to learn new tricks!

AREAL DIFFERENTIATION: 1930s TO THE 1960s

Retreat from Theory

"The simple faith in the determining influence of natural environment has almost disappeared," wrote Jan Broek in "Discourses on Economic Geography," which appeared in *The Geographical Review* for 1941. In the face of increased questioning, environmental determinism was abandoned by economic geographers, who began to look for new explanations based on the principles of economics. W. H. Carter and R. E. Dodge, for example, argued that economic geography "should analyze . . . universally applicable economic principles that underlie our whole industrial life."[17] There was some experimentation with industrial location analysis. O. E.

Baker made use of David Ricardo's rent theories in his studies of land use. Other American geographers became concerned with resources and the conservation of the environment during the Depression and the New Deal of the 1930s. Some geographers moved into problem-solving roles in President Franklin Roosevelt's National Resources Planning Board and in the Tennessee Valley Authority.

This initial flirtation with economic theory was short-lived, however. Rejecting not only environmentalism but also most attempts to theorize, the majority of economic geographers from the 1930s to the 1960s returned once again to a very descriptive approach. The tentative generalizations about commodity production and trade in George G. Chisholm's introduction to his *Handbook of Commercial Geography* and sweeping assertions about economy and environment in J. Russell Smith's *Industrial and Commercial Geography* were dropped. In their place came a variety of organizations of subject matter, each simply a "container" for facts.

Economic geography, according to two textbook authors, once again became

> an inquiry into similarities, differences and linkages within and between areas in the production, exchange, transfer, and consumption of goods and services.[18]
>
> The study of the areal variation of the earth's surface in mans' activities related to producing, exchanging and consuming wealth.[19]

Some economic geographers organized their books by regions or countries and described their principal products and exports. Some authors described world-scale maps of the spatial patterns of production and trade of particular commodities. Still others organized their works around "activity systems," such as primitive subsistence economies, commercial grain-livestock farming systems, and industrial-urban complexes.

There were, to be sure, some changes over the years. The regionally oriented approaches dominated the 1940s, although there was a gradual shift toward topical organization. But the described variety of phenomena and the increasing abundance of facts led the describers to despair of ever again having a unified field of economic geography. In 1954, a review of the field appeared in *American Geography: Inventory and Prospect,* and it noted:

[17]W. H. Carter and R. E. Dodge, *Economic Geography* (New York: Doubleday, Doran and Co., 1939), p. vi.

[18]Richard S. Thoman, "Economic Geography," *International Encyclopedia of the Social Sciences,* Vol. 6 (New York: Macmillan, 1968), pp. 124–128.

[19]J. W. Alexander, *Economic Geography* (Englewood Cliffs, N.J.: Prentice-Hall, 1963), p. 9.

General economic geography [has] ceased to exist as a research specialty. . . . More and more the scholar who claims penetration in his research thinks of himself as a specialist in land utilization, in resources, in manufacturing geography, in the geography of transportation, or some other special aspect, and he makes no pretense to competence in research in economic geography as a whole.[20]

On the other hand, it was admitted that

There is a central theme, however, common to all the topic specialities within the general limits of economic geography. Economic geography has to do with the similarities and differences from place to place in the ways people make a living. The economic geographer is concerned with economic processes especially as manifested in particular places modified by the phenomena with which they are associated.[21]

The tone of the subject of economic geography in this third phase is illustrated by one popular text that went through many editions, namely, Clarence Fielden Jones's *Economic Geography,* first published in 1935. The descriptive approach in the book was set by the opening sentences, which are in sharp contrast to those of the Chisholm and Smith texts quoted earlier. Jones began a chapter titled "The Distribution of People" quite simply: "Everyone likes to travel. Most of us wish to visit distant lands." What followed was a description of the work people do in various lands, organized on an activity basis. Eight main activities were identified: hunting and fishing, grazing, farming, forestry, mining and manufacturing, and commerce. These then become the main sections of the book. Each chapter typically included a map of a representative farm and farming region. The farm maps were at a scale of 1 inch equals 1/4 mile, and were accompanied by a detailed description of the farm itself and the annual rhythm of activity. Discussion of physical factors affecting production led into a map depicting the limits of the agricultural region represented by the farm. Where necessary, further maps at intermediate scales were included. Thus, a map of a farm village in hilly land in Kiangsu Province, China, showed how farm plots were allocated among village farmers. The descriptions went far beyond the detail offered in the early commercial geographies and stressed

economic geography as a field of study that should be directly involved in travel, observation, mapping, and original data collection, rather than one depending on governmental statistics, as Chisholm had suggested.

Ultimately, the areal differentiation approach in economic geography became bound up with the definition and mapping of *economic regions.* Regions had always been important in economic geography, but they had received less attention in earlier approaches. Commercial geographers had employed countries as convenient units to present data on world commodity production and trade. Environmental determinists employed physical regions based largely on climate. In both cases, regions were a means to an end. In areal differentiation, definition of regions became an end in itself, the ultimate in descriptive generalization.

To younger geographers in the late 1930s, this was problematic, and they began to complain about the sterility of the regional focus. Change was halted by World War II, however, and after the war economic geography took new and different directions.

POST-1950S: OTHER APPROACHES

Locational Analysis

Wartime military intelligence and economic planning required applied geographic studies in which inferences had to be drawn from limited data with the help of sound theory. Younger geographers recognized they had been poorly trained for this work, and after World War II they expressed their dissatisfaction with areal differentiation, and voiced the need for sound theory and reliable methods of inference.

The search for theory intensified in the 1950s and 1960s, a time when the social sciences were becoming increasingly interdisciplinary, when computer technology was beginning to revolutionize quantitative analysis, and when governments were subsidizing research, particularly for planning and policy-oriented studies. There were many suggestions and calls to action. Geographers rediscovered the classical economic theories of location of J. H. von Thünen, Alfred Weber, Walter Christaller, and the newly translated (in 1954) work of August Lösch (these theories are discussed in Chapters 9, 10, and 11). At the same time, an economist, Walter Isard, was sparking a renewed interest in the economics of location. Because he felt that both economics and geography had let the development and application of location theory fall into the gaps between them, he called for creation of a new discipline, *regional science,* to take a leadership role. Partly as a result of Isard's challenge, economic geographers' work became more highly ana-

[20]Raymond E. Murphy, "The Field of Economic Geography." In *American Geography: Inventory and Prospect,* ed. P. E. James and C. F. Jones (Syracuse, N.Y.: Syracuse University Press, 1954), pp. 242–243.

[21]Ibid., pp. 242–243.

lytic and quickly embraced location theory as an intellectual core.

So pervasive and swift were the results that by 1968 Richard Thoman could write:

> . . . the past decade has marked the emergence of a new school of thought. . . . This school has chosen an explicitly theoretical approach, emphasizing nomothetic (law-seeking) research and depending . . . upon mathematic abstracting.[22]

An assessment of the changes was made by the U.S. National Academy of Sciences' National Research Council in a 1965 report titled *The Science of Geography:*

> Several traditional subfields of geography, including economic, urban and transportation geography, are not discussed . . . as they once might have been. . . . It would appear that the three . . . subfields have been joined in a problem area which we entitle . . . location theory studies. . . . The development, testing and refinement of location theory, related studies of the geographic organization of economic life, and of urban and transportation systems, have been fundamental. . . . The applicable body of theory includes . . . abstract concepts concerning spatial distributions and space relations. . . . Very recently a new synthesis has begun to emerge based upon: (1) the identity of spatial concepts and principles developed in (several) subfields of geography; and (2) emphasis upon the interaction of economic, urban and transportation phenomena in interdependent regional systems that are the material consequences of man's resource-converting and space-adjusting techniques. *This emerging synthesis thus results from a concerted application of systems theory within geography* [italics added].[23]

What is systems theory? It deals, in Arthur Koestler's words, with economies

> as an organization of parts-within-parts, because all living matter and all stable systems have a parts-within-parts architecture, which lends them articulation, coherence, and stability.[24]

A system is simply an entity consisting of a set of interdependent and interactive parts: land uses, business firms, trade flows, regions, or, more abstractly,

> *movements,* that (produce) the channels along which the movements occur, the *network,* structured around *nodes,* organized as a *hierarchy,* with the interstitial zones viewed as *surfaces.*[25]

Some emphasized not only systems theory but *normative* considerations involving control of these systems to reach specific goals. Many geographers, both East and West, began to think of their discipline as

> a science concerned with the laws of development of dynamic spatial systems formed on the earth's surface in the process of interaction of nature and society, and with control of these systems . . . the science dealing with the laws of development of geosystems and their control.[26]

> . . . economic geography emphasizes the need of *control* in the spatial allocation of our resources. It . . . (involves) . . . *geocybernetics,* the study of spatial organization.[27]

Economic Person

This new theoretical economic geography involved not only a focus on location theory and on the spatial structures that resulted (Figure 2.3), but it implied a new image of humanity, and it led to a concern with a quite different set of geographic concepts. Of all of these components, none has caused more subsequent concern or dissatisfaction than the image of humanity it implied. This image has become known as "economic person."

"Economic person," quite simply, has perfect knowledge of present circumstances and future events so that he or she has powers of perfect prediction. This individual is also entirely rational and driven by a single goal—to maximize profits. In some cases this goal may be achieved by locating economic activity so as to minimize transportation costs. In other cases, profits are maximized by seeking the "highest and best" land use. But most location decisions with which this economic person must grapple involve tradeoffs. Higher land rents are charged for the most accessible locations where

---

[22]Thoman, "Economic Geography," p. 124.

[23]Edward A. Ackerman, Brian J. L. Berry, Reid A. Bryson, Saul B. Cohen, Edward J. Taaffe, William L. Thomas, Jr., and M. Gordon Wolman, *The Science of Geography* (Washington, D.C.: National Academy of Sciences-National Research Council, 1965), p. 44.

[24]Arthur Koestler, *The Ghost in the Machine* (New York: Macmillan, 1967), pp. 82–83.

[25]Peter Haggett, *Locational Analysis in Human Geography* (London: Edward Arnold, 1965), p. 18.

[26]Y. G. Saushkin and A. M. Smirnov, "The Role of Lenin's Ideas in the Development of Theoretical Geography," *Vestnik Moskovskogo Universiteta, Geografiya,* No. 1 (1970), pp. 3–12.

[27]Commission on College Geography, *A Systems Analytic Approach to Economic Geography* (Washington, D.C.: Association of American Geographers, 1968).

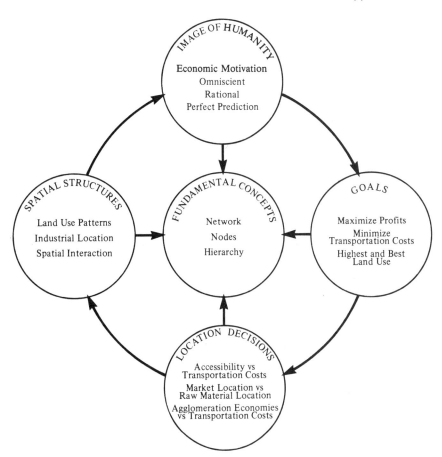

FIGURE 2.3 Building a normative economic geography. This conceptual framework was built upon an image of humanity as motivated solely by economic considerations, having particular goals, making locational decisions, and resulting in spatial structures of land use, industrial location, and settlement. Fundamental concepts in understanding these spatial structures include networks, nodes, and hierarchies.

transportation costs are lower, whereas less-accessible locations may involve higher transportation costs and lower rents. One set of tradeoffs may therefore involve accessibility—rents versus higher transportation costs. To cite a different example, an industrialist can minimize costs of obtaining raw materials by locating close to them, and can minimize marketing costs by locating close to markets. How should this person weigh a market location versus a raw material location? And how should he or she weigh tradeoffs relating to the scale of production? Unit costs of production tend to fall with increasing scale of output; larger industrial plants have lower unit costs than smaller plants, everything else being equal. But larger plants must serve a larger market area, which in turn involves higher transportation costs. Thus, economies of large-scale operation must be weighed against increased transportation costs.

Location theories that deal with these issues describe rational economic landscapes based on optimal decisions of economic people. These landscapes are not a product of differences in climate and soils, as the environmental determinist would have argued. Instead, they are constructed in an abstract space devoid of environmental differences. In this respect, the new economic geography of the 1960s represented a complete break with the past. George Chisholm stressed in his commercial geography the intrinsic physical advantages that each part of the world offered for the production of particular products. J. Russell Smith related production to climate. Clarence Jones described regional patterns. None of them would have predicted that complete economic landscapes could emerge out of rational decisions by profit maximizers, regardless of environmental considerations.

The completeness of the break with the past may be demonstrated by comparing four books, those of Chisholm, Smith, and Jones, already discussed, and a book titled *Readings in Economic Geography,* by Robert Smith, Edward Taaffe, and Leslie King. In this last book, regional studies are used to illustrate theory, and no attempt is made to provide systematic coverage of either all commodities or world regions. This work was a response to the growing interest of geographers in locational analysis and the increasing proportion of economic geography students completing courses in economics and quantitative analysis. The book was a substantial break from economic geographies based upon the idea of areal differentiation, and the editors noted that they were "quite aware that there are other approaches to the large and diverse subject of economic geography.'' Its closest affinity is with texts in regional economics, although the main thrust is a natural extension of ideas suggested as early as Chisholm's *Handbook*.

Coping with Uncertainty

Every theory in science implies a particular image of humanity. Changes in scientific theories involve changes in our image of ourselves. The new theoretical geography of the post-1960s thus involved a new model of how decisions are made about the location of economic activity. This model replaced the stimulus-response theory of people as robots dancing to the rhythm of their physical environment, which was developed by the environmental determinists, with the concept of rational scientific human beings in control, able to achieve goals and to maximize welfare.

One test of a theory is the acceptability of its particular image of humankind. All theory entails some simplification of reality. The image of humanity similarly entails some truncation of the complexity of human nature. Economic person simplified reality by removing uncertainty from life and by making us single-goal directed. The image was accepted in the 1960s, even though it is a gross simplification of reality, for two reasons. First, ''economic person'' provided a norm, or yardstick, with which to examine reality. Indeed, the great German location theorist August Lösch turned the argument around. The time had come, he said, to test reality against theory, not theory against reality. That is, we can judge people by how well they compare with economic person, not our image of economic person by how well it captures the reality of human behavior. This argument does have a certain appeal. Economic geographers can see some merit in knowing what the world would look like under the idealistic circumstances of omniscient, rational, profit maximizers, if only to know how far reality departs from the optimal. But they also know that individuals are not all-knowing—that they have to cope with uncertainty, even if a ''law of large numbers'' takes care of uncertainty for the population as a whole.

The collective ability of economic systems to deal with uncertainty was first explained by Armen Alchian in an allegory.[28] Imagine that thousands of motorists set out on a long journey picking their routes entirely at random. They are unaware that all the service stations are closed except along one route. The travelers who follow this route and so reach their destinations may appear to have acted rationally, and even with considerable foresight. In fact, the route of the survivors is just the same whether they act rationally or not. Similarly, the argument goes, the locational pattern of surviving firms will look much the same whether the surviving firms selected only the locations where they could survive (that is, economic *adaption* occurs) or whether they locate randomly and the economy *adopts* the lucky ones.[29]

The manner in which adoption and adaption occurs in real situations has been illustrated using game theory, a mathematics for optimizing under conditions of uncertainty.[30] The technique is discussed in Chapter 8, so here we need note only the nature of the problem, as illustrated by a Jamaican fishing village. Those who make their living from catching fish have two strategies: in-shore or off-shore fishing. Off-shore fish fetch a better price, but unpredictable currents can cause high losses. The trick is to go for a mixed strategy in which the proportions of in-shore and off-shore fishing are determined jointly by the risk of off-shore currents, and the premium that off-shore fish can earn (Table 2.1). Game theory demonstrates that the mixed strategy developed in this Jamaican village over years of trial and error is indeed the optimal one.

Behavioral Approaches

Many geographers were critical of the new theoretical economic geography. Some said that land-use patterns are not dictated by geometry and the cash register. The relevance of the new theory to understanding the real world was questioned. The validity of the statistical procedures employed was considered doubtful by some. And it was noted by others that even some economists were replacing the image of an economically motivated person with a new model in which the decision-maker was a ''satisficer.''

The Satisficer Concept

People do not necessarily achieve, or even wish to achieve, maximum profits.[31] They seek a variety of goals

---

[28] See Armen Alchian, ''Uncertainty, Evolution, and Economic Theory,'' *Journal of Political Economy,* 58 (June 1950), 211–221; Charles Tiebout, ''Location Theory, Empirical Evidence and Economic Evolution,'' *Papers and Proceedings of the Regional Science Association,* Vol. 3 (1957), 74–86.

[29] Alchian, ''Uncertainty, Evolution, and Economic Theory,'' pp. 214–215.

[30] William Davenport, ''Jamaican Fishing: A Game Theory Analysis,'' *Yale University Publications in Anthropology,* 59 (1960), 3–11; Peter Gould, ''Man Against His Environment: A Game Theoretic Framework,'' *Annals of the Association of American Geographers,* 53 (September 1963), 290–297.

[31] Julian Wolpert, ''The Decision Process in Spatial Context,'' *Annals of the Association of American Geographers,* 54 (December 1964), 537–558.

TABLE 2.1

People against the environment

| | | Fishing strategies[a] | |
		In-shore	Off-shore
Environmental conditions	Current	Win	Lose
	No current	Lose	Win

[a]Jamaicans who earn their living fishing have two possible strategies, in-shore and off-shore fishing. Conditions of the physical environment can be either with an off-shore current, or with no current. Knowing the chances of an off-shore current and the premium in price for off-shore fish, the individuals can develop an optimal mix of the two strategies, which maximizes their "wins."

and are prepared to trade off some income to achieve these other goals. Thus, they select, from among a set of satisfactory alternatives, that alternative which is most compatible with their aggregate goals.

Hazard and Choice Perception

The shift in the image of humanity accompanying this idea of "satisficing" has produced a shift in emphasis in economic geography. Rather than assuming economic person and building a theoretical geography, increasing emphasis has tended to be placed on how risks and opportunities are perceived and how these perceptions influence decision making. This new emphasis is particularly evident in studies of resource management.[32]

This research demonstrates that experience is a good teacher only when it is repetitive and consistent. Where risks are low, and perils infrequent, the decision-makers become prisoners of their own fragmentary experience and often underestimate the chances of disaster. Hence the paradox that increased expenditure on flood control in the United States has been associated with increased, not decreased, flood damage.

This new emphasis on the importance of how the perception of our uncertain environment influences the decisions we make is being reinforced by philosophical shifts in geographic thinking. Locational analysis of the 1960s was in tune with a prevailing philosophy termed *logical positivism*. Logical positivism involved empirical analysis within a normative (theory-building) framework. Data could be collected to test location theory, and the theory developed on the basis of many test results. However, in the 1970s, a number of influential articles appeared in geography that put forward the contrasting philosophy of phenomenology.

Phenomenology

Phenomenology stresses the importance of an individual's "lived-world" experience. It rejects economic person and the notion that there exists some "objective" world. Instead, there is the belief that life takes on meaning only through one's experience and needs. Thus, resources have no existence apart from human needs. Research must be guided, therefore, not by the preconceived notions of the researcher, but by an empathy between the observer and the observed, in which the researcher views the problem from the respondent's viewpoint.

Phenomenology argues for a step back from the location theory of the 1960s toward a more humanistic orientation within the discipline. Anne Buttimer warns that this approach offers no clear-cut operational procedures to guide the researcher. Rather, it offers perspectives that point to exploration of new facets of geographic inquiry. It is thus a preamble to theory.[33]

A simple illustration of the phenomenological approach is work on "mental maps."[34] When people are asked to rank places in terms of their personal preferences as to where they would like to live, some fairly clear patterns emerge. First, they tend to rank where they live highest. Places farthest from them rank lowest. This is similar to the results of Huntington's survey of civilization. Second, they are very discriminating in ranking areas around their home region, which they know best, but tend not to differentiate more distant places. But there is also a relationship between population density and rank. Perhaps people like to be at the center of things. Perhaps the density of population is high because these are desirable places to be. Whatever the reason, London ranks high among its residents, and New York high among American residents. The amenity factor is evident too, with high rankings for the southern coast of England, and in the United States, California and Colorado.

Such mental maps can be prepared at all scales, from local to global. Mental maps, drawn at the local scale by children, illustrate a fundamental distinction between the vertical world of children living in high-rise apartments and the horizontal world of children living in houses. William Bunge has made effective use of such maps in diagnosing problems in urban planning.

It is too early to judge the contributions that will flow from behavioral geography and the retreat from location theory and the concept of economic motivation

---

[32]T. F. Saarinen, *Perception of Environment* (Washington, D.C.: Association of American Geographers, Resource Paper 5, 1969).

[33]Anne Buttimer, "The Dynamism of Lifeworld," *Annals of the Association of American Geographers,* 66 (1976), 277–292.

[34]Peter Gould and Rodney White, *Mental Maps* (Harmondsworth, U.K.: Penguin Books, 1974).

that is involved. It is obvious that the shift has brought economic geography back to earth, and this return to reality was needed. Marvin Mikesell commented on how little attention geographers had given the debate on *Limits to Growth*, "this most relevant of all issues," and the social and philosophical aspects of resource use and environmental protection.[35] The normative economic geography of the 1960s, intellectually exciting though it was, had little to say about these problems. It assumed, rather, that the world is undoubtedly unfolding as it should.

CONTINUITY AND CHANGE

The history of economic geography, like that of all academic disciplines, is punctuated by major shifts in thinking. Four distinct economic geographies have emerged: commercial geography, environmental determinism, areal differentiation, and location theory.

The cycle of advance into theory and retreat into fact, with each stage involving changes in the content and organization of the subject matter, should be noted. Commercial geography was a practical geography serving the day-to-day needs of business and government for factual information on production and trade. Environmental determinism emphasized physical, particularly climatic, causal factors and painted people as "robots" stimulated and challenged by their environment. Areal differentiation required detailed field work and the preparation of maps delimiting regions of agricultural production such as the U.S. "cotton belt." Location theory sought to describe economic landscapes created by "economic person," in which areal differentiation results not from intrinsic differences in climate, soils, or physiography, but instead from accessibility, transportation costs, and economies of scale.

But this image of "economic person," omniscient, rational, and profit maximizing, no longer satisfies economists or economic geographers. In reality, human behavior displays "bounded rationality," in which profit maximizing must be weighed against competing objectives. Hence, a new image of the decision-maker is being developed, the "satisficer image," with decisions based on limited knowledge and bounded rationality.

Yet even as this is happening, some geographers argue that still another change in thinking is needed. Individuals, companies, and countries compete for position or rank in income level and command over the best goods and services, thus producing social limits to growth.

[35]Quoted in R. J. Johnston, *Geography and Geographers* (London: Edward Arnold, 1979), p. 157.

Among those calling for yet another radically different approach to the field are the Marxist geographers, who allege a sinister alliance between economic geography and the capitalist mode of production in each of the earlier approaches. Commercial geography, they say, served the imperialist needs of expanding empires for information on the resources of colonial territories. Environmental determinism was developed to justify the political dominance achieved by the United States and the European powers. Huntington's very definition of civilization included "the capacity to dominate the less-civilized parts of the world," and helped to support the position of the privileged. Areal differentiation and location theory ignored the real needs of society. The Marxist alternative they advocate emphasizes the impact of external political forces in shaping economic landscapes.

This restless search for new economic geographies may have involved a too-quick rejection of what is good in the old. Marvin Mikesell has been led to ponder whether such changes in approach reflect the fickleness of geographers seeking the latest fashion rather than the refinement of science (see Topic 7 at end of the chapter). Others have suggested that a progressive development is evident in the succession of approaches. What is probably the case is that the quest of economic geography is directed by both internal and external forces. The discipline must not only deal with the changing realities of the world but also satisfy the intellectual demands of its practitioners. The external forces are harder to document than the internal forces that have shaped the discipline, but it seems likely that these forces have been as much geographic and technological as they have been political. Not all locations are of equal productivity: They differ in resource endowment and accessibility. Technology is not constant: It becomes more sophisticated through time and diffuses out from centers of innovation, changing the relative value of resource endowment and geographic location. The combined result is suggested by Figure 2.4.

Environmental factors may provide a satisfactory explanation of economic activity and use of resources where geography and technology combine to restrict choice in small-scale and highly localized societies. As the range of options increases, nonenvironmental considerations can be expected to influence decisions as to resource use and economic activity. Determinism yields to possibilism. Given a range of satisfactory alternatives, optimization may yield to satisficer behavior, but the problems facing the world in this age of crisis make it evident that satisficing behavior is a luxury not available to all the people of the world. And even if all the basic human needs and wants could be fulfilled, we would still face social limits to growth. Not all of us can

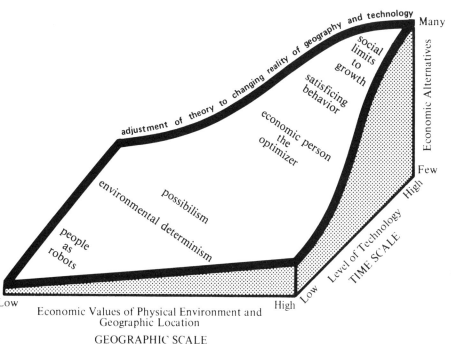

FIGURE 2.4 The changing nature of economic geography: a synthesis. The quest of economic geography required integrating the internal intellectual needs of the subject with the external realities about the location of economic activity, the spatial organization and growth of economic systems, and our use and abuse of the earth's resources. This diagram is intended to stimulate debate on the impact of external forces on the nature of the subject, and is not offered as a definitive statement of how the different approaches to the subject can be dovetailed.

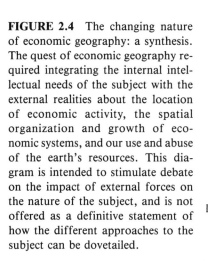

have the best jobs, highest incomes, and most attractive locations. And what is true for individuals is also true for countries. Countries compete for industry and none wants to be relegated to the position of "hewers of wood and drawers of water."

Whatever the correct interpretation of the changing nature of economic geography and the dual role of internal and external forces, we should not ignore the lessons and contributions of each of the four economic geographies described in this chapter. Hence, in organizing this book we have attempted to integrate the mosaic of ideas into their geographic and economic fundamentals, to elaborate the theories of location and interaction that result, and then to return to the problems identified by the movement for a New International Economic Order.

TOPICS FOR DISCUSSION

1. How similar in approach are the discussions of particular commodities or regions in current bank reports and business news to the accounts given in the old commercial geographies such as Chisholm's *Handbook?* Why have such accounts failed to satisfy the goals of economic geography as an academic discipline?

2. How essential are environmental differences to a geography of commodity production? How important are environmental influences to the existence of geography as a science? (You may want to reconsider your answer after reading Chapters 9 to 11.)

3. H. A. Innis argued the need for a "geography of geographers" [*Geographical Review*, 35 (1945) 301–311]. How far are the views of geographers influenced by where they live and when they live? Discuss this question in relation to a specific geographer or geographers.

4. Describe the dominant characteristics in approach and content during each of the four main periods in the history of economic geography.

5. Each school of thought in economic geography has favored a particular concept of region. Commercial geography used political regions; environmental determinism, climatic; areal differentiation, regions based on cropping patterns or analogous characteristics of areas; and location theory, regions based upon flows and interdependencies. How true is this generalization? Give examples and exceptions.

6. What is the image of humanity implied by each of the four schools of economic geography? Why is this image important?

7. "One is always tempted to ask whether the changing fashions of geography reflect the refinement of a science or simply the fickleness of human nature."[36] Examine

---

[36]Marvin Mikesell, in B. J. L. Berry, ed., *The Nature of Change in Geographic Ideas* (Dekalb, Ill.: Northern Illinois University Press, 1980), p. 19.

this assertion by reviewing representative economic geography textbooks of each of the four periods.

8. How were questions of world population and world food supplies assessed by each school of economic geography? Which school most closely reflects the thinking in *Limits to Growth?*

9. Give examples of economic "adaption" and "adoption" as observed at the local urban scale.

10. The contribution of "economic person" is as a norm against which to compare decision making in the real world. Discuss.

11. The potential links between economic geography and economics were weakened by the advent of environmental determinism. Determinism involved "taking each phenomenon in turn and relating it to the physical environment, whereby the mutual relationships between the phenomena have been underemphasized."[37] Discuss.

[37]Michael Chisholm, *Geography and Economics* (London: G. Bell & Sons, 1966), p. 24.

FURTHER READINGS

ALCHIAN, ARMEN A. "Uncertainty, Evolution, and Economic Theory," *Journal of Political Economy,* LVIII (June 1950), 211–221.

Economic systems cope with uncertainty through a process of adoption and adaption. The process is explained by an allegory.

CHISHOLM, GEORGE G. *Handbook of Commercial Geography.* London: Longmans, Green and Co. First edition, 1889; tenth edition, 1925; subsequent editions revised and rewritten by L. Dudley Stamp and others. Last revision, the twentieth, revised edition, 1980.

The main development in the first 10 editions was a progressive development of the introduction. It is well worth reading the introduction to one of these early editions to gain a feeling of the shift in thinking that occurred with environmental determinism.

CHISHOLM, MICHAEL. *Geography and Economics.* London: G. Bell & Sons, 1966.

Chapter 2, "Relations Between Geography and Economics," pp. 4–28, traces the history of development in and relationships between both geography and economics. This is an important and readable summary.

DAVENPORT, WILLIAM. "Jamaican Fishing: A Game Theory Analysis," *Yale University Publications in Anthropology,* Vol. 59 (1960), 3–11.

Brought to the attention of geographers by Peter Gould, this paper concluded that fishermen, as a group, maximize their income in the face of uncertainty, perhaps through trial and error over a long period of adaption and adoption.

FREEMAN, T. W. *The Geographer's Craft.* Manchester, U.K.: Manchester University Press, 1967.

Contains seven biographies, including Ellsworth Huntington (pp. 101–123), a geographer, it was said, many Americans would sooner forget.

HUDSON, JOHN C. (Ed.). *Annals of the Association of American Geographers Special Issue: Seventy-Five Years of American Geography,* Vol. 69 (March 1979).

A series of personal observations by 27 of those who were participants in events leading up to the present. It provides fascinating insights on differences in the approaches between leading centers of geography as well as changes over time.

JOHNSTON, R. J. *Geography and Geographers: Anglo-American Human Geography since 1945.* London: Edward Arnold, 1979.

The key for a more detailed overview of the changing nature of economic geography.

JONES, CLARENCE FIELDEN. *Economic Geography.* New York: Henry Holt & Co., 1935.

An example of areal differentiation in economic geography using the activity systems approach. This popular textbook was later published by the Macmillan Co. in three editions, 1951, 1954, and 1965, co-authored with G. G. Darkenwald.

MARTIN, GEOFFREY J. *Ellsworth Huntington: His Life and Thought.* Hamden, Conn.: Archon Books, 1973.

Huntington was a prolific and controversial writer. For a balanced view of his thinking and contribution read Chapter XIV, "The Geography of Ellsworth Huntington: Some Thoughts and Reflections," pp. 232–253.

POWELL, J. M. "T. G. Taylor: 1880–1963." In *Geographers, Bibliographic Studies,* Vol. 3, pp. 141–154. Edited by T. W. Freeman and Philippe Pirichemel. London: Mansell, 1979.

One of an excellent series of biographies. Contains a particularly useful chronology of events.

ROSE, JOHN K. "Griffith Taylor, 1880–1963," *Annals of the Association of American Geographers,* Vol. 54, No. 4 (December 1964), 622–629.

A concise summary of the highlights of Taylor's career.

ROWLEY, VIRGINIA M. *J. Russell Smith: Geographer, Educator and Conservationist.* Philadelphia: University of Pennsylvania Press, 1964.

Smith's *Industrial and Commercial Geography* is reviewed on pp. 49–60.

SMITH, JOSEPH RUSSELL. *Industrial and Commercial Geography.* New York: Henry Holt & Co. First edition, 1913; fourth edition (co-authored with M. Ogden Phillips and Thomas R. Smith), 1955; reprinted, 1961.

The first major textbook in economic geography in the United States, it presented in its early editions the environmental determinist viewpoint. Its aim was to interpret the earth in terms of its usefulness to humanity, but the first chapter, "Our Changing Environment," described civilization as the product of adversity. The environmental stand was much reduced by the fourth edition.

SMITH, ROBERT H. T., EDWARD J. TAAFFE, and LESLIE J. KING. *Readings in Economic Geography: The Location of Economic Activity.* Chicago: Rand McNally, 1968.

A most useful collection of classical statements, empirical studies, and theoretical restatements. It illustrates the fourth period of economic geography and reveals a sharp break with past economic geographies.

TIEBOUT, CHARLES M. "Location Theory, Empirical Evidence and Economic Evolution," *Papers and Proceedings of the Regional Science Association,* Vol. 3 (1957), 74–86.

Elaborates the argument of Alchian that the economic system adopts those industrial entrepreneurs who choose the correct locations, regardless of how those decisions come to be made.

CHAPTER 3

The Challenges of Population Growth and Change

Modern technological developments in the production and distribution of food and other human needs have made it possible to support large numbers of people even as medical advances have increased the survival rate and longevity of human populations. The result has been a remarkable acceleration in the rate of population growth in recent times.

A number of theories have arisen to help find meaning in the phenomenon of population growth and to aid in predicting its future course. One line of study has pursued the relationship between population growth and economic development. This work promises to help in coping with present and anticipated problems of population growth in the Third World and to provide an understanding of the problems of adjustment that population decline is beginning to raise in some industrialized countries.

Added to the strains of differential rates of population growth is the migration of peoples from one country or region to another. Great numbers of people still migrate from one region to another within countries, and the Third World is experiencing a growing rural-urban movement that is creating new metropolises that dwarf those existing in the older industrialized countries.

Objectives:

- to describe the processes by which populations grow or decline and to examine the theories that have been advanced to explain them
- to outline demographic transition theory, relating population growth and economic development
- to examine the causes and nature of human migrations and to note their social and economic effects upon supplying and receiving regions
- to explain the changing character and the consequences of international and interregional migration

POPULATION AND RESOURCES: THE BASIC VARIABLES

Whatever the approach taken to their subject matter by economic geographers, the most basic variables remain *population* and *resources*. In Chapters 3 and 4 we will deal with the population factor and then, in Chapter 5, we will turn to key resource issues: food supply, energy, industrial materials, and environmental quality.

Above all, people are the prime consideration. They are the consumers of what is produced; the workers who do the production; the investors and managers who organize the transformation of raw materials into finished products and the distribution of these products to their consumers. The circuits of interdependency may be local, as in the world's few remaining relatively isolated self-sustaining communities, but they are more likely today to be regional, national, and increasingly global.

People living in isolated communities, with limited technologies at their disposal, are closely tied to their immediate resource base. At any given level of technology, the resources will have a finite "carrying capacity," and if population approaches that limit, social, economic, and political strains are likely to reduce efficiency and even endanger existence. If population overshoots the carrying capacity, the consequences may be calamitous; famine, sickness, and premature death can still stalk the world.

Carrying capacity is dependent on technology, however. What at one time may be a problem of population pressure may subsequently become one of relative abundance, even in an isolated self-sustaining community, if new technologies become available, such as improved agricultural practices or new crops.

The narrow insecurity that stems from localized dependence on immediate resources may be offset in other ways, too—by increasing specialization and trade, and by widening radii of interdependence, thus providing everyone with access to a broader resource base and the security of more alternatives. Emerging global interdependence and rapid technological change make the question of the earth's ultimate carrying capacity highly speculative and quite contentious, as we saw in Chapter 1.

To be sure, numbers of people *are* important even in the global equation. Canada's labor-short economy produces and exports goods very different from those of Taiwan's labor-surplus economy, and the two countries have followed contrasting paths of economic development. An adequate labor supply is a recognized precondition for locating a new productive enterprise: Managers cannot safely assume that a large establishment will inevitably attract the necessary work force from distant areas. Likewise, regional and national economies may fail to attain their full growth potential if too few people are available to permit adequate exploitation of opportunities. In many parts of the world, however, the opposite problem is more common today; such countries as India, Egypt, and El Salvador find their economic development hindered by overpopulation and by the very rate at which their populations grow.

Yet the question is not limited to mere numbers of people. The particular qualities of human populations—education levels, age structure, the availability of crucial skills, health and longevity, social attitudes—are also important. A major consideration is the unevenness with which human populations and their essential characteristics are distributed in space, not only among countries but also within countries.

Both this chapter and the next deal with several related concerns. The first has to do with the processes of population change. What are the principal components of such change? What influences produce a rise (or fall) in numbers of people and cause them to move from one part of the earth to another? How does population change affect the material welfare of societies?

Based on this discussion of population dynamics, Chapter 4 will analyze the spatial distribution of populations. We shall be asking such questions as these: Where are particular kinds of people concentrated? Why is the spatial pattern so uneven? How do we expect future maps of world population to look?

NATURAL INCREASE

Two dynamic processes are responsible for the growth of populations and for regional variations in numbers of people: These processes are *natural increase* and *migration*. Natural increase results from an excess of births over deaths within a given area. Populations are growing throughout most of the world today, even though the rate of increase has slackened in the industrial countries and zero growth has been attained by a few maturer societies. The unprecedented rate of world population growth in the latter half of this century has aroused general concern, and widening regional disparities in rates of natural increase pose new dangers to world security and human welfare.

2.6 Million Years of Population Growth

Anthropologists believe that human existence on earth extends back at least 600,000 years and possibly more than 2 million years prior to that. Quantitative information before A.D. 1650 must be estimated from circumstantial evidence based on our knowledge of how early human beings gained their livelihood and of the capacity of the land to support primitive economies. We know, for example, that subsistence gathering and hunting and fishing, as practiced by primitive peoples today, require as much as two square miles per person. Even the most rudimentary agriculture, on the other hand, can normally support much denser populations. Supplementing such estimates as these are the scattered records of early communities, particularly those of the Roman Empire, together with other archaeological and historical evidence.

Accelerating Growth

These estimates of early populations, together with data accumulated from modern censuses and projections of current growth trends, provide enough information for us to construct curves of world population growth like that shown in Figure 3.1. The main impressions given by this curve are its persistent upward trend and its accelerating rise in recent times. Note that until the modern era, world population increased slowly, with periods of actual decline. Only within the past 300 years—a tiny fraction of human tenure on earth—has world population grown at consistently high rates.

During the preagricultural era, before 8000 B.C., when only rudimentary tools and weapons were in use, not more than 5 million people inhabited the earth. Numbers increased to between 200 million and 250 mil-

lion by the beginning of the Christian era and possibly as many as 257 million by the end of the first millennium. Within the next 300 years the population of Europe began to rise, and the world total may have reached as much as 384 million by A.D. 1300.

The following century brought a series of plagues that reduced Europe's population so drastically that the population of the world as a whole declined. From 1400 to 1650, however, European civilization enjoyed a rebirth, and European peoples began an energetic conquest of new lands. Although Europe's population likely rose at more than twice the world rate during this period, the indigenous population of the Americas probably declined sharply as a result of the impact of European invasion. Population estimates undertaken in 1650 indicated a world total of about 500 million. Within the next two centuries the total rose even more rapidly, doubling to approximately 1 billion people by 1850. By 1930 the population had reached 2 billion, and by 1970, 3.6 billion. This was a significant event considering that the world contains about 3.6 billion acres of arable land. In that year (1970), therefore, there was one acre of cropland for every person in the world. The amount of land per person has since diminished even further as world population has continued its climb, reaching 5 billion in 1986.

The Growth Curve

Accelerating growth has thus caused a continual steepening of the population curve. In A.D. 1300, the annual rate of growth for the world was perhaps 0.11 or 0.12 percent, but between 1650 and 1750 it was probably nearer −0.3 percent. By the 1930s the annual rate had reached 1.0 percent, and by the 1960s it had risen to 2.1 percent. Another way of looking at this is to note the number of years it takes for the world's population to double. Between 8000 B.C. and A.D. 1650 this doubling required 1500 years; but the next doubling, between 1650 and 1850, took only 200 years. Eighty years later, by 1930, population had doubled again, and it had once again doubled by 1975, a mere 45 years. You will recall the discussion of exponential growth and doubling times in Chapter 1.

If instead of plotting world population on an arithmetic scale as in Figure 3.1 we use a double-logarithmic scale (Figure 3.2), which emphasizes rates of change, we discover a number of details obscured in the previous diagram. We now find that three main surges of population have likely occurred during human history rather than only one, and that each surge was apparently associated with a technological breakthrough that increased the capacity of the world economy to support more people. The developments that

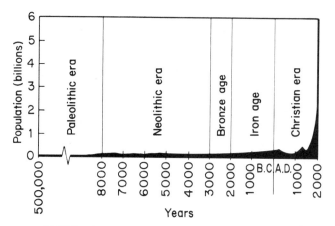

FIGURE 3.1 Growth of world population. Note that, after having gained but little during the thousands of years of early human life, population began a slow rise during Roman times, slipped backward during the Dark Ages, and began to rise again by the fourteenth century, when the bubonic plague brought a sharp but temporary decline. Since then, population growth has accelerated rapidly. [*Source:* After *Population Bulletin,* Vol. 18, No. 1.]

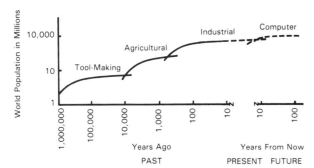

FIGURE 3.2 Technological revolutions and world population growth. Population growth for the past million years plotted on a log-log scale shows a series of surges, each associated with a technological revolution that has increased the earth's capacity to support human life. Some technological optimists have also suggested that widespread adoption of computers may lift productivity sufficiently to support a new surge of population growth in coming decades. [*Source:* Adapted with modifications from Deevey, "The Human Population." Copyright © 1960 by Scientific American, Inc. All rights reserved.]

fostered these bursts of population were the tool-making, agricultural, and industrial revolutions. Figure 3.2 also suggests a fourth technological revolution in the making, a possible result of advances in the use of computers and robotics and in knowledge use in an "information society," which promise quantum increases in productivity in the near future.

As we shall note shortly, population growth rates are not likely to continue indefinitely at recent high levels, despite increases in human efficiency that a computer revolution may bring. The threat to finite world supplies of food and nonrenewable natural resources and the growing effects of environmental pollution would seem to dictate upper limits to the number of people this planet can support. Indeed, for the first time in modern history, the rate of global population growth has apparently begun to slip, falling from 2.1 percent in the early 1960s to 1.7 percent by the end of the 1970s. Confirming this, the UN Fund for Population Activities suggested in a 1981 report that world population could stabilize at 10.5 billion within 30 years, depending upon the success of current national and international campaigns to limit growth.

Thus, the ordinary exponential curve may prove in the end to be less appropriate for describing the current phase of world population development than a logistic curve, one that eventually levels off and perhaps even declines. Precedent for this is seen in the experience of such mature populations as those of Western Europe. More recently, the curve of population growth in the

United States has begun to assume such a shape, as Figure 3.3 shows.

The Growth Mechanism

What are the components of natural increase (or decrease)? The basic ingredients of this process are numbers of births and deaths within a specified time. Whether a population increases or decreases (assuming no migration) depends upon which of these components is greater. A variety of events may influence the relationship between the two.

Birth Rates, Death Rates, and Rates of Natural Increase

Birth rates are commonly expressed in terms of yearly births per thousand people. For example, at the beginning of 1980, the population of the United States was 222,100,000 people, and the number of births in that year was 3,598,000. Dividing the number of births by the population and multiplying by 1000 gives a birth rate of 16.2 for the year. Similarly, we obtain the 1980 death rate for the United States by dividing the number of deaths, 1,986,000 by the population and multiplying by 1000, which gives a rate of 8.9. The rate of natural increase is the difference between the birth and death rates, or 7.3 per 1000. It is customary, however, to express the rate of natural increase as a percentage, that is, so many people per 100 per year, which in this case would be 0.73 percent. This rate for the United States is typical of industrialized countries, but it is well below the rate of 1.7 percent for the world as a whole. Note that the rate of natural increase can be affected by a rise or fall in either the birth rate or death rate.

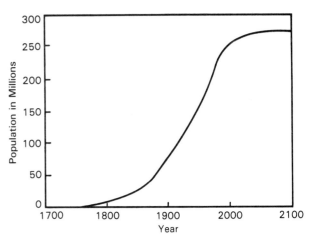

FIGURE 3.3 Logistic growth of the United States population from A.D. 1700 projected to A.D. 2100.

Although these are the most commonly used forms of birth and death rates, meaningful population analyses and predictions require more refined measures. The *crude birth rate* described above is not as revealing as the *fertility rate,* which is the number of births in a given year per thousand women of childbearing age (15 to 49). Thus, fertility rates are more useful for comparing anticipated changes in a young population having a large number of females with those of a more mature population. Fertility rates are also generally higher in rural areas than urban ones, among lower classes than upper classes, and among blue-collar workers than professionals, although these differentials have diminished in more advanced countries as educational levels and the quality of mass communications have risen.

Likewise, the *crude death rate* does not give as much information as the *age-specific death rate,* defined as the number of deaths per thousand in a particular age group. One widely used age-specific death rate is the *infant mortality rate,* or the number of deaths in the first year of life per thousand live births. This is one of the more valuable indices of socioeconomic well-being. Another measure that performs a similar function is *life expectancy,* that is, the average age at death of the inhabitants of a given area.

Events Affecting Population Increase

Although primitive peoples ordinarily have birth rates approaching 50 per thousand, these are generally balanced by similarly high death rates. Consequently, the rates of natural increase remain low in such societies unless some event alters the birth or death rates and tips the balance.

Until modern times the death rate was the more volatile of the two measures. The most dramatic effects on death rates have been those resulting from disease, famine, and war. The bubonic plague (A.D. 1348 to 1350), for example, quickly reduced Europe's population by at least one-fourth, and the London plague of 1665 eliminated one-third to one-half of that city's population. Endemic diseases, such as malaria, have been almost as destructive to certain populations, even in more recent years.

Many of the deaths attributed to disease in some parts of the world, however, are merely the indirect effects of hunger and malnutrition; indeed, the correlation between disease, hunger, and death rates is very high. Periodic famine, caused by floods, droughts, insect plagues, and war, was one of the earliest population controls. Between A.D. 10 and 1846, for example, Britain recorded approximately 200 famines. China had an estimated 1828 famines between 108 B.C. and A.D. 1911, an average of about one per year. Nine to 13 million Chinese died between 1869 and 1876 alone. Nor are famines unknown to this present century. In all, the USSR suffered 5 million to 10 million deaths attributable to famine between 1918 and 1922 and between 1932 and 1934. India lost from 2 million to 4 million in 1943, and similarly large numbers of famine deaths occurred during Bangladesh's struggle for independence from Pakistan and Biafra's attempt to secede from Nigeria.

Receiving more public attention, though, are the wartime deaths resulting directly from the fighting. The two world wars in this century reduced populations throughout Europe. Among some primitive peoples, as in the Indonesian province of West Irian, intertribal wars have been a major and customary cause of death.

Famines, epidemics, and war also affect birth rates, by reducing the ability to conceive and by disrupting normal family life; however, the voluntary means of reducing births have had the most pervasive and prolonged effects upon population growth. Although birth control has been the most effective means of population control in modern times, even early societies limited population growth by such means as infanticide, sexual taboos, killing the sick and aged, and marriage restrictions. Abortion has been illegal in most twentieth-century industrialized countries—Japan and Scandinavia have been the most notable exceptions—but these restrictions are easing. Contraception, an ancient practice mentioned in the Bible, is the most common way of preventing births. The extent to which birth control is practiced, as well as the choice of methods, is influenced by cost and the availability of information, within a framework of religions, customs, attitudes, technological development, and degree of urbanization.

Population Theory

The steeply rising curve of world population shows clearly that the balance between births and deaths has been seriously disturbed in recent times. This increasingly urgent problem has given rise to a body of population theory, the most familiar being that of Thomas Malthus. The eighteenth century had been a period of optimism concerning the perfectibility of humankind, combined with the view that a large population is a source of national strength. By the end of that century, however, a reaction had taken place. The Industrial Revolution in Britain had revealed the evils of the factory system, economic growth had brought with it a rapid increase in population, and the appearance of bad times soon caused these numbers to seem excessive. A period of poor harvests, high food prices, and much human misery provided the setting for Malthus's pessimistic statement of 1798.

Malthus

Thomas R. Malthus was an English clergyman, historian, and economist, born in 1766 to the English landed gentry and educated at Cambridge. In his famous *Essay on the Principle of Population,* intended originally as an answer to the Utopians, he strongly expressed the view that it is not desirable for a population to expand indefinitely without the assurance that the means for supporting that population can keep pace. Malthus concluded that population has a natural tendency to increase rapidly as long as food, or "subsistence," is available. If unchecked, population will go on doubling itself every 25 years, that is, it will increase at a "geometric ratio" (2, 4, 8, 16, 32, etc.). At the same time, however, even under the most favorable circumstances, the food supply cannot increase faster than at an "arithmetic ratio" (3, 6, 9, 12, 15, etc.). The number of people to be fed will thus quickly overtake and exceed the food supply.

Malthus believed that the *ultimate* check to population growth, as in the case of the lower animals, is exhaustion of the food supply at the point when the two growth curves cross. This ultimate check to population growth would, of course, cause death from starvation, but more usually either of two kinds of *immediate* checks intervenes. One is the *preventative* check, resulting from the ability of human beings to recognize the consequences of their behavior. This preventative check Malthus termed "moral restraint," by which he, being a good churchman, did not mean birth control. To Malthus, moral restraint meant postponement of marriage, "accompanied by strictly moral behaviour"—the purpose being to avoid having children before the parents are able to support them. The second intervening influence is the *positive* check, "all of those causes which tend in any way prematurely to shorten the duration of human life." These include "vice"—those misfortunes we bring upon ourselves, such as war and the various consequences of immoral behavior—and "misery"—unavoidable products of the laws of nature, especially plagues and famines. Note that the positive checks act to limit population growth by raising death rates, whereas the preventative checks accomplish this same result by reducing birth rates.

According to Malthus, the lowest stratum of society is most affected by positive checks. In mature societies these forces cause the population to rise and fall in a cyclical fashion. In times of prosperity the population increases, but this in turn causes the price of labor to fall and the cost of living to rise. The ensuing hard times bring the Malthusian checks into play, and the population decreases until once again the labor force is in balance with job opportunities. Prosperity then re-

turns, bringing with it complacency and a repetition of the population growth cycle. Malthus indicated that this cycle is not confined to advanced lands but is seen even in tribal societies, where populations are subjected to a whole range of positive checks upon reaching the limits of subsistence.

Malthus saw no lasting way out of this dilemma through charity or emigration, which can bring only temporary relief from population pressure. His proposed solution was the general adoption of "moral restraint," that is, postponement of marriage, together with mass education (including the teaching of population principles) and increased respect and personal liberty for single women.

Malthus was enormously influential. His basic ideas had a pervasive effect not only on philosophical, economic, social, and political thought but also on the physical sciences, legislation, and popular education. Out of his work grew a school of population study that, with modifications, persists today.

Later in the nineteenth century Malthus's population theory fell into disfavor as the populations of Western European countries and their colonies experienced accelerated growth while enjoying unprecedented improvements in their standards of living. This appeared to refute Malthus, who had failed to anticipate the important effects of the social, economic, and technological changes then taking place. Yet it has since become apparent that Malthus's perspective held some validity for the long run: Today, human populations do indeed threaten to increase to that point beyond which the world's resources can no longer support them.

Other Population Theories

As Malthus's predictions failed to be realized in Western Europe, other theorists attempted to correct the deficiencies in the Malthusian thesis. Like Malthus, many early theorists sought "natural laws" of population growth, but they tended to look more to the newly emerging social sciences for these laws. Michael Sadler, for example, maintained that as population densities increase, fertility rates will drop. Herbert Spencer suggested that the increasing complexity of modern life would divert human energies from procreation and cause a reduction in the capacity to produce children. And, as recently as 1929, Corrado Gini claimed that population growth is directly related to the rise and fall of nations.

Some nineteenth-century writers proposed population theories to substantiate their political and social ideas. For example, Karl Marx, who misinterpreted Malthus's writings, insisted that it was not overpopulation that produced poverty and hardship, but rather the failure of the economic system. Henry George maintained that his "single tax" would provide land for everyone who needed food and that this would increase agricultural productivity and expand the food supply indefinitely.

A more modern theorist, Alexander Carr-Saunders, suggested that the rate of population growth was determined by human perception of the densities that are economically desirable for a particular way of life. Although he agreed with Malthus's assessment of the growth trends of population and food supply, he believed that other checks operate to limit population. Contemporary theorists disclaim any "natural law" of population growth but attribute differences in birth and death rates to social, cultural, economic, and physical conditions.

Demographic Transition

As we observed earlier, the rapid growth of Europe's population confirmed Malthus's predictions, but the remarkable increase in European prosperity did not. Moreover, he did not anticipate the effects that development might have on those forces determining population size. Today we have come to recognize the close interrelationship between the processes of development or "modernization" on the one hand and those of population growth on the other.

The European Experience

The demographic history of modern Europe illustrates some of these relationships. Prior to the Industrial Revolution, when death rates and birth rates were very high, Europe's population was fairly stable. Urban death rates were especially high, and city growth was made possible only by heavy in-migration. The unwholesome urban conditions responsible for such mortality rates resemble those of many cities in less-developed countries today: uncertain food supply, contaminated water, inadequate housing, lack of sewage disposal, and poor medical service.

The Industrial Revolution that began in Britain during the second half of the eighteenth century had profound effects on both death and birth rates in Western Europe. The application of inanimate energy to mining and manufacturing greatly increased total and per capita output of goods. The rising incomes that resulted from greater production made possible the purchase of food in larger quantities and of higher quality. Incomes also provided financial support for better sanitary practices and for medical research. Although these improvements in food supply and public health evolved gradually, their cumulative effect was to reduce death

rates substantially and to make cities capable of sustaining their populations. Much of the total rise in population during the succeeding two centuries since the Industrial Revolution can be attributed to improved conditions in the cities.

Related to these urban and industrial developments, and essential to them, was the accompanying revolution in agriculture. Previously, British agriculture had consisted mainly of subsistence farms producing very little surplus for cash sale. Even the richest agricultural regions were unable to grow sufficient food to support more than 15 percent to 20 percent of their populations in urban activities, such as manufacturing, commerce, and government. Near the end of the eighteenth century, however, farmers began to breed higher-quality livestock, introduce new high-yielding crops, and develop farm techniques that increased the output of traditional commodities. Through the "enclosure movement," medieval open fields and common lands were reallocated into compact and individually owned farmsteads, and the many landless laborers who were displaced made their way to the growing cities. Thus, as the Industrial Revolution made larger urban concentrations necessary, new developments in agriculture supplied the additional food required to support a growing nonfarm population, and reorganization of the agricultural landscape forced surplus farm workers into the growing urban labor force.

Important innovations in transportation took place at the same time as these industrial and agricultural developments. The construction of roads, canals, and railways, and the invention of new types of vehicles, greatly expanded the range of distribution and collection. No longer was it necessary for communities, or even countries, to be self-sufficient in raw materials and foodstuffs. Local crop failures thus became far less likely to cause hunger and famine among European peoples. Not only goods but also people and ideas circulated freely over greater distances, thereby accelerating the rate of scientific discoveries, including those related to health.

As these events combined to bring about a steady decline in death rates, birth rates were also dropping, although at a slower rate. The Industrial Revolution influenced birth rates in ways not anticipated by Malthus. It did this first of all by concentrating people into towns and cities, where they no longer had the need for large families that they once had on the farm. At the same time, the decline in infant mortality removed an important incentive for large numbers of births. And as ideas of the French Enlightenment spread over Europe, more time was devoted to education and age at marriage rose. With effective changes in attitude toward family size, the practice of contraception spread. Beginning among upper-income groups in urbanized areas, contraception diffused to lower levels of society and into rural areas. Malthus could not have foreseen this, and he would not have approved of it if he had.

The development of contraception did not exert its full force until this present century, however. Most of the nineteenth-century reductions in birth rates came from increased age of marriage. Europe was only able to escape what might have been excessive population pressures because its surplus peoples migrated in large numbers to newly discovered lands in both the Western and Southern Hemispheres. These migrants in turn brought rich virgin lands into cultivation and shipped an ever-increasing supply of grain and other commodities back to the markets of their former homelands. In this century, the population of Western Europe has stabilized, as new low death rates and birth rates have come into balance. As the same demographic trends have diffused throughout the lands settled by Europeans, the advanced countries seem to have eluded the Malthusian trap. The real worry today is for the less-developed countries, where rapidly growing populations threaten to fulfill Malthus's gloomy prophesy.

Population Growth in the Less-Developed World

Some of the densely settled lands of eastern and southern Asia, especially China and India, likely reached their optimum population densities as agriculturally based peasant societies centuries ago. The Chinese population apparently fluctuated at a high level over an extended period, despite war, plague, and famine. Evidently it followed a cyclical pattern like that described by Malthus, rising in good times and falling in bad times. This equilibrium was disturbed by the coming of European colonial control, which brought a new burst of population growth in such lands as Indonesia and India. Colonial administrations reduced internecine fighting among native populations and introduced economic improvements, causing death rates to fall below persistently high birth rates.

Since World War II, however, much of the less-developed world has experienced a population crisis as improved public health delivery and better food distribution brought a rapid drop in mortality rates. Unlike the gradual reduction of death rates in today's developed countries, which had to await a whole series of medical advances over a period of two centuries, today's less-developed countries were able to import low-cost, highly effective death-control measures that were ready-made. Many primitive villages otherwise untouched by modernization have benefited from sophisticated medical technology. So successful have these

programs been that crude death rates in the less-developed world as a whole had fallen to only 14 per thousand in 1980, and in several Third World countries the crude death rates have dropped well below the rate of 9 per thousand prevailing in the developed world. In Costa Rica, which after years of runaway population growth has an unusually young population, the 1983 crude death rate was only 4.0.

Meanwhile, birth rates remain high throughout most of the Third World. As Figure 3.4 shows, crude birth rates exceeding 40 per thousand are typical of countries at the lower levels of development. Some African countries, Zambia and Kenya, for example, have crude birth rates estimated at 50 per thousand or more. Most of the Middle East and much of Africa and Latin America have rates of natural increase exceeding 3 percent. Nicaragua's population is currently growing 3.9 percent each year. The resulting "population explosion" in the Third World will add another billion people to the world total during the final decade of this century. Unlike the European colonial powers of the previous century, the less-developed countries of today cannot ship their surplus populations to new lands in other continents, although some, such as Indonesia, are attempting to send people from their overpopulated "heartlands" into lightly populated outlying regions. Growth rates are therefore exceedingly high—at least 2 percent per annum for the less-developed world as a whole and much higher in many regions. Meanwhile, rates of natural increase among the advanced countries have fallen below 1 percent, and several populations, notably those of Sweden and West Germany, have ceased to grow at all. Even in their periods of most rapid growth, during the nineteenth century, the advanced countries of today never attained rates of population increase approaching present rates in the Third World.

The already-crowded lands of East Asia and West Africa have felt the most immediate and obvious impacts of this growth, but the less densely populated Latin American countries also are seriously affected. Having achieved their independence from European powers a century or more earlier, they were free to begin the process of reducing their death rates sooner and have now progressed further in this respect.

One important consequence of high growth rates is a young age distribution. Figure 3.5 compares the age structure of a rapidly growing population, Costa Rica, with that of a mature population, Sweden. In Costa Rica, 38 percent of the population is below the age of 15, as opposed to only 19 percent in Sweden. Typical of the Middle East, Syria has 48 percent of its population in this dependent-age group, and the African countries of Botswana and Zimbabwe have more than 50 percent. The percentage of children under 15 is sim-

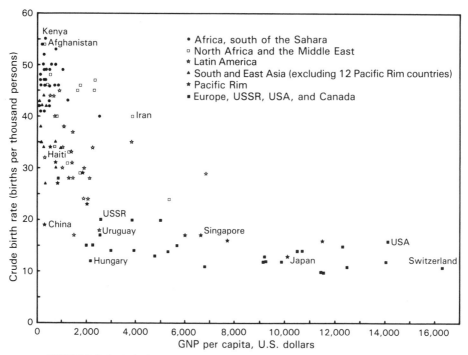

FIGURE 3.4 Relationship between birth rates and per capita GNP, 1983. Countries at the lowest levels of development tend to have the highest birth rates. Tightly clustered at the upper left of the diagram are a large number of African, Middle Eastern, and South Asian countries. When development is measured by per capita GNP, as in this illustration, the nonindustrialized oil-exporting countries such as Iran, Venezuela, and Trinidad appear as anomalies. The most extreme cases of this type—Islamic states on the Persian Gulf—have been omitted here. Note that the rapidly industrializing Pacific rim countries (see Chapter 14) have now achieved low birth rates, as has China. [*Source:* Data from World Bank, *World Development Report 1985* (New York: Oxford University Press, 1985).]

ilarly high throughout Central America and the Caribbean islands.

Transition Theory

This international comparison of demographic characteristics suggests that countries undergo a *demographic transition* as they rise in the scale of development. The study of this process has given birth to a *transition theory,* which serves as a tool for predicting future population changes of developing countries and offers a means for anticipating the problems that accompany these changes. According to this theory, a country passes through three demographic phases as it develops (see Figure 3.6).

In the first phase the population remains fairly stable. It is kept in equilibrium by the combination of a high birth rate and a similarly high, but fluctuating, death rate. This describes the demography of societies as diverse as preindustrial Europe, premodern China,

and contemporary primitive peoples in the rain forests of the Amazon and Congo basins.

When the development process commences, the country enters the second phase. As diets and health improve, the death rate drops; but the birth rate remains high throughout the earlier stages of the development process before it too begins to decline. During Phase II, therefore, the two curves diverge, producing a *demographic gap*. This is the period of rapid population growth, or "population explosion." Much of Latin America and the Middle East and parts of Africa and southern and eastern Asia are at this point. Subsequent maturing of the economy brings urbanization, higher per capita incomes, and various social changes, especially better-educated women, all of which favor smaller families. The accompanying changes in social attitudes therefore act to reduce the birth rate during the latter part of Phase II.

When at last the birth rate has fallen to a level approximating that of the already-low death rate, Phase

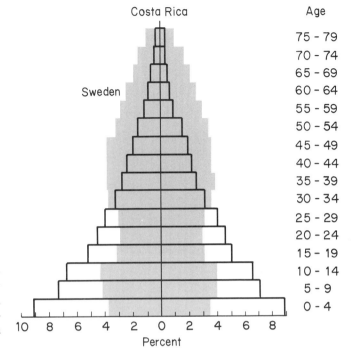

FIGURE 3.5 Comparison of age structures of Costa Rica and Sweden. Costa Rica's population, with large numbers in the dependent age groups, is typical of newly developing countries having high birth rates and low death rates. Sweden's population structure is representative of more-developed countries, whose death rates and birth rates are both low.

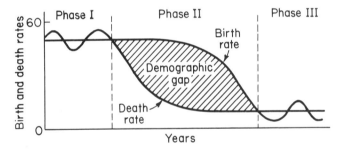

FIGURE 3.6 Transition theory. At the beginning of a country's development the death rate tends to drop quickly, whereas the birth rate remains high for an extended period before it too begins to decline. The divergence of these two rates creates a demographic gap, or "population explosion," which continues until equilibrium is finally reestablished during the later stages of development.

III has been reached. Note that in this final phase it is the birth rate that fluctuates about some mean, a response mainly to rises and falls in the business cycle. When times are good, families are more likely to contemplate an additional child. The countries of Western Europe, Anglo-America, and Oceania, as well as Japan, have attained this equilibrium.

Transition theory actually represents a generalization of the Western European experience. Recent events, however, have shown that the history of today's industrialized nations offers a less-than-perfect model

for predicting demographic change in today's less-developed countries. For one thing, current fertility rates in less-developed countries are much higher than they were in premodern Europe. This is a result of the religious beliefs, marriage customs, land tenure arrangements, and other cultural factors prevailing in much of the Third World. People will eagerly accept innovations that improve their health and increase their longevity, but they do not easily relinquish traditional attitudes toward marriage and the home.

Illustrating this problem, Figure 3.7a contrasts the demographic changes now taking place in Sri Lanka (formerly Ceylon) with those experienced previously by Sweden. Figure 3.7b similarly contrasts the experiences of the developed countries of the world as a group, with the developing countries as a group. After a century and a half of declining birth and death rates, Sweden has now reached the point of "zero population growth," where it will likely remain for the foreseeable future. Although Sri Lanka's demographic transition began only a few decades ago, it is progressing far more rapidly than Sweden's. Note that at the start of this process Sri Lanka's birth and death rates were both much higher than Sweden's had been and that the death rate has dropped more steeply, actually falling below that of Sweden because of Sri Lanka's very young population. The resulting population bulge will continue well into the next century.

Adding to the difficulties of applying transition theory to contemporary conditions is the fact that the largest of the less-developed lands, especially India and

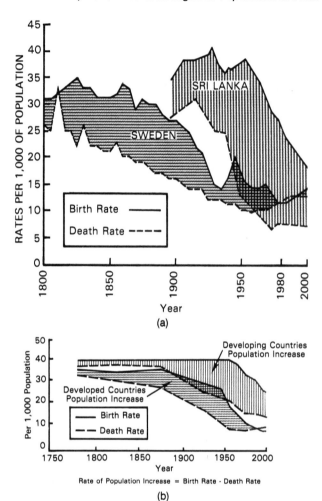

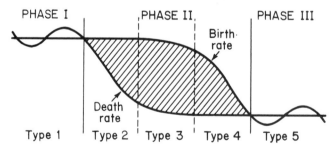

FIGURE 3.7 (a) Contrast between demographic transitions in Sri Lanka and Sweden. Sweden's transition extended over nearly two centuries and has now concluded with birth and death rates at a low equilibrium. Sri Lanka's transition began a century later and is proceeding rapidly. Note that Sri Lanka's death rate has declined steeply and is now actually lower than Sweden's because of Sri Lanka's much younger population. Sri Lanka's birth rate is still far higher than its death rate, resulting in continued rapid population growth. [*Source:* From Halfdan Mahler, "People," *Scientific American,* Vol. 243, No. 3 (September 1980), pp. 66–77. Copyright © 1980 by Scientific American, Inc. All rights reserved.] (b) The demographic transition in today's developed and developing countries compared. [*Source:* World Bank, *World Development Report 1982* (New York: Oxford University Press, 1982), p. 26.]

China, are more densely populated than was preindustrial Europe. A further complication is the differing demographic histories of some developed countries; Germany, for example, reached population equilibrium much later than did France.

Despite these problems, the central features of the transition theory remain valid. First, the death rate always begins its decline before that of the birth rate, except perhaps in totalitarian countries where individual choice is restricted. Second, changes in the death rate are the main determinant of population size in less-developed lands, but fluctuations of the birth rate are the principal determinant in advanced societies.

A Demographic Classification of Countries

Most population forecasts and regional analyses now make use of transition theory in some manner. The Population Division of the United Nations employs a classification system that subdivides the second phase of demographic transition into three parts. It is important to know whether a country is just entering this critical period of rapid population expansion and thus has the major part of its population growth ahead of it, whether it is in the middle or most explosive part of the phase, or if it is about to emerge from this part of the cycle.

The diagram in Figure 3.8 illustrates this application of transition theory, and Figure 3.9 shows how the countries of the world fit into the scheme. The shaded portion of the diagram (Figure 3.8), which indicates the dimensions of the demographic gap, has been subdivided into three subcategories designated with arabic numerals. Five population growth types result. Type 1 countries have high birth rates and high, fluctuating death rates, producing stable populations with growth rates generally under 1 percent. Although several densely populated underdeveloped countries had these characteristics at an earlier time, the combination is now rare. Most former Type 1 countries have now at least begun their demographic transitions.

The transition process commences with the Type 2 countries, which have high birth rates and high but declining death rates. The two curves are beginning to diverge (Figure 3.8), indicating the start of the expan-

FIGURE 3.8 United Nations' classification of countries according to population growth types. Phases I, II, and III correspond to the major stages of demographic transition, whereas Types 1 through 5 refer to classes of countries according to their demographic characteristics.

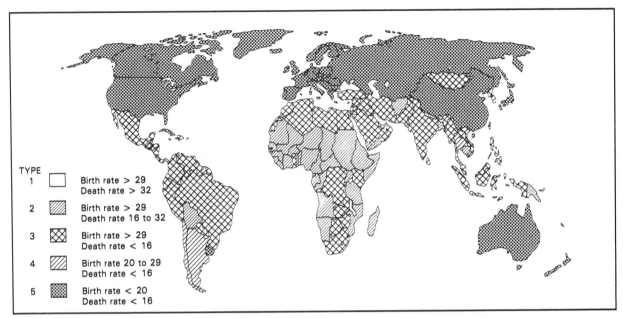

TYPE		
1		Birth rate > 29 Death rate > 32
2		Birth rate > 29 Death rate 16 to 32
3		Birth rate > 29 Death rate < 16
4		Birth rate 20 to 29 Death rate < 16
5		Birth rate < 20 Death rate < 16

FIGURE 3.9 World map of population growth types. During the past decade some of the more populous countries of Africa and South Asia have entered the most explosive phase of the demographic transition, and a number of others are approaching that condition. On the other hand, much of East Asia has now achieved population stability (Type 5), notably China, the world's largest nation. Type 1 appears in the legend for the sake of completeness only; the last countries falling in this category have now begun their demographic transitions. [*Source:* Based upon data from *United Nations Demographic Yearbook 1983* (New York: United Nations, 1985).]

sionary Phase II of the demographic transition. Population growth is well over 1 percent and climbing. Much of South Asia is at this stage, as are several parts of Africa.

Type 3 countries, with their high birth rates and fairly low death rates, are in the most explosive part of Phase II. This combination gives exceedingly high growth rates, often between 3 percent and 4 percent per year. Mexico, most of Central America and the Caribbean, parts of northern South America, and most of North Africa and the Middle East have these characteristics. Several African countries south of the Sahara, which were Type 2 countries a decade ago, have now firmly entered this period of most rapid growth.

The distinguishing marks of Type 4 countries are a declining birth rate and a fairly low death rate. The result is a slackening in their growth rates, which brings them closer to population equilibrium. The southernmost countries of South America—Argentina, Uruguay, and Chile—are in this category, along with Spain. Costa Rica and Egypt, two countries that only recently were in the high-growth class, have begun to bring their birth rates under control and have therefore now become Type 4 countries.

With their low but fluctuating birth rates and low death rates, Type 5 countries are in the final phase of the demographic transition. Growth rates are usually not more than 1 percent, and in many countries they are much less. All of the world's industrialized countries belong to this group, and several in Northern and Western Europe are at or near zero population growth.

Consequences of Population Growth and Decline

The relationship between population growth and food supply was Malthus's chief concern, and this subject continues to preoccupy most writers on population today. Vital as the question of feeding an expanding world population may be, however, this is by no means the only problem resulting from population increase. As most Third World countries have discovered, rapid population growth creates many other economic, social, political, and environmental problems that complicate the developmental process. Meanwhile, some mature industrial societies are having to adjust to another kind of demographic change—zero population growth, or even decline.

Problems of a Growing Population

All too frequently a less-developed country finds its developmental gains wiped out by overly rapid population growth. Arriving at the end of the year with increased output, it discovers that these additional goods must be divided among a still larger number of people. The problem of diminishing per capita food supplies is one of the most worrisome effects of excessive population growth, not only because of humanitarian concerns but also because of its political and economic consequences.

Figure 3.10 shows that many of the less-developed countries are finding it difficult to supply the daily nutritional needs of their people. The diagram suggests a fairly close relationship between daily per capita food energy (calories) and level of development (measured by per capita *gross domestic product,* GDP). Even so, the average Third World family spends a larger proportion of its income on food than does the typical family in advanced societies. Referred to as *Engel's law,* this relationship is illustrated by the case of Ghana, where half of family income goes for food, or Honduras, where a family spends more than two-fifths of its income in this manner. By contrast, a Danish family spends less than one-fourth of its income on food, and a Canadian family spends about one-fifth.

Not only do most people in the less-developed world consume less food per day but they are also more likely to suffer from dietary deficiencies. The poorer the population, the more dependent the people are upon starchy foods, such as grains and root crops. The es-

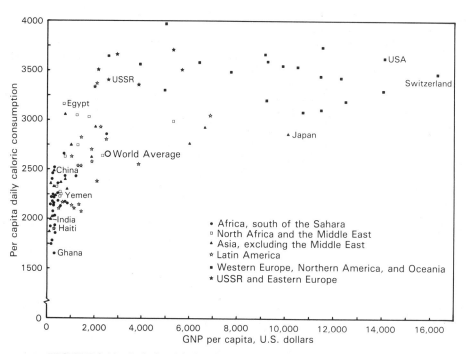

FIGURE 3.10 Relationship between per capita calorie consumption and level of development. This diagram lends support to Engel's law, which says that poor families allocate larger proportions of their incomes to food than do richer ones. Note that average food consumption rises with per capita GNP only up to a certain point, after which it rises but little. In many parts of the world people are eating better today than they did a decade ago. The green revolution has improved food supplies in parts of Asia, notably China and Pakistan, as well as in some Latin American countries. Several newly industrializing countries are also enjoying more food consumption, for example, Turkey, Egypt, and some Pacific rim lands. Much of Africa south of the Sahara, however, has slipped backward, and so have the poorest countries of South Asia. Cultural differences help to explain variations among countries at similar levels of development. [*Sources:* Based upon data from *FAO Production Yearbook 1984* (Rome: Food and Agriculture Organization of the United Nations, 1985); and World Bank, *World Development Report 1985* (New York: Oxford University Press, 1985).]

sential "protective" foods, which are most costly, are generally lacking in the diets of the poorest peoples, as shown by the relationship between GDP and consumption of proteins (Figure 3.11), and especially animal proteins (Figure 3.12). These associations between diet and development imply that a rise in per capita income should bring a drop in the percentage of income spent on food, an increase in the total amount consumed (until some optimal level is reached), and a shift from cheaper starches to more expensive and nutritious foods, especially animal products ("indirect calories").

Despite the difficulties of feeding their growing populations, most underdeveloped countries employ a majority of their labor forces in agriculture (Figure 3.13). Much of this agriculture is of an unproductive sort. Consider the plight of Asian or African peasants on their plots of exhausted land, which are so tiny that

they must be devoted almost entirely to grains and other foods for direct human consumption. In their poverty these peasant farmers are caught up in a vicious circle. Unable to afford machinery, fertilizer, or improved seeds, they can only apply increased quantities of human labor in their efforts to raise levels of output. This provides a motivation to have large families, which in turn means more mouths to feed. High rates of population growth in less-developed countries therefore tend both to reduce the quantity and quality of per capita food consumption and to affect adversely the conditions for producing that food.

In addition to its impact on food supply, rapid population growth causes economic stress. Inflation, once a localized problem affecting only individual countries, has now become a global phenomenon. Business cycles in the industrial world have become increasingly

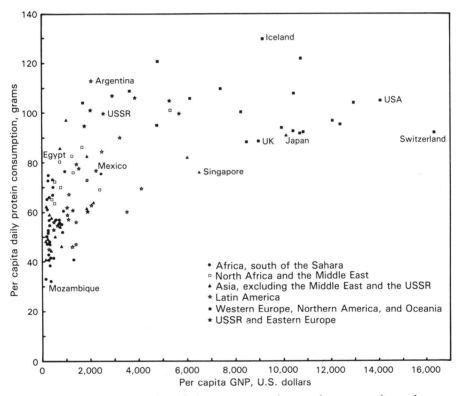

FIGURE 3.11 Relationship between per capita protein consumption and level of development. Not only are larger quantities of food available in many parts of the world (see Figure 3.10), but diets are improving in nutritional quality. Especially encouraging is the rising protein consumption in East Asia, including China, and in North Africa and the Middle East. A different trend has emerged, however, in the desperately poor countries of Africa south of the Sahara, where prolonged drought and overpopulation have caused already-meager diets to decline in quality as well as quantity. [*Sources:* Data from *FAO Production Yearbook 1984* (Rome: Food and Agriculture Organization of the United Nations, 1985); and World Bank, *World Development Report 1985* (New York: Oxford University Press, 1985).]

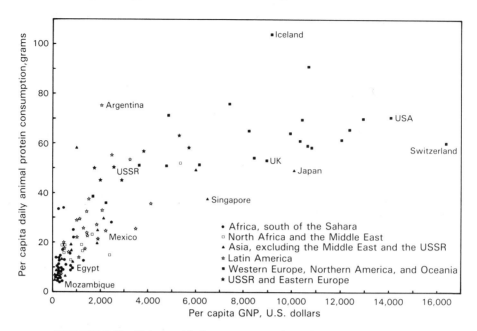

FIGURE 3.12 Relationship between per capita animal protein consumption and level of development. Consumption of animal proteins offers a better measure of nutritional quality than does the total amount of protein in the diet (Figure 3.11). Availability of the higher-quality proteins found in meat, fish, and milk products gives a different view of nutrition in several major world areas. Some of the world's poorest populations derive most of their protein from vegetable sources of inadequate nutritional value. This is true of the impoverished countries of Africa and South Asia shown tightly clustered in the lower left-hand corner of the above diagram. Many Latin Americans also rely upon vegetable sources for much of their protein (beef-producing Argentina is an exception). Most Western Europeans have increased their consumption of animal proteins, notably the Mediterranean peoples. An interesting case is Iceland, where fishing is the mainstay of the economy and supplies a principal item of diet. Total protein supplies have risen in the USSR and Eastern Europe, but animal-protein consumption has failed to keep pace owing to lagging farm economies. [*Sources:* Data from *FAO Production Yearbook 1984* (Rome: Food and Agriculture Organization of the United Nations, 1985); and World Bank, *World Development Report 1985* (New York: Oxford University Press, 1985).]

synchronized, creating a simultaneous growth in demand for finite supplies of resources and pushing up world prices. As the most accessible and highest-quality resources are used up, it becomes necessary to turn to less-productive farmlands, grazing lands, fisheries, and forests, and to mineral deposits that are more remote and of poorer quality. The resulting decline in output for each additional new unit of input—referred to as the *law of diminishing returns* (to be discussed in Chapter 9)—adds further upward pressure on global commodity prices. Growing scarcity provides opportunities for the creation of cartels, such as the Organization of Petroleum Exporting Countries (OPEC), which are able to set artificially high prices for the commodities over which they share effective oligopolistic control. Mean-

while, overexploitation of physical resources brings environmental deterioration.

Population growth underlies the worsening global problem of unemployment. In the industrialized lands, young people born during the "baby boom" era of the 1950s and 1960s are now entering the labor force more rapidly than jobs can be found for them; the result is abnormally high levels of unemployment among those age groups. The problem is far worse, however, in the less-developed countries, where high birth rates are flooding labor markets with millions of new workers. In these mainly agricultural nations, available farm land quickly becomes overcrowded, and fledgling industries cannot generate manufacturing employment rapidly enough to absorb the overspill from the countryside.

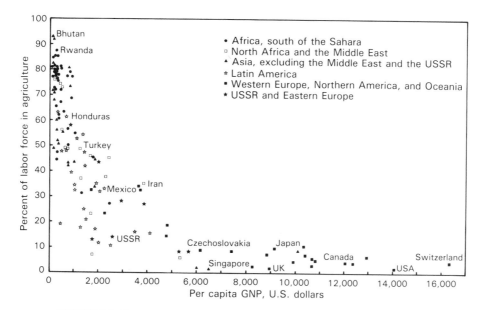

FIGURE 3.13 Relationship between percent of labor force in agriculture and level of development. In the poorest, hungriest countries, agriculture is usually the largest employer, as shown here by the concentration of low-income African and South Asian countries in the upper left of the diagram. Farming is also the leading occupation in another food-deficit region, North Africa and the Middle East. Paradoxically, most of the principal exporters of agricultural commodities—such as Canada, the United States, Australia, and Argentina—have relatively few farm workers. [*Sources:* Data from *FAO Production Yearbook 1984* (Rome: Food and Agriculture Organization of the United Nations, 1985); and World Bank, *World Development Report 1985* (New York: Oxford University Press, 1985).]

The result is high unemployment rates, which would be even greater if they included all the *underemployed.* These are the surplus workers who remain on the family farms even though their labor is not really needed there. Thus India, already burdened with massive unemployment and underemployment, has little hope of finding sufficient work for the more than 5 million young people entering the labor force each year. In neighboring Bangladesh at least one-third of the work force is unemployed.

Other related economic and social ills result from overly rapid population growth. With millions of jobseekers pouring into their cities each year, many Third World countries are wrestling with a host of severe urban problems: overcrowding, inadequate housing, and lack of sanitation and health services, in addition to severe unemployment.

A further burden for developing countries with high birth rates is the large number of people in the dependent ages. With one-third to one-half of their people under the age of 15, these countries find it exceedingly difficult to provide the necessary extra services, especially education. So many children are reaching school age each year that schools cannot be built or staffed fast enough to accommodate them. Compulsory education laws are thus of little practical significance, and literacy rates are in some cases actually falling. This, of course, diminishes the quality of labor forces.

Thus, plagued by excessive population growth, many less-developed countries are trapped in a vicious circle of poverty, malnutrition, and disease. Despite the relative improvements in public health delivery that have reduced death rates and therefore fueled the very population expansion that retards their development efforts, the countries of the Third World still lag behind the industrialized nations in quality of health care. Indeed, such indicators of health as life expectancy are strongly correlated with level of development, which is measured by GNP (see Figure 3.14). A direct link exists between birth rates and the health of women and children: After repeated pregnancies, mothers become increasingly debilitated and vulnerable to death in childbirth, and the mortality rates of their infants rise.

Finally, rapid population growth may have adverse political consequences. The many economic and social problems of rapidly growing populations are im-

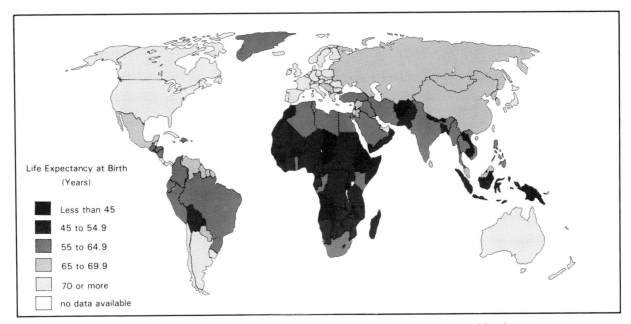

FIGURE 3.14   Life expectancy at birth. As a measure of the general level of health in a population, life expectancy ranges from less than 45 years in some poorer countries to more than 70 years in the richer ones. Note that the areas ranking lowest on this scale—Africa south of the Sahara and parts of South Asia—also appear in Figure 3.12 as the poorest nourished. [*Source:* Data from World Bank, *World Development Report 1985* (New York: Oxford University Press, 1985).]

portant sources of internal political instability in many developing countries. Declining domestic farm output, for instance, can undermine the stability of governments, as shortages and rising prices bring popular unrest. Food riots in Egypt during the 1970s and later in Poland underscored the political dangers of an inadequate food supply. Many countries are forced to divert ever-larger amounts of scarce foreign exchange from development needs to pay for food imports. At the same time, differential rates of population growth among countries often produce international political strains. If, for example, the population of one country is increasing faster than the populations of its neighbors, this may arouse fears that the overcrowded country may attempt to seize adjacent lands to relieve internal population pressures. The suspicious attitude toward Iran held by other Persian Gulf countries, whose populations are much smaller, stems partly from this source; Indochina has endured centuries of warfare between overpopulated neighbors contending for the rice-basket areas of the Mekong delta. History offers innumerable examples of wars of conquest prompted by the desire on the part of one country for relief from overcrowding.

Problems of Declining Populations

In the industrialized countries of Western Europe and North America, uneasiness is arising over an op-posite demographic trend—population decrease. Despite some disagreement about the precise consequences of population decline, it is generally conceded that these consequences are pervasive. The demographic effects are the most obvious. Population growth depends not only upon birth rates but also upon the number of women reaching childbearing age. Hence, until recently, the arrival of postwar babies into this age group has ensured a substantial growth in population, despite a continuing decline in birth rates. Even though family size in the United States has now dropped to a two-child average, which is below the replacement level, births will exceed deaths for the rest of the century. Meanwhile, the age structure of the United States population has begun to change, affecting the mix of goods and services demanded. Smaller and smaller numbers of children are entering the schools, whereas the proportion of the population aged 65 and above is growing. In these trends the United States is following on the heels of Western Europe, where some countries have already arrived at the point of zero population growth.

A declining population is an aging population. Any decrease in death rates among older age groups will further augment the increasing proportion of senior citizens that results from falling birth rates. As this dependent population grows, the society encounters a new set of problems. Figure 3.15 illustrates the contrasting

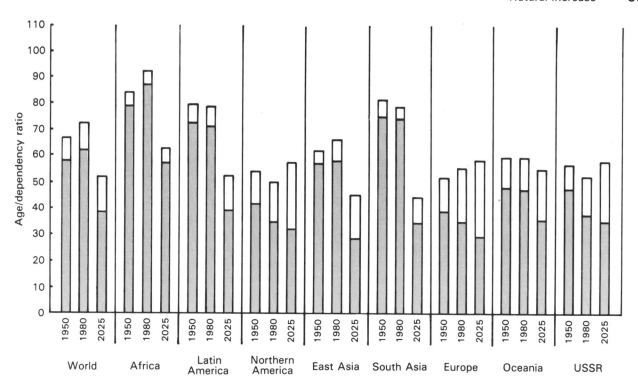

FIGURE 3.15 Age-dependency ratios for the world and for major regions, 1950, 1980, and 2025 (UN medium-variant projection). The age-dependency ratio is defined as the ratio of the combined child population less than 15 years of age and adult population 65 years or more, to the population of intermediate age, per 100. This measure indicates the relative number of dependents that persons in the economically active age groups must support in each of the regions shown. The shaded portion of each bar represents the dependency ratio for the under-15 age group and the white portion the ratio for the 65-and-over group. In the least-developed areas, the economically active population must support relatively large numbers of dependent children; in the most-developed areas, workers must provide for large numbers of retirees. [*Source:* Based upon *World Population Prospects: Estimates and Projections as Assessed in 1982* (New York: United Nations, 1983).]

nature of dependency in the developed regions, with their mature, stable populations, and the less-developed areas, whose populations are still very young. The dependency ratios (the combined child population under 15 and adult population 65 or more, expressed as a relationship to the number in the intermediate years) show that a comparatively small number of Africans and Latin Americans in the economically active ages of 16 to 64 must support large numbers of children but few elderly persons. In Europe and North America (Canada and the United States) a mainly middle-aged work force must provide for a large and increasing number of retirees 65 years and older. Note also that if population projections prove correct, the currently heavy burden of dependency in the Third World will diminish as population growth comes under control, especially in East Asia.

One effect of the aging of a population is to increase the burden of providing adequate national pension programs, as shown by the recent strains that have emerged in the U.S. social security system. A response to the longer-term problem of declining numbers of active workers has been to reverse a trend toward earlier retirement; in the United States, mandatory retirement has shifted from age 65 to age 70, and in many circumstances it has been eliminated altogether. Helping to compensate for higher pension costs, a falling birth rate may serve to hold education expenditures in check. But the educational level of the labor force is a major determinant of economic growth, especially in an era when new knowledge-intensive industries, such as computers and robotics, have begun to replace older industries that employ unskilled workers in assembly-line production. The need for adult education and retraining for older employees displaced from declining industries such as steel and automobiles is growing as fewer young workers, many of whom have above-average education levels, enter the labor force, and as a surplus work force of displaced workers in their fifties grows.

The product mix of consumer demand changes as the population shifts from the "Pepsi generation" to the "Geritol generation" and as needs shift from highchairs to wheelchairs. Adjusting production levels to changes in the demand mix is more difficult if the labor force is aging and the proportion of new, more mobile, workers is falling, although this may hasten the adoption of new computerized technologies: robots on the assembly line and computer terminals that enable information rather than people to be moved. Certainly, most current innovations in industry are substituting capital for labor in the production process, calling on smaller numbers of better-trained higher-quality workers.

Finally, a decline in population can have an impact on public opinion and policymaking. An older population generally holds more conservative views on public questions. Furthermore, as we discovered during the 1930s, when birth rates dropped steeply in North America and Europe in response to the Great Depression, many people react to zero population growth with feelings of extreme anxiety, fearing an adverse effect on national prosperity and security. Although population decline does indeed pose problems of adjustment, these merely signal the need for a creative public policy rather than call for a program to encourage higher birth rates. Students of such problems generally believe that the average person will be substantially better off economically if population growth follows a two-child family pattern rather than a three-child family, or more.

MIGRATION

The second dynamic population process is *migration,* the permanent movement of human beings from one place to another. Migration between continents and countries is far less important today than it was in the nineteenth and early twentieth centuries, but interregional migration within countries remains at high levels in many parts of the world. Migration is a complex phenomenon, and the study of it is all the more difficult because official data are so variable in quality.

The Migration Process

Viewed broadly, migration is similar to trade, with flows of people substituting for flows of merchandise. As in the case of commodity movements, one area supplies a surplus population, or at least provides some "push" that causes people to want to leave. At the other end of the journey, an area of demand exerts a "pull" because of a population deficiency or the presence of some other positive attraction. Between the regions of supply and demand, a variety of barriers interpose obstacles to the movement of people.

Here the analogy to trade ends. Goods are passive, whereas people are active agents ordinarily free to decide for themselves whether or not to migrate. Exceptions are numerous, however, and involuntary movements of people are not unusual. Many of history's large population transfers have taken place as a result of actions by governments or other official agencies, which offered little or no choice to the migrants. Then, too, children and other dependents usually have decisions about migration made for them.

Why People Migrate

Perhaps the most familiar explanation for migration is that offered by the classical economic model of *factor mobility.* Underlying this model are the assumptions that migrants are motivated by the desire to maximize their incomes and that they are fully aware of the opportunities for employment in other locations, as well as the wages prevailing in each place. A further assumption is that the workers are numerous and are identical in skills, values, and needs. Finally, the model assumes the absence of barriers to migration. Under these conditions labor will migrate from Region A to Region B as long as *real wages* (wages expressed in terms of how much they will buy) are higher in B than in A. The expected outcome is a labor market that is everywhere in equilibrium, with a job for every worker and all vacancies filled.

This focus upon economic reasons for migration finds some justification in both less-developed and advanced countries. In India, for example, one study found that the decisions of individuals to move hinge largely upon their expectations of job opportunities in the new area. In another case, it was shown that 85 percent of the labor movements between regions of the United States are associated with changes in unemployment levels. In other words, people tend to migrate to those places where new jobs are opening up most rapidly in relation to the number of persons entering the labor force.

Even so, the assumptions of the classical model have limited applicability. People have other than economic motives for moving, and few are able to decide with complete objectivity. Much rationalization is connected with most decisions to move, knowledge about conditions at the other end of the journey is usually imperfect, and there are many barriers in the way of the prospective mover. Prospective migrants must weigh their perceptions of their present locations against those concerning the proposed locations. In this evaluative process, economic reasons do not tell the whole story, and sometimes they do not even give the most important part.

Often the most compelling reasons for moving are of a cultural nature. Religion has been an important migration factor: Throughout history many individuals and groups have moved to new places where they could practice their beliefs unhindered. Kinship, friendship, and linguistic and ethnic ties have also played important parts in decisions to migrate.

Cultural groups have tended to produce "streams" of migrations into particular places. During the American colonial period large numbers of German migrants settled in Pennsylvania, where they came to be called "Pennsylvania Dutch." The Mormons, in their organized westward movement, followed distinct paths and settled in certain selected areas. In Canada, Finns chose to congregate at the head of Lake Superior and Mennonites in southern Manitoba. In the Italian migrations to the Western Hemisphere, those from southern Italy went mainly to the United States and those from the north of Italy tended to go to the Rio de la Plata region of South America. Meanwhile, some migrants changed their minds, or perhaps decided to return home to marry or to retire, thereby creating "counterstreams."

Political considerations have been prominent in decisions to migrate. Persons seeking relief from political persecution, expelled from their homelands because of unpopular beliefs, or fleeing because of war have figured importantly in migrations to new lands. In addition, governments have forcibly resettled large numbers of people and have sent sizable groups to colonize new areas.

Some demographers have attempted to classify the many possible explanations for migrating. Sociologist William Petersen devised a fivefold classification, further subdividing each category as to whether it is "innovating" or "conservative." Migrants whose moves are innovating are undertaking a new way of life; those whose moves are conservative are preserving their accustomed way of life in new surroundings. Petersen's five classes of migrants are as follows:

1. *Primitive migration* describes movements of peoples at very low levels of development in response to conditions of the physical environment over which they have little control. In its *conservative* form, primitive migration is exemplified by the wanderings of the herders of Central Asia, the subsistence farmers of Amazonia, or food gatherers in the Congo. The *innovative* form is indicated by the settling of Middle Eastern nomads into an urban way of life in Egypt or Syria.

2. *Forced migration* is the compulsory transfer of a people, usually by a political agency. The resettling of populations as a result of the westward shift of Poland's borders following World War II was a conservative type of forced migration, whereas the African slave trade was an innovative type.

3. *Impelled migration* is similar to forced migration in that migrants are under some form of duress, but it differs in that they retain some ability to decide whether or not to move. The flight of ancient Britons before the Saxon invaders was a conservative form of impelled migration; those who chose not to escape to the security of the Welsh mountains had the option of remaining behind to be enslaved. Jewish victims of the Russian pogroms, who could have stayed at home under subjection, elected instead to leave their rural homeland to pursue urban trades in American cities.

4. Individual movements for economic betterment or mere adventure are referred to as *free migration*. The westward migrations of pioneer farmers in the United States and Canada were a conservative type of free migration, whereas migrations of modern Americans or Canadians leaving their cities for the farms, logging camps, or mines of Alaska or the Northwest Territories are innovating.

5. As the name suggests, a *mass migration* involves large numbers of participants. In such movements the migrants tend to submerge their individual motives and may not even be fully informed of what to expect in their new settlements. Entire rural communities from the Westlandit region of southwestern Norway migrated to North America in this way. Some found opportunities to establish farms in their new environments, but others did not.

Migrations differ in the degree of governmental control to which they are subjected. Before World War I the United States accepted virtually all immigrants; following the war, however, it admitted immigrants according to a rigid quota system that excluded some nationalities altogether. Thus, a policy of *selective* immigration replaced one of *unrestricted* immigration.

Typologies of migration have more than academic uses: They aid policymakers and other agencies in dealing with the numerous problems created by emigration or immigration. In general, the analytical approach to this subject offers a better understanding of the pressures and motivations underlying the present global urbanization trend, the movement of people from the U.S. Northeast to the Sunbelt, and other contemporary migrations.

Barriers to Migration

The question of *why* people move must be distinguished from that of *how many* actually do so. Often many persons would, or should, move but are prevented from doing so because of certain barriers to migration. These are of three types: distance, political restrictions, and those characteristics of would-be migrants that reduce their mobility.

One of the most formidable barriers to migration is distance, which therefore figures prominently in most analyses. Such studies invariably show that most people move short distances and that the frequency of moves declines with an increase in distance from the migrants' original homes. Migrants may find that long-distance moves simply entail too much transport cost or that such moves exact too high an "opportunity cost"—that is, the income that would have to be foregone at the old locations.

A variety of noneconomic considerations further reduce the number of long-distance moves. For one thing, people's knowledge about other areas, and the opportunities that may exist there, grows dimmer with increasing distance from home. Moves to remoter places, especially to foreign lands, also cause many personal disruptions owing to the unfamiliar customs and languages and the lack of family and community ties in the new locations. These pose "psychic costs" for migrants.

Because distance has such an effect upon human migration, "gravity" models are often used for the study of this subject, following in the footsteps of Newton's laws in physics. The basic hypotheses underlying this approach are, first, that the propensity to migrate from region i to region j is inversely related to the distance separating them (or, more commonly, the square of the distance) and, second, that the number of persons moving to a particulate point is directly proportional to the population living at each end of the journey. In its simplest form, the following expression describes the relationship:

$$M_{ij} = \frac{P_i P_j}{d_{ij}^x} \times k$$

where

M_{ij} = number of migrants moving from region i to region j

P_i, P_j = size of population in regions i and j, respectively

d = distance separating regions i and j

x = a factor that describes that rate of decline of migration with distance

k = a measure of proportionality

Certain adjustments in this model are usually required. It is necessary to make some kind of allowance in the formula for the nature of employment opportunities in the new place. This provides a better measure than does population alone. Acount must also be taken of any intervening opportunities that may appear along the routes of travel from the place of origin. Studies of labor migration in Sweden, for example, have shown that proximity to other employment centers tends to siphon off sizable numbers of migrants from more distant places. Another useful variable indicates the number of friends and relatives who may already have moved to the new location, persons who can be depended upon to give information about opportunities in that place, and perhaps even to provide food and shelter at the outset. Finally, the model should allow for other attractive qualities of the destination, such as a benign climate. Studies of interregional migration in the United States have confirmed that this can be an important variable.

Because of the influence of distance, therefore, the areas nearest the prime source of migrants tend to fill up first. Migration thus usually takes the form of a diffusion outward from the center. This has been apparent in studies of local, regional, and international migration.

Political barriers may be especially difficult for migrants to penetrate. As in the case of trade, international movements encounter more obstacles of this type than do interregional ones. This has become increasingly true in recent years: Only in this century have national governments closely controlled immigration and emigration, but the trend has now proceeded to the point where free international migration has nearly ceased. Thus, while still accepting immigrants from some British Commonwealth and European lands, Australia has excluded nonwhite immigrants from overpopulated neighboring countries in southern Asia. During periods of high unemployment, the industrialized countries have become increasingly reluctant to issue work permits to foreigners.

Despite generally rising bars to immigration, Western countries do not ordinarily restrict emigration. By contrast, the Communist countries permit few of their citizens to leave. The most visible evidence of this policy is the Berlin Wall, built to prevent the East German economy from being weakened by the outflow of its best-trained young adults.

Where people are free to move at will, as in most interregional migration, some are prevented from doing so by still other, more subtle, barriers. Among the strongest are the family and cultural ties that bind would-be migrants to their home areas. Such links have prevented many unemployed people in depressed areas of Appalachia, the Ozarks, and the old manufacturing districts of the Northeastern United States from going to more dynamic areas where jobs are available. Home ties have likewise been strong deterrents to interregional migration in Britain and China.

Certain members of a society are less bound by such links than others. The most mobile persons are young adult males between the ages of 15 and 30. The more prosperous among the elderly, however, may retire to areas with warmer climates. Studies have shown that fewer women than men leave their home areas. Migrants also tend to be better educated and more skilled and to have better health than those remaining behind.

Not only are some people more likely to migrate than others, but they are also more inclined to move at certain times. Migration is much greater when the business cycle is ebbing in the source region and rising in the receiving region. The life cycle of the individual also affects migration decisions: People are more inclined to move upon completing their education and entering the labor market, when they are retiring, or when they are undergoing changes in marital status. During the long intervals between such landmark events in an individual's life, most people are reluctant to undergo the financial and emotional strains of leaving friends and accustomed surroundings for a new way of life in a strange place.

Effects of Migration

Because it is a selective process, migration can have important effects on both the supplying and receiving regions. Immigration and emigration frequently alter the age composition, sex ratios, literacy rates, and demography of the affected areas; they can also create social and economic problems.

For a region of heavy out-migration, the departure of predominantly young adults in their most productive years leaves behind a population consisting mostly of the very young and the elderly. Conversely, an area of in-migration usually has a preponderance of young and middle-aged adults. Exceptions are regions with warm, sunny climates, such as Florida and Arizona, which attract large numbers of retirees.

Migration also affects the sex ratio: the proportion of males to females in a population. This ratio is obtained by dividing the number of males by the number of females and multiplying by 100. High sex ratios, indicating proportionately larger numbers of males than females, are characteristic of newly settled areas. This is because men tend to be the most mobile members of the population. The relatively larger numbers of women remaining behind give low sex ratios to areas of heavy out-migration. The greater life expectancy of women further reduces the sex ratios of older, more stable, areas. The low ratio of the United Kingdom (93.6) is

typical of Western Europe, which has experienced continued emigration over a long period. By contrast, Australia's higher ratio (101.3) is representative of countries still receiving immigrants.

As time passes, the sex ratios of newer countries and regions gradually decrease. Throughout its earlier years the United States had proportionately large numbers of males owing to heavy immigration. In 1910 the sex ratio was 106.2, by 1940 it had fallen to 100.8, and by 1969 it was only 95.2. The lowest ratios in the country are those of New England, whereas the highest are in the West. In Alaska, for instance, the ratio is 132.3.

The loss of young adults results in lower birth rates in regions of much out-migration and correspondingly higher birth rates in the receiving areas. In this way the selectivity of migration accentuates the population losses and gains of the two areas. Ultimately, however, the influx of immigrants to a new region accelerates the growth of urbanization, which is normally attended by falling birth rates.

The effects of migration upon death rates are complex. Paradoxically, the influx of retirees to Arizona, many of whom are attracted by the reputed healthfulness of the desert climate, has given that state a higher-than-average death rate, simply because immigration has raised the age level.

The social effects of migration are likewise mixed. Although emigrants tend to be the more physically healthy members of a source population, their mental health and emotional stability often range from the very best to the worst. The problems of adjusting to a new environment may contribute to increased incidence of crime, lawlessness, and disintegration of families among in-migrants. Such stresses apparently underly many of our most difficult urban problems. In addition, cultural conflicts between newcomers and an indigenous population can produce antagonisms, social unrest, and even violence.

Economically, a region that receives large numbers of immigrants may benefit in many ways, at least in the earlier stages. This seems to have been true of the United States prior to World War I. The influx of immigrants during that era has been credited with increasing the growth rate of the country's total gross national product, and possibly even raising it in per capita terms. This apparently resulted from the addition of large numbers of persons mainly of working age who were healthy, skilled, conditioned to hard work, and possibly of better-than-average intelligence. As they prospered, these persons offered a rapidly expanding market for goods of all kinds and especially those of the newly developed manufacturing industries. These conditions in turn created an attractive investment market for the European capital required for further expansion.

The economic effects upon those regions supplying migrants have varied. For the Western European countries of the nineteenth century, emigration of their surplus peoples to the New World gave temporary relief during downward swings of the business cycle. The large numbers of farmers moving to agriculturally rich lands in the Americas also supplied Europe with abundant new supplies of foodstuffs at low prices. At the same time, the industrial nations gained rapidly expanding markets for their manufactured goods in these overseas areas.

For today's less-developed countries and regions, emigration is often detrimental, for the emigrants are the most enterprising, skilled, and educated members of the population. Many potential business leaders and professionals receive educations abroad, then elect to pursue their careers in advanced countries, where the financial rewards and opportunities are greater than at home. Because the developing nations often desperately need such skills, this type of migration has perverse effects. (Refer back to Figure 1.6.)

The recent migration of people from the United States Snowbelt to the Sunbelt of the South and Southwest offers many examples of the problems that such population movements can create. The out-migration of people and industries is not only costing the northern states some of their more enterprising people, but it is increasing the burden on local governments, which must try to maintain public services with diminished tax revenues from industry, property, and personal income, as well as retail sales. Meanwhile, the Sunbelt states, though benefiting from the influx of new business and industry, are hard-pressed to install new roads, streets, sewers, and other forms of infrastructure required by economic growth and the flood of new people. Local governments encounter new and unaccustomed problems of law enforcement and provision of social services.

Patterns of Migration

Let us now examine briefly some of the main patterns of migration that have contributed to the current distribution of populations, which will be the subject of the next chapter. Migration patterns are apparent at three scales of observation: worldwide, within continents, and within countries.

International

The earliest human migrations were group movements of clans and tribes; individual movements and migration streams appeared much later. The first primitive migrations were impelled mostly by climatic changes or by calamities, such as hostile invasions. Considering the comparatively small number of inhabitants on earth during the period of prehistory, it is paradoxical that one of the probable reasons for early migrations was population pressure. We must remember, however, that primitive means of livelihood were (and still are) highly extensive in their use of land. Because the support of every individual required so much land, primitive folk constantly had to adjust their activities to an uncertain food supply. When their numbers increased to the point that their traditional lands became inadequate, migration to new areas became necessary. Physical features of the landscape, such as mountain passes, ice bridges, and wide plains and valleys, dictated their routes of travel.

Modern migrations, however, have dwarfed all such primitive movements. Whereas earlier migrations often involved the encroachment of primitive peoples upon the lands of more advanced cultures, as with the Mongol invasions of China, most modern migrations have reversed this process. An estimated 60 million Europeans and Africans took part in the great migrations since A.D. 1500. These migrations began slowly. Although from 10 million to 20 million African slaves were transported to the new lands, relatively few Europeans moved permanently prior to 1800, probably no more than 2.5 million in all.

The European exodus accelerated during the nineteenth century, particularly after 1830, and reached a peak on the eve of World War I with an annual flow of 1.5 million. These persons were mainly escaping rural overpopulation in Scandinavia, Ireland, Scotland, Germany, and Italy, as well as political upheavals, religious persecution (such as the Russian pogroms), and economic depressions, although many came in a spirit of adventure. Most of the movements formed streams to particular locations. Of the total, almost two-thirds went to the United States, but large numbers moved to Canada and other British Commonwealth countries as well. South America attracted immigrants mainly from the Mediterranean lands.

Intracontinental

Changes in national policy following World War I quickly altered these familiar flow patterns. The Great Depression reversed migration flows during the early 1930s, when some Western European countries actually experienced net gains, mostly from returnees. For a time the United States, Australia, New Zealand, Argentina, and Uruguay had net losses of migrants. Since that period the most significant population movements have taken place within continental areas.

Intra-European migrations have been particularly

large since the beginning of World War II, the war itself being responsible for wholesale displacements of populations. Just prior to the war about 400,000 persons (mostly Jews) had escaped from Nazi Germany, and during the war the Germans imported 8 million foreigners as forced labor. In all, the Nazis uprooted an estimated 30 million or more persons. The postwar boundary changes produced large population shifts, especially the westward expansion of the Slavic area at German expense. This resulted in the displacement of 11 million Germans and a very large exchange of populations between the USSR and Poland along their new border. Another million Germans subsequently escaped from East Germany into West Germany. In all, 25 million or more people moved during the time of postwar resettlement.

Among the prospering nations of postwar Western Europe a new pattern of population movement emerged. Surplus labor from the southern Mediterranean region, North Africa, and Asia Minor streamed into labor-short Germany, France, Switzerland, and the Low Countries. When economic recession appeared in the late 1970s, it brought with it an alarming rise in unemployment in those countries. Losing their jobs, many of these "guest workers" from the south returned to their homelands, although some remained in their new locations, creating social and economic problems for host governments. Also during this period a great many unwanted immigrants from Commonwealth countries in the Caribbean, Africa, and Asia poured into already-overcrowded Britain, resulting in urban unrest and racial strife. Several countries of Africa and Asia, newly freed from colonial control, have had very large migrations, mainly unrecorded, of peoples uprooted by famine, intertribal conflict, and war.

Internal

Although migrations between countries and within countries stem from the same basic causes, internal movements are of much greater relative magnitude today because of rising international barriers to migration. The two main types of internal migration, *interregional* and *rural-urban,* are both still evident in the United States, although these are now taking some new turns. As the historically important westward movement continues, it is being joined by a southward flow from the Northeast and North Central states. Meanwhile, growth of the largest metropolitan areas appears to be nearing an end.

While the United States population as a whole was increasing by more than 10 percent between the censuses of 1970 and 1980, the populations of the Northeast and North Central regions remained virtually unchanged. This lack of growth resulted from a large and growing exodus from the old manufacturing belt, offsetting the natural increase of population in the area during the 1970s. This out-migration stemmed in large part from the decline of the region's mature industries—especially basic metals and motor vehicles—the victims of changing domestic and world economies. The primarily agricultural states of the West Central region also had net out-migrations. Except for the three states of northernmost New England, which grew at rates above the national average, these three regions of the North and Northeast represented population stagnation, in which they were joined by the adjacent border state of Maryland. Only two states, New York and Rhode Island, actually had net losses of population, however.

The overwhelming number of these out-migrants were destined for the states of the West and the South, commonly described as the Sunbelt. The main attractions here were mild climates, in a period of soaring energy costs, and greater prospects for employment in the new high-growth industries of these regions. Except for Delaware, all states of the South and West grew at rates well above the national average. Leading in numerical gains were California, which added 3.7 million people, Texas (3 million), and Florida (2.9 million). These three states alone accounted for 42 percent of the entire United States population increase between censuses.

Over a very long period there had been a persistent trend toward an increasing concentration of the United States population in metropolitan areas. This apparently ended with the 1970s, as it also did throughout Western Europe. Although the country's metropolitan areas as a group increased at about the same rate as the population as a whole between 1970 and 1980, the largest of the metropolises either lost population or failed to grow significantly. New York City lost more than 900,000 people, and Philadelphia, Detroit, and Boston likewise had significant losses. The principal gainers were smaller towns and cities, and nonmetropolitan areas, which increased half again as fast as the country as a whole. Smaller centers proved increasingly attractive to new manufacturing industries and other economic activities because of lower operating costs and taxes. As places to live, too, they were increasingly favored not only because of lower living costs but also because of better job opportunities as well as the perception that they were safer places and offered better environments. The interstate highway network and many other changes in transportation and communications have meanwhile made these smaller centers as accessible to national markets as formerly only the major metropolitan centers were.

Canada, too, has had important internal migrations, both interregional and rural-urban. Canada's interregional migrations have had two spatial components: east to west and hinterland to heartland. The east-west trend was prevalent until World War II, with the result that each province, with few exceptions, had a net gain of people from every province to its east and lost population to every province to its west. At the same time, streams of migrants converged on the Ontario industrial belt from resource-oriented hinterland regions. Increasingly since the war, both immigration from abroad and internal migration have tended to follow these trends.

Other advanced countries have had similar internal migrations, both rural-urban and interregional. Italy, for example, has experienced a substantial flow of Calabrians, Sicilians, and others from the overpopulated and economically depressed rural south to the prosperous industrial cities of the north. Large-scale internal migrations have likewise occurred in many less-developed nations, particularly rural-urban movements. As we shall see in the next chapter, the most rapidly growing cities in our present era are in the Third World.

AN ASSESSMENT: POPULATION GROWTH AND MIGRATION IN THE CONTEMPORARY WORLD

Though large-scale movements of people within countries continue in many parts of the world, permanent migrations between countries, as we have noted here, have become relatively minor in the latter part of the twentieth century. Despite growing population pressures throughout the Third World, migrants from less-developed countries are finding borders closed to them nearly everywhere. This declining role of international migration highlights the growing importance of differential rates of natural increase among countries as an agent of global population change.

The basic questions posed by Malthus and his successors are therefore being asked once again. Lending credence to the claim of early theorists that population growth is linked to the earth's carrying capacity, the evidence suggests that past surges of population increase occurred in response to technological breakthroughs that enhanced the productivity of earth resources. Some observers believe that the computer revolution now under way has the potential to power yet another such surge of population growth. Nevertheless, an eventual end to the long process of human multiplication seems likely, when at last the earth's finite supplies of resources approach exhaustion and environmental deterioration grows more threatening. Indeed, current indications are that the rate of natural population increase has already begun to decline, and experts at the United Nations are predicting that the global population will stabilize at about 10.5 billion people before the end of another century.

Yet, as we saw, Malthus did not anticipate the effects of development upon the basic factors of population growth, namely, birth rates and death rates. The theory of demographic transition holds that as development commences, death rates fall more rapidly than birth rates, causing a demographic gap, or "population explosion," which continues until equilibrium is finally reestablished in the later stages of development. Recent events, however, show that transition theory, which is based upon Europe's experience, has not accurately predicted demographic change in today's less-developed countries, whose fertility rates are generally much higher than in premodern Europe and whose death rates have fallen much more rapidly. Current population densities are also far greater. Nevertheless, transition theory retains some validity because it accurately predicts the sequence of demographic events, if not their precise magnitude and timing. It thus provides a useful basis for attacking the problems of population change.

Our examination of this subject has shown that the problems of growing populations are different from those of declining ones. Rapid population growth can wipe out the gains from development, reduce food supply, produce dietary deficiencies and disease, and cause poverty, inflation, unemployment, urban problems, and high levels of dependency, all of which contribute to political instability. The aging of a population, on the other hand, creates the need to restructure the economy in response to the changing nature of demand. It substitutes one kind of dependency for another and introduces new kinds of social, psychological, and political problems. In the long run, population stability appears to be the optimal state.

At present the disparities between countries in their rates of population growth are still widening. With most of the industrialized world approaching zero population growth, Third World nations are doubling their numbers every 20 to 35 years. Undoubtedly, therefore, the world population map of A.D. 2000 will look very different from today's, and international migration will have much less to do with these changes than will differential rates of natural increase. The existing pattern of world population, which evolved in response to past events, and the new patterns expected to result from trends now in motion, will be the topic of the next chapter.

TOPICS FOR DISCUSSIO

1. Why did world population grow so slowly prior to the seventeenth century, and why has its growth accelerated since? What gave rise to the three surges of population growth that occurred in the past? Describe the new developments that promise a quantum change in the world's productive capacity and explain why these developments are less likely to produce a renewed surge in world population growth.

2. Define the following: crude birth rate, crude death rate, rate of natural increase, fertility rate, age-specific death rate. Which of these measures are the most useful for assessing population change? What do they tell us about a society?

3. What did Malthus perceive as the "ultimate" check to population growth? Describe his "preventative" and "positive" checks. What solution to the problem of excessive population growth did he advocate? Why might we regard Malthus as a pioneer in the movement for women's liberation? Explain why Malthus's predictions for Western Europe failed to materialize. Where in the world today are his predictions apparently being borne out to some degree? Why?

4. Explain "demographic transition" and discuss the historical basis for transition theory. What is a "demographic gap"? ..ny is ti model for today's devel..

5. Show how transition theory serves ..dings United Nations' classification of countries according .. their demographic characteristics. Discuss the five U.N. demographic types, illustrating each with country examples. Which types of countries give the greatest cause for concern?

6. Explain Engel's law and show how it applies to less-developed countries. Discuss the economic, social, health, and political problems that these countries encounter because of rapid population growth.

7. Contrast the problems of dependent populations that face Mexico with those confronting West Germany. What are some of the other kinds of new problems that countries with declining populations must solve?

8. Explain the changing relative importance of natural increase and migration as determinants of national and global population patterns in recent times. Why do people migrate? Describe the various types of migration, giving examples.

9. How do the social, economic, political, and demographic effects of migration differ for supplying and receiving regions? Give some examples of migration streams.

FURTHER READINGS

BROWN, LESTER R. *The Twenty-Ninth Day: Accommodating Human Needs and Numbers to the Earth's Resources.* New York: W. W. Norton & Co., Inc., 1978.

The president of Worldwatch Institute and a leading thinker on world ecological issues describes the social, economic, and environmental consequences of continued rapid population growth.

DEMKO, GEORGE J., HAROLD M. ROSE, and GEORGE A. SCHNELL. *Population Geography: A Reader.* New York: McGraw-Hill, 1970.

A durable collection of geographical writings on the spatial distribution of populations and the nature and problems of population growth and human migration.

INTERNATIONAL BANK FOR RECONSTRUCTION AND DEVELOPMENT (IBRD). *World Development Report.* Washington, D.C.: IBRD, 1982.

Survey and analysis of developmental problems confronting the Third World, especially those stemming from recent demographic trends and the accelerating growth of cities in developing countries.

JONES, HUW R. *Population Geography.* New York: Harper & Row, 1981.

In this recent geographical treatise on population, the author emphasizes the spatial-temporal processes shaping current patterns of fertility, mortality, and migration at global, national, and subnational scales. He also discusses the social and economic consequences of contemporary trends and their policy implications, especially for developing countries.

MAHLER, HALFDAN. "People." *Scientific American,* 243 (September 1980), 66–77.

Comparing demographic trends in developed and less-developed countries, the Director General of the World Health Organization describes the adverse effects of rapid population growth upon the general level of health in a society and discusses the implications for development.

SMITH, ROBERT S., FRANK T. DEVYVER, and WILLIAM R. ALLEN. *Population Economics: Selected Essays of Joseph J. Spengler.* Durham, N.C.: Duke University Press, 1972.

This volume reproduces some of the more enduring works on population economics by a noted authority.

CHAPTER 4

Changing Patterns
of World Population

Human populations are spread very unevenly over the world: Great numbers of people concentrate within a relatively few regions, leaving vast land areas virtually empty. Today's population pattern is the cumulative result of countless human actions over a very long period of time. This pattern has been shaped by the physical needs of human beings for food, comfort, and opportunities for a livelihood, as well as their desires, perceptions, and social and cultural relationships. The world map shows four great population concentrations and several lesser ones. The spatial irregularity of population distributions extends also to subnational levels.

As rates of population growth diverge among regions, a very different population map of the future takes shape. Most developed areas are already at or near zero population growth, ensuring that their share of global population will continue to shrink. Though 95 percent of future population growth will occur in less-developed countries, some will grow faster than others. Within a century Africa will likely hold a quarter of all humanity, and most of the world's largest cities will be in less-developed countries.

Population projections are very uncertain for the world's poorest areas, however, and for some of these they are mere guesses. Such uncertainties underscore the question: Can the world support more than 10 billion people by the end of the next century?

Objectives:

- to examine both the existing spatial pattern of human populations and the factors that have caused that pattern to assume such an irregular shape

- to observe present demographic trends and show how these vary among countries at different levels of development

- to predict the changes in the population pattern that the twenty-first century will bring if current trends persist

- to consider the implications of these evolving patterns, noting the problems they will likely pose for future generations

PRESENT DISTRIBUTION
OF HUMAN POPULATIONS

The spatial pattern of world population is exceedingly uneven, as Figure 4.1 shows. This has led some people to question the growing concern with overpopulation. They note that large numbers of human beings are concentrated in a few relatively small areas whereas vast expanses of the earth's surface remain only lightly occupied or entirely vacant. Why, they ask, should we not settle our surplus populations in these little-used areas? In this chapter we shall look at some of the reasons why the problem is not so simply solved. The existing pattern of world population is a product of the dynamic processes of natural increase and migration described in the previous chapter. Let us now see how these processes, working together through the many ages of human existence, have favored certain areas over others. What are the characteristics of those regions that have attracted large numbers of people and of those that have been avoided?

The second main task in this chapter is to learn where current population trends are likely to lead us. With the increasing restrictions on international migration, the future map of world populations will be shaped largely by differences among countries in their rates of natural increase. How will that map differ from today's, and what problems are present population trends likely to bring in future years?

The circumstances that have produced the present spatial distribution of population reflect the whole range of human requirements, desires, perceptions, and social and cultural interrelationships. At the most basic level, the physical environment has tended to limit the range of habitation, based upon the biological needs of human beings as organisms, as well as the physical opportunities for them to gain a livelihood—the needs of people as economic beings. Within this material framework many other influences have helped shape the pattern we see today. In Chapter 3 we noted the ways in which political organization and control, the policing and regulatory powers exercised by governments over their territories, may directly or indirectly affect migration and demography. Also influencing population patterns are the divisive or cohesive forces resulting from racial, linguistic, and religious affiliation, the traditions associated with marriage and the family, and other forms of group behavior.

The population patterns we see today, therefore, represent the cumulative effects of innumerable human actions in the long past, including those dictated by a technology and social organization different from that of today. Despite the many new developments of recent times, however, past patterns persist because of the limited mobility of human populations, especially at the global scale. As is true of most geographical phenomena, the scale of observation affects the kinds of comparisons that are possible—whether between continents,

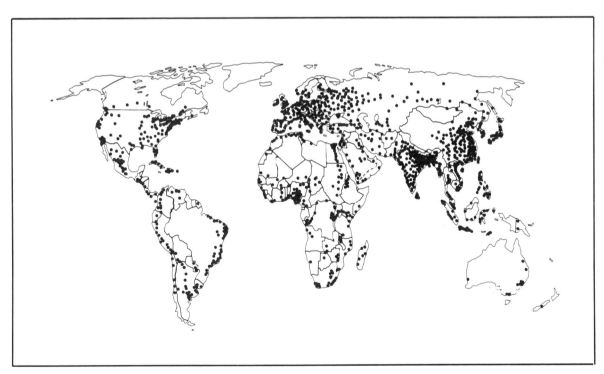

FIGURE 4.1 World population.

countries, or regions and localities within countries. The quality of population data also varies with scale, as well as from place to place.

Numbers of People: International Comparisons

The chief sources of population data are official records, especially those compiled by national governments and the United Nations. Some of this information is of doubtful reliability, however, particularly that relating to less-developed countries; for some states in Africa, Asia, and Latin America no dependable statistics exist at all. Interpreting data of such uncertain quality requires caution, all the more so when one is making temporal comparisons. Studies by the United Nations have disclosed, for instance, that official censuses in parts of Africa have suffered from underenumeration and that the populations of some of these countries are much larger than had been suspected. Only in 1982 did the People's Republic of China, which contains nearly a quarter of all humanity, undertake its first real census; only rough estimates had hitherto been possible. Complicating comparisons of data over time are the many boundary changes of recent decades, such as that resulting from the separation of Bangladesh from Pakistan. Furthermore, measures of population characteristics and definitions of urbanization are not standardized internationally.

Comparative analyses thus require judgment and careful qualification. The problem is less acute for developed countries, which have fairly reliable data. To minimize data problems among Third World countries it is often desirable to aggregate information by continental groupings.

Population Size

From the totals shown in Table 4.1 it is clear that the continents differ greatly in population size. Asia contains more than half of the world's people, even when we exclude the USSR, which is the third most populous country. Although Europe has the second largest population among the continents, it has only one-fifth as many people as Asia. Africa now has the third largest population and is rapidly gaining on Europe. Oceania, which includes Australia, New Zealand, and the islands of the South Pacific, has the smallest population of all the continental groupings. The USSR appears separately in Table 4.1 because of its large land area, nearly 15 percent of the world's total, and because it is partly in Europe and partly in Asia.

In Table 4.2 those countries having the largest populations are listed in rank order. Altogether, 79 percent of the world's people live in these 25 nations. Nearly one in every four persons lives in China, and one in seven lives in India. Note that 13 of the countries are Asian, not counting the USSR. It is obvious from Tables 4.1 and 4.2, however, that continental and country totals do not give an accurate impression of crowding. One reason for this is that the world's populous countries differ so greatly in areal extent (Table 4.2, column 3).

Population Density

Differences among countries become all the more apparent if we relate numbers of people to land area, to derive a measure of population density (Table 4.2, column 5). Thus, the USSR and the United States rank third and fourth, respectively, among the world's most populous countries, but the people in those two coun-

TABLE 4.1

World distribution of population by continent, 1982

Region	Population (thousands)	Percent of world population	Density (population per sq km)	Arable hectares per person	Total hectares (thousands)
World	4,368,486	100.0	29.1	0.3	1,455,251
Africa	448,042	10.3	14.8	0.6	253,817
Asia (excluding USSR)	2,536,201	58.1	91.2	0.2	455,077
Europe (excluding USSR)	483,653	11.1	98.0	0.3	153,578
North and Central America	369,292	8.5	15.2	0.7	256,584
South America	242,208	5.5	13.6	0.3	73,028
Oceania	22,602	0.5	2.7	1.5	33,609
USSR	266,542	6.1	11.9	0.9	230,085

Sources: Encyclopaedia Britannica Book of the Year 1982; and Food and Agriculture Organization of the United Nations, *Production Yearbook 1982* (New York: United Nations, 1983).

TABLE 4.2

Twenty-five countries with largest populations in 1984

Country (ranked according to size)	Population (thousands)	Area Sq km (thousands)	Area Percent of world	Density (population per sq km)	Percent of world population
1 China	1,051,551	9,561	6.4	110.0	22.1
2 India	746,742	3,288	2.2	227.1	15.7
3 USSR	275,761	22,402	14.9	12.3	5.8
4 United States	235,681	9,363	6.2	25.2	4.9
5 Indonesia	162,167	1,919	1.3	84.5	3.4
6 Brazil	132,648	8,512	5.7	15.6	2.8
7 Japan	119,492	378	0.3	316.1	2.5
8 Pakistan	98,971	796	0.5	124.3	2.1
9 Bangladesh	98,464	144	0.1	683.8	2.1
10 Nigeria	92,037	924	0.6	99.6	1.9
11 Mexico	77,040	1,958	1.3	39.3	1.6
12 West Germany	61,214	249	0.2	245.8	1.3
13 Vietnam	58,307	330	0.2	176.7	1.2
14 Italy	56,724	301	0.2	188.5	1.2
15 United Kingdom	55,624	244	0.2	228.0	1.2
16 France	54,559	544	0.4	100.3	1.1
17 Philippines	53,395	300	0.2	178.0	1.1
18 Thailand	50,584	514	0.3	98.4	1.1
19 Turkey	48,811	781	0.5	62.5	1.0
20 Egypt	45,657	1,001	0.7	45.6	1.0
21 Iran	43,799	1,648	1.1	26.6	0.9
22 South Korea	40,309	98	0.1	411.3	0.8
23 Spain	38,717	505	0.3	76.7	0.8
24 Burma	38,513	677	0.5	56.9	0.8
25 Poland	37,228	313	0.2	118.9	0.8
Total	3,773,885	66,750	44.5	56.5	79.2
World Total	4,765,000	150,157	100.0	31.7	100.0

Source: Population Newsletter No. 36, July 1985. Population Division, Department of International Economic and Social Affairs, United Nations Secretariat, New York.

tries are spread over very large territories, resulting in low density figures. The simplest measure of density is that used in Table 4.2, namely, *arithmetic density*, which is simply the total number of people divided by the total land area. Some of the greatest densities occur in tiny city-states such as Monaco, with 13,684 persons per square kilometer, or the Vatican City, with 2273 people per square kilometer. This is especially true of city-states that occupy small islands, as, for example, Hong Kong (5300 people per sq km) and Singapore (3869 per sq km). Excluding such cases, as well as all island nations smaller than 10,000 square kilometers, we find that the 25 countries listed in Table 4.3 are the most densely populated in the world. Nine of these are European, of which The Netherlands ranks third, Belgium fourth, West Germany seventh, the United Kingdom tenth, and Italy sixteenth. Except for The Netherlands and Belgium, these European countries ranked higher on the list a decade ago. Since that time, several Third World countries listed in Table 4.3 have substantially increased their population densities. These are Bangladesh, South Korea, Sri

Lanka, India, Vietnam, the Philippines, and North Korea—all in East or South Asia—Rwanda and Burundi in East Africa, and Jamaica, Haiti, and El Salvador in Latin America. Two small neighbors at the eastern end of the Mediterranean, Lebanon and Israel, also appear in Table 4.3. Note that seven of the 25 densest populations belong to island nations: Japan, the United Kingdom, Sri Lanka, the Philippines, Haiti, the Dominican Republic, and Jamaica.

The Food and Agriculture Organization of the United Nations (FAO) has estimated the proportion of land available for crops, that is, *arable* land, in each of the major regions. From this information it is possible to derive a measure of *physiological density*, which relates the size of a population to the amount of arable land available for its support. Table 4.1 lists this information for each of the continental areas and for the world as a whole. Note that in 1982 the average person in the world could draw upon only one-third of a hectare (0.8 acre) of cropland (column 5 in Table 4.1); 10 years earlier the amount available per person had been

TABLE 4.3

Most densely populated countries (1984 estimates)

Country (ranked according to density)	Density (population per sq km)	Area (thousands sq km)
1 Bangladesh[a]	683.8	144
2 South Korea[a]	411.3	98
3 The Netherlands	351.0	41
4 Belgium	323.0	31
5 Japan[a]	316.1	378
6 Lebanon	260.0	10
7 West Germany[a]	245.8	249
8 El Salvador	248.0	21
9 Sri Lanka	233.3	66
10 United Kingdom[a]	228.0	244
11 India[a]	227.1	3,288
12 Rwanda	219.2	26
13 Jamaica	209.1	11
14 Israel	195.0	21
15 Haiti	189.0	28
16 Italy[a]	188.5	301
17 Vietnam[a]	177.3	330
18 Philippines[a]	173.7	300
19 Burundi	160.7	28
20 North Korea	158.7	121
21 Switzerland	158.5	41
22 East Germany	154.6	108
23 Dominican Republic	122.4	49
24 Czechoslovakia	120.3	128
25 Denmark	118.6	43

Source: United Nations.

Note: Includes only those countries with areas having more than 10,000 sq km.

[a]Also appears on list of countries with largest populations, Table 4.2.

0.4 arable hectare (one acre). Three-fourths of the world's people live in areas having less than the world average of one-third hectare: Asia has only 0.2 arable hectare per person, and South America, with its rapidly growing population, has now fallen below the world average in arable land per person. Although Europe as a whole has a larger ratio of cropland to total land area than any other continent, its population densities are so great that the average European has only 0.3 hectare.

Physiological density is only a rough measure, however, for it does not take into account the variable quality of cropland. Although the per capita supply of arable land in Africa is well above the world average, the productivity of that land is generally much below that of North America or Europe. A large part of Latin America's cropland is of poor quality also. Similarly misleading is the large amount of land per person shown for Oceania, a sparsely populated region with only 2 percent of the world's total arable acreage.

Limits of Habitation

Population density figures for continents or countries can be deceptive, however. As Figure 4.1 demon-strates, densities are rarely consistent throughout national territories, and many major population concentrations cross national boundaries. Let us explore the reasons why certain areas are more heavily occupied than others.

For the most part, the pattern of world population we see today took form at a time when human beings gained their livelihood directly from the land. It is not surprising, therefore, that those parts of the earth's land surface with little or no human habitation—about three-fifths of the total—are physically unsuited to agriculture. Figure 4.2 provides a generalized view of those regions that are too dry, too wet, too cold, or too mountainous for the ordinary forms of cultivation. In some cases two or more of these negative conditions coincide in a particular area. Note, however, that few of the major world regions are entirely devoid of human beings. Within some broad nonarable areas are localities that have special conditions permitting the practice of agriculture—desert oases, for example. Some areas that lack farmland contain nonagricultural settlements, located near valuable mineral deposits, biotic resources (such as forest products), recreational facilities, or other special assets.

Excessive aridity virtually excludes farming from large portions of the world. The amount of moisture available to crops varies according to the evaporation rate in an area. At least 10 inches of annual rainfall are usually required in the middle latitudes, but 30 inches or more may be needed in the tropics to replace evaporation losses. Much of the earth's surface is either desert (less than 10 inches of rain per year) or steppe land (between 10 and 20 or 30 inches) and thus mostly unsuited to agriculture. Within such dry lands, however, exceptional circumstances may permit irrigated agriculture in certain favored localities. For example, "exotic" rivers such as the Nile or the Colorado, with sources in regions of high rainfall, pass through arid lands where their waters may support large agricultural populations. In some desert areas, oases grow up around local springs or wells drawing upon deep underground veins of water. Vast expanses of the Sahara and other major deserts, however, are either remote from water supplies or lack true soils to permit agriculture on their barren sandy or rocky surfaces. Arid regions with deposits of valuable minerals such as petroleum, nitrates, or metallic ores may attract some human habitation, but such activities normally require only small numbers of workers and rarely affect the general population pattern to an important degree.

On the other hand, some large regions support only small populations because they receive too much rainfall. The great equatorial basins of the Amazon and Congo rivers support a dense rain forest vegetation,

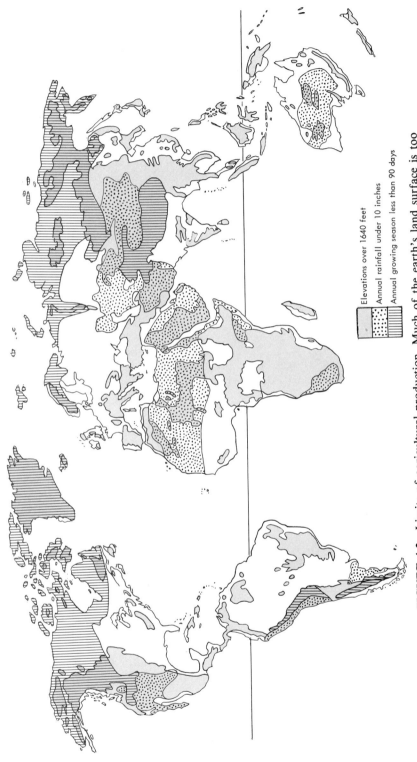

FIGURE 4.2 Limits of agricultural production. Much of the earth's land surface is too mountainous or too dry or has too short a growing season to support the usual forms of agriculture.

Elevations over 1640 feet

Annual rainfall under 10 inches

Annual growing season less than 90 days

leading some people to believe that these lightly populated areas could become productive agricultural lands suitable for resettlement of the world's surplus millions. Scientific evidence, however, does not support this idea, and the poor results of Brazil's recent large-scale attempts to develop Amazonia cast further doubt on it. The basic problem is the inherently low quality of tropical rain forest soils. Heavy rains throughout the year leach the soluble mineral plant food elements out of the soil and carry these to depths beyond the reach of ordinary shallow-rooted food plants. The deceptively lush growth of native trees results from the ability of these forest giants to send their taproots deep into underground deposits of nutrients. Most areas with tropical rain forest climates are thus lightly settled; Amazonia, for instance, supports only one person per square kilometer. Important exceptions are to be found in certain areas where local soil conditions permit successful farming despite heavy rainfall and rapid leaching. Thus, the Indonesian island of Java is able to support some of the world's highest rural population densities on its rich soils, which are periodically renewed by volcanic deposition. In some other places, sizable numbers of people obtain a livelihood from the cultivation of tropical tree crops such as rubber, bananas, and cacao.

Possibly the most forbidding of all climatic features is excessive cold. Ice and snow permanently cover great areas near the poles and on the higher mountains. Adjacent to the polar sheets are even greater expanses where low temperatures and short growing seasons prevent ordinary agriculture. Because most food plants require at least three months without frost to reach maturity, the limit of the 90-day growing season usually represents the poleward boundary of agricultural production (Figure 4.2). The colder climates, however, do support some human habitation: Exploitation of minerals employs limited numbers in certain favored localities, fishing provides a livelihood along the coasts of the northern continents, and forest products support scattered populations along the southern margins where temperatures are high enough for tree growth.

Farming is impossible in those mountainous areas with slopes too steep for soil to cling. The higher mountains are also too cold for ordinary crops because of the tendency for temperatures to drop with increasing elevation. In the middle and upper latitudes, forestry is confined to the lower slopes because temperatures at higher elevations are too low for trees to grow. Nearer the equator, however, the moderate temperatures and gentler slopes of highland basins provide ideal farming conditions; in tropical America these are the preferred places for human habitation (compare Figure 4.1 with Figure 4.2).

Grazing is often possible in areas that are too dry or cold for agriculture. With their sparse natural covering of grasses and herbaceous plants, the steppe lands are much used for this purpose, as are the basins and upper slopes of some mountainous regions. Reindeer herding takes place even in the far north of Eurasia and Alaska. Such lands have a meager carrying capacity for grazing animals, however, and they therefore support only scattered human populations.

Although such extreme climatic conditions tend to limit the spread of human beings into the more hostile areas, physical capabilities of the land do not bear a perfect relationship to the patterns of population density elsewhere. One important influence is length of settlement. In those parts of Asia and the Middle East where people have lived continuously since the emergence of human life on earth, rural overcrowding has become severe despite the submarginal quality of much of the land and poor agricultural conditions generally. In these places the steady growth of population over a very long time has diminished the capacity of the land to support human life. By contrast, farmlands of superior quality in the more recently settled Americas have far smaller population densities.

A further reason why maps of population density do not correspond perfectly with those of physical conditions is the governmental limits placed on immigration. Thus, sparsely settled Australia long excluded peoples seeking to migrate from the populous lands of nearby southern Asia.

Modern technology has further modified the influence of physical factors on settlement patterns. Today, if human beings have a compelling reason to live in an inhospitable area, they manage to create their own artificial environments. Heating, air conditioning, desalinization of water, and drainage are some of the costly measures that technology offers for residents of otherwise inhospitable surroundings. Perhaps the ultimate artificial environments are those found in great cities. These places develop an economic momentum of their own, attracting and providing for their populations regardless of the inherent physical characteristics of the land on which they are built.

The Empty Areas

Having noted the factors that limit human habitation, we may now examine some of those regions that have few people (Figure 4.1). One almost empty area is the enormous arctic region of North America, which includes northern Alaska, Canada, and Greenland. Also sparsely settled are the dry lands of western North America. Two virtually unpopulated regions in South America are the tropical rain forests of Amazonia and the great deserts of the south: the Atacama of Chile and

Peru and the Patagonian region of Argentina. Africa has three prominent empty areas: the vast Sahara Desert in the north, the tropical rain forests of equatorial Africa, and the Kalahari and Namib deserts of the south. Even Eurasia, the most populous of continents, has two extensive negative areas, the great polar fringes of the USSR and Scandinavia, and the deserts of central Asia and the adjacent highlands. Of all the inhabited continents, Australia, with its "dead heart," has the largest proportion of unoccupied land. Antarctica, which is covered by a huge ice sheet up to 2 miles thick, has no permanent human habitation at all.

The Major Population Nodes

Contrasting with these empty areas are four great population nodes, which dominate the world population map. The three largest, all in Eurasia, have at least half a billion people each; together they comprise more than three-fifths of humanity. Leading them all, the *East Asian* node includes Japan, Korea, and eastern China. Each of these areas has a middle-latitude location with generally favorable climatic conditions for agriculture. The inhabitants of this node are particularly concentrated within the large river floodplains and deltas on the Chinese mainland and the densely packed coastal plains and river valleys of mountainous Japan and Korea. As the birthplace of one of the principal human races, this region has an ancient history of habitation. Further contributing to the high population densities here are religious and cultural traditions that favor large families. Although intensive agriculture supports high rural densities, a large and efficient industrial economy enables Japan to sustain a population more than half that of the United States and to do so on a group of mountainous islands having a combined area less than that of Montana.

Second in size is the *South Asian* node, which includes most of India, Pakistan, and Bangladesh, in addition to the island of Sri Lanka (formerly Ceylon) and parts of Burma. Here the greatest population densities are in areas with a heavy monsoon rainfall. The only limit on the growing season is the availability of water, as warm temperatures prevail 12 months of the year. The largest cities and highest rural densities are found in the river deltas and floodplains and along the coastal plains, but even the drier interior of the Indian peninsula bears large numbers of people. Despite the generally poor quality of the soil—exhausted after several millennia of continuous use—agriculture remains the chief life support. High birth rates, however, continually strain food supplies.

Europe and the western Soviet Union constitute the third great population node. This region enjoys one of the most reliable of all agricultural climates, especially in its western portions. With moderate temperatures, a dependable supply of rainfall well distributed throughout the year (except along the Mediterranean), and a long growing season, Europe produces some of the world's best crop yields. Of all the continents, Europe also has the largest proportion of its land area devoted to agriculture. Despite their productivity, however, Western Europe's farms employ only a small proportion of the labor force. Relatively few people are engaged in exploiting Europe's ample mineral and biotic resources; most are employed in manufacturing and service activities; hence, the high degree of urbanization. Like the other population nodes of Eurasia, this is a region of long settlement, dating at least to the end of the last Ice Age.

The population node of *Eastern North America*, large as it is, has only a fraction of the people contained in each of the three major large concentrations. This region includes the "megalopolis" of the Middle Atlantic seaboard of the United States with its westward extension in the Great Lakes region of the Middle West and southern Ontario and Quebec, together with the associated rural populations of this important farming area. Despite a temperate climate, the growing seasons are decidedly shorter here than in most parts of the other three population nodes. Eastern North America also has important natural resources, including coal, iron ore, natural gas and oil, and a variety of other raw materials. Unlike the other three population nodes, this region was settled fairly recently and experienced rapid growth mainly through immigration and natural increase during its formative period. As in Western Europe, agriculture in Eastern North America is efficient and productive but occupies only a small percentage of the labor force.

Lesser Population Clusters

In addition to these major concentrations, at least 14 smaller population clusters appear on the world map. One is the *Los Angeles–Central Valley–San Francisco* area of California, until recently the fastest-growing concentration in the United States. The magnificent scenery and benign climate of this area have been prime attractions, but shortages of water and other environmental and economic problems threaten its continued growth. Another small cluster includes the *Vancouver* and *Puget Sound–Fraser River* areas of the Pacific Northwest, likewise a region of pleasant physical surroundings.

Mexico City and adjacent parts of the central plateau offer some of the most attractive climatic conditions in Mexico. Although agriculture is limited, this area contains a large part of the country's population and has become the center of a growing industrial district. The valleys of the *Central American highlands* contain most of the population of the isthmian region. Although widely separated from each other, the *islands of the Caribbean* are among the most densely populated areas of the Western Hemisphere.

The rapidly increasing population of South America is mainly concentrated at various points along the continental margins. Largest of these clusters is the *Central Plateau and Northeast Coast of Brazil,* the leading industrial area of Latin America and one of its principal agricultural districts as well, despite the difficult problems of supporting a swelling population. The *Rio de la Plata* district is the heart of Argentina's and Uruguay's populations; it contains most of the industry and is the focus of commercial agriculture. *Middle Chile,* another area of pleasant climatic conditions and productive agriculture, contains the majority of that country's people. The *Highland Basins of the Northern Andes,* extending from La Paz, Bolivia, northward through Peru, Ecuador, Colombia, and Venezuela, provide an attractive environment similar to that of the Central American highlands.

One of the most unusual population concentrations occupies the *Valley of the Lower Nile River* in North Africa. Here some of the highest rural densities in the world are compressed within the narrow confines of the irrigated floodplain and delta of an exotic stream that flows from the humid East African highlands through one of the driest of deserts (less than 1 inch of rainfall per year). The *Gulf of Guinea* coast of West Africa supports large numbers of people, especially in Ghana and Nigeria, where subsistence agriculture is the main occupation. In *East Central Africa,* potential overcrowding has been held in check by intertribal warfare. Another concentration of people in that continent is the *Republic of South Africa.* The coastal belt of this country has a pleasant Mediterranean-type climate and its interior is rich in valuable minerals, including gold, diamonds, coal, and iron. The final population node includes *Eastern Australia and New Zealand.* Australia's people live mainly along the southeast coastal lowland, which, by contrast with the arid center and west, receives adequate rainfall, has moderate temperatures, and offers most of the country's agricultural potential.

Intracountry Variations

Regional Concentrations

As we have seen, the national population figures for most countries obscure large internal variations in density. Even a country as small as Belgium, with an overall density of 323 persons per square kilometer, has its lightly populated Ardennes uplands. Though the United Kingdom as a whole has a high density, several regions, such as central Wales, the Pennine uplands, and the Scottish Highlands, have surprisingly few people. Even greater differences occur in Brazil, where the large and economically active population of the São Paulo–Rio de Janeiro region and the crowded rural northeast contrast markedly with the virtually empty Amazonian north. Likewise, the densely peopled Toronto–Golden Horseshoe district of Canada is entirely different from the nearly vacant Arctic lands of the Canadian north.

Some of the greatest regional variations are in China. Despite a huge population of 1005 million (1982 Census), China's overall density is only 110 persons per square kilometer. This is lower than the densities of most of its neighbors in eastern and southern Asia and much less than those of Western Europe. China's population is concentrated mainly in the coastal and central provinces, where most of the cultivated land is found. The Chengtu Plain in Szechwan Province supports exceedingly high rural population densities, whereas great areas in the arid west remain nearly unpeopled.

Why does the Chinese population remain so unevenly distributed after more than 40 centuries? One reason is the extreme variation in the physical capabilities of the land. Wide differences in soils, temperatures, and rainfall have profoundly influenced the locational choices of this predominantly agricultural people. Even where underused agricultural opportunities seem to exist, however, the Chinese have been unusually reluctant to move, owing to the influence of ancestor worship, of traditionally strong ties to family and village, and of regional language differences that hamper communication. Furthermore, extreme poverty has been endemic in China for centuries. Lacking savings, being vulnerable to a variety of natural calamities, and having little assurance of bettering themselves elsewhere, the Chinese have preserved a remarkably stable population pattern. Communist control appears to have had little overall effect in redistributing population among provinces, although important shifts have occurred locally.

Urbanization

The ultimate population concentration, of course, is in cities. One of the notable events of recent decades has been the rush of people from farms to cities and from smaller urban places to larger ones. By 1980, 78 percent of the people in the world's most industrialized countries lived in urban places, as opposed to 68 percent 10 years earlier.

Gregariousness among human beings appears to be instinctive: The survival of early peoples depended upon their living close to others of their kind. Throughout history, people have established cities for defense as well as for the various social and economic advantages of cooperative efforts. Both commerce and industry enjoy numerous savings by locating within urban areas, as later chapters will show. Among their other important roles, cities also serve as centers for administrative control, education, and culture, and as points of convergence for transportation routes.

Nevertheless, the very large city is a phenomenon of modern times; indeed, the word "civilization" is derived from the Latin term for city. Primitive human activities provided an insufficient surplus of food to support a large non-food-producing population. Subsistence gathering, hunting and fishing, herding, and agriculture supply barely enough food for tribal members and are very extensive in their use of land; migratory peoples may require five square kilometers or more to feed each individual. Although the well-organized Romans were able to mobilize production to support sizable urban populations, this capacity was lost in Europe when the Roman legions vanished. As Marco Polo discovered, however, the Chinese were able to maintain large cities throughout the period when medieval Europe's urban centers remained small.

Modern urban growth resulted from three essential developments. The first was the agricultural revolution of the late eighteenth century, which, for the first time, allowed European farms to feed a large nonagricultural population. Farm yields increased because of improved cultivation methods, new crops, scientific breeding of both plants and animals, consolidation of land holdings, and better communications and transportation. Transmitted across the Atlantic, the agricultural revolution brought similar results to the United States, where agricultural employment steadily declined as a percentage of the total labor force. In 1820, farm labor represented 72 percent of the gainfully employed, but by 1900 this figure had dropped to 37 percent; in 1980, only 2 percent of the labor force worked on farms, where they grew enough food not only to support the other 98 percent of the population but also great quantities for export overseas.

Beginning about the same time, the Industrial Revolution brought the factory system, which displaced the earlier cottage industry and hastened the growth of large concentrations of people. Simultaneously, the transportation revolution permitted cheap, fast, and dependable distribution of food, industrial raw materials, and other goods required by an expanding urban population. Meanwhile, these three developments helped expand the commercial hinterlands that acted as markets for the goods and services of the growing urban centers.

The ultimate result of the agricultural, industrial, and transportation revolutions has been the creation of great metropolises. The population of metropolitan London increased eightfold during the most recent century and a half, reaching a total of 9.8 million people in 1985. During that same period, New York's metropolitan area acquired a population of 15.3 million. Eclipsing New York's population today are the metropolitan areas of two Third World cities: Mexico City (18.1 million) and São Paulo (15.9 million).

The degree of urbanization in a country usually corresponds to its level of economic development: In general, the most urbanized countries also have the highest per capita gross national products (see Figures 4.3 and 4.4). Studies have shown that those countries ranking highest in urbanization also tend to rank highest on a scale of technology that combines indices of transportation, communications, energy production and consumption, national and per capita incomes, and foreign trade. In developed countries, urban pursuits—manufacturing and the services—employ most workers, including a majority of those actually residing in rural areas.

As Figure 4.3 shows, however, several developed countries are exceptions to this general relationship. Thus, among the richer industrialized countries, a few are less urbanized than their per capita GNPs would suggest. Switzerland, for example, is only 59 percent urbanized and Norway is only 55 percent urban. On the other hand, not counting such city-states as Singapore and Hong Kong, one of the most urbanized of all is Australia, with an urban population of 86 percent—hardly the picture of a nation of sheep growers and wheat farmers.

Within countries the degree of urbanization varies from one region to another. Urban development in the United States has produced dense concentrations of cities along each coast and on the shores of the Great Lakes. Elsewhere in the country, urban centers tend to be smaller and more scattered. In the lightly settled, largely rural plains and Rocky Mountain states, most cities exist in semi-isolation, although several urban centers in the intermontane west are growing very rapidly at present.

The typically lower levels of urbanization in less-developed countries stem mainly from their greater dependence upon agricultural employment. Even many of those persons living in cities and towns go daily into the countryside to work in the fields. Some of the lowest percentages of urbanization are in Asia, especially such remote, mountainous countries as Bhutan and Nepal, which have only 4 percent and 7 percent urbanization,

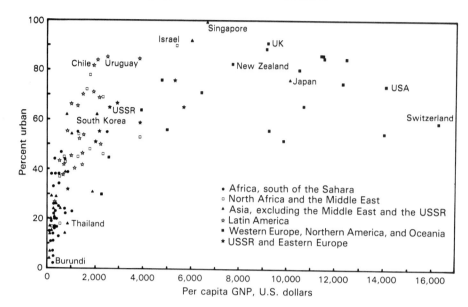

FIGURE 4.3 Relationship between urbanization and per capita gross national product. The correlation is very close at lower levels of development, but urbanization varies considerably among the more prosperous countries. In nearly all parts of the world, however, the movement to cities continues. [*Source:* Data from World Bank, *World Development Report 1985* (New York: Oxford University Press, 1985).]

respectively. Even in a country as large as Bangladesh, only 17 percent of the people live in cities. More striking yet is China, where 21 percent of a total population of one billion live in urban places. In India, 24 percent of the nation's 747 million people are urban. Levels of urbanization are likewise exceedingly low in sub-Saharan Africa; for example, Burundi (2 percent), Rwanda (5 percent), Mozambique (17 percent), and Tanzania (14 percent). On the other hand, in the semi-industrialized Republic of South Africa half of the population is urban.

Latin America has proceeded much further with its urbanization than have Asia and Africa. Indeed, the more prosperous countries of South America have higher levels of urbanization than many in Western Europe and North America. Venezuela, Uruguay, Argentina, and Chile all have more than 80 percent of their people in urban places, and semi-industrialized Mexico and Brazil are two-thirds urban. The least-urbanized Latin American lands are in parts of Central America and the Caribbean and in certain Andean areas.

Despite the mainly rural character of most lower-

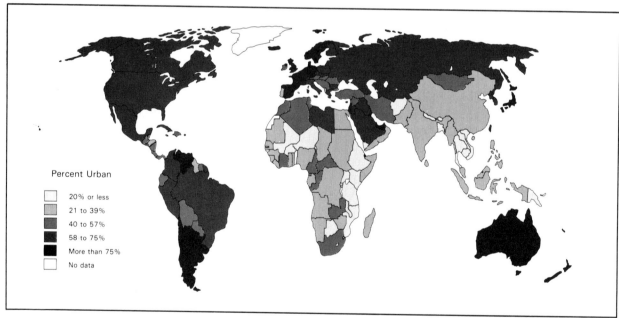

FIGURE 4.4 World urbanization. [*Source:* Data from World Bank, *World Development Report 1985* (New York: Oxford University Press, 1985).]

income countries, some of the world's great cities are in less-developed lands. Thus, the first-ranking metropolitan area is Mexico City, with 18.1 million people. Close behind are São Paulo (population 15.9 million), Shanghai (11.8 million), and Calcutta (11 million).

Only the most backward societies lack cities altogether. Typically, a less-developed country has only one truly large city and this dwarfs all other urban places in the land. For instance, Panama City contains 66 percent of the people in Panama. Other such "primate cities" include San José, where 64 percent of all Costa Ricans live, and Bangkok, home to 69 percent of Thailand's people. In addition to the usual commercial functions of a large urban place, the primate city of a less-developed land dominates the economically active parts of the country and is the focus of national political, social, and cultural life. In those countries at the lower end of the developmental scale, however, the functions of their principal cities tend to be limited in scope. Manufacturing, transportation, and communications are usually poorly developed, except insofar as they link demands of the developed world to the resources of the primate cities' hinterlands.

FUTURE POPULATIONS

Predictions

The spatial patterns of human population we have been describing are even now undergoing changes that will make tomorrow's world population map look very different from today's. Working to effect these changes are the dynamic forces discussed in the previous chapter: migration and differential population growth. With international migration now largely curtailed, however, the evolving population map increasingly reflects spatial variations in fertility and mortality rates. The kinds of demographic change now occurring create innumerable problems for the present and threaten even graver ones for the future.

If we are to devise strategies to cope with such problems, we must have forecasts of future population growth that are sufficiently reliable to pinpoint the trouble spots and to suggest the amount of potential danger. In the past, population forecasting was notoriously poor; most earlier projections greatly underestimated the rates at which growth was to occur. Thus, in 1949 Colin Clark forecast a world population of 3.5 billion by 1990, a figure that was exceeded before 1970. The main reason for such errors was the failure of demographers to anticipate the important declines in mortality and increases in life expectancy that advances in medical technology and the provision of public health care would

bring. Today's forecasts are much more accurate, as demographers sharpen their analytical tools and receive better information. The 1980–81 series of censuses around the world confirmed the accuracy of recent United Nations' projections. These projections have benefited from greatly improved data on fertility and mortality, especially from the larger countries such as China, India, Bangladesh, and Indonesia. Furthermore, the growth rate of world population has now peaked and has begun to fall off, thereby making demographic trends more predictable and reducing the range of forecasting error. No forecast, however, can allow for the unexpected: catastrophes such as global wars, massive famines, or environmental or agricultural crises that raise death rates, or unanticipated developments in technology or social organization that reduce birth rates, or medical breakthroughs that increase longevity.

The World in A.D. 2100

Barring such unforeseen catastrophes, the United Nations Population Division believes that future world populations will take shape in the manner suggested in Table 4.4. The evidence indicates that the world population is now at a turning point. Throughout the post–World War II era the global growth rate rose, as shown by the steepening curve in Figure 4.5. As of the mid-1980s, the slope of the curve is no longer increasing. World population growth has peaked and, judging by present demographic trends, it will slacken further in the future. Having grown from 2.3 billion people in 1940, global population currently stands at about 5 billion and should reach 6.1 billion by the end of this century (previous United Nations' projections had anticipated a population of 6.5 billion by the year 2000). The United Nations expects world population to stabilize during the latter part of the twenty-first century, reaching a total of about 10.2 billion by the year 2100 (Table 4.4). Thus, in Figure 4.5 the steeply rising curve in the first decades following World War II does indeed seem to confirm Malthus's prediction of exponential growth, but thereafter the curve assumes the typical S-shape of logistical growth, something Malthus did not expect.

Although, according to this scenario, the world as a whole will attain zero population growth (ZPG) by A.D. 2095, the various world regions are to reach this point at different times (Table 4.4; Figure 4.5). The more-developed regions, now growing at only 0.6 percent per annum, are already close to ZPG. The less-developed populations, however, are still growing at a very high rate of 2.2 percent annually, which means that for this group as a whole, ZPG will not arrive until the end of the twenty-first century. Nevertheless, a number of

TABLE 4.4

World population by regions. Estimates and projections, 1940–2100: United Nations medium variant (population in millions; percent of total in parentheses)

	1940	1960	1980	2000	2025	2050	2075	2100
World total	2,295 (100.0)	2,998 (100.0)	4,432 (100.0)	6,119 (100.0)	8,195 (100.0)	9,513 (100.0)	10,097 (100.0)	10,185 (100.0)
More-developed regions[a]	821 (35.8)	976 (32.6)	1,131 (25.5)	1,272 (20.8)	1,377 (16.8)	1,402 (14.7)	1,419 (14.1)	1,421 (14.0)
Less-developed regions[b]	1,575 (64.2)	2,022 (67.4)	3,301 (74.5)	4,847 (79.2)	6,818 (83.2)	8,111 (85.3)	8,677 (85.9)	8,764 (86.0)
Africa	191 (8.3)	273 (9.1)	470 (10.6)	853 (13.9)	1,542 (18.8)	2,166 (22.2)	2,507 (24.8)	2,591 (25.4)
Latin America	131 (5.7)	213 (7.1)	364 (8.2)	566 (9.2)	865 (10.6)	1,096 (11.5)	1,215 (12.0)	1,238 (12.2)
North America	144 (6.3)	199 (6.6)	248 (5.6)	299 (4.9)	344 (4.2)	364 (3.8)	378 (3.7)	382 (3.8)
East Asia (including Japan)	635 (27.6)	794 (26.5)	1,175 (26.5)	1,475 (24.1)	1,712 (20.9)	1,765 (18.6)	1,762 (17.5)	1,763 (17.3)
South Asia	610 (26.6)	865 (28.8)	1,404 (31.7)	2,075 (33.9)	2,819 (34.4)	3,198 (33.6)	3,306 (32.7)	3,284 (32.2)
Europe	379 (16.5)	425 (14.2)	484 (10.9)	512 (8.4)	522 (6.4)	509 (5.4)	503 (5.0)	504 (4.9)
Oceania	10 (0.4)	15 (0.5)	23 (0.5)	30 (0.5)	36 (0.4)	40 (0.4)	43 (0.4)	42 (0.4)
USSR	195 (8.5)	214 (7.2)	265 (6.0)	310 (5.1)	355 (4.3)	375 (3.9)	384 (3.8)	381 (3.7)

Sources: Data for 1940 and 1960 are from United Nations, *World Population Prospects, 1965–2000, as Assessed in 1968,* ESA/P/WP.37. New York: United Nations, 1970.

Data for 1980 through 2100 are from United Nations Secretariat, "Long-range Global Population Projections, as Assessed in 1980." *Population Bulletin of the United Nations,* No. 14-1982. New York: United Nations, 1983.

[a]More-developed regions are defined as North America, Europe, USSR, Japan, Australia, and New Zealand.

[b]Less-developed regions are defined as Africa, Latin America, East Asia (excluding Japan), South Asia, and Oceania (excluding Australia and New Zealand).

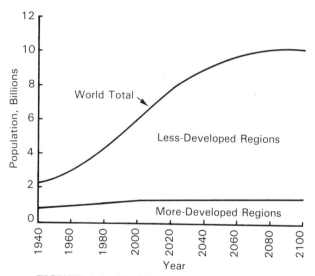

FIGURE 4.5 World population, 1940–2100. Nearly all industrialized countries will have achieved zero population growth by the end of the present century, but much of the Third World will continue to have rapid population growth until the latter part of the twenty-first century. [*Source:* Table 4.4.]

The United Nations bases these projections on a number of demographic trends, which are reflected in the contrasting age structures of populations in more-developed and less-developed countries. In Figure 4.7, the age structure of more-developed regions in 1980 displays the effects of low levels of both fertility and mortality. With only 23 percent of their populations below the age of 15 and more than 11 percent 65 years and older, these countries typify an old age distribution. On the other hand, the less-developed populations have much higher levels of fertility and mortality and hence much younger populations. The median age of this group is only 20 years; 39 percent of their populations are under 15 and only 4 percent are 65 and older. If the United Nations' predictions are realized, however, the age structures of the more-developed and less-developed countries will converge in the latter part of the next century, taking the forms shown in Figure. 4.7b.

One implication of all this is that most of the population growth of the next 100 years will be in less-developed areas. From Figure 4.8 we can see that growth is already slowing in Europe, North America, and the USSR, but that expansion continues elsewhere. This will bring important changes in the relative sizes of world regions during the next century. Although the less-developed regions held only two-thirds of the world's people at the time of World War II, they now have three-fourths and will have four-fifths by the year 2000 and six-sevenths at the end of the twenty-first century. In this period the more-developed regions will have de-

the more prosperous among the less-developed countries should achieve stationary populations much sooner than the rest. The close relationship between level of development and the year at which a country is expected to attain ZPG is apparent in Figure 4.6.

FIGURE 4.6 Relationship between per capita GNP and year of reaching stationary population. The years indicated here are not to be taken as actual predictions; they are merely estimates of when particular populations will stop growing if current trends continue. The estimates are based upon present age structures, together with assumptions concerning future mortality rates, fertility rates, and life expectancies. They suggest that some less-developed countries wll take a very long time to achieve stationary populations. If present trends continue, India will ultimately have the world's largest population, 1.7 billion people, surpassing China, the current leader. Mexico is to have 200 million, Brazil 300 million, the USSR 380 million, and the United States 290 million. Meanwhile, however, Japan's population is to increase only slightly before attaining its maximum, and some European populations are actually expected to shrink. [*Source:* Data from World Bank, *World Development Report, 1982 and 1985* (New York: Oxford University Press, 1982, 1985).]

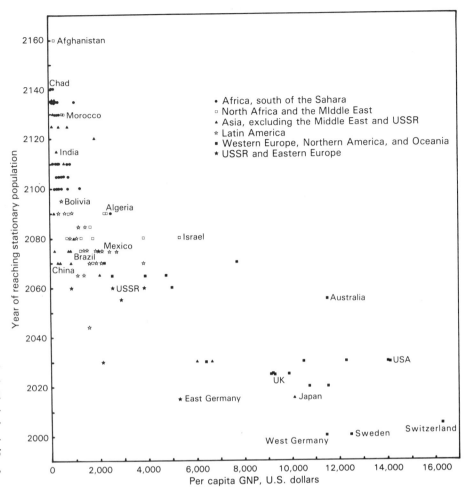

clined from one-third to only one-seventh of the world's population.

Another way of predicting how different growth rates are likely to affect future population distributions is to compare doubling times—the number of years it will take for populations to grow to twice their present size (see Chapter 1, page 3). Note from the map (Figure 4.9) that if current growth rates continue, nearly all African countries will have doubled their populations within 20 years or less. Similar doubling times prevail in the Islamic lands of the Middle East. Contrast these with Western Europe, where it will take up to 700 years for most populations to double in size. Now let us look more closely at current growth trends in major world areas.

The More-Developed Regions

With low birth rates closely balanced by low death rates, the more-developed regions are Type 5 countries according to the United Nations' classifications of population growth types (see Figure 3.8, Chapter 3). Fer-

tility rates remain generally below replacement levels because of the kinds of things that discourage having children: high incomes, urbanization, high levels of female education, large numbers of women in the work force, postponement of marriage, widespread use of contraception, delayed age of giving birth to the first child, and rising divorce rates. Life expectancy is rising at a slower rate because most diseases except those related to old age are largely under control.

Population stability has thus become universal in the industrialized regions, and the projected size of future populations is likely to change little (Table 4.4; Figure 4.5). The more-developed peoples now total a little more than 1.1 billion, and they will probably reach hardly more than 1.4 billion during the coming century. They will therefore become an ever-smaller proportion of global population. Although all the more-developed lands fall into this general pattern, their circumstances and the timing of demographic change vary.

The most mature region of all is Europe, where the first demographic transition occurred. Fertility is so low in some countries that their populations are begin-

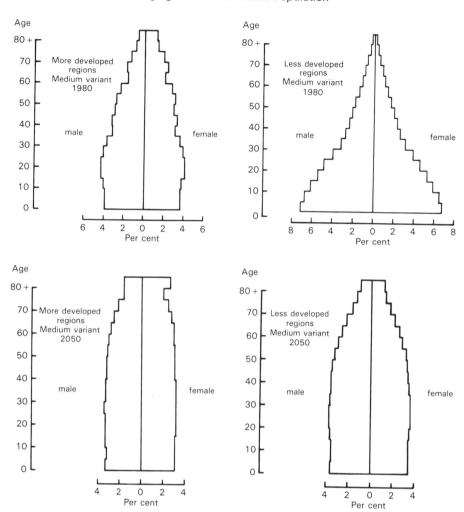

FIGURE 4.7 Age structures of more-developed and less-developed regions for the years 1980 and 2050. The less-developed countries have much higher levels of fertility and mortality and therefore have younger populations. By the second half of the twenty-first century, however, the two age distributions should become more similar. [*Source:* UN Population Division, *Population Bul.* No. 14, 1983.]

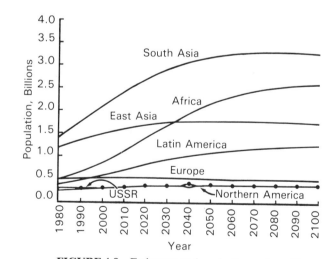

FIGURE 4.8 Estimates and projections of world population by regions, 1980–2100. Growth is slowing in Europe, Northern America, and the USSR, but populations continue to expand in the less-developed regions. [*Source:* After UN Population Division, *Population Bul.* No. 14, 1983.]

ning to decline absolutely. Between 1970 and 1980 slight decreases occurred in Austria, East Germany, and West Germany, and zero growth was the rule elsewhere in the region. According to United Nations' projections, Europe's population will be smaller at the end of the twenty-first century than at its start. Today Europe represents 11 percent of the world total; by A.D. 2100 it will likely be only 4.9 percent of an enlarged global population. The decline will come to Northern Europe before it comes to Southern Europe, and will arrive in Western Europe before it arrives in Eastern Europe. In the 1950s and 1960s some communist countries in Eastern Europe tried to avert population decline but have abandoned these efforts in the face of worsening food shortages.

In Northern America (Canada and the United States) societal changes have brought fertility levels to historic lows. Despite a growing number of women from the baby boom generation who have now reached childbearing age, birth rates have not risen proportionally. Northern America's population is therefore projected to increase at a rate of only 0.8 per annum during the

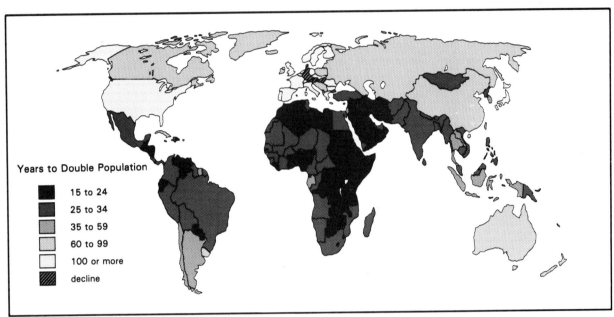

FIGURE 4.9 Number of years to double population. If current birth and death rates were to continue unchanged, much of Africa, the Middle East, and the tropical Americas would have twice as many people within another generation as they do now. Little future growth is expected, however, in Northern America, Europe, the USSR, or the industrializing countries of East Asia. [*Source:* Based upon data from *1986 Britannica Book of the Year* (Chicago: Encyclopaedia Britannica, Inc., 1986).]

1980s. Now 5.6 percent of world population, this region will probably be only 3.8 percent of the total at the end of the twenty-first century.

One of the most interesting cases is Japan, which had an exceedingly high birth rate until the end of World War II. At that time official policy changed abruptly, as the Japanese saw the difficulties of accommodating a rapidly expanding population within a small island nation no larger than California. Thus, they quickly brought population growth under control by using such means as contraception, abortion, and other measures. Small families are now the rule in Japan, and the growth rate and age structure are similar to those of the United States.

The USSR has also entered the ranks of UN Type 5 countries. Now growing at only 0.9 percent annually, the population of the USSR about equals that of Northern America (Table 4.4) and is following a very similar growth path. The USSR differs from other industrialized countries, however, in the unusual variability among its constituent republics (which are generally drawn up along ethnic lines). Births have fallen below replacement levels among the ethnic Russians comprising the largest Soviet republic, the Russian SFSR. In the USSR's Central Asian Republics, however, fertility remains surprisingly high—nearly double that of the Russian SFSR and comparable to rates found in less-developed lands. This puzzles demographers because the high-growth areas have literate female populations and low death rates. A likely cause is a firmly embedded cultural bias among these Muslim minorities favoring very large families. This disparity in population growth worries ethnic Russians, who currently dominate the country politically and economically. Another unique demographic feature of the Soviet population is its unusual age distribution. The 60 to 64 age group has a disproportionately small number of males, a result of heavy casualties during World War II. At the same time, the 35 to 39 age group is relatively small because these are the children of those who fought the war.

The Less-Developed Countries

As the populations of the more-developed regions stabilize, those of the less-developed areas continue to soar. The United Nations expects the poorer countries to account for 95 percent of world population growth between now and the middle of the next century. Although birth rates are beginning to decline in some important areas, they generally remain very high elsewhere. Meanwhile, throughout much of the less-developed world, mortality rates are falling and people are living longer.

Although continued population growth is the dominant trend among less-developed countries, each region seems to be taking its own path. Moreover, some of these paths are easier to predict than others, mainly because fertility rates vary greatly from region to region. Several less-developed countries have achieved surprisingly low levels of fertility, whereas others have fertility rates as high as ever. Fertility is a complex matter: Although high fertility is closely linked to poverty, it has deep cultural roots as well (see Chapter 3). Thus, we cannot be certain when it will start to fall in those areas where it is currently high, nor can we be sure how fast its decline will be.

Figure 4.10 shows the widely differing expectations for future total fertility rates (*total* fertility is the total number of children born to the average couple). Demographers at the United Nations predict that fertility will continue to decline rapidly in eastern Asia, that it will decrease more rapidly in southern Asia than in Latin America, and that it will lag far behind the others in Africa.

For the remainder of this century Asia will remain a serious problem area, not just because of its high rate of growth but because of the enormous population to which those rates apply. The situation differs from one country to another, however. Some countries have begun to make substantial progress and may attain zero population growth early in the next century; others are disappointingly slow. Both types are present in southern Asia. Fertility rates are dropping rapidly in the industrialized city-state of Singapore, where total fertility is now well below the replacement level of two children per family. Despite low incomes, the island nation of Sri Lanka is also progressing. On the other hand, sev-eral other low-income countries—Kampuchea, Bangladesh, Nepal, Afghanistan, and Pakistan—still have very high fertility and mortality rates. The same is true of the Muslim countries of Southwest Asia—both those that are rich in oil and those that are not. A notable exception among Islamic nations is semi-industrialized Turkey, which maintains a strict separation between religion and the state and is beginning to get its population under control. The other countries of southern Asia, nearly a billion people in all, are making only slow progress.

Perhaps the brightest spot in the developing world is eastern Asia. Even though China's recent census has forced an upward revision in the estimated total population, a dramatic reduction in population growth is taking place throughout the region. This is occurring not only in the middle-income industrialized countries—Taiwan, South Korea, and the city-state of Hong Kong—but most notably in China, a low-income nation that has made startling progress in population control. Prior to the 1949 revolution, China was truly a UN Type 1 country: a very high birth rate balanced by a similarly high death rate. The new government effected a remarkable reduction in the death rate by improving food distribution, raising literacy levels, and introducing health-care facilities in virtually every rural community. The result was explosive population growth, adding 400 million people—almost as many as in all of Europe—to an already-overpopulated agricultural country.

Influenced by Mao Tse-tung's utopian philosophy, China's ruler at first did nothing to stem this growth, believing that the more people the better. Subsequently, a more pragmatic leadership awoke to the fact that 30 percent of national income was being drained

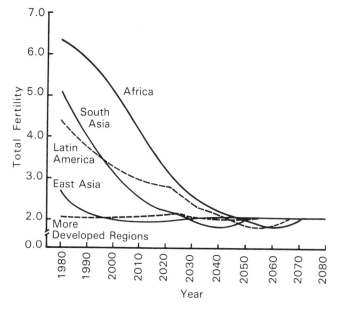

FIGURE 4.10 Projected total fertility rates by world regions—UN medium variant, 1980 to 2080 as assessed in 1980. The United Nations anticipates wide variation among regions in the timing of the decline in their total fertility (average number of births per couple during their lifetime). Rates will likely remain very high in Africa well into the twenty-first century. [*Source:* After UN Population Division, *Population Bul.* No. 14, 1983.]

off to support these new additions to China's population. A new official policy has therefore set a target of zero population growth by A.D. 2000, with a standard of one child per family, backed by a combination of rewards and penalties. Although difficult to enforce in the rural countryside, this policy has quickly reduced fertility, cutting in half the former birth rate of 40 per thousand. China thus appears to be compressing its demographic transition into an uncommonly short time span. This dramatic reversal of China's tradition of large families compares with similar changes achieved previously by ethnic Chinese populations living in Taiwan, Hong Kong, Singapore, and elsewhere in Asia. This has prompted demographers to speculate that the Chinese culture is particularly receptive to the idea of lower fertility. The abruptness of this change in mainland China is clear from the current age structure of that country, as shown in Figure 4.11. Note the broad-based pyramid typical of less-developed countries but with a sharp contraction in the youngest age contingent, showing the recent decline in birth rates. Trends such as these underscore predictions made by the United Nations that early in the next century East Asia's population will drop to third among world regions (Table 4.4).

Taking East Asia's place in second rank will be Africa, the only continent where population growth rates actually rose during the 1970s. Two-thirds of the world's poorest nations are in Africa, confirming the much-noted poverty-population link. Recent data suggest that Africa's fertility rate is now rising slightly. The United Nations has therefore had to revise upward its

estimates of the future size of this region, now expected to constitute one-quarter of all humanity 100 years hence. Even so, the United Nations has little confidence in this prediction because of the early stage of Africa's demographic transition and uncertainty over its timing.

The entire African continent is a demographic problem area, but the problems differ north and south of the Sahara. North Africa is a Muslim area with a strong cultural bias toward large populations. Yet, as urbanization and development proceed in the countries in the north, some signs of declining growth rates are appearing. Egypt, the most advanced country within this group, is leading the way with moderate decreases in fertility, especially in Cairo, Alexandria, and other large cities. Tunisia is following closely behind, suggesting that the remaining countries of North Africa, which now have very high fertility rates, will eventually take the same path. Yet the ultimate outcome in this region is not at all certain, given the Islamic cultural influence.

The most serious threat, however, comes from sub-Saharan Africa, as Figure 4.12 illustrates. Note that birth rates in these poorest parts of Africa show no sign of diminishing but that death rates, although generally higher than elsewhere in the world, are steadily declining. Throughout this region are some of the highest fertility rates ever recorded; in no country has fertility dropped, and in some countries it has increased. Many demographers have concluded that the populations of this region have a greater cultural propensity to high fertility than other peoples at similar levels of development. Tropical Africa has an exceedingly young pop-

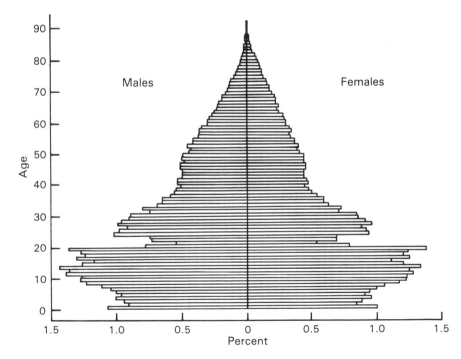

FIGURE 4.11 Population pyramid of China, 1982. This age structure is typical of less-developed countries except that the youngest age groups are proportionately smaller than usual, evidence of China's effective new population policy. The effects of past crises in the country's recent history are also apparent in the reduced numbers of people in their early twenties and late thirties. [*Source:* China, Population Census Office, 1983.]

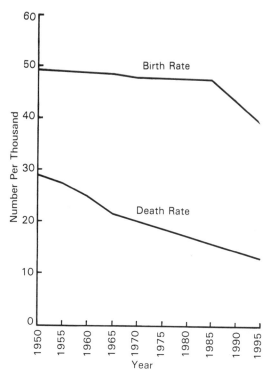

FIGURE 4.12 Birth and death rates in low-income Africa. Death rates, although still higher than elsewhere, are steadily declining. Meanwhile, birth rates remain uncommonly high, creating conditions for explosive population growth (the drop in birth rates after 1985 is conjectural only). [*Source:* After World Bank, *World Development Report 1981* (New York: Oxford University Press, 1981).]

FIGURE 4.13 Age structure of Tanzania. High fertility rates in sub-Saharan Africa are producing unusually young populations.

ulation, as Tanzania's age structure illustrates (Figure 4.13). Thus, Africa is only now entering the most explosive phase of the demographic transition. Although Africa's demographic future is clouded at this point, one thing is sure: The twenty-first century will see continued population growth, posing grave problems in a region where many peoples are already pressing the resources of the land. If Malthus is to be vindicated, it will be in Africa.

Latin America's population began to soar in the early post–World War II period, the result of successful programs to reduce death rates. Birth rates remained high, however, and most Latin American nations have exceedingly young populations. Latin America in general has all the conditions conducive to high fertility: widespread poverty, female illiteracy, and a cultural bias toward large families, reinforced by religious strictures against birth control. As life expectancy continues to rise, this region comprises an expanding share of total world population (Figure 4.8; Table 4.4).

Latin America is very diverse, however, and some parts fit this description better than others. A number of low-income countries—notably Honduras, Haiti, and several smaller island nations of the Caribbean—have persistently high levels of fertility and galloping population growth. Certain other high-fertility countries, somewhat less impoverished, have very low death rates and exploding populations. Prominent in this group is Mexico, together with Bolivia, Ecuador, Paraguay, and parts of Central America. On the other hand, a number of countries have achieved some reduction in fertility and thus moderated their rates of population growth. Among these are Brazil, Venezuela, Colombia, Peru, Costa Rica, Panama, and Cuba. Finally, in southernmost Latin America, semi-industrialized Argentina, Uruguay, and Chile have already attained low levels of fertility and mortality and should be reaching zero population growth early in the next century.

Despite this evidence of demographic change, Latin America's population is destined to rise from 8 percent of the world total now to 12 percent by the latter part of the twenty-first century. At the end of World War II, Latin America had fewer people than Northern America; in another hundred years it will have more than three times as many. As yet only a few countries in Latin America are actually overcrowded, notably El Salvador and several Caribbean islands. Although densities are otherwise well below those common in Asia and West Africa, present trends will doubtless change this. Furthermore, even those growing Latin American populations that have not experienced physical crowding are finding it increasingly difficult to feed, educate, and employ the new additions to their numbers. One troublesome result is the mounting spillover of Latin Americans into North America.

Changes in Structure and Spatial Distribution

In addition to their changing demography, the developing countries are experiencing profound changes in the structure and spatial distribution of their labor forces. As development proceeds, it substantially alters the occupational makeup of a population, which in turn reinforces the flood of people to the cities, as described previously. In this section we look at the expectations for structural change in developing economies and examine projections of future urban growth as it affects the major cities in those areas.

As we compare work-force structures of countries at different stages of economic development, a fairly consistent pattern of change takes place, as illustrated in Figure 4.14. Before industrialization, the primary sector—agriculture, forestry, and fishing—employs a major part of the work force. Secondary forms of production, mainly handicrafts, occupy relatively few workers. The non-goods-producing activities, likewise poorly developed, consist of two parts. The tertiary sector, including retailing and wholesaling, is often inflated in numbers by the inefficient nature of marketing and by the prominence of personal and domestic service in less-developed economies. The quaternary sector—administration, higher education, research and development, medicine, and other more specialized activities—is severely limited and rudimentary. Typical of such economies is Haiti, where 74 percent of the work force is in agriculture, only 7 percent is in industry, and the remaining 19 percent in the services. In some of the poorest countries of Africa and southern Asia, the primary sector accounts for nine-tenths or more of all employment.

When industrialization commences, demand for workers in secondary occupations grows at an accelerating pace until eventually manufacturing becomes a major employer. Meanwhile, increased efficiency in the use of farm labor leads to a steady drop in primary employment. The tertiary and quaternary activities develop less slowly because services and administration still come mainly from outside the country. One such newly industrializing country is South Korea, which now employs 34 percent of the labor force in agriculture, 29 percent in industry, and 37 percent in the services.

The late-industrial stage, which arrived in the United States during the 1920s, sees an accelerating decline in agricultural employment. Manufacturing employment continues to grow, although at a declining rate as labor productivity rises and finally reaches a maximum by the end of the period. Meanwhile, tertiary activities expand steadily to satisfy the proliferating demands of supporting services for manufacturing and to supply the growing requirements of an ever-more-prosperous population. Though initially slow to develop, the quaternary sector eventually expands and becomes increasingly sophisticated as the economy and society grow more and more complex. In Italy, which appears to be at this stage, agriculture now employs only 11 percent of the work force, whereas industry takes 45 percent and the services 44 percent.

The postindustrial stage, which began soon after World War II in the United States and arrived in Western Europe and Japan in the 1960s, is marked by a declining emphasis upon material goods and a growing interest in the quality of life. Agriculture becomes so capital-intensive and efficient that only a small number of farm workers provide the food and industrial raw materials needed by the rest of the population. Meanwhile, automation reduces labor requirements in industry. Tertiary activities, now more specialized than ever, begin to reach saturation; but the quaternary sector steadily expands, developing an elaborate division of labor and supplying a whole new set of societal needs. Thus, in the United States only 2 percent of the work force runs the farms that feed 235 million people and that produce a major share of the country's export earnings. Industrial employment has fallen to 32 percent,

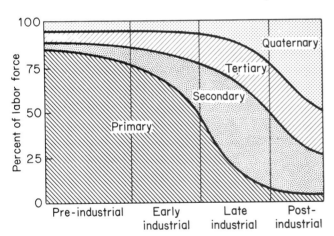

FIGURE 4.14 Effects of economic development upon the structure of the labor force. As a region rises in the scale of development, the proportion of its labor force engaged in primary activities diminishes. The percentage employed in secondary activities increases until industrialization is essentially completed, at which time it begins a relative decline. The proportion in the services, both tertiary and quaternary, consistently rises.

but the services now require 66 percent of the work force.

As newly developing nations follow along this path, presumably their labor forces will undergo the same kinds of structural changes as those that have taken place in the developed countries. The shift of workers out of primary employment, however, accelerates the flow of people into those large cities where jobs in industry and the services are concentrated. Hence, the pace of urbanization now under way in developing countries will likely continue well into the next century.

The effects of this trend are apparent from Figure 4.15, which lists in rank order the 35 largest cities in A.D. 2000, according to United Nations projections. For comparison, Figure 4.15 also shows the populations of those same cities in 1985. Note that 25 of the 35 are in less-developed countries and that only 2 of the top 10 are in more-developed lands. In 1950, seven of the 10 largest cities were in developed countries. As we have noted previously, the flight of people from the countryside in less-developed countries is proceeding more rapidly than jobs or services can be provided for them, posing enormous urban problems. Can these already-burgeoning cities really absorb the numbers predicted for them?

ASSESSMENT: WHAT TO DO WITH 10 BILLION PEOPLE

This is a crucial period for the issue of world population; much depends upon what happens between now and the end of the present century. By the 1980s the number of human beings inhabiting the earth had reached levels previously considered unthinkable, and most of this increase had occurred within the modern era. As we have seen in this chapter, today's population of 5 billion people is crowded into a comparatively small portion of earth space, mainly regions that in earlier times held special attractions to migrants and offered optimal conditions for the multiplication of human populations. Chief among these conditions was the presence of favorable agricultural environments for a people who obtained their livelihood directly from the soil. Today the largest population concentrations are in those regions with the earliest histories of habitation, but the areas most densely packed with humanity are the great urban metropolises that have evolved in modern times—end products of the agricultural, industrial, and transportation revolutions.

Evidence presented in this chapter suggests that the world has entered an important era of demographic change. The slope of the global growth-rate curve is no longer steepening, an indication that world population growth may have peaked. Indeed, United Nations experts anticipate a further slackening in the rate of growth and predict that the global population will have stabilized before the end of the twenty-first century. But these long-range projections are based upon unsure assumptions about a remote future. Forecasting techniques have improved sufficiently for us to be fairly sure about what will happen in the developed world, where detailed information is available and trends are well established. For the less-developed regions, however, the future is less clear because circumstances are so varied and cultural influences so important.

Demographers are already breathing easier about East Asia, where fertility rates are dropping much sooner and far more rapidly than any had dared to hope. Japan's success in reversing its high fertility at the close of World War II is being emulated today, three decades later, throughout the Orient, most notably in China. This is an important development, considering that East Asia's present population is so huge and densities are so great. The situation is less sure in Latin America and southern Asia, where some countries have made progress but several very large ones have done less well.

The greatest uncertainty focuses upon sub-Saharan Africa and the Islamic lands of the Middle East and North Africa. The social pressures for large families among Muslim peoples threaten to offset the moderating effects of urbanization upon fertility rates. When directed toward African countries south of the Sahara, however, predictions become mere guesses. Extreme poverty, illiteracy, and cultural propensities combine in those areas to create conditions for explosive population growth. United Nations projections for the entire region are hardly more than hopes; no one knows when the present high rates of fertility will begin to drop, or even whether this will happen at all.

We have also noted that the populations of developing countries are being transformed in other, related ways, especially the structural changes in their labor forces that take place as workers are shifted progressively out of primary occupations into manufacturing and service activities. A visible manifestation of this is the accelerating rate of urbanization within the Third World, which by A.D. 2000 will contain the majority of the world's largest metropolises, together with all the economic, social, environmental, and political strains these bring.

At every scale—global, regional, or urban—population predictions are horrendous, even if they prove correct. This chapter has shown that rapid population growth intensifies nearly every serious problem of humanity: unemployment, illiteracy, poor housing, ill health, political instability, and, most basic of all, in-

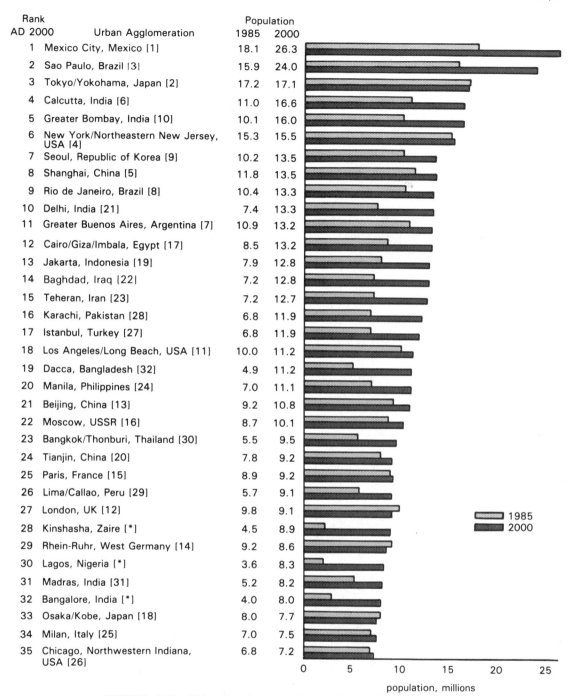

Rank AD 2000	Urban Agglomeration	Population 1985	2000
1	Mexico City, Mexico [1]	18.1	26.3
2	Sao Paulo, Brazil [3]	15.9	24.0
3	Tokyo/Yokohama, Japan [2]	17.2	17.1
4	Calcutta, India [6]	11.0	16.6
5	Greater Bombay, India [10]	10.1	16.0
6	New York/Northeastern New Jersey, USA [4]	15.3	15.5
7	Seoul, Republic of Korea [9]	10.2	13.5
8	Shanghai, China [5]	11.8	13.5
9	Rio de Janeiro, Brazil [8]	10.4	13.3
10	Delhi, India [21]	7.4	13.3
11	Greater Buenos Aires, Argentina [7]	10.9	13.2
12	Cairo/Giza/Imbala, Egypt [17]	8.5	13.2
13	Jakarta, Indonesia [19]	7.9	12.8
14	Baghdad, Iraq [22]	7.2	12.8
15	Teheran, Iran [23]	7.2	12.7
16	Karachi, Pakistan [28]	6.8	11.9
17	Istanbul, Turkey [27]	6.8	11.9
18	Los Angeles/Long Beach, USA [11]	10.0	11.2
19	Dacca, Bangladesh [32]	4.9	11.2
20	Manila, Philippines [24]	7.0	11.1
21	Beijing, China [13]	9.2	10.8
22	Moscow, USSR [16]	8.7	10.1
23	Bangkok/Thonburi, Thailand [30]	5.5	9.5
24	Tianjin, China [20]	7.8	9.2
25	Paris, France [15]	8.9	9.2
26	Lima/Callao, Peru [29]	5.7	9.1
27	London, UK [12]	9.8	9.1
28	Kinshasha, Zaire [*]	4.5	8.9
29	Rhein-Ruhr, West Germany [14]	9.2	8.6
30	Lagos, Nigeria [*]	3.6	8.3
31	Madras, India [31]	5.2	8.2
32	Bangalore, India [*]	4.0	8.0
33	Osaka/Kobe, Japan [18]	8.0	7.7
34	Milan, Italy [25]	7.0	7.5
35	Chicago, Northwestern Indiana, USA [26]	6.8	7.2

FIGURE 4.15 Thirty-five largest urban agglomerations in A.D. 2000, ranked by estimated population size. Populations for 1985 are also shown for comparison (1985 ranks appear in braces; asterisk indicates that city was not among the 35 largest agglomerations in 1985). Note the increasing prominence of Third World cities. [*Source:* Data from United Nations 1982 Assessment, UN Biennial, 1985.]

adequate food supply. The adverse impact of population growth afflicts most severely the poorest areas and most impoverished people. And, when these problems become sufficiently severe in one area, they spill over into others: Even the richest, most stable populations cannot escape their consequences in an ever-shrinking world. Thus, the question for us all is whether or not the world is able to support 10 billion people. The next chapter looks for answers to this.

TOPICS FOR DISCUSSION

1. What are the relative merits of each of the following measures for comparing populations: population size, population density, physiological density?

2. Discuss the various physical limits to human habitation, and explain how these have contributed to the shaping of contemporary population patterns. Why is the correlation between population density and physical conditions an imperfect one?

3. Describe the principal population nodes that appear in Figure 4.1, and discuss their relative importance. Why do lightly populated areas exist within the territories of some of the most densely populated countries? Give examples.

4. What causes human beings to congregate in cities, and why have truly large cities appeared only in modern times? In what countries does urbanization reach its highest levels today and why? Account for the current rush of people to the cities of Third World countries, and identify those cities most likely to be the world's largest by the end of this century.

5. Analyze the main demographic forces at work to change the world population map. Why has population forecasting failed so badly in the past, and why are demographers more confident of today's forecasts?

6. Describe and explain the differences in age composition of populations in advanced countries and those in less-developed ones. How do the occupational structures of these two categories of countries differ and why? What economic and social problems do these population characteristics create in each case?

7. How is a world population map for the year 2080 likely to differ from a map of today's population? Explain the wide variations in population growth projected for different Third World areas. Which world regions are of greatest concern to students of population? Explain.

FURTHER READINGS

BOGUE, DONALD J., and AMY ONG TSUI. "Zero World Population Growth?" *The Public Interest,* Spring 1979, pp. 99–113.

Explores the reasons for recent declines in birth rates and the implications of these for bringing world population growth under control.

BOUVIER, LEON F., with HENRY S. SHRYOCK and HARRY W. HENDERSON. "International Migration: Yesterday, Today, and Tomorrow." *Population Bulletin* 32, No. 4. Washington: Population Reference Bureau, Inc.

Looks at modern trends of international migration and envisions massive migrations of African workers to Western Europe similar to the legal and illegal migrations of Latin Americans to the United States.

COALE, ANSLEY J. "A Reassessment of World Population Trends." *Population Bulletin of the United Nations,* No. 14-1982. New York: United Nations, 1983.

Reassesses trends in mortality and fertility and their long-term implications for population growth, with special reference to earlier projections, one of which has proved very accurate. Using this latter method, the author examines trends in a large number of countries. He finds a great diversity of levels and trends of fertility among developing countries, and he concludes that future rates of increase in Third World areas depend upon the unpredictable timing and pace of the reduction of childbearing in those populations where fertility continues to be high.

COALE, ANSLEY J. "Recent Trends in Fertility in Less-Developed Countries." *Science,* Vol. 221, August 26, 1983, pp. 828–832.

Coale notes that in the 1960s the world birth rate began to decline more rapidly than the death rate, but that the rate of decline varied greatly among Third World countries. He predicts that the momentum of growth will bring continued population increase for several decades even in countries where fertility has fallen the most and that these increases will be very large in those populations whose fertility has not yet begun to decline.

DAVIS, CARY. "The Future Racial Composition of the United States." *Intercom* 10, No. 9/10, 1982, pp. 8–10.

Projects annual migrations, legal and illegal, to the United States and predicts a Hispanic-Black-Asian majority for the country by the middle of the twenty-first century.

KATES, ROBERT W. *The Human Environment: Penultimate Problems of Survival.* Natural Hazards Research and Applications Center, Special Publication No. 6. Worcester, Mass.: The Center for Technology, Environment, and Development, Clark University, 1983.

Considers three related sets of issues: population growth and resource use, income disparities and their potential for widespread unrest and conflict, and environmental problems resulting from technological change.

TSUI, AMY ONG, and DONALD J. BOGUE. "Declining World Fertility: Trends, Causes, Implications." *Population Bulletin* 33, No. 4. Washington: Population Reference Bureau, Inc., 1978.

Projects population growth rates for A.D. 2000. African populations are expected to continue growing very rapidly, but rates will be declining in Latin America and most of Asia.

VAN DE WALLE, ETIENNE, and JOHN KNODEL. "Europe's Fertility Transition: New Evidence and Lessons for Today's Developing World." *Population Bulletin* 34, No. 6. Washington: Population Reference Bureau, Inc., 1980.

Analyzes changes in marital fertility among European populations since the eighteenth century. The wide differences among countries in the timing of fertility decline suggests the influence of cultural factors.

CHAPTER 5

Resources:
Food, Energy, Materials,
and Environment

Continuing population growth brings into question the earth's capacity to provide the necessary food, energy, and industrial raw materials during the coming century. The Third World, being the last to achieve population equilibrium, will exert most of the new pressures upon resources. Thanks to new technology, the global food supply will probably be adequate for the near term; beyond A.D. 2000, however, the outlook is not yet assured. Already the Third World is a net importer of food.

Population growth and industrialization likewise exert pressures upon nonrenewable resources. The oil crises of the 1970s focused attention upon energy supplies. Like other minerals, the fossil fuels are concentrated in a few countries and regions, some politically unstable. Oil and gas output will peak early in the new century; coal should last much longer, although hampered by problems of pollution and shipping cost. In the longer run, new technologies will take over. The outlook for other minerals is less promising. Although a few are plentiful, many have limited life spans, and all draw upon other scarce resources in their production and use. It appears unlikely that the world as a whole can ever consume many of these at current U.S. levels.

The intensifying use of the earth's resources also threatens the quality of the environment. Pollution wastes valuable resources even as it poisons the atmosphere and water. Although costs of remedial measures are high, the future habitability of a crowded planet requires that these measures be taken.

Objectives:

- to understand the nature and availability of the earth's resources
- to appreciate the difficulties of ensuring an adequate supply and equitable distribution of food for future populations
- to distinguish between short- and long-run political, economic, technical, and environmental problems of global energy supply
- to evaluate future prospects for mineral raw materials and possibilities for extending their life spans
- to describe the impacts of population increase and industrialization upon environmental quality

CAN THE WORLD SUPPORT ITS FUTURE POPULATIONS?

Growing Pressures

Does the earth have enough material resources to provide for the 10 billion people expected eventually to live here? This is the much-debated question that closed the previous chapter. The answer depends upon what happens to the two parts of the resources/population ratio. In Chapter 4 we examined those elements influencing the denominator of this fraction—numbers of people. Here we consider the many complex issues affecting the numerator: the problems of how much food, energy, and raw materials the earth can be made to yield and whether the physical environment can remain habitable with intensifying human use.

The shape of future world populations is now beginning to emerge. Drawing upon better data and improved predictive techniques, demographers generally feel that we are approaching that turning point when the population growth curve, which has risen exponentially for so long, will start to moderate its rate of climb and will eventually assume the characteristic S-shape of the logistic curve. Although the world's population as a whole is expected to reach a steady state some time in the latter part of the next century, however, the timing

of this will vary greatly from one part of the world to another. Population equilibrium will arrive last in the poorest countries, where growth still remains high. Hence, it is safe to predict that the future drain on resources will come increasingly from parts of the Third World.

While population is assuming a new global pattern, the other side of the Malthusian ratio is likewise changing. Two things are happening to the resource part of the fraction: Per capita resource use is growing, and new kinds of resource needs are arising. The main reason for increased consumption of food, energy, and raw materials per person is the general rise in level of development. The *Global 2000 Report to the President of the United States* predicts that gross national product for the world as a whole will grow by more than 50 percent during the final two decades of this century (see Figures 5.1 and 5.2). This will not occur equally in all regions, however. As Figure 5.2 shows, the largest increases in per capita GNP are taking place in certain of the semi-industrialized countries, especially Brazil, Mexico, and the countries of the western Pacific rim. Growth in per capita GNP will continue to be lowest in southern Asia and sub-Saharan Africa.

Furthermore, as Robert Kates has noted in his book *The Human Environment: Penultimate Problems of Survival* (1983), the numerator of the Malthusian ra-

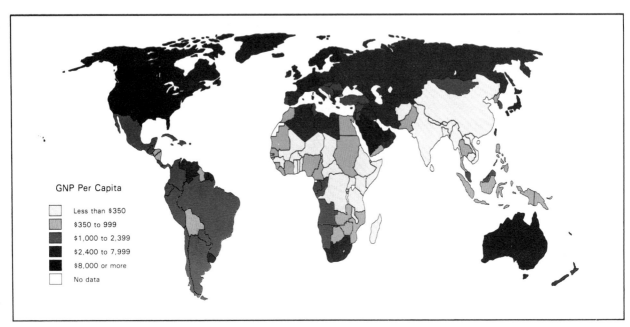

GNP Per Capita

- Less than $350
- $350 to 999
- $1,000 to 2,399
- $2,400 to 7,999
- $8,000 or more
- No data

FIGURE 5.1   Gross national product per capita, in U.S. dollars. The 29 poorest countries are in Africa south of the Sahara and in southern Asia. Several high-income oil-exporting countries stand out in otherwise low-income regions, notably North Africa, around the Persian Gulf, along West Africa's Gulf of Guinea coast, and in northern South America. [*Source:* Data from *Britannica Book of the Year 1986* (Chicago: Encyclopaedia Britannica, Inc., 1986).]

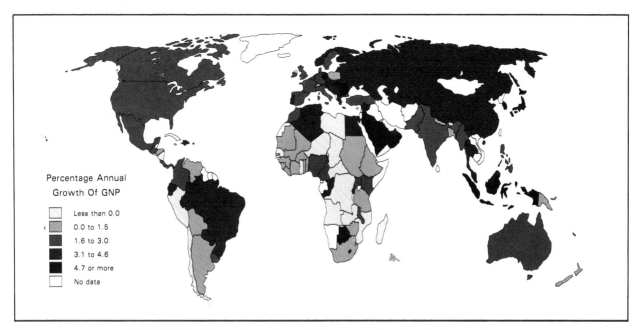

FIGURE 5.2 Percent annual growth in gross national product per capita, 1965–1983. Many countries were materially better off by the early 1980s than they had been two decades earlier. Per capita GNP grew rapidly in some parts of the Third World, especially Brazil and the newly industrializing countries on the western margins of the Pacific, together with certain oil-exporting countries in the Middle East, in Latin America, and around West Africa's Gulf of Guinea coast. Most of Europe prospered during this period also. More recently, growth has slowed in those Third World countries with huge debts and falling prices for their oil and other export commodities. (Data for the following countries are for the period 1960–1980: Bhutan, Chad, Mozambique, Yemen PDR, Angola, Iraq, Bulgaria, Czechoslovakia, German Democratic Republic, Poland, Romania, and the USSR. [*Source:* Based upon data from World Bank, *World Development Reports,* 1985 and 1982 (New York: Oxford University Press, 1985 and 1981).]

tio is changing in composition and in the relative importance of its constituent parts. When Malthus first posed the problem in 1798, food supply was the all-important factor limiting population growth. By the middle of the next century, however, the supply of mechanical energy had joined food as a necessary requirement for a society that was industrializing and advancing technologically. A century later, pollution control was added to the list in recognition that industrialization and urbanization are beginning to poison the environment. Then, in the 1970s, came evidence that intensive human use of physical resources threatens the biosphere and the basic life-support system of the biogeochemical cycles. During that same period, growing scarcities and rising prices of raw materials and energy raised new questions about the adequacy of world reserves (Meadows and others, *The Limits to Growth,* 1972).

Cyclical variations in the level of economic activity complicate the analysis of these changing relation-

ships between population growth and resource use; they also confuse public perceptions of these problems and hamper governmental responses to them. Periods of prosperity cause consumption to rise, straining available supplies of physical resources and intensifying environmental pressures. This heightens the general awareness of resource limitations, prompts greater research on such problems, and leads to official measures to minimize the impacts of shortages and rising prices. Succeeding times of economic recession reduce the demand for basic commodities, causing prices to fall and bringing relief from the scarcities that had earlier prevailed. Officialdom and the general public lose sight of resource problems, and long-term research and development suffer.

This vacillating response to resource questions is much greater at those times when business cycles converge worldwide. The evidence suggests that such coincidences of global prosperity and hard times have occurred at intervals of roughly 50 years ever since the

Industrial Revolution in the eighteenth century. The latest such "long wave" crested in the 1970s, temporarily enhancing the bargaining power of raw material- and energy-exporting nations and providing the conditions for the commodity price shocks and other global economic crises of that decade (see Chapter 14 for a discussion of their effects upon international trade). The wave thereupon collapsed, leading to the worldwide recession of the early 1980s and subsequently to a new upturn. Chapter 11 traces the history of earlier long waves and offers a theoretical explanation for them.

Changing Conceptions

Just as alternating periods of scarcity and abundance affect attitudes toward the relative importance of resources, so does technology change perceptions of what actually constitutes a resource. In a real sense, the term *resource* refers to the supply of anything that may be regarded as useful or necessary to human beings, a store upon which we can draw as we need it. This does not imply anything absolute or constant about a resource; indeed, it does not actually become a resource until human beings conceive it as such. Thus, what we class as a resource changes as our perceptions of it change, or as new technology or rising prices make its exploitation feasible. Oil bubbling from the ground in ancient Persia was a nuisance to some of its earlier inhabitants, but it is a vital source of energy and export earnings to modern Iranians. Uranium was a waste product of Canada's radium mining operations during the 1930s, but since then the old mine tailings have been reworked to recover the newly valuable uranium ore remaining in them. The abundant but low-grade Lake Superior taconite ores became a commercially exploitable resource only when the rich Mesabi iron deposits gave out.

At a given state of technology, the absolute supply of certain natural resources can be sustained at a given level or even increased. These are the *renewable resources*—those capable of replenishing themselves or being replenished by human beings. Most biotic resources, such as forests, animal populations, and fish, are of this type. Even soils can be made to recover from excessive use in some instances; indeed, many of the soils of Western Europe and southeastern Asia are essentially made by human beings.

Resources that cannot regenerate are referred to as *nonrenewable resources*. Most minerals fall into this category. The concentration of mineral ores in economically exploitable quantities relies upon physical processes that normally require many thousands or even millions of years. Once a given deposit has been mined out, that resource for all practical purposes ceases to exist. The accelerating demand for minerals as a result of ad-

vancing technology spurs a constant search for new deposits to replace the old. The total known world reserves of a particular mineral therefore tend to rise and fall as new deposits are discovered and old ones exhausted.

Flow resources—such as running water, winds, ocean tides, and solar rays—represent still another type. Ordinarily these do not become exhausted, but they must be used as they appear or they are lost. Each of these constitutes a potential or actual source of energy.

A Many-Sided Problem

To determine whether the earth's resources will be adequate for future populations is truly an urgent task. It is also a difficult one, considering the many uncertainties. Perhaps the most unpredictable aspect of all concerns the effects of what we might call the *politics of resources*. This problem arises from the fact that the principal areas of demand for many of the earth's resources are in one part of the world and the supply is concentrated in some other part. For instance, countries with stable populations possess some of the world's most productive agricultural lands, whereas the largest and most rapidly growing populations are in countries that have lost their capacity to feed themselves. Similarly, a number of countries with poorly developed industrial sectors control large reserves of minerals that are vital raw materials for factories in countries lacking these. In each case the have-not nations run grave political risks of being cut off from these essential imports.

Another uncertainty affecting the study of resource questions on a global scale is the nature of the data, which vary in quality from country to country. Information for some Third World countries is scanty, and data for the poorest areas are often full of gaps, forcing the analyst to rely upon estimates. Projecting future world supplies therefore requires making a number of assumptions: that no major changes will be made in governmental policies; that no wars or other major disruptions will interfere with production, consumption, and distribution; and that no revolutionary advances in technology will occur. With these warnings, let us now look at the problems of providing for future populations, taking into account the various elements affecting food supply, energy, raw materials, and environmental quality.

FOOD SUPPLY

Food as a Limit to Growth

The possibility that population growth might outstrip the earth's capacity to supply enough food is of as much concern today as it was in Malthus's time, although the immediacy of this problem is much debated. Two contrary trends are partly responsible for the uncertainty. On the one hand, soil erosion, urban encroachment upon farmland, and other human and natural processes are acting to diminish the food supply; on the other, technological developments are raising the efficiency of food production by increasing output per unit of physical resources. The answer to the problem also depends upon the level of dietary quality deemed acceptable. To raise the global average of food consumption to levels now prevalent in the richer countries would be a daunting task, considering the high proportion of animal proteins and fresh green vegetables entering into such diets and the drain on basic resources such foods impose.

These matters aside, the problem of maintaining the world food supply does not appear critical in the short run. Global food production has more than doubled since World War II, and the current total is more than sufficient to feed everyone on earth. Even by the end of this century the total supply seems likely to be adequate, assuming that productivity continues to increase at current rates. The outlook beyond A.D. 2000, however, is exceedingly cloudy. Predictions for the new century depend not only upon dietary standards but also

upon the possibilities for unfavorable climatic changes, containing loss of productive capacity through such factors as soil erosion, and achieving breakthroughs in food production technology.

Yet, even if total output should prove sufficient, the thorny problem remains of ensuring that all the world's inhabitants receive an equitable share of these supplies. Even now the regional differences in production and consumption are enormous: Food is just not reaching everyone who needs it and the disparities are widening. Early in the postwar era food output balanced population increase in the developed countries and even in the Third World as a whole, although particular regions were unable to keep up. More recently, North America and Europe have been overproducing—at a time when their populations have stabilized—whereas food output has lagged behind population growth in the USSR and the majority of less-developed countries (see Figure 5.3). Meanwhile, inequities in food distribution within the Third World have continued to worsen.

Countries deficient in food output are of two main kinds. One group includes the oil-exporting countries of the Middle East and the newly industrializing countries of the Pacific rim, which are able to make up for in-

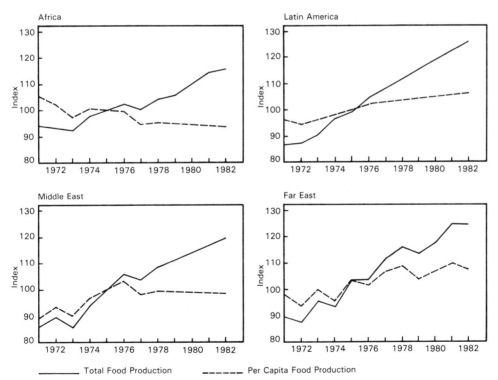

FIGURE 5.3 Food production in less-developed areas, indices (1974–1976 = 100). Although total production of food has risen in all four regions, per capita output has lagged because of population growth, especially in Africa. [*Source:* Data from *FAO Production Yearbook 1983* (Rome: Food and Agriculture Organization of the United Nations, 1983).]

adequate food production by selling abroad their petroleum and valuable manufactured goods to finance imports of needed foodstuffs. The USSR has likewise resorted to imports to compensate for its badly lagging food production.

The other group of food-deficit countries consists of the many less-developed countries too poor to buy needed food supplies abroad. Indeed, much of the Third World is suffering a food crisis at this time. Making news headlines are the famines in Ethiopia, the Sudan, Chad, and other countries of the drought-stricken region of Africa south of the Sahara; but even more common than famine today is chronic malnutrition. Hunger is a growing world problem, affecting possibly a billion people. Note from Figure 5.4 how widespread are low dietary levels throughout Africa and southern Asia and parts of Latin America.

Although the effects of hunger and malnutrition upon human beings are not fully understood as yet, we do know that they contribute to stunted physical growth, a lower resistance to disease, higher childhood death rates, and arrested mental development. Studies of this problem in Latin America have identified malnutrition as either the main or a contributing cause of 57 percent of all deaths between the ages of one to four. In Brazil, children in this age group accounted for four-fifths of *all* deaths. In the less-developed world as a whole, according to estimates of the United Nations Food and Agriculture Organization, more than two-thirds of the present group of children will develop illnesses related to malnutrition. Upon reaching adulthood many of the survivors will remain mentally or physically handicapped to the extent that they will either be dependent upon society for their support or will be able to contribute little to it because of their reduced productivity. Hunger and malnutrition are clearly a serious drag on the economic development of impoverished nations.

The main cause of hunger in the world today is simply poverty. The world still has enough food in total, and those who can afford to buy it eat very well, including such food-deficient areas as Japan and several other Asian countries, as well as certain food-short European lands. As a comparison of Figures 5.1 and 5.4 shows, the correspondence between low per capita food intake and low per capita income is very close. In addition, wide variations in food consumption occur within countries, especially those less-developed nations with great income disparities, and even in some of the richer industrialized countries, such as the United States, where a surprising number of people go to bed hungry every night.

Regional disparities threaten to widen still further in the years to come. Although food requirements are to change little among developed countries, demand in the less-developed nations will rise steeply through the remainder of the twentieth century. Income growth will add some of the new demand in the Third World, but the greater part of it will come from population growth. World food output will therefore have to double or even treble to meet the needs of less-developed countries by

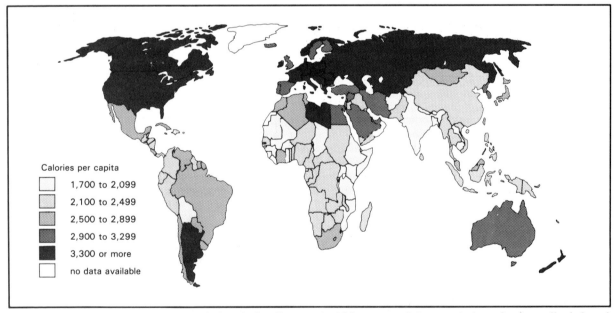

FIGURE 5.4 Daily dietary energy supply in calories. Twenty-six African countries currently have food supplies below the 2334 calories per person cited by the United Nations Food and Agriculture Organization (FAO) as the daily minimum requirement for that region. Similar deficiencies prevail in eight countries of South Asia and four countries in Latin America. Haiti's food supply, for example, represents only 80 percent of the FAO minimum for Latin Americans. [*Source:* Based upon data from the *1986 Britannica Book of the Year* (Chicago: Encyclopaedia Britannica, 1986).]

the turn of the century. Physical limitations will make it impossible for most African and Middle Eastern countries to produce the additional food they will be requiring; hence, consumption will fall below even present inadequate levels. Moreover, it seems likely that the real price of food will double by the end of the century and pressure on current food sources will intensify, requiring ever-greater use of costly capital-intensive methods to raise productivity.

Beyond A.D. 2000 the Third World's food needs will continue to rise, but the physical limits will become even more crucial in the struggle to increase global output. What are the prospects for overcoming those limitations? Let us now consider the opportunities for meeting future food needs from conventional sources and examine the possibilities offered by certain new food technologies.

Conventional Sources of Food Supply

All types of food trace their origins to solar energy that has been captured by green plants through the process of photosynthesis. The plants are then consumed by herbivorous animals, which may be eaten by carnivorous animals, or human beings. In the sea the food chain commences with the phytoplankton, tiny one-celled plants that are eaten by certain fish, which are themselves eaten by larger ones. More than 99 percent of the world's food supply currently comes from agriculture, and a mere 0.7 percent derives from the sea.

Agriculture and Grazing

As we approach the end of the twentieth century, only 36 percent of the world's land area is being used

for the production of food, and two-thirds of this small proportion is devoted to permanent pasture, which characteristically yields a relatively meager output per hectare (Table 5.1). This leaves only 11 percent of the world's land surface for field and tree crops. Major portions of total arable farmland are in Asia, North America, Africa, and the USSR (Figure 5.5). The figures can be misleading, however, because these lands vary greatly in their productive capacity and in the numbers of people they must support. A more revealing measure, therefore, is the amount of arable land per person (Table 5.1 and Figure 5.6). Thus, Asia, with nearly a third of the world's cropland, has only 0.17 hectare per person, whereas North America has nearly three-quarters of a hectare per person. Because of the large quantity and high quality of its arable land, North America has been a major surplus food supply area from the time of the first European settlement. Despite its small overall size, Europe has the largest proportion of its land area in crops of any region (almost 30 percent); and, through intensive use, this acreage contributes more than enough to feed that continent's very large population. Though Oceania would appear to be an important source area as measured by persons per hectare, we must keep in mind that this lightly populated region accounts for only 3 percent of the world's arable land (Figure 5.5).

Despite the great variety of food crops grown throughout the world, a surprisingly few of these crops carry the main burden of feeding the human and animal populations. The overwhelming leaders are the grains, especially wheat, corn, and rice (in that order), even though they are relatively low in protein. Being eminently transportable and having a multitude of uses, these commodities are staples of world diets. (The millets and sorghums, another large family of grains, are

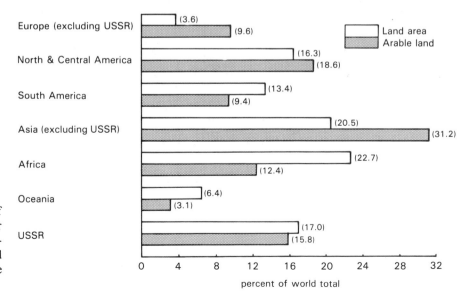

FIGURE 5.5 Regional shares of world land area and land under crops. [*Source:* Data from *FAO Production Yearbook 1983* (Rome: Food and Agriculture Organization of the United Nations, 1983).]

TABLE 5.1

World land use in million hectares, arable land per person, and percent regional share (parentheses)

Region	Land area	Percent	Arable land and land under permanent crops	Percent	Permanent pasture	Percent	Forested land	Percent	Other area	Percent	Arable hectares per person
World	13,077 (100)	100	1,469 (100)	11.2	3,172 (100)	24.3	4,090 (100)	31.3	4,347 (100)	33.2	0.32
Europe (excluding USSR)	473 (3.6)	100	141 (9.6)	29.8	86 (2.7)	18.2	155 (3.8)	32.8	91 (2.1)	19.2	0.29
North and Central America	2,136 (16.3)	100	273 (18.6)	12.8	354 (11.2)	16.6	682 (16.7)	31.9	826 (19.0)	38.7	0.71
South America	1,753 (13.4)	100	137 (9.4)	7.8	454 (14.3)	25.9	937 (22.9)	53.4	225 (5.2)	12.8	0.56
Asia (excluding USSR)	2,679 (20.5)	100	458 (31.2)	17.1	649 (20.5)	24.2	552 (13.5)	20.6	1,020 (23.5)	38.1	0.17
Africa	2,966 (22.7)	100	183 (12.4)	6.2	784 (24.7)	26.4	694 (17.0)	23.4	1,306 (30.0)	44.0	0.36
Oceania	843 (6.4)	100	45 (3.1)	5.3	470 (14.8)	55.8	150 (3.7)	17.8	177 (4.1)	21.0	1.92
USSR	2,227 (17.0)	100	232 (15.8)	10.4	374 (11.8)	16.8	920 (22.5)	41.3	701 (16.1)	31.5	0.86

Source: Food and Agriculture Organization of the United Nations, *FAO Production Yearbook*, 1983.

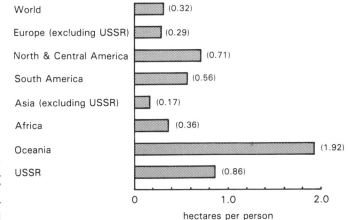

FIGURE 5.6 Per capita arable land, major world regions. [*Source:* Data from *FAO Production Yearbook 1983* (Rome: Food and Agriculture Organization of the United Nations, 1983).]

locally important sources of animal and human foods in much of the world but do not figure as importantly in the world grain trade.) The world grain supply is therefore a dependable barometer of the global food situation. The total output of grain has increased steadily since the end of World War II, but per capita production has risen only slowly. Population growth has effectively canceled much of the gain in total volume.

The pattern of the world grain trade has shifted ominously in recent years (Figures 5.7., 5.8, and 5.9). Although both South America and Asia were net exporters of grain prior to the war, both have since become net importers. Africa, never important as a source of world grain, has been a net importer since 1950. The USSR and Eastern Europe have barely produced enough

grain for their own needs, and in bad years they have had to import huge quantities. Western Europe has long had a substantial output of grain, mainly wheat, but generally had not produced enough to satisfy all of its needs. In recent years, however, the European Economic Community's Common Agricultural Policy, with its generous subsidies to farmers, has led to such an increase in output that Western Europe now faces an oversupply. Oceania (principally Australia) has relatively large grain surpluses, but these represent less than 1 percent of total world output of the three principal types.

It is increasingly apparent that the United States and Canada are destined to become the global breadbasket. With less than 6 percent of the world's people—and approaching zero population growth—these two

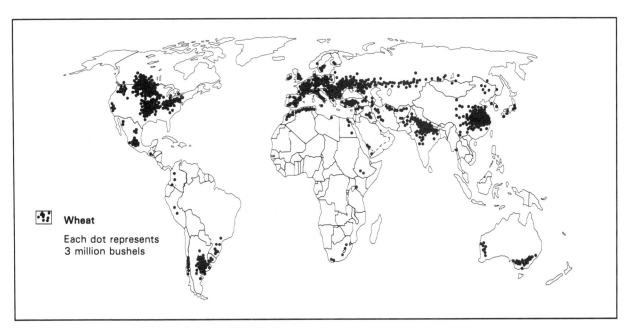

FIGURE 5.7 World wheat production. [*Source:* Data from *FAO Production Yearbook 1983* (Rome: Food and Agriculture Organization of the United Nations, 1983).]

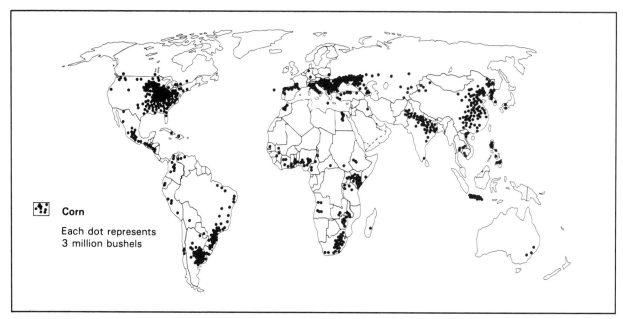

FIGURE 5.8   World corn (maize) production. [*Source:* Data from *FAO Production Yearbook 1983* (Rome: Food and Agriculture Organization of the United Nations, 1983).]

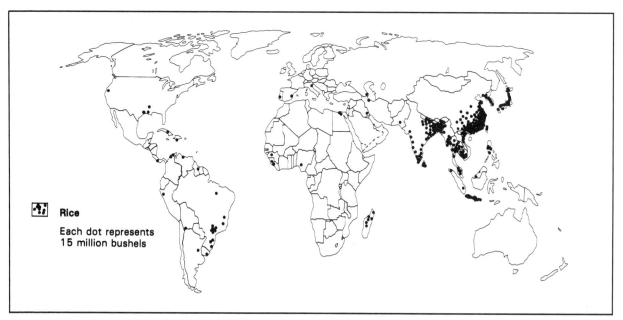

FIGURE 5.9   World rice production. [*Source:* Data from *FAO Production Yearbook 1983* (Rome: Food and Agriculture Organization of the United Nations, 1983).]

countries already account for one-quarter of all grain output. Consequently, they offer the main hope of future supplies for those countries whose production no longer keeps up with population growth. As Figure 5.3 indicates, many less-developed regions are losing the capacity to feed themselves and must turn more and more to the remaining surplus grain producers for help. As

Third World populations continue to expand, however, it seems doubtful that present sources of food will be able to sustain the pace into the twenty-first century unless important advances in agricultural production occur. What are the possibilities for this?

Two main ways exist for increasing world output of agricultural commodities: (1) expanding the cultivated area and (2) increasing the output per hectare (yield). In the modern era, however, bringing more land under cultivation does not offer an adequate solution for this mammoth problem. Some estimates suggest that the possibilities for expanding the world's cultivated land are very great, that perhaps twice the present total quantity of land in use is potentially arable. Expert opinion, however, is generally agreed that such estimates are misleading. One reason is that the unused land is generally not in the same places as the people with the greatest need for it; moreover, major economic, political, and social obstacles severely limit the wholesale transplanting of populations required to redress the imbalance. The Food and Agriculture Organization of the United Nations (FAO) anticipates, therefore, that no more than 10 percent or 20 percent of this potential cropland will be in use by the end of the present century.

The greatest need, according to a study conducted jointly by the FAO and the International Institute for Applied Systems Analysis (IIASA), is concentrated in a group of 57 countries, all of which lack sufficient arable land, at present levels of agricultural technology, to feed the populations projected for them for the year A.D. 2000 (Shah and Fischer, 1984). Of these "critical" countries, 27 are in Africa, the one region that does not as yet show signs of significant progress toward bringing its population under control during the twenty-first century (Figure 5.10). Most of these rank among the poorest lands on earth, with per capita gross domestic prod-

ucts less than $300. Ten critical countries are in Middle America: El Salvador on the mainland and nine island nations of the Caribbean. Five are in southern and southeastern Asia, Bangladesh being the most difficult case. All but four countries in the Middle East are on the list, and of these four only Turkey has substantial potential for further agricultural development. Elsewhere in the Mediterranean, and in most of Asia, reserves of unused arable land are essentially exhausted, and this point is quickly approaching in many other world regions.

Another reason that estimates of unused land are misleading is that in most major areas where potential arable land is supposedly available, formidable obstacles stand in the way of its development. One such obstacle is excessive aridity. One-fourth of the earth's land surface is classified as desert—areas where rainfall averages less than 10 inches per year. Most of the unused potentially arable land of Asia is desert. Only a small fraction of such land can be irrigated.

One problem with irrigating desert lands is that many of these are covered either by shifting sands or by "desert pavement," stony surfaces devoid of soil. Equally difficult is the problem of finding enough irrigation water in the right places. Much of the irrigated agriculture in desert areas occurs along "exotic" streams, such as the Nile or the Colorado, which flow into these dry lands out of rainy mountainous regions (see Chapter 4). Many other irrigation districts make use

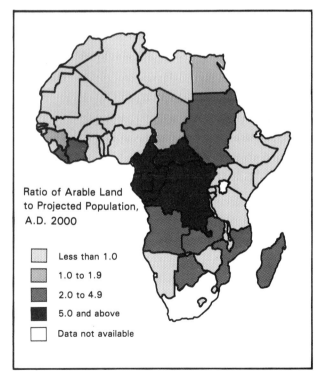

FIGURE 5.10 Land-short countries of Africa. Ratio of population-supporting capacity to projected population, A.D. 2000. Today, Africa as a whole is a food-deficit region, and many African countries depend upon food imports to sustain often-inadequate diets (compare with Figure 5.4). By the end of this century at least 29 African countries are expected to lack sufficient arable land to produce the food required by the populations they are projected to have by that date, according to a study jointly sponsored by the Institute for Applied Systems Analysis (IIASA) and the United Nations Food and Agriculture Organization (FAO). The land shortage is termed especially critical in 27 of the 29 countries. The Republic of South Africa was excluded from the study. [*Source:* Data from "People, Land, and Food Production: Potentials in the Developing World," by Mahendra Shah and Günther Fischer in *Options,* International Institute for Applied Systems Analysis (IIASA), 2 (1984), pp. 1–5.]

of ground waters available through an unusual combination of geological conditions that link such areas with rainy uplands. Besides being rather uncommon, these artesian systems have an exceedingly slow rate of natural recharge—usually thousands of years. In many places, such as the American Southwest, water tables in artesian basins are falling precipitously from overuse. A further problem with irrigating deserts is the very high cost of constructing dams, canals, and roads, preparing soils, and administering these systems. One of the most unsettling aspects of the aridity problem is the mounting evidence that some of the world's major deserts are growing, encroaching upon neighboring lands where large populations gain their livelihood from agriculture and grazing. For a discussion of this "desertification" process, see page 97.

In addition to the virtually rainless desert areas, nearly one-third of the earth's surface is steppe land, where rainfall averages between 10 inches and 30 inches per year. Because of high evaporation, steppe lands in tropical latitudes are usually suitable only for grazing, but in temperate areas commercial grain farming is often possible. Although the upper-latitude steppes have some of the world's best soils—excellent for wheat or grain sorghum—the lack of dependable rainfall makes the farming of these areas highly uncertain. The tragic dust bowl conditions of the American plains during the 1930s and the failure of Premier Nikita Khrushchev's "virgin lands" project in the USSR dramatize the problems of relying upon the steppe lands for substantial additions to the earth's total arable area. Nevertheless, as we shall see shortly, many areas of uncertain rainfall in the Third World have provided important opportunities for increasing the output of existing farmlands through the introduction of new agricultural technology, including irrigation.

Many of the lands commonly classified as potentially arable lie within the vast tropical rain forests of the Amazon and Congo basins. As indicated in Chapter 4, the agricultural capabilities of these areas is much overrated because the heavy downpours of rain leach essential plant food elements out of the surface layers of soil, rendering them unproductive for ordinary shallow-rooted crops. Perhaps an even more serious obstacle to the use of the tropical areas of Africa, where population pressures in neighboring lands are intense, is the prevalence of dread diseases, especially river blindness (onchocerciasis) and sleeping sickness (trypanosomiasis). Great areas in the valleys of the Volta, Niger, Congo, Gambia, and Upper Nile rivers remain unfarmed owing to fear of river blindness, which persists despite concerted efforts of governments and world organizations to eradicate it. Sleeping sickness, carried by the tsetse fly, has excluded the usual types of farming

from 1 billion hectares of tropical Africa. Experiments with insecticides have been largely unsuccessful because of their high cost and because of the fly's resistance to them.

The best hope for increasing the world food supply from agriculture, therefore, does not lie in expanding the amount of arable land, but in more intensive use of existing farmlands: applying more labor and capital in order to raise yields per hectare. Recent technological advances in North America, Western Europe, and Japan—as well as in certain developing countries—point the way. The problem of transferring agricultural technology to new areas, however, is an intricate one because every locality has distinctive soil and climatic conditions and its own combination of land, labor, and capital. Plant varieties that work well in one place usually have to undergo substantial modification before they can be introduced on the farms of another locality.

The appropriate strategy for raising yields differs for a country with an abundance of farmland but a small supply of farm labor—such as the United States—and a country with a relatively large number of farm workers but a limited amount of arable land—as in the case of Japan. The situation is still different for a less-developed country with large quantities of both land and labor but lacking management skills and capital. Nevertheless, Japan's solution offers much hope for Third World agriculture because, initially at least, that country's population/food supply problems so closely paralleled those of today's less-developed countries. During the first half of this century Japan's arable land area increased by only 18 percent, but average yields rose by two-thirds and total national farm output nearly doubled.

The intensification of agriculture entails two kinds of technologies, and Japan used both: mechanization and the introduction of improved plant varieties in combination with increased fertilizer use. In addition to adopting new high-yielding seeds and making optimal use of chemical fertilizers, the Japanese developed special types of machinery suitable for use on their tiny, garden-size farms. In this way they were able to maintain and increase output even as industrialization lured more and more farm workers to the cities. Thus, in Japan, farmers substituted machinery for labor, just as their counterparts did in the United States, except at a different scale. It should be noted, however, that Japanese agriculture has also benefited from governmental protection from import competition. This has kept domestic food prices very high, enabling farmers to continue operating despite high production costs (see Chapter 12, page 319).

Though most less-developed nations have little incentive to replace their abundant rural labor with ma-

Desertification

By attracting worldwide sympathy to their suffering, the victims of famine in sub-Saharan Africa have served to focus attention upon a worsening global problem: the continuing spread of deserts into adjacent populated lands, a process called "desertification." Though a severe, prolonged drought was the immediate cause of the crop failure and resulting starvation in Africa's Sahel in the 1980s, drought is a temporary condition that has come and gone many times in that part of the world; more worrisome is the evidence that drought is merely furthering the long-term, virtually irreversible process of desertification already under way in the region. Furthermore, the deserts of Africa are not the only ones that are advancing: Desertification is also proceeding at an accelerating pace in other subhumid areas of the world, especially the Middle East and parts of northwestern Asia (see Figure 5.11). Each year an additional 200,000 square kilometers are rendered useless in this manner—an area equivalent to all of New England plus New Jersey. Altogether, the threat extends to 20 percent of the earth's land surface, home to possibly 80 million people.

This destruction of productive land is largely a result of prolonged human use and misuse of a vulnerable natural environment. Soils form slowly in arid lands, and they are usually deficient in various important plant nutrients. Because of the scarcity of moisture, plant cover is sparse, and the shallow soils are susceptible to rapid deterioration through erosion and gullying. In these areas of ecological instability, the chief agents of land degradation are overcultivation, overgrazing, and deforestation. Over the ages poor farming practices, trampling and close cropping of vegetation by goats and sheep, and stripping of woodlands for timber and fuel have so reduced the natural ground cover that the soils lie exposed to erosion from sun and wind.

Human pressures upon this fragile ecological system are intensifying, for the rates of population growth in these areas are among the world's highest. As they struggle to feed their expanding numbers, the farmers and grazers of the semiarid lands struggle to get more and more out of the land until finally the soil is so exhausted that it yields nothing. The onset of a drought therefore finds the land stripped of its natural defenses, and the process of desertification quickens. Eventually the inhabitants must abandon their farms and seek food wherever they may hope to find it.

The most recent drought in sub-Saharan Africa began in the 1970s, abated slightly in 1980, then re-

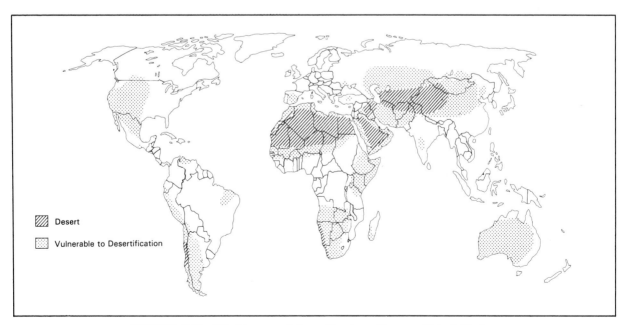

FIGURE 5.11 World map of desertification. [*Source:* United Nations Conference on Desertification, 1977.]

surged with new vigor in the following years to become the worst in a century and a half. In the process, an estimated 70,000 square kilometers succumbed to desertification each year. The band of most intense drought stretched uninterruptedly for 6,000 kilometers from Dakar on the Atlantic to the Horn of Africa on the Indian Ocean (Figure 5.11), an area twice the size of the continental United States. The severest impact fell upon Chad, Ghana, Mali, Ethiopia, Somalia, and Senegal. Farther to the southeast, Mozambique was among the hardest hit in still another area of drought.

The human tragedy was immeasurable: More than 150 million people lacked sufficient food, and countless numbers died of disease and starvation. By 1983, grain output in the affected countries had fallen 35 percent below normal, a decline further accentuated by severe insect infestations of crops. Adding

to the misery were outbreaks of cattle disease and brushfires, as well as wars and revolutions in Chad, Ethiopia, and Somalia.

If the past is a reliable guide, the recent siege of droughts in sub-Saharan Africa should not continue much longer. The record shows that, for reasons not yet well understood, droughts in this region occur in cycles averaging seven years in length, with especially severe episodes having reappeared in each of the past three centuries. An episode of intense droughts occurred between 1820 and 1840, according to historical records; and a still earlier one took place between 1773 and 1758, as indicated by geological evidence. It seems unlikely, however, that the end of the drought of the 1980s will return the sub-Sahara to previous levels of food output. The lands most recently swallowed up in the process of desertification are probably lost for good.

---

chines, they can increase farm output by introducing machinery for certain operations. For instance, at harvest time, when all workers are needed in the fields, a few trucks can transport the crop to market more quickly, economically, and with less spoilage than could any number of human porters and draft animals. Also, mechanical pumps are much cheaper and more effective in raising irrigation water than are primitive hand pumps and waterwheels.

The greatest opportunities for increasing yields, however, come from the second of these technologies: the introduction of new, higher-yielding varieties of plants, together with the chemicals and water supplies that these require for the full realization of their potential. The scientific selection and breeding of plants, which had done so much to raise farm yields in the industrialized countries since the beginning of plant genetics a century earlier, are now being applied successfully to increasing the output of wheat, rice, and other cereal crops in the Third World. International research centers have led the way by developing new plant strains and spreading them throughout the tropics and subtropics. This has required adapting these crops to an enormous variety of local soil and climatic conditions. Plant breeders have concentrated upon producing sturdy, short-stemmed plants capable of supporting the large cereal heads that yield greater output per hectare. They have also bred these plants to mature more quickly, to be resistant to pests and diseases, and to have better flavor and storage qualities.

Unlike the hardy but poor-yielding native varieties they are replacing, however, the new types require large amounts of fertilizer. Accompanying the introduction of the new seeds, therefore, has been a large increase in the use of chemical fertilizers in developing countries, where they were virtually unknown prior to the 1960s. Indeed, half the increase in grain yields in the past three decades is attributable to greater fertilizer use. The fertilizers are effective, however, only when sufficient moisture is present in the soil to dissolve these nutrients so that they can be taken up by the plant roots. Hence, the other part of this new agricultural technology is the provision of adequate water supplies. In much of the Third World, natural rainfall is either inadequate or comes at the wrong times. In southern Asia the timing and amount of the monsoon rains has been crucial to the success or failure of harvests in the past. Supplementary irrigation has therefore been a third essential element in the drive to raise farm output in developing lands.

In some tropical and subtropical countries irrigation has been the largest single contributor to improved yields. Under certain conditions it has doubled and even trebled yields during the main growing season and has made possible the growing of a second or third crop in the remainder of the year. The irrigated area has increased steadily since the 1960s until it now encompasses about a fifth of the arable lands in Third World countries. China and India alone account for half of this. Unfortunately, the extensive irrigation systems and storage reservoirs required for such projects are not feasible in many other areas, especially those parts of sub-Saharan Africa suffering from drought and famine.

On the whole, Third World agriculture has made substantial progress during the past three decades. As a result of internationally organized research and promotion, yields and total output of staple crops have risen markedly through the introduction of new seeds in combination with fertilizer and irrigation water. These advances have greatly improved the lot of millions of people in some less-developed countries, where it has been termed the *green revolution* (see page 100 for further discussion of the achievements of the green revolution).

This revolution, however, has not reached all parts of the Third World. Many poorer countries have been unable to avail themselves of this new technology, and even some regions within those countries profiting from these developments have not had access to it. Despite the spectacular achievements of some, therefore, the overall results hardly more than offset the growth of population that has occurred during this same period. Indeed, per capita food output rose only 0.4 percent per annum during the 1960s and 1970s. Moreover, the rate of increase was least in those regions with the most rapidly growing populations and the lowest incomes. Thus, while per capita output was rising by 1.4 percent a year in Southeast Asia, it was growing only 0.6 percent annually in Latin America and it failed to rise at all in most other areas. In Africa, for example, per capita food output increased by 0.2 percent per annum during the 1960s but has since declined at an annual rate of 1.4 percent.

As we confront the huge task of feeding future populations, the questions of time and cost arise. Enormous expenditures are required for opening new lands, building new fertilizer factories, and distributing the fertilizer and new seed varieties. Much time is needed to develop those seeds and to train farmers and technicians in their use; but time is very short. With the likelihood that the remaining supplies of potentially arable land are nearing exhaustion, and the possibility that further experiments in plant genetics will ultimately reach a point of diminishing returns, what are the prospects for supplementing future food supplies through alternative approaches?

Food from the Sea

The seas supply about one-fifth of the world's high-quality animal protein, and this source of food is particularly important to certain fishing nations such as Japan, the USSR, China, Norway, and Iceland. Yet the nearly 80 million metric tons of food obtained from seas, lakes, and rivers provide less than 1 percent of the world's total food. Public statements on this subject often overestimate the unused potential of food from the sea: Informed sources insist that the present catch cannot be increased by much more than 15 percent on a sustained-yield basis.

This last qualification identifies the real problem, for overexploitation today means reduced catches in the future. Indeed, we have already seen stocks of many varieties of food fish greatly diminished and some species virtually depleted. Certain types, such as salmon, are especially vulnerable. Overfishing is one result of the "open seas" principle, which treats the world's oceans as common property. This means that no one is responsible for maintaining the "fertility" of fishing grounds; indeed, the open-seas concept encourages intense competition among national fishing fleets, which develop increasingly sophisticated gear to capture larger quantities of dwindling stocks of fish. Another unfortunate feature of commercial fishing is the practice among less-developed nations of exporting their catches instead of retaining this valuable protein to feed their own undernourished populations. Currently, nearly one-seventh of the world catch is exported.

The seas thus contribute only a small part of global food needs, and the supply of conventional sea foods appears unlikely even to keep pace with the rate of world population growth. This realization is one of the factors spurring the search for unorthodox forms of food.

More Radical Methods of Increasing Food Supplies

From time to time the Sunday newspaper supplements report spectacular scientific discoveries that will multiply the world's food supply limitlessly. Many such claims are mere science fiction, but certain recent developments are genuinely encouraging to a world concerned with the daunting challenge of feeding future billions. Let us explore the possibilities offered by some of the proposals now being advanced.

One of the paradoxes of world agriculture is that some of the driest deserts are adjacent to huge bodies of water; however, the salinity of these oceans and seas precludes their use of irrigation. The technology of desalination is sufficiently advanced to provide large quantities of water for household use, but the process is still much too costly for ordinary agricultural or industrial purposes. One proposal is to construct large multipurpose nuclear installations whose costs are largely borne by the sale of the electric power they generate but that have sufficient additional capacity for the production of fertilizer and desalinated water for ad-

The Green Revolution

The dramatic development in world agriculture called the *green revolution* had its beginnings in the 1960s, when two international research institutes released new high-yielding varieties of wheat and rice to Third World farmers. The work of these organizations, CIMMYT (the International Maize and Wheat Improvement Center, sponsored by the Mexican government and the Rockefeller Foundation) in Mexico and IRRI (the International Rice Research Institute, funded by the Rockefeller and Ford Foundations) in the Philippines, represented the first worldwide efforts to extend the benefits of modern plant genetics to the problems of tropical agriculture.

Following introduction of the new varieties in 1966, India's wheat output doubled within six years. Previously the world's second largest grain importer, India had become self-sufficient by the end of the 1970s. Other countries quickly adopted the new types of wheat and several of these have experienced substantial increases in yields. China, Pakistan, Turkey, and Bangladesh are prominent examples of countries that achieved early successes from applying the new technology.

Meanwhile, the new rice strains were quickly spreading throughout southern and southeastern Asia, although certain areas were unable to adopt them because of their exacting water requirements. Those districts with suitable conditions, however, enjoyed very large increases in rice output. Not only did farmers gain from the high yields but they also benefited from the short maturity times of the new strains, which make it possible to grow two or more crops within a single year.

Figure 5.12 illustrates the remarkable success achieved by wheat and rice farmers in the Indian state of Punjab, which lies on the semiarid Indo-Gangetic Plain. Although this district is subject to frequent droughts, its progressive and energetic farmers have availed themselves of local supplies of irrigation water and have applied the chemical fertilizers required by the new plant strains.

Although the green revolution has had less dramatic results with maize (corn) and grain sorghums, notable gains have occurred here as well. Maize varieties that produce exceedingly high yields in one district often fail in other areas. Nevertheless, improved types have succeeded in a number of countries, especially Argentina, China, Kenya, and Zimbabwe. Sorghums initially presented special technical prob-

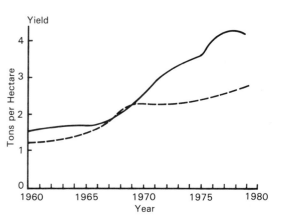

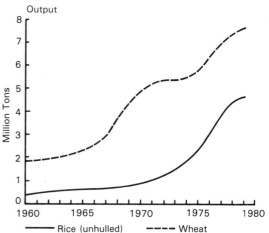

FIGURE 5.12   Results of the green revolution in the Indian state of Punjab (plotted as 3-year moving averages). Dramatic increases in yields and output of rice and wheat followed the introduction of new hybrid seeds in the mid-1960s. A brief decline in wheat yields during the early 1970s, owing to the appearance of wheat rust, was subsequently corrected by the development of disease-resistant strains. [*Source:* World Bank, *World Development Report 1982* (New York: Oxford University Press).]

lems and encountered some resistance from farmers, but they are now gaining wide acceptance in northeastern China, the drier parts of India, and some areas of Latin America.

The effects of the green revolution upon food output in the Third World as a whole have been startling. Average grain yields in developing countries have risen by 2 percent per annum, and wheat yields alone have gone up by 2.7 percent annually. Rice yields have increased at a yearly rate of only 1.6 percent in the Third World as a whole, but they have risen by 3 percent in the Philippines and Indonesia, countries that have the necessary conditions for the new types.

Despite the great benefits that the green revolution has brought to many less-developed countries, it has not succeeded in all places, hence the criticism of this technology that is sometimes voiced. Its failures are due to a number of special causes: inappropriate soil and climatic conditions, lack of sufficient water supply, inadequate transport and marketing networks, or distortions in local price and incentive systems. In some instances, too, the green revolution has succeeded very well but rampant population growth has overtaken the increase in food supply.

This was the case in Mexico, a pioneer in developing and applying the new technology.

Those cases where the green revolution has not met expectations must be weighted against the very substantial contribution it has made toward global food supplies in a time when Third World populations are still mounting. Important too is the fact that some of the greatest successes for the new technology have occurred in the most populous less-developed countries, particularly India, China, Indonesia, and the Philippines. Still another measure of its significance as an approach to the world food problem is the growing number of international research institutes since the appearance of CIMMYT and IRRI in the 1960s, as well as the proliferation of research programs in individual Third World countries.

jacent farmlands. Another alternative for seaside agriculture in dry lands is to breed food plants that tolerate salt water. Research on this problem has already shown some promise.

A second approach to augmenting the global food supply is for the world as a whole to adopt the traditional Oriental practice of bypassing animals in the food chain. Under this plan everyone would eat the products of the soil directly rather than first converting them into animal products. These "direct calories" are much more efficient in their use of the land because at best only 14 percent of the plant food value per hectare reaches the meat eater. This would require radically altering the eating habits of most people, especially in the richer nations, but it might also subject them to the same high-starch, low-protein diets that keep so much of the Third World malnourished.

A likely solution for this nutritional problem is to develop high-protein foods from plant sources. Research has focused upon soybeans, and to some extent cottonseeds, both of which are already important sources of nutritious animal feed. An acre of land can supply 10 times as much protein in the form of soybeans as it can in the form of beef and at a far lower cost. One difficulty has been to make soybean and cottonseed products sufficiently palatable for human beings. Thus far these products have served mainly as additives to meat and bread. Among other radical experiments are attempts to convert alfalfa leaves, forest leaves, pea vines, and other common green plant parts into high-protein human food. Scientists have also worked at developing a palatable human and animal food from single-celled organisms cultured on petroleum.

Possibly the greatest promise lies in the discovery of a complex chemical that is the medium through which the fundamental characteristics of all living things are transmitted—deoxyribonucleic acid, or DNA as it is more commonly called. As scientists gain a better understanding of this substance, they are able to create entirely new organisms by manipulating the genes of various species.

Although genetic engineering is only in its infancy, plant scientists have already succeeded with certain experimental techniques, notably *tissue culture.* This is a method for multiplying plants starting with only a single part—a piece of root or leaf—and developing completely new and genetically identical plants. Tissue culture is a much quicker way of multiplying plants than seeding or grafting, and the resulting clones are completely uniform in all important respects, such as yield, quality, and maturing times. The technique also permits the engineering of plants that are resistant to disease and that are adapted to particular environments. Considerable success has already been achieved with various temperate and tropical tree crops. The potential for quantum increases in world food supplies through these and other recently developed techniques of plant engineering offer much hope for the next century.

Meanwhile, other scientists are seeking ways to multiply the food-producing potential of the seas. One product attracting attention is *fish protein concentrate,* a flour made by grinding up whole fish and using it as an additive to fortify low-protein diets in poorer countries. Not only does this method employ more of the fish for food but it also makes possible the use of fish not ordinarily caught for human consumption. Thus far, however, fish protein concentrate has not been well received by consumers.

Despite the sophisticated techniques employed by some fleets, commercial fishing is still essentially little different from the activities of food gatherers and hunters. Modern fishing fleets merely seek out what nature has provided, with little or no thought for cultivating or replenishing the breeding stock. For the long run at least, it would seem logical for the fishing industry to follow the example of agriculture or animal husbandry by devising methods for commercial fish farming. Oriental rice farmers have traditionally cultivated carp and other fish in their irrigation ditches, ponds, and flooded fields as a source of much-needed protein in their starch-filled diets. In the same way, rice farmers in the lower Mississippi valley and delta successfully produce edible crayfish and catfish as byproducts of their irrigated rice growing. Oyster farming is a long-established industry in the brackish waters of Chesapeake Bay and various other coastal waters of the United States. These techniques are now being adapted to the cultivation of other relatively sedentary forms of sea life, such as lobsters, clams, and crabs.

Several fishing nations of Western Europe have begun to cultivate nonsedentary species, especially certain high-quality food fish found in the open seas. Norway's fish-farming program is already far advanced: By 1984 it was earning a substantial income from trout and salmon and had begun production of cod, turbot, and flatfish. Spain, France, and West Germany have developed techniques for growing fish and shellfish in aquaculture plants and releasing the hatchlings into their coastal waters for restocking. Japan and other fishing countries have long used such methods for rebuilding their salmon fisheries.

As in agriculture, opportunities exist for short-cutting the food chain of the seas. Harvesting seaweed is already a well-established industry, especially along the coasts of Japan and Canada's Atlantic provinces. The seaweed yields products widely used as food additives (ice cream stabilizers, for example) and in the chemical industries. One frequently voiced proposal is to harvest plankton directly instead of concentrating upon catching the fish that feed on it. Experiments have shown that this is an expensive operation, however, and consumers find the fishy flavor of the product distasteful. Moreover, some marine biologists argue that large-scale harvesting of plankton would merely deprive food fish of their main source of sustenance.

Feeding the World beyond A.D. 2000

The problem of feeding future populations raises many complex questions that lack sure answers. Just how many people will have to be fed, and how much food will it take? Where will the greatest demand for food come from? Who will have to produce it and how? As we have seen, the world population will probably continue growing at a fairly high rate into the twenty-first century before it tapers off, and the less-developed countries will account for virtually all of that growth beyond the year 2000. Moreover, the new additions to population will increasingly concentrate in the poorest of the poor countries.

Thus, the new demand for food will be confined almost solely to the Third World. The growth in demand will stem from two sources: (1) the increase in numbers of people to be fed and (2) greater per capita consumption as a result of rising incomes. Better diets for those Third World populations whose standards of living are improving probably mean more consumption of animal proteins, which in turn will substantially augment the demand for feed grains. This second source of demand increase—rising incomes—will center upon the middle-income less-developed countries. The poorest countries will probably continue subsisting on their accustomed high-starch diets and direct calories.

How will this new demand be supplied? The Third World as a whole is already a net importer of food: About 9 percent of current needs come from foreign sources. Only a select number of less-developed countries—notably the newly industrialized nations of the Pacific rim—could find the needed foreign exchange to pay for significant additional supplies of imported food. Many Third World countries already have burdensome trade deficits and large foreign debts. Realistically, therefore, most less-developed countries must count upon producing their new food needs themselves.

We have previously noted that future increases in food supplies will have to come predominantly from two sources: conventional agriculture and new developments in nonconventional food production. The seas currently contribute only a minor fraction of world food needs, and conventional fish catches have already leveled off. Agriculture remains the chief hope, especially with the encouraging rise in yields and output during the past two decades, which exceeded most predictions. Even so, the world food supply has little more than kept up with population growth thus far, and the task for the twenty-first century is immense. If world agriculture is to continue keeping up with population, it must achieve ever-greater technological improvements. It must also minimize future losses of arable land to competing forms of land use—urban, industrial, transportation, and so forth—and to soil deterioration from such causes as erosion, desertification, and alkalinity.

Agricultural experts concerned about the earth's future food supply have still another worry: the possibility of a major climatic change. This century has already seen unusual periods of global warming and cooling, leading some climatologists to speculate that this growing variability foretells the approach of another ice age, which they believe is about due. Others, however, note that human activities may actually be producing a countertrend that could bring a general warming instead. The combustion of fossil fuels causes carbon dioxide and other chemicals to accumulate in the upper atmosphere, where they create a "greenhouse effect" by trapping the incoming sun's rays and raising air temperatures. If either of these opposing trends were to materialize, crop production could be greatly affected, particularly in those areas that are unusually sensitive to temperature change: the higher latitudes, the upper elevations, and the semiarid regions. For instance, a 1°C decrease in mean annual temperatures, it has been estimated, would cut the potential wheat-growing area of Canada by one-third and would cause the U.S. corn belt to shift 140 km (85 miles) southward. Farmers in the South American Andes and other upland areas would have to abandon their lands at higher elevations and retreat to the lowlands.

Aside from the threat of environmental change, agriculturalists can expect additional yield increases to become ever more costly because these require larger capital outlays for irrigation and growing amounts for machinery and chemicals. Furthermore, most of the measures upon which we rely to augment world food supplies have the effect of intensifying the demand for other resources, most of which are nonrenewable. Minerals are essential for the manufacture of commercial fertilizers, for smelting metals used in making farm machinery and transport equipment, for the mechanical energy to propel this equipment, both on the farm and off, and for the construction of buildings, roads, dams, irrigation ditches, and other facilities. What are the prospects for maintaining an adequate supply of such resources?

ENERGY, MINERALS, AND OTHER EARTH RESOURCES

Resource Use and the Threat of Exhaustion

Soils can often be restored to fertility, plants and animal stocks can be replenished, and some barren wastes can be afforested; but a mineral deposit, once exhausted, is gone forever. The rate at which nonrenewable resources are being used is rising steadily throughout the world and especially in the industrialized countries. During much of this present century the United States alone has accounted for one-third to one-half of total world con-

sumption of these resources; U.S. mineral usage increased tenfold (reckoned in constant dollars) during the first 70 years of this century while population was rising only 2.7 times. By 1970 the United States, with fewer than 6 percent of the world's people, was thus consuming resources at a per capita rate seven times the world average.

The implications of this for future world resource use are apparent from Figure 5.13, which relates industrial output per person to levels of per capita resource use. The S-shaped logistic curve indicates that resource use rises steeply during the earlier stages of industrialization but eventually tapers off at some high level. Although U.S. consumption had reached that leveling-off stage by the third quarter of the century, the rest of the world was just entering the steepest part of the curve. This implies that other countries would follow the path already taken by the United States. In succeeding years Western Europe and Japan did indeed increase their consumption of resources, and the newly industrializing countries of the Pacific rim and Latin America have added further to the drain on global supplies. Thus, if the world as a whole were ultimately to attain the current American level of per capita production, vast quantities of energy and materials would obviously be required.

The important question to be addressed in the following pages, therefore, is whether or not the total sup-

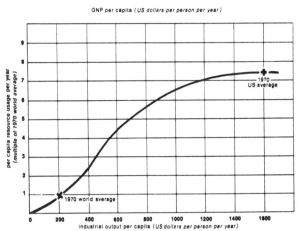

FIGURE 5.13 Per capita industrial output and resource use. With only 6 percent of the world's population, the United States was consuming resources at a rate seven times the world rate by 1970. If the rest of the world were to catch up with the U.S. level, massive additional quantities of raw materials and fuels would have to be found. [*Source:* Donnella Meadows, Dennis Meadows, Jørgen Randers, and William Behrens, *The Limits to Growth* (New York: Universe Books, 1972).]

ply of these resources will be adequate for a world consuming at the United States rate. The resources to be examined will be mainly of the nonrenewable kind; but a few are of the flow type, such as water, which are constantly being renewed by nature but are limited in total amount and subject to deterioration in quality as a result of human use.

The Nature of Reserves

Viewed in absolute terms, 88 known elements occur in the earth's crust in great amounts. Though some of these elements are indeed plentiful, others are relatively scarce (Figure 5.14). These less-abundant materials have become available to human beings only through the natural processes of concentration, which have caused comparatively large amounts of each to accumulate in a few places. This is the basis for the usual concept of a *reserve*, defined as that part of a known natural supply of a raw material that can be exploited commercially with existing technology and at current prices. A price rise makes it economically feasible to exploit deposits that are less accessible or poorer in quality. Thus, it took an OPEC crisis to add the high-cost deposits of Alaska's North Slope and Britain's North Sea to world oil reserves. Conversely, falling prices cause global reserves to decline as marginal deposits become uneconomical.

Considering the erratic, seemingly capricious way in which such concentrations have formed, what is the current state of world reserves? The consumption of most resources is growing more rapidly than the rate of population growth. Not only are more people consum-

ing resources but the average person is consuming larger quantities. According to most projections, the known resources of many vital materials would be used up within the next century, and some of the more important ones would become exhausted within only a few decades.

Rarely, however, are natural resources totally exhausted; usually their extraction is abandoned as a result of accelerating costs and prices. This does not usually happen suddenly. More often, rising prices cause the rate of use to diminish to the point where exploitation virtually ceases and substitutes are sought.

Among the variables affecting the cost of exploiting a resource are *quality* and *accessibility*. In the case of a mineral resource, accessibility includes both the depth of deposits in the ground and their distance from markets. As exhaustion of a material approaches, miners pursue reserves of increasingly poorer quality to greater depths and in more remote locations. Meanwhile, however, technological developments may slow the rise of production and processing costs, thereby postponing the exhaustion of a resource in this economic sense.

Spatial Distribution

Most natural resources are distributed very unevenly. This erratic spatial pattern results from the nature of the physical processes that cause such concentrations to form initially. In many cases a single country, or two or three, possesses a major share of the world total. The leading producers of a material, however, are not always those with the largest reserves. The most intensive production usually takes place in the most industrialized countries, which are the principal markets for those materials and for the products made from them. On the other hand, some of the largest reserves of certain vital nonrenewable resources are in countries with economies too small—such as Canada or Australia—or too underdeveloped to make full use of what they possess. The Communist Bloc countries, especially the USSR, and certain politically volatile areas, such as the Middle East and southern Africa, are leading producers of several essential fuels and raw materials.

This combination of spatial patterns of production and consumption holds many important implications both for world commerce and for global politics. These concerns will underlie our discussion of the present and future status of particular types of earth resources.

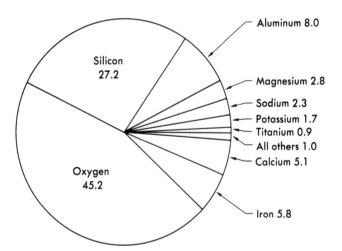

FIGURE 5.14 Elements in the earth's crust. Some of the most important industrial raw materials are included in the category "All others," which comprises only 1.0 percent of the earth's crust. [*Source:* Brian J. Skinner, *Earth Resources* (Englewood Cliffs, N.J.: Prentice-Hall, 1969).]

Energy

Ever since the dramatic events of the 1970s, energy has been a matter of intense international concern. When the Organization of Petroleum Exporting Countries (OPEC) seized control of global oil supplies and pricing late in 1973, it abruptly halted an era during which the world had come to believe that energy would remain cheap and abundant forever. The soaring prices and periodic shortages of oil in subsequent years raised urgent questions: Will the world have enough energy for continued economic growth? If so, will those who control these supplies share them with the rest of the world—and at what political and economic price?

Accelerating Demand

Considering the central role of mechanical energy in modern technology, this concern for future supplies seems warranted. Indeed, the spread of industrialization throughout the world has called for ever-growing amounts of energy. Although some of the poorest lands may still depend upon human porters, hand laborers, and crafts workers for power, this is no longer true—or even possible—for those countries where modernization is well advanced. A little more than a century ago, for instance, the United States still relied upon human labor for 94 percent of its industrial power; today less than 8 percent derives from this source.

As in other forms of resource use, the United States has led the way in the enormous expansion in energy consumption. How rapidly this growth took place in the United States is apparent from Figure 5.15, which shows the increase in total horsepower of the country's main prime movers (that is, the various devices for harnessing mechanical energy, such as electric motors and steam and gasoline engines). Between 1870 and 1970, U.S. nonhuman energy capacity more than doubled in almost every decade. This means that in 1870 the average resident of the country could draw upon only 0.4 horsepower, but a century later each American had access to 100.6 horsepower. Note, however, that the growth of energy consumption slowed sharply following the oil crises and economic recessions of the 1970s and early 1980s.

The United States still leads the world in total energy use, consuming one-third more than second-place USSR, but it no longer has the highest per capita use. Canada and Norway, both important surplus energy producers, now lead on a per capita basis. Although total world energy use has risen elevenfold since the beginning of the twentieth century, consumption rates vary greatly among countries at different levels of development. The relationship between energy use and economic development arises from the fact that the development process requires quantum increases in labor productivity. This is possible only through the replacement of human and animal power with inanimate energy. The closeness of this relationship is apparent from

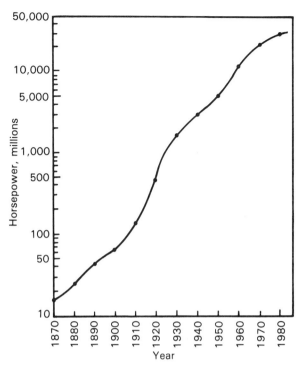

FIGURE 5.15 Total nonhuman energy of all prime movers, United States, 1870–1983 (horsepower). Capacity for mechanical energy use in the United States doubled in nearly every decade until the 1970s, when soaring prices and economic recession sharply curtailed the growth of energy consumption. [*Sources: Statistical Abstract of the United States, 1984* (Washington, D.C.: U.S. Government Printing Office, 1984); and *Historical Statistics of the United States* (Washington, D.C.: U.S. Government Printing Office, 1960).]

Figure 5.16, which shows how per capita energy consumption rises with increases in per capita national product. The world map of energy consumption (Figure 5.17) offers further confirmation of this.

Today, most of the industrialized world has caught up with the U.S. rate of energy use, having risen to that point on the logistic curve of resource use where further increases will be only moderate (refer again to Figure 5.13). As Figure 5.18 shows, the industrial market economies are consuming energy at an average annual rate of 4,985 kilograms of oil equivalent per year, a figure that exceeds energy use in the communist lands of Eastern Europe and the USSR by only 12 percent but is nearly 20 times as great as the average rate in the world's 34 poorest countries. In all, the Third World has about three-fourths of global population but consumes only one-third of all energy. But, with energy production concentrated in only a few parts of the world, most less-developed countries are forced to spend the greater part of their export earnings for energy imports. Altogether,

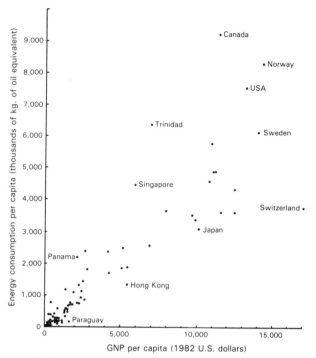

FIGURE 5.16 Energy consumption and per capita GNP. As countries rise in the scale of development, their per capita energy use increases proportionately. Note, however, that some industrialized countries use energy more sparingly than others. [*Source:* Data from World Bank, *World Development Report 1985* (New York: Oxford University Press, 1985).]

64 less-developed countries must rely upon imported oil for 75 percent or more of their total energy needs.

The various forms of inanimate energy upon which the world increasingly relies are drawn from five storage banks, all ultimately derived from that basic source, solar energy. The first of the five to be used by human beings was the *living-plant bank,* which was tapped through the domestication of herbivorous draft animals and the burning of wood. Exploitation of the *water-storage bank* came next, followed by development of the *fossil-fuel bank,* consisting of decayed and buried plant remains in the form of coal, oil, and gas. More recently the world has begun to draw upon the *nuclear-fuel bank* through the harnessing of the products of nuclear decay. In some favored localities, heat generated deep in the earth itself is providing the basis for commercial development of *geothermal power,* and in other places the power of ocean tides and direct solar energy are subjects of experimentation.

During the past century significant shifts have occurred in the relative importance of the different energy banks. Thus, in 1870, draft animals supplied the major part of the nonhuman energy of the United States, and these remained the chief source until the end of the nineteenth century (Figure 5.19). At that time electricity came into general use, followed quickly by the internal combustion engine. This meant increasing dependence first upon the water-storage bank for electric power generation and then upon the fossil-fuel bank, which subsequently gained overwhelming dominance. During this present century, however, the relative importance of the various fossil fuels has changed greatly. Coal was the principal fossil fuel prior to 1910, but oil and gas have since overshadowed it. Today our mounting needs force us to turn to the remaining energy banks, especially nuclear power.

In view of the accelerating demand for mechanical energy, we need to ask just how good are our reserves in each of the principal energy-storage banks, where these reserves are located, and who controls them. Considering our present heavy dependence upon fossil fuels, let us begin by reviewing the status of each of these and examining the possibilities for maintaining a future supply.

The Fossil Fuels

Today the United States obtains nine-tenths of its mechanical energy from the fossil fuels, and in many other countries the proportion is even greater. The figure was even higher prior to the early 1970s, when the sudden crisis in global oil supplies and prices gave added urgency to the search for alternatives. As Figure 5.19 shows, the share of other forms of energy (hydroelectric, nuclear, geothermal, and solar) has edged slowly upward during the late 1970s and 1980s. Nevertheless, the fossil fuels offer so many advantages in cost and convenience that they continue to dominate the short-run energy picture.

The fossil fuels are derived from the fossil remains of plants and animals and represent the energy products of organic decay. Normally these decay products escape into the atmosphere through radiation, but under certain special conditions they may be trapped and stored. This occurred ordinarily in swamps and bogs, where these materials later become preserved and concentrated under the pressure of layers of rock. The resulting hydrocarbons assume the form of solids (coal), liquids (oil), and gases. Although these formed in minute quantities each year, their total accumulation eventually became exceedingly great during the millions of years of the Carboniferous era (between 280 and 350 million years ago). Considering their slow rate of formation, the fossil fuels are essentially nonrenewable, which poses grave problems for future supply.

Oil and natural gas are more highly prized as fuels and as chemical raw materials than is coal because they

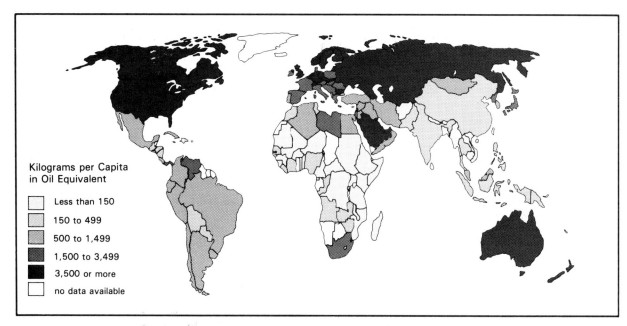

FIGURE 5.17 World energy consumption per capita. The least use of mechanical energy per person occurs in Africa south of the Sahara and in parts of southern Asia, areas at generally low levels of development. Several OPEC members, notably those on the Persian Gulf, rank with the industrialized countries in per capita energy consumption. Those countries at the highest levels of development differ in their energy consumption, depending upon a variety of economic and cultural considerations. [*Source:* Data from World Bank, *World Development Report 1985* (New York: Oxford University Press, 1985).]

are more easily transported and stored, have higher caloric content, and give more nearly complete combustion. Although oil is cheaper to transport than gas, which requires pipelines for overland shipment and specially designed vessels for movement by water, gas has the advantage of burning more cleanly. By contrast, because it is solid in form and has a high ratio of bulk to

heating value, coal is expensive to ship, and its combustion creates many pollutants.

Much of the crude oil (a liquid) and natural gas (mainly methane) occurring in nature are found in association, both apparently having been derived from decayed organic matter in ancient sea basins. Crude oil is a complex mixture of hydrocarbons—hydrogen and ox-

FIGURE 5.18 Per capita energy use (thousands of kg of oil equivalent) of major country groups (weighted average), 1960 and 1981, and percent increase (parentheses). [a]Oman, Libya, Saudi Arabia, Kuwait, United Arab Emirates. [b]Not available. [*Source:* Data from World Bank, *World Development Report 1984* (New York: Oxford University Press, 1984).]

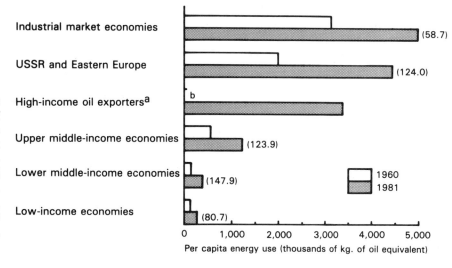

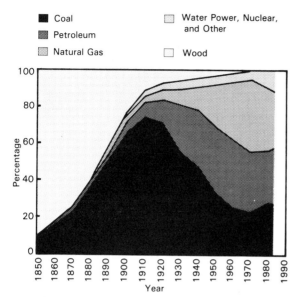

■ Coal
■ Petroleum
▨ Natural Gas
▨ Water Power, Nuclear, and Other
□ Wood

FIGURE 5.19 Percentage production of energy, by major sources, United States, 1850–1983. Wood, the most important source of energy a century ago, is little used for that purpose in the United States today. Its place has been taken mainly by fossil fuels—first coal, then oil and natural gas. The impact of the energy crises of the 1970s is apparent from the contraction in petroleum and gas output and the relative gains made by coal and such alternative sources as nuclear, geothermal, solar, and wind power. Falling oil prices in the 1980s threaten a reversal of these trends. [*Sources:* U.S. Bureau of the Census, *Statistical Abstract of the United States 1985* (Washington, D.C.: U.S. Government Printing Office, 1984); and *Historical Statistics of the United States, Colonial Times to 1970* (Washington, D.C.: U.S. Government Printing Office, 1976).]

ygen chemically combined in many ways. It therefore occurs in many grades, some light and others very heavy. The lighter grades are naturally richer in gasoline and other valuable fractions, but modern refining technology makes it possible to "crack" the heavy fractions into lighter forms. Unlike coal, oil and gas often migrate from the rocks in which they originated. Moving upward toward the surface, they become caught in "traps," rock formations that act as barriers. There they accumulate in pools, with the gas partly dissolved in the liquid and partly resting on top. Oil and gas are also capable of lateral migration, sometimes moving many miles from their origin. As the lightest fraction, natural gas often migrates still farther and may become entirely separated from the oil. In addition, some natural gas is derived from organic materials that are incapable of yielding oil. Hence, some countries lacking the geological conditions for oil have sizable reserves of gas.

Today, every barrel of crude oil brought to the surface is used completely. Not only does it yield gasoline, kerosene, jet fuel, lubricants, and fuel oil, but it also serves as a feedstock for hundreds of thousands of petrochemical products in direct competition with coal chemicals. Natural gas has a similarly wide range of uses. Modern urban-industrial economies have therefore grown heavily dependent upon these convenient and versatile fuels, which until recently were so cheap. As a result, these two energy sources, which have been exploited commercially for only a little more than a century, are being extracted and consumed at a profligate rate. How much is left, and where is it?

Proved reserves of crude oil are widespread, but they are unevenly distributed (Figure 5.20). The heaviest concentrations are in a select group of less-developed countries, most of which belong to the Organization of Petroleum Exporting Countries. The majority of OPEC's members are in the Middle East (Iran, Saudi Arabia, the United Arab Emirates, Kuwait, and Iraq), centering upon the Persian Gulf, and in North and West Africa (Algeria, Nigeria, Gabon, and Libya), but two are in South America (Venezuela and Ecuador) and another (Indonesia) is in South Asia. OPEC's reserves (1983) represent two-thirds of the world total, and 55 percent of reserves are in the Persian Gulf states alone. Saudi Arabia has more than a quarter of the world's known oil reserves, and Kuwait has almost a tenth. Not only are the Middle Eastern deposits vast, but the average output per well is many times that of North America, and costs of discovery, development, and production are only a fraction of those elsewhere.

The communist countries—mainly the USSR, Eastern Europe, and China—have another one-eighth of proved reserves. The USSR ranks third in reserves, having about 9.4 percent of the world total. Based upon recent discoveries, China is estimated to have about 3 percent of total reserves.

Western Europe, previously considered a have-not region in petroleum, has been the scene of important new finds. High prices, induced by OPEC's impact upon world markets, provided the stimulus for intensive exploitation of high-cost North Sea deposits, principally by the United Kingdom and Norway. Nevertheless, Western Europe still accounts for only 3.5 percent of total reserves.

The Western Hemisphere has also increased its oil reserves, which now constitute more than 18 percent of the world total. To a great extent, this is due to huge discoveries in Mexico, which is now fifth in world oil reserves. Elsewhere in the Western Hemisphere, substantial amounts occur along the Andean margins of South America, especially in Venezuela, which is still a sizable producer despite dwindling reserves after long

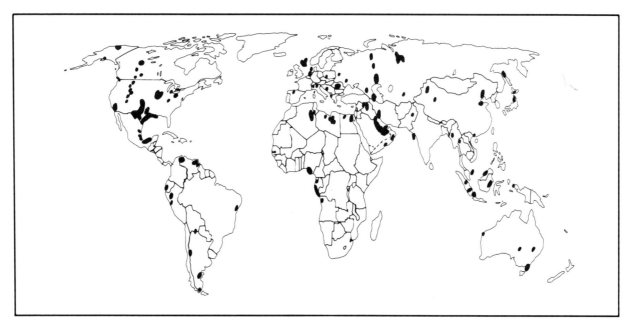

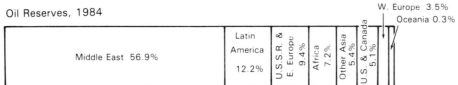

Oil Reserves, 1984

W. Europe 3.5%
Oceania 0.3%

| Middle East 56.9% | Latin America 12.2% | U.S.S.R. & E. Europe 9.4% | Africa 7.2% | Other Asia 5.4% | U.S. & Canada 5.1% | | |

FIGURE 5.20   Crude oil: world reserves and principal oil fields. [*Source:* U.S. Bureau of Mines, *Minerals Yearbook* (Washington, D.C.: U.S. Government Printing Office, 1985).]

years of exploitation. One-third of the hemisphere's reserves are in the United States and Canada. These are diminishing, however, despite the development of huge deposits along the North Slope of Alaska and continued exploration in the Arctic by both Canada and the United States.

The spatial patterns of global oil production and consumption correlate poorly with the locations of world reserves. With four-fifths of reserves concentrated in less-developed countries and another one-tenth in the USSR and its European satellites, only one-tenth of the total is left for the developed market economies. Yet the latter are exploiting their remaining reserves with growing intensity. This enables them to produce a quarter of the world's total output (Figure 5.21), but it also means that they are drawing down their dwindling reserves at a rapid rate. Even this is not enough to satisfy the enormous demand of this group; in all, these nations account for nearly half of global consumption. They must therefore make up the difference in imports from the less-developed countries and the USSR.

By the early 1980s, the United States had slipped to second place in oil production, although it continued to lead in consumption, taking more than a quarter of

world output. With each American citizen using oil at a rate five times the world average, the country has to rely upon imports for more than 40 percent of its needs. Even so, the United States has avoided the extreme degree of import dependence of most industrialized nations because of its generous supply of other fuels. With its smaller population, Canada has found its oil reserves sufficient to cover domestic consumption and provide a small surplus for export.

Other industrialized regions are less fortunate than North America. As a whole, Western Europe uses nearly one-fifth of the world's oil (Figure 5.21) and must import three-fourths of this despite the substantial production in the North Sea (the United Kingdom is now the sixth largest oil producer and the fifth largest exporter). Japan is much worse off than the other major industrial countries. Having negligible output, it is the third largest oil user and alone accounts for half of all Asian consumption.

Since 1983 the USSR has been the world's largest oil producer, supplying 23 percent of the total, and has become a leading exporter. Saudi Arabia ranks third among producers, and the Middle East as a whole accounts for 23 percent of global output. More than three-

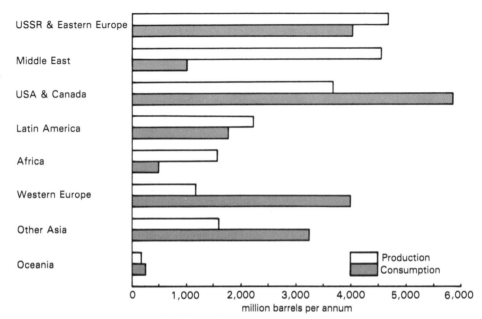

FIGURE 5.21 Production and consumption of crude oil, major world regions, 1983. Except for the USSR, the industrialized regions consume far more oil than they produce. Japan, the third largest user of oil, is mainly responsible for the big deficit for "Other Asia." [*Source:* U.S. Bureau of Mines, *Minerals Yearbook* (Washington, D.C.: U.S. Government Printing Office, 1985).]

fourths of this goes into world markets. Mexico has moved ahead of Venezuela, attaining fourth place as a producer of oil, more than half of which is exported. Latin America currently supplies 11 percent of the world's oil. Led by China and Indonesia, Asia excluding the Middle East and the USSR ("Other Asia" in Figure 5.21) produces an additional 8 percent. A like amount comes from Africa—mainly Nigeria, Libya, Egypt, and Algeria.

World oil consumption peaked at 64 million barrels per day in 1979, the year of the last big OPEC oil-price rise, and by 1983 it had dropped to 58 million barrels. The most highly developed countries were responsible for most of this decline; indeed, consumption actually continued to rise among the less-developed countries, especially the newly industrialized members of this group. The weakening demand for oil caused a supply reversal—from the shortages of the 1970s to the glutted markets of the 1980s. The accompanying fall in oil prices resulted in a slackening in exploration for new reserves and retarded the development of alternative sources of energy. These unfortunate effects of an otherwise welcome respite from the intense pressures on a dwindling nonrenewable resource merely raised the likelihood of future energy shortages when consumption resumes its inevitable rise.

Further helping to ease the pressures on world oil supplies is the growing availability of natural gas, which often occurs separately from oil and therefore has a somewhat different global pattern (Figure 5.22). In all, natural gas has been found in some 30 countries that apparently have no oil. Gas is much better represented in the USSR, North America, and Western Europe than is oil but is relatively less abundant in the Middle East, Latin America, and Africa. Indeed, the USSR, which has less than one-tenth of proved oil reserves, has nearly half (44 percent) of the world's gas supplies. Iran is second with 15 percent, and the United States is in third place with more than 6 percent.

Although proved oil reserves have been slipping in recent years, gas reserves have been rising as large new discoveries have been made in such widely scattered places as China, South Africa, and western Australia. In addition, estimates of reserves have been revised upward in the USSR, Norway, The Netherlands, and some other existing areas of production.

A comparison of Figure 5.21 and Figure 5.23 shows that natural gas also differs from oil in its spatial patterns of output and use. Some of the leading oil-producing regions—especially the Middle East and Africa—use only a fraction of their own petroleum output, whereas the major oil-consuming areas of Western Europe, the United States, and Japan have huge deficits. By contrast, quantities of gas produced and consumed are very similar at the regional scale (Figure 5.23). This close correspondence results mainly from the high cost

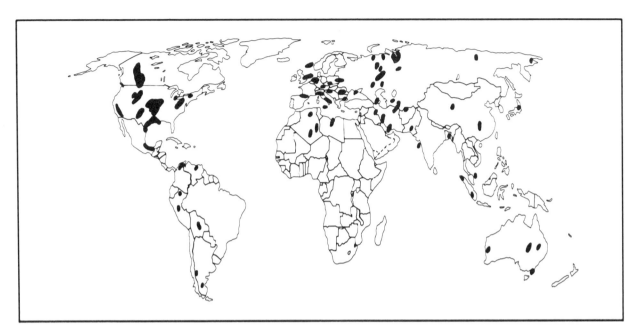

Gas Reserves, 1983

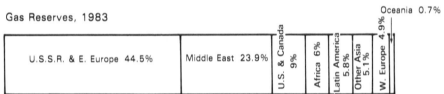

Oceania 0.7%

U.S.S.R. & E. Europe 44.5%	Middle East 23.9%	U.S. & Canada 9%	Africa 6%	Latin America 5.8%	Other Asia 5.1%	W. Europe 4.9%

FIGURE 5.22 Natural gas: world reserves and principal producing fields. [*Source:* U.S. Bureau of Mines, *Minerals Yearbook* (Washington, D.C.: U.S. Government Printing Office, 1985).]

of transporting gas by sea, which limits intercontinental movements. Within continental areas, however, this valuable fuel moves readily by pipeline and has become an important item of commerce between neighboring countries.

Pipeline distribution systems, however, are feasible only in high-income areas where urbanization and industrialization provide mass markets. Gas came to be widely used in the United States during the postwar years, and by the early 1970s it was supplying one-third of national energy needs. Conveniently served by an elaborate pipeline network direct from the producing fields, consumers obtained this clean, efficient fuel very cheaply because of government-regulated prices. The low prices discouraged the search for new reserves, however, so that the energy shortages resulting from the OPEC oil crisis of the 1970s forced a relaxation of price restraints. Higher prices thereupon caused gas consumption to slip to one-quarter of U.S. energy use (Figure 5.19), but they also stimulated new drilling. The resulting new supplies, plus imports from Canada and Mexico, have once more made gas plentiful, at least in the short run.

Meanwhile, production and consumption of natural gas have increased in other industrialized countries as new fields have been discovered and linked by pipeline to industrial and consumer markets. During the 1960s large finds were made in the British and Norwegian sectors of the North Sea and in Groningen Province of The Netherlands. As intra-European trade in this new energy source grew, the United Kingdom and neighboring lands on the continent switched from coal and oil to natural gas for many of their energy needs.

In recent years the USSR has found enormous quantities of natural gas, especially in northwestern Siberia. As pipelines are built, the USSR has begun converting more of its economy to natural gas and exporting the growing surplus to Eastern Europe. A further extension of these pipelines has brought a large flow of Siberian gas into Western Europe, adding to the growing domestic supply and causing gas prices to fall.

As Figure 5.23 shows, the Third World has lagged in its use of natural gas. Even the Middle East, which has nearly a quarter of world reserves, accounts for only 2 percent of consumption. Lacking effective consumer and industrial demand, producers in these countries

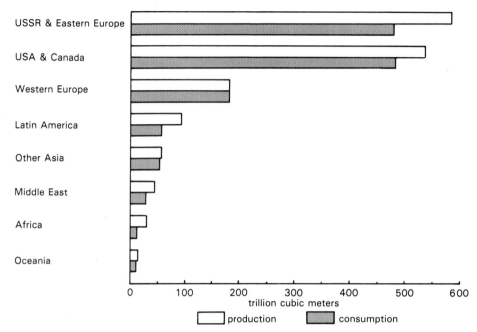

FIGURE 5.23 Production and consumption of natural gas, major world regions, 1983. Being less transportable by sea than is crude oil, natural gas is consumed mainly within the regions in which it is produced, although large quantities are exchanged among adjacent countries, especially in North America and Western Europe. [*Source:* U.S. Bureau of Mines, *Minerals Yearbook* (Washington, D.C.: U.S. Government Printing Office, 1985).]

merely burn off into the atmosphere much of the gas that naturally occurs in association with the oil. In the world at large about 6 percent of this valuable resource is lost in this manner, and nearly half of this waste occurs in the Middle East. Some progress is being made, however. Saudi Arabia, for instance, has constructed two great petrochemical complexes, one each on the Persian Gulf and the Red Sea, that use natural gas as a feedstock and an energy source.

New technology is also providing Third World countries with a way to export their natural gas to overseas markets. At special waterside installations this bulky product is converted to the liquid state by reducing its temperature to −259°F. The liquid natural gas (LNG) is very compact and can be transported long distances in tankers designed like thermos bottles. Algeria was one of the pioneers, exporting LNG to the United States, Britain, and other European markets. Japan, the most energy-deficient large economy, is receiving LNG from a growing number of sources. Pipeline transport is much cheaper, of course, and a number of Third World producers are finding ways to export their gas by this means. Algeria and Libya ship gas to southern Europe through a trans-Mediterranean pipeline, Mexico has direct pipeline links to its U.S. markets, and Malaysia now pipes gas to Singapore.

Although more natural gas is being used productively rather than being burned off and wasted, the rate at which it is being consumed hastens the time when global reserves of this valuable nonrenewable resource will begin to diminish, as is already occurring with oil. Later we shall look at the projected life span of this and other energy sources, but let us first consider the status of some competing forms of mechanical energy.

One form of energy that appears to face no immediate global supply problem is coal, the most abundant fossil fuel. Although coal was the energy that powered the Industrial Revolution, it has been eclipsed in this century by oil and gas, which are much more convenient to extract, transport, and use. Thus, coal accounts for 70 percent of the world's energy reserves, yet it comprises only one-fourth of current consumption.

Coal is a solid fuel that evolved from the burial, compaction, and aging of peat, a process that progressively increased its density and carbon content. The energy-giving qualities of coal therefore rise with increasing age. Hundreds of coal types exist, ranging from the highest-quality anthracite (hard coal) and bituminous (soft coal) to the lowest-grade lignite (brown coal). Although the major coal basins of the world have apparently been identified, the full extent of these is only now being determined with any accuracy. The projected life span of world reserves is estimated to be several hundred years at current rates of use. Very likely, however, the continuing preference for oil and gas will delay the final exhaustion of world coal supplies for some time. For this reason, and because they are much less plentiful, oil and gas will probably be exhausted first, after which coal will increasingly be converted into liquid and gaseous fuels until it too is finally used up.

Not only is coal more plentiful than the other fossil fuels but it is more evenly shared by the major world regions (Figure 5.24). The USSR leads, with slightly more than one-fourth of global reserves, although the greater part of these is inconveniently located in Siberia. Even the USSR's East European satellites, which are generally lacking in the other fossil fuels, have sizable amounts of coal, especially Poland and East Germany. North America is the second largest source area, and the United States alone has a quarter of world reserves, only slightly less than the USSR. Asia (excluding the USSR and the Middle East) likewise has very large supplies, most of these being in China (which ranks third behind the United States) and India. Western Europe, too, is well endowed with coal, despite its continuous heavy use

of this energy source since the eighteenth century. Only one-tenth of global reserves are in the Southern Hemisphere, but this is more than had earlier been thought. Both Australia and South Africa have large amounts—indeed, Australia's reserves rank fourth in the world.

Because of high transport costs, coal consumption has always been greatest in those regions where it is mined (compare Figure 5.24 and Figure 5.25). Changes are beginning to take place in the world patterns of production and consumption, however. Several major coal-producing areas are either developing other fossil fuels or are gaining better access to them, and high oil prices have brought a resurgence of coal use in certain other regions. At the same time, intensified exploitation of coal deposits is occurring in some places in response to industrialization and in others because of export opportunities.

Figure 5.25 shows the resulting patterns of production and consumption. The prominence of Asia (excluding the USSR and the Middle East), for instance, stems from the surge of coal use by China, which passed the United States as the leading producer in 1983. Both China and India have had substantial growth in energy-

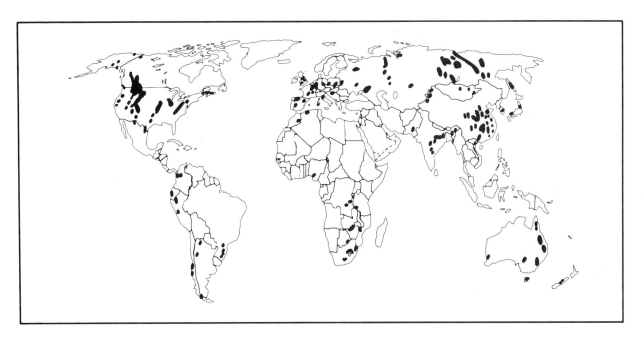

Coal Reserves, 1984

U.S.S.R. & E. Europe 36.2%	U.S. & Canada 25.3%	Other Asia 15.5%	W. Europe 11.9%	Oceania 6.6%	Africa 3.7%	Middle East	Latin America

FIGURE 5.24 Coal: world reserves and principal coalfields. [*Source:* U.S. Bureau of Mines, *Minerals Yearbook* (Washington, D.C.: U.S. Government Printing Office, 1985).]

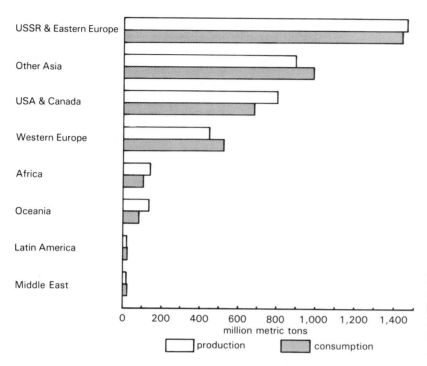

FIGURE 5.25 Production and consumption of coal, major world regions, 1983. [*Source:* U.S. Bureau of Mines, *Minerals Yearbook* (Washington, D.C.: U.S. Government Printing Office, 1985).]

intensive heavy industries that draw upon their large coal reserves. Although the United States and Canada have more coal reserves than do the Asian lands, they rely more upon other fuels. As oil and gas have become more expensive, however, their dependence upon coal has risen somewhat. The same is true in Western Europe, which is not only a large producer of coal but also a major importer. The growing availability of natural gas, however, has prevented an even greater increase in Europe's coal use. Coal consumption in the USSR and Eastern Europe has always been very great, but during the past two decades it has been declining because of increased availability of gas and oil. Since 1960 coal has fallen from 71 percent of total energy consumption in Eastern Europe to only 61 percent, and in this same period it has dropped from 44 percent to 31 percent in the USSR. Another country that has relied heavily upon coal is South Africa. A pariah nation, isolated from the world community because of its racial policies, South Africa has intensively exploited its sizable coal reserves as a way of achieving energy independence. To make up for its lack of oil, it has successfully synthesized liquid fuels from coal and has even become an exporter of its synfuel technology, as well as an important supplier of coal.

The United States still leads in coal exports, although its share of the world market is shrinking. Australia, whose northeastern coalfields are well located near major sea lanes, ranks second. Poland has now slipped to third place among coal exporters because of internal political problems that have reduced output.

Other major suppliers to the world are the USSR and Canada.

Coal production and use in the industrialized world would be still greater were it not for the harmful effects of coal combustion upon the atmosphere. Newly developing countries that rely upon coal, such as China and India, have yet to become concerned with this problem. Ironically, with all its problems as a pollutant, coal is the leading fuel for the generation of electricity, which is the cleanest form of energy.

Electricity

Of the conventional forms of energy, electricity has experienced the steadiest growth in demand during the modern era. Indeed, electric energy requirements have at times risen so fast that new generating capacity could not be installed quickly enough in some areas to avoid power shortages at peak periods of use. The popularity of electricity stems from its many special advantages. One of these is its mobility, which has given a new locational freedom to its users, especially light industry. It is clean to use, even though generating it can create a great deal of pollution. It also can be used in precisely the quantities needed, unlike the big steam engines that supplied power for factories in earlier times.

Because it is so flexible and versatile, electricity is ideal for an infinite variety of energy applications. In the United States more than one-fifth of all electricity is consumed by private households and commercial establishments; another quarter is used in transportation;

and the rest goes to industry. In many parts of the world the percentage used by manufacturing is much larger. Electric motors account for much of the industrial consumption, but electrometallurgical and electrochemical companies also require great amounts of power.

Electricity is difficult to categorize, for it is really a hybrid. An electric current is essentially a movement of electrons and it therefore has many characteristics of a flow resource, except that it is used up. Also, unlike other flow resources, electricity is hard to store and most of the output, except for transmission losses, is consumed as it is produced. It is easy to transmit over short distances, but long-range transmission entails higher costs and greater losses. The difficulty of storing electricity requires that the power industry attempt to anticipate demand, which can vary seasonally, daily, and even hourly.

Electricity is a derived form of energy rather than a primary source in itself. It is produced by generators that are powered by other (primary) energy forms. Thus, the force of falling water drives turbines, which generate hydroelectricity. In the production of thermoelectricity, heat from the burning of coal, oil, or gas is used to raise steam, which in turn drives the turbines. Generators may also be powered by internal combustion engines, which may burn either gasoline or diesel fuel. More recently,

new types of primary power for generating electricity have appeared. Two thermal sources—nuclear and geothermal energy—are in commercial use, whereas solar and tidal energy are still experimental.

Per capita consumption of electricity varies widely (Figure 5.26), and so does the source of primary energy employed to produce it. The richer countries use far more electricity per person than do the poorer ones. For instance, in 1982 Ethiopia used only 20 kilowatt hours (kw/hr) per person, Chad only 14, and Haiti 49, whereas semi-industrialized Argentina consumed 1367 kw/hr per capita and the United States 10,074. In most less-developed countries, per capita electricity use is considerably lower than total energy consumption, much of which is in the form of motor fuels for transportation.

The correlation of electricity consumption and level of development is not perfect, however, mainly because advanced countries differ so greatly in their use of power. How much electricity a high-income country uses depends upon its industrial structure, whether or not a particular cheap source of power is available, and the frugality of the populace. Thus, Canada uses 40 percent more electricity per person than does the United States, and Norway uses more than twice as much. Both Canada and Norway have small populations and unusually abundant supplies of inexpensive hydroelectric-

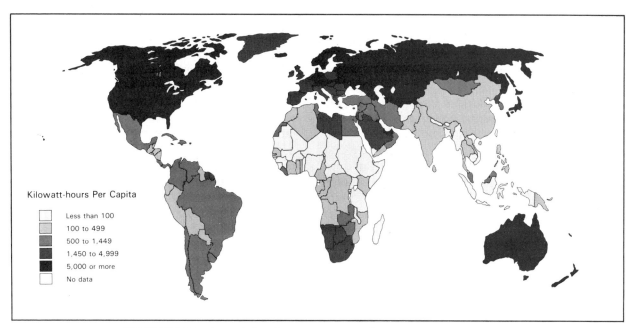

FIGURE 5.26 Annual electric power consumption per person. Northern America and Scandinavia have very high levels of per capita electricity use, and the remainder of Western Europe is only slightly lower. The least consumption takes place in sub-Saharan Africa and southern Asia, where many countries have usage levels of less than 100 kilowatt-hours per person. [*Source:* Data from *1986 Britannica Book of the Year* (Chicago: Encyclopaedia Britannica, Inc., 1986).]

ity, which has attracted large electrometallurgical and electrochemical manufacturers requiring huge blocks of power.

Yet, on the whole, the preferred fuel for generating electricity in most of the world is coal, despite the environmental problems it creates. Because of the cheapness and availability of this form of primary energy, the United States and the majority of Western European countries rely upon coal for three-fourths or more of their generating capacity. The proportion is much higher in Eastern Europe, Australia, and South Africa.

Petroleum is a leading fuel for electric generation in many places, especially the Persian Gulf countries, which rely almost entirely upon this locally abundant resource for their electricity. Moreover, Japan produces nearly two-thirds of its electricity with oil-fired generators; and the United Kingdom, which obtains four-fifths of its electric power from fossil fuels, uses dual generators designed to burn either coal or oil, depending upon availability and market conditions.

Water power is a main source of electricity in those countries fortunate enough to have the requisite physical conditions and the large supplies of capital needed to develop such resources. Norway obtains 99.9 percent of its electricity in this way, Switzerland 71 percent, Iceland 93 percent, and Canada 67 percent. Hydroelectricity is especially important in certain parts of the Third World. A prominent example is Brazil, which, to reduce its burdensome dependence upon imported energy, has embarked upon an ambitious dam-building program; at present the country relies upon falling water for 93 percent of its electricity. Brazil's latest major project is the world's largest hydroelectric dam, Itaipu on the Paraná River, which began delivering power in 1984. Among other large hydroelectric facilities in the Third World are Zambia's huge dam on the Zambezi River and Egypt's Aswan Dam on the Nile. Africa as a whole has 27 percent of the world's hydroelectric potential but only a tiny proportion of that has been harnessed. This is true also of Southeast Asia, which has 16 percent of the potential, and Latin America with 20 percent. In each region the problems are lack of necessary capital and lack of a present market for the power. In the industrialized countries, on the other hand, the largest and most accessible sources of hydroelectricity have mostly been used up, especially in Western Europe, North America, and Japan.

In those countries lacking fossil fuels or water power, the second most common primary source of energy is uranium. At present levels of technology, nuclear energy appears to be the only source that has sufficient potential to satisfy the rising demand for electricity in future years. The power of the atom is harnessed in two

ways: nuclear *fission* (the process used by the atomic bomb), and nuclear *fusion* (the hydrogen bomb method). The former entails capturing the energy released by fissioning radioactive elements, a process that can be controlled to release steady amounts of heat for generating electricity. One pound of nuclear fuel can produce as much electric power as 5900 barrels of oil. This fuel is uranium 235, a rare and costly element with the potential to create dangerous levels of radioactivity in the environment. Nuclear fusion, on the other hand, relies upon cheap and plentiful raw materials, and the process is nearly pollution free. Fusion reaction presents formidable technological problems, however, and it is therefore unlikely to become a commercial source of energy before the twenty-first century.

Despite its high cost and the hazards it poses, nuclear fission is gaining widespread use throughout much of the world. By 1984 France had taken the lead in fostering this energy source, upon which its state-operated utility system relies for 55 percent of its electricity. Altogether the system operates 38 nuclear installations. The United Kingdom, which pioneered in the commercial development of atomic power, depends upon this source for 16 percent of its electricity. Indeed, atomic energy has become a major supplier of electric power to nearly all parts of Europe, both West and East. Even Japan, the only country to experience wartime atomic destruction, depends upon nuclear power for 18 percent of its electricity. Among Third World countries with atomic power installations are India, South Korea, and Taiwan. The USSR obtains 6 percent of its electricity from this source, and the United States, despite its many problems with nuclear power, generates 13 percent of its electricity in this manner.

Still another new technology that contributes significant amounts of electricity in several countries is *geothermal* energy. This method of generating power relies upon heat that occurs naturally inside the earth; temperatures rise with increasing depth, reaching 5000°C at the core. Over most of the earth's crust this heat remains too deep for it to be tapped in any useful way, but in a few areas abnormally hot rocks approach the surface. Where groundwater comes into contact with these rocks it forms geothermal pools, which overflow as hot water or steam to create hot springs and geysers. Among countries successfully harnessing this earth heat to generate commercial quantities of electricity are Iceland, Japan, Mexico, New Zealand, and the United States (in California).

Today, increasing amounts of electricity are traded among countries as power-surplus nations sell their excess supplies to power-short neighbors. Regional and national power grids link adjacent countries in order to balance differing peak loads and to provide extra reservoirs in case of emergency. The continental countries of Western Europe have interconnected power systems of this sort, and a two-way cable linking the United Kingdom and France under the English Channel is nearing completion. The leading exporting country is Canada, which sends large amounts of its cheaply produced hydroelectricity to nearby power-deficient areas of the United States. In Western Europe the chief exporters are Switzerland, Norway, and Austria—all with great surpluses of hydroelectricity—and France, which is rapidly expanding its supply of nuclear-generated power for export. A similar exchange of electricity takes place in Eastern Europe, the USSR being the largest supplier. Some trade in electricity is even taking place among less-developed countries. Zambia, for example, finds sizable markets for its abundant hydroelectricity in neighboring Zimbabwe and South Africa.

Noncommercial Energy

In the Third World as a whole, much of the inanimate energy comes from noncommercial sources. Ironically, it is in these lands that perhaps the most critical energy shortages of all are taking place, threatening not only local economies but also the physical environment itself, along with all of those people who depend upon it for support. The amount of energy obtained from fuel wood, agricultural wastes, animal dung, and other noncommercial fuels is immense. For instance, in India and Indonesia, two of the most populous less-developed countries, these sources contribute almost as much to total energy consumption as do commercial sources. In all, possibly 1.5 billion people rely solely upon firewood for heating their water and cooking their food. Most have no access to alternative forms of energy and could not afford them even if they did. The total amount of firewood used in a year is likely more than a billion metric tons.

Although noncommercial energy constitutes a diminishing proportion of total energy consumed in the Third World—a result of increasing industrialization in some developing countries—the number of people still relying upon traditional fuels remains very great because of the high rates of population growth in these lands, especially the poorest ones. Indeed, severe population pressure is a prime cause of the worsening energy crisis now facing major parts of the Third World. With growing numbers of people scavenging for wood, the forest cover is disappearing at an alarming rate over vast areas. Wood gatherers have to range farther and farther each day in search of wood, and in some countries they are forced to take every sapling and twig and even the litter on the ground. As the forest floor becomes denuded, trees and shrubs are no longer able to

reseed themselves and the bare soil is left to erode in the wind and rain.

When the firewood disappears altogether, as it has in much of Africa south of the Sahara and in southern Asia, the population must turn to the dried dung of their livestock for fuel. This deprives their fields of vitally needed animal fertilizers and thus reduces crop yields. Hence, the crisis in noncommercial energy adds to the crisis in food supply of poorer lands. This Third World energy problem is little noticed in the general effort to ensure future supplies of commercial energy for the industrialized countries.

The Energy Future

Having examined the characteristics of conventional energy forms, and the spatial patterns of their reserves, production, consumption, and exchange, we now turn to the most pressing question: Is the supply of energy adequate for future needs? Public complacency on this subject gave way to deep concern after the oil price shocks precipitated by the Arab oil embargo of 1973–1974 and the Iran-Iraq War beginning in 1979. As oil prices rose, the prices of gas and other competing fuels rose in sympathy, introducing a new era of more costly energy and greater uncertainty. It brought with it economic recession and slower economic growth and it aggravated income and social inequities.

Considering the immense transfer of wealth among oil-importing and oil-exporting countries, the world has on the whole made a surprising adjustment. Energy consumption has fallen in response to the higher prices and slower economic activity. And new sources of petroleum have been vigorously sought and found in the North Sea, Alaska, Mexico, and other non-OPEC areas. Indeed, the adjustment has been sufficient to lull many people, and their political leaders, into a false sense of security. Great uncertainties remain, however, and future shortages are entirely possible.

Looking to the future, we ask: What are the predicted life spans of the conventional types of energy? What can be done to postpone their exhaustion? Given that these nonrenewable resources will ultimately be used up, what are the prospects for new kinds of energy to replace them? Is it possible to avert future energy crises? When considering the question of future supplies, however, we must not forget the other side of the problem—the directions of future demand. The demand side is often neglected because it is not as glamorous as the supply side, which entails the search for exciting new scientific discoveries. Before taking up the prospects for future supplies, therefore, let us first see how much energy the world is likely to need.

Anticipating future world demand is difficult because countries at various levels of development use energy differently and react differently to price changes. Less-developed countries generally spend a higher proportion of their gross national products on energy than do advanced countries, and this proportion continues to diminish at the highest levels of development. Though per capita energy consumption is very low among the least-developed countries, this climbs steeply with rising GNP, later tapering off at high levels of GNP (refer back to Figure 5.16).

The effects of price on energy demand are complex. In the short run the price-elasticity of demand for energy is low in advanced countries; that is, a rise in price is not immediately reflected in reduced consumption (see Chapter 6, pages 144–145, for a more detailed explanation of price-elasticity of demand). Consumers do not instantaneously trade in their gasoline-wasting big automobiles for more energy-efficient ones when fuel prices rise, nor do factories immediately install new machinery or homeowners insulate their houses. More likely, a quick, sharp rise in energy prices will merely precipitate an economic recession. In the longer run, however, the price-elasticity of demand is much higher: The next car purchased gets much better gasoline mileage, and so forth. On the whole, citizens of the richer countries have many opportunities for saving energy merely by making discretionary changes in lifestyle—living closer to work and recreation, traveling less, and turning off electric lights and appliances. The effects of price rises on the economic growth of advanced countries are generally less, too, because a larger part of GNP is derived from the services and high-technology industries that consume little energy.

The cost of energy and its availability impact on the economic growth of less-developed countries, however, because of the nature of their industrial and transport needs. Any rise in their level of development is directly reflected in increased demand for energy. High rates of population growth add further to this demand.

Projections for the remainder of the twentieth century therefore suggest that total energy demand in the industrialized nations will double but that demand in the Third World will increase fivefold to sevenfold. Nevertheless, current levels of energy use in the less-developed countries are so low that even this gain in total amount will by the year 2000 leave their per capita consumption six or seven times smaller than that of the richer ones.

Finding sufficient additional quantities of energy to supply this growing demand raises still other uncertainties. Although reserve estimates such as those appearing in Figures 5.20, 5.22, and 5.24 give some indication of near-term prospects, the more distant future is clouded by questions of data quality and changes in

costs. Added to this is the problem of uneven world distribution and the political risks this poses for energy-importing countries, all of which carry great potential for future price fluctuations.

Based upon what we know now, and assuming a minimum of political intervention in world commerce, we may expect oil production to peak during the final decade of this present century. Thereafter, supplies will likely diminish gradually and production costs and market prices will rise accordingly. Because such a large proportion of known reserves is concentrated in the USSR and the politically volatile Middle East, however, the political uncertainties surrounding this current prime energy resource are especially troublesome.

Natural gas production should rise substantially toward the year 2000, reaching a peak within the first two or three decades of the new century. Gas supplies are thus likely to last a little longer than oil. As in the case of oil, however, a major part of the world's natural gas is in the USSR and the Middle East (although this time the USSR has the greater share). North America and Western Europe are relatively better off in gas reserves than they are in oil, and the United States has a very large potential from high-cost sources. As we have seen, however, the sharing of this resource between have and have-not nations is more difficult than oil because gas is so costly to ship by sea.

As the most abundant fossil fuel, coal should be plentiful throughout the next century. Moreover, its reserves are more widely distributed, including very large stocks in the United States and China, as well as the USSR, Europe, and Australia. This pattern is therefore much more favorable for the noncommunist industrialized nations than other conventional fuels. Yet, those countries lacking coal are at a disadvantage because of its high shipping costs. Widespread future use of coal also requires finding an economical solution to the problem of atmospheric pollution now associated with coal combustion.

The remaining energy sources now making a significant contribution all pose problems for future expansion. With current technology, nuclear fission is unlikely to last beyond the turn of the century because of limited supplies of low-cost uranium. Environmental constraints are also a serious deterrent, especially in the United States. Hydroelectricity has a limited future among developed countries, where most of the existing waterpower potential has been exhausted. A very large unused potential remains in parts of the Third World, but obtaining the capital required to develop this resource will continue to be a great obstacle.

Beyond this present century, projections of energy demand and supply become increasingly uncertain. The distant energy future is easier to foresee in the case of the present group of industrialized nations because their populations have stabilized and their levels of resource use appear to have peaked and even to have begun a decline. The less-developed countries present an entirely different set of problems. We cannot be sure of their future demand for energy without knowing how far their development will proceed and what form their industrialization will ultimately assume. What we can be sure of is that the potential demand will inevitably rise as Third World populations continue to climb before peaking in the latter part of the twenty-first century. At that point, the number of potential users of energy will probably have reached 10 billion or 12 billion. With the output of today's preferred forms of energy expected to dwindle soon after A.D. 2000, the search for new kinds of energy is already pressing. This is especially so because of the long lead time required for a new form of energy to supersede an older one; in the past this has usually required about 50 years.

Experience gained from the energy crises of the 1970s has shown that one sure way of gaining additional time for developing radically new kinds of energy is to stretch out existing supplies of conventional energy. Conservation is now generally recognized as the cheapest and quickest method of obtaining energy in the short run. The OPEC crises slowed the rate of energy use far more than the most optimistic predictions of the time. The reaction was worldwide; between 1979 and 1983 consumption in the noncommunist countries actually fell by 13 percent, reversing the steady rise in energy consumption that had prevailed for decades previously.

This reversal in consumption trends was especially dramatic in the United States, long a profligate user of energy. By 1983 the country was using less energy than it had in 1973 on the eve of the first OPEC crisis, yet gross national product had risen at an average annual rate of 2.5 percent during that 10-year period. The United States achieved its 1983 GNP with 22 percent less energy than if 1973 levels of energy efficiency had continued unchanged.

The trend toward energy saving acquired a momentum of its own when people came to realize that the days of cheap oil were gone forever. Thus, energy efficiency now has a built-in quality. Consumers will not return to gasoline-wasting motor cars to any great extent (the U.S. average in 1974 was only 14 miles per gallon; in 1984 it was 28 miles per gallon), and their energy-efficient home furnaces and insulation are in place for good. Most encouraging, when economic recovery came in 1983 it did not cause a spree in energy use. The ratio of energy use to GNP continues to fall, although at a slow rate.

Industrial users, who account for 40 percent of the U.S. total, have made a special effort to increase energy efficiency. Industrial use of energy by 1982 was one-third less than would have been the case if 1973 consumption trends had continued. This was achieved in part by installing new equipment, but it also reflected slower industrial growth as the services assumed a larger part of the economy. At the same time, changes in the industrial structure have brought the decline of old energy-intensive industries and have forced old, less-efficient plants to shut down. Nevertheless, a huge potential for further improvement apparently remains: According to the Department of Energy, American industries could actually turn out the same amount of product with 50 percent less energy than at present. The United States still lags behind Japan and Western Europe, where energy has always been more costly. American industry has taken the easy steps; the more difficult ones are mostly ahead. Undoubtedly the greatest opportunities for energy conservation, viewed globally, however, are in the USSR, where energy consumption far exceeds world levels. The USSR's energy use is actually 2.5 times that of Europe, largely because of outdated plants and equipment and excessive use of energy-intensive materials.

Although in the short run conservation has proved unexpectedly effective, in the longer run substantial new supplies will have to be found. One way of doing this is to intensify exploitation of existing reserves and exploration for new ones in order to extend the life spans of conventional fuels. Those producing countries that are net importers of energy are already pursuing this policy with considerable effect. Thus, the United States, which has only 4 percent of the world's proved oil reserves, accounts for 16 percent of total production, whereas the Middle East, with 57 percent of the reserves, yields only 23 percent of world output. Additions to U.S. production now come mainly through horizontal and vertical expansion of existing fields, that is, drilling new wells on the margins and going to greater depths.

The only truly important U.S. finds in recent times were in Alaska, and that region (which holds one-third of U.S. reserves) continues to be the country's main hope for new supplies to replace the now-dwindling output at Prudhoe Bay. An equally intensive and costly search for oil and gas is under way in the Canadian Arctic. Elsewhere in the world the effort to locate new supplies has continued since the first OPEC crisis, yielding important finds in the North Sea, southern Mexico, China, Australia, and Colombia. The USSR, though known to have some of the world's largest energy resources, has had to put massive new investments into oil exploration to compensate for declining output. The USSR's main problem is that thus far the country has been relying upon only the richest and most accessible deposits, thus skimming off the cream of its huge energy wealth. As these older fields decline, new exploration has led ever deeper into remote and frozen areas of Siberia, where high costs and technical difficulties have slowed development. Meanwhile, the Middle East maintains its status as the richest area of all: Recent additions to Kuwait's reserves, for example, alone equal all the known reserves of the United States. The net effect of all this intensified exploration since 1973 is that the world has located more oil than it has used since the first oil crisis. In 1979 the noncommunist countries were calculated to have a 30-year supply of oil; today they have a 40-year supply.

The success of this feverish search for new energy has reduced the oil cartel's hold on world markets and has postponed the time when fossil fuels will become exhausted. Nevertheless, the experts consider it unlikely that any new "Middle Easts" will appear to provide a quantum rise in world reserves. Given the long lead time for developing new types of energy, where do our best hopes lie for the more distant future?

All the options for other energy sources involve the development and refining of new technologies. One such option concerns the perfection of techniques for recovering the great amounts of oil left underground in an oilfield after the usual extraction methods have ended. When pumping of an oil pool ceases, as much as 60 percent to 70 percent of the oil remains behind, trapped in pockets and holes in the rock. The industry has developed secondary recovery techniques that can bring up some of the remaining oil, and so-called enhanced recovery contributes additional amounts; but these methods still leave possibly half of the total behind. The remainder represents an enormous resource, but finding ways of tapping it poses great technical difficulties yet to be solved.

Another great resource that awaits further technological development before it can be fully utilized is coal. Its combustion releases into the atmosphere dangerous impurities that pose serious environmental hazards, but a truly effective treatment is costly because of the number and complexity of the pollutants that must be driven off. Present techniques—washing, fluidized beds, scrubbers—add 20 percent or more to the cost of generating electricity and therefore place this valuable fuel at a competitive disadvantage with respect to other forms of energy, especially in locations remote from coalfields. Developing an economical method that would give clean-burning coal should be of highest priority to the United States, which has such large reserves. Although such techniques appear within grasp, this type of research has been unable to attract the funding needed for a quick solution.

On the other hand, during and immediately after the energy crises a great deal of attention focused upon synfuels. These are produced by converting solid fuels to gaseous or liquid forms suitable for use in internal combustion engines. The most common raw materials are coal, oil shales, and tar sands. For at least 150 years coal has been used for generating a low-grade fuel called "coal gas," or "town gas," which was common in Europe and North America until it was superseded by cheaper, hotter natural gas. More recently, attention has turned to obtaining liquid fuels from coal, to be used as substitutes for oil and gasoline. Processes developed in Germany during World War II are the bases for existing methods, which South Africa has adopted and further refined for its drive to achieve energy independence as described earlier. Several experiments with these techniques were undertaken in the United States in the late 1970s but languished with the decline in world oil prices in subsequent years.

North America is likewise well endowed with two other resources used for making synfuels—tar sands and oil shales. So plentiful are these that they have the potential for nearly doubling the world's fossil fuel stores. Tar sands contain large-molecule hydrocarbons like those of crude oil, but they do not migrate as do oil and gas. Instead, this thick bituminous material adheres firmly to the sand grains among which it has lodged. Tar sands occur in limited quantities in several parts of the world, but the most important known deposits are in western Canada. The Athabaska tar sands of northern Alberta are 200 feet thick and extend over 30,000 square miles. Other large occurrences are the Orinoco deposits of Venezuela and the Olenek deposits in the USSR. Recovery of this resource requires mining the sands and then heating them to cause the asphaltic hydrocarbons to flow. Commercial extraction of the Canadian deposits is already well under way.

Oil shales are rock formations that contain concentrations of bitumen that can be converted into valuable petroleum products. Vast reserves of rich oil shales occur in the Rocky Mountains of the United States, extending over much of Colorado, Utah, and Wyoming. These Green River shales can be made to yield from 0.5 to 1.5 barrels of oil per ton; in total the country's oil shales probably exceed the amount of its conventional oil reserves. Pilot plants have proved the technical feasibility of mining oil shale, but it is too costly to exploit at present price levels. In addition, current processing techniques threaten the vulnerable western environment with atmospheric pollution, water contamination, and problems of waste disposal. Nevertheless, both tar sands and oil shales represent potentially important supplements to future energy supplies.

To many experts, nuclear power is the ultimate answer to the energy problem. The realization of these expectations, however, depends upon the success of some exceedingly difficult research. The form of atomic power now in commercial use, nuclear fission, is the basis for rapidly growing power programs in several countries. At today's prices energy from this source continues to be competitive except in the United States, where elaborate and costly measures to ensure safety have made nuclear power plants less economical. The future of nuclear fission therefore encounters grave environmental concerns.

A second problem with nuclear fission is that uranium is a scarce element—only 0.00016 percent of the earth's crust—and high-grade ores of U-235 are severely limited in occurrence, despite the most intensive search ever conducted for a metal. Leading noncommunist sources, in order, are the United States, South Africa, Canada, and Australia; Communist reserves are a closely guarded secret. The apparent solution to this problem of supply is the breeder reactor, which uses a lower-grade fuel and actually creates new fuel at the same rate or greater than the fissioning atoms are used up. When perfected, this would seem to be the final solution to the long-sought goal of perpetual motion; but it does not end concerns about radiation.

Fusion research is the promised answer to the environmental problems surrounding atomic power. Unlike fission, however, nuclear fusion has not yet been successfully controlled to permit its use for generating electricity, even in the laboratory. If and when research on this technology succeeds, nuclear fusion could supply limitless amounts of electric energy using one of the cheapest and most plentiful raw materials, hydrogen. It would present no radiation dangers. Success in this research effort is not yet assured, and few would predict that nuclear fusion will become a commercial reality until some time after the turn of the century.

The oil crises of the 1970s directed attention to many other energy options, several of which may well achieve commercial success in the long run. One of the most attractive of all is solar energy, which is renewable, clean, and available in boundless quantities. As yet, however, solar research has not produced a technology that is suitable for widespread commercial application. Many solar heating devices are now in use, but for most areas they are too inefficient and costly. Research on solar generation of electricity is more promising, although for dependable commercial operation it would be confined mainly to regions with cloudless skies, such as Israel and the southwest deserts of the United States.

Another energy alternative that has attained a degree of success under specific conditions is alcohol used to fuel internal combustion engines. Alcohol made from corn and mixed with gasoline to produce "gasohol" has become a popular motor fuel in the grain-producing American Midwest. Faced with unbearably high bills for imported oil, Brazil has undertaken an urgent national program to replace gasoline with alcohol made from sugar cane, which is grown cheaply in that country. Further options under consideration or development are hydrogen gas (used directly as a motor fuel), geothermal energy (already operating commercially in a few favored localities), wind power, and power from ocean tides, waves, and thermal convection.

Clearly, then, we have many options for keeping the world supplied with mechanical energy in the future. This present period appears to be one of transition, a time when the end of the familiar and conventional forms of energy is approaching and newer forms are not yet ready to replace them fully. The transition is filled with uncertainties relating to consumption trends, investment levels, technical questions, and political hazards.

In the short run, we may have to contend with crises. Political crises in the form of wars, revolutions, and embargoes may suddenly cut off supplies, although presumably these would create only relatively brief interruptions. Crises could also arise if producing countries and companies fail to make the necessary investments to sustain necessary levels of output. Some exporting countries, for instance, could decide that it is in their own best interest to keep their surplus oil in the ground for future sale. Finally, we may encounter crises of reserve supply, occurring when the physical supplies of nonrenewable resources are finally exhausted. Some predict that this crucial transitional period could continue through the first quarter of the next century.

The long-run situation is another matter. After the transition is past, the world energy supply is not likely to be limited by an insufficiency of resources. After the oil and natural gas are gone, large amounts of coal, tar sands, and oil shales remain to be used as environmental problems with these fossil fuels are solved. Meanwhile, nuclear fusion and other radically new forms of energy await only the application of human ingenuity for their potentials to be realized.

Industrial Materials

If the long-run outlook for energy is optimistic, the situation is less promising for another class of nonrenewable resources, the industrial raw materials. The future is especially uncertain with respect to maintaining a continuing supply of certain metallic ores that must be teamed with mechanical energy if the modern economic system is to function.

The Metals

Metals are a class of elements that are hard, heavy, and opaque, have a "metallic" luster, and are capable of being drawn into fine wire (ductility), hammered into thin plates (malleability), and melted by heat. Moreover, they are able to conduct both electricity and heat (conductivity). Each metal, however, possesses these qualities in different combinations and degrees and therefore has its own set of uses. The versatility of many metals is enhanced by a capacity for *alloying,* that is, for combining with other metals in varying proportions. This multiplies the already extensive range of special purposes that these elements are able to serve.

An intimate relationship exists between metals and the consumption of mechanical energy. Indeed, metals are indispensable to all sectors of the modern economy. Although obvious in the case of manufacturing and transportation, this is equally true of the extractive industries, including modern agriculture. Not only do the metals contribute to high agricultural yields through their use in farm tools, machinery, and transport equipment but also in the production of agricultural chemicals. A great many metals are required by an increasingly complex modern technology, in which subtle differences in metallic qualities can be vital. Although some substitution of materials is possible, no feasible substitutes have been discovered for certain key metals.

For these reasons, a continuing supply of metals is vital. But how good is this supply? The answer is different for each metal: Some are still plentiful whereas others are nearing exhaustion. But all are nonrenewable. One of the first things we discover when examining our metallic reserves is that some of the most "common" metals are not really common at all. Of the so-called common metals only iron and aluminum are among the first 10 elements in the continental earth crust, and these 10 represent 99 percent of the total crustal weight. Relatively speaking, therefore, the other commercially important metals exist in only small quantities. Considering the great mass of the earth's crust, however, the absolute amounts are in fact much greater than this would seem to indicate and a realistic dividing line between the abundant and the scarce metals is nearer the 0.01 percent level. The most plentiful metallic elements, therefore, are iron, aluminum, manganese, magnesium, chromium, and titanium, whereas the least plentiful include such familiar metals as copper, lead, zinc, and nickel. In many cases, the scarce elements are being extracted in large quantities despite severely limited reserves.

Some metals are much more widely distributed over the earth than others. In some instances this results from a generally greater crustal occurence, but in others it reflects the essential character of the ores from which they are extracted. Certain ores—such as iron, aluminum, and copper—have a metallic content that varies continuously from very rich to the very lean. This variability is a boon to the mining industry, for the limits to practical exploitation are set simply on the basis of cost and available technology. Many other metals, however, are discontinuous in concentration; they either occur in a place or they do not. This is true of such important metals as lead, zinc, tin, nickel, tungsten, mercury, manganese, gold, and silver. Certain of these are concentrated in only a few places.

Still another problem of world mineral supply is the fact that the countries consuming the largest quantities are not necessarily the ones that are best endowed with resources. The United States is the outstanding consumer of metals, but it lacks many vital metallic resources. Similarly, most European industrial nations are conspicuously deficient in metallic ores. Some of the largest reserves occur in less-developed countries and in those advanced nations with large territories and small populations, especially Canada and Australia.

Among those metals required by world industry in very large quantities are iron and its close partner, manganese. Of the metals, iron is the overwhelming leader in total annual tonnage of output—constituting 95 percent of all metals extracted—and the quantity rises each year. One reason for the heavy production and consumption of iron is that it is plentiful and very cheap (only a few cents per pound). Another reason for its popularity is its great strength and its readiness to form alloys with many other metals. When added to iron in even minute quantities, these elements can cause it to assume a variety of desirable properties that contribute still further to the versatility of this metal. Iron technology is relatively easy, too, for the metal can be removed from its oxides (the most common occurrence in nature) by means of chemically simple processes.

Since the first discovery of a technique for making iron, about 2000 B.C., this metal has been one of the most important materials, used by virtually every society today. Nevertheless, per capita consumption of iron bears a decided relationship to level of development. The S-shaped curve of Figure 5.27 demonstrates this. Usage is exceedingly low in such underdeveloped countries as Indonesia, Ecuador, and India, but it climbs steeply with rising per capita income. Note, for example, the positions on the curve of moderately developed Spain and somewhat more prosperous Italy. Ultimately, however, per capita usage reaches a saturation point, as shown by the similar rates of consumption among the most in-

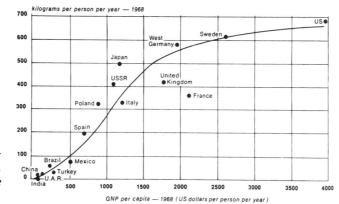

FIGURE 5.27 World steel consumption and per capita GNP. [*Source:* Meadows and others, *The Limits to Growth.*]

dustrialized countries. This relationship is also apparent in the changing rates of consumption by a particular country. Note that the United States (Figure 5.28) reached this point of saturation by the 1950s. (The lower figure for 1960 reflects the economic recession of that year.)

Rates of iron and steel production are likewise related to level of development, but this relationship is changing. Although the USSR, Japan, and the United States still lead in steel output, many newly industrializing countries in the Third World are now acquiring their own steel-making capacities. With new facilities using the latest technology, and with cheap labor, China, Brazil, and Mexico, among others, are challenging the leaders in world markets.

Many important steel-making nations, however, have little ore of their own. This is particularly true of Japan, Italy, and certain other European producers. Even the United States, which originally had large reserves, now imports much of its ore and growing amounts of finished steel. The richest Lake Superior deposits have long since been exhausted and lower grades of American ore are now being developed. Indeed, low-grade taconite iron deposits now contribute a major part of the ore mined in the United States. Today the 10 largest producers of iron ore are the USSR, Brazil, Aus-

tralia, China, India, the United States, Canada, South Africa, France, and Liberia (Figure 5.29). Note the prominence of less-developed countries as well as advanced nations that have large areas and low population densities. Many of these countries are important exporters of ore.

Because iron is the second most plentiful metal in the earth's crust, and because nearly all types of iron ore are now successfully treated by iron technology, total reserves of this element are enormous. Consequently, iron is cheap for its bulk. Transportation costs and accessibility to market are therefore important determinants in the selection of deposits for exploitation, more so than for any other metal. But the smelting of iron ore also requires great tonnages of other ingredients, especially coal for fuel and for driving off oxygen, and limestone to carry off other impurities. Hence, transportation costs and accessibility of these other materials are likewise important locational considerations for the steel industry. For these reasons many large known deposits in remote areas remain ignored, whereas ores of indifferent quality but close to market and to other iron-making materials are actively pursued.

The projected life of world iron ore reserves is thus much greater than that of most mineral resources. In addition, vast resources of lower-grade iron ore are

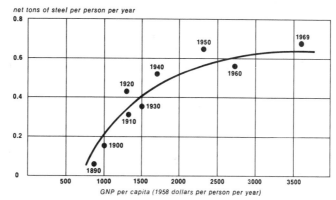

FIGURE 5.28 United States steel consumption per capita, 1890–1969. During the earlier stages of industrial growth in the United States, per capita steel consumption rose sharply and steadily. As the economy matured, steel use eventually leveled off at a fairly high point around which it has since fluctuated with the business cycle. [*Source:* Meadows and others, *The Limits to Growth.*]

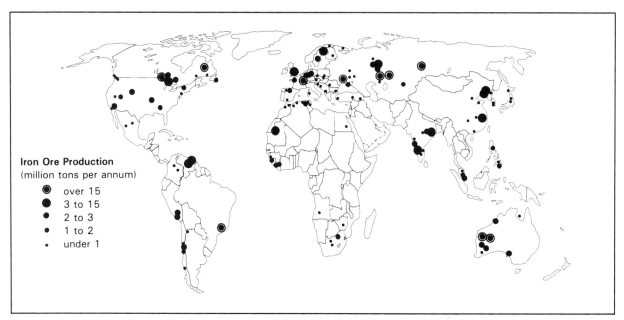

FIGURE 5.29 Iron ore: world production. [*Source:* U.S. Bureau of Mines, *Minerals Yearbook* (Washington, D.C.: U.S. Government Printing Office, 1985).]

available. The main effect of future iron ore usage, therefore, will be to cause prices to rise as richer, more accessible reserves become exhausted. Because iron resources are in no immediate danger of depletion, the basic supply problem for iron becomes the adequacy of companion resources upon which its production and use depend, namely energy and alloying elements.

Manganese is a vital alloying metal for steel manufacture. It serves a dual function in the steel industry: (1) a process material acting as a "scavenger" to carry off sulfur and oxygen, an essential use for which there is no known substitute, and (2) an alloying element that imparts toughness to the metal. Although manganese has other industrial applications, they are minor. Because manganese is a relatively plentiful element in the earth's crust, its total world supply presents no immediate problem. Indeed, so large are current supplies that the metal tends to be overused.

The main difficulty of manganese supply is the spatial distribution of reserves: The best deposits are not always in the places where the metal is most needed (see Figure 5.30). The United States, in particular, has virtually no domestic reserves of high-grade manganese ore and an inadequate supply of low-grade ore. Other big industrial nations also lack manganese, except for the USSR, which has at least one-half of the known world supply. The remaining reserves are mainly in the less-developed nations of Africa and Asia. Consequently, a major part of the world output of manganese moves between continents. Fortunately for the United States,

very large quantities of manganese occur on the ocean floor. Nodules of manganese have been found at depths of 500 feet to 3000 feet off the southeastern coast of the United States and at depths of 5000 feet to 14,000 feet in the eastern Pacific. Commercial extraction, using dredges and vacuum devices, has proved feasible. Thus, the supply problems of iron and its close companion, manganese, are not immediately pressing.

The prospect is less promising for a second class of high-volume metals, the nonferrous group. Several nonferrous metals essential to technologically advanced countries are in relatively short supply. The members of this group—aluminum, copper, lead, and zinc—are widely used and consumed in very large quantities, often with little relationship to the total reserve supply available. Moreover, the rate of consumption of each of these four metals has steadily risen, as shown by the history of copper use in the United States (Figure 5.31). All of the nonferrous metals normally occur in low-grade ore, except aluminum. These elements are also erratically distributed in the world, resulting in a large volume of world trade both in the metals and their ores. All four metals are more costly than iron, owing to the complexity of their ores, intricate technology of extraction, and expensive processing methods.

Aluminum is an exception in this group in several respects. First, it is the only nonferrous metal that appears abundantly in the earth's crust (8 percent of the total). Moreover, it is the only one of the four that occurs in high-grade ores, mostly over 32 percent metallic

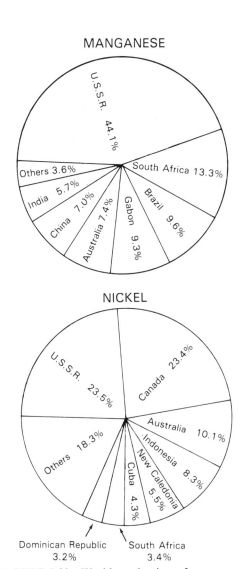

FIGURE 5.30 World production of manganese and nickel ores, 1984. [*Source:* U.S. Bureau of Mines, *Minerals Yearbook* (Washington, D.C.: U.S. Government Printing Office, 1985).]

content (Figure 5.32). Although consumption of this metal grew very rapidly throughout the postwar period, demand has slackened in recent years, lessening worries about its long-term prospects. Very large supplies of low-grade aluminum ore exist, but these are not commercially feasible to exploit with today's technology.

The other nonferrous metals are rare in crustal occurrence, copper being only 0.0058 percent, lead 0.0010 percent, and zinc 0.0082 percent. These three have become sufficiently concentrated for commercial extraction only through fortuitous acts of nature. Their world supply, though adequate for the near term, is cause for concern in the more distant future. Of the three, only copper occurs in continuously variable concentrations, which means that lower grades may be mined. Copper is already being extracted from exceedingly lean ores: only 0.9 percent metallic content in the United States, 1 percent to 2 percent in Canada and Chile, 4 percent in Zambia, and 6 percent in Zaire. Moreover, turning to still lower grades appears feasible, in view of the cheap open-pit mining that prevails in the copper industry. But this alternative does not apply to lead and zinc, which usually occur together. Their ores are generally much richer than those of copper, but their deposits are small and require costly underground mining. This cost tends to be partially offset by the valuable by-products, such as copper, gold, and silver, that are frequently obtained in lead and zinc mining operations.

Unlike many minerals, a substantial proportion of the nonferrous metals comes from advanced nations, especially Canada and Australia (Figure 5.32 and Figure 5.33). Even so, consumption rates in those lands are so great that domestic output must be supplemented with imports from certain less-developed countries. Australia has more than one-third of the known reserves of the chief aluminum ore, bauxite (aluminum hydroxide), and the industrialized countries as a whole have about one-

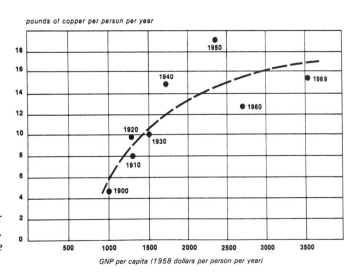

FIGURE 5.31 United States copper consumption per capita, 1890–1969. [*Source:* Meadows and others, *The Limits to Growth.*]

BAUXITE

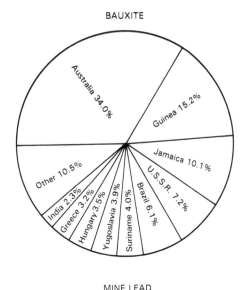

MINE COPPER

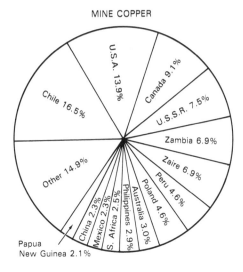

MINE LEAD

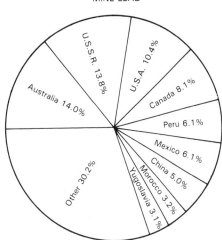

MINE TIN

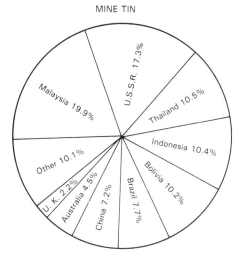

FIGURE 5.32 World production of bauxite and lead. [*Source:* U.S. Bureau of Mines, *Minerals Yearbook* (Washington, D.C.: U.S. Government Printing Office, 1985).]

FIGURE 5.33 World production of copper and tin. [*Source:* U.S. Bureau of Mines, *Minerals Yearbook* (Washington, D.C.: U.S. Government Printing Office, 1985).]

half of the total. Africa and the Caribbean have most of the rest, while South America and Asia possess lesser quantities. Nearly half of the world's copper reserves are also in the developed countries, particularly the USSR and the United States. The rest is mainly in South America (principally Chile and Peru) and Africa's rich copper belt (Zambia and Zaire). Most of the world's larger deposits of zinc and lead are found in the United States, Canada, and the USSR.

Although these metals cost more per pound than iron, they are surprisingly cheap, considering their relative scarcity. Nevertheless, their cost has risen as reserves have declined in size and richness. The pressures on these supplies continue to grow as more and more vital uses appear for the nonferrous metals. Copper and aluminum are virtually indispensable in electrical ap-

plications because of their high conductivity. All four metals are used variously in the manufacture of important alloys such as bronze, brass, monel metal, solder, bearing metal, type metal, casting metal, and special alloys for aircraft applications. Aluminum, because of its lightness, is valuable as a structural metal. Copper and aluminum are much used for cooking utensils, owing to their heat-conducting properties. Copper, lead, and zinc each have their special applications because of their resistance to corrosion: sheathing, storage batteries, and galvanizing, for example. All four have essential uses in the production of chemicals.

The nonferrous metals thus have a multitude of vital applications and have become interwoven into modern production in a variety of ways. With the possible exception of aluminum, their supplies are limited, however. Some substitution is possible, as, for example, the increasing use of aluminum in the place of more expensive copper in applications requiring conductivity; unfortunately, such substitution is not always feasible. Note also that the production of nonferrous metals is a drain on other resources. In particular, a great deal of mechanical energy is used in their extraction and processing. Zinc processing requires much heat, and copper and aluminum refining use large amounts of electricity.

Most of the metals produced and consumed in small volumes are also limited in crustal occurrence, and all are relatively expensive. Several of these low-volume metals are obtained as joint products of mining operations designed to obtain simultaneously other metals occurring in the same ores. Despite their low levels of use, these metals are essential to modern industry. Among the many elements fitting this description, two categories are especially prominent: the alloying metals and the precious metals.

The alloying metals have many individual characteristics and a multitude of uses, but they all share one kind of application: their use in combination with other metals, especially steel, to give special properties to the finished product. For most of them this is their main application. Because this is a derived use, their demand structures and price levels are usually derived also. If the price of one of the alloying metals should fall, for example, it is unlikely that any additional amounts of it would be consumed, for the quantity required depends upon the current level of steel production. Pricing is further complicated for those alloying metals obtained as joint products. Because their output is tied to that of other metals with different demand conditions, changes in price have little effect on quantities produced. Although the alloying metals are often used in minute quantities, they have such an essential function that they are often referred to as *vitamin elements.* Some substitution among them is possible, but in many cases it is not.

Although a few of the alloying elements are plentiful in the earth's crust, others are rare. It is important here to distinguish between *rarity,* which is determined by an element's relative physical abundance in the earth's crust, and *scarcity,* an economic concept that refers to the costs of acquisition at a particular time and place. Three alloy metals appear to present no immediate problems of scarcity: chromium, titanium, and magnesium.

Because chromium helps steel to keep a sharp cutting edge even at high temperatures, it is employed in high-speed steels, a use for which chromium has no satisfactory substitute. Together with iron and nickel, it is also one of the principal constituents of stainless steels, a large and particularly important family of alloys.

Chromium is fairly plentiful, four-fifths of total output coming from South Africa, the USSR, Turkey, Rhodesia, and the Philippines. Another abundant alloying element, titanium, comprises 0.86 percent of the earth's crust, and most of its current output is in Canada, Japan, the United States, Australia, and Brazil. It is a lightweight, high-strength, corrosion-resistant metal used as an alloy of steel as well as in aerospace applications and in paint pigments. Magnesium is the lightest of all the metals, yet it is very strong. It is used to produce lightweight, corrosion-resistant alloys and in chemical production. It, too, is widespread in occurrence. Magnesium is consumed in only small amounts and total output is not great. At present, most of the world supply is obtained through electrolysis of seawater. At current levels of demand, therefore, magnesium poses no supply problems.

Supply is more critical for most of the other alloying elements, especially nickel, molybdenum, tin, and tungsten. Shortages of tin and tungsten are possible in the near future. Occasionally these four elements occur separately; but these individual occurrences are in special metallogenic provinces—regions that have undergone a rare combination of geological events. More often they occur as by-products or joint products with other elements, which means that a shift in demand and price may have little effect on the supply.

Most of the nickel that is mined is used in stainless steels and high-temperature and electrical alloys. Its crustal occurrence is small and it is found concentrated in only a few places: Canada (half the world's output), the USSR, New Caledonia, and Cuba (Figure 5.30). Molybdenum imparts toughness and resilience to steel, and this is its chief use. Like nickel, its occurrence is highly erratic. Some of it is obtained as a by-product of copper, but most comes from a metallogenic province that extends north and south through the Canadian and United States Rocky Mountains.

Tin, long valued for its corrosion-resistant properties, is used for plating iron and steel and as an alloy of copper in the production of bronze. Most of its output comes from two metallogenic provinces—one in Southeast Asia and the other in the Andes of South America (Figure 5.33). The tin supply from these sources is dwindling, however. Tungsten often occurs together with tin in its main source region, which extends from Korea to Malaysia in East Asia. It makes exceedingly hard alloys with steel and is also used to manufacture tungsten carbide for cutting tools.

The precious metals—silver, gold, and the platinum group—are another important class of elements whose supply is diminishing. Since ancient times silver and gold have been prized for their beauty and indestructibility. The precious metals have always been rare but they are becoming critically scarce today as their demand increases. Silver has a number of very useful properties, and much more would be used if it were less costly. Its principal applications are in coinage, household silver, and jewelry, but industrial applications constitute its greatest market. Silver is the main ingredient of photographic film, and it is also used in critical electrical applications because of its conductivity, which is even greater than that of copper.

Silver is naturally rare (only 0.000008 percent of the earth's crust by weight). The world's major source area is the Great Cordillera of the western Americas; smaller amounts are found in the USSR and Australia. Today, most of the newly mined silver is obtained as a by-product of lead, zinc, and copper operations. Very little is mined for its own sake, as the ore is rarely rich enough. Because of its growing scarcity, silver has risen in price in recent years; yet its output has increased but little in response, so inelastic is its supply.

Because it occurs in the native state and is easily worked, gold was used for coinage and shaped into jewelry by the earliest civilizations. The antiquity, beauty, and rarity (0.0000002 percent of the earth's crust) of gold have endowed it with a mystical aura. This esoteric quality of gold is apparent in the tenacity with which modern governments cling to it as a basis for their currencies in the face of a steadily dwindling natural store of the metal. One of its principal commercial uses continues to be in jewelry making, where it is highly regarded for its lustrous appearance and great value. However, gold's inertness and resistance to corrosion account for many of its growing number of industrial applications. Although some gold is produced in 71 countries, 90 percent of the total output comes from South Africa (two-thirds), the USSR (one-eighth), Canada, the United States, and Australia.

In modern times, gold and silver have been joined by another group of precious metals, the platinoids. In addition to platinum, the main member of the group, these include five other closely related metals that invariably occur together in nature. They are not quite as rare as gold, and the world supply seems fairly secure at present rates of consumption. The platinoids are acquiring a growing number of industrial applications, in addition to their use in jewelry, and current projections could prove excessively optimistic. The USSR, South Africa, and Canada are the principal sources.

Another valuable element that does not fit into any of these categories is the industrial metal mercury, which appears in the liquid state at ordinary temperatures. Although mercury is generally regarded as indispensable to any number of industrial applications, its supply is dwindling. The ancient Spanish mines remain the leading source but their expected life is limited.

Other Nonrenewable Resources

Two other classes of nonrenewable resources remain to be considered: (1) the mineral raw materials used for the manufacture of fertilizers and other chemical products, and (2) the nonmetallic-mineral building materials. Both of these are essential to the functioning of a modern economy, and they affect every member of society either directly or indirectly. Will the supply of these be adequate to support a growing population?

As we noted earlier in the section on food supply, the best hope for feeding the expected additions to the world population is to increase the yield of land currently under the plow. Chemical fertilizers are essential to achieving this increase, along with improved seeds and more water. Although every plant type has its own particular combination of requirements, all crops must have nitrogen, phosphorus, potassium, calcium, and sulfur. These are natural constituents of some soils but not all. Moreover, some plants make unusually heavy demands on certain elements and quickly deplete them from the soil. These nutrients must be replaced for subsequent plantings.

Farmers have traditionally restored plant food elements to the soil either by *fallowing*—that is, resting the soil so that it can recuperate naturally—or by *crop rotations* that alternate soil-depleting crops with soil-restoring ones such as the legumes. But these practices are not always effective and they are too extensive in their use of land under conditions of increasing population pressure. One way of restoring nutrients to the soil is through the application of organic fertilizers, especially animal manures and, in the Orient, "night soil," or human wastes. This is inadequate for today's needs, however, and the use of manufactured fertilizers is accelerating rapidly.

The mineral raw materials for manufacturing fertilizers are also used to produce other chemical products and have a variety of other industrial applications. However, fertilizer manufacture is the largest single market for these materials. The United States is still the leading producer and consumer of chemical fertilizers, but other parts of the world are catching up.

The original source of nitrogen for fertilizers was from naturally occurring compounds, the most important deposits being those in Chile's Atacama Desert. Today, Chile supplies only minor amounts. Much of the remainder is extracted directly from the atmosphere, of which nitrogen is the largest constituent element. In addition to large quantities of electricity, the other major requirement for synthesizing nitrogenous fertilizers is hydrogen, with which the nitrogen is combined to produce a water-soluble ammonia compound that plants can readily assimilate. Ammonia is also obtained as a by-product of coke-oven operations, most of which are associated with the steel industry.

Phosphorus is essential to plant growth, but it is easily exhausted by intensive cultivation. The chief commercial source of phosphorus is phosphate rock (apatite), which is treated with sulfuric acid to make it water-soluble and thus accessible to plants. The resulting superphosphate is very concentrated. Phosphorus is an abundant element, constituting 0.1 percent of the earth's crustal weight, but most phosphate rock is found among the marine sediments of old sea beds. Despite the large global reserve of this mineral, deposits of commercial size and quality occur in only a few places (Figure 5.34). The United States produces nearly half of the total world output, most of the rest coming from the USSR and North Africa. One consequence of the unequal distribution of this vital material is the large quantity of it that moves in international trade.

Another abundant element that produces a vital fertilizer is potassium, which comprises 1.68 percent of the earth's crust. Potassium is widely distributed throughout the world, but not in a readily usable soluble form. Most of it is obtained commercially from salts resulting from the evaporation of seawater. Total reserves are very great, but the chief source areas are western Canada and the United States, Europe, and the USSR (Figure 5.34).

Calcium is important to certain crops, especially corn and other grains. It is a natural constituent of certain soils in sedimentary regions and it reaches high levels of concentration in subhumid lands, such as the plains and prairies of western United States and Canada and the steppes of the USSR. These are all extremely productive soils. The calcium content of many other soils is inadequate, however, and easily exhausted by intensive cultivation in humid areas. Lime needed for replacement of this lost element is easily obtainable in many parts of the world wherever limestone is available. Calcium is one of the most plentiful elements, and processing is simple.

The most basic chemical raw material is sulfur, which has an endless number of uses in chemical production and manufacturing in general. The largest single application, however, is fertilizer production, which consumes two-fifths of total output. Sulfur is used both in the manufacture of superphosphates and ammonia sulfates. In addition, much of the chemical industry's use of sulfur goes eventually into agricultural applications, including insecticides and herbicides. Sulfur is widespread and abundant, being united in nature with many other elements (Figure 5.34). Relatively pure elemental sulfur is also available in limited quantities and in specific places. Volcanic cones in Japan, Sicily, and the Chilean Andes provide a certain amount, but the largest sources are coastal salt dome deposits along the margins of the Gulf of Mexico. Native sulfur reserves cannot be expected to last long, however, and increasing output is coming from fossil fuels, where it is obtained in the purification of oil and gas and collected from coal smoke. It also constitutes a by-product from the processing of sulphide metallic ores. These and other similar occurrences assure an ample supply of sulfur, though possibly at rising costs.

Total reserves of all the principal fertilizer raw materials are thus very large. No world shortage is apparent for the foreseeable future despite increasingly heavy demands for agricultural, chemical, and general industrial applications. The resource problem resulting from consumption of these minerals concerns the drain that their use imposes indirectly upon other resources. Because the nations of the world are unequally endowed with fertilizer materials (except for atmospheric nitrogen), much long-range transporting of bulky commodities is required, thereby consuming much energy and other resources. Moreover, fertilizer production in-

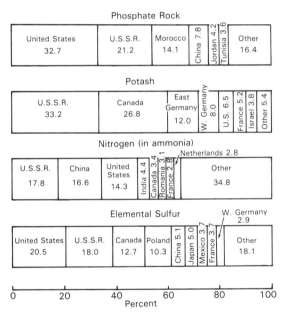

FIGURE 5.34 World production of mineral fertilizers. Three of the four principal fertilizer raw materials are mineral products; most of the fourth, nitrogen, is extracted from the atmosphere and combined with hydrogen to form ammonium nitrate. Only one-fourth of the world's sulfur now comes from native sulfur deposits. The remainder is extracted from mined pyrites or is obtained as a by-product of the oil and natural gas industries, coal treatment, and metal smelting. [*Source:* U.S. Bureau of Mines, *Minerals Yearbook* (Washington, D.C.: U.S. Government Printing Office, 1985).]

volves large inputs of capital and draws heavily upon fossil fuels, electric power, and other chemicals.

The rocks and earthen materials that are used for building purposes are so common that their true importance is often overlooked. In volume of output they lead all the minerals, and in value they are second only to the fossil fuels. Some of the building materials—such as sand and gravel, crushed stone, and dimension stone—are used directly with almost no further treatment after extraction. Others—including asbestos, clays, and the raw materials for glass and cement—receive considerable processing before final use.

Some of these commodities are among the most plentiful natural resources, and, with special exceptions, tend to be found in a great many places. As in the case of the fertilizer raw materials, therefore, the main long-run supply problem that the mineral building materials present is their effect on other resources. Their extraction is highly mechanized, using power machinery made of metals and burning fossil fuels. Most of the building materials are heavy and bulky, and their transportation makes further demands on the mechanical energy supply. Their processing, too, in some instances consumes large amounts of heat. Any projections of future use of these commodities must therefore take into account their substantial effects upon the energy supply.

Solutions for Mineral Supply Problems

Every mineral resource has its ultimate limit, yet the demand for minerals continues to grow steadily. In the past, the Americas, Africa, Asia, and Australia quickly yielded up fabulous finds of rich ores occurring in deposits at or near the earth's surface. Today, exploration must proceed more painstakingly in the search for hidden deposits. Ultimate exhaustion of the nonrenewable resources would thus appear to be inevitable.

How, then, is the end likely to come? For a given mining operation the final day may appear very suddenly, but it is not likely that all mines will fail simultaneously. Rather, they will probably give out one by one and the total amount of the commodity appearing on the world market will gradually diminish. For this reason, noted earlier in the cases of silver and gold, it is probable that the life spans currently being predicted will actually be exceeded as annual output falls and as the amount demanded is reduced by accelerating prices. Approaching exhaustion will be signaled well in advance when growing shortages force prices upward until they finally become prohibitive.

If eventual depletion of reserves thus seems unavoidable, do we have any way of postponing that final day? The optimists answer yes to this question and some

confidently predict that technology may prevent that day from appearing at all. Those who place their trust in technology cite the impressive accomplishments of the past, when one spectacular breakthrough often followed on the heels of another. Let us consider, therefore, some of the ways in which technology may come to our aid, either by stretching out the life spans of resources or by conserving the existing supply.

Among the new developments that are helping to keep known reserves from dwindling too soon are new methods for discovering, mining, extracting, and refining minerals. In the past, such technological advances have had the effect of reducing costs (or at least preventing prices from rising unduly). They have also made feasible the exploitation of materials that had not previously been classified as resources because of their remoteness or poor quality.

Some optimists are predicting that technology will eventually provide such an abundance of very cheap electricity from new sources, including breeder reactors and nuclear fusion, that it will become feasible to use this to extract and process minerals from sources now considered unorthodox. One such source, it is suggested, could be the oceans, which cover 71 percent of the earth's surface to an average depth of nearly 2.5 miles. This great volume of salt water contains much dissolved material—as much as 160 million tons of solids per cubic mile. Salt, magnesium, sulfur, calcium, and potassium constitute 99.5 percent of this. Other, more valuable, elements in a cubic mile of seawater include 47 tons of zinc, 14 tons of copper, 14 tons of tin, 1 ton of silver, and 40 pounds of gold. Sodium, chlorine, magnesium, and bromine are already being extracted electrolytically from the sea and the idea of removing some of the others is very tempting. One of the problems with the proposal is that the disposal of the enormous tonnages of waste materials would make this a formidable undertaking. Even more serious is the fact that the valuable metals are contained in extremely dilute solutions, which would require that huge quantities of water be treated. The most serious problem of all is the amount of energy needed to do the job.

Fanciful as such ideas may appear, certain other radical methods are being actively pursued with some success. One is the development of techniques for seeking out ores deep beneath the earth's surface and for determining the most promising areas in which to concentrate exploration. Many people insist that more resources are yet to be found, both in areas that have already been explored and in some that have not yet been thoroughly surveyed. These individuals believe that better exploration techniques and an improved knowledge of regional geology will substantially expand reserves of many commodities. Remote sensing of the earth's environment from orbiting satellites has had some success in accomplishing these ends.

Even the most confident of the technology optimists, however, are coming to agree that we should take better care of the mineral resources available now. The recent success in conserving energy described above has stimulated interest in this approach to enhancing other earth resources. A promising place to begin is the reduction of waste in extraction and processing. Indeed, surprisingly large quantities of valuable mineral materials are lost in the earlier stages of production. Underground mining is especially wasteful. Pillars left to support mine roofs are often rich in minerals, but these have traditionally been left behind after the mine is abandoned. Many minerals are overlooked, owing to ignorance of irregularities in the shape of the ore body; others are ignored because the ores are considered too lean for economical extraction. Although improved techniques may subsequently allow these residues to be of use, reopening an abandoned flooded mine is usually difficult.

Open-pit or strip-mining operations are ordinarily far more efficient in extracting most of the valuable mineral. Perhaps the best example of this is the mining and processing of porphyry copper ores, which result in virtually 100 percent recovery of the copper from ores averaging below 0.9 percent in the United States. In addition, these techniques yield valuable by-products, such as gold and silver.

Several techniques permit resources to be used more efficiently in manufacturing. The quantity of a metal that is required for a given application can often be reduced, for example, by producing the metal to closer tolerances or by adding alloys to increase its strength. Today, a ton of steel gives about 43 percent more structural support than the same amount would have provided a few years ago. Because of this, it is possible to make structural members and sheets thinner than before. This is one reason why the United States produces relatively less tonnage of steel than does the USSR, where steel products tend to be heavier than necessary in order to fulfill official quotas specified in terms of total weight.

In addition to these advances, certain others are equally feasible but require changed social attitudes and goals. Thus, one way to husband large quantities of valuable resources would be to increase the durability of manufactured products. This is desirable not only for goods employing scarce materials but even those using abundant ones, for valuable energy resources are required for their manufacture in either case. Most advanced societies have innumerable opportunities for changes in lifestyle that would deemphasize high per capita levels of resource use.

The idea of reusing valuable metals and other materials has received much attention recently, but the notion is by no means a new one. Today, approximately 40 percent of the copper consumed each year has been reclaimed from discarded objects, as has a high proportion of the tin. Nearly half of the lead is recycled, most of it from old automobile batteries. Far more reclamation of metals and other materials is desirable and possible, especially the reusable materials from abandoned vehicles and household wastes.

To an ever-increasing extent the substitution of one material for another has been forced upon us by growing scarcities and rising costs of certain commodities. More aluminum is replacing copper in electrical applications, and aluminum is beginning to substitute for tin-plated steel in the container industries. Tinplated cans are also being replaced more and more by lacquered ones. Plastics are increasingly substituting for metals in a great many uses, from plumbing pipes to automobile fittings.

It must be accepted, of course, that these and other conservation techniques may raise resource costs. Recycling of most materials is expensive, and so are improved product designs and more intensive mining methods. Moreover, the recovery of metals is only partial after each cycle of use. Some metal is essentially lost altogether, and all of it is therefore due to be permanently consumed in the long run.

Although past achievements may seem to justify continued faith in the ability of technology to bring salvation, previous experience is no longer a reliable guide to the future. As more and more developing nations join the ranks of the industrialized lands, and as levels of prosperity rise still further in the richer countries, global consumption steadily rises. Many authorities therefore recognize that excessive optimism diverts attention from the real problem of ultimate exhaustion of our nonrenewable resources.

What will the final depletion of our natural resources mean to us as individuals and citizens? Ultimately it will touch each of us, but in the near term, people living in industrialized lands will be affected differently from citizens of less-developed countries. High levels of consumption affect advanced countries in several important ways. They show up first in the intensive exploitation of domestic reserves, such as the Lake Superior iron ores, followed in time by depletion, or the threat of it. Even prior to exhaustion, consumption may greatly exceed the resource endowment and the country will begin to rely more and more upon imports. The United States used to be a net exporter of minerals, but since World War II it has been a net importer. By 1970 the country was importing five-sixths of its nickel, three-fourths of its bauxite, nearly half of its zinc, more than a third of its iron ore, and almost all of its tin and manganese. As world reserves of a particular resource diminish, however, those countries still possessing reserves may be unwilling to export to deficit countries. Some mineral-rich nations in the early stages of development may prefer to retain their raw materials for use in domestic industries.

With a few exceptions, the known world reserves of even the most abundant mineral resources would not be sufficient for global consumption at per capita rates now prevailing in the richest lands. Burdened by large and growing populations, the Third World as a whole can hardly expect to attain the current rate of United States consumption. It thus follows that the possibilities for industrialization of many underdeveloped nations are dim. Already some voices in the Third World are expressing concern that the industrialized lands are using up their heritage, and they wonder what resources will be left when the time comes for them to need them.

Contrary to common belief, growth can actually increase inequality. And as the gap between the rich and poor widens, high rates of population growth exacerbate this difference. With increasing numbers and rising consumption, distribution may become less equitable; those who have anything of value hang onto it. Because dwindling resources ultimately affect everyone, the need for a coordination of resource policies is becoming clearer.

ENVIRONMENTAL QUALITY

Thus far our attention has focused upon the quantitative results of the increasingly intensive exploitation of our physical environment. The main question has been whether sufficient resources exist to support large numbers of people at ever-higher levels of per capita consumption. Now we consider the qualitative aspects: How are rising levels of human activity affecting the world as a place in which to live?

The Physical Environment

Pollution is a problem with many facets. At the least, it concerns aesthetics; at the most, it poses a threat to the ecosystem involving the survival of human life itself. Pollution wastes important resources during the process of contaminating the air and water. Thus, the compounds of mercury and lead entering the atmosphere and water supplies are serious pollutants, but they also represent the loss of critically scarce metals. And just as

resource use is growing even more rapidly than the population, so also is pollution rising at ever-increasing rates. This is evidence of the relationship that pollution bears to agricultural activity and industrialization.

The impact of pollution tends to be delayed, raising the danger that it will exceed the limits of safety before we become aware of the problem. Many long-lived toxic substances travel great distances and accumulate in unforeseen places. Besides the problems of mercury and lead poisoning, chemicals such as DDT pose serious threats. Thus, DDT evaporates and is carried long distances in the air, precipitating out of the atmosphere, entering the food chain, and persisting in the tissues of living organisms. At least two decades may be required for it to lose its potency.

Contamination of the Atmosphere

Air pollution occurs when waste gases and solid particles enter the atmosphere and spread. In the form of smog (smoke plus fog) it hangs visibly over large industrial cities, so thick at times that it shuts out much of the sunlight. It assails the other senses too, irritating the eyes and lungs and issuing repulsive odors. Some other common effects of air pollution are corrosion of paint, steel, rubber, nylon stockings, and statuary.

To a major extent, air pollution is a product of the consumption of energy, especially the combustion of fossil fuels, and of many industrial processes. Among the greatest offenders are the internal combustion engines that power passenger cars, buses, trucks, and aircraft, all of which emit great quantities of noxious gases: carbon dioxide, carbon monoxide, sulfur oxides, nitrogen oxides, particulate matter (soot), and tetraethyl lead. The most serious industrial offenders are pulp and paper mills, iron and steel mills, petroleum refineries, smelters, and chemical plants, which contribute enormous tonnages of carbon monoxide, sulfur dioxide, nitrogen oxide, and fly ash to the atmosphere.

Oddly enough, the cleanest form of energy, electricity, is the source of some of the worst pollution. Thermal generating plants contribute one-fifth of all the particulates and nitrogen oxides and half the sulfur oxides sent aloft from the United States annually. Sulfur compounds emitted from coal-burning plants become dissolved in particles of moisture within the upper atmosphere to form sulfuric acid. Drifting with the prevailing winds from its industrial source, this airborne moisture subsequently falls as "acid rain," which is accused of destroying forests and other vegetation and of killing water life in ponds and lakes. Increasingly, this is becoming the subject of international disputes. Canadian provinces downwind of the Ohio River Valley's coal-burning industries protest the environmental damage attributed to this source, and several Western European countries are in contention over the acid rain that crosses their borders from elsewhere to kill forests and water life. Nuclear power plants, which contribute a growing proportion of the world's electricity, avoid the atmospheric pollution problems of conventional power plants but add new environmental hazards of their own.

A further source of atmospheric pollution is *space heating*. The use of fossil fuels to heat homes, offices, and factories adds much to the total load. The burning of trash by householders and also by municipalities, commercial junk dealers, and others is an additional source.

Each of the principal contaminants of the atmosphere is capable of becoming extremely hazardous to human beings. These toxic substances in the atmosphere tend to be slow-acting with people of normal health, but they may affect with tragic suddenness the very old, very young, or those with respiratory ailments.

Evidence is mounting that atmospheric pollutants may even affect the weather and perhaps alter climatic patterns. Because all energy is ultimately dissipated as heat, the cumulative effect of energy consumption on a large scale is to warm the atmosphere. It has been estimated that by the year 2000 the amount of heat released by human activities may be equal to 18 percent of incoming solar energy. This may eventually impose a limit to the amount of mechanical energy that can be safely used.

Probably the most valuable resource of all is water. The total amount on the earth's surface, below it, or above it, is vast; but 99.35 percent of this is in the oceans or locked in the polar ice caps and thus not directly accessible for human consumption. The remaining 0.65 percent is all that we have to use (except for navigation); this occurs as ground water or is in lakes or streams. When viewed on a global scale, water is a renewable resource; at the local level it can be a vanishing resource.

During its stay on earth, water is often used and reused many times for municipal purposes, industrial cooling, process water, or irrigation. Almost every time that water is used, contaminants are added to it. Flowing water has natural recuperative powers, but these can easily be exceeded under intensive use. It must usually then be treated before reuse, but much of the water that contains municipal and industrial wastes is incompletely treated, and some is dumped into streams with no treatment at all.

The Cost of Growth

The accelerating pace of modern living has thus brought with it a multitude of problems whose dimensions we are only now beginning to comprehend. Increasing numbers of people and rising volumes of industrial production have resulted in contamination of the atmosphere, pollution of water, disfiguration of the landscape, and deterioration of human relationships within an environment that is being used with ever-greater intensity. These are the complications that have accompanied our efforts to reach successively higher levels of material well-being measured in terms of more and better transportation, housing, appliances, clothing, recreation, medical care, and other specialized services of a proliferating variety—in other words, all that is contained in that familiar measure called the gross national product (GNP). More formally defined, GNP represents a country's total annual output of goods and services.

Today, some people are saying that the GNP has been misleading us, that it does not take into account hidden costs exacted by problems of the kinds just described. Such costs, it is said, actually reduce the total benefits gained from rising output. As a more realistic index of how well off a population may be, economists William Nordhaus and James Tobin have proposed a Measure of Economic Welfare, MEW. This is derived by adjusting the GNP to allow for the costs to a society resulting from environmental deterioration and the problems of contemporary urban life. More euphoniously, and perhaps more accurately, Paul Samuelson has relabeled this measure Net Economic Welfare, or NEW.

Figure 5.35 illustrates the relationship between GNP and NEW as this evolved during a four-decade period. Note how steeply per capita GNP climbed following World War II. On the other hand, NEW rose much more slowly, owing to the cumulative effects of modern urban problems. Because the two curves are rising at different rates, the gap between them is widening. If effective steps should be taken to solve the problems caused by growth, NEW would begin to rise more steeply; however, the costs of such remedial measures—for example, sewage treatment plants and devices for precipitating pollutants in factory stack gases—would reduce the slope of the GNP curve. In this way the gap between the two would begin to close and GNP would thereby gain increased reliability as a measure of a society's well-being.

HUMAN NEEDS IN THE TWENTY-FIRST CENTURY

Our assessment of the problems of supporting an increasing population at higher levels of material comfort, while attempting to minimize the distorting effects of growth, has reinforced our impressions of a world sys-

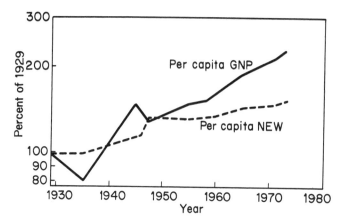

FIGURE 5.35 Differential growth of net economic welfare and gross national product. Note that as per capita GNP dropped during the Great Depression, net economic welfare (NEW) remained little changed. When war production brought a sharp rise in GNP during the 1940s, NEW lagged behind until the period of postwar readjustment. Since that time GNP has continued to rise more rapidly than NEW. (Drafted from trends suggested by Paul Samuelson.)

tem that is intricately interrelated. We have seen that an increase in population requires larger supplies of food, clothing, shelter, transportation facilities, services, and an ever-expanding array of other needs. Satisfying these enlarged demands in turn calls for heavier investments of capital. Greater allocations must be made for the production of fertilizer, farm machinery, and chemicals; for the construction of irrigation works and farm-to-market roads; for building textile and clothing factories; for constructing dwellings and so forth. But these uses of capital make rising demands upon nonrenewable resources: fertilizer and chemical raw materials and other metallic and nonmetallic minerals, as well as fuels.

Some of these resources, we have learned, are plentiful; but a great many others are not. Yet exploitation and use of even the abundant resources makes demands on other resources more limited in supply. Iron is plentiful, but steel production requires carbon and heat, provided by fossil fuels, together with a variety of scarce alloying metals. The raw materials of cement are abundant, but their manufacture consumes much heat. The ultimate solution to the energy problem appears to be electricity obtained from unconventional sources, but scarce nonferrous metals are needed to transmit and use this electricity.

Moreover, the consumption and final discarding of resources results in pollution, which adversely affects both population and production. Not only does pollution present severe health hazards but it also imposes a mounting cost burden on the economic system. Its ultimate effects we cannot anticipate with accuracy because of the time lag in its impact. Yet it is most certainly a grave problem that cannot be avoided, because both the United States and world populations are now too large to survive without intensive and mechanized agriculture, industry, and an integrated transportation system. It is no longer possible to retreat entirely to a simpler era. There are too many of us.

All projections thus point to continued growth in population, investment, resource use, and pollution, at least in the near term. Yet, considering the ultimate limits to the total supply of food and resources and to the amount of contamination the environment can absorb, where will these projections of growth take us? How long can the world system continue to expand without tempting disaster?

Before we can reasonably address this question, we must examine more closely a variety of important facets of the world economic system as it is structured and functions. These will be the subjects of the next several chapters, and the information presented there should enable us to think more analytically about the issues of growth and change.

TOPICS FOR DISCUSSION

1. Explain the general trends affecting the numerator and denominator of the Malthusian resources/population ratio. What do these trends tell us about the future spatial pattern of resource use? Why are government policymakers and the general public unable to sustain a long-range view of resource problems and to adopt the necessary measures to solve them?

2. What is meant by the term "resource," and why must any given resource be regarded as a changing concept? Define the various categories of resources. Why do the spatial patterns of supply and demand for most resources differ, and what political and economic problems arise from these differences?

3. Most experts no longer fear that the global food supply will be exhausted before the end of this century. What has happened to allay those fears? Why, then, do 1.5 billion people nevertheless remain hungry? Discuss the nature and spatial pattern of world hunger.

4. Give the reasons why many estimates of the world's potential cropland are misleading. Describe the process of "desertification" and examine the various dimensions of the food problems of sub-Saharan Africa. Where must the world look for additional supplies of food that will be required beyond the year 2000?

5. Discuss the relationship between resource use and development, and suggest the implications this holds for future supplies of nonrenewable resources. Define "reserve," indicate why reserve estimates fluctuate from time to time, and describe the process of resource exhaustion.

6. How do oil, natural gas, and coal differ in their spatial patterns of occurrence, exploitation, consumption, and trade? Account for these differences. How was OPEC able to gain command over world oil markets, and what caused this control to slip by the mid-1980s?

7. Where is future demand for energy likely to be greatest and why? What sources of energy are likely to predominate in the short-run future? In the longer run? Explore the various measures available to us for extending current supplies of energy and for ensuring future supplies. Should we be optimistic or pessimistic about the short-run and long-run prospects for energy?

8. Why are many observers more worried about world supplies of industrial raw materials than they are about energy? What classes of industrial materials give the greatest cause for concern and why? Discuss the political and economic implications of the erratic spatial distribution of minerals. Why have OPEC-like cartels failed to develop in the case of industrial materials?

9. Not only does pollution poison the physical environment and threaten human health but it also constitutes a waste of scarce and valuable physical resources. Explain. Discuss the implications of pollution for international politics and for economic development. Interpret Samuelson's concept of Net Economic Welfare.

FURTHER READINGS

DARMSTADTER, JOEL, HANS H. LANDSBERG, and HERBERT C. MORTON, with MICHAEL J. COADA. *Energy Today and Tomorrow: Living with Uncertainty.* Resources for the Future. Englewood Cliffs, N.J.: Prentice-Hall, 1983.

This concise review and analysis of contemporary energy issues is based upon the authors' work at the Center for Energy Policy Research at Resources for the Future. Included is a useful examination of the contrasting views of "limitationists" and "expansionists" on resource questions.

KATES, ROBERT W. *The Human Environment: Penultimate Problems of Survival.* Natural Hazards Research and Applications Center, Special Publication No. 6. Worcester, Mass.: The Center for Technology, Environment, and Development, Clark University, 1983.

Thoughtful analysis of three related sets of issues: the Malthusian question regarding the adequacy of resources for a growing population, the problems of growing income disparities and their potential for widespread unrest and conflict, and the contrast between the growing technological capability for change (and destruction) and the meager ability of society to control it.

MEADOWS, DONELLA H., DENNIS L. MEADOWS, JØRGEN RANDERS, and WILLIAM W. BEHRENS III. *The Limits to Growth: A Report for the Club of Rome's Project on the Predicament of Mankind.* New York: Universe Books, 1972.

A very influential study commissioned by the Club of Rome, an international group of prominent industrialists, scientists, and economists. Using a dynamic world model linking population, pollution, resources, land, and capital generation, Dennis Meadows and co-workers at MIT predict that exponential growth will ultimately result in global collapse.

SHAH, MAHENDRA, and GÜNTHER FISCHER. "People, Land, and Food Production: Potentials in the Developing World." *Options,* International Institute for Applied Systems Analysis (IIASA), 2, 1984, pp. 1–5.

Assesses the output of particular food crops and their population-supporting potentials in the Third World. Synthesis of a study conducted by IIASA in collaboration with the Food and Agriculture Organization of the United Nations. This work finds that, of the 117 countries analyzed, 57 do not have sufficient land resources to feed the populations that have been projected for them A.D. 2000.

SKINNER, BRIAN J. *Earth Resources,* 2d ed. Englewood Cliffs, N.J.: Prentice-Hall, 1976.

Succinct discussion of the geology of existing and potential sources of energy and industrial raw materials. Describes the spatial pattern of their occurrence in the earth crust, and provides estimates of reserve size and relative scarcity.

U.S. COUNCIL ON ENVIRONMENTAL QUALITY. *The Global 2000 Report to the President.* New York: Penguin, 1982.

Report to the President of the United States on a three-year interagency study designed to project changes in population, resources, and the environment through the end of this century. These projections were intended to serve as the bases for future governmental policymaking. The report concludes that by A.D. 2000 current trends would produce a world "more crowded, more polluted, less stable ecologically, and more vulnerable to disruption."

VAN LENNEP, EMILE (Ed.). *Interfutures, Facing the Future: Mastering the Probable and Managing the Unpredictable.* Paris: Organization for Economic Cooperation and Development (OECD), 1979.

A report on the three-year INTERFUTURES project conducted by the OECD. This work examines the possibilities for ensuring the future prosperity and balanced economic and social development of advanced industrial countries in harmony with less-developed countries, giving special attention to the physical limits to growth and to current trends and their implications for the future.

CHAPTER 6

Price and Other Mechanisms for Regulating Exchange

This chapter deals with one of the central issues raised in the previous chapters. This issue is the nature of the mechanisms by which limited supplies of resources and products are shared among the growing demands of an escalating world population. Two sets of mechanisms are described: traditional and modern. In traditional, smaller-scale, preindustrial economies, sharing is based on social rules, established rights, and customary obligations. In modern economies, exchange occurs in response to the profit motive and is regulated by a price mechanism. In both traditional and modern economies, distinct variations on the basic mechanism exist.

The chapter is introduced by a preamble on the relationships among economics, geography, and economic geography. This preamble describes a gap in theory that results from the divergent goals of economics and geography. Economists deal with an abstract, homogeneous world in which space is collapsed to a point, whereas geographers ignore economic fundamentals. This chapter helps to bridge this gap by explaining the basic economic concepts of price and applying them to the geography of price found in modern economies.

Objectives:

- to describe the householding, redistribution, and reciprocity mechanisms for regulating exchange in preindustrial economies
- to explain the mechanisms by which price regulates exchange in more complex, modern economies
- to define and interpret the basic economic concepts underlying price theory and illustrate how they can be extended to apply to actual data and the real world
- to provide a foundation for the discussion of theories of location, exchange, and interaction

ECONOMICS, GEOGRAPHY, AND ECONOMIC GEOGRAPHY: A PREAMBLE

Divergent Disciplinary Goals

Economic fundamentals are becoming important in modern economic geography after a long period of neglect. Their neglect by past geographers reflects the divergent goals of economics and geography. Economics is concerned with how scarce resources are allocated among competing users, with how prices are determined and incomes distributed, and with policies for promoting economic growth. Geography is concerned with humanity's use of resources, to be sure, but from the perspective of the spatial distribution of phenomena, patterns of spatial interaction, and the regionalisms that result.

Recently, economists who study what they call *regional economics* have become interested in spatial patterns as well. But their literature deals in a highly abstract way with patterns that can arise in homogeneous space, devoid of differences in climate, soils, and vegetation or in the social, cultural, and economic characteristics of its population. In their highly mathematical formulations, regional economists rarely use real-world data.

It is modern economic geography that therefore has come to occupy the middle ground between economics and geography. Economic geographers examine the interplay of abstract economic principles and real-world geographic factors. More specifically, modern economic geographers study the locations of centers of economic activity, the trade flows to and from hierarchies of these centers, and the transport networks over which the trade moves, patterns of resource use, regions of production and consumption, and the spatial dynamics of growth and decline. In other words, modern economic geography is concerned with such spatial building blocks as *points of focus, lines and channels of movement*, and *areas of organization*, and with their changes through time.

Historically, economic geographers have disregarded the contributions that economic principles can make to their disciplinary goals. Some elementary probes into the economic fundamentals of the subject were made by G. G. Chisholm (see Chapter 2). Geographers abandoned these attempts, however, when they espoused environmental determinism. The subsequent rejection of determinism led to the highly descriptive diversions of areal differentiation rather than to the pursuit of more satisfactory economic principles.

This failure of economics and geography to integrate their theory clouds the thinking of social scientists and policymakers on many current world issues. One example is the conflict between the environmentalist and economist views on resources (Chapter 1). Are resource shortages an indication of underpricing (the economist viewpoint) or of real, absolute shortages (the environmentalist view), or a bit of both? And are the most crucial world problems those of limits to growth or disparities in distribution? Unfortunately, we cannot even begin to examine these problems adequately, much less resolve them, until we have developed an integrated approach involving both geographic and economic fundamentals.

It is this interdependence of economic life and environment to which Erich Zimmermann referred in his classic study titled *World Resources and Industries* (1933, 1951, p. xi). There is, he argued, a need for economists to incorporate physical realities into their theory, and for geographers to incorporate basic economic theory into their explanations of areal differences. This section on economic fundamentals lays the foundations on which this borderland theory, so long ignored by geographers and economists, must be built.

The Role of Theory

Theory plays the same role in economics, geography, and economic geography, notwithstanding differences in disciplinary goals and in the levels of theoretical development achieved. The objective of theory, whatever its content, is to reduce a hodgepodge of details to an intelligible pattern of consistent relationships among phenomena. The development of theory requires preselection of which characteristics are to be examined, which relationships are to be explored, which aspects of total reality are to be explained, and what assumptions are to be made.

The first beginnings of theory may be prompted by casual observation and experience. In these first probes toward theory, description of fact makes up the preponderant share of the effort. Increasing sophistication and rigor leads to a growing concern with testing tentative theories using carefully selected data and a variety of statistical techniques. In these later developments, the subject matter of a discipline becomes increasingly theoretical and deductive, rather than empirical and descriptive.

Specifically, the objective of theory in modern economic geography is to explain the geography of economic systems using a relatively small number of variables. Among the items to be explained are the spatial distributions of production and consumption, the spatial interactions evidenced by data on communications and trade, and regional differences in growth and development. The economic geographer's concerns begin at the individual level, for ultimately it is individual decisions and behavior that create spatial systems and that change them. Humankind is both producer and consumer. As producers we engage in employment that results in the creation of materials and services and yields income. As consumers, we have needs. Our values, embedded within a culture, translate these needs into *wants* for materials and services that we obtain with the income we earn. To develop these concerns, however, economic geographers must devise theoretical structures that can be applied to economic planning as well as to the satisfaction of individual and social needs.

TRADITIONAL AND MODERN ECONOMIES

The question of *scale*, one of the most fundamental questions in economic geography, arises out of this need to establish a bridge between the individual and society. For some individuals, the relationship between production and consumption is local. For example, an individual in an isolated village in the highlands of New Guinea may be part of a local, essentially closed, and self-sustaining system. On the other hand, the spatial domain of Westerners is worldwide: The world economy is a complex network of flows of people, money, energy, goods, information, and ideas, and changes in any part affect the whole. Between these two extremes of local and worldwide systems, a whole range of types and scales of social groups and socioeconomic systems can be identified, many of which will be discussed in detail in later chapters.

Sociocultural Bases of Traditional Economies

This variety of socioeconomic systems is, of course, a product of the long period of sociocultural evolution of humanity. Recently, American anthropologists have tried to develop a classification of cultures that charts this evolutionary process. They argue that change has been expressed in two fundamental ways: (1) a steadily rising level of sociocultural development throughout human history, expressed in increasing economic and social control of the environment; and (2) progressively more complex development of organizational resources to permit larger and larger groups to work together to mutual advantage. Furthermore, they argue that, up to the modern transformation of the world beginning in the Industrial Revolution, human social systems evolved through four stages, examples of which have persisted to the present:

1. hunting and gathering societies,
2. seminomadic groups engaging in simple slash-burn agriculture without animal husbandry,

3. settled villages of tropical agriculturalists with animal husbandry,
4. the larger-scale Eurasian plow agriculture dominated by urbanized central governments and complex forms of social stratification.

Sociopolitical Bases of Modern Economic Systems

Fundamental transformations in these basic cultural systems occurred in the past three centuries as the result of a succession of industrial, political, and social revolutions. As a result, world economic organization should be described today in terms of five basic *sociopolitical systems*, among which there are significant differences in how growth takes place, and how locations and land use are determined:

1. *Free-enterprise, decentralized, market-directed systems.* In such systems decisions are made by individuals, groups, and corporations. These decisions interact in the market through the interplay of the forces of demand and supply. Economic power and political power, vested in the claims of ownership and property, are widely dispersed and competitively exercised, leading to pluralistic societies in which many groups exercise influence. Collective or government action protects and supports the central institutions of the market and maintains the decentralization of power. These systems are found in North America, Western Europe, Australasia, and westernized South America and southern Africa, but in the past several decades these market economies have tended to change into either Type 2 or Type 3 economies, discussed below.
2. *Organizational market-negotiated systems.* Modern industrial and postindustrial societies are a recent outgrowth of the decentralized free-enterprise systems in the West. Major developmental decisions are made by negotiation among large-scale autonomous organizations. Pitted against each other, these voluntary associations, which are profit-oriented but not necessarily maximizers, bargain together and exist in a context of negotiated relationships. Decision-making power is determined as a matter of policy or is agreed upon by counterbalancing powers. Listing the characteristics of these systems, we obtain the following:

(a) Organization of production is by large corporations run for the benefit of stockholders. Labor negotiates wages through large-scale unions.
(b) Consumption of end products is determined

partly by individual choice, and partly by governmental policy.

(c) The power of organizations, the collective power of the government, and the free choice of individuals are all part of the system. A classic case is the alliance in Japan among business, labor, and government in what is often called "Japan Incorporated."

3. *Redistributive welfare states.* In such states, the free-enterprise system has been modified by government action to reduce social and spatial inequities, to provide every citizen with minimum guarantees of material welfare—medical care, education, employment, housing and pensions—usually achieved through differential taxation and welfare payments, but sometimes, too, by nationalization of industries and by direct governmental investment. Throughout the world, but particularly in Western Europe, there has been a progressive increase in the welfare functions of governments, with an associated extension of more centralized decision making designed to make the market system satisfy social as well as traditional economic goals.

4. *Socialist economies.* An outgrowth of twentieth-century political revolutions, this group consists of single-party political systems, in which there is state operation of nonagricultural industries (in some, agriculture too), centralized direction of the economy (with experiments in decentralization), semi-industrialized production structures, per capita incomes more variable than in the West, and strong commitment to economic growth. This group includes the USSR, the Eastern European countries, China, Cuba, Vietnam, and North Korea (although the latter countries share many features with Type 5, discussed below). In particular, in such systems:

(a) The *plan* rather than the free movement of market prices controls production, consumption, and distribution.

(b) The essence of the plan is centralized decision making; the few decide for the many, and the activities of the many are carried on under the directives of the few.

(c) Centralized action requires a complex apparatus for gathering basic data needed for decision making, for formulating goals and alternatives, and for enabling the feedback necessary to adapt processes and expectations to changing circumstances.

5. *Less-developed economies.* A collection of partly preindustrial and partly modernizing societies,

this group is characterized most commonly by one-party governments or military dictatorships, political instability, with limited capacity for public administration, small public sectors, fragmentation of the economy along geographic and modern-versus-traditional lines, imperfection of markets and limited development and continued predominance of agriculture, lower per capita product, and market dependence on foreign economic relations. This group comprises many of the nations of Central America and South America, Africa (except South Africa), Asia (except Japan), and many small island economies.

No single theory can bridge the fundamental differences between the several kinds of traditional economies and the equally diverse range of modern economies. Indeed, the shift from traditional to modern economies has been called by Karl Polanyi "the great transformation." In traditional economies, the economy was submerged in social relationships. Laboring was motivated by social mores and custom, and it was not for income. Trade was not primarily undertaken for economic gain, but to acquire prestige items. Life was not directed by principles of economic efficiency or distinct economic institutions. The great transformation changed all this. Market economies developed in which price regulated exchange, and social motivations yielded to economic imperatives. These two groups of systems will be discussed separately, after first introducing elementary concepts in a "Robinson Crusoe" case.

ROBINSON CRUSOE: A SIMPLE CASE

Consider Robinson Crusoe before his man Friday came along. He was responsible for satisfying all his own demands. That meant he had to decide what he wanted, *extract* his raw materials and crops, *transport* them to his workshops, *process* them to create desired products, *store* the products at some convenient place until the need for them arose, and finally *distribute* them in the proper proportions to wherever they were to be consumed. His *productive process* (embodying the stages of extraction, processing and distribution, and the attendant operations of transportation and storage) thus led to final satisfaction of his needs in *consumption*.

Crusoe was a complete *economic system* unto himself, for he originated the *demands*, created the *supplies*, and so organized his work that his demands and supplies were maintained in overall *equilibrium*, consistent with his needs and capabilities and the resources available to him. Clearly, equilibrium was in his best interest, because to produce too much would be wasteful of time and effort, and to produce less than he needed would be dangerous, and potentially fatal.

Both historically and in the less "Westernized" parts of the world today, examples may be found of small groups of people subsisting in communities with simple, self-sustaining "Crusoe-like" economies in which the proper quantities and varieties of products are distributed among the members without the need for markets, money, or prices. In many of these communities, a primitive form of affluence also may be seen: Many hunters and gatherers, for example, satisfy their needs with only a two- to four-hour workday. To the extent that there is production above subsistence levels, this is elicited by kinship organization and the institution of chieftancy, which serves to generate effort, output, and movement of goods in excess of the limited desires of the domestic group.

In Crusoe's case the decision as to how much to produce and how to distribute the output was his own *individual* one. In Crusoe-like economies the decision is *social*; the rules, obligations, traditions, and group decisions of the community determine who shall produce what and how it will be distributed. Three such patterns of social control have been identified: *householding*, *redistribution*, and *reciprocity*.

HOUSEHOLDING, REDISTRIBUTION, AND RECIPROCITY IN SMALLER SCALE SOCIETIES

Householding

Householding is a literal translation of the Greek word *oeconomia*, the etymon for our word "economy." Householding means "production for one's own use." The economic historian Karl Polanyi has described householding in his book *The Great Transformation* as follows:

> Whether the different entities of the family or settlement or the manor form the self-sufficient unit, the principle is invariably the same: that of producing and storing for the satisfaction of the wants of the members of the group. . . . Production for use as against production for gain is the essence of householding.[1]

The householding unit is a self-sustaining entity. The medieval *manor*, the Roman *familia*, and the South Slav *zadruga* are all comparable examples of such householding economic systems. Large numbers of these independent economic units were the basis of feudal society in Europe.

[1]Karl Polanyi, *The Great Transformation* (New York: Octagon Books, 1975).

The householding unit is closest to the Robinson Crusoe example in both pattern and organization. Instead of a single consumer, there are several, with division of labor based upon age, sex, social standing, and tradition. Only when kinship or political organization demanded it was *Chayanov's rule* overridden. This rule states that "the greater the relative working capacity of the household, the less its members work." The rule indicates that householding production is designed to meet the household's needs, and nothing more.

Thus, the medieval manor consisted of a series of families who worked cooperatively in cultivating their communal fields, woods, pastures, and ponds. Each family had an established right to the output from certain strips of land, to pasture a certain number of animals, to use a certain amount of wood, and so forth, but it also had the responsibility to produce a surplus for the feudal lord, who in turn was responsible for security. Equity was maintained by these rights. Local demands and supplies were kept in balance.

Redistribution

In some societies equity is maintained through the institution of a strong central authority, whose function is *redistributive*. Products are delivered to this head person, or chief. They are then parceled out by this person to members of the social group as determined by custom.

Many of the ancient empires, such as the New Kingdom of Egypt, were founded upon this principle of redistribution. It is also common among many of the cattle-raising tribes of East Africa. One interesting manifestation was found in the *potlatch* of the *Kwakiutl* Indians of the Pacific Northwest, in which the chief assembled the wealth of the tribe and redistributed it by giving to others in elaborate gift-giving ceremonies.

Redistribution by government is, of course, also the fundamental difference between modern market and socialist societies, and it is the organizing principle of the contemporary communist state.

Reciprocity

The third pattern of exchange is *reciprocity*. Needs are met by exchange between complementary producers. In the Trobriand Islands of Western Melanesia, for example, inland communities are paired with coastal villages in a pattern of exchange of inland breadfruits for coastal fish. The pairing extends to particular individuals being responsible for the direct exchange, in symmetrical arrangements of remarkable regularity and persistence. Many such exchanges are disguised in the form of reciprocal giving of gifts, but the principle is the same.

Karl Polanyi (1975), who has contributed greatly to our understanding of small-scale, self-sustaining, preindustrial societies by his pioneering work, draws the following conclusions about them. Most important is the subordination of economic life to social rules and tradition. All economic systems known up to the end of feudalism in Western Europe were organized either on the principles of reciprocity, redistribution, or house-holding, or on some combination of the three. The orderly production and distribution of goods were secured through a great variety of individual motives disciplined by general principles of behavior. Gain was not prominent among these motives. Custom and law, and magic and religion cooperated in inducing the individual to comply with the rules of behavior that, eventually, ensured one's functioning in the socioeconomic system. Further, Polanyi argues that as long as social organization ran in the ruts of tradition, no individual economic motives needed to come into play. Nor was the shirking of personal effort to be feared. Division of labor was automatically ensured. Social and economic obligations were duly discharged. Material means for an excellent display of abundance at all public festivals were guaranteed. Such are the basic considerations guiding the simplest forms of exchange, not simply in feudal Europe, but in all societies in which the marketplace is absent.

BARTERING AND HIGGLING IN PEASANT SOCIETIES: A STAGE IN THE EVOLUTION OF MARKETS

The gradual emergence of both local and long-distance trade between social groups was responsible for the transition of many self-sustaining groups into peasant societies and, in turn, the transformation of peasant societies into full-fledged exchange economies. A *peasant society* is one in which the household or local social group remains relatively self-sustaining with respect to necessities such as food and shelter, but trades a surplus or a specialty product for outside manufactured goods or luxuries. A full *exchange economy* is one in which the principles of the division of labor apply to every producer. In an exchange economy, very few producers, even farmers, consume more than a small part of their own specialized output, for they come to produce only that for which they have a comparative advantage, not everything.

Perhaps the earliest long-distance trade was exploration beyond the limits of the local area. Such exploration might involve warlike forays or irregular trading,

often for ritual goods associated with the temple, the early focus of society, and the god-king who maintained social controls. As long as the resulting exchange of goods was sporadic, market centers did not develop. Only when regular trade connections emerged was there justification for the establishment of permanent market places.

One regular form of long-distance exchange was between complementary production zones, for example, between plains dwellers and hill folk, each trading surpluses of their own specialty for those of the other. Market sites would often develop along the territorial boundary zone, on neutral ground. At the appropriate season, often in conjunction with religious festivities, people from surrounding areas would converge upon the market sites to barter surpluses. Where relations between the different groups were strained, a truce would be called and the market site would constitute neutral ground.

Local trade emerged on the basis of regular intercourse between peasants, local craftsworkers and specialists, and town merchants and intermediaries. Local surpluses would be traded for such necessities as salt, iron, or durables, and merchants would have available some luxuries and trinkets obtained from the great fairs. To fit in with work on the land, the markets would be held periodically. Links connecting long-distance trade, great fairs, and local periodic markets were provided by the town merchants, whose travels would transport the goods from one place to the other.

It was only with the emergence of local and long-distance trade that market sites and trading posts became widespread in peasant societies. For example, in Yorubaland in West Africa, the earliest markets were located along with contact zone between forest and savanna, along coastal lagoons and creeks, or at the boundaries between different peoples. The larger markets were situated along the chief trade routes, and changed in importance with these routes. One important origin of Yoruba markets was the resting place where local populations provided services to passing groups of traders. If such resting places became popular, a market into which farmers brought their wares sprang up, and periodic market days developed. Extra-large meetings would be held less frequently, when large numbers of traders converged.

Initially, at these meeting-places *bartering* was the dominant means of exchange. But gradually, some form of *money* took over as the medium of exchange, and goods began to move at prices determined by *higgling*, that is, face-to-face bargaining between buyer and seller with both trying to maximize their advantages, ultimately agreeing upon mutually satisfactory payment. Under such conditions prices are highly variable and flexible from time to time and place to place, although in each case they reflect a balance or agreement between buyer and seller that transfers a commodity or a service from one to the other.

THE GEOGRAPHY OF PRICE IN FREE-ENTERPRISE SYSTEMS

Basic Economic Concepts

Now consider the problem in a much larger-scale free-enterprise economy in which there are many buyers and sellers who cannot meet face to face to bargain, yet for whom some type of balance between demands and supplies ultimately must be achieved. It is to this case that the classic economic theory of price applies. Three important concepts drawn from this theory will enable us to develop a *geography* of price. These three concepts are the nature of *price* itself, the relationship of *supply and demand* to price, and *market equilibrium*, the price at which supply equals demand. The concept of *elasticity*, the rate at which supply and demand change with price, also is introduced.

Price

According to *price theory*, price is the rate at which a good, service, resource, or factor of production can be exchanged for any other good, service, resource, or factor of production in a manner that clears the market of available goods and satisfies consumer demand at that price. Goods have prices because they are *useful* and *scarce* in relation to the uses to which people want to put them. When something has no use, it does not command a price; when it is useful but available to all in unlimited amounts, like air, it cannot command a price.

Whether or not a good is useful is determined by consumer demand. Scarcity, on the other hand, is determined by the capacities and willingness of producers to generate the supplies needed at the prevailing price. Price, then, is determined by the demands and supplies of many consumers and producers jointly interacting in a market where goods and services are exchanged for each other.

The most fundamental characteristic of such free-enterprise markets is that, because there are large numbers of equally small producers and consumers, the individual buyer or seller is a "price-taker," having no control over the price he or she must pay or can receive. The prices are determined competitively in the market, and the actions of any particular individual cannot change them. Indeed, very elaborate legal safeguards (antitrust legislation) have been developed in free-enterprise societies to preserve this situation as the way of conducting business. In some types of businesses, because of the possibility of achieving economies of scale, there has today been the transition to market negotiation, while markets continue to work best in agriculture, the precious and nonferrous metals industries, the stock exchanges, and the markets for land, homes, and other kinds of property.

Demand and Supply

The relationship between demand and price is quite simple. The theory of demand postulates that, *as the price of a product falls, more of it will be bought.* This is because some people who could not buy at the higher price will begin to make purchases as prices fall and because many buyers are likely to increase their purchases of the cheapening commodity in place of alternative goods that have become relatively more costly. In addition, if nothing else changes, the price decline will increase people's real incomes, and they will consume more because they are relatively better off.

The theory of supply postulates that *the higher the price is, the more of a good that will be offered for sale* because existing sellers are eager to sell while conditions are good, and rising prices will make it attractive for more producers to enter the market. If prices fall, supplies will be withheld in the hope that prices will rise again, and marginal producers may go out of business. Supply is also affected by the relative efficiency of different producers and production units. If prices are low (or demand drops) only the more efficient, lower-cost mines, power-generating plants, railroad rolling stock, and so forth will be used. When prices are high, less-efficient products and facilities will be brought into use because the higher prices will cover the higher costs.

Demand and supply can be represented in tables (or schedules) or by graphs. Hypothetical data are given in Figure 6.1 to illustrate how the demand and supply for "thingamabobs" might react to price changes, and the typical downward-sloping demand curve and upward-sloping supply curve that result.

An example, using real data, may help to emphasize that demand, even of such basics as specific food items, can be very sensitive to price. The U.S. Department of Agriculture has attempted to estimate demand for a variety of meats, based on prices for 1948–1962. The simplest case to emerge is that for chicken. There was a fairly progressive drop in the price at which chicken was offered for sale throughout this entire period. And as prices fell, demand increased, apparently tracing out a smooth downward-sloping demand curve (Figure 6.2). Chicken consumption doubled in just 15

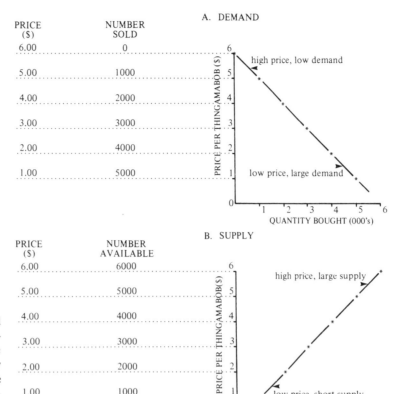

A. DEMAND

PRICE ($)	NUMBER SOLD
6.00	0
5.00	1000
4.00	2000
3.00	3000
2.00	4000
1.00	5000

B. SUPPLY

PRICE ($)	NUMBER AVAILABLE
6.00	6000
5.00	5000
4.00	4000
3.00	3000
2.00	2000
1.00	1000
0	0

FIGURE 6.1 Demand, supply, and price. Demand has an inverse relationship to price: the higher the price, the lower the demand. Supply has a direct relationship to price: the higher the price, the greater the supply. These relationships are illustrated in table form (the demand and supply schedules) and by graphs.

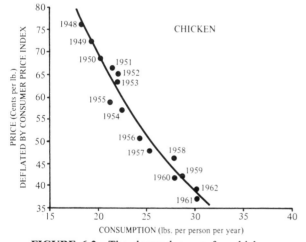

FIGURE 6.2 The demand curve for chicken, United States, 1948–1962. The demand curve for chicken remained constant in the United States over the study period: 1948–1962. The supply curve, however, kept shifting, because producers were able to produce more chicken at lower prices (in constant dollars) as the years went by. The demand curve is traced out as a sequence of market equilibrium points (see Figure 6.3). [*Source:* U.S. Department of Agriculture, Economic Research Service, Neg. ERS 2147-63(7).]

years in response to a halving in price (adjusted for cost of living).

It is unusual to find empirical data that trace out a demand curve as neatly as the U.S. chicken example. It occurred in this case because the demand curve for chicken remained constant over the entire study period, whereas the supply curve shifted progressively. By contrast, the same study shows that the demand and supply schedules for other meats both shifted.

Market Equilibrium

In order to understand how demand and supply are brought into balance, it is helpful to plot supply and demand curves back to back on a single graph. The results for the "thingamabob" example are shown in Figure 6.3.

If suppliers are prepared to increase the quantity of a good they market as price increases, and if consumers reduce the amount they buy as price increases, then there should exist a *price at which supply equals demand*. This price, which "clears" the market of available supply and also satisfies demand, is the point of *market equilibrium*. Market equilibrium is identified on a graph of back-to-back supply and demand curves as the point of intersection (*E* on Figure 6.3).

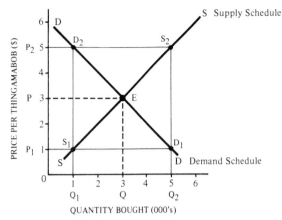

FIGURE 6.3 Market equilibrium. The market equilibrium is the point of intersection of the supply and demand curves (*E*). The market equilibrium determines the price (*P*) of the good, the quantity (*Q*) bought and sold, and total demand (*P* × *Q*). At price *P*, buyers and sellers match purchases and sales and are just able to clear the market of available supplies. In the case of thingamabobs *P* = \$3.00 and *Q* = 3000, so that total demand is \$9000. If the price were \$1.00, demand would rise to 5000, and supply fall to 1000, leaving a deficit (*S₁D₁*) of 4000 thingamabobs. Disappointed customers would bid up the price. If the price rose to \$5.00, demand would fall to 1000 and supply would increase to 5000, leaving a surplus (*S₂D₂*) of 4000. The market glut would force down prices. Thus, the market price will tend to remain at the market equilibrium level.

Price will tend to fluctuate around the market equilibrium in a free-enterprise economy. If the price rises above the equilibrium, price reductions will be needed to clear the market of excess supply resulting from the price rise. If demand rises above supply, disappointed customers will scour the market, offering higher prices. Any deviation from the market equilibrium price thus triggers corrective action that pushes the price back toward the market equilibrium level.

The natural tendency of prices to hover around the market equilibrium level makes it difficult to observe the full demand-and-supply schedules in real market conditions. Hence, the chicken example (Figure 6.2) is of special interest. Actually, what Figure 6.2 shows is a series of market equilibria, one for each year! These market equilibria join to pick out the demand curve because the shifting supply curves intersected an unchanging demand curve at a progression of different price-and-quantity equilibrium levels.

Elasticity

The magnitude of response in demand or supply to changes in price can vary a great deal depending on the good. For some items, such as tobacco, there is little drop in demand with increase in price. But consumers are conscious of the seasonal swings in the prices of fresh fruits and vegetables and are highly responsive to these changes (see Tables 6.1 and 6.2).

Elasticity is a measure of response to price changes. *Elasticity of demand* is the percentage fall in demand for a product that results from a 1 percentage point increase in price. *Elasticity of supply* is the percentage increase in supply of a product that results from a 1 percentage point increase in price. If there is no change in demand with a change in price, the elasticity of demand is zero. If small changes in price produce massive shifts in demand, the elasticity of demand approaches infinity, as is shown in Figure 6.4. An elasticity of 1.0 means that a 1.0 percent change in price results in a 1.0 percent change in quantity. Actual computed demand elasticities for a variety of goods and services are shown in Table 6.3. They vary from close to zero to as high as 4.6. For staple commodities the elasticity tends

TABLE 6.1

Seasonal variations in apple prices

Oct.	Nov.	Dec.	Jan.	Feb.	Mar.	Apr.
5.00	4.25	4.25	4.38	4.35	4.38	4.60

Source: U.S. Department of Agriculture, *Prices and Spreads for Apples, Grapefruit, Grapes, Lemons and Oranges Sold Fresh in Selected Markets, 1962/63–1966/67* (Washington, D.C.: USDA Economic Research Service, Marketing Research Report No. 888, 1968).

Note: Prices are *shipping point price (FOB),* the simple average of the midpoint range of daily prices for a specified container of apples of specified grade and size received by a broad sample of shippers in representative shipping districts during a specified week. FOB means *free-on-board,* and signifies that the price excludes transportation charges.

TABLE 6.2

Retail price variation of selected food items,
New York City, 1936–1940

	Average monthly variation in prices (percent)		Average monthly variation in prices (percent)
Fresh beets	31.0	Fresh milk	4.0
Fresh tomatoes	28.7	Butter	3.5
Cooking apples	17.5	Dried navy beans	2.0
Grapefruit	14.3	Canned tomatoes	1.2
Potatoes	12.0	Canned peaches	.7
Large white eggs	9.7	Rice	.5
Oranges	8.3	Dried prunes	.5
Fresh carrots	6.2	Cheese	.2

Source: 738, Department of Agricultural Economics, Cornell University, June 1950.

Note: What is the relationship between (1) price variation and length of season?, (2) perishability and price variation?

to be low, but for luxuries and discretionary items it is much higher.

To be useful in economic geography, each of the basic economic concepts (supply and demand, price, elasticity, and equilibrium) has to be extended by introducing ideas of the market as a *place*, of location relative to this place, and of transportation costs. The result is a *geography* of supply, a *geography* of demand, and a *geography* or market equilibrium in free-enterprise economic systems.

The Geography of Supply

Basic Concepts

The supply curves of the economist ignore the systematic impact of transportation charges on the delivered cost of any good. Transportation costs can be expected to increase directly with the distance a good has

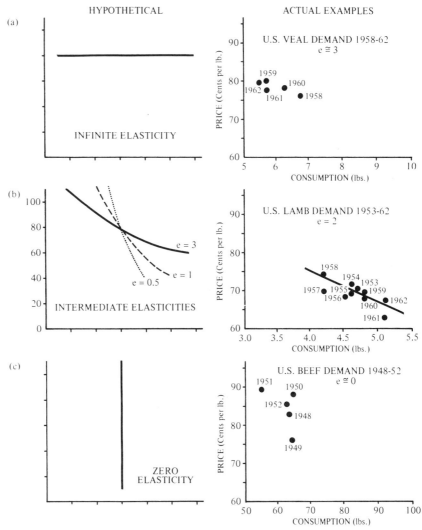

FIGURE 6.4 Elasticity of demand. This figure shows a variety of elasticities from zero to infinity. Note that the more sensitive consumers are to price, the higher the elasticity and the gentler the demand curve is.

Note: Price is deflated by Consumer Price Index.

TABLE 6.3

Elasticity of demand for selected goods

	Estimated elasticity		Estimated elasticity
FOOD ITEMS		DURABLE GOODS	
Cabbage	0.4	Kitchen appliances	0.6
White potatoes	0.3	China & tableware	1.1
Sweet potatoes	0.8	Jewelry & watches	0.4
Green peas, fresh	2.8	Automobiles	0.6
Tomatoes, fresh	4.6	Tires	0.6
Watermelons	1.5	Radio and television receivers	1.2
OTHER NONDURABLE GOODS		SERVICES	
Tobacco products	0.0	Physicians' services	0.6
Shoes	0.4	Legal services	0.5
Stationery	0.5	Airline travel, short run	0.06
Newspapers and magazines	0.1	long run	2.4
Gasoline and oil, short run	0.2	Foreign travel, short run	0.7
long run	0.5	long run	4.0

Source: Adapted from Daniel B. Suits, *Principles of Economics* (New York: Harper & Row, 1970), p. 287. Copyright © 1970 by Daniel B. Suits. Reprinted by permission of Harper & Row, Publishers, Inc.

to be transported. Because price therefore increases with distance from the point of production, the result is a *supply-price funnel* as can be illustrated with the example of "thingamabobs" (Figure 6.5).

August Lösch (1954), who introduced the term *price funnel*, has provided maps and data to illustrate such price variations in space for a wide variety of goods. Agricultural products were cheapest, he found, in the centers of production and increased in price outward from these centers. Potatoes in 1936 were 18 cents a pound in Prince Edward Island, for example, but 25 cents a pound in Toronto. Orange prices were 16 cents a pound in California, but 37 cents a pound in Chicago. Lösch also examined nonagricultural goods and found significant price funnels for newspapers with large market areas, automobiles, and soap, for example. Similarly, and quite surprisingly, given the large number of small producers and the short distances milk is transported, even for milk, there was in 1957–1958 a single, countrywide price funnel centered on Eau Claire, Wisconsin, at the heart of the dairy belt (Figures 6.6 and 6.7).

The Role of Central Markets in Setting Prices Received by Suppliers

Lösch's price funnels, upward and outward from supply regions, do not tell us what individual suppliers receive for their output, however. Within the supply region there will be one or more *central markets*, and the price received by a given supplier will be the price established in that market *minus* the costs of transporting the product to that market. The farther the supplier is

from that central market, the lower the price, as shown in Figure 6.8.

Suppliers have a choice of selling to consumers in their local market, or to dispose of their supplies in the central market. The supplier will sell to local consumers only if the price they are willing to pay exceeds the central market price less transportation costs. Prices in the central market minus costs of transportation therefore set a *producer's price floor*, the price that may be obtained by selling in the central market when local demand is weak.

Each central market has its own *supply area*. Individual producers will sell to the central market that offers them the greatest *on-site return* (on-site return is another way of saying central market price minus transportation costs). The supply area boundary is located where the producers' price floor gradients intersect, as at *X* and *Y* in Figure 6.9. The boundary between the supply areas of competing central markets traces out the locus of minimum on-site returns. How low that minimum is depends upon the locations of the central markets, the prices in those markets, and how rapidly the price floor falls with distance. Compare the prices at boundaries *X* and *Y* in Figure 6.9.

Why Did Central Markets Emerge?

Why did central markets emerge to set the spatial patterns of prices? Central markets are a creation of modern economies and transportation systems. In the United States until the 1850s, agriculture was characterized by small production units. Transportation, communication, and marketing were local, and trading was

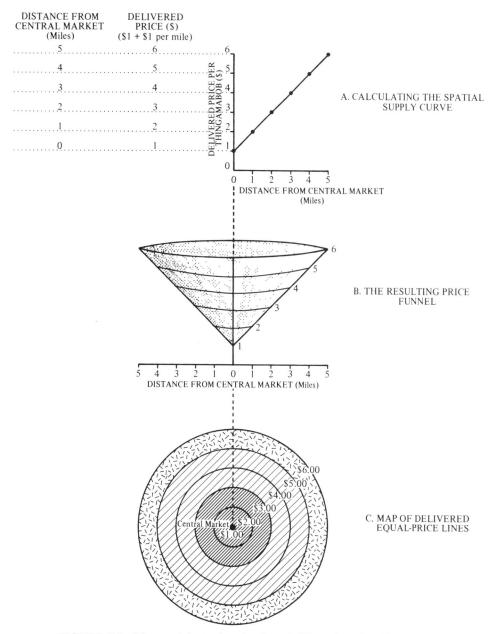

DISTANCE FROM
CENTRAL MARKET
(Miles)

DELIVERED
PRICE ($)
($1 + $1 per mile)

A. CALCULATING THE SPATIAL
SUPPLY CURVE

B. THE RESULTING PRICE
FUNNEL

C. MAP OF DELIVERED
EQUAL-PRICE LINES

FIGURE 6.5 The spatial supply-price funnel. The price of a thingama-bob is $1.00 at the market plus a transportation charge of $1.00 per mile. The result can be shown in four equivalent ways: table, graph, price funnel, and map. Becoming familiar with all four is helpful in understanding the economic fundamentals of economic geography. Note that a price funnel shows price against distance, whereas an ordinary supply curve shows price against quantity.

very often a face-to-face matter between producer and consumer in a weekly market. In the last half of the nineteenth century, many changes took place that led to the development of a nationwide, commercial marketing system. Cities grew rapidly, western lands were brought into production, railroad mileage expanded quickly, and communications improved. These devel-

opments facilitated the long-distance flow of commodities from specialized production regions to food-deficit areas, but required that some other institution replace weekly face-to-face trading.

Trading therefore progressed from the informal weekly markets to formal clubs that provided a common meeting place for traders. The next step was for

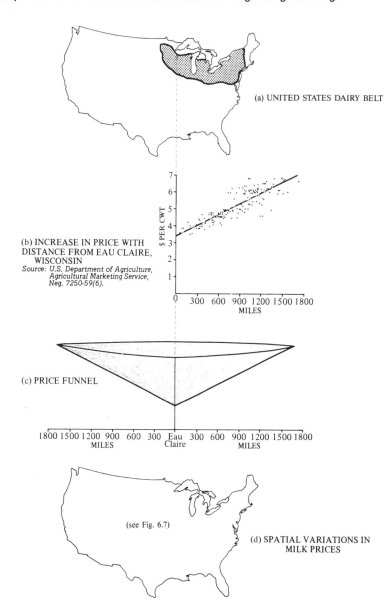

(a) UNITED STATES DAIRY BELT

(b) INCREASE IN PRICE WITH DISTANCE FROM EAU CLAIRE, WISCONSIN
Source: U.S. Department of Agriculture, Agricultural Marketing Service, Neg. 7250-59(6).

(c) PRICE FUNNEL

(d) SPATIAL VARIATIONS IN MILK PRICES

(see Fig. 6.7)

FIGURE 6.6 Milk prices in the United States, 1957–1958. The center of milk production in the United States is Eau Claire, Wisconsin. Milk prices increase regularly with increasing distance from Eau Claire, creating a price funnel. Prices climb from less than $4.00 per hundredweight (cwt) to more than $5.00 in California and nearly $7.00 in Florida. Prices increased on average by 2.2 cents per 10 miles. For spatial variations in milk prices (d), see Figure 6.7.

commodity exchanges to emerge and provide organized trading. Commodity exchanges are nonprofit association of persons acting as principals or agents in the transfer of ownership of agricultural or other primary commodities. *Futures* markets are the major part of most exchange activities, trading contracts for future deliveries at agreed-upon prices. *Cash* or *spot markets*, where available commodities are sold and delivered within a few hours, also are part of the commodity exchange function.

What do such commodity exchanges do? Both spot and futures markets provide continuous market trading for those who wish to buy or sell. They involve large numbers of buyers and sellers, maintain quality standards, and permit a free flow of information, so that competitive prices can be determined. In effect, they are

the prime example of "the market" in classical free-enterprise economies.

Commodity exchanges functioning as central markets exist for many products including livestock, grains, fruits and vegetables, wool, cotton, hides, and tobacco. For example, in the United States, corn prices are set by the price of No. 3 Yellow Corn on the Chicago Board of Trade. The prices of oats and soybeans are also set there. Barley prices are set by the quotations for No. 3 Barley in Minneapolis. Sorghums are based on No. 2 Yellow Milo at Kansas City. American cheese at factories in Wisconsin is priced at the Wisconsin Cheese Exchange. On the world scene, many metals are priced on the London Metals Exchange. Rotterdam now functions as the world's spot market for petroleum.

Chicago and London are examples of the large *ter-*

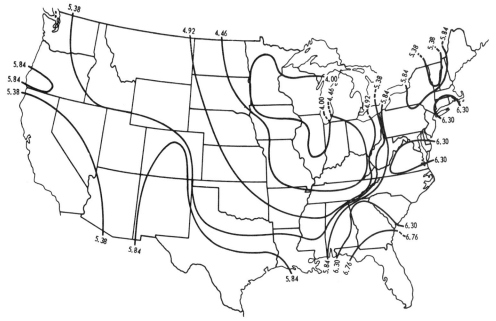

FIGURE 6.7 Spatial variations in milk prices, 1957–1958 [see Figure 6.6(d)]. Dealers' buying prices, per cwt, 3.5 percent butterfat for fluid use, based on prices in 185 markets. [*Source:* U.S. Department of Agriculture, Agricultural Marketing Service, Neg. 7215-59(6).]

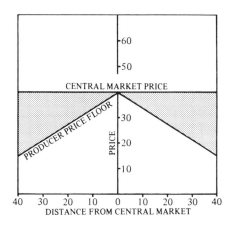

Transportation Costs to Central Market

FIGURE 6.8 Producer price floors. For many agricultural products and industrial raw materials, a base price is competitively determined at one or more central markets. The supplier receives the central market price *minus* transportation and related charges, but may be able to sell locally at a price higher than this price floor.

minal markets where products from wide areas are concentrated, and it is for this reason that they developed their market concourses. Another example is that of Liverpool, which prior to 1940 was the major international market for wheat. Wheat prices registered on the Liverpool market were looked upon as the world price.

The United Kingdom was the largest single importer of wheat, and Liverpool was an ideal world market as prices were little affected by special conditions in one or another of the world's producing areas, but reflected the general tendencies in all producing areas.

Logically, of course, the world price of wheat should be determined chiefly by the world supply of wheat and the general level of world commodity prices. From 1924 to 1938, virtually all the variation in the price of wheat at Liverpool, commonly referred to as "British parcels," was tied to variations in the world supply of wheat and British wholesale prices. A 1 percent change in supply in this period was associated with a 1.4 percent change in the price of wheat in the opposite direction. A 1 percent change in the index of prices was associated with a 1.2 percent change in the index of wheat in the same direction.

United States wheat prices tended to depend directly on British wheat prices. Thus, from 1922 to 1939, three-quarters of the variation in the price of wheat in the United States at the domestic wheat-price basepoint, Kansas City, was associated with variations in the price of British parcels of wheat at Liverpool. Prices elsewhere in wheat-producing areas of the United States reflected transportation charges to Kansas City. In most years since then, however, U.S. domestic prices have been determined chiefly by the level of price support established by the government or by other governmental policies.

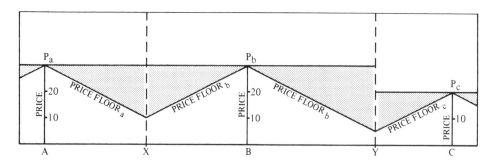

A, B, C : Locations of Central Markets

X, Y : Supply Area Boundaries

AX : Primary Supply Area of A

XBY : Primary Supply Area of B

YC : Primary Supply Area of C

P_a, P_b, P_c : Prices at Central Markets

☐ : Transportation Costs to Central Markets

FIGURE 6.9   Supply areas of central markets. The boundaries of supply areas are set by the intersection of producer price floors from competing central markets. The boundaries are thus lines of indifference along which producers receive the same price from competing central markets. The lower a central market's price is, the smaller its supply area will be. Thus, C's primary supply area (CY) is reduced and B's (BY) is extended.

The Liverpool market ceased to exist as a free market from October 1939 through November 1953. During that period, trading in futures did not exist and all wheat purchases were handled by government agencies. On December 1, 1953, the grain trade in wheat was returned to private hands and the futures market reopened for trading. Since 1955, the price of futures at Liverpool probably represents the closest approximation to a "world price" once again. It no longer reflects world supply and demand conditions as closely as in the interwar period, however, because of the growth of governmental regulation, particularly in the United States.

Role of the Market Traders

It is the market traders who make the whole process of balancing demands and supplies work. To illustrate, consider a trader who has been put in charge of a grain "desk" at the Continental Grain Company. A cable arrives from one of Continental's overseas offices—say, Paris. A buyer has bid for 10,000 tons of soybeans for July delivery in Rotterdam. Before accepting or countering with an offer, the trader considers future prices, world news, freight quotations, vessel bookings, the crop outlook, and the competition.

Then the trader makes a simple calculation. The basis for the final price is the "futures" quotation on the Chicago Board of Trade for July soybeans. The trader adds in the barge freight to New Orleans, the cost

of handling at Continental's grain elevator there, and the ocean freight to Rotterdam. Then the trader cables the Paris office with a CIF price offer—cost, insurance, and freight.

If the trader gets an "accept" from the other side, the trader begins the task of seeking out a profit. First, the trader "hedges" by buying July futures in Chicago. Because the futures price is the basis for the actual soybean sale, the trader can limit losses this way. Then the trader tries to find cheaper soybeans. If he or she does, the trader can sell his or her July futures, and the trader's speculative profit will be the difference between the Rotterdam contract price and what the trader paid for the cheaper soybeans, less any cost of reselling the July futures.

The chartering department, meanwhile, will be speculating on shipping, trying to get the best deal possible for the July delivery in Rotterdam. It may take a section of a ship under charter by another company. Or it may charter a tanker for the 10,000-ton sale; 30,000 tons excess may be filled by another sale, or it may figure on selling the space later to a competitor at a profit.

All these facts, and more, determine what Continental's profit on the sale will be. At any rate, it will be months before the trader will know if the sale to Rotterdam was a success, but it is the possibility of making speculative gains that motivates the traders who keep the free-enterprise system of buying, selling, and price determination operational.

The Geography of Demand

Under perfect competition, the price paid by a *consumer* increases with distance from a central market, in the manner of Lösch's price-funnels (Figure 6.5). Central market price plus transportation costs from the central market sets a ceiling on the price that local consumers have to pay. They can always buy from local suppliers if prices are lower, but they need never pay more than the ceiling price determined by the central market plus transportation (Figure 6.10).

Where goods or services are available from competing central markets, consumers will buy from the market offering the lowest ceiling price if they do not buy locally. Market prices plus transportation costs thus lead to ceiling price gradients that trace out *market area* boundaries where they intersect (as at *X* and *Z* in Figure 6.11). Such boundaries trace out the locus of maximum ceiling prices between adjacent central markets, leading to the conclusion that there is a direct relationship between welfare and distance: The most distant consumer pays the highest prices (Figure 6.11), just as the most distant producer receives the least (Figure 6.9). Those on the periphery are doubly disadvantaged!

The Spatial Demand Cone

Demand for a good sold at a central market can be expected to drop progressively outward from that market as transportation costs add to the price of the

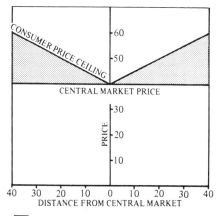

Transportation Costs from Central Market

FIGURE 6.10 Consumer price ceilings. Under perfect competition, the maximum delivered price equals the central market price plus transportation. This price sets a *consumer price ceiling*. The consumer may be able to buy locally for lower prices, but will not pay more. Figure 6.10 can be thought of as the top half of Figure 6.8. Combined, they show two price gradients fanning out from central markets, a consumer price ceiling and a producer price floor.

good. This relationship follows from the basic relationship of demand to price (see Figure 6.1). Using the demand schedule, which indicates the amount bought at each given price, and the delivered price at each distance

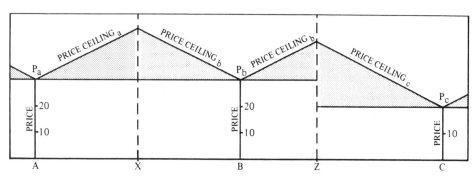

A, B, C : Locations of Central Markets

X, Z : Market Area Boundaries

AX : Primary Market Area of A

XBZ : Primary Market Area of B

ZC : Primary Market Area of C

P_a, P_b, P_c : Prices at Central Markets

Transportation Costs from Central Market

FIGURE 6.11 Definition of market areas. The market area of a central market is the area in which central market price plus transportation is less than (or equal to) the delivered price from competing central markets. The lower the price at the central market area, the larger the primary market area. Thus, *C*'s primary market area (*CZ*) is increased at the expense of *B*'s (*BZ*).

band from the market, one can draw a *demand cone* centered on the market. The outer perimeter of the cone, where demand drops to zero, would be the market area boundary in the absence of competitive centers, and is called the *range of the good*. (See Figure 6.12)

Consider the case of thingamabobs discussed earlier (Figures 6.1 and 6.5). The price of these delicate

widgets increases from $1 at the central market to $6 at a radius of 5 miles. Each dollar increase in price produces a decline in demand of 1000. Demand drops from 5000 at the central market to zero at 6 miles distance.

A map of the market area can be drawn showing the demand contours for thingamabobs. The demand at the market boundary itself is zero. A succession of con-

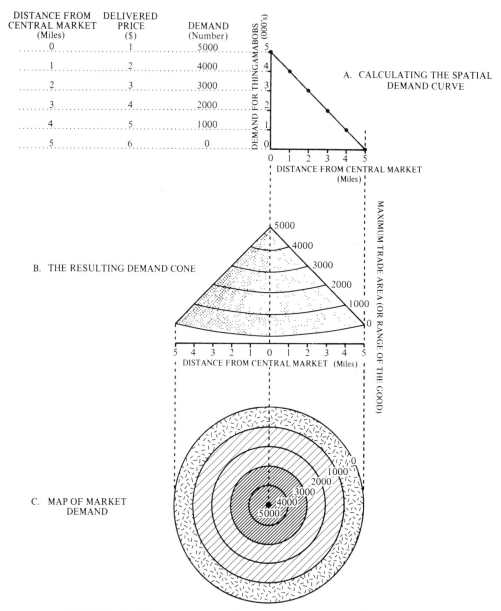

DISTANCE FROM CENTRAL MARKET (Miles)	DELIVERED PRICE ($)	DEMAND (Number)
0	1	5000
1	2	4000
2	3	3000
3	4	2000
4	5	1000
5	6	0

A. CALCULATING THE SPATIAL DEMAND CURVE

B. THE RESULTING DEMAND CONE

C. MAP OF MARKET DEMAND

FIGURE 6.12 The spatial demand curve, or demand cone. The construction of a demand cone requires data on the delivered price with increasing distance from the market (the price funnel) and the quantity bought at each price (the demand schedule). Delivered price at each distance band is then translated into demand at each distance band. The maximum market area in the absence of competition (called the *range of the good*) is set by the radius at which demand falls to zero. It is important to understand that the table, graph, demand cone, and map are four equivalent ways of presenting the same information. Compare this figure with Figure 6.5.

TABLE 6.4
Variation in expenditures by income level

Annual family income	Coffee (lb)	Soft drinks (number)	Alcoholic beverages (dollars)	Clothing Men's (dollars per person)	Clothing Women's (dollars per person)	Dried beans (lb)
			Weekly expenditure			
Under $2,000	0.67	1.67	$0.06	$1.25	$1.42	1.00
2,000–2,999	0.74	2.64	0.12	1.55	2.10	0.69
3,000–3,999	0.82	3.19	0.12	2.13	3.00	0.62
4,000–4,999	0.88	3.23	0.23	2.68	3.20	0.52
5,000–5,999	0.89	3.49	0.39	2.72	3.27	0.72
6,000–7,999	0.94	3.58	0.42	3.21	4.05	0.61
8,000–9,999	0.97	4.23	0.60	4.38	5.15	0.11
10,000 and over	1.02	5.17	1.83	6.70	11.00	0.43

Sources: Data on foods and beverages from U.S. Department of Agriculture, *Household Food Consumption Survey, 1955.* Clothing data adapted from U.S. Bureau of Labor Statistics, *Clothing the Urban American Family: How Much for Whom?* BLS Report 238-16, January 1968. From Daniel B. Suits, *Principles of Economics* (New York: Harper & Row, 1970), p. 290. Copyright © by Daniel B. Suits. Reprinted by permission of Harper & Row, Publishers, Inc.

tours at $1000-thingamabob intervals can be drawn with a spot height of 5000 at the central market itself. The table, graph, demand cone, and map are equivalent. They all show the same information, but in different forms.

Incomes and Demand

Demand for most goods is sensitive to income. Purchases of many items increase with higher income. Exceptions are food stuffs such as dried beans, which are cheap but take time and trouble to prepare (Table 6.4), and which are replaced by more convenient substitutes as incomes rise. These exceptions are called *inferior goods*. By contrast, expenditures on luxury items such as women's clothing increase very rapidly as income increases.

The sensitivity of consumers to price changes for any good also differs with income level. It is believed that, in general, lower-income families are more sensitive to price than higher-income families. Demand curves can, therefore, be drawn according to income. An example using our familiar "thingamabobs" is provided by Figure 6.13. In this example, the demand curve for low-income families, D_L, has a greater elasticity than that for high-income families, D_H. The total demand curve is formed by adding up the quantities demanded at each price by high- and low-income families.

FIGURE 6.13 Income level and market demand. Aggregate demand schedules, such as those presented in Figures 6.1 and 6.2, ignore differences in income level among consumers. Disaggregating the schedule for low- and high-income areas reveals in this hypothetical example that low-income areas are more sensitive to price. They stand to gain most with any fall in price (as in Figure 6.2), but conversely to suffer most with any increase in price. Note that the market equilibrium remains at *E* as in Figure 6.3 with the low-income area purchasing 1200 and the high-income area 1800 thingamabobs, to make a total of 3000 as before.

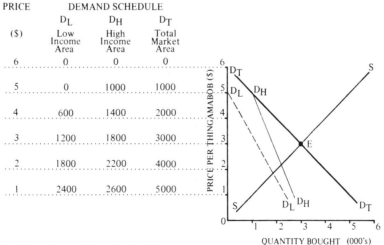

PRICE ($)	DEMAND SCHEDULE D_L Low Income Area	D_H High Income Area	D_T Total Market Area
6	0	0	0
5	0	1000	1000
4	600	1400	2000
3	1200	1800	3000
2	1800	2200	4000
1	2400	2600	5000

D_T D_T Demand Curve for Total Area
D_H D_H Demand Curve for High Income Area
D_L D_L Demand Curve for Low Income Area
S S Supply Curve
E Market Equilibrium Price

Demand cones can therefore be constructed that are sensitive to the special characteristics of each part of a market area. Suppose the market for thingamabobs is divided into high- and low-income sectors. The demand cone is steeper and the market area smaller in the low-income sector. (Figure 6.14). This example demonstrates the general principle that the higher the income-level is, the farther out the market area can extend.

Spatial Market Equilibrium

The balancing of supply and demand in the economic textbook case depicted in Figure 6.3 is a straightforward

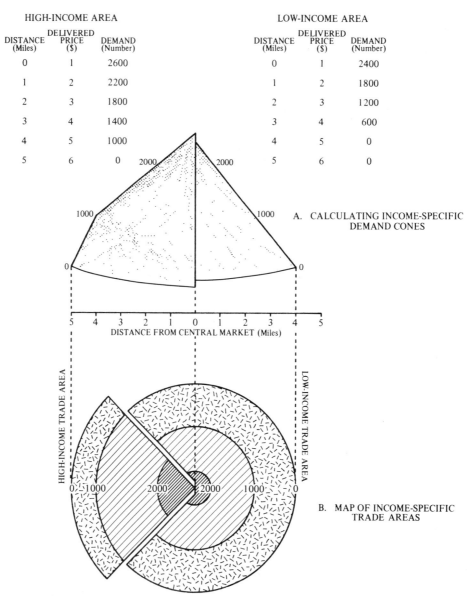

HIGH-INCOME AREA

DISTANCE (Miles)	DELIVERED PRICE ($)	DEMAND (Number)
0	1	2600
1	2	2200
2	3	1800
3	4	1400
4	5	1000
5	6	0

LOW-INCOME AREA

DISTANCE (Miles)	DELIVERED PRICE ($)	DEMAND (Number)
0	1	2400
1	2	1800
2	3	1200
3	4	600
4	5	0
5	6	0

A. CALCULATING INCOME-SPECIFIC DEMAND CONES

B. MAP OF INCOME-SPECIFIC TRADE AREAS

FIGURE 6.14 The demand cone for high- and low-income market areas. The demand schedules differ between high- and low-income areas (Figure 6.13). Therefore the demand cone will be different for high- and low-income areas. The trade area is larger for the high-income area and smaller for the low-income area. Aggregate demand for a good within any given distance-band of the central market equals the sum of the demand in the high- and low-income areas shown separately in this figure. The market boundaries occur at the price where demand falls to zero.

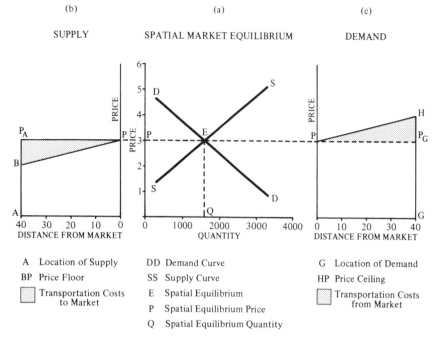

(b)   (a)   (c)

SUPPLY   SPATIAL MARKET EQUILIBRIUM   DEMAND

FIGURE 6.15 Spatial market equilibrium: simple case. Under perfect competition, buyers and sellers are price-takers. The equilibrium price is set by the equation of demand and supply at the market. Suppliers receive this price minus transportation. Buyers pay this price plus transportation. There is not, however, a one-way determinism of price at the marketplace without regard to transportation costs. Instead, the spatial market equilibrium price reflects the transportation costs of buyers and sellers as a whole, as well as setting their individual price ceilings and price floors.

A   Location of Supply
BP   Price Floor
▨   Transportation Costs to Market

DD   Demand Curve
SS   Supply Curve
E   Spatial Equilibrium
P   Spatial Equilibrium Price
Q   Spatial Equilibrium Quantity

G   Location of Demand
HP   Price Ceiling
▨   Transportation Costs from Market

exercise. The supply and demand curves are drawn back-to-back and the equilibrium price and quantities indicated by the point of intersection. This exercise is repeated every day in central markets throughout the world (Figure 6.15a). Suppliers can expect to receive, at the minimum, central market price *less* transportation costs (Figure 6.15b). Consumers can expect to pay, at the maximum, central market price *plus* transportation costs (Figure 6.15c).

The total supply and demand curves at the central market (Figure 6.15a) are, however, an amalgam of many individual supply and demand curves. If you wish to understand how a combined supply curve is derived, refer to Figure 6.16. Suppose there is a central market at *M*. In the manner of Figure 6.15a the right-hand side of the graph in Figure 6.16 shows how the combined supply curve of two producers is derived at the central market. The producers are shown at *A* and *B* on the left-hand side of the graph (Figure 6.16), which corresponds to Figure 6.15b. The problem is one of combining the two producers' individual supply curves, taking into account transportation costs. This process is described in the caption accompanying Figure 6.16.

MANAGED PRICES IN IMPERFECTLY COMPETITIVE SITUATIONS

The foregoing discussion refers to free-enterprise dynamics. But what about less-competitive situations? A market is imperfectly competitive when the actions of

individual buyers or sellers can affect the equilibrium price. Such individuals are not "price-takers" forced to accept the price collectively determined by the free play of market forces. On the contrary, in the extreme case just one or two sellers or buyers set the market price themselves.

A situation of *monopoly* exists where a single *seller* sets the selling price, and a situation of *oligopoly* exists where relatively *few sellers* determine the price. This may be the case where a large proportion of total output of some product is accounted for by just one, or a few, manufacturing firms. *Monopsony* is where a *single buyer* dominates the market for the product and so dictates the purchase price. *Oligopsony* is where a *few buyers* dominate. A firm may be both monopsonist and monopolist. It may dominate the market for some raw materials, or components, hence setting the purchase price for them. It may also dominate the market for the finished product and so set the selling price. An automobile manufacturer, for instance, may dictate the price to parts manufacturers at which components such as tires will be bought, and, as a price leader, the price at which cars will be sold on the market. Or one large firm acting as a monopsonist may *countervail* the power of another large firm, as where a retail chain accounts for a large proportion of sales of household appliances and is thus able to bid down the manufacturer's price of these items.

In conditions of imperfect competition the industry may follow a price leader, or engage in price collusion or in other discriminatory practices. Smaller firms with a local market must follow the price lead set by a

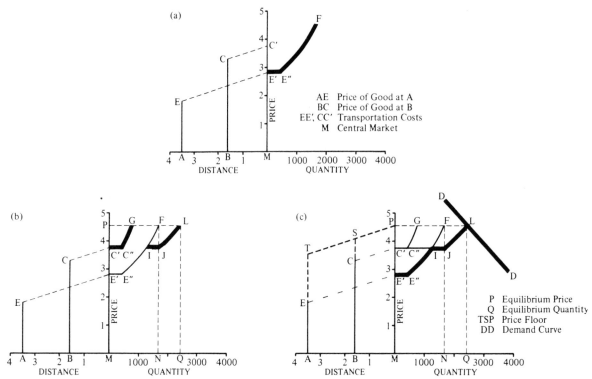

FIGURE 6.16   Spatial market equilibrium: a more complex case. The spatial market equilibrium price must take into account transportation costs of all suppliers and consumers as a whole. To simplify, imagine there are just two producers, at *A* and *B*, respectively. The local price at which *A* is able to start production is *AE*. At *B* it is *BC*. Notice that although *A* is more distant from the market, it can supply *M* more cheaply (*ME'* rather than *MC'*).

As price increases above *ME'* and *MC'* , each supplier will be willing to produce and ship more to the market. Assume that the supply curve for producer is *E'E"F* (in [a].) (This takes into account transport costs from *A* to *M,* at *A,* the supply curve would be lower because no transportation costs need be added in at the point of supply.) As the price at *M* increases, a level will be reached at which *B* becomes willing to supply the market, in competition with *A.* That price is *C'.*

Once the price at *M* exceeds *C'* , *B* begins to supply the market. *B*'s supply curve is shown in (b) by the upward-sloping line *C'C"G.* Since both *A* and *B* supply the market at prices above *C'* , their *combined supply curve* in the market has to be derived. This is *EE" IJL* and it is formed by adding *B*'s supply curve *C'C"G* to *A*'s supply curve *E'E"F* horizontally, to show the total amount the two producers are willing to supply at each price level. *EE" IJL* is the combined supply curve.

The combined demand curve in the market is *DD* (*note: DD* can be derived in a manner analogous to the foregoing). The point of equilibrium is *L.* The resulting market price is *MP.* The total quantity *MQ* will be supplied. *PST* is the local producer's price floor. At the price *MP, A* supplies the quantity *MN* (given by the intersection of *A*'s supply curve *E'E"F* and *PL*) and *B* supplies the balance, *NQ.*

dominant firm with a national market. To do otherwise would be to invite lethal retaliation, because the large firm can wipe out local competition by undercutting prices in that local area. Large firms in competition with each other realize they must restrain competition or be ruined by it. But whatever the precise circumstances, the general objectives are always the same, namely, to maximize returns either by manipulating the firm's sale price or negotiating its purchasing prices, and to stabilize the prices and volumes of goods bought or sold.

The Basing-Point System

The most common form of noncompetitive pricing is the *basing-point system*. Consumers pay a price set at a given place, the *basing-point*, plus a transportation charge from that location—even if the good is produced and shipped from a nearer and lower-cost site. The purpose of the basing-point system is, of course, to entrench the advantages of the site selected as the basing point, and the producers whose facilities are concentrated there.

An example may be used to clarify the details of basing-point pricing. We have selected the British cement industry as described in a study by A. Moyes (1980). Prices are administered by the Cement Maker's Federation (CMF), an industry association to which all producers of any consequence belong. The price at the nominated basing-points varied in March 1978, from £ 22.51 to £ 26.90 per ton, reflecting to some degree differences in production costs. Delivery charges were added to the basing-point using a standard formula based on 5-mile steps. The first four steps cost 20.7 pence each. The next three cost 18.1 pence, after which all steps cost 12.9 pence each. The result was a regular concentric pattern of delivered prices radiating out from each basing point (Figure 6.17).

These results look very similar to the base-point pricing of central markets discussed in the previous section. The two should not be confused, however. They differ significantly in the way in which prices are set. In

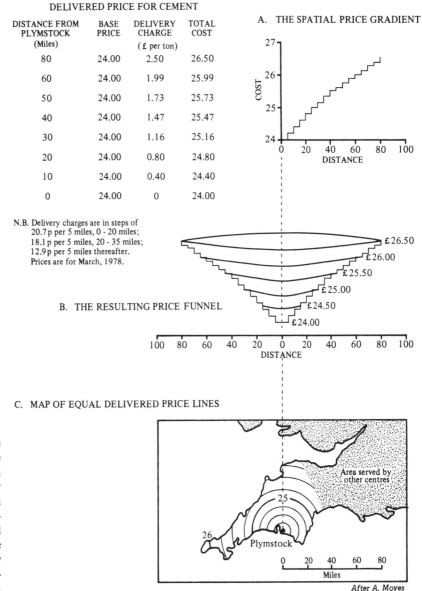

DELIVERED PRICE FOR CEMENT

DISTANCE FROM PLYMSTOCK (Miles)	BASE PRICE	DELIVERY CHARGE (£ per ton)	TOTAL COST
80	24.00	2.50	26.50
60	24.00	1.99	25.99
50	24.00	1.73	25.73
40	24.00	1.47	25.47
30	24.00	1.16	25.16
20	24.00	0.80	24.80
10	24.00	0.40	24.40
0	24.00	0	24.00

N.B. Delivery charges are in steps of 20.7p per 5 miles, 0 - 20 miles; 18.1p per 5 miles, 20 - 35 miles; 12.9p per 5 miles thereafter. Prices are for March, 1978.

A. THE SPATIAL PRICE GRADIENT

B. THE RESULTING PRICE FUNNEL

C. MAP OF EQUAL DELIVERED PRICE LINES

FIGURE 6.17 The delivered price of cement in southwest England. The price of cement was £24 a ton in Plymstock in March 1978. Delivery charges were based on distance from Plymstock. The result was the regular concentric pattern of delivered prices shown in the map. For more details see: A. Moyes, "Can Spatially Variable Prices Ever Be 'Fair'?," *Regional Studies,* Vol. 14, 1980, 37–53.

After A. Moyes

basing-point systems the price level at the basing point, the transportation cost schedule, and the number of basing points are all preset by the industry. With the free-enterprise base-point system, these three elements of delivered cost—the price level at the central market, freight rates, and the number of central markets—are all determined by the free play of supply and demand.

Industry-determined basing-point price systems were used as early as 1880 in the United States, but they did not come into widespread use until after 1901, when such a system was applied to steel by the U.S. Steel Corporation.

The U.S. Steel scheme was known as "Pittsburgh plus." Under it, delivered prices for steel and steel products were quoted throughout the United States as the sum of a basing-point price at Pittsburgh plus a transportation charge from Pittsburgh, regardless of the actual plant price or freight costs incurred from the actual producing point. Nearer or lower-cost plants, which could actually deliver at lower cost than Pittsburgh plus, thus were able to earn extra profits. These profits were called "phantom freights" (Figure 6.18). The overall effect was to raise prices, reduce demand, and protect U.S. Steel's Pittsburgh investments.

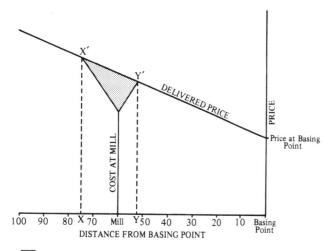

■ Phantom Freight

XY   Distance from Basing Point over which Delivered Cost from Mill is less than Quoted Delivered Price.

FIGURE 6.18 Phantom freight with basing-point pricing. Under the basing-point price system, customers pay price at basing point plus transportation costs from that point. A local mill may not undercut basing-point price structure. Its delivered price is boosted to the basing-point price level, yielding it a "phantom freight." The phantom freight negates any locational advantage of the mill. Thus, the market area *XY* is shared between the local mill and mills at the basing point. Under FOB pricing, the local mill at *M* could expect to dominate the market area *XY*.

Soon after the adoption of the basing-point plan by the steel industry, the practice was extended to the cement industry. Then, after 1912, the single basing-point practice spread rapidly to a variety of other industries; for example, cast-iron pipe, glucose, malt, maple flooring, welded chain, zinc, lead ("St. Louis plus"), and copper ("Connecticut Valley plus"). The practice became worldwide. In Russia, for example, before the communist revolution, steel was priced according to a "Chelyabinsk plus" basing-point system.

In some industries multiple basing points were established. The principle is the same, except that two or more producing centers are quoted as bases, and the market was divided among them according to base-price-plus-freight charges. Some of the industries adopting multiple basing points have been iron and steel (in 1924, following U.S. government antitrust action declaring a single basing point illegal), cement, hardwood lumber, gasoline, sugar, chemical fertilizers, milk and ice cream cans, asphalt roofing material, small-arms ammunition, corn products, gypsum products, hard-surface floor coverings, linseed oil, rigid steel conduit, firebrick, lubricating oil, and plate glass.

An example of basing-point pricing on the international scale is provided by petroleum (Melamid, 1962). The United States was the largest petroleum exporter at the turn of the century and its major producers set world prices on a "Gulf-plus" system. Delivered prices anywhere in the world equaled the price at the Gulf of Mexico plus transportation costs, regardless of the origin of the oil. Iranian oil shipped to the United Kingdom was priced at the U.S. Gulf price plus transportation rates from the Gulf of Mexico to the United Kingdom. Today, the world petroleum price is set by OPEC on the basis of Saudi Arabian light crudes at Dhahran, on the Persian Gulf, plus transportation.

Uniform Pricing

Under basing-point systems, consumers may be quoted prices FOB (free on board), meaning they pay the basing-point price and whatever they can arrange for transportation charges, or CIF (cost, insurance, and freight), in which case the supplier guarantees the delivered price at the consumer's location.

Another form of price quotation is *uniform pricing*, according to which suppliers quote consumers the same delivered price regardless of location. Such pricing is much more common than is generally realized. A number of good reasons exist for its use. Transportation costs are often a very small fraction of total delivered price, and improvements in transportation make the scheme more logical (see Figure 6.19). Uniform pricing is also sensible when a commodity is moved in very small

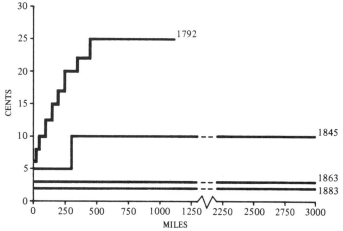

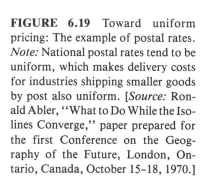

FIGURE 6.19 Toward uniform pricing: The example of postal rates. *Note:* National postal rates tend to be uniform, which makes delivery costs for industries shipping smaller goods by post also uniform. [*Source:* Ronald Abler, "What to Do While the Isolines Converge," paper prepared for the first Conference on the Geography of the Future, London, Ontario, Canada, October 15–18, 1970.]

quantities to a large number of places, if transportation costs themselves vary little or not at all with distance, and if the administrative costs of determining the proper transportation charges are high.

Uniform pricing may also be used to extend the market area. Customers near the plant are charged more than FOB prices to subsidize customers beyond the FOB market area. Industries sometimes argue that advertising campaigns are more effective where a uniform price can be quoted, and that the additional sales achieved permit economies of scale. The practice is widespread in, for example, the United Kingdom, even in cases where transportation costs are substantial. British Oxygen, which accounts for virtually all oxygen and acetylene sales in the United Kingdom, charges uniform prices even though transportation costs average one-fourth of total delivered price. Studies have shown that the practice is becoming more widespread, especially as improvements in transportation and communications reduce the share of delivered price accounted for by these factors.

PRICE REGULATION BY GOVERNMENT

Regulation by Western Governments

Strengthening Perfect Competition

Governments as well as industry associations try to influence prices. Western governments intervene in the marketplace under two opposite circumstances: (1) to strengthen the free play of market forces where free-enterprise is considered beneficial, if the prices resulting from perfect competition are appropriate; and (2) to modify the ordinary price mechanism where perfect competition is deemed inappropriate. The result of the latter intervention has been a growing body of govern-

ment regulations that may have the detrimental side effects of adding significantly to the cost of doing business and weakening the effectiveness of market signals. The goals of all these regulations are often summarized in broad policy objectives such as encouraging economic growth, stabilizing prices, increasing productivity, and guaranteeing social welfare. But virtually all government regulation explicitly or indirectly affects the supply and demand for goods and the prices at which they trade as well as the size and even the location of supply and market areas.

Governments strengthen market forces by three sets of policies. First, all Western governments are concerned with the degree of concentration of production or purchasing of goods, and the danger of price-fixing (as in basing-point systems) that may result. Where there is sufficient evidence of price-fixing, governments may seize company documents and initiate legal proceedings against the companies involved.

Second, governments strengthen the competitive market mechanism by increasing market information. Labor exchanges provide both employed and unemployed persons with job information. A wide array of information is made available to industrialists, ranging from technical, to general management, to trade information. One function of census-type surveys is to provide information on labor and markets that can be used to improve the working of the economy.

Third, special attention is given by governments to ease adjustment to secular (long-run) change. Industry may be locked into obsolete technology, regions overreliant on declining industries, and workers immobilized in declining regions. Government may offer industry investment incentives to retool. Research and development incentives are also sometimes available. Labor-retraining programs and relocation benefits may be introduced. Rural land-use programs may be developed where farmers have locked into inefficient practices.

Such programs are intended to substitute long-run gain for short-term pain.

In each of the above cases, the objective of government intervention is to bring market prices closer to what they would be under perfect competition, free from oligopoly and oligopsony, and to ensure more perfect knowledge and an economy that adjusts freely to market changes. Such government intervention strengthens the working of the price system as a mechanism for regulating production and exchange.

Economic Problems with Market Prices

Governments may, however, want to modify the free play of market forces where these fail for reasons that are economic, social, or regional. Economic issues arise: in pricing goods with a high social cost; in paying for collective goods; where maintaining quality takes priority over minimizing price; and in countervailing seasonal and cyclical fluctuations for particular commodities or for the economy generally. Governments find that free-market prices are undesirable under these circumstances.

The clearest case is where producers can pass some production costs onto society. One example is what Hardin calls the "tragedy of the commons" (Chapter 1). The market price does not include the costs of industrial pollution or resource depletion. Government may then regulate pollution levels or set production levels, or it may tax the industry to recover part or all of the social costs involved. A particular problem arises in transportation. Subsidies for public transportation are justified because road and fuel taxes may fail to recover the full social cost of private travel to work. Similarly, subsidies for rail haulage are justified because rail companies must build and maintain their own lines, whereas road haulage companies do not. In each case, the concern is that optimizing on the basis of private plus social costs may lead to different decisions and prices than optimizing on the basis of private costs alone.

Some goods are collective and are not purchased in individual market actions. Examples are national defense forces, police and fire protection, meteorological services, city parks, and the cost of government itself. The cost of collective goods cannot be recovered effectively on a "user" basis. Thus, governments are elected in part on the level of such services that they promise to provide and they pay for them by taxes and public borrowing. The cost of these services to the individual is based on ability to pay (where taxes are progressive, that is, increase with income) and not on use or need. The price is determined by the level and quality of the service set by government policy.

Government also establishes the quality of service and regulates price when consumers cannot be expected to judge quality of service for themselves, as in the case of goods and services for which minimum standards are essential for consumer protection. Many regulations come under this third category, whether government-imposed or industry-controlled: fire protection, building codes and zoning ordinances; regulations controlling foods and drugs; transportation services and equipment, whether automobiles, airlines or ships; professional services and trades, whether medical, legal, insurance, electrical, or plumbing.

The fourth economic circumstance where free-market prices are considered inappropriate is where there are serious fluctuations in supply or demand, with concomitant fluctuations in price. To stabilize welfare in face of recessions or booms, the government may, for example, set minimum prices for farm products and store surpluses. Countercyclical measures also may be taken: These include *fiscal*, as when tax rates are reduced to stimulate demand, or *monetary*, as when interest rates are raised to curb excessive demand and to relieve inflationary pressures.

Social Needs versus Economic Efficiency

In certain cases governments may conclude that the ordinary price mechanisms are inappropriate because they put economic efficiency above social need. Governments identify three broad cases of such social priority: the provision of minimum living standards and of social security; the distribution of benefits and responsibilities; and the maintenance of cultural levels. As Western countries industrialized, they found that the existing mutual-aid schemes failed to meet the needs of urban, industrial workers. Five basic sets of welfare policies were introduced in country after country, and generally in this order: for (1) injury related to employment; (2) sickness and maternity; (3) old age; (4) unemployment; and (5) family income supplements. Governments have added regulations on working conditions, housing, education, and health and welfare, all of which affect the supply and cost of labor. Location decisions in the case of labor-intensive industry may well be influenced by the level and cost of such regulations in regions competing for the industry.

Social equity may also override market considerations where goods are in short supply. In times of war, particularly, governments and the public are not prepared to accept the allocation of food and other supplies on the basis of the ability to pay. A rationing system then is used to hold prices below their free-market level and to allocate supplies equitably, without regard to income. Duties such as military service are parcelled out on the basis of ability, and individuals are not permitted to buy out. At such times even the most free-enterprise country is prepared to abandon the very economic principles on which its society is based and argue instead, "from each, according to one's abilities; to each, according to one's needs."

Governments also feel a need to support cultural activities that could not survive the rule of the market place. The young writer seeking the wherewithall to write her first novel, the symphony orchestra that has established an international reputation, and live theater groups are all dependent on public funding to some extent. They give artistic expression to the sentiments of a nation and add to its culture and traditions in ways that cannot be measured in the market place. In such cases, it is agreed that support should be based on excellence and not commercial viability.

Regional Goals

Finally, the free play of market forces may be incompatible with the desires of Western governments for balanced regional growth and development. This set of goals may take three forms. Initially, in the case of New World countries, the concern may be with the spread of settlement and the development of resources across the entire national territory. Governments are sensitive to the dangers of large empty tracts of national territory and historically have encouraged immigration, settlement, and the building of railways. We saw in Chapter 2 how Griffith Taylor got into trouble with the Australian government over the settlement potential of the outback by returning World War I veterans. Canada is very sensitive about the presence of any foreigners in its Arctic regions and concerned that oil and gas developments there involve a much higher degree of Canadian ownership and control than in previous Canadian oil developments.

More recently, governments in all Western countries have become concerned with the problems of lagging or depressed regions. Until the 1930s or even later, governments believed that if they maintained strong national economic performance, then the regions would be able to take care of themselves. The reality of severe and persistent regional disparities forced a change in this attitude and the adoption of policies, often tied to the location of manufacturing activity, to diminish regional disparities. As with social policies, the argument is one of equity, not efficiency.

In other cases, governments are concerned with locational aspects because of the nature of the specific activity. In wartime, governments may give higher priority to security than to economic efficiency in the location of industry. In peacetime, the recreation needs of the population may dictate the setting aside of lands for park use that may have a much higher economic value as industrial or commercial land. Beaches, cross-country ski trails, camping grounds, and adventure playgrounds are all established by government on the basis of geographic supply and demand rather than economic laws. Governments are finding that they must be even more sensitive to location issues when dealing with hazardous or potentially hazardous activities. The location of nuclear power stations close to, and upwind from, large urban concentrations is hard to justify on grounds of cost efficiency. The regulation and control of the dumping of industrial waste products is another example where safety must be given precedence over convenience and cost.

Augmented Government Impact

The impact of government regulations on the economy and its regions is augmented by direct involvement of governments in the economy. Three measures of this direct involvement are the amount of spending by all levels of government in a country; the percentage of labor force employed in the civil service; and the surface area of the national territory owned by government. Usually the first measure is employed, with government spending quoted as a percentage of gross national product or of total consumption expenditures. Western governments usually account for about a fifth of consumption expenditures and about a quarter to a third of gross national expenditures. Shifts in government expenditure patterns can therefore have a very significant impact on the economies of the regions affected, and indeed on the national economy as a whole.

The direct impact of government is further augmented and complicated where industries are owned by the government. Such industries are generally considered to make some special contribution to the nation, over and above their direct economic worth. Hence, their survival may not depend entirely on profitability as in private enterprise. In the United Kingdom, for example, most nationalized industries, including steel, ship building, automobiles, and rail transportation, have lost great sums of money, notwithstanding heavy government investment, and would not have survived on their present scale without the umbrella of government ownership coupled with heavy subsidies.

Diminished Effectiveness

Both public and governmental attitudes on the effectiveness of government regulation of the economy underwent rapid change in the 1970s. Theoretical analysis and actual experience suggest that government regulation is far less effective than was previously thought. Far from correcting economic failures in the marketplace, government regulations can suffer their own failures. Far from achieving a wide range of economic, social, and regional goals, these goals can sometimes conflict with each other and policies can sometimes prove countervailing rather than reinforcing. And far from improving the working of the economy, government regulations can sometimes run into jurisdictional and administrative problems, consume resources, and sap enterprise.

The economic failures of government regulations are drawing increasing attention. The basic economic problem is that government regulations to control price inevitably affect quantity or quality, and regulations to control quantity or quality affect price. Economists have discovered that such regulations create a *transitory-gain trap*. The regulations create advantages or disadvantages that are quickly identified and capitalized. The advantages (or disadvantages) are temporary or "transitory." Three examples, taxi regulation, housing policy, and transportation regulation, illustrate how this trap undermines government efforts to achieve economic, social, and regional goals in cases where free competition was considered inappropriate.

In many cities, local governments regulate the taxi business and limit the number of taxis by use of permits or medallions, to protect users and provide some security for drivers. But the number of permits issued is usually below the competitive level, giving them a scarcity value. As a result, taxis can earn an extra income. That extra income can be converted into a capital value (based on current interest rates) or "capitalized." The price of a license is then equal to the city fee plus this capitalized value. The price varies from city to city depending on the level of undersupply. Thus, one study of the Canadian taxi industry found 1972 going prices of $18,000 in Toronto, and $30,000 in Vancouver. The extra profits accrued to the original holders of permits (often taxi companies). The taxi driver, burdened with the cost of renting a licensed vehicle, or of buying a license, may find it as hard or harder to earn a living than it was before the regulations were introduced. The advantage was indeed transitory. But to deregulate the business would cause unfair losses to those who paid high prices for permits in good faith that the regulations would remain in force. On the contrary in 1980, Montreal taxi drivers, misunderstanding the nature of the problem, complained that there were too many taxis to make a decent living, and wanted a reduction in the number of licenses granted.

The same fundamental supply relationship between price and quantity has triggered a transitory-gain trap in rent controls. Government attempts to help low-income families by imposing rent controls create increasing distortions in the marketplace. In the short run

the supply of rental housing is inelastic, although rent controls do reduce supply as apartments are converted into condominiums and sold, and as construction rates fall. The frequent market response to price controls where supply is inelastic is to allow quality to fall. Thus, profit levels can be redressed by postponing or eliminating customary maintenance. The demand for rental accommodation, however, can be expected to increase as rental controls make home ownership less attractive. In this case families must vie with one another for possession of apartments on grounds other than rent. These grounds may include paying key money, offering to buy or rent furniture from the owner at high prices, agreeing to paint the apartment or provide other work at no income, or at less than market wage, or simply waiting in a long queue with little hope of success. Where key money is the principal factor, the amount paid will be related to the capitalized value of the subsidy. It is thus equivalent to the medallion price paid by prospective taxi drivers.

The transitory-gains trap also afflicts regional policy, and has become a particularly contentious issue in the case of statutory grain rates in Canada. The development of western Canada after confederation of the British North American colonies in 1867 was based on a National Economic Policy of railway building, agricultural settlement, and tariff protection for industry. The railways were granted land rights and subsidies, but in return promised to accept government-imposed freight rates for wheat. These statutory rates, often called *Crow rates* after a pass through the Rocky Mountains used by the railways, are the same today as when they were first set at the turn of the century. A temporary increase imposed by the federal government during World War I was rolled back by order of the Supreme Court of Canada in 1925.

The result of Crow rates on wheat shipments is that it costs a farmer less to ship a bushel of wheat to Vancouver or Thunder Bay than to post a letter. Controlled prices have reduced the quality of service as the railways are understandably reluctant to invest in rolling stock or line maintenance for shipments that pay about a quarter of their real transportation costs. But farmers resist any attempt by the Canadian government to raise rail rates, even if new rates are coupled with major improvements in speed and quality of service.

The problem is that the price of farmland in the Canadian prairies is related to yield, to wheat prices at central markets, and to the costs of shipment to those central markets (formerly dominated by Liverpool, as we saw earlier). The value of the Crow rate has already been capitalized and included in the price of farmland. The subsidy has thus created a sort of "key money" that farmers have to pay to gain access to the land. If the freight rate for wheat is increased, the capital worth of farmers will be reduced, perhaps seriously. The failure of grain freight rates to keep in step with inflation created capital values that were captured primarily by the original farm owners. The gain was transitory and imposed the trap of increasing government subsidies to the railways and diminishing quality of service to the present farmers.

These examples of government regulations suffering market failures of their own are very specific, but the principle of the transitory-gains trap is very broad. It applies, and has geographic implications, whenever quotas are set on farm acreages for specific crops, or minimum prices are established for commodities. It applies when industries are subsidized with grants or special loans, or protected by tariffs. It applies within cities where development is regulated by zoning or other controls. And it applies as well to all regulation of transportation and of fuel charges. Regulations tend to create special profits that can be capitalized, sometimes by the owners of the resource, sometimes by labor and sometimes by a third party. The benefits cannot always be held by those intended to gain from the regulations. They can end up serving private interests rather than the common good.

Regulation in Socialist States

The economic theory and political objectives that govern prices in socialist states are quite different from those in Western countries, based as they are on pervasive government regulation. The economic principles, and even the definition of economics presented in this chapter, are not relevant to socialist economies. Recall how these "command" economies were described at the beginning of the chapter. Monolithic, authoritarian governmental systems are dominated by a single party. The state owns the means of production, operating nonagricultural industries, and in some socialist countries, agriculture too. There is centralized direction of the economy. In the classic socialist scheme, each industry is supposed to produce according to preset physical targets. Performance—at least until the late 1960s—was measured by output rather than sales, which meant that commodity movements were managed through rationing systems rather than the interplay of demand and supply. Prices have played little, if any, role in economic management. Finally, socialist economies have been geared to ensuring rapid growth above all else.

The Example of Czechoslovakia

For example, when the communist regime came to power in Czechoslovakia, the economic system of that country was reshaped to conform to that of the USSR. Czechoslovakia adopted a program of expanding production along the entire spectrum of raw materials, metals, and heavy equipment, often at the expense of the high-value precision machinery that had been the mainstay of prewar Czechoslovakia's foreign trade.

Enforcement of these investment decisions required a hugh party-controlled bureaucracy. The bureaucrats devised economic plans, determined the allocation of resources, set production quotas, fixed prices on 1,500,000 different categories of goods, decreed their distribution, and conducted all foreign trade.

Ota Sik, who played a leading role in this design, and who fled to the West after the abortive attempt to liberalize Czechoslovakia in 1968, has commented that all the economic problems that arose in the country can be traced to the removal of prices as the "thermostat" controlling the economy. The central role of market prices is too little appreciated, even in the United States, among business interests who thoroughly understand the central function of prices in the operation of their own enterprises. As Sik states,

> The situation is beyond the control of the best manager, planners, and government departments. Involving, as it does, such a multitude of contradictory processes, no planning mechanism even with the aid of the most sophisticated computers, can possibly function successfully. It has been demonstrated that, despite its deficiencies, the market mechanism is the sole medium capable of dealing with the complex interrelationships in a modern industrial economy.[2]

Destruction of the market-price mechanism had a devastating effect on the Czech economy. Planners fixed prices on the basis of their notions of social utility, and in some cases this resulted in heavy losses for producers—or would have, if anyone had been keeping accurate accounts. And industrial managers, judged solely on their ability to meet production quotas, churned out great quantities of goods so shoddy that they could not be sold even at subsidized prices. In 1967, Sik says, Czech warehouses were bulging with many billions of dollars worth of unsold goods.

Even worse, over the long run, elimination of market prices left the planners without any sound way of determining where to invest the country's resources. Funds were poured into new factories—often in low-profit, low-technology industries—and huge construction projects. Little or nothing was devoted to modernization of existing plants.

[2]Ota Sik, *Czechoslovakia: The Bureaucratic Economy* (White Plains, N.Y.: International Arts and Science Press Inc., 1972), p. 11.

Soviet Pricing Schemes

To repeat, in free-enterprise economies, prices limit demand for each product to available supplies. But in socialist countries, following the lead of the USSR, prices have been set differently. In the USSR, apart from collective farm markets, foodstuffs and manufactured goods are made available to the consumers entirely through publicly or cooperatively owned retail shops. In these shops, the actual prices charged are determined directly by the all-union Council of Ministers, or executive agencies working on its behalf, usually as a fixed markup over wholesale prices, which are also dictated.

In general, these "official" or "administered" prices have not been set at clearing levels. Rather, for some commodities they have resulted in rapid buildups of unsold inventories, while for others they are so low that persistent shortages exist and many demands go unmet.

The reason for these divergences is that the Soviets have tended to relate prices ultimately to production costs and to some concept of "social value" rather than to the interplay of demand and supply. In the case of manufactured goods, for example, retail prices are ultimately related to the pricing of labor and of industrial materials, taking into account standard markups, and a turnover tax that varies between commodities to reflect social desirability. Industrial materials are, in turn, priced so that the return equals the average production cost plus a limited planned profit. Because average costs change with the scale of output, this pricing policy has the effect of ultimately relating all prices back to the nature, scale, location and efficiency of production—all of which are set by the command structure of economic planning in the state. Demand plays no role whatsoever in price determination in this scheme.

Since the 1960s, Soviet economic planners have relied increasingly on methods of mathematical programming in order to provide ways of estimating more efficient relationships among planned targets, output levels, and commodity flows, as a substitute for the free market's prices. These methods produce what the Soviet planners call "objectively determined values" for products. Similar values are called by Western scholars "shadow prices" that, if charged, would ensure that the economic relationships that are sought are achieved. Such shadow prices can be calculated in ways that reflect both scarcity and productivity, and they would avoid some of the problems of shortages and surpluses that now exist in the USSR. However, because consumption targets have to be preset by the planners before the mathematical methods may be used, the prices still reflect only production-and-supply considerations. The free play of consumer preferences and demands that characterize Western societies play no role in determining the mix of things produced.

SUMMARY

Human beings regulate the exchange of goods and services that they require by mechanisms that are primarily social, economic, or political (Figure 6.20). *Social* mechanisms were dominant in the traditional small-scale economies before the Industrial Revolution. These economies were largely self-sufficient, either at the level of the household, the region (with *redistribution* among households), or a set of regions (with *reciprocity* between regions). Reciprocity involved trade, often disguised as gift-giving. The expansion of trade to include more goods shipped over greater distances was associated with the gradual emergence of *peasant economies*. Peasant economies are intermediate in nature. Necessities are home-produced and are distributed according to social custom. Surpluses and specialty goods are traded on economic principles.

Full-exchange, *free-enterprise economies* use price to regulate exchange. Goods command a *price* when they are both useful and scarce. The *market equilibrium price* attracts just enough output to meet demand and just enough buyers to clear the market of output. *Supply* and *demand* come into balance because they have opposite relationships to price. Supply increases with price; demand decreases. If supplies are short, the price tends to rise, augmenting supplies and cutting demand. The rate of response of supply and demand (or elasticity) varies for different goods, and for market conditions such as income levels and consumer and producer preferences.

Price, supply, and demand vary systematically across supply and market regions because of transportation costs. Prices increase outward from production or market centers generating *price funnels*. The price funnel is the consumer *price ceiling*. Consumers pay central market price plus transportation costs unless local producers can sell at lower prices. Demand drops, in step with price increases, producing corresponding *demand cones*. The outer limit of the market area is the base of the cone, where demand falls to zero. The *price floor* for producers is the central market price minus transportation costs. The limit of the central market supply area is where the price floor is too low to attract supplies. The spatial market equilibrium price brings aggregate demand and supply over the market and supply areas into balance. The economic principles and resulting geographies can be severely distorted, however, in conditions of imperfect competition. Producers

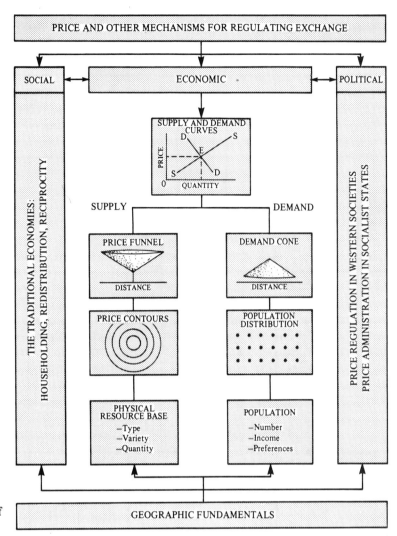

FIGURE 6.20 The geography of price: A synthesis.

or consumers can distort prices at a market and across its region using basing-point price systems or uniform pricing.

Government regulation of free-enterprise economies has risen sharply since the 1930s, either to strengthen the competition or, conversely, to modify it, as deemed appropriate. Some regulations have explicit regional goals, such as diminishing income disparities and high unemployment in lagging regions. All other policies, though not explicitly regional, have regional impacts, because of the regional concentrations of the target commodity or population of any policy.

Government regulation of the economy, intended to correct failures in the pricing mechanism, falls victim to failures of its own. Prominent among these is the *transitory-gains trap*. All regulations give advantage to some group at the expense of others. Often, that advantage can be converted into a value capitalized by some group. This group is not necessarily the group in-

tended to benefit from the legislation. Examples are premium prices paid for taxi medallions, apartment key money, inflated land values. Regulations then become entrenched in the price system.

Political administration of the economy reaches. its extreme in socialist countries. In principle, socialist economies have no private ownership or profit. The economic principles applying under perfect competition are irrelevant. Prices are set by a central authority on the basis of some assumed average costs, without taking demand or market equilibrium into account. The emphasis is on the achieving of production levels set by planners rather than satisfying the demands expressed by consumers.

No comparative assessment of various mechanisms of regulating exchange can be offered. Different mechanisms reflect different goals. Traditional societies were not oriented to growth, producing only what was needed. Chayanov's rule applied: the greater the productivity, the less the hours worked. Western and socialist countries do place a high premium on economic growth, among other goals, but differ fundamentally in how they price and distribute goods. They consequently differ in how they measure the total value of goods and services (or gross national product). Any comprehensive comparison of economic versus social or political regulation of economies would need to take account of the actual performance of particular countries. But actual economic performance may depend as much or more on geographic fundamentals and the human and physical resources on which the economy must be structured as on how the economy is regulated. Furthermore, no country follows the dictates of theory without modification. Socialist societies have some free enterprise, are granting some autonomy to factory management, and introducing some Western microeconomic principles into their planning. Western countries have varying degrees of public ownership, provide social welfare benefits, and engage in national and regional planning. But the differences between Western and socialist countries remain fundamental, for society selects the theories that suit its self-image and its goals, but is then molded by the theories. The theories then become embedded matters of belief rather than open questions for debate.

TOPICS FOR DISCUSSION

1. Plot the demand curve for a selected commodity. (You may use annual data on price and quantity in the U.S. Department of Agriculture (*Annual Statistics*). Is the demand relatively elastic (that is, greater than 1.0) or inelastic (less than 1.0)?

2. Draw a map of regional variations in price for some commodity. (One good data source is the table in Lösch, p. 487; see Further Readings.) What is the relationship between the spatial price pattern and centers of production?

3. Draw a graph showing the relationship between prices for beans and kerosene and distance from Kano, Nigeria, on the basis of the maps in Figure 6.21. How do spatial variations in price relate to areas of surplus and deficit?

4. The greater the costs of transportation, the less impor-

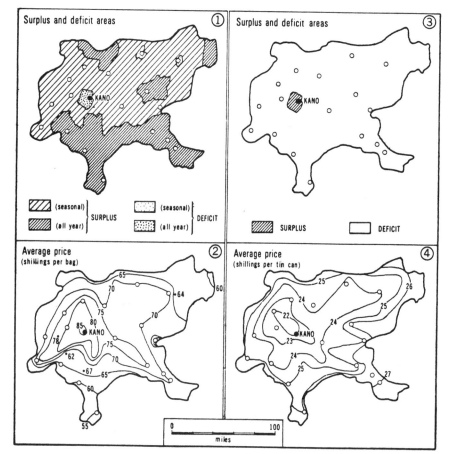

FIGURE 6.21

tant are differences in central market base prices in determining the boundaries of market areas. Demonstrate this assertion by redrawing the consumer price ceilings for central markets *B* and *C* in Figure 6.11 with slopes at 10°, 25°, 40°, and 55°. Note the location of the supply market boundary at each of these gradients.

5. Continue to test the assertion in Topic 4 by determining the boundaries of the supply areas for central markets *B* and *C* given producer price floors at slopes of 10°, 25°, and 55°, on the same diagram in Figure 6.11.

6. How low can transportation costs get before central market *C*, with its lower prices, loses all of its supply area to central market *B*? At this price, which central market loses its market area, *B* or *C*? Evidently a central market can attract supplies from a competing central market, paying higher prices, only if the transportation costs are greater than the price difference between them. What is the corresponding conclusion regarding the existence of separate market areas?

7. Assume that demand within the market area of central market *C* in Figures 6.9 and 6.11 increases. What happens to the price at *C*? How does this price change affect the supply and market areas? Now describe the reverse

process where there is a large surplus at central market *C*. How might this affect prices at central market *B*? Where central market prices are in spatial equilibrium are they then dependent of one another?

8. Explain how a price funnel results where a market is in spatial equilibrium, even when there are no formal central markets, as in milk. (You may wish to consult the map of optimum interregional dairy product movements in Bressler and King, p. 191, see Further Readings, as well as Figure 6.6).

9. Draw demand cones for two hypothetical goods that have very high and low elasticities, respectively. Assume that a very large area must be supplied with both goods. What is the approximate spacing needed for plants producing these goods, assuming FOB pricing? Why might a plant wish to use CIF pricing to market a good with high elasticity?

10. Describe the various mechanisms attempted in a POW camp to regulate exchange, including redistribution, reciprocity, bartering, and a price system. Why did the price system prove most effective? (See R.A. Radford, "The Economic Organization of a P.O.W. Camp," as cited in Further Readings.)

FURTHER READINGS

BRESSLER, RAYMOND G., and RICHARD A. KING. *Market, Prices, and Interregional Trade*. New York: John Wiley & Sons, 1970.

A description of economic development and regional specialization in the United States from colonial settlement to mid-twentieth century is provided (pp. 3–70), as an introduction to an advanced theoretical treatment.

CHISHOLM, MICHAEL. *Geography and Economics*. London: G. Bell & Sons, 1966.

Provides a key reading on the economic fundamentals of economic geography. For this chapter, see "Relations Between Geography and Economics," pp. 4–28, and "Pricing Policies," pp. 173–204.

GREENHUT, MELVIN L. "When Is the Demand Factor of Location Important?" *Land Economics*, 40 (1964), 175–184. Reprinted in *Locational Analysis for Manufacturing*, Gerald J. Karaska and David F. Bramtrall (Eds.). Cambridge, Mass.: MIT Press, 1969, pp. 339–348.

Greenhut has published extensively on location theory and the theory of spatial pricing, often at a very advanced level. This article presents a basic nonmathematical treatment of the three industrial pricing systems: CIF, FOB, and basing point.

GROSSMAN, GREGORY, *Economic Systems*. Englewood Cliffs, N.J.: Prentice-Hall, 1967.

A succinct statement of modern political-economic systems. A case study of the command economy of the USSR is included (pp. 73–97) together with a review of ideologies, including Marxism.

LÖSCH, AUGUST. *The Economics of Location* (Translated from the 2d revised edition by William H. Woglam). New Haven, Conn.: Yale University Press, 1954.

This great classic always makes rewarding reading. See particularly Chapter 26 on "Price Levels in Space," pp. 452–495, which demonstrates the continuing importance of regional differences in prices, notwithstanding reductions in freight rates and many cases of uniform pricing.

MELAMID, ALEXANDER. "Geography of the World Petroleum Price Structure," *Economic Geography*, October 1962, 283–298.

A most interesting account of the basing-point price system from before World War II (Gulf plus), and the changes made following World War II.

MOYES, A. "Can Spatially Variable Prices Ever be 'Fair'? Some Observations on the Price Commission's Judgments on British Cement Prices," *Regional Studies*, Vol. 14 (1980), 37–53.

Not only an excellent case study of the basing-point price system, but also an exemplary geographic analysis.

POLANYI, KARL. *The Great Transformation*. New York: Octagon Books, 1975.

An impressive and wide-ranging work of synthesis that emphasizes the social and economic changes wrought by the Industrial Revolution, and the fundamental differences between traditional and modern economies. See particularly Chapter 4, "Societies and Economic Systems," Chapter 5, "Evolution of the Market Pattern," and Chapter 6, "The Self-Regulating Market," pp. 43–76.

RADFORD, R. A. "The Economic Organization of a P.O.W. Camp," *Economica*, XII (1945). Reprinted in *Readings in Economics*, Paul A. Samuelson and others (Eds.). New York: McGraw-Hill, 1964, pp. 179–186.

As a prisoner of war in World War II, Radford saw in microcosm the emergence of a price system based on cigarettes. Samuelson notes that, "The very simplicity of the story he tells has made this article a minor classic in economics. To understand its full flavor is to know the world around us better."

REYNOLDS, LLOYD G. *The Three Worlds of Economics*. New Haven, Conn.: Yale University Press, 1971.

A very readable account of organization of capitalist, socialist, and less-developed economies, together with a review of economics itself and the question of theory and reality.

SUITS, DANIEL B. *Principles of Economics*. New York: Harper & Row, 1970.

An economics textbook makes a useful adjunct to these chapters on economic fundamentals. Suits is much better than most because he is an exception to the rule about the use of hypothetical data. His treatment of "Consumer Demand," pp. 276–300, is enlivened with many actual examples and provides a fuller treatment of the basic economic concepts introduced in this chapter.

WAGNER, PHILIP. *The Human Use of the Earth*. London: The Free Press of Glencoe, 1960.

This book is primarily concerned with the ecological expression of different cultures and social arrangements. Chapter 5, "The Economic Bond" (pp. 60–87), restates and develops Polanyi and presents a geography of economic forms. The themes of the text are summarized masterfully in Chapter 10, "A Geographic Outlook," pp. 228–237.

WARNTZ, W. *Toward a Geography of Price*. Philadelphia, University of Pennsylvania Press, 1959.

An innovative study of supply and demand in space and time, which links physics, economics, and geography. The concepts are illustrated with four crops (wheat, potatoes, onions, and strawberries) in the United States, 1940–1949.

ZIMMERMANN, ERICH W. *World Resources and Industries*. New York: Harper & Brothers, 1951.

This text popularized the economist view of resources among geographers.

CHAPTER 7

Costs and Output: Economies of Scale

Why do supply curves slope upward to the right? Why is it that in some manufacturing industries there are only a few plants serving large market areas, whereas in other industries many local markets each have their own producers, and in yet others many small producers cluster together and compete to serve wide market areas? These and related questions are the focus of this chapter, which probes the relationships of production costs to scale of output, and scale of output to industrial organization. An understanding of the basic principles is an essential foundation for reading Chapters 9, 10, and 11, on theories of location.

Objectives:

- to explain the reasons for increasing and decreasing returns to scale
- to differentiate between short-run and long-run cost curves
- to describe both internal and external economies of scale
- to analyze the relationship among scale, industrial concentration, and barriers to entry in oligopolies

WHY ARE ECONOMIES OF SCALE IMPORTANT?

The textbook picture of the way in which costs of production vary with scale of output is one in which average costs per unit of output initially fall with increasing production as economies of scale are achieved until some *minimum efficient size* (MES) is achieved. Unit costs of production are at a minimum at the MES. They may also rise if output expands beyond this point, although an important distinction must be drawn between the relationship of cost per unit to increasing scale of output in the short run and the long run. In the *short run,* capital investment is assumed to be fixed and greater output is achieved by using existing facilities more intensively. In the *long run,* firms may add new capital investments (machines, production lines, buildings) to achieve greater output levels. Increasing output in the short run generally results in diseconomies of scale above the MES; more is produced, but the cost per unit goes up. In the long run, changes in the capital stock may enable the firm to expand output without experiencing such scale diseconomies.

Why is it, then, that the classical supply curve slopes upward to the right? If firms are operating at or near the MES, and their selling prices are set accordingly, greater quantities will only be offered for sale if prices increase, because increased output results in greater unit costs. In addition, when prices are low only the most efficient producers can sell profitably. If prices rise, other facilities with a higher MES can be brought into production.

Why is it that some industries have only a few producing firms while others have many? This is because unit cost curves vary among industries, and there are wide resulting variations in the MES.

Why is it that some supply curves are quite elastic (that is, highly responsive to price shifts) whereas others are inelastic? Why is it that long-run supply responses are more elastic than short-run responses to price changes? The answers, again, are to be found in the shape of unit cost curves, and therefore in the nature of economies and diseconomies of scale (Figure 7.1).

Economies of scale are an important consideration in many kinds of governmental policy. One argument raised in favor of Britain joining the European Economic Community was the economies of scale in serving a larger market. Canada, more recently, carefully considered potential economies of scale offered by a larger population in the debate on immigration policy. Where there are "natural monopolies" (that is, where a market is most efficiently served by a single company, as in the case of a city served by a gas or electricity utility), governments may need to regulate the industry to

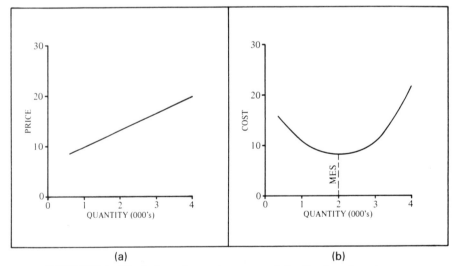

(a) (b)

FIGURE 7.1 The industry's supply curve and the firm's unit cost curve. (a) The supply curve. Supply curves such as were used in Chapter 6 show how industries respond to price changes by offering more or less goods. Higher prices are needed to cover the increased costs of additional output by existing firms, and to attract new producers into the field. (b) A unit cost curve. Unit cost curves show the relationship of production costs to scale of output. Initially, increasing output is accompanied by economies of scale, and unit costs fall to a minimum efficient size (MES)—in this case at an output level of 2000. Thereafter, costs per unit of output may rise if diseconomies of scale are incurred.

ensure that prices are fair and profits are not excessive. Economies of scale are important considerations both in a government's antitrust activities and in the evaluation of merger and takeover proposals where the likely consequence is greater concentration of corporate power.

The pervasive importance of the subject has stimulated a continuing flow of research with detailed studies of a wide range of industries and with instructive international comparisons. These studies have sought to *identify* the factors responsible for economies of scale, to *measure* the MES for various industries, and to *evaluate* the economic, geographic, and policy consequences that follow.

This chapter, therefore, begins by identifying the economies of scale that occur in manufacturing and other economic activities, dealing first with economies internal to the firm, and then with external economies of scale.

The chapter next reviews the *measurement* of economies of scale. Important differences are noted between short-run and long-run cost curves.

Economies of scale set barriers to entry for new entrepreneurs and may affect pricing policy. If the MES is high, a great deal of capital may be required for a new firm to enter and, by achieving the MES, to be competitive. Existing firms may try to prevent such an entry by artificially lowering their prices for a time. From the measurement of economies of scale, we turn, therefore, to evaluation of the results. The consequences of economies of scale for industrial organization and conduct are noted. We also review some consequences of economies of scale for the location of industry and the emergence of urban hierarchies.

IDENTIFYING INTERNAL ECONOMIES OF SCALE

Economies of scale are the reductions in average production costs that result from increased scale of output. They include all increases in efficiency and improvements in productivity that occur with increasing size. These efficiencies may result, for example, from better, faster workmanship; the use of specialized machines; concentration on the production of a single, standard item; and longer production runs. A distinction must be drawn, however, between economies of scale and *pecuniary advantages*. A large corporation may be able to obtain special rates for raw materials, energy, transportation, advertising, and bank loans as a result of the bargaining power bestowed by size. Where such price advantages involve no physical resource saving or change in productivity but only a redistribution of in-

come between buyers and sellers, the advantage is *pecuniary*, rather than a *real* economy of scale.

Economies of scale are pervasive and can be cross-classified in a variety of ways. They are sometimes distinguished by the level in the corporate hierarchy at which they are achieved. That is, economies of scale can result from the concentration of resources on the manufacture of particular *products*, within specialized *plants*, integrated in a single *corporation*. Economies of scale are often described according to the function involved: labor, technical, managerial, marketing, and finance. Economies of scale for these functions are achieved largely at some given level of the corporate structure. The corporate hierarchy thus generates a function hierarchy of economies of scale (Figure 7.2).

Product-Specific Economies

Product-specific economies are associated with spreading start-up costs over a large output, with product standardization, with improved labor efficiency as production runs increase in *length*, and with technical efficiencies as production runs increase in *rate* of output.

Product Development Costs

The production of any good requires initial development and design costs. These may be very small, as in the case of shoes, or may be an important element of total cost, as in aircraft manufacture. Economists call these costs *indivisible* with respect to output. That is, the cost required for development and design cannot be reduced by reducing output. Development and design costs can be averaged out, however, and the larger the output, the smaller the average will be (Figure 7.3). The economies of averaging such fixed costs over increasing scale of output are tending to increase in importance over time, as products become more sophisticated. However, such economies quickly become insignificant at the output levels involved in most industries. The newspaper industry is a special exception. Total "first copy" costs are sometimes a higher proportion of total costs for newspapers with larger circulations, as managers use circulation to justify improving the quality of coverage by widening the range of items covered, the depth in which they are reported, and the amount of investigative reporting.

Labor Economies

Specialization of production on a single good permits *labor efficiencies*. These efficiencies arise from the division of labor. The division of labor was described by Adam Smith over two centuries ago in his *Wealth of Nations* (see page 173). If instead of each worker mak-

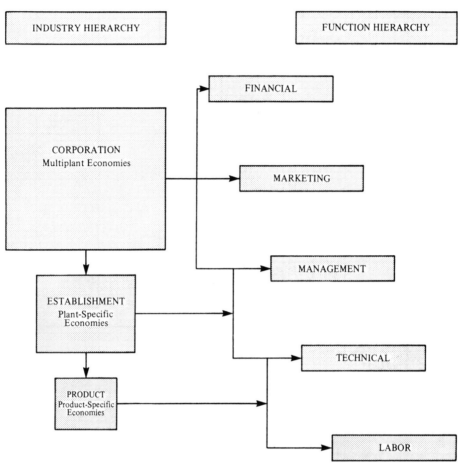

FIGURE 7.2 The dual hierarchy of economies of scale. Economies of scale can be arranged into two hierarchies. Industries have a three-level hierarchy: the corporation, the establishment, and the product. Functions within industry can be ranked from financial, to marketing, management, technical, and labor according to the industry level where they apply. Labor and technical economies of scale are exhausted first, and at the lowest level. Marketing and financial economies persist longest, and at the highest level.

ing the entire good, production is divided into particular processes, output can be substantially increased. There are three reasons for this. First, there is increased dexterity in performing the work. Second, time is not lost in passing from one process to another. Third, machinery can be specialized, adding technical economies of scale to labor economies.

Practice makes perfect. Experienced workers gain a rhythm and an economy of motion. Output tends to follow a *learning curve* (Figure 7.4). Labor costs in aircraft production during World War II were found to fall by 20 percent for each doubling of output. The British

Textile Council reported that output per worker increased by 167 percent when average rayon cloth-weaving runs increased from 3800 to 31,000 yards. The most dramatic examples of increased output are in highly technical industries such as integrated electronic circuits, where much experience is needed before good parts exceed rejects. And, of course, division of labor facilitates the allocation of workers to jobs at appropriate skill levels.

The second economy in the division of labor is the time saved in passing from one job to another. The manufacture of a relatively simple product like a pair

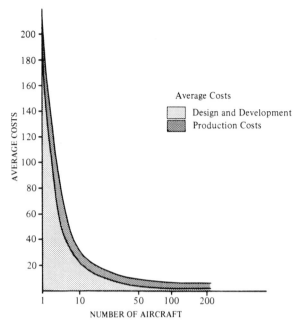

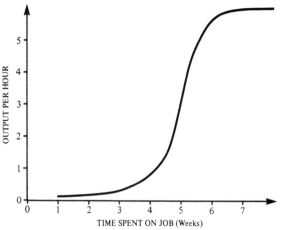

FIGURE 7.3 Economies of scale in the aircraft industry. Development costs include research and development, and the cost of special tools. These figures are representative of aircraft costs in the early post-World War II period. Development costs quickly fall to a small fraction of total production costs. [*Source:* After C. Pratten, *Economies of Scale in Manufacturing Industries* (London: Cambridge University Press, 1971), p. 152.]

FIGURE 7.4 The learning curve. The longer a worker remains on the job, the higher is his or her productivity. Productivity tends to rise at an accelerating rate to the average level of efficiency, and from then on at a decelerating rate. The importance of experience is dramatic in highly technical activities. In the manufacture of large-scale integrated circuits, fewer than 2 in a 100 made by an inexperienced worker may function properly. With experience this proportion may rise to 80 out of 100.

of shoes requires a hundred or more distinct operations, divided into five sets. First is "clicking"—the highly skilled work of cutting the uppers. Decoration, stitching, and cementing of the uppers takes place in the "closing" room. The bottoms are made in the "preparation" room. Twenty different machine operations are employed in the "making" room, completing the shoe. The final shoe process is inspection and packing.

The work is passed from room to room on conveyor belts, or on trolleys or trays (Pratten and Dean, 1965).

Third, the division of labor, concentrated on the production of a single commodity, justifies the development of special machines that would be quite uneconomic unless kept continuously in production over long periods of time. For instance, the decoration of the uppers in the closing room of a shoe factory may involve a pattern of perforations. Where a small number of shoes is to be made, this work must be done by hand. Press stamping is much faster, but the machine cost can be justified only for long production runs.

Adam Smith on Producing a Pin

A workman not educated to this business . . . could scarce, perhaps, with his utmost industry, make one pin in a day, and certainly could not make twenty . . . but it is divided into a number of branches. One man draws out the wire, another straightens it, a third cuts it, a fourth points it, a fifth grinds it at the top for receiving the head; to make the head requires two or three operations; to put it on is a particular business, to whiten the pins is another; it is even a trade by itself to put them into the paper. . . . I have seen a small manufactory of this kind where ten men . . . could make among them upwards of forty-eight thousand pins in a day. Each person, therefore, . . . might be considered as making four thousand eight hundred pins in a day.

The Wealth of Nations, 1776.

Ball-bearing production provides an example of three technology levels according to output volume. On the largest runs of standard size bearings (perhaps a million a year), a computer-controlled, fully automated process is justified. At intermediate levels (about 10,000), simpler automatic equipment can be used, but unit costs may be double. Even so, unit costs are much less than for very small runs (of perhaps a 100). These small runs must be done on general-purpose lathes by skilled operators because the eight hours it takes to set up an automated machine cannot be justified.

Plant-Specific Economies

It is at the level of the establishment, or plant, that most economies of scale can be attained. Many *fixed costs* are incurred at the plant level and can be averaged down, the greater the scale of the output. Major technical economies come into force, involving a number of different principles. These technical economies produce concomitant labor economies. Management economies are achieved with larger operating scale as well.

Averaging Down the Fixed Costs

Operating a factory incurs *fixed costs*. The magnitude of these costs is unaffected by the volume of output. Fixed costs include property taxes and rents, interest payments, depreciation of buildings and equipment, maintenance costs, and insurance. All functions, from labor and maintenance, to marketing and finance, involve some component of fixed costs (Table 7.1). The larger the factory output, the lower are the average fixed costs per unit.

Economies of Scale on Variable Costs

Plant-specific economies of scale are also achieved for *variable costs*. Variable costs are those costs that vary in magnitude with the level of output. These economies of scale occur when an increase in variable cost is less than proportional to the increase in output. Most of these economies are technical and involve three principles. These principles are the *cube-square law, the principle of multiples,* and the *massing of reserves.* A fourth principle, *bulk transactions,* may also apply.

The cube-square law states a simple and obvious relationship between the volume of a container and its surface area. Surface area increases as the square of the dimensions. Volume increases as the cube of the dimensions. Double the dimensions and the area is four times larger (2^2), but volume is eight times greater (2^3) (Figure 7.5). The "container" may be a blast furnace, a storage tank, a compressor, a turbine, or even a ship (Figure 7.6). The cube-square law (or *two-thirds rule* as it some-

TABLE 7.1

Examples of fixed costs in manufacturing industry

Type of cost[a]	Partly or wholly indivisible with respect to
Financial	
Issuing a prospectus to raise capital	Size of issue
Marketing	
Preparation of advertisements	Size of area over which advertisement is shown, and number of times used.
Calls by salespeople	Number of lines carried, and amount sold.
Managerial	
Office records on product specifications	Output
Management personnel	Output
Technical	
Capital cost of equipment	Output
Labor	
Maintenance	Output

Source: C. Pratten, *Economies of Scale in Manufacturing Industries* (London: Cambridge University Press, 1971), p. 11.

[a]Fixed costs are organized by industry function. Product-specific fixed costs (research and development) and some plant-specific costs (building-related costs) are not shown.

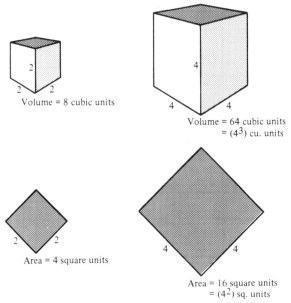

Volume = 8 cubic units

Volume = 64 cubic units = (4^3) cu. units

Area = 4 square units

Area = 16 square units = (4^2) sq. units

FIGURE 7.5 The cube-square law. This is also called the *two-thirds law.* It states that area increases at a rate of two-thirds the increase in physical volume of the equipment. In industries where output is proportional to volume, and capital costs are proportional to area, substantial economies are offered by scaling up equipment. Chemical engineers thus sometimes use a "rule of 0.6" to estimate the ratio of capital cost increase to volume increase when scaling up equipment.

FIGURE 7.6   The cube-square law in action. Adding a deck to this British Columbia Ferries Corp. ferry doubles its car capacity from 192 to 400. The ferry was cut horizontally, and the top deck, weighing 2500 tons, was raised by using 108 jacks. The job cost about $10 million, compared with $29 million for a new ferry. The cube-square guideline suggests that doubling capacity increases capital costs about 60 percent. The additional capacity in this case cost only 30 percent, because the equipment and engines remained unaltered, apart from extra stabilizers, new bulbous bow, and extra bow thruster and new generators.

times called) still holds. If costs increase in proportion with area, as they can be expected to do, and output increases in proportion with volume, then significant economies can be achieved by scaling up equipment. Thus, chemical engineers often apply "the 0.6 rule," which states that if equipment is scaled up, capital cost increases at a rate of 0.6 (rather than the 0.66 of the cube-square, or two-thirds rule). The same rule applies to breweries. Of course the figure (whether 0.6 or 0.66) is only a rough guide and the specific characteristics of

the industry modify the actual economies of scale substantially.

The *principle of multiples* is also straightforward. The design of special equipment for each specific process in making a commodity raises a problem. The machines are not all likely to run at the same rate. Those that complete their step in the production chain at the slowest rate will hold all faster machines back to their speed unless a principle of multiples is applied. This principle states that the minimum efficient scale (MES) at the technical level is the lowest common multiple (LCM) of the individual machines. If three steps are involved, with machines processing 4, 3, and 6 units per hour, the LCM is 12. The MES requires three of the 4-unit, four of the 3-unit, and two and two of the 6-unit machines, respectively, to produce 12 units per hour (Figure 7.7).

The actual output figures are rarely as convenient as in our example above. In the making room of the typical shoe factory, 20 different machines are used, capable of producing anywhere from 480 pairs of shoes in a day to 2,400 pairs (Table 7.2). Furthermore, some of the machines with very high output rates are very expensive and therefore should be kept running as much as possible. It is not feasible to reach a full multiple of every machine; what is important, however, is to approach an output level approximating the lowest common multiple of the *expensive* machines—numbers 4, 6, 8, and 17 in Table 7.3, and Figure 7.8. This minimum is 1200 pairs of shoes a day, and costs fall at each multiple of this output level (Table 7.4).

The third principle explaining greater efficiency at higher output levels is the *massing of reserves* (or massed reserves). The smooth operation of a plant, including production and marketing, requires maintaining some minimum level of reserves. Raw materials, fuel, spare parts for equipment repair and maintenance, and perhaps even spare machines are needed if plant stoppages are to be avoided. These savings are harder to document although their existence is easy to understand. They are most evident where equipment must be taken out of service at regular intervals for maintenance. A basic oxygen furnace in the steel industry must be relined with refractory bricks every 25 to 40 days. Two furnaces are

TABLE 7.2

The problem of balancing output in the making room of a shoe factory

Type of machine	Output per day per machine (pairs of shoes)	Machine utilization to produce 1200 pairs of shoes per day
1	1800	0.7
2	1440	0.8
3	1260	1.0
4	1800	0.7
5	1260	1.0
6	480	2.5
7	600	2.0
8	1440	0.8
9	1860	0.6
10	1980	0.6
11	840	1.4
12	1860	0.6
13	1320	0.9
14	1860	0.6
15	1200	1.0
16	1200	1.0
17	720	1.7
18	1200	1.0
19	960	0.7
20	2400	0.5

Source: C. Pratten and R. M. Dean, *Economies of Large-Scale Production* (Cambridge, U.K.: Cambridge University Press, 1965), p. 49.

Note: The making room is where the uppers (which have been through the clicking and closing rooms) are combined with the bottoms (made in the preparation room). Twenty different machines are used, with many different output rates.

needed to keep a steady flow of steel. Adding a third furnace, however, increases output by 50 percent for a 33 percent increase in cost.

Finally, a *principle of bulk transactions* sometimes applies. Economists distinguish between the case where size is used to bargain for better rates, which is a pecuniary advantage, and where real increases in efficiency occur. Shoe manufacturers often sell their shoes through their own outlets. A complete range of sizes in each color for each style must be carried. Where sales are large, the size distribution of the stock can more nearly approximate the size distribution of the market. Volume sales thus reduce overhead costs and the risks of being left with extreme sizes at the end of the season.

Management costs, not all of which are fixed, also rise less than proportionately with size. Management economies at the plant level are very much like labor economies at the product level. Division-of-management tasks permit allocation of duties according to aptitude. The principles of the learning curve, specialization of duties, and development of specialized management aids become feasible in larger plants. Management economies are thought to continue beyond the scale where technical economies are exhausted and continue on up to multiplant firms.

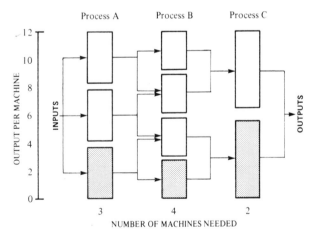

FIGURE 7.7 The principle of multiples. Given a number of processes involving machines operating at different rates, the technical minimum efficient size is the lowest common multiple of the rates.

TABLE 7.3

The principle of multiples at work in the making room of a shoe factory

Expensive operations	Output rate	Possible combinations of machines and operatives at different outputs					
		600	800	1000	1200	1500	2400
4	1800	1	1	1	1	1	2
6	480	2	2	3	3	4	5
8	1440	1	1	1	1	2	2
17	720	1	2	2	2	3	4
Total no. all operatives		21	23	25	26	37	48
Average output per operative		29	35	40	46	41	50

Source: Pratten and Dean, 1965, p. 49.

Note: One operative is required for each machine. The figures apply to both the number of machines and the number of production workers in the making room. Output figures are in pairs of shoes per day. Average output rises steadily to output levels of 1200 pairs per day, and then falls until production is doubled to 2400 pairs.

FIGURE 7.8 Economies of scale in the making room of the shoe industry. Twenty operations are involved in joining the uppers and bottoms of a shoe in the typical shoe factory. Each operation involves machines, some of which are very expensive, and each of which has different production rates (Table 7.3). Technical and labor economies are achieved by increasing output toward the lowest common multiple of the different rates. This is the principle of multiples (or balance of processes). Without such economies at the plant level, the economies of the division of labor can be seriously offset.

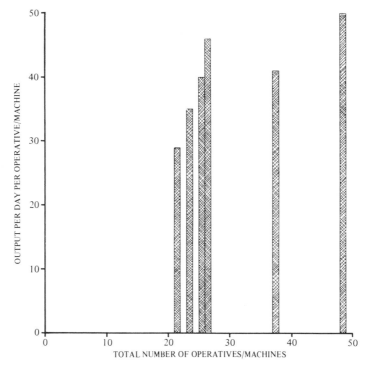

TABLE 7.4

Average costs at various output scales in the shoe industry

Output capacity (pairs per day)	Labor and equipment	Total production costs including materials
300	100	100
600	94	97
1200	90	95.5
2400	87	94
4800	85	93

Source: Pratten and Dean, 1965, p. 52.

Note: These estimates, based on British factories making women's medium-priced shoes in the 1960s, are representative of economies of scale in the shoe industry generally.

Multiplant Economies

The organization of industry into multiplant firms permits production economies over and beyond those attributable to the sizes of the individual plants. These economies of scale for multiplant firms involve primarily the financial and marketing functions.

Production Economies

Multiplant firms can allocate particular products to specific plants, increasing product-specific economies. The 1969 merger of three British companies manufacturing antifriction bearings provides an example of just how great such economies can be. Two of the companies had manufactured overlapping lines of general-purpose bearings. The merger permitted production assignments that ended duplication and permitted longer production runs. Output per employee jumped 50 percent in one year, and even greater improvements in productivity were expected with the introduction of new equipment justified by longer runs. Two Canadian companies, each making broad lines of home appliances, merged in 1971, ending duplication and achieving major, if less spectacular, economies.

Marketing Economies

Multiplant firms can also achieve important marketing economies. Companies sometimes spend large amounts on advertising to hold or extend their share of sales, or to market a new product. Advertising costs are particularly high in the case of soaps and detergents. A new enzyme detergent which cost £200,000 to develop was launched on the British market in the mid-1960s with a £1 million advertising campaign. A similar sum would have been needed for any new company to launch its product. That is, some threshold level of expenditure must be made on advertising before the product catches public attention, word spreads, and sales take off.

An effective sales campaign can reshape an industry, as it did in the case of the United States brewery industry. After the repeal of Prohibition in 1933, a few breweries chose to set their prices high relative to local and regional beers, and to promote a national image as "premium" Milwaukee beers. The big three, Anheuser-Busch, Schlitz, and Pabst, captured an increasing share of the market. The consequent economies of scale then enabled them to reduce their prices and to start driving out smaller-scale local producers, thus enlarging their market share still further.

Financial Economies

Multiplant firms also achieve important financial economies of scale. They can concentrate their financial resources on the expansion of each plant in turn as the market grows. This strategy is impossible for single-plant firms. Where an industry is composed largely of single-plant firms, all firms will try to expand competitively, usually resulting in initial overexpansion and then of failure by the least efficient.

Multiplant firms can also raise capital through stock issues at lower interest rates because the financial community views them as better risks. Many of the costs of negotiating a loan are fixed, and it has been found that costs can vary from as little as 5 percent of share value to as much as 44 percent according to the size of the corporation.

Underlying these multiplant economies are the same set of principles as in the plant-specific and product-specific cases, and they apply to all functions. First is the principle of averaging down the fixed costs over larger volumes. Next are the sets of principles applying to variable costs: the cube-square law, multiples, massed reserves, and bulk transactions (Table 7.5). The last two are particularly important. The economies of scale at the firm level depend in part, however, on the relationship among the plants. This relationship in turn depends on any mergers by which the plants were acquired.

The Merger Movement in the United States

Multiplant corporations dominate most industries in most Western countries. A 1963 U.S. survey of 417 industries revealed only 22 industries in which the four leading sellers operated only single plants. This dominance of the market by multiplant firms is the result of three great merger waves. The first wave was dominated by horizontal integration, the second by vertical inte-

TABLE 7.5

The principles of economies of scale by manufacturing function

	Fixed costs	Variable costs			
	Averaging down	Cube-square law	Multiples	Massed reserves	Bulk transactions
Financial	*	•	•	•	*
Marketing	*	•	•	•	*
Management	*	•	X	•	•
Technical	X	*	*	*	•
Labor	○	•	*	•	•

*, Very important; X, important; ○, weak; •, not applicable.

Note: These assessments are based on many published studies and do not necessarily pertain to any individual industry.

gration, and the third by conglomerate mergers. Let us look at each of these in turn.

The first wave, which lasted from 1887 to 1904 in the United States, saw the consolidation of thousands of firms into relatively few multiplant corporations dominating the market they supplied. The wave was triggered by changes in transportation, communications, manufacturing technology, and legal institutions. Standard Oil captured 90 percent of the petroleum market by acquiring competitors. U.S. Steel was formed in 1901 by the merger of 785 plants accounting for 65 percent of the country's steel capacity. The American Can Company, organized the same year, involved 120 firms with 90 percent of the national market. Other leading corporations established during the great merger wave are U.S. Rubber (Uniroyal), Pittsburgh Plate Glass (PPG Industries), International Paper, United Fruit (United Brands), Eastman-Kodak, and International Harvester. Almost all industries were affected: copper, lead, railroad cars, tobacco, chemicals, and shoe machines among them. The wave was halted only by a combination of a depression and the enactment of antitrust laws, but some significant mergers still occurred. IBM was established in 1911. General Motors was formed from Buick, Cadillac, and Oldsmobile, added Chevrolet a few years later, but was unable to raise the cash to buy out Ford when Henry Ford offered to sell out in 1908 and 1909.

The second great merger period, from 1916 to 1929, involved more companies but created fewer industrial leaders. It did, however, create important "number two" firms, such as Bethlehem Steel and Continental Can. One authority distinguished this second period as "mergers for oligopoly" as compared with first-wave "mergers for monopoly." In addition, the second merger period saw much more *vertical integration* of industry than the first, during which *horizontal integration* predominated.

Horizontal mergers (integration) involve the combination of firms producing similar items and selling in the same market. Industry concentration is involved. The leading firms may account for most of the sales in a given industry. Competition is reduced as former competitors become integrated partners in a single firm.

Vertical mergers (integration) combine successive production activities into a single firm. The firm's plants now serve each other in sequence as the product is carried through a progression of processes. In steel, the succession of steps involves making pig iron, converting it to steel, and shaping the steel into semifinished products. In other cases, vertical integration involves separate components of a good, as when a soft-drink producer buys out a bottle manufacturer. Vertical integration is *backward* when a firm buys out its suppliers. A steel company may acquire coal and iron ore mines, to secure raw materials. Vertical integration is *forward* where the purpose is to secure markets and outlets for the production of the dominant partner in the integration. Breweries in Britain own their own pubs, the film industry operates its own cinema chains, automobile companies sell through franchised dealerships.

The impact of vertical integration on competition is more subtle than in the case of horizontal integration, and it can involve clear economies where the production steps are technologically complementary, as in the steel industry. Mergers that produce sizable shifts in market shares are increasingly frowned on, however. As a result, the post–World War II period has witnessed a third wave of *conglomerate mergers,* in which the firms that join together have no obvious complementarities other than those of financial and tax manipulation. A case in point is the 1982 acquisition of Marathon Oil Co. by U.S. Steel (recently renamed USX). Where some small complementarities do exist, the mergers are described as *lateral integration.* The British aircraft industry has thus moved into a variety of engineering ventures.

The urge to merge springs from a variety of motives. Among these are the search for financial security, the instinct to jump at a good business opportunity, tax advantages, and hoped-for economies of scale. Horizontal integration increases security by reducing competition, vertical integration reduces vulnerability by controlling supplies and markets, and conglomerate mergers spread product and financial risk by diversity. Integration may be good business where another company's stock is underpriced, where new management can revitalize a lagging corporation, or where its physical plant can be acquired at a low price. But mergers also offer economies of scale (Table 7.6). These are most obvious in horizontal mergers. Vertical integration can im-

TABLE 7.6

Economies of scale by type of industrial merger

	Horizontal	Vertical	Conglomerate
Financial	*	*	*
Marketing	*	*	X
Management	*	*	*
Technical	*	*	•
Labor	*	•	•

*, Very important; X, important; •, weak.

Note: Economies of scale are most easily achieved in horizontal integration. But horizontal integration is the very kind that most obviously restricts market competition. Vertical integration offers the greatest scale economies where the sequence of processes are technologically complementary. Conglomerate mergers achieve financial and management economies of scale but such mergers are motivated primarily for other reasons.

prove the flow of output through the sequence of processes and facilitate the management of quality and design of components, and size always bestows financial and marketing advantages. Indeed, a company may be acquired for its good will, even if the physical plant is not needed. An extreme example is in the case of U.S. breweries when the G.W. Heileman Co. paid $10.7 million for the Blatz trademark, 32 trucks, and the Blatz marching band. In the case of commodities with high transportation costs, where the market area that can be served by any one plant is as a result restricted, horizontal integration offers nationwide sales: Several factories in different market areas produce and sell the same nationally advertised product. This is an important factor in cases like beer (not all "Milwaukee" beers are produced in Milwaukee), cement, petroleum refin-

ing, and the soft-drink industry. Coca-Cola, Pepsi-Cola, and others are bottled in a myriad of small plants serving particular urban-regional markets. The importance of the financial and marketing advantages are clearly evident in 12 industries analyzed by Scherer (1975) (Table 7.7).

EXTERNAL ECONOMIES OF SCALE

In addition to the internal economies of scale that a firm obtains through the scale of output of specific products, the size of individual establishments, or of the firm itself, *external* economies of scale may contribute to lower average production costs. External economies of scale are the gains in efficiency and productivity resulting

TABLE 7.7

Advantages of multiplant operations

Industry	Minimum number of plants to achieve multiplant economies	Main basis for advantage	Disadvantages of single-plant operation
Beer brewing	3–4	National brand image and advertising; coordination of new plant investments	Slight to severe, depending upon inherited brand image
Cigarettes	1–2	Advertising and image differentiation	Slight to moderate (borderline)
Fabric weaving	3–6	Integration into finishing; broad-line sales force and advertising	Very slight to moderate, depending upon product line
Paints	1	Integration into raw materials production	Slight
Petroleum refining	2–3	Risk spreading on crude oil ventures; coordination of plant investments; advertising and national image	Very slight to moderate, depending upon regional market position and crude oil access
Shoes	3–6	Broad-line sales force and advertising	Slight to moderate, depending upon product line
Glass bottles	3–4	Need for central engineering and design staff	Slight to moderate depending upon location and products
Cement	1	Risk spreading and capital raising	Slight
Ordinary steel	1	Capital raising; plant expansion coordination	Very slight
Bearings	3–5	Broad-line customer preferences affecting lot sizes; central engineering	Slight to moderate, depending upon product line
Refrigerators	4–8 (incl. other appliances)	Image and market access, affecting production run lengths; warehousing and transportation	Moderate
Storage batteries	1	Market access	Slight

Source: F. M. Scherer, Alan Beckenstein, Erich Kaufer, and R. Dennis Murphy, *The Economics of Multi-Plant Operation: An International Comparisons Study* (Cambridge, Mass.: Harvard University Press, 1975), pp. 334–336.

TABLE 7.8

Internal and external economies of scale: The continuum

	Type of economy of scale	Economy of scale depends on	Example of an economy of scale achieved
EXTERNAL (Different firms)	Place-specific (urbanization) Industry-specific (Localization)	Size of city Size of industry	Range of urban services Research and development
INTERNAL (Same firm)	Firm-specific Plant-specific Product-specific	Size of firm Size of plant Length and volume of production run	Advertising and marketing Larger machines (cube-square law) Division of labor

Note: External economies are in part a continuum on the range of economies of scale. They are industry- or place-specific, rather than specific to a particular firm, or to a plant or product within that firm. Sometimes they are a partial substitute for internal economies. Firms internalize economies of scale by integration, and they externalize them by disintegration.

from the concentration of different firms in a single location (Table 7.8). External economies derive from *spatial association* rather than corporate integration. They may be *industry-specific* and depend on the concentration in one location of different firms involved in the manufacture of similar products (called *localization economies*), or they may be *place-specific* and result from efficiencies in the provision of services to industry that are dependent not on the particular nature of the industry, but on the local scale of output of all kinds (called *urbanization economies*).

Localization Economies

Localization economies arise from the clustering of plants engaged in similar activity in a restricted geographical area. The local scale of the industry that results benefits individual plants within the group and tends to perpetuate the localization of the industry. Several kinds of economies exist:

1. The reputation acquired by goods produced in a given locality leads to *product differentiation.* Goods produced in some localities, whether or not they meet the standards of that locality, carry with them the aura of high standards of workmanship and quality. A typical case is that of the cutlery and steel produced in Sheffield, England; others are Brussels lace, Irish linen, and Milwaukee beer. Whether or not the products are superior, the image is that they are and their product is therefore differentiated from the same goods produced elsewhere, giving a distinct market advantage.

2. The consequences of the industrial atmosphere pervading the localized area stemming from the close association of manufacturers who meet frequently. Rivalries among these manufacturers breed innovation; at the same time there can be interchange of personnel and information and, where necessary, cooperative action to preserve or enhance the locality's reputation. Knowledge under such circumstances is more rapidly diffused among firms located within the cluster. Firms in the same industry but outside the cluster operate at a disadvantage. This factor of geographic association was, of course, more important during the nineteenth century than the twentieth. It is of less importance today because of the growth of nationwide selling organizations and of a trade press that diffuses ideas rapidly. Nonetheless, it has been of real significance in the localization of computer firms in California's "Silicon Valley" and around Boston's Route 128.

3. The creation of a pool of skilled labor, which thereby strengthens localization economies, results in the local labor force becoming uniquely adapted to the needs of the local industry, which enhances local productivity.

4. The adaptation of local utilities and services to the particular needs of the industry also produces efficiencies that reduce costs. Banks, insurance agencies, and transportation companies supplying special facilities appropriate to the needs of the industry dominate the kinds of service provided in the locality, and their costs are lower because they become expert in the problems and needs of the industry.

5. Most important, the local scale of industry permits the subdivision of operations between plants. Auxiliary specialists emerge, meeting the requirements of several firms. The specialists provide components or needed services more cheaply than if the individual firms

had to provide their own. With a localized industry, then, vertical *dis*integration is important. It arises from the close geographical association of firms, short hauls, speedy delivery, and the lessening of stock requirements. The resulting interdependence facilitates those real economies of subdivision that are exhibited by the most localized activities. The outstanding examples are the clothing industry and the cutlery trades. Examples include the garment districts of New York and the East End of London. In the metal trades of the West Midlands of England, three main types of activity constitute the localization: (a) a large number of firms performing common metal processes, but not producing finished goods; for example, the foundries, rerollers, forgers, welders, galvanizers; (b) a large number of firms making common components, screws, bolts, nuts, tools, springs; and (c) service trades; for example, small establishments making wooden patterns or machine tools, the scrap merchants, and so on. These three main types of activity support the highly localized metal goods manufacturers who engage in assembly and the further processing of the components made by the three main types of activity. Good examples are motor vehicles, bicycles and motorcycles, guns in Birmingham, locks at Wolverhampton, and so on.

Localization economies thus accomplish through geographic juxtaposition the same kinds of linkages as those achieved through corporate integration in internal economies of scale (Table 7.9). P. Sargent Florence (1949) described the four main types of industrial linkages that characterize localizations as follows:

1. *Vertical linkages.* In this arrangement, a series of processes linked to each other in succession contributes to the gradual transformation of raw materials into finished products. If there is *vertical disintegration* of an industry, each of the successive stages is carried on by different plants within a localization. By contrast, in *vertical integration,* successive steps in the transformation of raw material into finished products are brought

within the ownership of a particular company and within the confines of a particular plant.

2. *Diagonal linkages* characterize trades that serve a number of different industries and need contact with all of them to maintain viability. Examples are the engraving, plating, and polishing activities in the jewelry district of a city.

3. *Lateral linkages* characterize industries producing parts, accessories, or services that feed into an assembly-type industry at different stages of the assembly process. Thus, industries converge upon the flow of the assembly line at different stages.

4. *Common-service linkages* help industries using the common processes and skills provided in a local area. For example, each of the metal trades draws on the same skills and common processes; the nut and bolt industry, nuts, screws, buttons, chains, cables, locks and bolts, and so forth.

Economies of localization are *acquired advantages* that an industry develops out of its historical evolution in a particular area. Over the years the initial advantages that first attracted the industry may disappear. The persistence of the industry in the area then results from the advantages of the environment it has created for itself. Very often industrial *inertia*—the failure to respond to growth of new markets or the opening up of new resources—is tied up with acquired advantage; the question of survival becomes one of economies derived from agglomeration and persistence rather than lower costs of labor, raw materials, or transportation.

Urbanization Economies

Urbanization economies derive from the close association of many different kinds of industry in large cities. The cost advantages derive from several sources, the most important of which are:

1. *Transporation costs.* A large city usually has superior transportation facilities offering significantly lower transportation costs to regional and national markets. A city located at a focal point on transportation networks is especially suited for easy assembly of raw materials and for ready distribution of products. There are thus market advantages for speedy and cheap distribution that may be accentuated by the advantages arising out of the size of the local consuming market. The local population may in fact form a large part of the total national market. Greater London, for example, has one-fifth of the British consumer market, and the New York metropolitan area has been called "one-tenth of a nation." In both cases, these markets account for a significantly larger proportion of the higher-quality and fashion-oriented demands. Thus, the large city

TABLE 7.9

A classification of external economies of scale by linkage

Urbanization economies	Place-specific	Lateral and common-service linkages
Localization economies	Industry-specific	Diagonal and vertical linkages

Note: The economies of scale achieved through corporate integration in large firms can be achieved equally by locational integration of smaller firms. The principles and the categories are the same. They involve horizontal and vertical, and lateral and conglomerate linkages. A distinction is made between economies due to the concentration of similar industries—the industry-specific economies—and the concentration of economic activity generally in large metropolitan areas.

may be the ideal plant location: Local demands are substantial and the rest of the plant's output is easily distributed.

2. *Labor costs.* The large city labor market is diverse and dynamic, and the labor demands of single firms are only a small part of the total demands for labor. This labor pool is especially important where firms have seasonal variations in labor needs. The big-city labor market also offers a wide range of skills. Facilities for workers that are readily available in the large city may also have to be provided by the firm in the small town, which raises the real labor costs.

3. *Quality of services.* The larger the city the higher the scale of services it can supply. Services such as firefighting, police, gas, electricity, water, waste disposal, education, housing, and roads are generally better in the larger city than in the small town, and they are provided publicly. Firms located in otherwise unindustrialized areas may be forced to spend much more of their capital on infrastructure and social facilities. These kinds of advantages first came into play in the industrial development of the largest metropolitan areas in the period following World War I. Service economies had a magnetic effect on industries in which coal was replaced as motive power by electricity, and in which rail and water transportation was replaced by the truck. Light industry, that is, manufacturing consumer goods, was attracted to large cities not only by their markets and marketing facilities but also by their services. In turn, the accumulation of light industry in large cities further enhanced the attractiveness of the cities, creating positive conditions for further growth. In this way, urbanization economies have fed on themselves in a process of "circular and cumulative causation." (This process is discussed in more detail in Chapter 16.)

INDUSTRIAL COMPLEXES

When a set of activities involves production processes so closely interlinked that their production, marketing, or other operations can be coordinated at a given location, *economies of an industrial complex* may be said to exist. In the extreme case, the activities may be so closely interdependent that they can be operated as a single plant; more often they involve a variety of plants and companies, but with very closely coordinated interdependence involving raw material, product, and byproduct flows.

Types of Linkages in Industrial Complexes

Several types of linkages create different kinds of industrial complexes:

1. When successive stages in the manufacture of given end products are linked at a single location, as in the case of vertically integrated iron and steel mills;

2. When there is joint production of several products from a single class of raw materials, as when foodstuffs, fertilizers, and industrial products are made from cattle;

3. When raw materials are processed to yield intermediate products that may combine to form end products. An example is where acetylene and hydrogen cyanide can be produced from alternative sources of hydrocarbons (oil, natural gas, coal). These intermediates can be used to manufacture other intermediates—for example, acrylonitrile, which can be turned into final-stage intermediates such as Orlon fiber, and ultimately into such final products as textile fabrics. Three industries are represented in these industrial linkages: petroleum refining, chemicals, and textiles. But what is important about the complex is that the particular production sequence is interdependent, demanding joint locational evaluation of each of the elements to derive the best location for the complex.

Kolossovsky's Territorial Production Complexes

Walter Isard pioneered joint locational analysis for industrial complexes in the United States. In 1947, a Moscow geographer, N. Kolossovsky, provided a general classification of the circumstances in which industrial complexes might arise in a centrally planned economy such as that of the USSR, calling them "territorial production complexes." His classification was based upon the energy involved in the production process, and he argued that each type of production complex produced a distinct type of economic region. He described, for example, what he called the "pyrometallurgical cycle of ferrous metallurgy," including coking coal and iron ore mining, enrichment of metals, coking of coals, blast-furnace processes, recasting of pig iron into steel, rolling processes, heavy-machine building, and, to some extent, machine and tool making.

Another example was the "petrochemical cycle" of oil, power, and chemical production, including extraction and processing of natural deposits of oil, natural gas, common potassium, and other salts. To this cycle belong the oil refining industry, and organic synthesis of alcohols, rubber, plastics, and other products of the chemical industry.

Kolossovsky's other cases involve nonferrous metallurgy, hydroelectric power, timber industries, consumer-goods industries, and industries based upon agriculture and irrigation.

Kolossovsky's typology of industrial complexes was developed for describing the economic regions of the USSR rather than for analyzing the interdependencies involved in the location of industrial complexes. However, his classification does provide a concise overview of the circumstances under which such complexes might arise, as seen through the eyes of a Soviet scholar concerned with the central planning of industrial locations. In each case, joint location of several closely related activities can produce a different set of locational advantages and industrial patterns.

DISECONOMIES OF SCALE

Average costs of production tend to fall with increased scale of output because of economies of scale, but there is reason to believe that once a minimum efficient size of production has been reached (the MES), costs may not fall any further, and may rise, at least in the short run (see Figure 7.1).

Internal Diseconomies of Scale

Labor Diseconomies of Scale

The reductions in labor costs per unit of production end when all the economies of the division of labor have been achieved. As workers become skilled in operating their equipment, the learning curve flattens out and no further economies can be expected from this source (Figure 7.4). There is a one-time savings in keeping workers at a single specific task using specialized equipment. Overspecialization of jobs makes the work repetitive and boring. As workers find their jobs less satisfying and challenging, they must be paid higher wage rates to keep them interested. As a result, many industries have been reorganized to make work more varied and interesting. The sales offices of Rowntree & Co. in York, England, reintegrated the handling of correspondence and the granting of credit into a single division, thus giving wider responsibilities for fewer customers to each section head. Their tasks thereby became less monotonous, and as section heads became familiar with their own batch of customers, the time lost on consulting records was reduced. In Sweden, long assembly lines have been replaced in some industries by smaller work groups carrying the product through to completion, resulting in greater worker commitment and higher-quality products.

The sheer size of the labor force in a single plant

also produces problems. Workers in large plants tend to find their work less satisfying than workers in small plants for reasons not yet properly understood by psychologists. Large plants find they must therefore pay a wage premium. Furthermore, as the size of the labor force grows, it must begin to attract workers from greater distances. The added transportation costs faced by workers are reflected in wage rates. A point will be reached when increases in wage rates associated with increasing size of plant cannot be offset by increased efficiency. At that point, labor economies of scale give way to labor *dis*economies of scale.

Technical Diseconomies of Scale

In the case of technical factors, many firms find that a size is reached where technical economies of scale are exhausted. The cube-square law faces sheer size limits beyond which technical problems and costs exceed possible economies. Cement lime kilns experience unstable internal aerodynamics above 7 million barrels per year capacity. Machines and equipment become increasingly unwieldy. Parts may have to be strengthened in proportion to volume rather than size once strength limits are approached, offsetting any possible scale economies. Where the size of a new plant is above the usual size range for the industry, there may also be substantial design costs and initial difficulties in getting into production.

The principle of multiples confers fixed rather than continuous economies of scale. Costs are a minimum where the product of output per machine times number of machines is the same for each step in a process. If output is increased beyond this level, costs rise until production reaches a new multiple of machine capacity (Figure 7.8). But the average costs per multiple may be the same unless increased scale permits larger and more efficient machines to be introduced.

The other principles underlying technical economies of scale also run into diminishing returns. The *massing of reserves* principle may not apply fully if several smaller production lines are replaced by a single large production line. In the chemical industry, for example, continuity of production is essential. Supplies are more vulnerable for a large single-stream plant than for many small ones. The danger of disruption can be reduced by storage, but the storage costs reduce the economies of scale of a larger plant.

A firm may run into actual technical difficulties in increasing scale of output. Limited physical space available for expansion may cause increasing congestion. There may be physical limits imposed by availability of water for production or cooling processes from nearby rivers and lakes. Environmental pollution may become more difficult to cope with at larger output levels. In sum, technical considerations tend to set a minimum efficient scale of production, but once this scale has been reached, further technical economies of scale may be hard to win. Technical diseconomies of scale can be avoided by operating a number of separate plants. In this case, however, the firm is still faced with management diseconomies of scale.

Management Diseconomies of Scale

Management diseconomies of scale occur because of the increasing difficulty of coordinating larger firms. These management diseconomies have been described in different ways and from different viewpoints. One writer has argued that the cube-square law works against economies of scale in management (Haire, 1959). Using a simple biological analogy, Haire argued that supervisory and management personnel grow disproportionately with output, in fact, at a $\frac{3}{2}$ power of the growth in production. Many functions that can be taken care of informally in small plants must be organized formally in larger organizations. Parking, eating facilities, medical care, and security are examples. Coordination becomes more complex with increasing size and division of labor. What was managed by a worker as part of the job routine becomes a new and wholly separate function. Hierarchies of management control evolve, with the attendant danger that top management becomes increasingly remote from day-to-day production problems. Decision making becomes more difficult, takes longer, and becomes less flexible. Bad decisions are harder to detect but may be more damaging and difficult to reverse. One need only to look at the giant corporations in difficulty today to see examples of this.

Marketing Diseconomies of Scale

The most serious diseconomies of scale may be in marketing. More output requires more sales. Advertising can be used to promote additional sales, but too much advertising can backfire. Budweiser found that advertising increased its sales of beer up to a maximum, beyond which further advertising appeared to reduce sales. Scherer (1980) notes that consumers deluged with Budweiser ads asked their liquor dealers to give them anything *but* a Bud (Figure 7.9).

Sales may be increased by extending the market area, but more distant sales incur greater delivery costs. Beyond a certain distance, these increased costs can be expected to exceed the economies of scale.

Of all the factors contributing to internal economies of scale, only finance appears to be more immune to diminishing returns, and hence to diseconomies of scale.

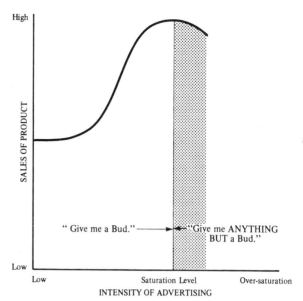

FIGURE 7.9 Diseconomies of advertising. Saturation advertising of a product beyond consumer tolerance levels can turn off potential buyers, as Budweiser found. [*Source:* Suggested by F. M. Scherer, *Industrial Market Structure and Economic Performance* (Chicago: Rand McNally, 1980), p. 109.]

External Diseconomies of Scale

External diseconomies of scale set in once the costs of urban congestion begin to exceed the benefits of industrial concentration. Precise definition is more difficult than in the case of internal diseconomies of scale. The general nature of these diseconomies is not, however, difficult to understand. Some cause industries to seek lower-cost regions, as when big-city wage rates force labor-intensive industries such as textile producers to exploit lower-wage labor forces elsewhere. Others produce a shifting of activities between central and suburban locations. High land values in inner-city areas, cramped and restricted sites, parking difficulties, deficiency of light and air, and environmental pollution lead industries that seek space, light, and air to go to the periphery of the big city, to smaller towns, or to nonurban areas; often a relocation is planned to bring the plant closer to the owner's or manager's preferred place of residence. The peripheral area avoids the diseconomies of centrality while retaining the advantages of proximity. There the best of both worlds can often be obtained.

This movement to the fringe took place slowly in the industrial areas of the United States and Western Europe before World War II. Despite more widespread use of electric power and the development of road transportation and of improved highways, reducing the locational pull on industrial locations of rail terminals and docks in central areas, a long period of economic depression prevented wholesale relocation or many new suburban plant locations, although new outlying planned industrial estates were pioneered in many countries. The great change came after World War II: Highways were further improved, and new large-scale trucks came into operation, often in combination with rail transport ("piggyback"). Rapid decentralization of industry from the central cities began in force.

It operated selectively. For some kinds of activities, central locations remained so crucial that they outweighed the disadvantages of congestion. Industries decentralizing were those using road transportation and preferring single-story facilities or expansive sites. Industries moving out of big cities altogether have done so in sequence: First were those seeking low labor costs (especially textile producers and a variety of assembly operations), next were the machine tool industries serving those that left first, then integrated production complexes that were capable of standing alone, and then a variety of new computer- and communications-based industries that were relatively immune from the pulls of the central city but highly dependent on being able to attract skilled scientists and technicians to attractive residential environments.

MEASURING SCALE ECONOMIES

The Theoretical Approach

The many ingredients contributing to economies and diseconomies of scale can be usefully melded into a composite picture by focusing on the relationships of costs to output. Costs can be measured in various ways, but if these various measures of cost can be identified for a particular industry, then the most efficient size can be identified very precisely. Actual cost data for a comprehensive range of outputs and industries are not generally available. Even if they have such comprehensive data, industrialists are naturally reluctant to part with information that might help competitors. The cost curves shown in most books are, therefore, based more on the theoretical understanding of economies of scale than on actual cases. In this text, too, the data are hypothetical and employed only to illustrate the key relationships between cost, output, and economies of scale.

Costs can be classified in two distinct ways. First, there is the distinction between *fixed costs* and *variable costs:* This distinction was noted in describing plant-specific economies. Second, there is the distinction between *total, average,* and *marginal costs.* It is this second classification that is crucial to the theoretical approach to understanding economies of scale.

Total costs of operating a plant at a given output level are equal to the fixed costs plus the total variable costs. If fixed costs are $100, and total variable costs are $180, then total costs are $280. Fixed costs do not change with output. However, variable costs must always *increase* with output (Figure 7.10). If they did not, an industry could find itself in the enviable but bizarre position where it cost less to produce more.

Economies of scale are easier to identify from average costs than total costs. Average costs are simply total costs divided by output (Table 7.10). Average fixed costs always decrease with higher output (Figure 7.11). Average variable costs decrease until diseconomies of scale come into play. Diseconomies in variable costs may be offset by continuing economies in fixed costs. Thus, the output level with minimum average total costs may be higher than for the minimum average variable costs. It is the output level with *minimum average total costs* that marks the point of *maximum economies of scale.*

OUTPUT	TOTAL COSTS ($)		
Number of Units	FIXED	VARIABLE	TOTAL
0	100	0	100
1	100	50	150
2	100	90	190
3	100	123	223
4	100	152	252
5	100	180	280
6	100	210	310
7	100	252	352
8	100	311	411
9	100	405	505
10	100	550	650

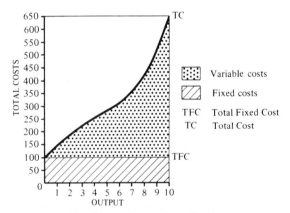

FIGURE 7.10 Change in total production costs with scale. Total production costs comprise two components, fixed costs and variable costs. These figures are entirely imaginary and are chosen to display, first, increasing economies of scale and then increasing diseconomies of scale in the figures that follow.

TABLE 7.10

Calculating actual production costs: A hypothetical example

	OUTPUT LEVEL		
	5 units	6 units	7 units
FIXED COSTS			
Total	100	100	100
Average	100/5 = 20	100/6 ≃ 17	100/7 ≃ 14
VARIABLE COSTS			
Total	180	210	252
Average	180/5 = 36	210/6 = 35	252/7 = 36
Marginal		210 − 180 = 30	252 − 210 = 42
TOTAL COSTS			
Total	100 + 180 = 280	100 + 210 = 310	100 + 252 = 352
Average	20 + 36 = 56	17 + 35 = 52	14 + 36 = 50
Marginal		310 − 280 = 30	352 − 310 = 42

Note: This table should be followed using Figures 7.10, 7.11, and 7.12. Note that marginal costs are less than average variable costs at an output of six units: Economies of scale therefore prevail. But marginal costs exceed average variable costs at an output of seven units: Economies of scale are exhausted.

OUTPUT Number of Units	AVERAGE COSTS ($)		
	FIXED	VARIABLE	TOTAL
1	100	50	150
2	50	45	95
3	33	41	74
4	25	38	63
5	20	36	56
6	17	35	52
7	14	36	50
8	13	39	52
9	11	45	56
10	10	55	65

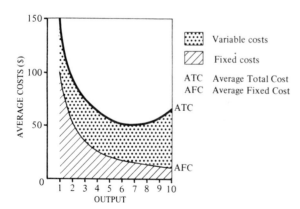

FIGURE 7.11 Change in average production costs with scale. These figures are obtained simply by dividing the totals in Figure 7.10 by the output levels involved. The total fixed cost for five units is $100, so the average is $20. Total variable for five units is $180, so the average is $36. The average total cost for five units is then $50. Thus, average cost is cost divided by output.

There is a simple test of whether output has reached the point of maximum economies of scale, which depends on calculating *marginal cost*. Marginal cost is the added cost of producing just one more unit of output (Table 7.10; Figure 7.12). As long as the marginal cost is less than the average total cost, producing more will lower the average. For example, if the average cost of six units is $50, and the marginal cost of producing one more unit (the seventh) is $42, it pays to do so. The average cost for seven is less than for six (Table 7.10). But it turns out in the example that the marginal cost for the eighth unit jumps to $60, which is higher than the average. Hence, the average cost starts to rise. The rule is, therefore, that *average total cost is a minimum where it equals marginal cost.* At lower output levels, marginal cost is less than average cost and pulls average cost down. At higher levels, it pulls average cost up (Figure 7.13). Thus, economies of scale are maximized where average total cost equals marginal cost.

In summary, costs can be classified into fixed, variable, and total costs, and further classified into total, average, and marginal costs (Figure 7.13). The behavior of the cost curves in this two-way classification identifies the point of maximum economies of scale. This point is the MES (minimum efficient scale). The point occurs *after* marginal costs have started to rise, and *after* average *variable* costs have started to rise. The MES occurs where average *total* costs are minimized.

Complicating Factors: Transportation Costs

A number of complications need to be considered. Increased output may require a larger market area and

OUTPUT Number of Units	TOTAL VARIABLE COSTS ($)	MARGINAL COSTS ($)	INCREASE IN OUTPUT from
0	0		
		50	0 to 1
1	50		
		40	1 to 2
2	90		
		33	2 to 3
3	123		
		29	3 to 4
4	152		
		28	4 to 5
5	180		
		30	5 to 6
6	210		
		42	6 to 7
7	252		
		60	7 to 8
8	311		
		93	8 to 9
9	405		
		145	9 to 10
10	550		

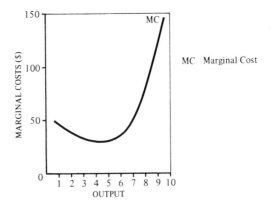

FIGURE 7.12 Change in marginal production costs with scale. Marginal cost is the additional cost of producing one more unit. It can be calculated as the difference in variable costs, in increasing output by one unit. The result is the same if total cost is used. The figures above are derived from Figure 7.10. The marginal cost of increasing production from five units to six is $30. The marginal cost is $210 in variable costs for six units minus $180 for five. Equally, it is $310 in total costs for six minus $280 for five.

involve higher transportation costs. If transportation costs are substantial, they can reduce the MES. Each marginal unit sold involves higher and higher transportation costs, forcing up average total costs (Table 7.11). Another layer of costs is added to production so that average costs comprise average fixed, average variable, and average transportation costs (Figure 7.14). Comparing the output levels with and without transportation costs thus permits an exact determination of the impact of transportation costs on the point of maximum economies of scale (Figure 7.15).

Hoover's Margin Lines

Edgar Hoover introduced the concept of *margin line* to deal with the effect on economies and diseconomies of scale of extending the marketing area and in-

curring transportation costs. The concept is fairly straightforward. At each distance from a plant a calculation is made of what the delivered price would be at that point when transportation costs are added. As long as economies of scale outweigh transportation costs to each given distance, the margin line slopes down and it pays to extend the market area. Once the transportation costs outweigh the economies of scale, the margin line begins to slope up (Figure 7.16). The actual delivered price at each location is determined by the margin line at the actual market boundary. The price paid at each location is this price at the boundary, less the savings in transportation.

The Age and Scale of Equipment

Actual calculations of operating costs are affected by the age, or *vintage*, of equipment used and the scale of the operation. The age of factory equipment affects capital costs for a variety of reasons. Newer equipment tends to be relatively expensive because of inflation and added controls (whether for pollution, safety, or comfort). New equipment sometimes runs into teething problems, which can take years to correct. And the impact of these costs may be aggravated by accounting practices of heavily depreciating equipment in the early years. On the other hand, old equipment may be inefficient, raising labor costs. Based on his survey of British industry, C. F. Pratten thus found the structure of industry varied with the age of equipment in a characteristic way (Table 7.12; Figure 7.17). Moreover, the characteristic change between labor and capital costs with age of equipment was the same whether the equipment had a short life, as some machine tools and textile equipment, which can wear out within 10 years, or a long life, as in the case of cement or soap where machinery can continue to operate for over 40 years.

The newer the equipment is, the lower the average total costs tend to be, and the higher the output at which minimum average costs are achieved (Figure 7.18). Thus, the vintage of equipment affects not only the structure of operating costs but also the average level of operating costs, and the minimum efficient scale.

Long-Run versus Short-Run Unit Costs

Most of the previous discussion refers to the shape of *short-run* unit cost curves. *Long-run* average cost curves (also called *planning curves*) differ from these, because the assumption of a fixed investment in a given plant is dropped; all costs can be considered variable. In the short run, it is assumed that one is dealing with cost variations from operating a *given* farm or factory at different levels of output. In the long run, the business can

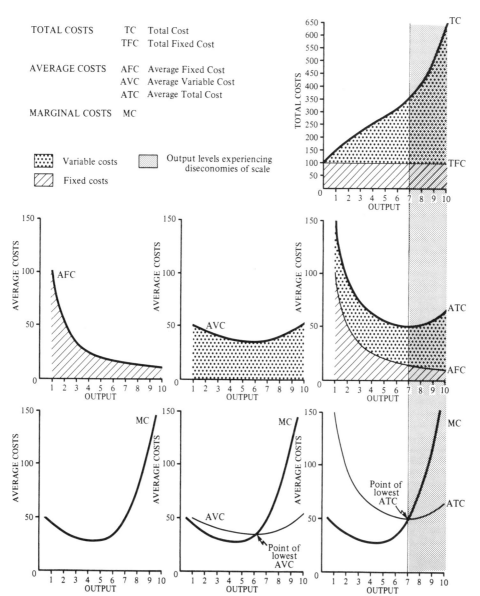

FIGURE 7.13 Finding the divide between economies and diseconomies of scale. This figure essentially brings together Figures 7.10, 7.11, and 7.12. Note that the marginal cost curve *MC* for a product always intersects the average variable cost curve *AVC* where *AVC* is a minimum. It also intersects average total costs *ATC* where these costs are a minimum. The divide between economies of scale and diseconomies of scale is at this point of intersection, where *ATC* is a minimum and where there is an inflection in total costs. Total costs are rising at a decreasing rate if there are economies of scale, and at an increasing rate if there are diseconomies of scale.

be modified or sold, or a new unit with a different amount and configuration of investment can be planned and built for a different scale of output.

In actual practice the distinction between short run and long run is not as clear and simple as the foregoing might indicate, however. For example, Rhys (1971–1972) has estimated that in heavy commercial vehicle manu-

facturing only 5 percent of total costs are variable within a week's time, but in a six-month period 80 percent may be variable (Table 7.13).

One way of looking at the long-run average cost curve is by comparing average cost levels for a variety of different facilities, as in Figure 7.19, which deals with the costs per patient per day for hospitals in Chicago in

TABLE 7.11

Adding in transportation costs

Output Number of units	Transportation costs		Variable costs plus transportation		Total costs plus transportation	
	Unit	Total	Total	Average (AVC')	Total	Average (ATC')
	(1)	(2)	(3)	(4)	(5)	(6)
1	0	0	50	50	150	150
2	5	5	95	48	195	98
3	10	15	138	46	238	79
4	20	35	187	47	287	72
5	35	70	250	50	350	70
6	50	120	330	55	430	72
7	65	185	437	62	537	77
8	80	265	576	72	676	85
9	95	360	765	85	865	96
10	120	470	1020	102	1120	112

Note: (1) Unit transportation costs are the costs of shipping a particular unit of output. The fifth unit cost $35, the sixth $50; (2) Total transportation costs are a running total of column (1). It costs $70 to ship the first five units of output, $120 to ship the first six; (3) Total variable costs are given in Figure 7.10. These figures include the total in column (2). Total variable costs for five units are $180 and total transportation costs are $70. Hence, total variable costs plus transportation for five units are $180 + $70 = $250; (4) AVC' is total average variable costs, including transportation. AVC' is calculated from column (3) divided by output. AVC' for five units is $250 ÷ 5 = $50; (5) Total costs plus transportation are total variable costs, column (3), plus the $100 fixed costs; (6) ATC' is average total costs plus transportation. ATC' is column (5) divided by output level. ATC' for five units is $350 ÷ 5 = $70.

the late 1960s. But each of the individual facilities representing different investment "packages" will have its own short-run cost curve, and the relationship between the two is more properly expressed by a relationship in which the long-run cost curve appears as an "envelope" embracing the many possible short-run curves, as in Figure 7.20.

The "Lazy-J" Long-Run Unit Cost Curve

An outstanding feature of Figure 7.20 is that it shows that the long-run returns to scale of investment may not be U-shaped, but rather that the envelope may take the shape of a reverse- or "lazy-J." The graph in Figure 7.20 shows the short-run cost curves for each of

several types of dairy farms in Minnesota and the characteristics of the least-cost farm are described in each case. For example, the least-cost three-person dairy farm (farm D) is one with an investment of $325,000, working 623 acres of land with a 100-head herd, and producing a net return of $16,925 per annum on a gross income of $80,000. The long-run curve traces out the best achievable cost per unit of output at each scale of production by forming an envelope beneath each of the short-run curves. Note how the long-run curve continues to slope downward to the right, indicating continuing cost advantages of increasing farm size. Each individual type of dairy farming has short-run unit cost curves that are U-shaped, with economies and diseconomies of scale, and an MES where costs are minimized.

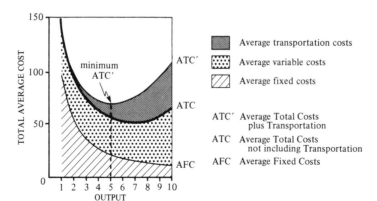

FIGURE 7.14 Average total costs with transportation added. Average total costs plus transportation are given in Table 7.11, column (6). This figure adds one more layer of costs to the average production costs presented in Figure 7.11. Note that the minimum average costs occur at an output level of 5 units when transportation costs are added in.

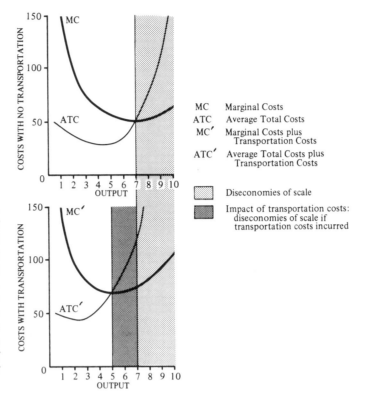

FIGURE 7.15 The impact of transportation costs on economies of scale. The upper figure, repeated from Figure 7.13, shows the output level at which diseconomies of scale set in without transportation costs. The lower figure shows that diseconomies set in at a lower production level if transportation costs are incurred. The difference between the two levels indicates the impact of transportation costs on economies of scale.

The long-run curve does not reveal any diseconomies of scale when farm sizes and management practices can be changed, however. Similar behavior of the long-run curve has been observed in many industries (Table 7.14).

Agriculture is pursuing these long-run cost advantages, resulting in rapid decline of smaller farms and a progressive increase in numbers of larger operations. Such results of cost advantages to larger-sized farms, accruing as they did throughout most of American agriculture, were responsible for the decline in the U.S. farm population from 15 million in 1960 to 10 million in 1970 as the small-scale farmers moved into urban occupations.

Returns to Scale and Threshold Size

Lazy-J long-run cost curves indicate a particular pattern of returns to investment. First, for the reasons cited in the case of short-run curves, there will be economies of scale, and the long-run unit cost curve will fall with increasing output. But only if there are long-run constraints will there be diseconomies of further increases in scale, producing a U-shaped long-run unit cost (LRUC) curve. What occurs with the lazy-J is that the zone of increasing returns to scale terminates at a critical *size threshold,* the minimum size at which the lowest attainable unit costs are achieved. There is no onset of decreasing returns beyond this point because of the flexibility of different investment configurations that may

be designed and built. Instead, beyond the threshold, average costs per unit of output tend to be relatively stable, and there is no apparent cost advantage of operating at either one scale or another. The *threshold size* sets the *condition of entry* for new firms to be able to compete. Entry at smaller scales means higher costs, lack of competitiveness, and ultimate failure, but firms may grow to several multiples of the threshold without cost penalty.

TABLE 7.12

Vintage of equipment and structure of costs in brick production

		Old works (percent)	New works (percent)
Clay		2.6	2.6
Fuel and power		31.5	28.6
Wages and salaries		41.4	20.1
Repairs		9.6	10.5
Rates (local taxes)		2.6	2.8
Office expenses		5.5	5.6
Depreciation		6.8	30.0
	Total	100.0	100.2

Source: Pratten, 1971, p. 97.

Note: Costs include depreciation but exclude interest on capital. Total costs are approximately the same for the two works. The new works has a capacity of about three times the old works, which is 40 years old.

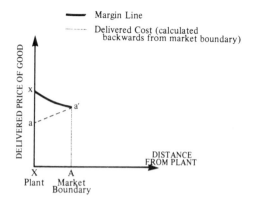

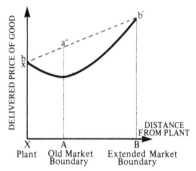

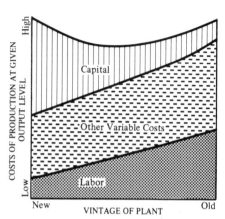

FIGURE 7.17 The effect of age of equipment on the structure of costs. New plant involves heavy capital costs, which in economic terms are incurred when it is installed, but which, for accounting purposes, may be depreciated over a number of years. Older plant is likely to have higher variable costs, for a given level of output. The structure of costs, therefore, varies according to the vintage of the equipment. [*Source:* Adapted from Pratten, 1971, pp. 306–307.]

FIGURE 7.16 Diseconomies in extending the market area. Edgar M. Hoover introduced the concept of *margin line* to deal with the economies and diseconomies in extending the market area. The margin line shows what the delivered price would be at each distance from a plant taking into account the economies of scale given the market available within that distance, and the transportation costs of shipping the good that distance. Given a plant at *X*, which ships as far as *A*, the delivered price at *A* is *Aa'*. If the market is extended to *B*, transportation costs outweigh economies of scale. The price at *B* is *Bb'*, and the price at *A* rises to *Aa"*. The price at any location is the price at the market boundary minus the transportation costs from that boundary.

The Relationship of Threshold Scale to Industrial Concentration

Measurement of Scale Thresholds

One economist, J. S. Bain (1956), has identified the size thresholds associated with lazy-J cost curves in a variety of industries in North America. By expressing the scale of individual manufacturing plants as a percentage of the total national capacity of an industry, costs were shown to decrease with increasing scale, and then to level off. This enabled threshold size to be measured in relation to the proportion of national industrial capacity contained in one plant of minimal efficient size, by selecting as the threshold the point at which costs

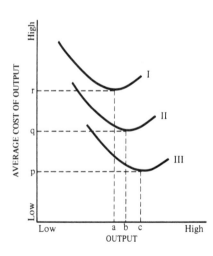

I	Oldest Equipment
II	Newer Equipment
III	Newest Equipment

a	MES of I
b	MES of II
c	MES of III
p	Minimum Average Cost of I
q	Minimum Average Cost of II
r	Minimum Average Cost of III

FIGURE 7.18 Vintage of equipment and economies of scale. Newer equipment tends to achieve its most efficient scale at higher output levels than older equipment. Thus the vintage of equipment affects not only the structure of operating costs but also economies of scale. [*Source:* After Pratten, 1971, p. 5.]

TABLE 7.13

Cost flexibility in heavy commercial vehicle manufacture

Proportion of total costs variable within		
1 week	1 month	6 months
5	35	80

Source: D. G. Rhys, "Heavy Commercial Vehicles: The Survival of the Small Firm," *Journal of Industrial Economics,* XX (1971–1972), p. 233.

Note: Cost flexibility is not symmetric. If orders increase in a six-month period, then 80 percent of costs will increase directly in proportion with output. If orders fall, the manufacturer may become locked into some costs.

leveled off. It also enabled the capital requirements for a new plant to enter the industry at the minimum efficient cost threshold to be calculated. The threshold conditions for entry in many of the industries that Bain studied were substantial.

Emergence of Oligopolies and Administered Prices

There are several consequences of such reverse-J long-run cost curves with high conditions of entry. Gen-

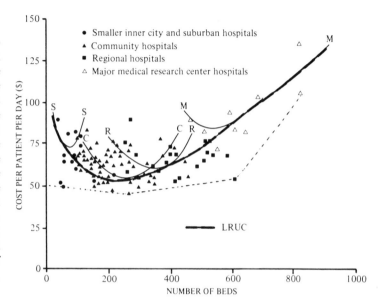

FIGURE 7.19 Cost data for hospitals in metropolitan Chicago. Each point in this graph shows the average patient-day cost for a hospital in the Chicago region. The solid line shows the average relationship for all the hospital averages. The dotted line is an envelope tracing out the silhouette of the best possible long-run average cost curve suggested by the data. The degree to which a hospital's costs lie above this silhouette is an indication of that hosptal's relative inefficiency. [*Source:* Adapted from Gerald F. Pyle, "Heart Disease, Cancer, and Stroke in Chicago," Department of Geography Research Paper No. 134, University of Chicago, 1971.]

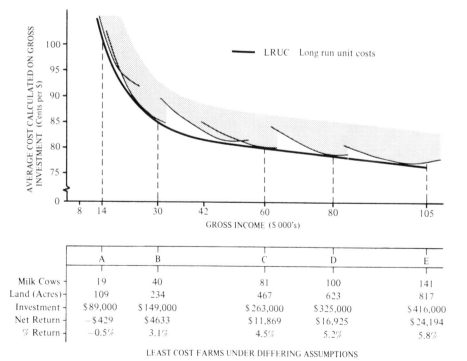

FIGURE 7.20 Short-run and long-run cost curves in dairy farming. The cost curves are a "lazy-J" shape in this example rather than the "U" shape of the earlier discussion of economies and diseconomies. The principles are the same, however. For each investment package there is an optimal output, as shown by the short-run unit cost curve. Alternative farm sizes reveal that the long-run unit cost curve favors larger farms. Farms of 100 acres operate at a net loss. [*Source:* After Buxton and Boyd, Minnesota Dairy Farming, Fig. 4, p. 20.]

	A	B	C	D	E
Milk Cows	19	40	81	100	141
Land (Acres)	109	234	467	623	817
Investment	$89,000	$149,000	$263,000	$325,000	$416,000
Net Return	−$429	$4633	$11,869	$16,925	$24,194
% Return	−0.5%	3.1%	4.5%	5.2%	5.8%

LEAST COST FARMS UNDER DIFFERING ASSUMPTIONS

TABLE 7.14

Long-run economies of scale: Cement industry

Item	Capacity (1000 tons)	100	200	500	1000	2000
	Number of kilns and mills	1	1	2	2	2
Fuel, power, and materials		100	98	97	96	95
Wages and salaries		100	70	55	40	35
Depreciation and return on capital		100	80	70	58	47
Overhead		100	90	82	75	70
Average total costs		100	85	77	69	62

Source: Pratten, 1971, p. 92.

Note: Costs are given as an index of production costs in the smallest plant (100,000 tons per annum). Costs of transportation and selling are excluded. All plants are new.

erally, high conditions of entry limit potential new competition and tend to create oligopolies in which the industry is controlled by a small number of multiplant firms.

An example of a typical oligopoly in which a few firms have consistently controlled a large share of the market is that of the sulfur industry, in particular the Frasch sulfur industry, which produces sulfur from brimstone deposits found in the salt domes of the United States and Mexican Gulf coasts.

The Frasch sulfur industry is oligopolistic because of the high conditions of entry, and the LRUC is reverse-J. The difficulties faced by potential new competitors in gaining entry to the industry are threefold:

1. *Absolute cost barriers.* Established firms control existing Frasch sulfur deposits, and there is great competition for new deposits when discovered. A new sulfur firm enters this arena by having to raise capital for the cost of entry at the same time that it competes with existing producers owning less costly deposits. The effect is to raise the price that must be paid for the new deposits.

2. *Product differentiation barriers.* Firms who have an established reputation with their customers have a sales advantage over new competitors.

3. *The economy of scale threshold.* The minimal scale at which a new firm may achieve the lowest attainable cost is a significant fraction of the total capacity of the industry. The entry of an additional firm may induce established firms to lower their price to preserve their market share. In this case, the newcomer must compete against a price that is even lower than the prevailing price when the firm entered.

This discouragement is often sufficient to turn away potential new entrants.

Relatively free from new competitors, Frasch sulfur producers let their prices be determined by administrative decisions rather than allowing them to fluctuate with market conditions. First, prices were determined by the industry in response to long-run criteria, rather than with respect to short-run economic changes. Second, the industry practiced price discrimination, charging one price in domestic markets and a second, higher basing-point price for foreign markets. The higher price was quoted FOB vessels, Gulf port through the Sulfur Export Corporation, to which all Frasch producers belonged. The domestic price was established competitively by producers; the foreign price, however, was an arranged one producing a world pattern of Frasch sulfur prices rising with transport costs from U.S. Gulf ports.

Product Differentiation as a Barrier to Entry

In most such oligopolistic circumstances, product differentiation is as powerful a force in restricting entry as is the condition of entry itself. The most obvious sources of product differentiation are differences in quality of design among competing outputs. For example, one brand of shoes may have better materials and workmanship than another, or one make of clothes may be fashionable whereas another may not. In either case, different buyers may rank the competing products differently. One buyer may be fashion conscious, looking for the latest styles. Another may be quality conscious, willing to pay a considerable premium for quality shoes. Yet another may be price conscious, accepting the lower quality if there is only a relatively small price concession.

A second source of product differentiation is the ignorance of buyers regarding the essential characteristics and qualities of the goods they are purchasing. This is likely to be an important consideration particularly with durable consumer goods, which are infrequently purchased and complex in design or composition. In this situation, the buyer is likely to rely on the "reputations" of the various products or their sellers—on popular lore concerning the product's performance and reliability, or on whether or not the seller has successfully remained in business for a long time.

Third, buyer preferences for certain products are developed or shaped by the persuasive sales-promotion activities of sellers, particularly by advertising of brand names, trademarks, or company names.

J. S. Bain has classified industries according to degree of product differentiation. He concludes that product differentiation is generally negligible in the producer-good segments of the agricultural, forestry, fisheries, and mining industries. Because goods produced by these industries are likely to be standardized at various grades and qualities, the sellers' efforts to introduce product differentiation have generally been unsuccessful. Moreover, these industries have many small sellers, thus providing a close approximation to the theoretical "pure competition."

On the other hand, in manufacturing and processing industries—particularly those producing consumer goods—product differentiation becomes very important. The consumer-buyer tends to be poorly informed, especially when faced with choosing among goods with complex designs. Even when the goods are not complex, buyers are susceptible to persuasive advertising campaigns that emphasize the sometimes nominal differences among products. In addition, producers can purposely vary the designs or quality of their goods in ways whose significance is not easily understood by consumers.

In some consumer-goods manufacturing industries, however, product differentiation is relatively unimportant. This seems to be especially true of basic necessities—food, clothing, and household supplies. Thus, in these industries the efforts of competing sellers to differentiate their products significantly have not been too successful. Thus, the establishment of brands and their support by advertising has not been automatically efficacious in creating strong product differentiation within a consumer-goods industry.

In manufacturing industries making producer goods, product differentiation is most frequently slight or negligible, and for the usual reasons—expert buyers, and goods that may be produced to standards or specifications. Basic industrial chemicals, for example, clearly come under this heading. Buyers purchase to

specification or rely on established grades and generally do not prefer one seller's output to another sufficiently to induce them to pay a higher price for it. The slight buyer preferences that do introduce some product differentiation generally depend on ancillary services that the seller performs for buyers, such as promptness in filling orders or making deliveries. But with producer goods for which the provision of services by the manufacturer is an important element of the transaction (often when the producer-buyers represent rather small firms) and with large, complex producer goods (specialized machinery of various sorts), product differentiation may become as important as it is in consumer-goods categories. This would be true, for example, of farm machinery and business office machines of various sorts.

Other sectors of the economy may be characterized more briefly with respect to the incidence of product differentiation:

1. Wholesale and retail trade (groceries, clothing stores, pharmacies, and so on). In retail distribution, product differentiation based on type and quality of service offered by the retailer and on the convenience of location to the buyer is generally quite important. Product differentiation is evidently less important in wholesale markets in which retailers purchase from wholesale distributors.

2. Service trades (barber shops, dry cleaners, entertainment enterprises, and so on). Product differentiation is again important, for the same general reasons as those that apply to retailing.

3. Contract construction. On large-scale construction for industry or government where contracts are awarded after a process of bidding to specifications, product differentiation is a minimal factor. In residential construction, product differentiation based on design and location is generally quite important.

4. Finance (real estate firms, insurance companies, banks, and so on). Product differentiation is important in some cases and not in others.

5. Public utlities and transportation. In most utility industries, including suppliers of electricity, gas, and communications services, local monopoly by a single firm typically forestalls the emergence of product differentiation. In the transportation field, product differentiation among the services of competing types of carriers and between competing car-

riers of the same type is present, but is evidently more important in passenger transportation than in freight transportation.

Conditions of Entry and Pricing Behavior

The degree of difficulty that a new firm has in entering a field of industry determines how much the already established firms can raise their prices above the defined competitive level without attracting new competition. In effect, the established firms administer a geography of price, with their selling prices restrained according to the barriers of entry. In industries where the conditions of entry are not difficult, the established firms can exceed only slightly the competitive selling price before new competitors will enter; if entry conditions are difficult, the established firms can perhaps attain a monopolistic price—substantially higher than the competitive level—without attracting competitors; if entry conditions are moderately difficult, the established firms can only raise their prices moderately to keep out new competitors.

Thus, J. S. Bain found in his studies that

1. When barriers to entry are either high or moderate, then
    a. among industries of high seller concentration, *limit pricing* to exclude entry is likely.

This will result in higher prices and greater monopolistic output restriction according to the height of the barriers to entry.
    b. among industries of moderate to low seller concentration, the preceding tendency is likely to be modified or obscured because intraindustry competition will frequently keep price fairly close to the competitive level.
2. When barriers to entry are low, then
    a. among industries of high seller concentration, periodic high prices and monopolistic output restriction are likely to emerge, followed by induced entry, and further followed by excess plant capacity. The ultimate result may be a significant decrease in seller concentration, an increase in intraindustry competition, and a lessening or elimination of monopolistic tendencies.
    b. among industries of moderate to low seller concentration, the pressure of entry plus the inherent tendencies toward strong intraindustry competition are likely to produce close approximations to competitive pricing and output.

Costs, prices, and the degree of concentration of production are thus closely interdependent.

TOPICS FOR DISCUSSION

1. How do the principles of multiples, bulk transactions, massing of reserves, and the engineering principle apply to a particular local industry?
2. Distinguish between the economies of scale owing to large plant size and economies of scale relating to large firm size.
3. Prepare a questionnaire that would be appropriate for the study of economies of scale of a local industry.
4. What advantages does joining a franchise offer to the entrepreneur of a small firm?
5. What are the external economies of scale that accrue to a firm as a result of locating in or near the central business district?
6. What are the external economies of scale offered by industrial parks?
7. What do the size and spacing of plants in different types of industries reveal about the tradeoffs between increasing economies of scale and increasing transportation costs? Does Hoover's margin line help in understanding these tradeoffs as a basis for intrafirm location policy?
8. What are the relationships among the following: minimum efficient scale of operation of an industry, the number of plants in a country, the ubiquity of the industry, and the urban hierarchy?
9. What are the implications for public policy of increasing firm size?
10. If economies of scale are so important, how do you explain the growing relative prominence of small firms?

FURTHER READINGS

BAIN, JOE S. *Barriers to New Competition*. Cambridge, Mass.: Harvard University Press, 1956.
    A pioneering work that laid an intellectual foundation for much that followed on the engineering approach to measuring minimum optimal scale as a percent of national capacity, and on product differentiation and other barriers to entry.

GORECKI, PAUL. *Economies of Scale and Efficient Plant Size in Canadian Manufacturing Industries.* Toronto: McGraw-Hill Ryerson, 1980.

A comprehensive description of economies of scale and the tariff is provided (pp. 67-90) for a country that is concerned about the inefficiencies of an industrial structure that is a miniature replica of the United States.

HAIRE, MASON. "Biological Models and Empirical Histories of the Growth of Organizations." In *Modern Organization Theory,* Vol. I, M. Haire (Ed.). New York: John Wiley, 1959, pp. 272-306.

HOOVER, EDGAR M. *Location Theory and the Shoe and Leather Industry.* Cambridge, Mass.: Harvard University Press, 1937.

One of the great classics on location theory, this book is in two distinct parts: Part I, pp. 3-111, provides a systematic review of location theory within the framework of Alfred Weber (with the developments of Wilhelm Launhardt and Tord Palander). The rest of the book is devoted to two case studies. Economies of scale, discussed in Chapter VI, "Economies of Concentration," pp. 39-111, focuses upon Hoover's concept of the margin line and on the balance of additional production economies less additional delivery costs.

MUND, V. A., and R. H. WOLD. *Industrial Organization and Public Policy.* New York: Meredith Co., 1971.

Like F. M. Scherer's *Industrial Market Structure,* this book is a text for economics courses in market structure, conduct and performance, and their implications for public policy. The authors discuss many topics of interest to economic geographers, such as pricing policies and how prices are set in central markets, in addition to economies of scale.

PRATTEN, C. *Economies of Scale in Manufacturing Industries.* London: Cambridge University Press, 1971.

A detailed study of some two dozen industries, which, together with the 1965 study below, describes the production process, the structure of the industry, cost components, and economies of scale. An excellent source book to use as a foundation for further field study.

PRATTEN, C., and R. M. DEAN. *The Economies of Large-Scale Production in British Industry: An Introductory Study.* Cambridge, U.K.: Cambridge University Press, 1965.

An exemplary study of economies of scale in four industries: book printing, footwear manufacture, the steel industry, and oil refining.

RHYS, D. G. "Heavy Commercial Vehicles: The Survival of the Small Firm." *Journal of Industrial Economics,* XX (1971-1972), pp. 230-252.

A well-documented case study of economies of scale.

ROBINSON, E. A. G. *The Structure of Competitive Industry* (rev. ed.). Chicago: University of Chicago Press, 1958.

A lucid statement of economies of scale and their impact on industrial structure, written for the layperson.

SCHERER, F. M. *Industrial Market Structure and Economic Performance* (2d ed.). Chicago: Rand McNally, 1980.

See Chapter 4, "The Determinants of Market Structure," pp. 81-150. A readable, well-referenced book intended for courses in industrial organization and public policy. Chapter 4 covers economies of scale and mergers, providing many examples and brief reviews of key articles on the subject.

SCHERER, F. M., ALAN BECKENSTEIN, ERICH KAUFFER, and R. DENNIS MURPHY. *The Economics of Multi-Plant Operation.* Cambridge, Mass.: Harvard University Press, 1975.

See Chapter 2, "The Economies of Multi-Plant Operation: Interview Evidence," pp. 237-355. A thorough and systematic discussion, enriched with a continuous stream of examples that bring the topic alive. A useful supplement to the industrial market structure chapter (above).

CHAPTER 8

Preference Structures
and Uncertain Environments

In Chapter 2 we introduced the concept of an omniscient and single-minded rational being, Economic Person, who—with perfect knowledge of present circumstances and future alternatives—is able to maximize utility by building an optimally scaled factory in an ideal location, or to combine resources and technology to achieve the "highest and best" land use. But different social scientists have come up with quite different images of decision-makers, and correspondingly different answers to how decisions are made about which crops to grow, where to produce our industrial goods, or where to locate retail activities. Prominent among these are ideas of "satisficers" working with bounded rationality, and "strategists" competing with a fickle environment. These three images are discussed in the following pages.

Objectives:

- to learn about preference maps and principles of choice among alternatives by an economic maximizer
- to explore ideas of bounded rationality and satisficing behavior
- to explain strategic choices when the "law of requisite variety" holds and the theory of games can be utilized

THREE IMAGES OF DECISION-MAKERS

Classical economic theory tells us what decisions will be made and the economic landscapes that will result if decision-makers know all the answers and act rationally to maximize profits. At the microscale, for instance, the optimal mix of crops needed to maximize income on an individual farm can be calculated. We can even calculate how that optimal mix progressively changes with the distance that an imported farm input such as grain has to be transported, as we shall see. At the macroscale, a later section of the book explains, according to land-use theory, how land is allocated to various urban uses within a city, and to competing rural uses beyond in such income-maximizing fashions.

But what if a decision-maker is not all-knowing, and is confronted by a variety of uncertainties about resources, technology, and markets? It is possible to postulate what such a decision-maker might do if the model of Economic Person prevailed, to compare actual decisions with those that are theoretically optimum, and to find reasons for the differences. Where such comparisons have been made, part of the explanation is usually found to be lack of knowledge, part to lack of access to the best alternatives, and part to uncertainty. What investigators have concluded is that where such differences prevail, decision-makers (working in a framework of *bounded rationality*) tend to be *satisficers*, seeking the certainty of guaranteed returns rather than exposing themselves to risk and uncertainty in the search for maximum profits.

Decision-makers are not omniscient. Information is never complete. Judgments about uncertain environments are often nothing more than "guesstimates." But researchers have come up with a startling conclusion: *Risk and uncertainty do not necessarily rule out maximizing profits.* They do make decision making a little more interesting. The rule is that each risk can be neutralized by a counterstrategy. Is it sometimes too dry? Then irrigate. Too wet? Then drain. Insects bad? Spray. Cold? Get out the smudge pots. Each environmental risk is a strategy that must be regulated and controlled by a counterstrategy. The greater the variety of strategies played by the environment, the greater must be the variety of strategies available to the decision-maker.

For only variety can destroy variety and nothing else can.[1]

This quote explains the *law of requisite variety.* Provided this law is satisfied, an optimal solution exists

[1]W. Ross Ashby, *Introduction to Cybernetics* (London: John Wiley, 1956), p. 207.

to counter any set of risks. That solution can be found by applying the *theory of games.* Without the requisite variety, the decision-maker stands to lose. Nature and the market can combine to play strategies for which there are no satisfactory replies. And such cases do occur: Witness all the uninhabited regions of the world shown on the population maps. With requisite variety, variety in the environment can be controlled by changing the structure and organization of production, however; observe the map of world agricultural regions where each change in climatic type is countered with a change in land use and farming type. Here then is a third image of the decision-maker, the decision-maker as *strategist,* controlling and regulating the risks and uncertainties of the environment, whether physical or human, to optimize output.

We shall now examine each of these three models of decision making in turn, the decision-maker as *maximizer, satisficer,* and *strategist.* And in connection with the discussion of maximization, we shall show, in addition, how demand curves may be constructed, and what the major consequences of spatial variations in prices are, as decision-makers adjust to them.

THE DECISION-MAKER AS MAXIMIZER: OPTIMIZING OUTPUT WHEN AN ECONOMIC PERSON HAS ALL THE ANSWERS

Consider the case of Farmer Jones, engaged in dairying in the state of Iowa. He wants to know what combination of grain and hay he should feed his cattle to maximize milk output and he wants to be able to determine how to crop his land to feed his cattle in an optimal manner. He decides to ask Professor Smith, an agricultural economist at the Iowa State Agricultural Experiment Station, for advice. Professor Smith suggests an experiment. Farmer Jones has a herd of larger-sized Holstein and Brown Swiss cows, each of which has an expected output capacity of 300 to 400 pounds of butterfat annually. The professor suggests that Farmer Jones feed the cattle different combinations of legume hay, corn silage, and grain, and chart the resulting variations in milk output.

This Farmer Jones does, and later on he brings the results to Professor Smith for analysis. The professor begins by plotting Farmer Jones's data in a graph, as in Figure 8.1. The two axes record amounts of grain and hay fed to the cows. Each dot represents one cow, with the milk output noted beside each dot. The next step is to interpolate contour lines showing combinations of feeds resulting in identical levels of output. For example, the 8500-pound contour traces out those combi-

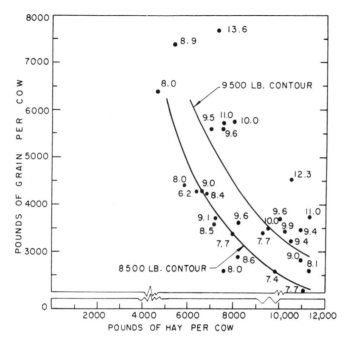

FIGURE 8.1 Equal product contours (feed combinations), at 8500 and 9500 lb of milk per cow. Contours interpolated using the production function, $Y = 3.56X_1^{0.5035}X_2^{0.4}$, where Y is the output of milk and X_1 and X_2 are hay and grain, respectively. Thus, for 8500 lb of milk, the input combinations yielding the 8500 lb contour are given by $X_2 = (8500/3.56X_1^{0.5035})^{2.5}$ [*Source:* Earl O. Heady and Russell O. Olson, *Substituting Relationships, Resource Requirements and Income Variability in the Utilization of Forage Crops* (Ames, Iowa: Research Bulletin 390, Agricultural Experiment Station, Iowa State University, 1952).]

nations of grain and hay that yield 8500 pounds of milk per cow. From a production standpoint, the professor tells Farmer Jones that if he wants this level of output per cow he can feed each of his cows 6000 pounds of grain and 5000 of hay or 3000 pounds of grain and 9000 pounds of hay, or indeed any combination of feeds along the line between. What is important, the professor says, is that Farmer Jones should be *indifferent* to these combinations of feedstuffs from a milk-production standpoint along any particular indifference curve. Each combination on a given curve works equally well, yielding equal milk outputs. The contours can therefore be called *equal-product curves,* or *indifference curves.*

Indifference Curves and the Preference Map

In Figure 8.1, a second indifference curve has been drawn at a higher level of output (9500 pounds). Clearly, many such curves could be interpolated in the graph, and one thing Professor Smith calculated was the mathematical equation describing the shape of the curves so that he could visualize them on the figure. This equation appears in the caption for Figure 8.1. A whole set of curves in a tradeoff graph, such as Figure 8.1, describes Farmer Jones's *preference map,* with higher levels of achievement moving upwards to the right. The curves are all convex to the origin because grain and hay are not perfect substitutes for each other in feeding the cattle. For example, if a cow is producing 8500 pounds of milk, and it is being fed 5000 pounds of hay and 6154 pounds of grain, 1 pound of hay can be substituted for

1.55 pounds of grain and the milk output will remain the same. At the other extreme, however (reading along the indifference curve), if 11,000 pounds of hay and 2281 pounds of grain are being used to produce 8500 pounds of milk, 1 pound of hay only does the same job as 0.26 pounds of grain. When a great deal of any one item is being used or consumed, its relative worth is much less than if a little of it is being used (the principle of decreasing marginal utility of resources as the amount used increases).

The Production-Opportunity Line and the System of Isoquants

The preference map is the first ingredient that Professor Smith needs to answer Farmer Jones's question about feed mixtures and cropping patterns. The second ingredient relates to what Farmer Jones can produce on his land. Let us suppose that he has 100 acres at his disposal to grow hay, grain, or some combination of the two feedstuffs. He might be able to produce, say, 200,000 pounds of grain (2000 pounds per acre) or 500,000 pounds of hay (5000 pounds per acre) by using the land entirely for one or the other, or he could grow some combination of the two.

What should he produce, he asks Professor Smith, to maximize milk yields if he restricts his herd to 8500-pound milk-yielders? And what size herd should he maintain? Professor Smith makes some rapid calculations. Ten times the figures that can be read off the 8500-pound contour in Figure 8.1 shows feed needed for 10

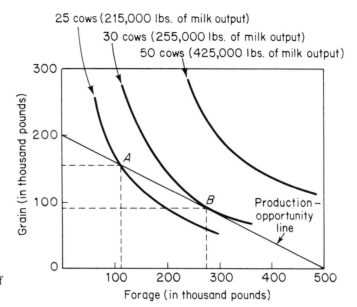

25 cows (215,000 lbs. of milk output)

30 cows (255,000 lbs. of milk output)

50 cows (425,000 lbs. of milk output)

A

B

Production-opportunity line

Grain (in thousand pounds)

Forage (in thousand pounds)

FIGURE 8.2 Determination of cropping pattern and herd size.

cows; adding a zero to that obtains the input requirements for 100 cows.

The professor then draws another graph—Figure 8.2—with the results of these calculations in it. First, he plots Farmer Jones's *production-opportunity line,* which shows what feeds he can produce on his 100 acres: either 200,000 pounds of grain, or 500,000 pounds of hay, or some combination of the two, depending on how much land he uses for one or the other. Second, he plots contours for the results of his calculations showing total input requirements for different herd sizes. These contours are called *isoquants,* and they were the ones produced by the calculations described above. Each isoquant records the input combinations that will produce an equal quantity of output. Thus, the lowest isoquant in Figure 8.2 charts the varying combinations of inputs required to support a 25-cow herd of 8500-pound milk-yielders. The highest isoquant is for double that herd size, and the middle one is for 30 cows, which will together yield 255,000 pounds of milk.

The professor then shows Farmer Jones why it is impossible to feed a herd of 50 cows and expect 8500 pounds of milk per cow. The highest isoquant in the graph requires far more feed than can be produced on 100 acres of land. Similarly, although the farmer could crop his land in a way that would just feed a 25-cow herd of 8500-pound producers (point *A* in Figure 8.2), he can do better than that. The production-opportunity line extends above the 25-cow isoquant in places, so that by producing somewhat more hay and less grain on his 100 acres he can still get 8500 pounds of milk per cow and support a herd of 30 cows (point *B* in Figure 8.2). At this point—the highest isoquant reachable with the

production-possibility line—some 270,000 pounds of hay and 90,000 pounds of grain are produced on the farm and result in a total output of 255,000 pounds of milk. This, Professor Smith tells Farmer Jones, is the way to maximize milk output in any *given* year.

The Effect of Complementary Production Relationships over Time

But Professor Smith points out that Farmer Jones can do even better than this if he grows his crops in rotation, managing his farm properly over a *period* of years. In Figure 8.2 it was assumed that the crops were *competitive,* that is, that any increase in acreage of one resulted in a correspondingly proportional decrease in acreage—and therefore in output—of the other. But crops grown in rotation may be *complementary* in that growing one may increase the yields of the other in the following year. Grasses and legumes, for example, accumulate nitrogen and therefore increase yields of the subsequent year's crops. Professor Smith provides a simple example to Farmer Jones (Figure 8.3). This was drawn from experimental data he had previously obtained from rotations grown on Marshall silt loam soil at the Page County Experimental Farm in Iowa. In Figure 8.3, the curve *CabcdR* indicates the output of grain and forage derived from 100 acres of land when the two crops are grown in rotation. The production-opportunity line is not straight, but convex upwards, indicating that the farmer might be able to crop his land and support a 35-cow herd of 8500-pound producers, giving a total output of 300,000 pounds of milk, if he practiced proper

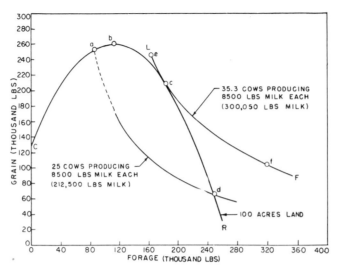

FIGURE 8.3 Substitution of forage for grain in crop production and milk production. [*Source:* Heady and Olson, 1952.]

crop rotations. Farmer Jones, seeing that point *c* is higher up in his preference map than, for example, points *a* and *d,* at either of which he could only support a herd of 25 cows, readily agrees that he should find the right crop rotation for his soils and climate.

What rotation scheme should then be used? Farmer Jones inquired next. The professor provided a series of examples of three-, four-, and five-year rotations, compared with single-cropping corn (Table 8.1). From such data, he and the farmer quickly determine an appropriate cultivation plan. Farmer Jones has the

information he needs to make the best choices among the alternatives available to him.

Price Changes and the Price Consumption Curve

If Farmer Jones operated a feed lot instead of cultivating the land, and bought his forage and grain on the open market, his herd size and feed mix would be determined by the funds available to purchase feeds, rather than the cropping capability of his land. Herd size and

TABLE 8.1

Complementary and competitive relationships in forage production for two soil types (data for 100 acres of land)

Rotation[a]	Acres of land out of 100 in		Total production (pounds)		Pounds of grain sacrificed for each pound of hay added over previous rotation
	Grain	Hay	Grain	Hay	
Wooster and Canfield silt loams, Wooster, Ohio, 1937–1943[b]					
C	100	0	217,840	—	
C–C–C–W–A	80	20	229,776	128,800	Complementary
C–W–A	67	33	215,480	203,200	0.19
C–C–W–A–A	60	40	190,672	316,000	0.22
C–W–A–A	50	50	165,928	363,000	0.53
Clarion-Webster silt loam, Ames, Iowa, 1945–1948[c]					
C	100	0	180,320	—	
C–C–O–Cl	75	25	217,360	85,000	Complementary
C–O–Cl	67	33	182,333	132,660	0.71

Source: Earl O. Heady and Russell O. Olson, *Substitution Relationships, Resource Requirements and Income Variability in the Utilization of Forage Crops* (Ames, Iowa: Research Bulletin 390, Agricultural Experiment Station, Iowa State University, 1952).

[a]C, corn; O, oats; W, wheat; Cl, clover; A, alfalfa.

[b]See Yoder, R. E., "Results of Agronomic Research on the Use of Lime and Fertilizers in Ohio," Ohio Agr. Exp. Sta. Agron. 96 (Mimeo), 1945.

[c]From unpublished data, Dept. of Agronomy, Iowa Agr. Exp. Sta. Ames, Iowa, 1915–1948.

feed mix would also be subject to fluctuations in grain and hay prices. The effects are illustrated in Figure 8.4. The graph shows a succession of isoquants. For purposes of this example, it is assumed that the farmer spends a fixed sum on forage and grain. If all the money is spent on forage, *OF* can be purchased.

Now, let forage prices remain constant, but grain prices change. When grain prices are high, only G_4 can be bought, and the farmer's *price-possibility line* is G_4F. This line, in a manner analogous to the production-possibility line discussed earlier, describes what can be purchased with the funds (or resources) available. The optimal herd size and mix of input purchases is given by point *A*. If the grain price falls, however, purchases of grain can be increased to G_3, G_2, etc. The equilibrium moves from *A* to *B*, *C*, and *D* on higher isoquants. Because grain prices are lower, more milk can be produced, and relatively larger shares of grain will appear in the feed mix. The line charted by the successive points *A*, *B*, *C*, and *D* is a *price-consumption curve* (or "satisfaction path").

Price Effects, Income Effects, and Substitution Effects

Movement along the price-consumption curve as prices fall is called a *price effect*, which has two parts:

1. An *income effect;* that is, as price falls, the farmer moves on to a higher isoquant, maintains a larger herd, produces more, and becomes better off.
2. A *substitution effect;* that is, because the relative price of grain and forage changes with a move along the curve, the farmer tends to use more of the input that has become relatively

cheaper, substituting it for the other in his input mix.

Construction of Demand Curves

It is from the price-consumption curve that the farmer's *demand schedule* or *demand curve* can be constructed. For example, each of the points, *A*, *B*, *C*, and *D* in Figure 8.4 shows how much grain will be purchased at different grain prices. If this information is plotted in a price-quantity graph, the farmer's demand schedule for grain will be apparent: As the price falls, the quantity consumed increases.

CONSEQUENCES OF SPATIAL VARIATIONS IN PRICES

In Chapter 6 we saw how many prices increased with increasing distance from market centers because of the effect of transportation costs. What are the consequences? Restricting ourselves for the moment to the agricultural example presented above, if grain is shipped in from some central market, the more distant farmers

1. use more forage, substituting the cheaper input for the more expensive one;
2. have smaller herds, and produce less on a given acreage, that is, they are less intensive;
3. earn less.

Because there are both income and substitution effects of price changes, as prices increase with distance, quantity consumed decreases, producing as a result, *spatial demand cones* of the kind discussed in Chapter 6.

Regional Variations in Welfare

The price effects of increasing distance include both income effects (people are less affluent) and substitution effects (activities are less intensive). The resulting regional variations appear and reappear in a variety of aspects of life throughout the world, where one of the most marked spatial differences is between affluent, growing activity in core regions where prices are determined, and lagging peripheries, less advanced, with greater poverty populations, and with far more extensive production patterns.

To illustrate, Figure 8.5 presents a series of graphs constructed as part of a study of regional development in the United States using data from the 1960 census. The horizontal axis in each of the 12 cases covers the 270 miles from Dallas to Houston-Galveston, Texas. The vertical axis of each shows how different characteristics

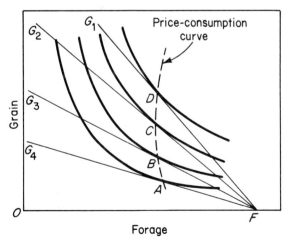

FIGURE 8.4   Effects of relative price changes.

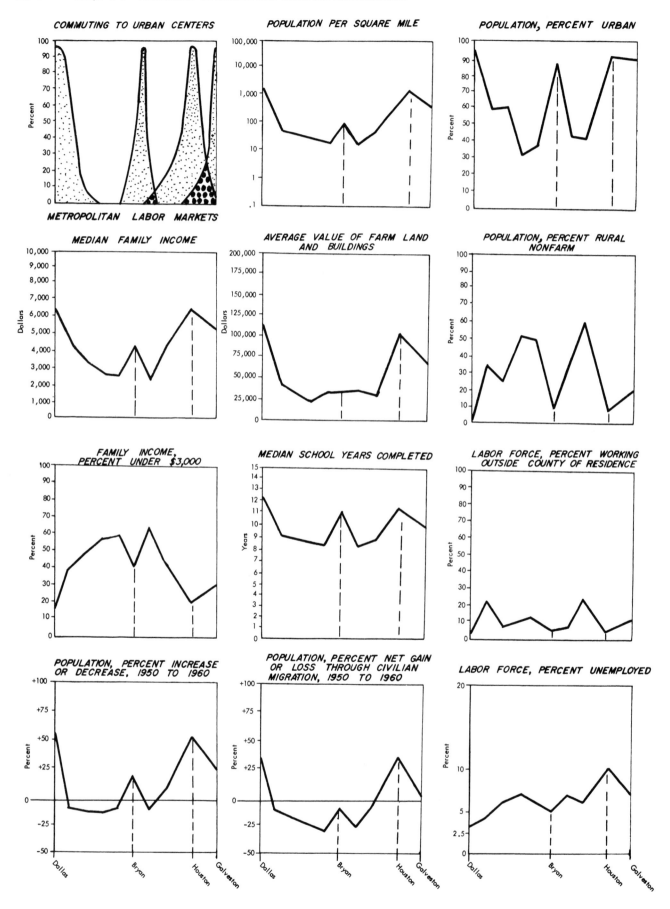

COMMUTING TO URBAN CENTERS

POPULATION PER SQUARE MILE

POPULATION, PERCENT URBAN

METROPOLITAN LABOR MARKETS

MEDIAN FAMILY INCOME

AVERAGE VALUE OF FARM LAND AND BUILDINGS

POPULATION, PERCENT RURAL NONFARM

FAMILY INCOME, PERCENT UNDER $3,000

MEDIAN SCHOOL YEARS COMPLETED

LABOR FORCE, PERCENT WORKING OUTSIDE COUNTY OF RESIDENCE

POPULATION, PERCENT INCREASE OR DECREASE, 1950 TO 1960

POPULATION, PERCENT NET GAIN OR LOSS THROUGH CIVILIAN MIGRATION, 1950 TO 1960

LABOR FORCE, PERCENT UNEMPLOYED

vary from place to place along this 270-mile stretch. The first graph on the second row shows that income levels drop with increasing distance from Dallas, rise around Bryan, fall again, then rise toward Houston. This is the income effect described above. Similar patterns will be found in each of the other graphs. In each case the *distance-gradients* reflect spatial adjustments resulting from the income and substitution effects of price increases. For example, as the extent of commuting to jobs in the metropolitan centers declines with distance from the metropolises (top left-hand graph), population densities, the proportion of the population classified as urban, the value of land and buildings, income, amount of schooling, rate of population increase, and percent change in the population through migration all decline. The percentage of the population classified as *rural nonfarm* rises and then falls. Both the percentage of families with incomes less than $3000 (the 1960 poverty line) and the unemployment rate increase with distance from the central city.

The rhythmic changes rise and fall like the tune of a well-known song. This rhythm symbolizes a *regional welfare syndrome* in which the lowest levels of welfare are to be found at the peripheries of major metropolitan regions, where prices are highest and economic opportunities are least.

That the population is responding to these systematic variations in welfare is also implied, for population is generally decreasing at the outer edges of the metropolitan regions, responding to differences in incomes and opportunities by migrating from areas of low opportunity to the metropolitan centers that are perceived to offer greater advantages.

Market Potentials and the Geography of Demand

It follows from the foregoing that areas more accessible to central markets are more likely to have a higher density of population and a higher per capita demand than less-accessible areas, and that distance reduces demand and incomes. This idea has been used to develop measures of *market potentials,* designed to show spatial variations in the demands that can be served from different locations.

The computation of market potentials is relatively simple. Quantity demanded drops off with distance in

any spatial demand cone. Total demand at any center can be calculated by finding the area under the spatial demand cone—that is, by adding up the quantity demanded at each point within the market area traced out by the demand cone.

Now imagine a map that plots the *results* of such summations.

In places with higher population densities and incomes, the market potential will be higher; in the inaccessible peripheries it will be lower. The data can be contoured and a map of market potentials can be produced.

Because the exact quantity likely to be demanded by consumers at all locations is unlikely to be known for all locations, approximation methods are used to indicate likely variations in market potentials, however. One such approximation uses population numbers rather than quantities demanded; another uses total incomes. The approximation techniques thus result in maps of *population potentials* and *income potentials* as conveniently calculated substitutes for exact market potentials.

Population potentials measure the influence of population at a distance. They are calculated on the assumption that the strength of the *gravitational influence* V of a population P, at some other point c located r miles away, is

$$V_c = \frac{P}{r}$$

where
V_c = population potential V at point c
r = distance to some other point

In other words, the attraction varies directly with population and inversely with distance. But there are many other places for which an attraction exists. Therefore the expression becomes

$$V_c = \Sigma_i \frac{P_i}{r_{ic}}$$

where
V_c = population potential V at point c
P_i = population at point i
r_{ic} = distance from i to c

and Σ_i signifies that each "bit" of gravitational influence on c of all i points surrounding c is being added

FIGURE 8.5 Socioeconomic gradients along a 270-mile traverse from Dallas to Galveston, Texas. The graphs have been plotted using U.S. census data from 1960. Each graph illustrates the same 270 miles from Dallas through Bryan, to Houston and Galveston. Locations of the towns are indicated at the bottom of each column. Note how incomes rise and fall in relation to the intensity of commuting to urban centers. Other characteristics rise and fall in the same manner.

together. If I_i, the total income at point i, is substituted for P_i in the last equation, one calculates income potentials in a directly analogous manner.

Potentials are easily mapped. This is simply a matter of joining all points of the same potential on the map, just as contours on a physical relief map are made by joining all points of the same elevation above sea level.

An example is given in Figure 8.6, a map of income potential for the world. Two important peaks of potential appear. The first of these summits is the New York–Chicago axis, the North American industrial heartland, and the second is the Western European peak extending from southern Great Britain to West Germany and thence to northern Italy. Observe that the peaks are sharply delineated and are surrounded on all sides by steeply declining gradients. Both peaks are enclosed by a single $300 million isopotential line.

Two much smaller high points on the income potential map also appear. One of these is defined by the $300 million isopotential line encircling the main Japanese island of Honshu and the other is the small area of southeasternmost Australia enclosed by an isopotential line of $150 million. Note the absence of peaks cor-

responding to the East Asian and South Asian population clusters. Despite their enormous populations, China and India have per capita incomes so low that they are unable to generate concentrations of income potential. Only the world's modern urban-industrial core regions stand out. They are, of course, the centers of demand on a world scale, the world's "heartlands."

HUMAN BEINGS AS SATISFICERS: THE DECISION PROCESS WHEN RATIONALITY IS BOUNDED

Economic Person is a theoretical ideal, in which human beings are perceived as organizing themselves and their activities in space so as to optimize utility. But in reality, decision-makers may operate in a context far from the theoretical optimum. For example, farmers in the developing countries rarely achieve the record yields attained in developed countries or in the controlled research conducted by agricultural research stations. Most of this gap in yields is a result of common-sense decisions by farmers or of circumstances outside their con-

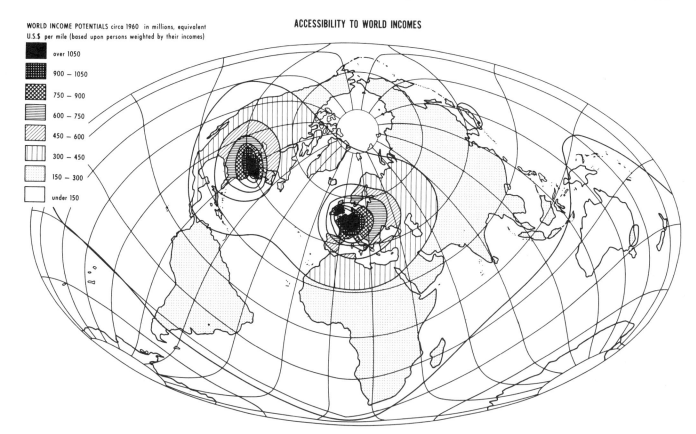

FIGURE 8.6 Income potential of the world. [*Source:* William Warntz, *Macrogeography and Income Fronts* (Philadelphia: Regional Science Research Institute, 1965), p. 92.]

trol, rather than lack of skill or initiative on their part. In some cases, it may not pay farmers to buy inputs that might help improve yields. In others, the poor quality of the land or a lack of resources may make it impossible for them to use the cultivation practices that maximize yields.

What are some of the factors that cause yields at research stations and in farmers' fields to differ? They are suggested in Figure 8.7.

First, the *technical ceiling* for on-farm yields is lower than that for research stations. The latter use technologies that are not feasible at the farmers' usual scale of production. Research stations are usually located on choice land and can depend on irrigation if it is needed. The farmers' environment is rarely as kindly.

Second, the on-farm *economic ceiling* is often much lower than the on-farm technical ceiling. Farmers' profits are often highest at input levels lower than those necessary for maximum yields, because of diminishing returns on investment in inputs.

Third, farmers' *actual yields* are usually below even economic ceilings. This may be because key inputs such as fertilizer, water, and labor are not available when needed, because farmers may not know about best cultivation practices, or because volatile output prices and unreliable rainfall reduce expected returns. These factors may force the farmer into a "safety-first" strategy, producing to assure guaranteed returns (*satisficing*) rather than risking all in a vain attempt to maximize.

Even in more-developed countries, satisficing is common. In a study of middle Sweden, Julian Wolpert (1964) compared actual labor productivity in agriculture to the theoretically optimum level of productivity calculated by using mathematical programming methods to simulate Economic Person. He found that, on av-

erage, middle Sweden's farmers achieved only two-thirds of the potential productivity their resources would allow, with substantial variations from place to place within the region. He concluded that one or both of the prerequisites for economic rationality (perfect knowledge and optimizing behavior) were lacking.

But which? Wolpert went on to explore the knowledge situation and discovered that, to a very great extent, information about recommended farm practices, new agricultural machinery, new seed varieties, expected costs, and market prices originated for middle Sweden's farmers among institutions in the Stockholm-Uppsala area. Although information was disseminated in a rapid and reasonably efficient manner, the communication process affected farmers unequally, and this unevenness was significant spatially. The diffusion process proceeded by steps, from the experts in the core zone of Stockholm-Uppsala to the disseminating organizations' central offices, then to the local county offices, which are situated typically in the county's leading city. This initial process took place rather rapidly without significant differences from one county to another in middle Sweden. The transmission then proceeded in stepwise fashion, directed at first to the larger farmers and those situated within the major agricultural districts of each county. An intracounty diffusion process was set in motion that involved filtering and imitation through the farmers' ranks so that considerable lag intervened until small farmers who are isolated were made aware of new information. Farm size, membership in the farmers' organizations, and location with respect to other farmers all influenced the network of communication over the surface. The communication stream was fastest in the areas of highest potential productivity (responding to the greater demand for information) and the spatial lag was greatest where the relative advantages of shifting in the direction of rationality were least (where there is less demand for information).

The farmers also worked in a climate of uncertainty that included: (1) personal factors; for example, farmers' health and ability to work; (2) institutional arrangements; for example, government policy, landlord-tenant relationships; (3) technological changes; (4) market structure; and (5) physical factors; for example, weather, blight, and other environmental variables. Many of these sources of uncertainty were reduced through social insurance, legal tenant contracts, and long-term government price policies in the agricultural sector, but yield variability arising from weather uncertainty remained as a significant unknown in the planning environment, and its impact was spatially differentiated. To spread this risk, the farmers tended to diversify their crops, preferring safety to the greater risks of the more lucrative crops. Where environmental risk

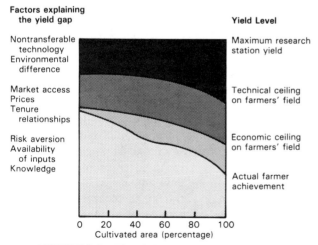

Factors explaining the yield gap

Nontransferable technology
Environmental difference

Market access
Prices
Tenure relationships

Risk aversion
Availability of inputs
Knowledge

Yield Level

Maximum research station yield

Technical ceiling on farmers' field

Economic ceiling on farmers' field

Actual farmer achievement

0   20   40   60   80   100
Cultivated area (percentage)

FIGURE 8.7 The yield gap in Third-World agriculture.

was greatest, so was crop diversification; only in the most favorable environments did farmers opt for specialization in profit-maximizing crops—and even then, not all farmers. In short, the presence of environmental uncertainty precluded profit maximization, and even if the intention had been to maximize profit, imperfect knowledge prevented its realization. The existence of risk and uncertainty about the consequences of alternative courses of action made it necessary for the farmers to consider not only the desirability of outcomes but also their probability of occurrence. Courses of action had to be determined, the outcomes of which were both sufficiently certain and desirable to satisfy the decision-maker. The quest for income stability was apparently at least as important to middle Sweden's farmers as the pure profit motive, and it was this preference for guaranteed security of outcomes that identified them as satisficers.

OPTIMIZING OUTPUT
IN UNCERTAIN ENVIRONMENTS

Environmental Uncertainty

Geography, by its very nature, is concerned with interrelationships between human beings and their environment. The environment is thought of as being primarily the physical environment: climate, soil, vegetation, and physiography. For the economic geographer, economic environment is important, too, including sources of raw material, location of markets, availability of labor, transportation facilities, and price levels. But whether the environment affecting production is primarily physical or economic, environmental conditions inevitably vary from time to time and from place to place, and these variations can create risks for the producer. Climate, for instance, has been described as average weather conditions, not long-term averages. Average rainfall, for example, is just that, and the variability tends to increase the lower that is the average. But the lower the average is, the smaller the margin may be between adequate and inadequate rainfall and the greater the risk to crops and livestock posed by any shortfall.

Risk and uncertainty may appear on first consideration to reduce decision making to a blind game of chance. The reader may well argue that if we cannot be certain of environmental conditions we cannot determine an optimal decision. Decisions based on average conditions may be wrong more often than right as actual conditions constantly fluctuate. To base decisions on averages is to ignore variety. And what if the data

are not adequate to provide meaningful averages? What, in fact, if the environment is quite unpredictable? Surely that spells an end to rational decision making. Not really. A way of taking account of such risk, predictable or otherwise, is provided by the *theory of games*. This approach, first brought to the attention of geographers by Peter Gould (1963), provides a powerful tool for optimizing decisions in the face of uncertainty. This theory, and the *law of requisite variety* on which it is based, calls for a number of changes in the way that environmental uncertainty is viewed.

First, implicit in the theory of games and the law of requisite variety is the idea that the *number* of types of uncertainty is more important than any single quantitative measure of the aggregate *level* of risk. The distinction between number and level of variations in the environment is therefore critical. Variations in environmental conditions are viewed qualitatively, not quantitatively. For example, if the minimum rainfall for a successful wheat crop is 10 inches, then 6 inches may be as bad as 4 inches. A miss is as good as a mile. And if the wheat needs 90 days to mature, and there was an early frost killing the crop, it scarcely matters whether it was one week or two weeks before harvest. Similarly, it is more important to know that sometimes farmers lose their crops because of drought and sometimes because of frost than to know that any one farmer has lost it on average one year in seven. If drought is the farmer's only problem, then only one set of solutions is called for. But if there is also a problem of frost, then a second, and separate, set of considerations is called for. And once environmental variety has been turned from adversity into diversity and neutralized from risk to event, then the frequency of these events loses its economic impact.

The list of environmental elements that may vary significantly is specific to the group of products, the time, and the place involved. For the farmer they may be physical factors such as drought, frost, soil conditions, and danger of hail, and economic factors such as interest rates, market prices, prices of farm equipment, and transportation rates. For the industrialist, they may be past prices and supply of components, changes in market tastes, obsolescence due to technological breakthroughs, and changes in government legislation affecting taxes, consumer protection, competition from imports, and permitted increases in wages and prices. The important thing is for the decision-maker to know which elements of the environment may vary, and to have a countervailing strategy to control and regulate the impact of each of them, whatever the risk. Only if the risk is so slight and predictable that it can be insured against, would the decision-maker ignore it in the decision making. Otherwise it should be considered and a strategy-mix developed to cover all possibilities. Strangely enough, the theory of games does offer a strategy-mix that optimizes output even when the probability of each event is unknown.

It follows that we should think in terms of environmental variety rather than environmental risk. The environment poses risks only if our decisions make certain environmental conditions a risk to our output. A particular amount of rainfall is not an intrinsic risk to agriculture. It is the actual decision as to what crops to grow that makes any particular rainfall level a potential risk. If our decisions are taken to accommodate the possibility of low rainfall, then low rainfall is one variety of environmental condition, and no more.

Time and Place in the Strategy-Mix

Variety in the environment must be regulated and controlled if we are to regulate output, wherever and whenever it occurs. In this sense variety between locations at one point in time is as important as variety at one location over time. Variety between locations in climate, mineral deposits, and market accessibility may be regulated by producing different goods. From this standpoint, economic geography is the study of how human beings take advantage of variety in the environment to satisfy the full variety of human needs and wants, by turning environmental variety into advantage rather than risk. Similarly, the decision-maker can control the impact of environmental variety over time in one location by following a mixed strategy rather than concentrating on some single product. There is, however, an important difference between the two situations. Variety across space can be countervailed by location-specific strategies tailored to the conditions at each location. Variety through time is less predictable in the short run and must be countervailed by a mixed strategy that accommodates variety at the location over time. For instance, if in one location the optimal strategy were to allocate 70 percent of the land to sheep and 30 percent to wheat, it would add up to the same thing statistically in the long run if farmers proportioned their land use each year or if farmers divided themselves into sheep specialists and wheat specialists and proportioned out the land aggregatively, or if the farmers allocated all the land to sheep seven years in 10, and to wheat the other three. Practical decision-makers, concerned with the here and now rather than long-term statistical averages, are likely to opt for an annual proportionment. The point is that diversity over time is more difficult to regulate than variety across space. It is precisely in this sit-

uation, then, that the theory of games has its biggest contribution to make.

THEORY OF GAMES

The Rules of the Game

The *theory of games* is a rigorous and sophisticated mathematical approach to decision making in the face of uncertainty. It was developed primarily by the Hungarian-American mathematician John Von Neumann. The approach received wide attention in the social sciences with the publication by Von Neumann and O. Morgenstern of their book *Theory of Games and Economic Behavior* (1944). Geographic examples were provided earlier in this text by Peter Gould. The simplest interesting applications involve two adversaries although the theory can be applied no matter what the number.

The theory assumes that there is a specific, predetermined outcome, or payoff, for every combination of strategies used by the players. Assume two players: a farmer versus the physical environment. The farmer (and in theory the environment too), know just what the yield will be for each crop under each set of climatic conditions. For instance, I plant corn, and the climate plays its short, cool, dry summer. Result: The corn does not grow quite as high as Rogers and Hammerstein's elephant's eye. Often the loser pays the predetermined amount to the winner, but whether this is so or not, it is assumed that each player wants to maximize winnings, or at least minimize losses.

The application of the theory of games to geographic examples involving the physical environment personifies nature. Nature becomes an unyielding opponent, relentlessly trying to outwit people in the vital task of earning their daily bread. This implied personification does not invalidate applications of the theory of games to geography but it does raise questions about the meaning of the results, which are presented as a conclusion to this section.

To see how the theory of games applies let us begin with a simple hypothetical example where the producer's strategy collapses to a single dominant choice. Imagine a farmer trying to decide whether to produce wheat or corn (or some combination of the two). The choice is dependent on the growing season, which can be wet or dry. Furthermore, rainfall has proved to be completely unpredictable so that the farmer has no way of knowing which it is likely to be. The farmer, an enthusiastic fan of Von Neumann, draws up a payoff matrix (Table 8.2). The farmer observes that the yields are

TABLE 8.2

Hypothetical payoffs in farmer versus environment

Farmer's strategies	Environment's strategies		Row minimum
	Wet	Dry	
Corn	45	1	1
Wheat	35	10	10
Column maximum	45	10	

Note: Figures are in bushels per acre and are hypothetical. The important point is that the highest row minimum (10 bushels) is the same as the lowest column maximum. This strategy is then the best for each player.

lower for both corn and wheat in dry years. Nevertheless, the 10 bushels of wheat is better than 1 bushel of corn. But in a wet year the 45 bushels of corn is much better than the 35 bushels of wheat. So which should the farmer choose?

Assume each player is trying to do the best one can. If the farmer consistently goes for corn, the environment would consistently go for a dry-year strategy to minimize its losses. The farmer, realizing this was a sequence of dry years, would switch to wheat. But even with this switch to wheat, the environment would be better to stick with the dry strategy. The environment's minimum maximum, namely 10 bushels, equates the farmer's maximum minimum. The strategies, given a miserly environment, will lock into this single wheat-dry strategy. It does not pay either player to change even though both players will have guessed the other's strategy. Prior knowledge does not benefit either player. One strategy dominates the others. The collapse of the farmer's corn strategy suggests the need for alternative strategies—perhaps growing millet or sorghum or perhaps introducing livestock. The single wheat strategy fails to meet the requisite variety imposed by the environment. Let us now, then, take a real example that does meet the requisite variety and where a mixed strategy has evolved.

A Jamaican Fishing Village

The anthropologist William Davenport (1960) has provided a vivid example of how the theory of games can be applied to understanding humanity's struggle against the environment with a study of the problems faced by 200 villagers on the south coast of Jamaica. The men of this village are all fishermen and make their living entirely by fishing in the local waters by canoe and selling their catch on the island. The fishing grounds extend 22 miles out to sea with the inshore (or "inside") banks extending out as far as 5 miles to 15 miles. Beyond are the offshore (or "outside") banks. This distinction is important. Very strong currents flow at frequent intervals in either direction across the offshore banks. The seas can be much rougher too. But the rewards for successful fishing on the offshore banks are considerably greater. Is it worth the risk?

The decision of where to fish must be made by each fishing captain. There are 26 of these, each with his own crew. In coming to a decision, a good many factors have to be considered. The outside banks yield fish of higher grade and larger size. But if strong currents flow for several days on end, the floats become waterlogged and the pots and their catch are lost. Even short periods of currents can cause havoc by dragging pots against rock outcrops and coral and by killing the catch with sudden water temperature changes. Equipment costs for offshore fishing are higher too because, in addition to a higher rate of pot replacement, stronger canoes are needed, which after a few years use are suitable for inshore use only and so must be replaced. The method of paying the crew also has to be considered. Two methods are employed. Either the crew are allowed to set some pots for themselves or they are given part of the catch plus a small wage. But on days when the crew with pots catch nothing, the captain is obliged to pay them a wage even if he has caught nothing himself. Now how can all this be set out in a form that will permit us to calculate their optimal strategy? The answer is to reduce the toil, risk, and heartbreak of the different outcomes to the common denominator of hard cash profit or loss. Davenport concludes that a fisherman opting to work the offshore banks exclusively for a month (in fact none do) could stand to make £20 profit if there were no currents, but to lose £4 if currents flowed throughout the month.

The exercise must now be repeated for the inshore option. Profits here are much lower, but the risks are less. This strategy yields its highest income when things go badly for the offshore fishermen. With the offshore catch lost, competition is reduced and inshore fishermen can earn as much as £17 a month. But better times for the offshore fishermen brings in a supply of better-quality fish, thus forcing their income down to a monthly equivalent of £12. A mixed strategy is also possible with captains locating pots both inshore and offshore.

The results of the alternative strategies are summarized in Table 8.3. The figures are Davenport's, and they show three separate strategies for fishermen: inshore, offshore, and mixed. We can now calculate the proper strategy for the fishermen.

First note that a 2 × 3 game should reduce to a 2 × 2 game. For the fishermen should use the very best available countervailing strategy for each environmental strategy. Two environmental strategies exist. The two best countervailing strategies only should be used. A

TABLE 8.3

Jamaican fishermen versus the sea: The payoffs

Fishing strategies	Environment Strategies		Row minimum
	Current	No current	
Inshore	17.3	11.5	11.5*
Mixed	5.2	17.0	5.2
Offshore	−4.4	20.6	+
Column maximum	17.3	17.0**	

Note: The figures are from William Davenport (1960) in £ sterling and are computed on the basis of a one-month period. Davenport uses the terms *inside* and *outside* rather than *inshore* and *offshore*.

+, The offshore strategy is dominated by the mixed strategy. *, The highest row minimum is different than the lowest column maximum (**). A mixed-strategy of inshore and mixed inshore-offshore fishing will be best.

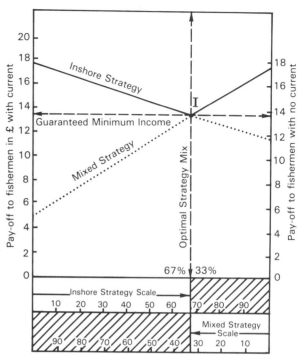

FIGURE 8.8 Graphical solution to the Jamaican fishing village strategy problem. Plot the income for each fishing strategy on the axes for current and no current, and join corresponding points. The maximum income under various mixes of current-no current conditions is given by the upper *V* above the intersection point *I*. Assume environment will force income to a minimum. Then the minimum maximum is the best obtainable solution, yielding about £13 income a month with two-thirds inshore, one-third mixed fishing. Point *I* is thus the "minimax" solution to the fisherman's problem.

third is redundant and is included in the study by Davenport only for the sake of completeness and to illustrate how one strategy can sometimes dominate another. In the case of the Jamaican fishermen, none uses the offshore strategy. Compare the offshore and mixed strategies in Table 8.3. The row minimums are £5.2 and −£4.4. If fishermen picked the mixed strategy, the worst they can do is £5.2. The column maximums are £5.2 and £20.6. The environment might have to pay out £20.6 if it picks the no-current strategy. The worst it does is a £5.2 payout with the current strategy. So given only these two sets of choices the game would reduce to a mixed/current play with a £5.2 payoff to fishermen. We shall return to the interpretation of environment in this context later. For the moment, note that the theory of games confirms the simple lesson learned long ago by the fishermen through trial and error: Offshore fishing is too risky to be practised exclusively.

Compare the inshore and offshore strategies in Table 8.3. Neither strategy dominates the other; both should be used. There are two approaches to calculating the proportions: graphical and mathematical. The graphical approach helps us to understand the basic philosophy of the theory of games. Plot to scale the payoffs from the two fishing strategies using, say, the left vertical axis for current and right axis for no current (Figure 8.8). Connect corresponding points to produce an inshore strategy line (going from £17.3 to £11.5 on the two axes) and a mixed strategy line (connecting £5.2 on the current axis to £17.0 on the no-current axis). It turns out that where the two strategy payoff lines intersect gives the optimal "minimax" strategy. Scaling the horizontal axis to provide the percentage mix for the two strategies indicates that 33 percent of canoe fishing trips should allocate some pots inshore, some offshore: the mixed strategy. The balance, 67 percent, should play it safe and put all pots inshore. The theory of games does not solve the problem for an individual fisherman on an individual day. He still has to make the decision, but on

balance, the village as a whole will expect to do best if the 26 canoes are allocated in this way and, using the mixed strategy, 18 stay inshore.

This graphical solution helps us to visualize what the theory of games does. Assume the environment wants to reduce the individual fisherman's catch to a minimum. Then the minimum maximum is the best the fisherman can hope for. Using this mix, the minimum payoff will be £13.3. And if the environment turns out to be more benevolent than portrayed in the theory of games, the payoff would be higher.

The mathematical solution is not complicated; however, it is not obvious either. The formula is set out in Table 8.4. The steps are these:

1. Calculate the difference between the two payoffs. The smaller the difference the smaller the risk attached to that strategy.

TABLE 8.4

Formula for allocating competing strategies

Your strategies	Payoff given the opponent's strategies		Difference in payoff	Proportion of turns to use each strategy
	A	B		
I	a	b	$(b - a)$	$\dfrac{(d - c)}{(b - a) + (d - c)}$
II	c	d	$(d - c)$	$\dfrac{(b - a)}{(b - a) + (d - c)}$

ratio of turns to use strategy I $= \dfrac{d - c}{b - a}$

Note: (i) $a, b, c,$ and d are the payoffs for each combination of strategies.

(ii) The differences in your payoffs are $(b - a)$ and $(d - c)$.

(iii) Use strategy I: $(d - c)/[(b - a) + (d - c)]$ proportion of the turns.

(iv) Use strategy I: $(d - c)/(b - a)$ ratio of the turns.

(v) In calculating differences, ignore minus signs.

2. Risk is minimized by playing each strategy more frequently the lower its risk, and the greater the risk of the alternative strategy. The ratio with which any strategy should be used is the difference in the payoff of the competing strategy, divided by the difference in the strategy itself.

Applying the formula gives the same results as the graphical, of course, with a few decimal points thrown in as a bonus. The results for the fishermen's optimal strategy mix, that for the environment and the income that results are set out below. (Tables 8.5 and 8.6.)

The Meaning of the Results

How do the results obtained by using the theory of games compare with reality? Davenport found they were very close indeed. Over the years, the fishermen have found the ideal solution to the allocation of their pots. For the village as a whole, fishermen do allocate their pots, inshore and mixed, on the two-to-one ratio predicted. And the currents do flow with about the frequency to be expected from a vindictive adversary, carefully weighing the payoffs associated with each fisherman/sea strategy, and scheming to minimize its losses. So how are these results to be interpreted?

The optimization of the mix of inshore and mixed inshore-offshore fishing by the canoe captains is not surprising. Indeed, it may well be that a good many economic systems have come, through trial and error over the years, to be guided by an intuitive grasp of the same principles that underlie the theory of games. Producers may well have learned through experience which mix of strategies will, in the long run, provide the highest net return for their efforts. Stability of the basic production techniques over long periods of time may, in this way,

TABLE 8.5

Fishermen versus the sea: Optimal strategies

Fishermen	The Sea		Differences along rows	Fishermen's optimal strategy mix	Percent ($\times$ 100)
	Current	No current			
Inshore	17.3	11.5	5.8	$\dfrac{11.8}{5.8 + 11.8}$	67.04
Mixed	5.2	17.0	11.8	$\dfrac{5.8}{5.8 + 11.8}$	32.95
Column differences	12.1	5.5			
Environmental strategy mix	5.5/17.6	12.1/17.6			
Percentage	31.25	68.75			

TABLE 8.6

Fishermen's payoff

Fishermen/sea strategy	Payoff rate	Played by fishermen (percent)	Played by sea (percent)	Actual payoff
a	17.3	0.33	0.31	1.77
b	11.5	0.33	0.69	2.61
c	5.2	0.67	0.31	1.08
d	17.0	0.67	0.69	7.86
Total payoff complete strategy mix				13.31

confer great advantages. Lack of sophistication may be more than compensated by the simple direct links between management of production and marketing. The integration of all these functions by a small crew of fishermen in a Jamaican village, for instance, provides immediate, direct feedback on the risks and payoffs of each strategy mix.

But what of the environment? We must now drop the interpretation of environment as some animate, scheming, calculating, determined player, unremittingly struggling to reduce yields and output to a minimum. A more realistic interpretation, particularly of the physical environment as a player in the theory of games, must be sought. Are most economic systems drawn to a "minimax balance" in which the environment reduces returns to the minimum maximum as exemplified in the Jamaican case study? Is it possible that necessity, the mother of invention, stimulates the development of strategies by human beings that hinge on the environmental mix of strategies? For instance, were the Jamaican fishing captains driven to experiment until they dropped offshore fishing and developed the mixed inshore-offshore fishing strategy as the only workable alternative to exclusive inshore fishing? Or is it the other way around? Does the exploitation of natural resources, for instance, drive environmental conditions back to the "minimax" balance?

Imagine that some new and improved technology were developed that allowed offshore catches on some days when currents prohibit it with existing technology. The proportion of offshore fishing would increase, thereby reducing the offshore catch in quality and size. This would in turn reduce the income line for that strategy down to some new minimax balance.

Or perhaps the relationship is one of mutual interdependency, environment influencing the ways in which we seek to earn our living, and consume the benefits of our efforts, but these in turn influencing the kinds of rewards for our efforts obtained from our environment. Or perhaps it is quite wrong to try to understand the interdependence between people and the

physical environment from the models of that interdependency. It may be safest, in conditions of uncertainty, simply to meet the environment as though it were a clever adversary trying to minimize people's winnings. But the main lesson of the theory of games for the geographer may have less to do with the nature of the environment than with the law of requisite variety, which underlies all efforts to regulate systems.

The Law of Requisite Variety

The *law of requisite variety* was formulated by Ross Ashby in his book *An Introduction to Cybernetics* (1956). Cybernetics is the science of regulation and control in all systems, animate and inanimate. Regulation and control of a system entails maintaining the performance (or output) of the system within predetermined limits by compensating for changes in inputs (from the environment). Some systems are designed to be self-regulating. Central heating systems are an example. The heating unit is switched on and off automatically by a thermostatic control. Cybernetics is concerned with how such automatic controls can, through "negative feedback," keep a system in a "steady state." Ashby's law of requisite variety draws attention to the need to compensate for greater complexity, or variety, in inputs from the environment with greater complexity, or variety, in the system's control mechanism. With a single strategy, mainly to increase the temperature, a central heating system can deal with one source of variety—cold—and it works well in winter when the environment uses this strategy with monotonous regularity.

Conversely, in summer, when it may be too hot, a different environmental input, or strategy, calls for a different countervailing strategy by the householder. If an air conditioner is added, the temperature can be regulated summer and winter. Do we want to regulate humidity as well? Then more equipment and controls are needed. For each element of variety in the environment we wish to regulate, we need one more variety of control to our system. In the words of Ashby, "Only variety can destroy variety, and nothing else can." This deceptively simple statement applies to all systems and has contributed to the solution of regulation and control problems in very sophisticated engineering systems.

Applications of the law of requisite variety are very straightforward in the case of agriculture. Agriculture must cope with a great spatial variety of climatic conditions from arctic to tropical, and from desert to rain forest. The environment cannot be significantly changed to meet the needs of any single agricultural system, so the global spread of agriculture has required the development of an equal variety of production strategies. The empty areas on the world population map indicate where we have failed. These areas are too cold or too dry, or too wet or too rugged, or perhaps too remote for existing agricultural systems.

The relationship between agricultural types and climatic types was an important theme of some earlier economic geographies. The definition of climatic types was guided by the response of natural vegetation to climate. Significant changes in vegetation suggested a meaningful subdivision of apparently unbroken gradations of climatic elements. Vegetation thus changes with changes in climatic type, and so too does agriculture.

Successful commercial agriculture has required an adjustment to variety not only in the physical environment but also in the human environment. Improvements in transportation and advances in agricultural science have changed the economic environment, opening up new areas to production, but thereby submitting older areas to new competition. The steamship and the Suez Canal helped to open up Southeast Asia to commercial plantation agriculture, including rubber, but in doing so undermined rubber production in Brazil. The facts of such developments were central to earlier economic geographers. What is being stressed here, however, is that the survival of commercial agriculture has depended on finding answers to variety in the physical and economic environment. If a solution could not be found to a new change in the economic environment, then the law of requisite variety was no longer satisfied. The margins of settlement might then retreat, as in northern Canada, or the frontier of settlement might become a hollow one, as happened in parts of Brazil.

Requisite variety applies equally to minerals and mining. The "neutral stuff," as Erich Zimmermann called the minerals found in the earth's surface, had to be converted into *natural resources* by knowledge, capital, and labor. The discovery of the limits to each development in that conversion from neutral stuff to natural resources went hand in hand with the discovery of their variety and qualities. Thus, products could be tailored to specific needs. High-speed steels that retain their cutting edge at high speeds could be achieved by adding tungsten, chromium, and vanadium. Manganese and chromium made tough steel for rail lines. Chromium makes steel resistant to corrosion. The tables are, in fact, turned. Variety becomes advantage, because controlled variety in system output helps to meet variety in market needs. The game changes. It is not so much a game of the industrialist against the physical environment as it is a game of the environment and industrialist against the needs posed by an advanced society, where they must compete with many alternative products. But however the players line up, that same law of requisite variety applies.

Requisite variety establishes the minimum level of alternative strategies needed to regulate system performance. Fall below that level and system performance is jeopardized. Rise above it and different strategies are available. If economic principles are applied, the strategy that maximizes income is selected. Many locations meet the requirements for any given industry. The one selected to locate a new plant will, according to location theory, be the one that minimizes transportation costs, or maximizes market accessibility, or, more simply, is likely to maximize profits. But it is precisely where the requirements of the law of requisite variety are surpassed, and where the decision-maker has a choice of decision, that the problem of defining an appropriate image of the decision-maker and model of decision making arise.

TOWARD AN INTEGRATED MODEL OF DECISION MAKING

Three decision models have been presented to illustrate how the choices that shape the geography of economic systems can be made. *First,* the decision-maker was described as an economic maximizer, aiming for the highest possible income. Location theories are built on this model. So, too, are farm management models. Whether the actual decisions observed in any given study conform to the predictions of this model or not, it can provide a norm, or yardstick, against which to compare reality. It may well be that actual decisions often fall short of income maximizing. Hence, a *second* approach, the *satisficer model,* is needed. Suboptimal decisions may be selected for a variety of reasons. These include aversion to risk, regional cultural differences, and incomplete knowledge of the options available. But whatever specific reasons apply in any particular case, spatial patterns emerge in the decisions made that mirror the regional diffusion of information. These differences are missed by the economic maximizer model. The satisficer model also leaves room to consider aversion to risk, something the economic maximizer model ignores. But neither of these two models meets risk in a satisfactory way. Nor is the problem an easy one. How are two alternative land uses to be ranked, for instance, that offer not only different income levels but also different risk levels? Is a higher income level with greater risk of failure necessarily preferable to a lower income at lower risk? Hence, a third model has been presented, which was developed specifically to deal with this problem.

The *third* model treats the decision-maker as a strategist and uses the theory of games. It treats risk as variety, and adversity as diversity, both of which must be regulated and controlled. Prior knowledge of which particular environmental conditions will occur is not required or expected, only a knowledge of what range of environmental conditions can occur. The model minimizes losses under what would be the worst possible combination of conditions in the environment, whatever the environment includes, whether physical, economic, technical, cultural, or political factors. The solution is therefore sometimes called the "minimax" solution, that is, the minimum maximum, of a set of possible maximums, assuming that the environmental forces will conspire to drive the decision-maker's payoff down to this minimum of the maximums. The mathematical technique is the theory of games. This theory may appear to employ an improper personification of the physical environment. Some may prefer to think of nature as a neutral stage on which is acted out the drama of economic production, trade, and consumption. It is possible, however, that the sheer pressure of population on resources may drive the physical environment to respond as though it were a scheming opponent seeking to reduce production to a minimum.

The three decision models differ in many respects. These include the decision-maker's assumed knowledge of the environment and of the strategies to deal with environmental uncertainty, the aversion of the decision-maker to risk, and whether a maximum or satisfactory income level is sought. Two of the models provide a *determinate* solution, one an *indeterminate* solution. All three models have implications for the spatial patterns of production that result, but the factors underlying these patterns are different. These differences are summarized in Table 8.7. Notice that the maximizer and strategist models appear very similar. The difference in their approach to risk is, however, crucial.

The three models of decision making are not necessarily disparate, competing decisions of how choices are made. The separate concepts on which each are focused apply to some extent to all models of decision making and provide a comprehensive conceptual framework within which to set each model. In doing so, decision making is seen as a selection process influenced by different circumstances. Thus, the way in which decisions are made that shape the geography of economic

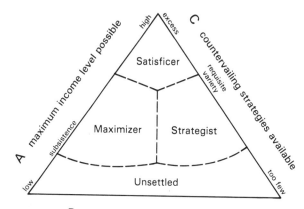

FIGURE 8.9 Decision process as a response to environmental circumstances, personal preferences, and choices available.

systems is in turn shaped by the physical, economic, and technical environment in which those decisions are made. The approach to decision making is not autonomously determined without regard to environment, but it must take the environment into account.

All three models of decision making assume some assessment of the economic consequences of each possible choice (Figure 8.9). Whether the decision-maker is a maximizer, satisficer, or strategist, the choices are listed and the income for each estimated. Thus, all choices can be ranked on an income scale from high to low (scale A, Figure 8.9). If the maximum possible income in an area is below the subsistence level, that area can be expected to remain unsettled. The higher the income levels provided by the better choices, the more likely it must be that the decision-maker will feel free to opt for a satisficer approach.

Likewise, all three models can be integrated according to how they are affected by environmental uncertainty and requisite variety. The ideal situation is low environmental uncertainty coupled with an excess of good countervailing strategies. Under these circumstances, the satisficer model is most likely to apply. The worst situation is a combination of high environmental variety without appropriate countervailing strategies and

TABLE 8.7

Three models of decision making

Model	Knowledge of environment	Environment risk (variety)	Income level sought	Solution	Factors controlling spatial pattern
Maximizer	Complete	Not considered	Maximum	Determinate	Economic
Satisficer	Incomplete	Considered	Satisfactory	Indeterminate	Diffusion process
Strategist	Incomplete	Regulated	Minimax	Determinate	Cultural and others; total environment

a low maximum income potential. A cycle of settlement, abandonment, and resettlement may occur, but without the requisite variety needed to regulate the environment, no foundation exists for lasting settlement.

Interest focuses on the intermediate cases where requisite variety is achieved. If the environment is stable, with few variations of any significance, the decision-maker can ignore risk and go for the maximum possible income. If, however, a number of environmental factors are subject to unpredictable change, decision-makers must hedge their bets and opt for a mixed strategy. The games theory approach is called for, the decision-maker becomes a strategist, and the highest income level achievable in the long run is the minimum maximum rather than the simple maximum.

The three different models of decision making are different aspects of a single, more comprehensive, model. Decision making in economic production ultimately involves at least three factors: (1) environmental conditions in competing locations; (2) the range of activities and technologies available to cope with environmental variety in any given location; and (3) the range of income levels promised by competing activities in the same place, or the same activity in competing places. The decision-maker may play one or more different roles in different places at different times, perhaps now the strategist combatting a complex variety of environmental changes, now a simple maximizer going for the jackpot, now a satisficer prepared to sit back and enjoy the nonmonetary benefits of an alternative, satisfying activity.

TOPICS FOR DISCUSSION

1. Draw to scale the graphical solution of the Jamaican fishing village using the data provided in Table 8.3 and including the offshore option. Does your figure confirm that the fishermen should not use the offshore fishing option? What would the minimum payoff for the offshore fishing strategy with a sea current have to be to make it competitive with the mixed strategy?

2. What does the application of the theory of games to geographic cases imply about relationships between humanity and physical environment? Do these implications affect the validity of the application?

3. "Game theory is applicable only to a few highly unrealistic situations; the greater the complexity, the more difficult it is to solve the mathematics required to generate a solution" (Smith, 1981). Discuss Smith's assertion and consider whether the theory of games can make any contributions to economic geography if the assertion is correct.

4. The Barren Middle Zone of Ghana, a belt which for environmental and historical reasons has a very low population density, has one of the most severe agricultural climates in West Africa, with heavy precipitation followed by the extreme aridity of the harmattan, which sweeps south from the Sahara. A further problem is that the high degree of variability of the precipitation makes it difficult for the farmers to plan effectively. The farmers of Jantilla, a small village in western Ghana, may use the land to grow the following crops, each with different degrees of resistance to dry conditions, as their main staple food: yams, cassava, maize, millet, and hill rice. They are faced by two different environmental conditions: dry years and wet years. Given the payoff matrix in Figure 8.10, what is the farmers' optimal cropping strategy? (Example from P. Gould, 1963.)

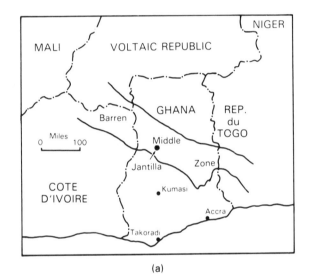

(a)

FARMERS OF JANTILLA	CROP CHOICE	ENVIRONMENT MOISTURE CHOICES	
		Wet Years	Dry Years
	Yams	82	11
	Maize	61	49
	Cassava	12	38
	Millet	43	32
	Hill rice	30	71

(b)

FIGURE 8.10 (a) The Barren Middle Zone of Ghana of low population density and extreme variability of rainfall. (b) Payoff matrix for two-person-five-strategy-zero-sum game; crop choices against moisture choices. [*Source:* Peter Gould, "Man Against His Environment: A Game Theoretic Framework," *Annals of the Association of American Geographers,* 53, 3 (1963), 291.]

FURTHER READINGS

ASHBY, W. ROSS. *Introduction to Cybernetics*. London: John Wiley, 1956, pp. 202–218.

Ashby's *law of requisite variety* states simply that only "variety can destroy variety." The full implications of this powerful law have yet to be properly considered in geography.

BEER, STAFFORD. *Designing Freedom: Massey Lectures, 1973*. Toronto: CBC Publications, 1974.

One of the few published applications of the law of requisite variety.

DAVENPORT, WILLIAM. "Jamaican Fishing: A Game Theory Analysis." *Yale University Publications in Anthropology,* 59, 1960, 3–11.

Brought to the attention of geographers by Peter Gould, this article is the source for the theory of games example in this chapter.

GOULD, PETER. "Man Against His Environment: A Game Theoretic Framework." *Annals of the Association of American Geographers,* 53, 3 (1963), 290–297.

Two examples from Ghana illustrate decision strategies to optimize economic decisions in the face of environmental uncertainty. A good place to begin. But ignore the mathematical calculations; they have typographical errors.

RAPAPORT, ANATOL. "Critiques of Game Theory." In *Modern Systems Research for the Behavioral Scientist,* Walter Buckley (Ed.). Chicago: Aldine, 1968, pp. 474–489.

Rapaport gives a generally favorable review of the theory of games.

SMITH, DAVID M. *Industrial Location: An Economic Geographical Analysis.* New York: John Wiley, 1981, pp. 121–123.

A concise, useful, and readable review of the application of games theory in industrial location.

VON NEUMANN, JOHN, AND O. MORGENSTERN. *Theory of Games and Economic Behavior.* Princeton, N.J.: Princeton University Press, 1944.

The classic study that introduced the theory of games to social scientists.

WOLPERT, JULIAN. "The Decision Process in Spatial Context." *Annals of the Association of American Geographers,* LIV, No. 4, December 1964, 537–558.

The key reference on the decision-maker as a satisficer.

CHAPTER 9

The Spatial Organization
of Land Use

The uses to which people put the land resources available to them reflect, in part, differences in physical factors, such as soil fertility and climate in rural land use, and amenities, such as high elevation with imposing views in urban land use. Historical and cultural factors—including the timing of settlement and the cultural traditions of a population—also affect land use. But even on a homogeneous plain, where there are no physical differences, the efforts of farmers or city residents and developers to maximize their returns produce systematic land-use patterns. The exciting discovery of these spatial patterns was first presented by J. H. von Thünen in his study *The Isolated State* in 1826. The importance of von Thünen's contribution cannot be overemphasized. He provided the earliest theory of the spatial economic organization of land use. Although world economic geography has changed dramatically in the century and a half since von Thünen made his seminal contribution, the basic principles that he stated still apply to the zonation of agricultural land use at scales from that of the village to that of the state itself.

Likewise, von Thünen's principles have provided the basis for understanding patterns of urban land use, and population densities within cities.

Of course, transportation costs on a featureless plain provide only a first approximation to the factors patterning land uses. Physical factors are important in rural land use, and cultural differences play a major role in differentiating urban space. Thus, in this chapter we probe not only the powerful effects of transportation in spatial organization but also explore how resources and culture add a textured richness to human use of the earth.

Objectives:

- to develop an understanding of the laws of returns
- to explain the concept of rent, and why differential rents arise
- to present the problem posed by J. H. von Thünen, the deductive model he developed to solve the problem, and the application of his principles to the modern world
- to extend von Thünen's model to urban land use

218

We have now described the distribution of population and resources and explained some economic principles, such as optimizing scales of output and combinations of inputs. Both of these, the geographic and the economic fundamentals, help to explain the location of economic activity. Land resources and relative location are both important determinants of land use; and although the location of manufacturing industry is to some extent related to the location of raw materials, the size and spacing of industrial plants is also related to the economies of scale and the barriers to entry. In the next three chapters, therefore, we introduce formal theories of the location of economic activity, beginning with the theories of rural and urban land use.

THE LAWS OF RETURNS

J. H. von Thünen's principles rely on ideas developed in Chapter 8, particularly those of how Economic Person seeks to optimize production to maximize returns. We now need to develop the *laws of returns* in more detail. Recall the manner in which Farmer Jones learned from Professor Smith how to combine inputs to achieve maximum output by preparing a preference map on which were plotted isoquants and production-possibility curves. Figure 9.1 is such a preference map in which there are two inputs, X and Y, and the isoquants show the combinations of these inputs needed to produce 10, 20, or 30 units of output, respectively.

Now assume that there is a fixed supply of one of the inputs (X), so that Farmer Jones can increase output only by increasing the use of the other input (Y). Let OA be the input in fixed supply (say, land). Then AB traces out the different scales of output that may be obtained by increasing inputs of Y (by using more capital or labor on the fixed amount of land). For example, increasing Y from 2 to 3 units enables Farmer Jones to

increase output from 10 to 20 units, but the next unit increase in Y, from 3 to 4, produces a lower increase in output, as does the one following, from 4 to 5, because of the way the line AB intersects the isoquants. The increase in output that results from adding a unit of the variable input Y is called the *marginal* increase in output, or the *marginal productivity* of Y—marginal *physical productivity* if it is measured in physical units of output, such as bushels of wheat, and *marginal revenue productivity* if it is measured in the dollar value of the output. The concept of marginal productivity is central to understanding the laws that govern returns to changing scale of output. The example just given illustrates decreasing returns to scale. (Refer back to the discussion in Chapter 7.)

Now consider the example provided in Figure 9.2. It is assumed that Farmer Jones has a fixed amount of land in grain production, and the output of grain can be changed by using more labor. Column 1 in Figure 9.2 shows the dollar value of the inputs of labor that could be used (per acre) in increments of $10.00; column 2 shows the resulting yield in bushels per acre; column 3 shows the dollar value of output per acre; column 4 shows the marginal value of output per acre for each successive $10 of inputs applied—the marginal revenue productivity of each labor unit—and column 5 shows the average value of the output per acre per $10 of inputs. The three lines in the graph show how the total (TV), average (AV), and marginal (MR) values of output per acre change as the total value of the labor inputs per acre increases. As more labor is applied to the land, the value of output first increases (that is, there are *increasing returns to scale*) and then decreases (that is, there are *decreasing returns*).

At what point should Farmer Jones stop trying to increase output? This depends upon both the marginal cost of the inputs and their marginal returns. As long as each successive $10.00 worth of labor input produces a greater marginal increase in the value of output, Farmer Jones should add inputs. But if an extra $10.00 of input produced less than $10.00 worth of output, it should not be made. The general rule is that Farmer Jones should keep on adding labor inputs to the point where *the marginal cost of the inputs equals the marginal revenue produced,* but no further. At this point, returns are maximized. Go beyond this point, and returns will decrease. Can you find this point in Figure 9.2? Subtract from the total value of output the cost of inputs needed to produce that output. The resulting net returns (profits) will increase from $5.00 to a maximum of $87.00 when $90.00 of inputs are used. But the next $10.00 of input yields only $9.00 in output and, indeed, total value ($186.00) less total inputs ($100.00) produces only $86.00 in net returns.

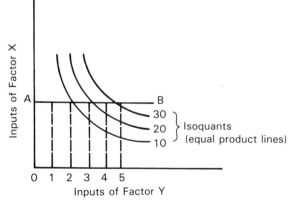

FIGURE 9.1 Production possibilities with one fixed and one variable input.

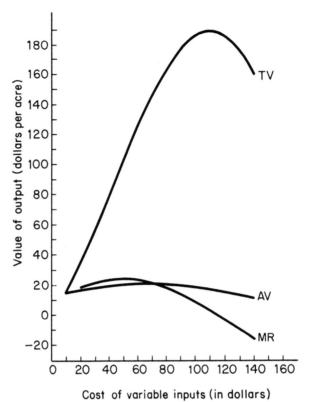

Cost of variable inputs (in dollars)

FIGURE 9.2   Total, average, and marginal value of output per acre under conditions of increasing and decreasing returns. This figure compares the cost of variable inputs with total value of output, the average value of output at the scale of output reached, and the marginal value of the last $10.00 increase in outputs. The data from which the graph is plotted are shown below.

Cumulative cost of inputs of variable factor (labor, per acre)	Yield (bushels per acre)	Total value of output at $1.50 per bushel	Value of additional output per $10 input per acre (marginal value of product)	Average value of output per acre per $10 input of variable factors
$ 10.0	10	$ 15.0		$15.00
			18.0	
20.0	22	33.0		16.50
			21.0	
30.0	36	54.0		18.00
			24.0	
40.0	52	78.0		19.50
			24.0	
50.0	68	102.0		20.40
			23.0	
60.0	83.3	125.0		20.83
			21.0	
70.0	97.3	146.0		20.86
			17.5	
80.0	109	163.5		20.45
			13.5	
90.0	118	177.0		19.67
			9.0	
100.0	124	186.0		18.60
			3.0	
110.0	126	189.0		17.18
			−3.0	
120.0	124	186.0		15.50
			−9.0	
130.0	117.3	176.0		13.54
			−16.0	
140.0	106.6	160.0		11.43

The marginal revenue productivity curve can also be interpreted as the demand curve for the variable factor. In Figure 9.2, if labor costs $10.00 per unit, then the farmer will maximize returns by consuming 9 units of labor at a cost of $90.00. If the price of labor were to double, two things would happen. First, all the numbers in the first column of Figure 9.2 would double. But, reading down column 4, so would the point at which Farmer Jones could maximize returns: By consuming only 7 units of labor at a cost of $140.00, the resulting maximum net returns would be $6.00. In other words, the marginal revenue productivity curve also records how many units of an input should be used to maximize revenues as the price of the input changes. The relationship between quantity demanded and price is the demand curve for the input.

THE CONCEPT OF RENT

We can now use this relationship to develop the idea of the marginal revenue productivity of land (that is, the demand curve for land), and from this the concept of land rent. To do this we will turn the analysis around and treat land as a variable input and other inputs as fixed. The concept of land rent is basic to the development of theories of agricultural and urban land use, because the core idea of land use theory is that land use is determined by land rent.

Rent as a Scarcity Payment

Assume we are dealing with an island that contains a fixed amount of homogeneous land available for cultivation (*OS* in Figure 9.3). The first farmer settles on the island, bringing a fixed amount of capital and labor. How much land will be used, and what rent will be paid?

Suppose this is a grain farmer selling wheat on the world market. Because of the nature of that market the farmer must be a price-taker, accepting a fixed world price. Let the marginal revenue productivity curve for land (demand curve) be *NM* in Figure 9.3, as output is increased by increasing inputs of land. The price paid by the farmer for the land (the land rent) and the quantity of land consumed will be determined by the intersection of the demand and supply curves for land. The demand curve is the marginal revenue productivity curve *NM*. The supply curve is the line *OST*. Thus, the farmer will use *OM* land. The rent will be zero. This is because there is land to spare. The farmer could always move if a landlord tried to charge rent.

Rent is payment to a landowner for use of his or her factor of production, land, which arises solely because land is *scarce*. This can be seen in Figure 9.3, if we let additional farmers arrive on the island. The total demand curve increases as each individual's marginal revenue productivity curve is added to that of the others. For example, *PQ* might be the total demand curve for land of one group of farmers (the summation of their individual marginal productivity curves). *PQ* intersects the supply curve *OST* at *Q*. Since there is only *OS* land available, farmers compete for the land, balancing demands and supplies at price *OR* (= *SQ*). The marginal cost curve for land is thus the price line *RQ*, and our first farmer, maximizing profits by equating marginal revenues and marginal costs, will cut land consumption to *OF*. The other farmers will cultivate the rest of the island, *FS*.

Differential Rents Due to Productivity Differences

Although the preceding example suggests that rents are uniform across the island, in reality rents do differ. Differential rents arise because

1. the productivity of different parcels of land varies
2. land is located at different distances from market.

Both types of variation are central to the theory of agricultural location, in which the basic idea is that each parcel of land is used for the activity that can pay the highest rent. If we can understand the reasons for the variations, we will have gone a long way toward understanding one of the basic problems of economic geography—that of explaining land use.

First, let us take the question of productivity differences. The idea of rent variations being attributable to productivity of the soil was first discussed by David Ricardo in his *Principles of Political Economy and Taxation* (1817). Ricardo said that high rents were due to the "niggardliness of nature" (to scarcity) and were re-

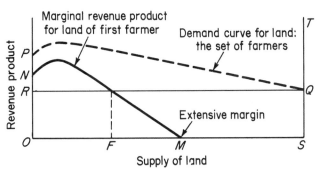

FIGURE 9.3 Marginal revenue product and the emergence of land rent.

lated to the "original and indestructible power of the soil" (to productivity differences). Further, he said that the most fertile lands are put to use first, with production extending to less favorable lands only as demands increase.

Why is this so? Productivity differences change the marginal revenue productivity curve for land because they change marginal physical productivity. For example, in Figure 9.4 the marginal revenue productivities of two grades of land, *A* and *B,* are shown. Assume situations in which both are in equal supply *OS*. The lower-quality land will not command a rent, whereas that of higher quality will command rent *OR*. In agricultural terminology, the lower-quality land is "marginal" because it does not pay any rent, and the rent charged for the superior-quality land is entirely due to its greater productivity.

A generalization of Ricardo's idea has been provided recently by geographers H. H. McCarty and J. Lindberg in the form of an "optima and limits" scheme (see Figures 9.5, 9.6). In Figure 9.5, two variables—temperature and moisture—provide the basis for their hypothesis. In some restricted area, those variables are presumed to combine ideally for producing a particular crop. That area is identified as having "optimum" conditions. Outward from it, conditions become less and less favorable until, finally, the physical limits are reached, beyond which production of that crop is impossible. In most cases, however, greater significance attaches to the "economic limits," which appear in Figure 9.6. When the productivity data of Figure 9.5 are translated into unit-costs of production and when those unit-costs are converted into rent (per unit of output), the areas of production that would appear in response

to various price levels for that commodity can be estimated. Assume that a price of "7" will cover costs in the four inside zones of the model. No production will occur outside that zone (in the "no-rent" areas). Further, rent will increase toward the optimum.

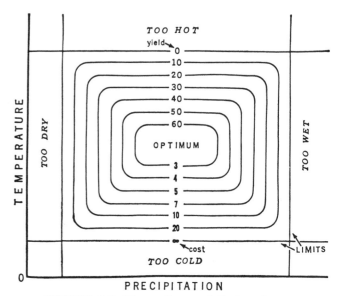

FIGURE 9.5 The optima and limits schema. [*Source:* H. H. McCarty and James B. Lindberg, *A Preface to Economic Geography* (Englewood Cliffs, N.J.: Prentice-Hall, 1966), pp. 61–62.]

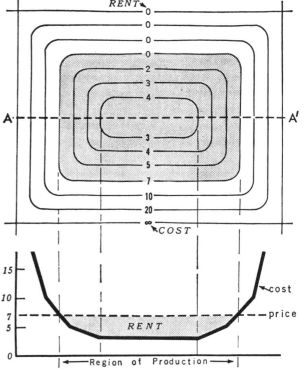

FIGURE 9.6 Rents in the productivity schema. [*Source:* McCarty and Lindberg, 1966.]

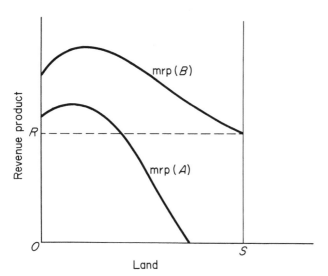

FIGURE 9.4 Marginal revenue product differences for differing land qualities.

What will happen if the price rises for the products of the land because of increasing demand? Marginal revenue productivity will rise, and the extensive margin of production will move into uncultivated lands. By the same token, the higher-rent land will also be used more intensively, because—recalling the earlier discussion of input substitution—if rents are higher for better-quality land, and if other factors are constant, it will pay farmers to substitute inputs of the other (cheaper) factors for inputs of the more expensive land to achieve the same resulting output.

Differential Rents Due to Locational Differences

The same relationship holds in the case of rent differences due to transportation cost. Marginal revenue productivity is defined in terms of market prices. Yet as we saw in Chapter 6, the at-farm price involves market price less transportation costs. Holding land quality constant, the effect of increasing transportation costs therefore progressively reduces the more distant farmer's marginal revenue productivity curve (even though marginal physical productivity remains unchanged), and thus reduces the rent he pays for a given amount of land. See Figure 9.7, in which a farm of size OL pays OR_1 at the market, declining to OR_3 20 miles away. The difference (R_1, R_3) is accounted for by the reduction in revenues due to the cost of transporting output the 20 miles to the market.

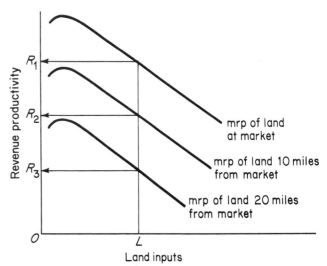

FIGURE 9.7 Marginal revenue productivities (mrp) of land of identical quality at different distances from market.

In such a situation, rents display a pattern of distance-decay from the market center. Further, just as higher-quality land will be used more intensively, so will more accessible land. We should expect to see both farm costs and returns decline with increasing distance from markets, and this is exactly the case in the agricultural example depicted in Table 9.1. Note that as rents fall with increasing distance, farm size increases because farmers substitute the cheapening factor of production (land) for others in their productive process.

TABLE 9.1

Some variations in agricultural characteristics with increasing distance from Louisville, Kentucky (1918)

Distance from Louisville (miles)	Rent of land per acre	Value of land per acre	Percentage of receipts from		
			Truck and potato	dairy	other
8 or less	$11.85	$312	68%	10%	22%
9–11	5.59	110	35	12	53
12–14	5.37	106	34	20	46
15+	4.66	95	20	27	53

Distance from Louisville (miles)	Average area of improved land (acres)	Operating expense per acre	Gross receipts per acre	Land earnings per acre	Value of fertilizer used per acre
9	44	$73	$96	$23	$19.25
12	121	36	45	9	6.50
13	212	15	20	5	5.20
16	420	14	18	4	4.25

Source: J. H. Arnold and Frank Montgomery, *Influence of a City on Farming,* Bulletin 678 (Washington, D.C.: U.S. Department of Agriculture, 1918).

Relationship of Land Rent to Everyday "Rents" and to Land Values

Is land rent the same thing as the rent paid to a landlord for an apartment? There is an important difference that must be clearly understood. What we call *rent* in an everyday sense is a payment to a landlord for a variety of things: land, building, furnishings and other services. Only a portion of this payment is the land rent. The rest is a "rental" for the capital, labor, and enterprise involved in constructing and maintaining the apartment. The difference is clearly seen on local property tax bills, which separate assessments for the land from those for the "improvements."

The assessor talks of land and building *values,* not rents, however. What is the difference? Land value is the price paid to purchase the land; land rent is the payment to an owner to use the land. There is a simple accounting relationship between the two: Land rent capitalized at the current rate of interest equals land value, or the price of land is the present or capitalized value of the rent the land will earn during its useful life.

VON THÜNEN'S ISOLATED STATE: THE FIRST ECONOMIC MODEL OF SPATIAL ORGANIZATION

This simple idea that rents decline with distance was the basis of the first economic model of spatial organization, Johann Heinrich von Thünen's 1826 classic *Der Isolierte Staat.* It is worth spending some time with von Thünen's model, not simply out of historical curiosity but because of the systematic way he linked the economic logic of rent theory to the spatial organization of land use.

Von Thünen had a university education in philosophy, biology, economics, and languages, and in 1810, when he was 27, he bought an 1146-acre estate at Tellow, southeast of Rostock in Mecklenburg, Germany. As he operated and managed Tellow he kept meticulous records, and his early training led him to speculate about the best way of using his land.

Nature of the Abstraction from Reality

Von Thünen found it most helpful to develop the abstract ideas underlying the everyday operation of Tellow, pointing out to the readers of *Der Isolierte Staat* that "the reader who is willing to spend some time and attention" to his work should not "take exception to the imaginary assumptions . . . because they do not cor-

respond to conditions in reality" since the reader will find that they allow him "to establish the operation of a certain factor, whose operation we see but dimly in reality, where it is in incessant conflict with others of its kind." This is to be said of all location theories, which are abstract because they seek to understand the basic processes at work shaping the complex reality of the everyday world, and it also explains why we spent so much time with rent theory at the beginning of this chapter.

Von Thünen was unremittingly logical. He stated his assumptions, posed his problem, deduced the consequences, and tested the deductions with empirical evidence that he collected on his estate over many years. As such, he was a model scientist.

The Assumptions

The assumptions enabled von Thünen to focus on spatial differences, and in particular upon the effects of transport costs on land use:

> Imagine a very large town, at the centre of a fertile plain which is crossed by no navigable river or canal. Throughout the plain the soil is capable of cultivation and of the same fertility. Far from the town, the plain turns into an uncultivated wilderness which cuts off all communication between this State and the outside world.
>
> There are no other towns on the plain. The central town must therefore supply the rural areas with all manufactured products, and in return it will obtain all its provisions from the surrounding countryside.
>
> The mines that provide the State with salt and metals are near the central town which, as it is the only one, we shall in future call simply "the Town."[1]

These assumptions are severe: a plain with complete physical homogeneity; a single market, the "Town"; a single source of food supply, the plain; transportation costs related only to volume and distance shipped; and decisions made by Economic Person, relentlessly organizing space in an optimal way. But these assumptions are needed in order to establish the role of distance, whose operation in reality is in constant conflict with other factors affecting land use, including variations in climate, soil fertility, management, and the transportation network with its freight-rate structure.

[1]Peter Hall (ed.), *Von Thünen's Isolated State.* Trans. Carla M. Wartenberg (Oxford: Pergamon Press, 1966), p. 7.

The Problem

Von Thünen then presented the problem that concerned him.

> The problem we want to solve is this: what pattern of cultivation will take shape in these conditions?; and how will the farming system of the various districts be affected by their distance from the Town? We assume throughout that farming is conducted absolutely rationally.
>
> It is on the whole obvious that near the Town will be grown those products which are heavy or bulky in relation to their value and which are consequently so expensive to transport that the remoter districts are unable to supply them. Here also we find the highly perishable products, which must be used very quickly. With increasing distance from the Town, the land will progressively be given up to products cheap to transport in relation to their value.
>
> For this reason alone, fairly sharply differentiated concentric rings or belts will form around the Town, each with its own particular staple product.
>
> From ring to ring the staple product, and with it the entire farming system, will change; and in the various rings we shall find completely different farming systems.[2]

What von Thünen is suggesting is that locational differences alone are sufficient to cause a complete system of spatial organization of land use, embodying concentric circles of crop production and farm types. But he did not stop there. Once the effect of distance had been observed, the assumptions were relaxed, and other variables introduced into the model to see how they modified the "ideal" pattern of rural land use that results from distance effects alone.

Location Rent for a Single Crop at a Single Intensity

Let us proceed stepwise through von Thünen's model. He recognized that land inputs embody two different goods, *space* (physical area) and *location* (accessibility). The basic assumption in *Der Isolierte Staat* is that space is physically homogeneous, so that all variations in land quality involve the second quality, accessibility to the Town. The impact of diminishing accessibility on net income per unit land area is thus measurable as total income minus production and transportation costs. Be-

cause production costs for any single farm commodity were also assumed to be virtually invariant with distance from the Town, variations in net income could then be attributed to differences in accessibility alone. Income net of all costs von Thünen called *location rent*. The question he then asked was how location rent differences were related to transport costs.

Von Thünen essentially calculated location rents as follows. Where

R = location rent per unit of land
E = output per unit of land
p = price per unit of output
a = production expenses per unit of land (including labor)
f = transportation costs per unit of output per mile
k = miles from market

then

$$R = E(p - a) - Efk$$

To illustrate the change in rent gradient with distance, let us assume production of a crop such that E = 40 bushels per acre; price (p) = \$2.00 per bushel; and the transportation rate (f) = 2 cents per bushel per mile. For farm *A,* directly at the market and with no transportation costs, $k = 0$, and the equation reduces to:

$$R = E(p - a)$$

Substituting gives

$$R = 40(\$2 - \$1)$$
$$= \$4 \text{ per acre}$$

For a second farm *B,* 25 miles from the market:

$$R = 40(\$2 - \$1) - 40(\$0.02 \times 25)$$
$$= \$20 \text{ per acre}$$

At 25 miles the rent has fallen to half. At what distance will it fall to zero? If

$$R = E(p - a) - Efk = 0$$
$$k = \frac{(p - a)}{f}$$

Substituting our hypothetical values gives

$$\frac{2 - 1}{0.02} = 50 \text{ miles}$$

[2]Ibid., p. 8.

A rent gradient, sloping downward with increasing distance from the Town, can be identified by applying the rent formula to different distances as in the above example. Figure 9.8 shows how the components of gross farm income will vary with distance from the Town. Then, as in Figure 9.9, we plot only the spatial variations in rent with distance. Rotating the rent gradient around the Town, we find it becomes a rent cone, the base of which maps out the extensive margin of farm land, as demonstrated by Figure 9.9.

Who receives the location rent? Imagine that all the farms are rented out each year on a fully competitive basis at an auction. The farmers know that net return increases with accessibility and bid up the rents for farms closer to market. It pays to continue bidding until the bid rent equals the location rent; indeed, it is necessary for the farmer who wants to occupy the land to do so. At that price the farmer just recovers production expenses (including what he expects to receive for his own labor) and transportation costs, and the landowner receives the location rent as a payment for his land. The competitive bidding eliminates the income differential to farmers that otherwise would be attributable to accessibility; and the bid rent, or contract rent, is the location rent. This bid rent produces a spatial equilibrium situation in which bid rent falls just enough from market to cover additional transportation costs so that the farmer is indifferent as to the distance from market. In essence, there is a tradeoff between transportation costs and accessibility rent.

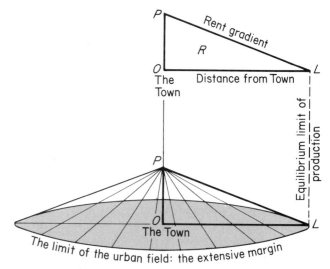

FIGURE 9.9 The rent cone and the extensive margin of production. The components of gross farm income in Figure 9.8 have been reversed to display the rent gradient. Economic rent at the Town is *OP*. At *L*, the equilibrium limit of production, *O*. The △*OPL* is rotated to describe the rent cone and to map the extensive margin, where farm land gives way to wilderness.

Location Rent for a Single Crop at Differing Intensities

The higher location rent paid for land with greater accessibility is an incentive to increase output per unit of land by increasing inputs of capital and labor. Even in von Thünen's day when technology was limited, distinct intensities of grain production existed involving different proportions of the three factors of production—capital, land, and labor. As noted earlier, however, factor substitution is imperfect. The incremental output for each additional unit of input of labor and capital is not uniform. At some point in the intensification of production extra units of labor, machinery, or fertilizer add a smaller amount of product than the previous unit. Total physical product may continue to rise, but marginal physical product begins to fall.

This law of diminishing returns has important spatial ramifications. Consider the location rent formula again, $R = E(p - a) - Efk$. The difference between market price (p) and production costs (a) diminishes per bushel as intensity increases, and the transportation cost per bushel (fk) increases with distance. The optimal level of intensity occurs where the marginal addition to yield by the final increment of capital and labor just pays for the transportation of that marginal yield to market. The lower the transportation costs are, the lower that marginal addition to yield need be to pay for itself. The

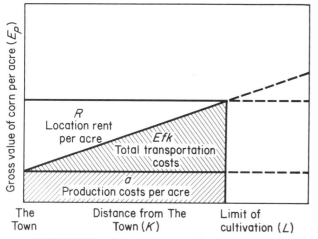

FIGURE 9.8 Components of gross farm income with increasing distance from the Town. Gross income per acre is invariant with distance from the Town. The residual amount, *R,* left after production costs, *a,* and transportation costs, *Efk,* are paid, diminishes with distance. This residual is termed *location rent* and is a measure of market accessibility.

closer the farm is to market, the further along the marginal physical product curve the farmer can proceed and the more intensive his farming system can be.

The spatial ramifications in the case where two intensity levels reflect two different types of farming organization (the *improved* and the feudal *three-field* systems) were explored in some detail by von Thünen. The data came from the Tellow accounts for 1810–1819, but were standardized for an area of 100,000 rods, or 217 hectares, an area slightly smaller than Tellow, and for soils a little poorer.

The improved system yielded a gross product of 3144 bushels of grain with costs of 1976 bushels and 641 thalers. Location rent fell to zero at 28.6 miles, at which distance the 1168 bushels of grain for sale (3144 minus 1976 bushels) just fetched enough to pay the town-based costs (641 thalers).

The three-field system produced a much smaller gross product—1720 compared with 3144 bushels—but both farm-based and town-based costs were smaller. A 45 percent reduction in yield contributed a 48 percent reduction in grain costs and a 49 percent reduction in town-based costs. The economic rent was lower, but it fell more slowly with increasing distance because the ratio of the 327 thalers of town-based costs to the 696 bushels for sale at the market in the three-field system was smaller than the corresponding ratio for the improved system. Plotting these data indicates that at 24.7 miles from market the three-field system provides the same location rent as the improved farming system (Figure 9.10). The improved system is better up to 24.7 miles from the market, and the three-field system from there to the extensive margin at 31.4 miles.

A spatial separation of the two farming systems occurs, with an inner circle of more intensive grain farming and an outer ring of more extensive farming. This separation illustrates the principle of highest and best use, which states that land is allocated to that use earning the highest location rent.

Land Use Organization in the Multicrop Case

The most prominent contribution of von Thünen's study was the determination of land use organization for the multicrop case. Activities are ordered according to the principle of the highest and best use as measured by their location rent at each distance from the market. Market price, transportation costs, and production expenses vary between crops so that the simple intensity law that applies to any single commodity is inappropriate. Instead, the general rule becomes that land uses are sequenced outward from the market in the order of the price spreads they achieve between market price and production plus transport costs. The site nearest the market will be appropriated by the product that can pay the highest location rent.

The details are complex but the basic operation of

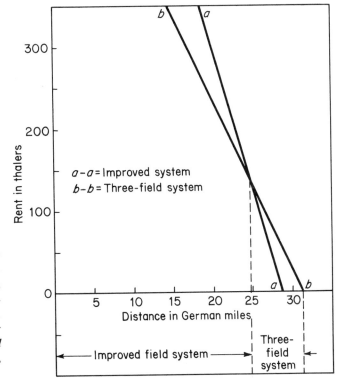

FIGURE 9.10 Rent gradients for the improved and three-field systems. The improved system yields a higher rent up to a distance of 25 miles, beyond which the three-field system is more profitable. The improved system has a steeper rent gradient. [*Source:* Data are derived from Peter Hall, ed., *Von Thünen's Isolated State* (Oxford: Pergamon Press, 1966), p. xxvii.]

a–a = Improved system
b–b = Three-field system

TABLE 9.2

Location rent for competing crops

	Milk	Potatoes	Wheat	Wool
Annual yield, E	725 gal	150 bu	50 bu	50 lb
Market price, P	$ 0.65 per gal	$ 1.75 per bu	$ 1.70 per bu	$ 0.60 per lb
Production cost, a	$ 0.05 per gal	$ 0.25 per bu	$ 0.20 per bu	$ 0.10 per lb
Transport rate per mile, f	$ 0.05 per gal	$ 0.075 per bu	$ 0.025 per bu	$ 0.005 per lb
Location rent at town	$435.00	$225.00	$75.00	$25.00
Rent at $0.00 at	12 mi	20 mi	60 mi	100 mi

Note: The data are hypothetical.

these principles may be illustrated by using hypothetical data for four commodities—milk, potatoes, wheat, and wool (Table 9.2). To graph the rent gradients, only the rent at the market and the limit of cultivation need be computed. Thus, wheat commands a rent of $75 per acre at the market and can extend 60 miles from market.

The rent gradients for the four crops, based on their market rent and distance values shown in Table 9.2, are superimposed to construct the rent diagram, Figure 9.11. In accordance with the law of highest and best use, the land use with the largest location rent at any given distance from market outbids the others. The four competing land uses are sequenced outward from the market to form concentric zones of milk, potato, wheat, and wool production.

Von Thünen's Farming Systems

Von Thünen described six farming systems in the *Isolated State,* ordered outwards as follows (Figure 9.12):

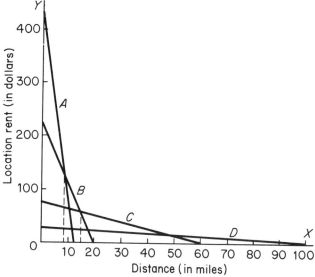

FIGURE 9.11 Rent gradients for competing crops.

1. *Free cash cropping* included horticulture and dairying for which perishability dictated a location as close as possible to market. Land use is intensive involving large labor inputs, multicropping, and heavy fertilizing; its outer limit of four miles is the maximum range of manure shipments from the city, where horses provided the principal motive power in von Thünen's day. The land is too valuable for open grazing and the milk cows are stall-fed.

2. *Forestry.* The location of forestry in the second zone comes as a surprise from the perspective of modern technology. It was logical at a time when forestry products were in great demand for both building and fuel and when transportation costs, by the primitive means available, were high so that it achieved a substantial cost reduction by proximity to market.

3. *Crop Alternation System (Belgian System).* Rings 3, 4, and 5 represented decreasing intensities of crop and livestock farming modified by von Thünen from contemporary agricultural practice. The crop alternation system involved a six-year crop rotation without fallow in which a given field was devoted for two years to rye, the staple grain crop, and for one year each to potatoes, barley, clover, and vetch (a legume fed to livestock). Rye and potatoes were cash crops, and the others used for livestock production, which also provided some cash income. Soil fertility was maintained under this intensive crop system by the rotation which included two soil-builders, clover and vetch, and by farm manure.

4. *The Improved System (Mecklenburg-Koppel System)* and

5. *The Three-Field System* were used to illustrate von Thünen's crop intensity theory earlier. The improved system involved a seven-year rotation, six of crops and one year fallow. The crops were rye, barley, and oats for one year each and three years of pasture. The three-field system commonly entailed the division of the farm area into a permanent pasture and an arable area with a rotation of winter grain, spring grain, and fallow. Production costs and yield were about halved in this system compared with the Koppel system (ring 3).

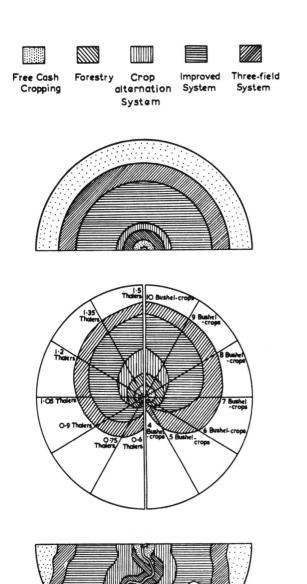

Free Cash Cropping   Forestry   Crop alternation System   Improved System   Three-field System

small town with its own region

MILES
0   40

FIGURE 9.12 Agricultural regions in the isolated state, showing effects of changing prices or yields, and of a navigable river and a small second town. [*Source:* Hall, 1966, pp. 216–217.]

Cash income in both systems came from rye and livestock products, the same commodities as the crop alternation system, with the exception of potatoes.

6. *Grazing,* the farthest zone functionally linked to the town, extended outward to a 50 German mile radius (230 English miles). In von Thünen's day this zone

was too distant for economic shipment of most grain and other crops and beyond it the land was wilderness. The grazing zone was devoted primarily to permanent pasture, although surprisingly, it could successfully market some intensive cash crops such as oilseeds, hops, tobacco, and flax.

Interestingly, zones 1, 3, 4, and 5 also tell us about economic history. The zones closest to the town were reserved for the most modern "improved" agricultures of the early nineteenth century, whereas those farthest away were the most traditional: Feudal agriculture still persisted in the more remote regions.

Modified Patterns with Relaxed Assumptions

Von Thünen recognized that his assumptions needed to be relaxed to approximate actual conditions more closely, even in 1826. He wrote:

> Actual countries differ from the Isolated State in the following ways:
> 1. Nowhere in reality do we find soil of the same physical quality and at the same level of fertility throughout an entire country.
> 2. There is no large town that does not lie on a navigable river or canal.
> 3. Every sizeable state has in addition to its capital many small towns scattered throughout the land.[3]

What changes in spatial organization result from taking account of these factors? And what effects do increasing prices or yields have on the pattern? The central diagram in Figure 9.12 represents von Thünen's description of the effects of increasing prices and yields on crop zonation. The effects maintain the concentric zones.

An irregular pattern of natural soil fertility, on the other hand, might completely disrupt the ordered pattern of concentric land-use zones. A pocket of fertile soil beyond the limit of cultivation for low-yield soil might support the intensive crop alternation system. Such variations in soil fertility distort the spatial pattern of interaction and the simple rent gradients.

Finally, as shown in the bottom diagram of Figure 9.12, substantial reorganization in the land-use pattern occurs with the introduction of a navigable river, for which von Thünen assumes a transportation rate of only one-tenth the land rate. A farm 100 miles from the Town but located on this river has the same relative accessibility as a farm 10 miles from the Town by road. A farm 5 miles from that riverside farm has the same relative

[3]Ibid., p. 171.

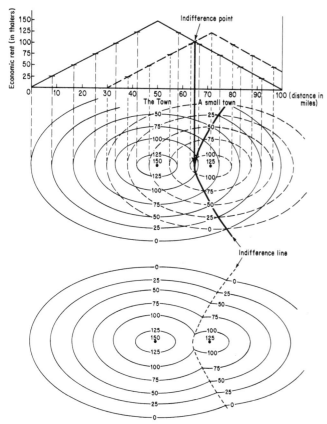

FIGURE 9.13 The impact of a second town on rent gradients and supply areas in the isolated stage. The data are hypothetical and assume a single-crop, single-intensity land use with simple transportation cost-to-distance relationships.

accessibility as one 15 miles by land from the Town. Von Thünen pictured the crop alternation system that results extending along the banks of the river to the limit of the cultivated plain with the land-use zones changing from a concentric to a sectoral pattern. One can imagine, of course, radiating highways of superior quality producing a "starfish" pattern.

Von Thünen also raised this question: What determines the relative position of the towns in the Isolated State in respect of size and distance from each other? For example, towns of one size, distributed evenly throughout the country would support higher location rents and farm population density. But a number of disrupting factors are discussed by von Thünen. Mineral deposits, notably ore, salt, and coal, are unevenly distributed resulting in an irregular distribution of mining towns and of the manufacturing towns processing raw materials of little value in relation to their bulk. The largest town, on the other hand, as the focal center of the country, would attract those industries enjoying large economies of scale, as will the functions and amenities, such as government administration, institutes of higher

learning, and art collections associated with the capital city of a state.

Von Thünen was satisfied, then, to leave the Isolated State with one primary center, introducing only one small town to illustrate the effect resource-oriented centers would have on land-use pattern, as in the bottom of Figure 9.12. The small town would compete with the large town for food supplies, and have a region skewed away from the big towns.

How might one determine the market area boundary between the large and small town? Figure 9.13 provides the answer. First, market price is lower in the small town because of lower population and, hence, demand. Rents fall with distance from each town, as in the top diagram of Figure 9.13. The spatial pattern of rents is shown in the middle figure, as is the market "indifference" line (that is, that line along which rents from selling in the two centers are equal). The bottom diagram thus illustrates the subdivision of the plain into market territories, and the rent patterns that result.

VON THÜNEN'S PRINCIPLES, THEN AND NOW

Great changes have occurred in agricultural and transportation technology, and world population has grown considerably since the *Isolated State* was written. At that time in many parts of the world, broad distance-related production zones could be distinguished not only in agriculture, but in other kinds of resource exploitation. W. R. Mead, for example, has described how exploitation of the forest resources of Scandinavia responded to "the discipline of distance" in the early nineteenth century (see Figure 9.14). The sailing vessel, with complementary horse haulage or riverboat transport, gave rise to the distinctive regional zonings of farmland and woodland use. There was a sharp gradient in softwood timber values from coast and tributary waterway to the interior, with corresponding differences in their use. In general, accessible woodlands tended to provide the bulkier, less-refined materials, whereas less-accessible woodlands produced the refined more transportable commodities. Norway, closer to Western European demand, produced relatively more of the transport-sensitive forest products than Finland.

Similar examples have been reported in many other historical instances, and at many scales, from the agricultural village to zonation of activity in the global economy itself. Even today, in those parts of the world where people still walk or use animals for their principal motive power, distance-related adjustments of land use take place. One example explored by P. M. Blaikie involves villages in north India, where minute adjustments

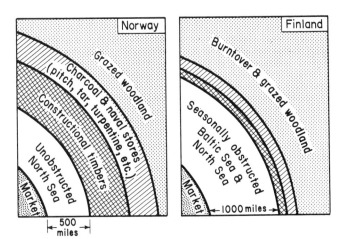

FIGURE 9.14 Zones of softwood exploitation in Scandinavia in the early nineteenth century. [*Source:* W. R. Mead, *An Economic Geography of the Scandinavian States and Finland* (London: University of London Press, 1958), p. 95.]

of land use to distance have come about because self-sustaining farmers existing close to the basic survival level have to economize upon use of their own time traveling to and from their fields (Figure 9.15).

Zonation characterizes dairying industries throughout the world. For example, in the United States, a hundredweight of 4-percent milk can be converted approximately into (1) 10 pounds of 40 percent cream, and 8 pounds of skim milk powder, or (2) 10 pounds of American cheese, or (3) 5 pounds of butter and 8 pounds of skim milk powder. These differences in densities cause substantial differences in the costs of shipping milk in the different forms. In addition to density, weight and perishability cause transportation costs to vary directly with the value of the product. Thus, the ratio of transportation costs of milk to an equivalent amount of cream is roughly 7 to 1, to skim milk powder 15 to 1, to American cheese 12 to 1, and to butter 25 to 1. Concentrated dairy products, whose values are high

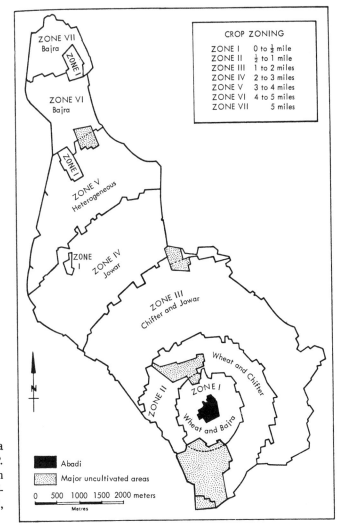

FIGURE 9.15 Crop zoning in a northern Indian village. [*Source:* P. M. Blaikie, "Organization of Indian Villages," *Transactions of the Institute of British Geographers,* No. 52, London (March 1971), p. 15.]

relative to their weight, can be shipped economically for longer distances than relatively bulky and perishable fluid milk. The result is a concentric zonation of milk specialization around central markets, as illustrated in Figure 9.16.

In Western Europe, the intensive cash-cropping areas that extended only four German miles from the Town in 1826 have expanded far beyond Mecklenburg to encompass much of Europe, and some authors see a single von Thünen pattern for this area (see Figure 9.17).

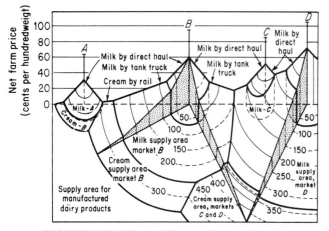

FIGURE 9.16 The net farm prices and supply areas for fluid milk, cream, and manufactured milk products, four-market model. Relative to base price for milk sold in manufacturing outlets. [*Source:* William Bredo and Anthony S. Rojko, "Prices and Milksheds of Northwestern Markets," University of Massachusetts Agricultural Experiment Station Bulletin No. 470, Amherst, 1952.]

The stock farming belt and the extensive grain production regions have migrated largely to the New World and the Southern Hemisphere. More traditional peasant agricultures remain in remoter regions, and hunting and gathering moieties only in the world's remotest peripheries. In a sense, then, the Isolated State has become the world, and the urban-industrial complexes of northwest Europe and northeast North America great "world Thünen-Towns," albeit affected by major world-scale differences in resources. Relaxing his initial assumptions did not lead von Thünen to anticipate this ultimate scale in the hierarchy of spatial organization, however, or the growing importance of urban centers and of manufacturing activity that have accompanied it.

Von Thünen did probe urban matters—indeed he suggested that his model was applicable to urban land use—but it was not until some 80 years ago that his principles began to be applied to an understanding of urban land use and that significant extensions to location theory were made by formulation of a theory for the location of manufacturing activity by Alfred Weber. On the other hand, it will be agreed that von Thünen's propositions—or more generally, those of rent theory—attach to every kind of resource use. Every resource commands a price, determined by scarcity commensurate with its quality and accessibility. The higher quality and the more accessible resource will be used first. Each price level calls forth a particular intensity of use. In the case of human resources, the argument extends to wages and incomes; the better educated and more skilled the worker, the higher the price (wage).

In the case of natural resources the argument is the same: As exhaustible supplies of higher quality and

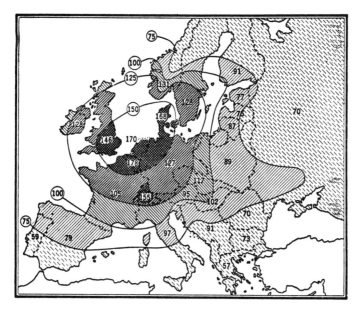

FIGURE 9.17 Intensity of agricultural production in Europe. The index of 100 is the average European yield per acre of eight main crops: wheat, rye, barley, oats, corn, potatoes, sugar beets, and hay. 1937 political boundaries. [*Source:* Michael Chisholm, *Rural Settlement and Land Use* (New York: John Wiley, 1967), p. 108, reproduced from S. van Valkenburg and C. C. Held, *Europe* (New York: John Wiley, 1952).]

more accessible resources are used, scarcity pushes up the marginal revenue productivity of lower-quality and less-accessible items, but at any time, the less the accessibility and the lower the quality, the lower the price.

THE ORGANIZATION OF URBAN SPACE

Although von Thünen's study captured at best only a fleeting reality in its empirical details, his work presents principles of lasting value that today still serve as the foundations of land-use theory. His conception of economic rent as a standardized measure of accessibility was, of course, his most important single contribution. Combined with the principle of highest and best use, the concept of economic rent identifies the three most fundamental components of the spatial organization of economic systems:

1. *concentric-circle arrangements* around centers of activity defining points of greatest accessibility
2. *development axes* along major transportation routes
3. *multiple nuclei,* with the introduction of additional points of interaction.

The relevance of these components becomes more apparent when we turn to the case of urban land use.

Von Thünen noted that rural land values increase toward a large town, but that this increase is only a prelude to a far greater rise in land values within urban areas. He went on to suggest that his principles govern this determination of land values and the allocation of land use in urban areas, just as they do in rural areas.

The first applications of the principles to urban land use were not provided until the classic statements of R. M. Hurd in 1903 and of R. L. Haig in 1926, however, just 100 years after *Der Isolierte Staat* was published. Hurd wrote:

As a city grows, more remote and hence inferior land must be utilized and the difference in desirability between the two grades produces economic rent in locations of the first grade, but not in those of the second. As land of a still more remote and inferior grade comes into use, ground rent is forced still higher in land of the first grade, rises in land of the second grade, but not in land of the third grade, and so on. Any utility may compete for any location within a city and all land goes to the highest bidder. . . . Practically all land within a city earns some economic rent, though it may be small,

the final contrast being with the city's rentless and hence, strictly speaking, valueless circumference. . . .

Since value depends on economic rent, and rent on location, and location on convenience, and convenience on nearness, we may eliminate the intermediate steps and say that value depends on nearness.[4]

Haig's principles, following on from Hurd, were:

1. Each activity seeks the location of maximum accessibility; *rent* is the charge which the owner of a relatively accessible site can impose because of the saving in transport costs which the use of his site makes possible.
2. The activity which can most successfully exploit the locational attributes of a given site will probably gain it through competitive bidding in the real estate market.
3. Land-use organization reflects the evaluation of the relative importance of accessibility to particular land uses.
4. The efficiency of urban spatial organization is inversely proportional to the aggregate costs of friction in overcoming spatial separation of urban functions.

A land economist, Richard Ratcliffe, succinctly restated these principles as "the structure of the city is determined by the dollar evaluation of the importance of convenience."

Concentric zones of urban land use were reported in 1923 by E. W. Burgess, who believed that these zones, illustrated in Figure 9.18, developed because (1) cities grow outwards from their original center, with the newest housing always found at the edge of the developed area, and (2) socially mobile individuals move outwards geographically as they move upwards in the socioeconomic system. Thus, higher-income families build new houses on the periphery of the city where open land is available and sell their old homes to lower-income families. The market provides housing for lower-income families not by building for them directly, but by a "filtering" process, letting higher-income families absorb depreciation costs before the house is handed on. This, in turn, produces very definite patterns of urban development and community change as the city grows and as new immigrants on the lowest rungs of the socioeconomic ladder find initial residences in "ports of entry" in the oldest neighborhoods closest to the city center.

[4]R. M. Hurd, *Principles of City Land Values* (New York: The Record and Guide, 1924), pp. 12–13.

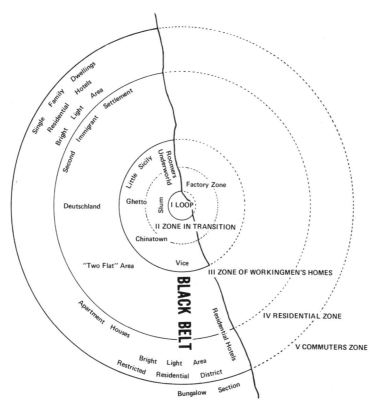

FIGURE 9.18 Burgess's spatial model. [*Source:* Robert E. Park and Ernest W. Burgess, *The City* (Chicago: University of Chicago Press, 1925), pp. 41–53.]

The five zones E. W. Burgess said characterized the internal structure of the city were:

Zone I: The Central Business District. At the center of the city as the focus of its commercial, social, and civic life is situated the Central Business District. The heart of this district is the downtown retail district with its department stores, its smart shops, its office buildings, its clubs, its banks, its hotels, its theatres, its museums, and its headquarters of economic, social, civic, and political life. Encircling this area of work and play is the less well-known Wholesale Business District with its "market," its warehouses, and storage buildings.

Zone II: The Zone in Transition. Surrounding the Central Business District are areas of residential deterioration caused by the encroaching of business and industry from Zone I. This may therefore be called a Zone in Transition, with a factory district for its inner belt and an outer ring of retrogressing neighborhoods, of first-settlement immigrant colonies, of roominghouse districts, of homeless-men areas, of resorts of gambling, bootlegging, sexual vice, and of breeding-places of crime. In this area of physical deterioration and social disorganization studies show the greatest concentration of cases of poverty, bad housing, juvenile delinquency, family disintegration, physical and mental disease. As families and individuals prosper, they escape from this area into Zone III beyond, leaving behind as marooned a residuum of the defeated, leaderless, and helpless.

Zone III: The Zone of Independent Workingmen's Homes. This third broad urban ring is largely constituted by neighborhoods of second immigrant settlement. Its residents are those who desire to live near but not too close to their work. It is a housing area neither of tenements, apartments, nor of single dwellings; its boundaries have been roughly determined by the plotting of the two-flat dwelling, generally of frame construction, with the owner living on the lower floor with a tenant on the other. While the father works in the factory, the son and daughter typically have jobs in the downtown area, attend dance halls, and motion pictures in the bright-light areas, and plan upon marriage to set up homes in Zone IV.

Zone IV: The Zone of Better Residences. Extending beyond the neighborhoods of second immigrant settlements, we come to the Zone of Better Residences in which the great middle class of native-born Americans live, small business men, professional people, clerks, and salesmen. Once communities of single homes, they are becoming apartment-house and residential-hotel areas. Within these areas at strategic points are found local business centers of such growing importance that they have been called "satellite downtowns." The typical constellation of business and recreational units includes a bank, one or more United Cigar Stores, a drug store, a high-class restaurant, an automobile display row, and a so-called "wonder" motion picture theatre. With the addition of a dancing palace, a cabaret, and a smart hotel, the satellite Loop also becomes a "bright-light" area attracting a city-wide attendance. In this zone men are outnumbered by women, independence in voting is frequent, newspapers and books have wide circulation, and women are elected to the state legislature.

Zone V: The Commuter's Zone. Out beyond the areas of better residence is a ring of encircling small cities, towns, and hamlets, which, taken together, constitute the Commuter's Zone. These are also, in the main, dormitory suburbs, because the majority of men residing there spend the day at work in the Central Business District, returning only for the night. Thus, the mother and the wife become the center of family life. If the Central Business District is predominantly a homeless-men's region; the rooming

The growth of the city increases the space needs of residents of each zone causing an *invasion* by each zone into the next outer zone so that at any given distance from the city center there is a "succession" of land uses. Burgess called this the *process of invasion and succession*.

Later, in 1939, Homer Hoyt advanced an axial model of urban development. He had been studying block data on rents for 64 medium to small American cities, provided by the Works Progress Administration of the United States federal government, supplemented by his own surveys of New York, Chicago, Detroit, Washington, and Philadelphia. He discovered that high-rent residential areas occupy only certain segments of an urban area, extending outward like slices of a cake. The high-grade residential area has its point of origin near the retail and office center where the higher-income groups work and farthest from the industries and warehouses where the lower-income groups work. Expansion can be outward only, because other growth points having a different character also grow, thus preventing lateral expansion. Hoyt noted that higher-priced residential construction tends to expand long the fastest existing transportation lines and toward the homes of community leaders. It is also attracted toward high ground and to waterfronts and riversides free of industrial use. It tends to follow the same direction of growth for long periods but is influenced by the location of new office buildings, banks, and stores. Hoyt noted, finally, that the direction of the growth of better residential neighborhoods may be changed by estate developers.

Soon after Hoyt, in 1943, Chauncy D. Harris and Edward L. Ullman suggested that models of urban land use must recognize the existence of more than one nucleus within a city around which growth occurs. The nuclei may date from the origin of the city as in London where "The City," the center of finance and commerce, and Westminister, the political focus, were at one time separated by open country. In addition, new centers may develop with city growth, as in Chicago where heavy industry, at first localized along the Chicago River in the heart of the city, migrated to the Calumet District, serving there as the nucleus for extensive new development.

The emergence of separate nuclei and differentiated districts are related by Harris and Ullman primarily to three centrifugal and one centripetal factors. The centrifugal factors are the rent gradient coupled with space requirements, the need for specialized facilities, and incompatibilities among different land uses. The centripetal factors that convert simple dispersion to multiple nuclei are the functional convenience, magnetism, and prestige that are not entirely restricted to the central nucleus.

The number of nuclei, Harris and Ullman said, may vary according to the historical development and localization forces involved. Typically, however, five distinct nuclei occur: the central business district, wholesaling and light manufacturing, heavy industrial, specialized nuclei, and suburban and dormitory satellites. The resulting internal structure of the city is suggested by Figure 9.19.

The strongest pattern is that of the decline of land prices with distance from the city center. That population densities repeat this pattern should be no surprise: As land prices fall relative to the prices of other inputs, households will substitute land for capital and labor. Because per-household land consumption increases, there will then be less households per unit of area, and population densities must fall.

The population density gradient has a very particular shape. This was the conclusion of Colin Clark in 1951. He argued that the pattern was one of negative exponential decline from the city center and could be expressed by the formula

$$d_x = d_o e^{-bx}$$

where

d = population density
x = distance from city center
d_o = density at city center
e = natural logarithmic base
b = density gradient (a measure of city compactness)

or $\ln d_x = \ln d_o - bx$ when the natural logarithm (ln) of density is used.

Clark provided 36 examples of cities for which this equation provided a good fit of population-density gra-

house district, the habitat of the emancipated family; the area of first-immigrant settlement, the natural soil of the patriarchal family transplanted from Europe; the Zone of Better Residences with its apartment houses and residential hotels, the favorable environment for the equalitarian family; then the Commuter's Zone is without question the domain of the matricentric family. The communities in this Commuter's Zone are probably the most highly segregated of any in the entire metropolitan region, including in their range the entire gamut from an incorporated village run in the interests of crime and vice, to exclusive villages with wealth, culture, and public spirit.

[*Source:* Ernest W. Burgess, "Urban Areas" in T. V. Smith and L. D. White, eds., *Chicago: An Experiment in Social Science Research* (Chicago: University of Chicago Press, 1929), pp. 114–123.

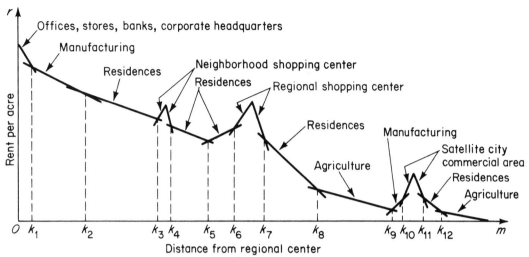

FIGURE 9.19 Hypothetical land rent profile in a multicentered urban area. [*Source:* William Goldner, *A Model for the Spatial Allocation of Activities and Land Uses in a Metropolitan Region* (Berkeley: Bay Area Transportation Study Commission, September 1968).]

dients. These examples ranged in time from 1801 to the contemporary period and from Los Angeles to Budapest. Subsequent research has added a myriad of cases, and repeated testing has not overturned Clark's basic claim that the negative exponential pattern is universally the simplest and best-fitting description of urban densities.

What the researchers have found, however, is that: (1) the gradient is steeper in lower-income sectors than in sectors occupied by higher-income residents (see Figure 9.20); and (2) that as transport costs decrease, or the technology of transportation improves, or affluence increases, the gradient flattens.

TOPICS FOR DISCUSSION

1. If, when the fixed factor Y is equal to 1, a firm's production functions are

$$\text{total product (TP)} = 6x^2 - x^3$$
$$\text{average product (AP)} = 6x - x^2$$

   (a) What is the marginal product (MP) function?

   (b) From the three production functions, construct a table and a figure showing graphically the three production functions for six successively larger increments to the variable factor X.

   (c) It should be possible then to divide the figure into three stages, a phase of increasing average returns to the variable factor, a phase of diminishing average returns to the variable factor, and a phase of negative marginal returns. Give the characteristics of each function in each stage.

2. Holding land quality constant, what is the effect of increasing transportation costs on marginal revenue productivity? In such a situation, what kind of a pattern do rents display? What happens to farm size with increasing distance? Why?

3. In what sense has von Thünen's Isolated State become the world? Is there anything wrong with this interpretation? If so, what?

4. Consider the location rent formula, $R = E(p - a) - Efk$:

   (a) As intensity of land use increases, what happens to the difference between market price (p) and production costs (a)?

   (b) What happens to transportation costs per unit as distance increases?

5. *Economic rent* of a good is the portion of the price that does not influence the amount of that good in existence. Consider the following statement: "The rent for land in Chicago is not a payment that is necessary to produce that land. It is a necessary payment to obtain use of the land. From the first point of view, it is an economic rent; from the latter point of view, it is a cost." Do you agree? If so, why? If not, why not?

6. In what aspect does Hoyt's model of land use differ from Burgess's, and how do both Hoyt's and Burgess's models differ from Harris's and Ullman's model?

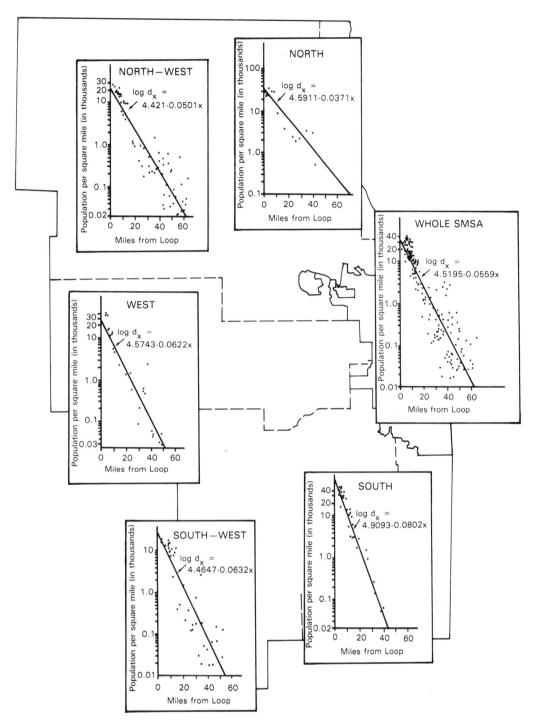

FIGURE 9.20 Density-distance graphs: The Chicago SMSA and five sectors, 1960. The urban gradient is steepest along the lowest-income sector, to the south, and is flattest in the high-income (northern) sector. [*Source: Philip H. Rees, The Factorial Economy of Metropolitan Chicago* (Master's thesis, University of Chicago, 1968), Appendix B.]

FURTHER READINGS

BECKMANN, MARTIN. *Location Theory.* New York: Random House, 1968.

A succinct treatment of the theories of industrial location, land use, and central places, together with the locational impact of economic growth. See especially Chapter 4, "Allocation of Land," which summarizes von Thünen's main ideas and extends these to include the effects of changes in demand, wage differentials, the appearance of urban rings, the introduction of transportation routes, and other complicating elements.

CHISHOLM, MICHAEL. *Rural Settlement and Land Use: An Essay in Location.* New York: John Wiley, 1962.

Simply and interestingly written, this introduction to the theory of rural land use is abundantly illustrated with empirical examples taken from many parts of the world.

GREGOR, HOWARD F. *Geography of Agriculture: Themes in Research.* Englewood Cliffs, N.J.: Prentice-Hall, 1970.

A general treatment of the geography of agriculture. Chapter 4, "Spatial Organization," contains a brief exposition of rural land use theory.

HALL, PETER (Ed.). *Von Thünen's Isolated State.* Trans. Carla M. Wartenberg. Oxford: Pergamon Press, 1966.

This translation of von Thünen's classic work on agricultural land use theory covers the essential portions of the original. The book provides invaluable access to von Thünen's seminal writings for English-speaking students of location theory. A substantial introduction by the editor supplies revealing background information on von Thünen and his times and includes an especially helpful guide to the main features of his theory.

HAUSER, PHILIP M., AND LEO F. SCHNORE. *The Study of Urbanization.* New York: John Wiley, 1966.

In this general study of urbanization, Chapter 10, "On the Spatial Structure of Cities in the Two Americas," interestingly contrasts the typical urban land use patterns of two distinct cultural realms.

HOOVER, EDGAR M. *The Location of Economic Activity.* New York: McGraw-Hill, 1948.

An influential and comprehensive statement of location theory for four decades, this very readable work remains a valuable sourcebook on the subject. See particularly Chapter 6, "Land Use Competition."

MAYER, HAROLD M., AND CLYDE F. KOHN (Eds.). *Readings in Urban Geography.* Chicago: University of Chicago Press, 1959.

Section 10, "General Nature of City Structure," is a convenient source of information on competing theories of urban spatial structure.

CHAPTER 10

Locational Decisions and Choice by Manufacturing Industry

From land use, let us now turn to industrial location. This chapter will review the basic elements entering into plant location decisions, and industrial location theory, which describes those circumstances determining successful locations under competitive marketplace conditions. Complementing the theoretical discussion is presentation of case studies of locational change in manufacturing industries, to illustrate how the principal forces determining industrial location have worked as technology has changed and market conditions have shifted.

The questions we want to answer are: Why are plants in the manufacturing industries located where they are? What factors and decisions enter into the firm's initial choice of plant location? To what extent are the locational patterns of plants within any manufacturing industry determined by the initial location decisions of the firm? To what extent do such locational patterns represent successful survivors, after competition has weeded out those plants initially located with least concern for, or awareness of, marketplace conditions? We look at the firm's plant location decisions first and then turn to industrial location patterns and the factors apparently entering into successful performance in the marketplace.

Throughout the discussion we will use the term *plant* to refer to the individual producing unit, *firm* to refer to the corporate management and decision-making unit, which may be single or multiplant, and *industry* to refer to a group of firms engaged in creating the same or similar types of product.

Objectives:

- to appreciate the processes involved in plant location decisions, differentiate *adoptive* from *adaptive* behavior, and understand the difference between the short-run and long-run consequences of decisions

- to learn the importance of the prices received by producers for their output and the prices they pay for their needed inputs on locational strategies

- to understand and explain the different forms of transport and labor orientation, the theory of the downward filtering of industry and its consequences, and the differential role of locational factors from one level of the urban hierarchy to another

- to learn the essential features of Weber's theory of industrial location, and of Palander's market area analysis

PLANT LOCATION DECISIONS AND INDUSTRIAL LOCATION PATTERNS

When manufacturers are asked why they locate their plants where they do, the answers are quite surprising. For example, in a survey of Michigan manufacturers made by Eva Mueller and John Lansing in 1960, firms were asked why they located in Michigan, and then why they chose the particular site within Michigan. The dominant response was "personal reasons" or "chance" or "opportunity—found a good site."

This hardly speaks for the careful prior analysis of locational alternatives that one might expect from rational businesspeople attempting to select the most profitable locations for their plants. One possible conclusion might be that because so many personal reasons enter into individual plant location *decisions,* theories of manufacturing location that assume rationality of choice are not appropriate.

Yet many students have observed that there is an apparent rationality to industrial location *patterns.* How can we reconcile what industrialists say they do with what researchers say they see? One answer is that we must distinguish between rational industrial location patterns created by the "guiding hand" of the market and the haphazard plant location decisions of the firm. Another answer is provided by study of actual management behavior of large-scale multiplant firms. The Lansing and Mueller surveys cited above show that "personal reasons" account for a very small percentage of the location and selection of plant sites by larger firms, which do, in fact, engage in systematic locational analysis in the search for an optimal location.

Adoptive and Adaptive Locational Behavior

The difference between the two cases has been highlighted by Armen A. Alchian and Charles M. Tiebout, two American economists. They distinguished two circumstances leading to the apparently rational industrial location patterns about which people think they can theorize. These circumstances were termed *adoptive* and *adaptive* locational behavior.

The idea of adoptive economic behavior has its intellectual roots in the "survival of the fittest" philosophies of the nineteenth century. The plant location choices of individual firms, it is acknowledged, may appear quite random when viewed case by case. But, it is argued, this random behavior takes place within a competitive economic environment. Thus, although many businesspeople pursue their activities without investigating alternative locations and choose plant locations for many strange reasons, the conditions imposed by the economic environment do make locations matter in the long run, because some locations are by their nature more profitable than others. The initial or individual location decisions of the firms may turn out to be *irrelevant* to the emergence of spatial regularities, because locational differences affect the ability of firms to survive in a competitive environment. In the long run, if a plant's location is inconsistent with the calculus of economic advantage it will find itself threatened by more favorably located competitors. The competitors will grow and the unprofitable plant will finally shut down. Such differential growth leads to apparently rational locational patterns of plants within the industry, made up of the successful survivors. The theory of industrial location with which we will be concerned later on in the chapter basically helps explain what happened and why the locational patterns emerged. In this sense, it is a *positive* theory that helps explain economic history's success stories, a tool for *understanding what is.* As marketplace conditions change, it also explains why locational change takes place, and what the resulting patterns are likely to be.

The adaptive viewpoint is somewhat different, focusing on rational decision making and locational choice. Large firms with substantial investment in market research and with systematic processes of internal decision making analyze the economic environment to find out how to locate themselves in the way that best achieves corporate goals. This automatically creates a "rational" economic geography consistent with predetermined goals: By design and analysis, firms ensure that they will be successful as the competitive process operates. To these firms, location theory provides the necessary guidance for analysis and selection of the optimal location; to the systematic analyst it is a *normative* theory *suggesting what ought to be.*

Now clearly, this is a very different point of view from that of the survival of the fittest. Whereas the adoptive viewpoint says that there is irrationality in individual decision making and that competition within the economic system determines who will be successful, the adaptive viewpoint says that optimal locations can be determined by analysis and that rational decisions can guide the individual business to the location that will result in the greatest economic advantage.

Locational Research by the Large Corporation

What factors enter into the locational decision process of the large corporation seeking an optimal location for a new manufacturing plant? Summarizing the results of several studies, John Rees, a British geographer, has developed a decision-making model. He argues that branch plant locations are determined in a specific decision-making environment that involves the short- and long-term goals of the firm, and he builds into the model perceptions of need, aspirations, and motivations of the decision-makers, and the fruits of past experience.

The firm becomes concerned about possible branch plants either because potential demand is perceived in its various sales territories, or in untried territories, or because growth has produced difficulties in expanding on site. A location problem is recognized that can be met by a short-term response of on-site increases in output, or by a long-term response of one of three kinds: relocation of the existing plant; acquisition of a plant from someone else; or construction of a new branch plant.

If the firm chooses to construct a new branch plant, it begins to seek location alternatives. There are three stages: (1) the selection of a potential sales *region* within which sufficient demand is thought to exist to warrant a branch plant; (2) the selection of a *community* within this region, using a comparative cost approach, to find the place most likely to satisfy the firm's profit goals; and (3) the selection of a *site* or sites for the plant within the community, often based on social, rather than economic, grounds (for example, where it is thought the probable manager would prefer to live).

Then the decision is finally ratified, and the firm's resources are allocated to build the plant. Whatever is learned from the decision process, and from later evaluation of the plant's performance "feeds back" to the decision-making environment within which future decisions will be made.

Similar models have been developed by P. M. Townroe in his studies of locational decision making by British firms. He found it necessary to distinguish three kinds of firms: the private capitalist, the corporate capitalist, and the state. For all three profit, security, and growth are basic goals. In Britain, however, the state, on its own behalf and by restrictions placed upon others, also insists that social goals be served.

Two different profit motives also are present. In the short run, firms may try to maximize their profits, but often in the long run they seek the greater security of *satisficing.* As we saw in Chapter 8, a satisficer is one who seeks a more-likely-to-be-guaranteed rate of return on investment rather than trying always to reach the maximum.

Townroe also points to the other elements in the complex decision environment: responsibility to shareholders, employees, and the public; the management structure of the firm; management and investment policy. All serve to illustrate the complex context of locational decision making. He also cautions that the search process and generation of alternatives was characterized in many of the cases he studied by lack of any systematic approach, by the ample opportunity for subjective as-

sessment, and by the frequency with which, in retrospect, even the largest companies felt that important aspects of the new location had been overlooked before the choice had been made.

Types of Locational Strategies

Both Rees and Townroe point out that the prime consideration in locational choice of the modern large manufacturing firm is demand (that is, whether there exists a potential market area of sufficient size to consume the output of a manufacturing plant). Such an assessment depends on the computation of *market potentials* for different locations, as was demonstrated in a classic study of the market as a factor in industrial location in the United States, completed by Chauncy D. Harris in 1954.

Harris first constructed a map of income potentials, such as that already discussed in Chapter 8. He then showed that manufacturing potentials, calculated in the same way, had the same spatial pattern in the United States. Finally, he demonstrated that manufacturing employment was increasing most rapidly where national market access, as measured by income potentials, was greatest. One exception was where the textile industries were expanding close to sources of cheap labor in the Piedmont of the Carolinas and Georgia. Later, Allan Pred confirmed Harris's results and emphasized that the demand factor was apparently most significant for high value-added manufacturing (that is, for those activities, such as the engineering trades, that convert simple inexpensive raw materials into complex costly products using large inputs of capital and labor).

Why should this be so? One useful insight has been provided by another location economist, Martin Beckmann. Beckmann points out that the prices received by producers for their output can be either the same from place to place, or they may vary spatially. The same is true for the prices paid by the producers for their needed inputs. This leads to four different types of locational choices (Table 10.1).

If both input and output prices are uniform from place to place, the firm is *locationally indifferent.* If, however, output prices are uniform from place to place but input prices (costs) vary locationally, then the firm can optimize by *minimizing cost.*

If input prices are uniform from place to place but selling prices vary locationally, the obvious strategy for the businessperson is to locate where he or she can *maximize revenues;* this implies getting into the position that is most sensitive to the variations in output prices. Finally, if both input and output prices vary locationally, the optimum location behavior—that which *maximizes*

TABLE 10.1

Beckmann's classification of location types

	Selling prices	
	Locationally variable	Do not vary with location
Production costs Locationally variable	*Type B* Optimal locations maximize difference between prices and costs to maximize profits	*Type A* Optimal locations minimize costs to maximize profits
Do not vary with location	*Type C* Optimal locations maximize sales to maximize profits	*Type D* Plants are locationally indifferent ("footloose")

profit—is to find the location that maximizes the spread between revenues and costs.

Now recall what was said about the relationship of costs and prices to firm characteristics in Chapter 7. Where goods are highly complex, there is substantial product differentiation and selling price variability. But such high-value producers purchase simple semiprocessed parts at input prices that vary little. In other words, the revenue maximizers in Beckmann's scheme will, in general, be the high value-added producers who seek out demand-maximizing locations rather than cost-minimizing locations. On the other hand, the cost-minimizers are likely to be price-takers in highly competitive industries who compete by minimizing costs.

Emergence of the different types may be understood historically. The earlier phases of the Industrial Revolution involved the growth of large numbers of small manufacturing firms converting raw materials to finished products that were sold in highly competitive markets. As price-takers, these firms depended upon minimizing production costs for their successful competition and long-term survival. Toward the end of the nineteenth century, scholars began to observe that survival of the fittest had produced quite distinctive locational patterns in these industries. Industrial location theory developed as these scholars codified their understanding of the market's guiding hand: The first theories sought to explain Beckmann's Type A locational choice (Table 10.1). The first of these theories was that of Alfred Weber (1909).

As the Industrial Revolution progressed, plant sizes increased along with scale of industrial organization and the ability of oligopolies to manipulate prices in different markets. Type A locational choice was joined by Type B behavior, and then by Type C decisions in industries creating high value-added products from standardized components produced by other manufacturing industries. By the middle of the twentieth century, as a consequence of this economic evolution, location theorists such as August Lösch and Melvin

Greenhut were adding demand, price, and markets to their extensions and reformulations of Weber.

Since World War II in particular, economic evolution has progressed to even higher levels of technology with the creation of products selling at uniform prices in national markets, using inputs and manufacturing processes that cost the same wherever the plant is located. Type D situations have emerged where qualitative factors not entering into the plant's cost or profit equation seem to have dominated locational choice; predominant of these have been the regions and the environments where businesspeople and their key personnel prefer to live.

The remainder of this chapter and Chapter 11 that follows trace this sequence of economic evolution and its accompanying bodies of location theory. We begin with cost-minimizing strategies and Type A locational choice.

COST-MINIMIZATION AS A DETERMINANT OF MANUFACTURING LOCATION

A manufacturing firm must go through several stages in getting its product onto the market:

1. procurement of raw materials;
2. processing of raw materials into finished products;
3. distribution of products to the consumer.

The first and third of these stages involve transportation costs. The second involves the productive operations—capital inputs and scale, for example—plus labor costs.

A variety of situations has been studied in which plant location is affected by variations of procurement, processing, and distribution costs. For example, cases have been noted in which plants are all very much alike in their labor requirements and scale of operations wherever they are located, so that these costs do not vary much spatially, but which incur substantial transportation costs that do vary considerably from one location to another. Under these conditions plants have to minimize transportation costs to maximize their competitive advantage. Such plants have been called *transport oriented*. Two forms of transport orientation have been noted: (1) where procurement costs are large and variable, in which case the plant is *raw-material oriented,* and (2) where distribution costs are large and variable and the plant is *market oriented*. As we will see later, there are strong pressures for transport-oriented plants to be either raw-material or market oriented rather than being located between raw materials and markets.

Industries in which plants are quite insensitive to transport cost variations also have been studied. Transport costs for these industries played a minor role in determining final cost and competitive position. Location analysts speak of plants in these industries as being *footloose*. For some footloose plants, however, processing costs often have been a large and variable part of total cost, leading to other kinds of locational patterns. One type arises from short-run differences in processing costs. Labor costs and taxes, for example, may vary locationally in the short run. Plants whose competitive advantage has depended upon minimization of labor costs are called *labor oriented*.

Other processing cost differentials persisting in the long run have been studied. Among these are economies of scale. When the threshold scale of plant alone determines cost levels, and the degree of concentration is substantial (as discussed in Chapter 7), plants are relatively insensitive to location. In such cases the advantages of an *early start* have often determined which firms achieve a superior ability to compete whatever their initial location.

Other long-run differences in processing cost have been attributed to *external economies* (the so-called economies of agglomeration) of which several kinds were identified in Chapter 7:

1. *Economies of localization,* which result from similar plants clustering together and achieving benefits from joint use of subsidiary facilities, such as a common pool of skilled labor or uniquely specialized financial institutions.
2. *Economies of urbanization,* which result from many businesses of many kinds serving a common market, drawing on a large pool of labor, and making joint use of public facilities (housing, transport, recreation).

3. *Industrial complex economies* in which closely related productive processes are linked together by materials and by-product flows.

Some of these economies strengthen the snowballing effect that the biggest cities have upon otherwise relatively footloose kinds of industry, and together they produce *hierarchical organization* of industrial locations. Industrial complex economies, in particular, have also been shown to produce major industrial groupings in rural areas.

Let us now attempt to probe more deeply into the findings of actual locational analyses of each of these factors.

The Forms of Transport Orientation

When transportation costs form a high proportion of total costs, research has confirmed that the plant tends to be transport oriented, minimizing transport costs so as to be able to put its products on the market at lowest cost. Transport-oriented firms survive in such circumstances, whereas their competitors falter and sometimes fail altogether.

Dispersion

The earliest form of transport orientation emerged under circumstances in which consumers were widely scattered and raw materials were available everywhere as ubiquities. If products were, in addition, expensive to transport, a locational pattern comprising many small, widely diffused firms resulted. Each plant would have to be small, sacrificing economies of large-scale production to save transport costs and serving a small market area with a radius effectively limited by rapidly escalating transportation costs.

Figure 10.1 illustrates this situation, recalling the presentation in Chapter 7. The plant has a U-shaped cost curve. If transport costs were zero the optimal scale of production would be S_p, with average production costs C_p. But as scale of production increases, the size of market area and the average transport cost burden must also increase. Hence, the combined production and transport cost curve, although still generally U-shaped, lies much higher. The optimal scale of output is lower (S_A) and average costs are much higher (C_A), the amounts depending upon the steepness of the transport cost gradient.

This industrial pattern was common in Western Europe and North America prior to the development of cheap transport by canals and railroads during the nineteenth century. Transportability of goods was low and production was local, intended only to serve local needs.

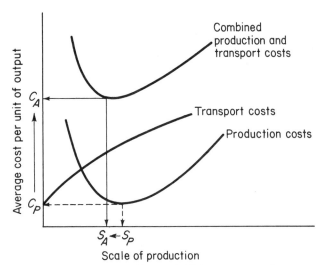

FIGURE 10.1 Effect of high transportation costs on the scale of output.

During the nineteenth century, however, several basic changes occurred as the Industrial Revolution ran its course. Market areas were widened by transportation improvements that slashed overland shipping costs; production was concentrated in larger plants that made use of newly developed technologies and tended to cluster in areas with superior resource endowments; industrial areas with associated urban complexes developed, and industry was therefore also effective in creating major centers of consumption. In many kinds of industrial activity—for example, production of iron—small diffused plants failed as the new large-scale producers put superior products on the market at lower cost. A new industrial order and pattern was created.

Thus, in Figure 10.2 we see how the lowering of

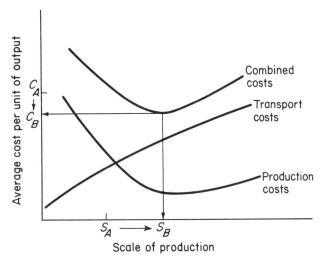

FIGURE 10.2 Consequences of improved production and transport technology for the scale of output.

the production and transport schedules leads to expansion of the optimal scale of output to S_B, together with a lowering of cost to C_B. In consequence, plants and market areas become larger and fewer. As scale increases, however, diffusion declines for other reasons. Larger and fewer modern firms have been shown to seek out and use superior sources of raw materials, to serve national markets from points central to these markets, but seldom to locate at some intermediate point.

Raw Material Orientation

Raw material orientation arises when:

1. there is a great deal of loss of weight or bulk of raw materials in manufacturing, so that if the plant is raw-material oriented a lighter and more compact product can be shipped to market;

2. when raw materials are more perishable or fragile than the finished products.

Raw-material-oriented industries are characteristically the "heavy industries": iron and steel plants, chemical plants, and so on. They may be identified by the following features: Costs of raw materials form a large percentage of the value of gross output; the value of products per ton is low; high weights of raw materials are used per operative; and the labor force is predominantly male. These are industries of low mobility, tied to sources of raw materials, which produce commodities that are heavy and bulky in relation to value and add substantially to the price of finished products if they are transported. Such were the industries that created the first large industrial towns during the Industrial Revolution.

Market Orientation

Manufacturing plants, on the other hand, are market oriented when:

1. there is a weight or bulk gain in production, so that products add more to price if transported than do the raw materials;

2. products are perishable or fragile;

3. frequent or rapid contact with consumers is required;

4. raw materials are simple and homogeneous and can be carried in bulk but there are several complex products that must be conveyed separately, as in the case of crude oil and separate refinery products;

5. there are differential transport rates such that more is charged to ship higher-value finished

products than lower-value raw materials (called "charging what the load will bear").

This type of transport orientation has been of increasing importance during the twentieth century, even for such traditionally raw-material-oriented industries as iron and steel.

Also, more and more industries are of the assembling kind, procuring semiprocessed raw materials and converting them into bulky products. By their very nature, these industries are market oriented and increasingly sensitive to demand rather than cost factors, as we saw earlier. Some examples are the American Can Company and Continental Can Company, both of which have experienced distinct economies from diffusing branch plants to many local markets. Because their products are bulky and expensive to ship, costs are minimized by minimizing the distances over which cans are shipped. Growth of the industry has occurred by establishing branch plants wherever the demand in a market area justifies it.

Indeed, the entire branch plant movement in the United States, Canada, and Western Europe has been promoted by decentralization. Although decentralization forfeits some of the internal economies of scale, it produces great savings in transportation costs and speedy servicing of customers. An example is in the soft-drink industry, where flavors and essences are shipped in liquid, or syrup, form to many local bottlers who add a ubiquity (water) and bottle. The economy is in shipping the end product, which consists mainly of water and bottles.

'Intermediate' Transport Orientations

Market orientation is increasing. But what of locations intermediate between raw materials and markets? Such orientations have been shown to be generally unfeasible, as illustrated by the combined cost curve in the upper half of Figure 10.3. One exception is where "processing-in-transit" privileges are granted by the railroads, as in the example of the U.S. flour-milling industry concentrated at Buffalo or where there is a break-of-bulk in the course of transportation, a situation illustrated in the bottom part of Figure 10.3. Ports, for example, are favorable spots for processing of raw materials that have been shipped by water. In Western Europe flour mills and sugar and oil refineries are concentrated at port locations. Most "colonial" raw materials brought in from the world's hinterland regions are processed at ports in Western Europe. Such transshipment centers are called *break-of-bulk* points. Other kinds of transshipment centers are *collection points,* where agricultural or other products are assembled prior

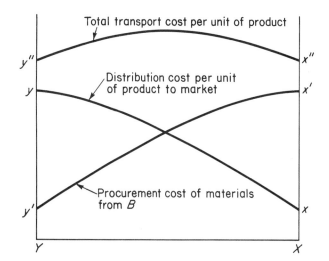

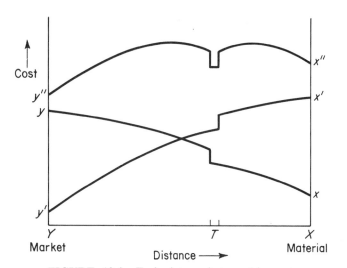

FIGURE 10.3 Endpoint and transshipment point locations. This figure illustrates a plant that uses a single material at X and sells its product at the market Y. The transfer-cost gradients xy and $x'y'$ indicate, respectively, the cost of moving material away from X and the cost of distributing to the market at Y. The vertical distance X to x is the terminal or loading charge at the material source, and Yy' is the cost incurred in distributing if the factory is at the market. The curve $x''y''$ is the total transfer cost (the sum of xy and $x'y'$), and shows the least-cost location at Y. With convex gradients, the total cost is bound to be more between Y and X than at these points, as indicated in the upper diagram. The effect of a transshipment point is illustrated by assuming a town, T, at which additional transfer costs are incurred through, perhaps, unloading from railroad to canal, as shown in the lower figure. Both curves xy and $x'y'$ take a jump here. A location in this town avoids these transshipment charges and is in fact as advantageous as being at the source of material X.

to shipment, or *distribution points* central to diffused markets. In the United States much wheat is processed into flour at collection points. The flour is then made into bread at distribution points. Many other examples will occur to the reader.

Transport Orientation: Cases

Sand and Gravel, Bricks and Cement: Reasons for Dispersion and Concentration

One interesting portrayal of the effects on locational patterns of transportation cost and production cost differences was provided by the Swedish economist Tord Palander, in *Beiträge zur Standortstheorie*.

Palander first took the case of two identical producers, and asked where the boundary between their market areas would occur. This is illustrated in Figure 10.4a. *A* and *B* are two plants serving a market distributed along the horizontal axis of the diagram. The plant cost, or price charged for the product at source, is given by the vertical distance A^p for firm *A*, and B^p for firm *B*. Away from the plant, the price the consumer has to pay is raised by the cost of transportation, as shown by the lines rising in both directions, A^f and B^f. Thus, at any point, the price charged includes a fixed plant cost and a variable cost of transportation. The boundary between the market areas of the two firms will be at *X*, where the delivered price from both producers is equal and customers will be indifferent as to which firm they buy from.

Figures 10.4b through 10.4e illustrate variations on the theme, in which Palander changed the relative values of plant price (*p*) and freight charges (*f*). Figure 10.4b shows equal freight rates but lower plant price at one location (*B*), enabling it to control more of the area between the two firms than *A* can. *B* should then have a greater output level than *A*. In Figure 10.4c, firm *B* has both a higher plant price and higher transport costs per unit of distance than *A* has, but it is still able to control a small market area by virtue of the higher delivered price from *A* near *B*. Figure 10.4d shows that where one firm (*A*) has a lower plant price but higher transport costs it is able to control a fairly extensive section of the market. To the left of *A*, however, there comes a point where *B* regains control by virtue of its lower freight cost. Finally, Figure 10.4e shows a more extreme version of the case at Figure 10.4d in which firm *B* cannot serve the market immediately adjoining its factory because the price at the plant is so high; it is only at some distance to the right that the relatively low freight rate from *B* allows the firm to sell at a lower price than that of *A*.

Some excellent examples of the above cases can be

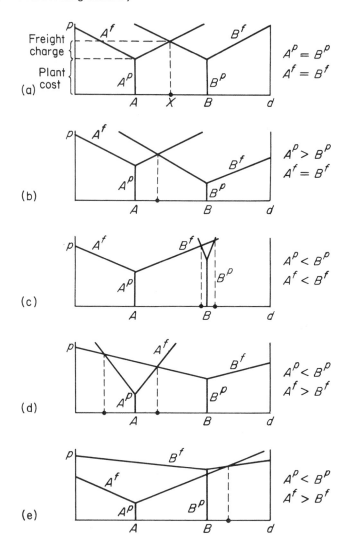

FIGURE 10.4 Market-area boundaries in different situations.

drawn from Britain's Labor government's post–World War II White Papers on the sand and gravel, brick, and cement industries. These examples reveal increasing concentration of production as relative transport and production costs decline from one case to the other.

Sand and gravel are widely available in superficial deposits in Britain. They are usually worked together, because gravel aggregates are found surrounded by sand. The product has a very low value in relation to bulk: In 1948 the pit price was five shillings per ton, including all costs of excavation and dressing. Pit price does not vary much from one part of the country to another. Transportation costs loom large in final delivered prices: Transportation of only two miles increased selling prices by 30 percent (the markup being for the fixed costs of loading and the variable costs of carriage) and shipment of 13 miles doubled the pit price. Because consumers make their purchases on the basis of final delivered price it is easy to see how small sand and gravel pits multiply, each serving small market areas limited by increasing transportation costs. Few pits sold sand and gravel farther than 30 miles from the pit in Britain; the few exceptions are where cheap water transportation is available.

In 1950 there were almost 1500 brick-making plants in Great Britain. There are very few clays in the country that have not been worked for brick making. Transportation costs were lower in relation to production costs than for sand and gravel. Prices increased 20 percent with shipment of 50 miles, and doubled if shipped 150 miles. Lower transport costs imply larger market areas, and more latitude in location of the brick-making plants, as suggested in Figure 10.4b. Thus, plants tended to concentrate on the best brick-making clays. One-third of the productive capacity of Great Britain was found at the time of the White Paper in 46 plants at Bedford, Bletchley, and Peterborough in the Midlands where the superior Oxford clays were used to make "Fletton bricks," the familiar red bricks that characterize the English landscape. This concentration was made possible because production costs on the Oxford clays were lower than elsewhere. Peculiar advantages are thick homogeneous beds that reduce excavation costs, the fact that 5 percent of the volume of the clay is carbonaceous, which reduces the amount of coal that has to be purchased to bake the bricks, and the plastic qualities of the clay, which eliminate pretreatment, such as pulverization, normally required before bricks can be molded. The Fletton producers sold over longer distances by virtue of lower production costs.

A third case is illustrated by the British cement industry. There are two kinds of cement: (1) Portland cement, formed by burning clay and chalk together until they fuse in a clinker, which is crushed to make cement, and (2) blast-furnace cement, a by-product of the steel-making industry. The former is most common in England, and provides this third example of the joint role of transport and production costs in reducing the diffusion of industry.

Several raw materials are needed to produce Portland cement. To obtain 100 tons of cement requires 225 tons of chalk, 75 tons of clay, 60 tons of coal, and 5 tons of gypsum. Clay and chalk are usually found close together in England, and because chalk inputs are greatest, cement plants tend to be tied to sources of chalk. But because costs of transporting cement are high, cement plants tended to be small, located centrally to small scattered markets. Price increases with overland transport are such that the cement was not sold farther than 25 miles overland from the cement plant.

In spite of such obvious pressures for diffusion, however, 50 percent of Britain's Portland cement was produced in the Thames-Medway area, southeast of London. Why should there have been this concentration? First, the Greater London market, accounting for 25 percent of Great Britain's consumption of cement, lay within a 25-mile radius of the Thames-Medway cement plants. Second, the chalk of lower Thamesside is pure, easily extracted and converted into cement so that production costs are lower than elsewhere. As in the use of Fletton bricks, this led to increases in the market area of the cement plants. Third, the plants were located by the river Thames, and cheap water transport was available to cement markets around the coasts of England. Thamesside was able to dominate the coastwise cement trade for several hundred miles, in the manner suggested by Figure 10.4e. The lesson is that the size and shape of market areas, and amount produced in any area, may be modified by the size of local markets and by differentials in transportation rates.

Changing Transport Orientation in the Iron and Steel Industry

The foregoing cases suggest that as transportation and production conditions change, the preferred transport orientation of an industry may change through time. If we trace the effects of technological development on the changing locational patterns of the iron and steel industry, the complexity of the relationships involved can be illustrated. It will be useful to begin during the eighteenth century—even though the iron industry dates much further back—because at that time processes became clearly defined and certain regional patterns had emerged.

Diffusion during the eighteenth century: During the eighteenth century, the industry produced pig iron. Furnaces tended to be found in wooded areas near the sources of iron ore. About 8 to 9 tons of pig iron could be produced using the charcoal obtainable from one acre of woodland. The largest furnaces could produce 20 to 30 tons of pig iron each week, consuming 150 to 200 acres of woodland each year. It was uneconomical to transport charcoal more than 15 miles. The amount of iron produced in any area was therefore limited by the available charcoal supplies: If the entire 15-mile radius were completely wooded and produced charcoal on a self-sustaining 50-year cycle, it could only support 40 furnaces making 60,000 tons of iron per year. Local concentrations of industry were out of the question, and in Europe and the settled parts of North America the industry had a highly diffused locational pattern. The industry could only grow by becoming more scattered. Perhaps the biggest iron producers of the time were Sweden and Russia.

Blast in the furnace was produced by direct water

power, which had replaced foot bellows a century earlier, and most furnaces therefore tended to seek streamside sites. Because the amount of power available from a water wheel was necessarily limited, reliance on water power had the same effects on the industry as charcoal; it kept the scale of operations small and the industry scattered.

During the eighteenth century, markets were also scattered, and the costs of transporting the finished products of the industry—castings, blooms, bars, and strips—were also very high, and these considerations reinforced diffusion trends.

Transformation of techniques and locations during the industrial revolution: This early iron industry was transformed by a series of major innovations at the end of the eighteenth century. Abram Darby had used coal to smelt iron as early as 1709, but his invention had limited application, because the process he proposed resulted in a "cold short" pig iron, a very brittle product of little general value. The ultimate triumph of coal as a source of fuel awaited inventions that would permit it to be forged into a valuable and desirable commodity like wrought iron. Such an invention became available in 1789 when the patents on Henry Cort's "puddling" furnace lapsed. Puddling was a means of processing iron as it was being smelted to reduce the carbon content and transform the brittle pig iron into more malleable wrought iron. The impact of Cort's process was immediate and widespread. In England, for example, charcoal was replaced as a fuel by coal within one decade. Simultaneously, the industry was freed from ties to water sites, because of the harnessing of steam to provide the blast in the furnaces and to rotate the rollers in the puddling furnace. Between 1790 and 1800 the scattered charcoal-iron industry was replaced by a more competitive coal–wrought-iron–steam industry. These changes made possible substantial increases in iron production at the same time as demands for iron were increasing because of industrialization, construction of the railroads, and other developments reflecting the increasing momentum of the industrial and transportation revolutions.

The net effect of these changes was the development of a larger scale industry, concentrated on coalfields where both fuel and clayband iron ores were available. Wrought iron could be made at lowest cost on the coalfields because the assembly costs of the requisite raw materials (coal, iron ore, and refractory materials) were lowest. As concentrated iron-producing districts developed, so did some of the first industrial towns of Western Europe and the United States.

This pattern was not allowed to crystallize, however. A series of additional technological changes took

place during the first decades of the nineteenth century and these also had marked effects upon the locational pattern of the industry. First, local iron ores on the coalfields were worked out rapidly and the industry had to reach further afield for iron ores. In England in particular this problem became critical: In 1850, 95 percent of the ore used was from coal measure sources; by 1880 this had declined to 30 percent, and by 1913 to 6 percent. Overseas sources of ore became increasingly important, first from northern Spain, and later from Sweden after a railroad was built from Kirunavaara to Narvik in 1894. Increasing ore imports gave importance to intermediate (port) locations at which ore had to be transshipped. Otherwise empty railroad cars coming back from carrying ore to the coalfield iron mills could be used to carry coal on the return haul to the port. By keeping some of the imported ore, the ports could develop iron plants. This was especially apparent in the United States with the westward movement of the country, the development of the Lake Superior ores, and the subsequent growth of the various lakeside steel plants (for example, at Cleveland and Chicago).

A second change was a steady decline in coal consumption, coming about because of introduction of the hot blast, which allowed furnace temperatures to be increased and lowered inputs of coal. In 1829, 8 tons of coal were required to produce 1 ton of pig iron; by 1850 this had been reduced to between 2 and 2.5 tons, and the pull of coalfields on the iron industry was relaxed accordingly.

The third and perhaps most basic change was the introduction of large-scale methods of producing cheap steel, a product superior to wrought iron for most purposes. Until the 1850s, steel was an expensive item produced in small batches by the Huntsman crucible process at places like Sheffield in England and Solingen in Germany, and wrought iron was used for most purposes. After 1880 the era of wrought iron had passed. The first steel converter was invented by Bessemer in 1856. This was followed by the invention of the open-hearth converter by Siemens and Martin in 1864.

At least two new elements were introduced into the locational calculus by the introduction of steel converters. In addition to the pulls of raw materials and markets, scrap could be used in the open hearth furnace, implying that cheap scrap locations could become feasible competitive locations for the industry. Further, invention of the basic Bessemer process by Gilchrist Thomas in 1879 enabled phosphoric ores to be used in steel production. This was of particular importance in Europe where vast iron ore deposits such as those of Lorraine in France are phosphoric. The discovery that lining the steel furnace with a limestone flux would remove the phosphorus immediately made these ores available to the steel industry. Basic Bessemer converters were introduced rapidly in France, Belgium, Luxembourg, and Germany. Acceptance was less rapid in Britain, where acid (nonphosphoric) ores were produced locally in Cumberland or imported. However, during the twentieth century Britain has made increasing use of the low-grade phosphoric iron ores of Oxfordshire, Northamptonshire, Lincolnshire, and Yorkshire. Even today most of the steel produced in the United States is acid. Only at Birmingham, Alabama, is there a basic Bessemer plant. Thus, a regional differentiation of steel-producing facilities emerged, based upon the types of ores used. The ability to use the new sources of ore led to new locational opportunities, particularly in Western Europe. In France today the greatest part of the iron and steel industry is ore-field oriented.

After this wave of technological change, concentrations of new steel mills were to be found in urbanized coalfield locations, at intermediate port locations, and at low-grade phosphoric iron ore deposits. This pattern persists, although continued relocation has taken place as availability of raw materials has changed, and a new strong pull of markets is evident.

The modern steel industry: Today there are three major stages in the steel-making process between the time that raw materials are assembled and finished products are available for consumers (Figure 10.5). The first of these stages centers on the blast furnace, in which three basic raw materials are placed: iron ore, coke, and limestone. Coke provides heat, which releases carbon monoxide and carbon dioxide from the limestone. The carbon monoxide acts on the iron ore so that the iron is separated from the sands and clays and other impurities that are also present in the ore; the carbon dioxide can be led off to the coke oven to assist in converting coal to coke. Impurities combine to form a slag, which can be used for construction or, as in the United States, a raw material for the cement industry. The iron is led off into *pigs*—hence the name pig iron—and may be used by forges, which produce wrought iron, by foundries which make castings, or it may be transferred to the second stage of the steel-making process, the steel converter, and transformed into steel.

Pig iron is a brittle product because of its high carbon content (3 percent to 4 percent), and is therefore relatively useless. Cort's puddling furnace provided a means to reduce the carbon content (to 2.5 percent), and the resulting wrought iron—a tougher and more malleable product—was of correspondingly higher value. The invention of the steel converter was revolutionary because it facilitated drastic reductions in carbon content (to 1.4 percent) and, accordingly, allowed a stronger, tougher product to be made.

Until the invention of the basic oxygen process, there were three types of steel converters in use in the world, all over a century old. The first was invented in 1856 by Henry Bessemer. This *Bessemer converter* required an input of hot pig iron, through which air is blown to burn off carbon. It is a small batch process (converters average 20 tons), and it is quick (a batch can be "cooked" in 20 minutes). Although it has low capital and operating costs, it provides relatively poor quality control. If the converter is lined with dolomite, it is ideal for removing phosphorus from ores, and hence phosphoric ores are charged into Bessemer converters to produce so-called basic or Thomas steel (after the inventor of the phosphorus-removing process). The *open hearth converter* was invented in 1864. Hot and cold pig and scrap iron can all be placed into this converter. It produces large batches (100 tons and over) and works slowly as air and methane are passed over the metal to provide heat (14 hours is an average). Exact quality control is possible. One advantage of the converter is the ability to charge cold scrap metal without prior heating, because in an average steel mill possibly 40 percent of the metal moving through is scrap that arises within the plant, so-called circulating scrap. A third, but special-purpose, steel converter is the *electric arc*. This converter is used mostly for producing special alloy steels. It uses large amounts of electric power, plus scrap, pig, and alloy metals such as chrome (for resistance to abrasion, stainless steel), vanadium (for flexibility), manganese (for hardness), tungsten (for high-speed steels), and molybdenum (for toughness).

From the converter, steel moves on to the cogging mill and forging press, where it is shaped into wheels, axles, and so on, or it moves to the finishing mill where plates, sheets, strips, tubes, rails, and so on are produced. These products then go to the automotive, construction, container, and engineering trades, which constitute the main consumers of the products of the steel industry.

Successful locations of blast furnaces, throughout the history of the industry, have depended upon cheap assembly of raw materials. Coal-to-iron ratios of 8:1 were powerful enough to pull the wrought-iron industry to the coalfields in the early nineteenth century. Economies in coal consumption reduced this pull, however, by lessening the extent to which minimization of transport costs on coal determined the least-cost location of blast furnaces. Since the middle of the nineteenth century, coke rather than coal has provided the charge for the blast furnace. In the early days coke was produced near the pit head and shipped by rail to the blast furnaces. Approximately 2 tons of coal were needed to yield 1 ton of coke. "Beehive" coke ovens were used. These beehives needed special coals, which would swell into a

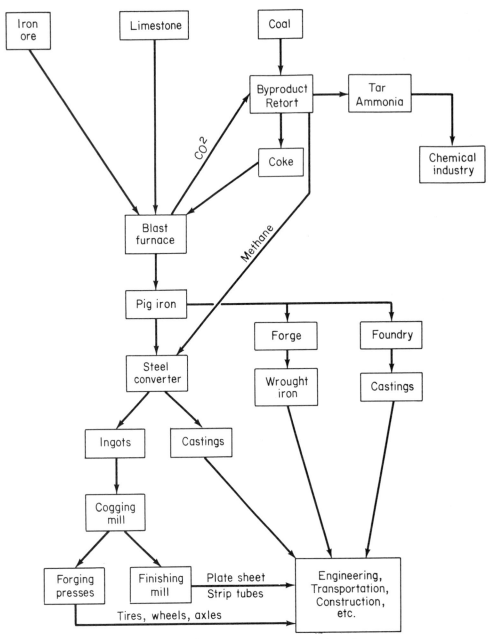

FIGURE 10.5   Production of iron and steel.

coke strong enough to let iron filter down through it as it was separated from impurities in the iron ore. The coals also had to be both phosphorus-free and sulphur-free, because the early steel industry had no means of eliminating these impurities. Such coals were only available in limited localities: Connellsville in Pennsylvania; Durham, South Wales and West Yorkshire in the United Kingdom; the Ruhr in Germany. Great concentrations of beehives therefore developed on these coalfields. In the beehives, all volatile materials were wasted, and no by-products were recovered.

To the developing chemical industries, however, by-products proved too valuable to be wasted, and after the turn of the twentieth century a dramatic change took place in coke production. In 1900, 80 percent of British and 84 percent of American coke capacity was beehive; by 1953, 96 percent of British and 97 percent of the United States' coke was produced in by-product retorts. These new retorts could use a wider variety of coals, freeing the industry from reliance on a few coalfields. By-products provided bases for chemical and, later, for artificial fiber industries. Also, instead of coke being shipped, it became common to ship coal to blast furnace locations, where the new coke ovens were constructed.

Methane produced in the coke ovens provided heat for steel converters. Economies in by-product ovens reduced the coal-to-coke ratio to 1.5:1.

Until Gilchrist Thomas invented the basic steel-making process in 1879, all ores used in steel making were of necessity acid, or phosphorus-free, for the industry had no means of removing phosphorus, which made steel brittle. After this invention large reserves of lower-quality phosphoric iron ores became available to the basic Bessemer steel industry—particularly the Lorraine ores of France. The Bessemer converter, rather than the open hearth, is used to produce basic steel because the dolomite lining placed in a converter to facilitate the basic process doubles the length of time needed to produce a batch of steel. Increases in the cost of heat required for this longer period of time are substantial in the open hearth, but the Bessemer converter just requires air to be blown through hot metal for a longer period.

Today the three stages of steel making tend to be located together in *integrated* steel mills. Many benefits accrue in such industrial complexes. Intermediate transport and handling is eliminated. Hot metal may be transferred from one process to another, eliminating costs of reheating. Wastes may be transferred from one stage to another and become items of real value. Transfers of carbon dioxide from the blast furnace to the coke oven and methane from the coke oven to the open hearth are examples.

On the other hand, three forms of *disintegration* persist:

1. market-oriented forges and foundries
2. rerollers producing tinplate, wire and nails, and similar products, which are also market oriented because they use compact pig iron inputs, and convert them into bulky products without weight loss
3. cold-metal shops.

Cold-metal shops usually start out with an open hearth or electric arc furnace, charging scrap and only a little pig. They lose the economies of integration and their locations are not determined by the same considerations as for hot metal plants. Cold-metal shops tend to be tied to cheap sources of market scrap, which does not compete with coal and iron ore as a location factor, and they are able to compete in outlying locations because scrap is sold at lower prices at greater distances from major industrial regions: Moreover, in such places the spread between raw material costs and the price of finished products tends to be higher, as Figure 10.6 suggests. This figure is reminiscent of Figure 10.4c. The pattern is noticeable in the United States, where Penn-

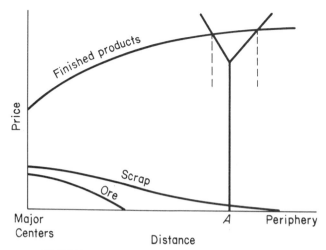

FIGURE 10.6 Success of a peripheral cold-metal shop at a great distance from major integrated producers. Producer *A* is located at a great distance from major centers but is able to compete because: (1) scrap is cheaper on the periphery (price at major centers of demand less transport costs) and (2) cost of finished products is greater (price at centers plus transport costs). Therefore, in spite of smaller scale and higher production costs, *A* works against a greater pricespread and is able to control a small market area at the periphery, provided, of course, the demands in the small market area are large enough to absorb *A*'s output.

sylvania steel mills charge 40 percent scrap ("circulating" or in-plant scrap) whereas plants in California charge 85 percent and in Texas charge 97 percent scrap.

Location of integrated steel mills has traditionally been governed by a least-cost balance between locating blast furnaces (involving raw material assembly costs) and location of finishing mills (involving least-cost distribution of products to markets). Costs of labor and taxes, until recently, varied much less from place to place than procurement and distribution costs and, accordingly, were of lesser impact upon locations.

Table 10.2 illustrates how the transport cost equation worked in the United States on the eve of World War II. An ideal location was where ore, coal, and markets are juxtaposed, and the markets are large enough to consume the output of a "threshold" plant. Seldom, however, did plants find this fortunate situation. Note how Birmingham, Alabama, benefited from very low assembly costs of juxtaposed sources of raw materials, but had extremely high costs of distributing finished products. Similarly, Pittsburgh had relatively high ore costs, while Duluth had the reverse. Each factor "pulled" the plant, with the strongest pull exerted by the factor contributing most to reduce the transport bill:

TABLE 10.2

Costs of steel production in alternative locations

Location	Assembly costs on raw materials per ton of finished steel for selected locations in 1939 (in dollars)			
	Ore	*Coal*	*Limestone*	*Total*
Sparrows Point	$7.16	$ 5.65	$1.05	$13.86
Bethlehem	1.81	5.93	0.51	8.25
Buffalo	3.57	4.78	0.45	8.80
Pittsburgh	6.24	.50	0.62	7.36
Youngstown	5.61	2.71	0.34	8.66
Cleveland	3.57	4.11	0.45	8.13
Detroit	4.12	5.15	0.31	9.58
Chicago-Gary	4.12	5.79	0.37	10.28
Duluth	1.77	5.54	0.37	7.68
Birmingham	1.46	2.39	0.15	4.00
Pueblo	4.47	3.06	0.79	8.32
Provo	3.55	3.86	0.26	7.67
San Bernadino	3.89	11.68	—	15.57

Producing center	Transportation charges for supplying certain markets with 1 ton of finished steel from selected producing centers, 1939		
	Assembly cost	*Freight charge on steel*	*Total*
Chicago			
Chicago-Gary	$10.28	—	$10.28
Cleveland	8.13	$ 1.68	9.81
Pittsburgh	7.36	6.16	13.52
Birmingham	4.00	12.54	16.54
New York			
Bethlehem	8.25	3.81	12.06
Buffalo	8.80	3.64	12.44
Pittsburgh	7.36	8.06	15.42
Sparrows Point	13.86	1.68	15.54
Seattle			
Birmingham	4.00	15.46	19.46
Provo	7.67	16.24	23.91
San Bernadino	15.57	9.41	24.98
Sparrows Point	13.86	11.20	25.06

Source: The Economics of Iron and Steel Transportation, U.S. Senate Documents, No. 80, 79th Congress.

By minimizing transport costs the greatest reduction in total costs is achieved.

Coal has traditionally exerted the strongest pull upon locations and led to the early concentration of industry in the Pittsburgh area of the United States, the Midlands of England, central Scotland and south Wales, the Ruhr region of Germany, the Nord-Sambre-Meuse region of France, Belgium and Luxembourg, and the Donbas region of the Ukraine in the USSR. In the twentieth century the pull of coal lessened because of blast furnace economies and heat transfers in integrated steel mills. Whereas the coal-to-iron ratio of the early industry was 8:1, the coal-to-steel ratio of the modern industry is now 1.3:1.

Ore sources have been of increasing importance with the decline in the pull of coal, particularly in Western Europe. For ore, the strength of pull depends upon its quality, or percentage iron content; the higher this percentage, the more iron is carried per ton of ore and the more transportable it is. Discovery of the high-quality Lake Superior iron ores and the westwards movement of the center of gravity of the United States together enabled the steel industry to decentralize from Pittsburgh to Cleveland and Chicago-Gary: intermediate locations at break-of-bulk points between water and land transport where coal could be carried back to transshipment points in the same railroad cars that had carried iron ore inland to the coalfields.

In Europe, steel mills were built during the late nineteenth and early twentieth century at intermediate point locations. But in England, France, and Germany, in the years surrounding World War II, ore sources exerted an increasing pull upon the location of integrated steel mills as low-quality phosphoric ores (with less than 40 percent iron content) were used. Advantages, therefore, accrued to ore field locations. Examples were the Scunthorpe and Corby steelworks in eastern England, the Salzgitter mills in Germany, and the Lorraine mills in France. More recently, reliance upon high-quality imported ores has given the cost advantage to central locations, and many of the inland orefield plants have been closed.

Markets also have had an increasing pull on the location of integrated steel mills. Modern low-cost mills have to enter production at a definite minimum size (approximately 800,000 tons of pig capacity) if they are to obtain economies of large-scale production. Mills usually locate in an area if the market is large enough to consume this output. Freight rates on finished steel tend to be at least twice as high as those on coal and iron, because transportation agencies tend to charge according to the value of the item carried rather than according to the cost of service. This means that for the same outlay of funds outputs can be shipped less than half the distance of inputs, a compelling motive for market orientation, incurring costs of shipping raw materials rather than of shipping finished products. Markets also tend to be sources of cheap scrap metal, which may be substituted for pig iron in the steel converter. Hence, orientation to scrap supplements the other pulls of the market.

In the past, the iron and steel industry has been highly mobile as raw material sources, markets, and technical characteristics of the industry have changed. Two decades ago, however, authorities could be heard arguing that the industry displayed considerable *inertia,* persisting in old localities long after these localities had lost their initial cost advantages, failing to grow in new locations where costs may be lower. Two cases were distinguished: when the industry is competitive and when competition is absent.

Inertia may exist in competitive steel industries because original advantages have been lost but new advantages have been acquired. For example, in Sheffield,

England, advantages of low assembly costs have long passed, but the industry persists because it now uses market scrap, and has tied to it a large specialized local market for special grades of steel. The specialized steel industry in Sheffield therefore remains competitive. On the other hand, inertia may exist because of artificial restraints upon the competitive process that restrict new centers and maintain old ones. Steel mills are enormous capital investments. In the U.S. in 1950, $250 million were required to develop a mill with ingot capacity of 1 million tons. Such investments are not easily abandoned. Because of the scale of plants in the industry, there was a very limited number of firms. Ten companies accounted for well over 90 percent of U.S. steel output. Capital requirements were such that entry of new firms into the U.S. industry was not easy. In most industries entry of new firms in better locations pushes old firms to the margin, but in the iron and steel industry a limited number of firms controlled development, and they had a stake in old locations that they were unwilling to sacrifice. This meant that existing concerns had in mind the effects of new developments on present capacity involving durable, specific, and immobile investment. A shift involved considerable financial loss that firms were understandably unwilling to bear. The industry had a desire for stability, because costs could only be minimized when the large plants were running to capacity and fixed costs were spread over large amounts of output. New developments were only undertaken in these circumstances when demands were increasing rapidly and old capacity was not affected adversely by new construction. Social and political pressures also promoted inertia, for many steel plants dominate one-industry towns. The closing of a plant would have calamitous local effects, which were inadvisable both socially and politically.

There were two consequences: Plants in new areas are the property of major concerns in old, and their operations were designed to have least impact upon the affairs of the older plants; pricing systems reflected interests in stability. The old "Pittsburgh plus" pricing system that protected Pittsburgh against competition from lower-cost producers in new locations (until it was finally declared illegal by the Supreme Court in 1948) was a good example of a pricing system developed in an industry for which stability was the major goal.

In the past two decades, steel production has spread to many developing countries, and competition has become global rather than national. The ability of steel producers to ensure stability within their home-country markets has fallen victim to significant worldwide cost differences. Several forces have come together. Continued technological advances have further reduced the locational pulls of raw materials, and improvements in transportation have reduced the overall importance of transport orientation as long as coastal sites are available for integrated steel mills. Demand shifts for specialty steels have led to rapid growth of smaller-scale, market-oriented electric furnaces. And on a global scale, labor costs, governmental subsidies, and taxes have loomed much larger in the delivered cost of steel. Particularly disadvantaged have been the heavily unionized U.S. and European producers, who had protected older technologies in one-industry mill towns. There, in the past decade, the industry has collapsed (just as the early woodland iron industry collapsed in the eighteenth century), with new centers of production arising in such developing countries as South Korea.

Weber's Theory of Plant Location

The original theory of plant location was formulated in 1909 by a German location economist, Alfred Weber, in a book entitled *Über den Standort der Industrien* (Theory of the Location of Industries) and was basically a theory of transport orientation. Weber sought a theory of industrial location that, he believed, would represent "one of the keys to understanding the current general social phenomenon of population concentration along with a host of other social and cultural changes which characterize our period." Because transport orientation was, for him, the primary key, it is appropriate that we conclude this section by examining his ideas (which shaped the analysis on which the findings already presented were based).

Assumptions and Definitions

The assumptions upon which Weber's argument is based are as follows:

1. A uniform country like that of von Thünen's uniform plain;
2. The locations of sources of raw materials were assumed to be known;
3. The location of points of consumption also were assumed to be known;
4. Labor was geographically fixed. Weber assumed that there exists a number of places where labor at definite, predetermined wages could be had in unlimited quantities;
5. Transportation costs were assumed to be a function of weight and distance and were the key locational determinant. Differences in topography are allowed for by appropriate additions to distance and differences in transportability by additions to actual weight.

Limited by the science of his time, Weber conceived of his model as a mechanical system of pulleys and weights.

Terms defined included the following:

1. *Ubiquities*—materials available practically everywhere, and presumably at the same price everywhere.
2. *Localized materials*—materials obtainable only in geographically well-defined localities.
3. *Pure materials*—localized materials that enter to the extent of their full weight into the finished product. Thread to be woven into cloth is perhaps an example of this category.
4. *Gross materials*—localized materials that impart only a portion of, or none of, their weight to the finished product. Fuel is the extreme type of gross material, for none of its weight enters into the product.
5. *Material index*—indicates the proportion that the weight of localized materials bears to the weight of the finished product. A productive process which uses pure material has an index of 1.
6. *Locational weight*—the total weight to be moved per unit of product. An article made out of ubiquities would have a locational weight of 1 because only the product itself would be moved; if it were made from pure material the locational weight would be 2 because for transportation of the product an equivalent weight of materials would be required.
7. *Isodapane*—the locus of points of equal transportation cost. The meaning of the term will become clear in the discussion.

Working with these assumptions, employing these terms, and seeking in the first instance to measure the effect of transportation upon location, Weber then imagined certain cases and developed conclusions about them. Let us look at these cases, reformulating Weber's initial arguments where modern theorists have improved upon them.

Case 1: One Market and One Source of Raw Materials

The first case supposes a raw material to be produced at *A* and the finished product made out of the material to be consumed at *B*. The problem is to determine where the manufacture or processing is to take place. Weber states four possibilities:

1. If ubiquities only are used, the processing will occur at point of consumption *B*, because the selection of *B* will make transportation unnecessary.

2. If one pure material is used, processing may occur at *A*, at *B*, or at any point between *A* and *B*. This conclusion is based upon the fact that the weight to be transported and the distance to be covered is the same in all instances.

3. If pure material plus ubiquities is used, the processing will occur at the point of consumption *B*, because the pure material will be without influence, and the ubiquities will govern.

4. If one weight-losing material is used, processing will occur at point of production, because the weight that is lost will not have to be transported.

Case 2: One Market and Two Raw Material Sources

Weber's second case assumes that raw materials are available at two places, *A* and *B*, at equal prices. The finished product is to be consumed at *C*, and the problem as before is to determine where manufacture or processing is to take place. Three possibilities are now considered:

1. If ubiquities alone are used, manufacture will occur at the point of consumption for the same reasons as when only two points were involved.

2. If several pure materials are employed, manufacture will also take place at point of consumption. On this supposition, the weight of materials exactly equals the weight of the product. All weights, whether in the form of materials or in the form of product, have to be moved from their deposits to the place of consumption. They should not deviate unnecessarily; therefore each material will proceed along the straight line that leads from the origin to the point of consumption. Unless the way of one should lead, by chance, through the deposit of another, all of these ways will meet for the first time in the place of consumption. Because the assembly of all materials at one spot is the necessary first condition of manufacture, the place of consumption is the location where manufacturing will be carried on; a productive enterprise, using several pure materials alone, will always locate at the place where its products are consumed.

3. The conclusion is different if several localized weight-losing materials are used. In analyzing this case Weber sets up what he calls a "locational figure." Let us suppose a process which uses two weight-losing materials produced at *A* and *B*, and let us suppose that the product is to be consumed at *C*. Manufacture will not take place at *C* because it is undesirable to transport from *A* and *B* to *C* the material weight that does not enter into the weight of the finished product. It will not, according to Weber, occur at *A* or *B* unless the importance of one material happens to be so great as to overcome the influence of all other elements. Instead, it will usually be found somewhere *within* the triangle, at that location determined by the relative balance of the locational weights.

The 'Distortions'

Weber treated labor costs as "a first distortion" of the industrial locations determined by transport costs. The second step of his locational analysis, then, was to plot the spatial variations in transport cost away from the optimum transport-cost location in order to observe the background against which differences in labor cost operate. If, at some other place in the region, the cost of labor per unit of product is less than it is at the optimum transport location, perhaps because an established industry closed down or an unusually high rate of population growth occurred, or a pool of particularly skilled workers is available, and if the increment to transport costs at this alternative location is less than the labor savings, a "deviation" from the "optimum" least transport cost location will arise.

Having combined the effects of transport and labor costs, Weber then turned to the problem of determining how that location may be deflected within the region by the tendency of firms to agglomerate. In Weber's view, there are two main ways in which a company can gain the benefits of agglomeration. First, it may increase the concentration of production by enlarging its factory, thus obtaining savings through a larger scale of operation. Second, it may benefit by selecting a location in close association with other plants. This "social" agglomeration yields benefits from sharing specialized equipment and services, greater division of labor, and large-scale purchasing and marketing.

As a "second altering force," agglomeration acts to divert manufacturing from either a least transport-cost location or a least labor-cost location, depending upon which was originally the dominant locating influence in a given instance. For an establishment that would normally be transportation-oriented, the savings from locating close to other firms may be sufficient to justify some sacrifice of transport cost. To determine whether or not such a diversion from the least transport-cost was feasible, Weber employed a similar logic to that previously used for weighing the counterattractions of transport and labor locations.

Because the attractions of agglomeration and labor-cost savings both represent deviations from the least transport-cost location, however, in Weber's view, these two influences may conflict. The decision will go to the one that provides the greater savings. Weber indicated that the winner is more likely to be the labor location because that is a place where "accidental" agglomeration may be expected to occur as a result of a concentration of population or the presence of special transport features. "Pure" agglomeration, he felt, would prevail only with industries having very low labor requirements, such as oil refining or chemical manufacture. The main effect of the conflict, then, is to increase the tendency of industry to collect at only a few locations.

Types of Labor Orientation

Labor costs and external economies are hardly mere distortions of transport orientation, however; they are dominant locational forces in certain types of industries. If transport costs are a low proportion of total costs, if the ratio of labor to total cost is high, and if labor costs vary a good deal from place to place, plants tend to be most competitive when they are located in areas in which labor cost is least. It is under such conditions that plants are described as being *labor-oriented*. In the world today, there are major industrial shifts taking place in labor orientation as part of a global scramble for cheap labor. Accelerating wage inflation in established industrial areas is pushing manufacturers into new efforts to tap the vast pool of willing and cheap labor in poorer countries. Manufacturers are farming out production of component parts, subassemblies, and even finished products sometimes for export to other areas but often for use back home. In the process they are not only cutting their own costs but speeding the industrialization of underdeveloped countries, some of which are coming to relish the role of workshops for distant, richer lands.

Tradeoffs between Money Wages and Skills

What are the bases of this movement? Clearly, the prime reason is labor costs, but studies of labor costs show how important it is to recognize that labor costs involve not only money wages. There are many situations where money wages vary apparently without effect on industrial locations because the benefits of lower wages are offset by a lack of skill and lower productivity of the lower-wage labor force. In such cases, skills are far more important in determining the least labor cost location than money wages alone. However, the importance of labor orientation to skills may be offset by technological advances that make unskilled and semiskilled workers as productive as the skilled workers who previously dominated the industry. For example, in 1970 it cost $2 million less on Taiwan to employ 1000 women than in the United States, and they took one-third the time to train. In such cases, an orientation to low wage areas rather than to skills has arisen, and is apparently the source of the world trend noted above. Labor costs, therefore, vary first in terms of money wages, and second in terms of productivity and skills.

Short- and Long-Run Labor Advantages

If the supply of labor is great relative to local demands for labor, wages will be low compared with areas where competition for labor is relatively greater. But research has shown that low wage conditions tend to be ephemeral: If industry comes to an area in search of the low wages, the very act of movement changes the local supply and demand schedules for labor and raises the price. Also, labor tends to migrate from areas of low opportunity to areas of higher opportunity, tending to equalize geographic differentials in wages for that reason, too. Thus, labor cost variations due to money wages tend to be short-run differentials that can only persist in longer periods of time either because there is a substantial immobility of labor due to ignorance, poverty, or local social ties, or political barriers between countries that inhibit the free movement of labor. But even such immobilities will tend to be eroded in longer periods of time.

Persistent long-run money wage differentials have been studied in two types of conditions. First, are those cases in which money wage differences do not represent differences in real wages; for example, in areas where the cost of living is low. Second, there can emerge those dynamic conditions described by Gunnar Myrdal in *An American Dilemma* for the United States or in his work *Asian Drama* for conditions on an international scale. Myrdal argued that processes of "circular and cumulative causation" can be identified such that labor cost differentials, rather than being equalized in the long run, tend to increase over longer periods of time. The principal reasons that he cited were the differential nature of the migration flows from areas of low to areas of high economic opportunity. Put simply, the most able people move to find better jobs, leaving behind an older and less able population group. This migration decreases the economic viability of the home area, although it increases the quality of skills available in the reception area. These skills impart advantages for further growth, so that the reception areas gain more and more relative advantages.

Regions with Money-Wage Advantages

Money wages have been shown to be low in four kinds of areas, which therefore represent the most attractive zones for industry decentralizing in search of low labor costs.

1. *Where the supply of labor is increasing more rapidly than the demand for labor.* This is typical in rural and backward areas where net reproduction rates are substantially greater than elsewhere. Such a condition is typical of the rural parts of the United States in which particular minority groups live. Today, the net reproduction rate of native Americans, for example, is much higher than that of any other group in the population. On an international scale, this is the characteristic of the Far Eastern countries. In each of these cases, migration rarely tends to offset the natural increase completely, so that a persistent labor surplus develops, which keeps the price of labor at a minimum.

2. *Where economic opportunities are declining in relation to a sizable local labor force.* Such a condition is typical of any kind of economically depressed area. The coalfields, for example, were in this position during the peacetime between the world wars. For a long time the anthracite towns of eastern Pennsylvania have faced this situation, as have many other mining areas. This was the history of the cotton textile towns of New England when the cotton textile industry moved to the Piedmont area of the Carolinas and Georgia. Of course, where economic opportunities are declining in relation to the labor force, wage rates will drop.

3. *Where employment opportunities are available only for part of the population.* This has been a general characteristic of female labor in heavy industrial areas where the demand is traditional only for male labor—in the coalfields, in mining areas, in fishing towns, or in railroad towns. In these areas of heavy industry, female labor has traditionally been available at very low wage rates. Where the size of the local female labor pool is large, however, labor-intensive, low-wage industries have been attracted.

4. *Where the cost of living is low so that real wages are high relative to money wages.* For example, housing prices in the American South and Southwest are much lower than in the Northeast because homes in the Northeast must be protected against the very severe winters. Lower housing prices mean that people can maintain the same real level of living at lower money wage rates because they need to put less into the housing that they purchase. A similar situation is where superior residential amenities create a substantial "psychic income" that people are willing to take instead of the higher wage rates offered in areas with fewer residential advantages. In such conditions, of course, money wages will tend not to reflect the real level of living, and the money-wage differential will act to the competitive advantage of labor-oriented firms.

Technological Change and the Ties of Localized Skills

We made the point earlier, however, that money wages are only significant locational factors where skills are relatively insignificant. We will turn later to instances in which the advantages of certain highly localized skills lead to the long-term ties of particular industries to particular locations, and we will discuss the reasons for the development of these localized skills. What is significant is the condition under which skill factors have been shown to exert a diminishing pull on industries. Localized skills are usually relevant to only one industry and are relatively immobile. They are thus very powerful causal factors in geographical inertia. Many operations can only break out of the bonds of localization in a skilled labor area by diminishing reliance upon the skill factor. Only when higher productivity is not related to skills will lower labor cost mean lower wages.

Industry has been shown to shift into areas of lower money wages most generally only under conditions of technological change, when increased mechanization, routinized operations and processes have tended to diminish the importance of skills. The introduction of line methods of production facilitates the use of relatively "green" labor, for example, so that operations can become routinized and can be performed efficiently with only a short period of training. Thus, when semiskilled labor force requirements become increasingly uniform, decentralization of routinized operations is facilitated in the direction of low-wage areas, and a wider source of labor is available. But, of course, we have to repeat that this movement to low-wage areas is essentially a movement of routinized operations. Quality products have to stay in the traditional areas, for style cannot be routinized and the skills required for production of high style are localized. In the clothing industry, for example, ready-made clothing production has moved to cheap labor areas, but style lines remain in the world style centers—New York, London, Paris, and so on.

In routinized operations, on the other hand, low-wage areas may even have an advantage in productivity. First of all, a new plant coming into a previously non-industrialized area can "skim the cream" off the local labor force by offering higher wages than those offered by the alternative occupations of the previously non-industrialized area. This new labor force in general, having no previous experience in factory employment and no preconceived notions about the organization of the industry, or about work loads, is more plastic to requirements of a changed technology, and will be willing to operate with more pieces of machinery than the worker in the traditional industrial areas. Also, too, low-wage areas tend to be those areas that have the least restrictive labor codes—we are all well aware of the substantial differences in legislation relating to employment and labor conditions among the states. The areas that have the most restrictive forms of legislation also tend to be the areas in which the trade union movement is strongest. In the United States this reflects, in general, the differences between North and South and between large city and small town. The relative abundance of labor in the South and in small-town locations means the inability of trade unions to establish themselves. Smaller towns, too, will tend to be dominated by one producer, who controls whatever he or she does not own locally. There, work loads are likely to be higher, employee benefits lower, and employers much freer to adapt the productive process to their wishes.

Labor Costs as a Locational Factor in the Textile Industries

The textile industries provide an ideal example of the emergence of labor costs as a location factor in modern industry, as well as providing insights into the locational dynamics that accompanied the technological changes of the Industrial Revolution. Because most of the early changes took place in Britain, we will look at the experience of that country first. Thereafter, the analogous American experiences will be described, and then current world dynamics will be analyzed.

The Early British Textile Industry

As late as 1851, British textile industries employed far more workers than the iron and steel industries. In 1851, 1 in every 19 workers was engaged in textile production, although the growth of other industrial sectors in later stages of the Industrial Revolution reduced this figure to 1 in 37 by the end of the nineteenth century. As the textile industry grew, its distribution changed.

Growth was accompanied by increased concentration in particular locations and then increasing shifts of one such concentrated location to another. For a beginning, however, as in the case of the iron and steel industries discussed earlier, we can go back to the eighteenth century. In the late eighteenth century, cotton could only be used in the textile industry when combined with other fibers, notably linen, to produce fustians. The early locations of the industry, as in the case of woolens and fine worsted production, were determined by the medieval organization of production.

In the Middle Ages, the textile industry was closely connected with farming. The peasant families cultivated and harvested their own foods; the spinning and weaving of animal fibers were done by hand. During the fifteenth and sixteenth centuries, settlements extended from the neighboring lowlands into the central mountainous spine of the British Isles, the Pennines, proceeding on a copyhold basis by a process of "intaking" of 15 to 25 acres per family. Because these holdings afforded inadequate support, farming families had to seek ancillary employment in the production of textiles. Indeed, the spread of new farms into the Pennines into previously manorial cattle-breeding areas was specifically governed by industrial opportunities. One act of Parliament, called the Halifax Act in the sixteenth century, for example, talks explicitly of settlement taking place on the basis of growing opportunities in the textile industry. Farming in such areas was essentially secondary to textile output. Agricultural produce was not sold but was consumed by the household, and the rent paid by the household for its land was paid in kind by the output from the loom.

With such a wide diffusion of textile production throughout the central mountains and moors of England, neighboring towns functioned as the marketing centers of large parishes from which they drew their trade. The towns were commercial, rather than manufacturing centers, and the characteristic pattern of urban settlement involved a large number of small towns, the most important building of which was the "piece hall" where the textile pieces were brought in for sale. Only Manchester grew larger because it had an urban cottage textile industry as well as a service function and also because it had finishing trades to which the produce of the countryside was brought for bleaching and dyeing. Only one branch of the textile industry—fulling, drawing the cloth from the local areas—was mechanized at this time.

New techniques in the first phase of the Industrial Revolution transformed this local medieval industrial pattern. The change came in spinning before it came in weaving. In 1785 the patent was withdrawn on Arkwright's water frame. Then, in 1813, Horrock's power loom was invented, although it was not widely used until after 1820. The result of the first of these changes was that hand spinning was replaced by machine spinning, thirty years before hand weaving was replaced by machines. The techniques were applied first in the cotton industry, in the woolen industry after 1820, and in very fine woolens and the worsted industry after 1810. Therefore there was a time lag between the emergence of mechanized spinning and weaving and in the pace of mechanization in the cotton, woolen, and worsted industries.

Initially, the only source of power was water. In the period from 1718 to 1825, the spinning industry was mechanized, and the new factories were located at water-power sites, surrounded by a cottage hand-loom weaving industry associated with the scattered farmsteads on the hillsides. The cotton industry spread to take up most of the available water-power sites, moving from the most accessible sites to more and more inaccessible spots, so that the manufacturing industry diffused quite widely throughout the British countryside. The limitation of the water-power source meant that local scale of industry was impossible. Spinning was undertaken by a very large number of small dispersed factory units, and a much wider spread of the cottage hand-loom weaving industry also took place, although without the ties to agricultural "intakes" that had characterized its earlier scatter.

After 1825, hand-loom weaving was gradually replaced by power-loom weaving, first in the cotton industry and then in the woolen industry. At the same time, water power was replaced by the use of steam. New towns grew around the new large-scale textile mills, generating the first phase of large-scale urbanization associated with the industrialization of the early nineteenth century. By 1840, the change from water to steam was relatively complete. In 1838, only 11 percent of the total horsepower was still drawn from water.

Because the pace of change was slower in the woolen and worsted industries than in the cotton textiles industries, it meant different rates of change obtained for each part of England where each type of textile industry was concentrated. The cotton textile industry, for example, was concentrated west of the Pennines in Lancashire from Blackburn south to Manchester, Stockport, and Oldham. Initially, this industry was not of pure cotton textiles, but of fustians, a mixture of cotton and linen. A subsidiary concentration of cotton textile production was in the Lanark area of Scotland; however, this area declined during the cotton famine of the American Civil War and its capital and labor shifted to iron production and shipbuilding.

Worsted had been produced in East Anglia and in the West Riding of Yorkshire during the eighteenth cen-

tury. During the early nineteenth century mechanization and expansion of worsted, the agriculturally based industry of East Anglia declined and by 1851 over 90 percent of the labor force in this industry was in the West Riding of Yorkshire, especially in the Bradford-Halifax area. A good deal of the decline in East Anglia was attributable to the fact that the industry shifted from water power to steam. The West Riding of Yorkshire was located on the coal outcrops where coal was readily available, whereas East Anglia had to ship in coal at great cost. The increasing coal costs raised the cost of worsted output in East Anglia and the industry lost in the competitive process to the coal-oriented West Riding producers.

The woolen industry was much more scattered than either cotton or worsted production, although much wool was produced in the West Riding of Yorkshire, in Wales, and in the southwest of England. During the early nineteenth century, each of the outlying centers maintained their importance so that by 1851 only 45 percent of workers in the woolen industry were found in the West Riding of Yorkshire. However, the West Riding grew faster, and the Tweed Valley arose as another production center in the mid-nineteenth century. These changes were attributable to the shifts in locational patterns associated with replacement of water power by steam power. First, the costs of coal became dominant in the productive process. Prices of the final product rose quite steeply when coal had to be transported over any great distance. Therefore, the steam mills were located on the coalfields. The large scale of the coalfield steam mills meant that they required a very large labor force. The workers' cottages clustered around the mills contributed to the growth of coalfield towns in which not one but a variety of mills were located. These towns became the dominant centers attracting labor flowing out of the countryside where economic opportunities in the declining cottage industries were vanishing.

Ancillary advantages also induced the steam mills to concentrate increasingly in towns, particularly in the larger towns. The towns provided many public facilities, such as the local gas plant that supplied light and local schools (meeting the terms of the earlier factory legislation) that provided a work force with basic levels of education. In towns, manufacturers could easily share costs of facilities with others, while in the country they had to provide these services for themselves. Moreover, manufacturers could pass on many of the costs to the workers. For example, rather than having to build housing out in the countryside, they could rely upon developers to build the housing and to rent it to the workers. The textile towns as we know them thus emerged. Great specialization developed from one town to another.

Some towns emphasized cotton, woolens, or worsted; some emphasized spinning or weaving; some made relatively coarse products, while others produced relatively fine material.

There is no satisfactory answer to explain why these very substantial differences in local specializations developed. In general, the initial spark was some historical accident. However, when specializations did develop, the whole town became adapted to the requirements of the specialty—the schools, the productive processes, the ancillary services, the merchants' associations, the forms of banking, the provision of capital. In this way, the phenomenon of industrial localization emerged, involving higher productivity based upon the particular skills founded in some local specialization.

The Early American Textile Industry

A similar history characterized the American cotton textile industry. There the initial concentration of the industry developed in New England. The start had a double origin—the 1793 invention of the cotton gin and the 1812 War blockade that prevented British imports from reaching North America and providing the impulse for new machinery to be imported from Europe.

The early start in New England was favored in several ways. Factories were established on the Merrimac, Connecticut, and Blackstone rivers at such towns as Concord, Lawrence, and Lowell. Each of these was a fall line site where an ample water supply was available. Capital was forthcoming for this stage of industrialization from the merchant classes and the shipping interests of Boston, and there was a substantial rural population available to supply the labor force. Furthermore, these locations were at the heart of U.S. markets and they also had easy access elsewhere by sea.

As in Britain, shifts in location came with the application of steam power. Fall River and New Bedford were the principal coal importers, and they became centers of the coal-steam textile industry, although the quality of the water-power sites in North America led to a substantial lag behind similar changes in Britain. By 1870, 25 percent of the U.S. industry was steam powered, and only by 1900 did it become 67 percent. The coastal locations obviously were ideal for the coal-oriented textile industry because they had the lowest assembly costs of coal. In 1870 Lowell's coal costs were 15 percent greater than those at the coastal sites. New Bedford was especially favored because after the Civil War it experienced a substantial decline in its whaling and shipbuilding industries. The surplus labor force was absorbed by the growing textile industries. After 1840

as well, it recruited substantial new immigrant labor, and as late as the 1920s New Bedford was the center of the U.S. yarn-spinning industry.

Changing Orientation to Areas of Lower Labor Cost

However, the twentieth century saw a fundamental shift in the location patterns of the textile industry. In the United States, the regional shift was from New England to the Piedmont fall line sites of the Carolinas and Georgia. As in the case of the early industry, the first shift came in cotton followed by woolens and worsteds, and spinning moved ahead of weaving. First of all, there was a relative decline in the New England textile industry, followed by an absolute decline and even a physical shift of many plants southwards. In 1880 the Piedmont fall line had only 5 percent of the U.S. spinning capacity. By 1900 this had increased to 22 percent; in 1920 it was 42 percent, and in 1952 it was 81 percent. New England, on the other hand, had 95 percent of the capacity in 1880, 78 percent in 1900, 58 percent in 1920, and 19 percent in 1952. The change came because of the labor cost advantages of the South.

In the late nineteenth century the New England industry had to compete for labor with a variety of other industries, for example, the boot and shoe industry and a variety of commercial activities. As a result of this competition, wage rates rose. Also, the new immigrants tended not to stay in New England but to head West. Because of this westward expansion and because of the intensity of union activity in New England, labor became increasingly expensive. In 1881 through 1886, Fall River had 15 strikes. Consequently, the wage rate increased very rapidly, while productivity of labor was relatively low because of the very strict labor codes that also resulted. The South, on the other hand, had much cheaper labor that was more easily available and more productive.

Of course, the initial money-wage advantage of the South has not persisted, because as industry moved South it raised southern wages. If we call the 1900 wage rate in New England 100, then in the South it was 50. In 1925 the ratio was 100 to 75, but by 1950 it had become 100 to 90. There was little initial competition for labor in the South. Mechanization encouraged the standardization of labor at a relatively low skill level, so that small-town locations became feasible for the new decentralizing industry. And in these small towns the textile mills tended to be the only industry. Because the mills could pay a slightly higher wage than that of the agricultural activities of the hinterland, they could command the cream of the local labor force.

As operations in the textile industry became increasingly routinized, productivity of the skilled labor in New England and the unskilled in the South was first equalized, then gradually shifted in favor of the South. First, there was little unionization in the work force. This meant that, in the Piedmont weaving industry for example the average load per worker was 18 looms, whereas in New England it was less than 12. Moreover, the factory exerted its command over the local community to oppose the organization of unions and the enforcement (and even in some states, the enactment) of labor codes. Another very substantial contributing cause to the industry's shift to the South in the period 1919 to 1939 was a technical revolution in the textile industry: Northrop looms were introduced in the southeast whereas the New England weaving industry remained concentrated in the older technology. These new looms reduced production costs by 40 percent.

The advantages of the South tended to diminish from 1940 onward. The coming of new industry meant a gradual increase in economic opportunity in the South, and a tendency for equalization of labor costs. After spinning came weaving, after cotton came woolens, then worsted. Thereafter came the textile machinery industry and the plants producing synthetic fibers. More recently, a range of electronic and engineering industries have located in the South. An increasing tightness of the labor supply in the Piedmont areas of the South has resulted.

This has led to a continuing trend for the industry to migrate further afield: into the Deep South; to Puerto Rico; over the Mexican border; to locations in the United States where "by product" female labor persists, for example, in the anthracite towns of eastern Pennsylvania or in the mining and forest cities of the upper Great Lakes, where heavy industries employ mostly male workers. In addition, of course, the United States is facing very substantial competition from textile production of the Far East. Initially this competition was from Japan, followed by that from Hong Kong, followed increasingly today by products moving out of Taiwan and South Korea.

This trend has been even more profound in northern Britain, the traditional center of the mechanized textile industry. In 1882, 80 percent of the world's textile exports came from the United Kingdom, and these amounted to 60 percent of Britain exports by value. In that year 4 billion yards of fabrics entered world trade. By 1949 to 1951, 14 billion yards were produced, but only 18 percent of this was made in the United Kingdom. In that year, 35 percent of the world output in textiles came from Western Europe, over a quarter from Southeast Asia, and 20 percent was accounted for by

Japan. Except for Japan, Southeast Asia remains the great growth area in the textile industry.

In both Europe and the United States, the pattern that has emerged is that of the very specialized high-skill products remaining concentrated in the old areas of production, whereas mass production for the textile markets of Western Europe, America, and indeed, for the world, is produced in the Far East. The reason for this is clear. It is to be found, first of all, in the replacement of coal as a locational factor by labor, once the coal-steam powered industry changed over to electric power during the early twentieth century. By 1953, the average cost of production of cotton textiles in the United Kingdom was 108.1 pence per pound. Of this, the average cost of raw cotton was 45.5 pence ± 3. Power costs were 4.8 pence per pound, with insignificant variability from place to place. Capital costs averaged 39.6 pence per pound and again varied insignificantly, while distribution costs averaged 3.5 pence and again varying insignificantly from place to place. However, labor costs, 16.7 pence per pound on the average, varied regionally from half to double that amount (8 pence to 32 pence per pound). Thus, with raw material costs not varying greatly with location, a product with high value per unit of weight, no weight loss, variable distribution costs, and electric power costs with little locational pull, capital costs perhaps offering some advantage to already developed areas because of lower interest rates, and labor costs varying greatly from location to location, labor became the factor conducive to low processing costs. Cheap labor became the critical location factor that determined success, particularly because mechanization had already eliminated the advantages of skill in the industry. Cotton textiles could then spread very rapidly, often becoming the springboard for further industrial growth. The relatively inexpensive machinery meant low capital thresholds, and very simple repetitive skills meant that a very poorly educated mass labor force could be employed. The growth of the industry in India, China, Japan, and South Korea thus reflects the low labor costs and ease of entry in the industry.

The history of textiles chronicles an industry that shifted very rapidly from a very widely scattered eighteenth-century cottage handicraft industry to a nineteenth-century mechanized industry that concentrated on the coal fields of Western Europe after initial spread of factories seeking water power, to a twentieth-century industry transformed by electricity, in which labor costs became the dominant locational factor. During the last half century, there has been continuing decline of traditional areas and rapid growth of the industry in those parts of the world where labor supplies are abundant and cheapest. The industry remaining in the traditional areas (for example, the linen industry in Belfast, the very fine worsted industry of Yorkshire, or the lace industry of Brussels) involves the highest skill lines and the prestige based upon historical localization. Elsewhere, as routinized textile operations based upon natural fibers continue to diffuse into low labor cost areas, the residual industry in Europe and the United States concentrates on lines of production using the artificial fibers, such as rayon, nylon, or dacron. The forces operating in these cases are the great capital requirements and substantial economies of scale involved in the production of artificial fibers.

Internal and External Economies of Scale and the Economies of Urbanization

Where neither transport costs nor labor costs vary significantly, other processing-cost differentials may determine the least-cost location. These differentials include internal and external economies of scale, especially localization and urbanization economies. Localization economies arise from the clustering of plants engaged in *similar* activity in a very restricted geographical area. The local scale of the industry that results from this close association tends to perpetuate the localization of the industry.

Urbanization economies, on the other hand, derive from the clustering of many *different kinds* of industries within large cities. In Chapter 7 we discussed at some length the various cost advantages that stem from these two types of agglomeration. We now look at the most extreme form of spatial association among industries, the concentrations that occur in and around urban centers.

Central Area Industries

The industries that typically remain in, or close to, the central areas of large cities are those that find the greatest advantage or necessity in high accessibility to the central business district (CBD). As the point of convergence for all city and regional transport routes, the CBD has traditionally offered unusual convenience for buyers as well as for workers. But industry in central business districts also faces severe competition for sites from many other functions seeking the same advantages of centrality. They compete through the prices they are willing to pay to occupy space. Hence, as we saw in Chapter 9, a hierarchy of land usage is found in the city. The "highest" uses are those that derive the greatest advantage from centrality and that can therefore pay

most by turning the advantage into profit and rents. Housing is generally low on the hierarchy, except for high-income apartment houses. Most types of industry are also driven out of the core of the city because for them the advantages of centrality are relatively small whereas production costs are lower on the periphery of the city. Therefore, as the process of land use competition takes place, the higher uses occupy the central area and the only industries that remain localized within the boundaries of the central business districts are of the following kinds:

1. The *financial district* of banks, brokers, and the like, relying upon speedy personal contact within a closely intertwined set of activities and relationships.

2. A variety of *specialized retail functions,* including department and specialty stores that require large population support at the point of convergence of population.

3. A variety of *social and professional functions,* including the *headquarters and main office function.*

These activities tend to squeeze out housing and industry from the most accessible points. The industry that survives in the city has very special features. It tends to be found on the edges of the central area in the back streets where land values are lower. For this kind of industry central location is imperative; there is no alternative. The industry must be in central areas because of its marketing needs in meeting demands. Marketing and manufacturing functions cannot be separated. A simple showroom in the central area will not do. Also, many of these industries have been long established in the inner areas because these areas support relatively immobile skilled labor forces and because the industry is part of the extreme subdivision of processes within the cluster of interdependent firms. The scale of operations of such firms is generally small. They use ground very intensively, their space requirements being very low in relation to their level of output. In this sense, they can adapt relatively obsolete multistory building space in a variety of ways. This kind of space is, of course, available at the lowest rents until it is cleared and rebuilt for some other more intensive higher-paying use. Industry in central areas thus tends to move from building to building, being displaced as those buildings are cleared for reuse. Two good examples of central area industries are printing and clothing.

For printing, the marketing factor is important. Generally it is involved with so-called job printing for rush jobs that must be completed in a very short time. Firms are generally located on the margins of the professional and financial districts. Newspapers also tend to be produced in central locations, usually in very large modern buildings near the zone of highest land values. Here, centrality is essential to speedy newsgathering. There has to be close contact among the reporters who gather the news, the editorial staff, printers, and the truckers for speedy delivery of the newspapers. On the other hand, periodicals, books, and standardized kinds of job printing are not found in cities but tend to decentralize into the suburban areas and rural and small town locations.

Central area clothing industries involve those branches where fashion and style are important; for example, ladies' dresses, gowns, coats, and so on. More than 50 percent of the labor force in these activities in England in 1950 was concentrated in London. More than 60 percent of all such garments made in the United States are made in New York. In the New York garment center there are three types of employers:

1. *Manufacturers,* who have an "inside" shop—that is, besides buying the cloth and selling the final product they run their own production plant, in which workers cut and sew the material into apparel.

2. *Jobbers,* who buy the raw materials, design the garments, and later sell them, but do not actually manufacture them. (In knit outerwear such a person is called a "converter" rather than a jobber.) The jobber has a showroom and usually a cutting room, but sends the fabric to "outside" shops to be sewed into apparel.

3. *Contractors,* who run the "outside" shop, where the fabric is sewn into garments. They hire the workers and are, in effect, labor contractors. They produce to specification, never take title to the goods, and are in no way involved with the marketing of the product.

The jobbing-contracting relationship has become a solidly established method of operation because it conveys two strong advantages. First, it permits specialization; the jobber concentrates on the merchandising while the contractor is a production expert. Second, it adds flexibility to an industry where uncertainty reigns; it provides a means of keeping down the unused plant capacity of all concerned.

This second advantage offers a key to understanding the business organization in the women's and chil-

dren's apparel industries. Although aggregate demand for these products is predictable, the style factor prevents any single firm from knowing what its volume of sales for the season will be; thus, the use of contracting relieves each firm of the need to maintain factories large enough to fill maximum orders. Jobbers can find additional contractors to produce for them when their orders rise, and the contractor, in turn, is not dependent upon orders from only one jobber, but may turn to others to keep the plant occupied. Contracting even helps the manufacturers who operate their own plants, because those plants need only be large enough to handle normal demand; peak demand can be contracted out.

Contracting is used most in women's outerwear and least in undergarments. Children's outerwear falls between the two. In only one industry, corsets and brassieres, as many as two-thirds of the establishments are those of manufacturers. This industry, producing more standardized products than the other types of women's and children's apparel, differs in many respects from the rest of the garment industries. On the other hand, blouses and unit-priced dresses are subject to frequent style changes and in these two industries, only about one-quarter of the establishments are those of manufacturers.

The crucial consideration is *style,* which involves rapid changes in design. Large cities are the places from which new designs are disseminated. The style factor means that output for stock is impossible, large varieties and small quantities of output are essential, and small scale of activity is appropriate. There is no division of processes or line methods of production, and only a few persons work on a single garment. The work is highly skilled. Thus, in central London there are more than 2000 firms making women's clothing. Women's outerwear firms have small space requirements; they can use converted obsolescent buildings. The industry's demand for skilled labor, as well as its demand for capital, coincided in the 1880s with the influx of Jewish refugees from Eastern Europe into London and New York. The garment trade thus became highly localized with interdependence of specialized subcontractors that produced accessories, such as embroidery, belts, and buttons. Reliance on common specialists arises out of the fashion nature of the trade.

The crucial point binding the industry to central locations is marketing: The industry has to be localized where buyers can cluster and have the garments immediately displayed to them. Therefore, the women's outerwear firms are close to London's West End and to the style centers of Manhattan. On the other hand, branches of the clothing industry manufacturing standardized products by line methods where there is a subdivision of processes and no skilled labor force requirements have decentralized to small-town locations.

Hierarchical Location Differences

The locational orientations and dominant location factors of industries vary by size of city: There are *hierarchical* location differences (for a discussion of theories of urban hierarchies, see Chapter 15). The reasons are not hard to find. Large cities have larger local markets and provide greater ease of access to regional markets than smaller cities. Likewise, smaller cities offer labor at lower wage rates than larger cities, because competition for labor is less. And the very idea of urbanization economies is one associated with city size. Because the cost factors in plant location vary systematically with city size, it is expected that plant location should vary significantly with the position of cities in the urban hierarchy, as follows: First, industries concentrated in large metropolitan areas serve national markets. They derive their locational advantages from externalities (economies of urbanization and localization), and from national market access. At the other extreme, small-town industry is of two kinds: (1) raw material-oriented processing industry related to agriculture, fishing, and forests and located to ensure maximum weight-reduction before the product is shipped to national markets; and (2) activities finding their locational advantage in the low labor costs of small towns. In between, medium-sized cities appear to have concentrations of larger-scale agricultural processers, and a broad range of large- and medium-scale industries engaged in fabricating intermediates and producers' goods from metals.

Costs, Infrastructure, Innovation, and Filtering Processes

What are some of the reasons for the differential importance of cost factors from larger to smaller cities? An urban economist, Wilbur Thompson, offers one set of reasons. He argues that the larger urban areas are places of creative entrepreneurship, continually inventing or adopting new activities, and enjoying the rapid growth characteristic of the early stage of an industry's life cycle when a new market is exploited. Thompson says that the economic base of the large metropolis derives from the creativity of its universities and research parks, the sophistication of its engineering firms and financial institutions, the persuasiveness of its public relations and advertising agencies, the flexibility of its transportation networks and utility systems, and all the dimensions of infrastructure that facilitate the quick and orderly transfer from old dying economic bases to new

growing ones. But when an industry matures, the rate of job formation in that industry slows, and the local rate of job formation in the large city may slow even more as the maturing industry begins to decentralize—a likely development, especially in nonunionized industries, because with maturity the production process becomes rationalized and often routine. The high wage rates of the innovating area, quite consonant with the high skills needed in the beginning stages of the learning process, become excessive when the skill requirements decline and the industry, or parts of it, "filters down" to the smaller, less industrially sophisticated areas where the cheaper labor is now up to the lesser occupational demands.

A filter-down theory of industrial location would go far toward explaining the small towns' lament that they always get slow-growing industries feeding on lower wage rates. The smaller, less industrially advanced area struggles to achieve an average rate of growth out of enlarging shares of slow-growth industries, originating as a by-product of the area's low wage-rate attraction.

The larger, more sophisticated urban economies can continue to earn high wage rates only by continually performing the more difficult work. Consequently, they must always be prepared to pick up new work in the early stages of the learning curve, inventing, innovating, rationalizing, and then spinning off the work when it becomes routine. In its early stages an industry also generates high local incomes by establishing an early lead on competition, and thus smaller towns receiving "filtered-down" industries are, almost by definition, destined to have lower income levels than those prevailing in metropolitan areas.

In support of his formulation, and to illustrate the consequences for the welfare of the citizenry, Thompson reports on a variety of analyses that show that median family income in American cities is a positive function of local educational levels, degree of manufacturing specialization, city size, the male labor force participation rate, and percentage of the population foreign-born. Thus, larger cities have higher educational levels, more diversified occupational skills, and more culturally enriched environments. These qualities combine with the higher-skill mix in manufacturing—more capital per worker and greater productivity—kept high at the margin by union control of the labor supply, and by the combined product and factor price power of oligopolies and unions. Such a nexus of oligopoly, unions, and capital-intensive production, particularly in heavy industry, contributes to the higher income levels of the metropolitan resident.

Economic growth benefits the smaller town only through the downward "filtering" of industry in this scheme. The mechanics of filtering are as follows: The higher the capital-labor ratio in a region, the higher the wage rate of the unskilled. The implication of this is that, in any economic expansion, the high-income region experiences rising wage rates first. Some industries will be priced out of the high-income labor market and there will be a shift of that industry to low-income regions, increasing their employment and incomes. If the boom can be maintained, industries of higher labor productivity will shift into the growing regions and some industries will be driven even further into the countryside. At any point in time, then, industries will be differentially located in urban areas and labor markets of different sizes. And the shifts can be seen operating not only in the United States but throughout the world today. Although newer forms of market-oriented industries tend to be centralizing toward major population centers, manufacturing—particularly such sectors as apparel and textiles and electrical machinery—is moving interregionally and internationally from rich to poor areas, and from larger to smaller urban centers.

The Case of the Apparel Industry

In the apparel industry in the United States, to consider one example, locational shifting has consisted of a continual process of "peeling off" particular branches of production from the body of the New York metropolitan region's employment. The process began in men's work clothing and women's housedresses. Both industries employ relatively unskilled female labor, and their products are highly standardized. Producing on a large scale, and not governed by rapid style changes, these firms do not require the external economies available in the New York metropolitan region. At the same time, labor cost is a crucial factor for survival. As the immigration laws cut off the influx of cheap labor, and as improved transportation made it feasible to locate in low-wage labor markets, these industries began to leave the region. While New York firms declined, the production of work clothing and housedresses expanded in Pennsylvania, in the southeast, and in the low-wage urban labor markets of St. Louis and Kansas City.

But the wage-oriented shifts in location were not confined to these cheapest products. In the 1920s, New York City emerged clearly as the highest wage area in women's and children's garments. At the same time, it appeared as the highest wage area in men's clothing, except for Chicago, which specialized in quality production. As a consequence, producers in other lines of garments—lines less standardized than housedresses or work clothing—began to search for locations with lower labor costs. In the two main branches of women's cloth-

ing—women's and misses' dresses, coats and suits—the shifts were facilitated by two factors that gained in importance during the late 1920s. One was the physical separation of the actual production—the sewing of the garments—from the merchandising and cutting operations. The other was the rise of "section work," which required relatively unskilled labor. As a consequence of these developments, contractors producing cheaper types of dresses, coats, or suits could locate outside New York City and still provide the jobbers with quick truck delivery. In this way it was possible for firms to retain many of the advantages of proximity to the center of fashion and skilled labor in New York City while enjoying lower labor costs in the sewing of the garments.

The search for cheaper labor thus did not always push the garment firms entirely out of the region. Many firms moved to the region's suburban counties; indeed, in women's coats and suits the bulk of the city's loss has been made up by employment in those counties. But the labor available in the mining communities of Pennsylvania and the textile towns of New England has been even cheaper than that available in the region's outlying counties. Overnight by truck from New York City, these communities could maintain close ties with Manhattan's garment center. Under the "section work" system, the producers could employ local women who had had no previous experience in the needle trades. As a consequence, dress contractors in the lower price lines moved increasingly to these communities. The relative decline of inexpensive dress production in the metropolitan region has been accelerated by expansion in still other areas in the South and Midwest.

Locational changes in other New York clothing industries displayed many similar features. In the more standardized and cheaper branches of women's undergarments, children's outerwear, and men's clothing, the New Jersey counties of the region gained at the expense of New York City; but the search for lower labor costs again led eventually outside of the New York metropolitan region. In men's clothing, for instance, the first outside gainers were the competing urban centers of Philadelphia and Baltimore; but in the 1930s relative gains were registered by smaller communities in Pennsylvania, Maryland, and the Midwest. A more recent expansion of employment took place in the low-wage Southeast in the manufacture of children's outerwear and women's undergarments. Among other industries showing the beginnings of "filtering-down" as mass production operations are separated from activities demanding higher skills are, for example, book manufacturing, which is decentralizing while composition and printing remain highly concentrated in major metropolitan areas, consistent with the high-skill component and the continuing need for specialized external services and close contacts with customers and supplies. The filtering industries moving into the smallest towns have been those traditionally displaying the least dependence upon urbanization economies, generally involving mass production of goods for final consumption. On the other hand, industrial complexes of highly interdependent activities producing intermediate products and capital and producers' goods are showing some tendency for increased concentration in moderate-size markets.

OVERVIEW: CHANGING CHARACTER OF THE INDUSTRIAL LOCATION PROBLEM

The nature of plant location decisions has gradually changed with the development of the manufacturing economy since the Industrial Revolution, and, as we have seen, so has the theory of industrial location that has evolved as a way of interpreting that process and its spatial manifestations. Hence, industrial location theory can be better understood if it is viewed from an historical perspective. To the extent that locational decision making has been of an *adoptive* kind—in which many decisions were made randomly, leaving behind a spatial pattern composed of those surviving firms lucky enough to have been well located—the theory is designed to help in understanding *what is*. To the extent that other, mainly large firms have engaged in an *adaptive* kind of locational decision making—which entails careful, systematic analysis of alternatives, leading to the creation of rational industrial landscapes—location theory serves as a guide to decision-makers and thus becomes a normative theory: a prescription for *what ought to be*.

During the early years of industrial development and throughout much of the nineteenth century, locational choices available to decision-makers were mainly of the Type A variety described earlier in this chapter: Optimal locations were those that minimized costs in order to maximize profits. One of the early theorists, Alfred Weber (1909), offered a widely accepted explanation for the locational problems of the period. It was a time that saw the growth of many small manufacturing firms engaged in converting raw materials into finished products sold in highly competitive markets. Weber and his contemporary theorists emphasized the locational importance of transportation cost for assembling materials and distributing products. Firms thus tended to locate their productive facilities at raw-material sources, at markets, or at certain intermediate points, depending upon which of these alternatives min-

imized total aggregate transportation costs. Weber regarded labor costs and other locational considerations as "distorting influences," representing deviations from the least-transport-cost points. The early iron and steel industry of Britain exemplified the locational problems with which nineteenth-century theorists were preoccupied.

With continued industrial development, new manufacturing technologies evolved, plants grew larger, and industrial organizations increased in scale and gained the ability to manipulate prices in various markets. Type B locational behavior—in which the optimal location maximizes the difference between prices and costs in order to maximize profits—therefore arose as an addition to those cases still calling for Type A decision making. The subsequent appearance of firms making high value-added products from standardized intermediate components obtained from other industries caused still a third kind of decision-making behavior, Type C, to appear. This type requires choosing that location which maximizes sales as a means for maximizing profits. The need to gain the patronage of as many customers as possible by expanding market size brought companies into competition with similar firms motivated by the same goal. By the middle of the twentieth century, therefore, this kind of locational interdependence among firms had become the concern of such theorists as August Lösch and Melvin Greenhut.

Continued technological development in recent decades has led to the emergence of a new kind of industrial firm, one that is truly locationally independent. The Type D locational behavior that characterizes many such high-technology companies may be described as "footloose." Enjoying prices that are uniform in national markets, and with costs of inputs and processing that are the same everywhere, such firms are free to locate wherever managers and key personnel find the most congenial living conditions.

Even as the types of optimal locational behavior have grown more varied with the evolution of modern industrial landscapes, theorists have come to recognize a greater variety of locational influences—such as internal and external economies. They have also focused increasingly upon the dynamic aspects of industrial location, including the differences between short- and long-run labor-cost advantages and the filtering-down process by which industries migrate from metropolitan areas to smaller towns when the industries mature and cheap labor becomes the prime locational attraction. The textile and apparel industries have undergone such locational shifts, not only interregionally within countries but also internationally, migrating from richer, high-labor-cost nations to poorer ones offering abundant cheap labor.

TOPICS FOR DISCUSSION

1. Table 10.3 shows the results of a survey undertaken by Mueller and Lansing in 1960 in an attempt to explain given plant locations in Michigan. How can one reconcile what industrialists say *they do* with what researchers say *they see?* Can anything be inferred from the different responses larger firms gave from the responses of smaller firms? If so, what?

2. In the world today, major industrial shifts are taking place in labor orientation as part of a global scramble for cheap labor, yet there are many situations where money wages vary apparently without effect on industrial locations. Why? Why do labor cost variations due to money wages tend to be short-run differentials? In what circumstances can these differentials persist in longer periods of time?

3. What kind of industries tend to remain localized within the boundaries of the central business districts (CBDs) of America's cities? Do these industries tend to conform with a hierarchy of land usage in the city? What is the basic principle involved in this land-use hierarchy? Explain with an example.

4. What are the mechanics of the downward "filtering" of industry as outlined by Thompson? What are the wage-rate implications of this theory?

TABLE 10.3

Explanations given for location of plant by number of plants operated by firm (percentage of employment represented)

	All Michigan	Number of plants operated by firm		
		One plant	2–4 plants	5 or more plants
Main Reasons for Locating Plant in Michigan[a]				
Personal reasons; chance	50%	63%	52%	32%
Opportunity-found good site, etc.	19	23	20	14
Proximity to customers; central location	15	17	20	4
Proximity to auto industry	8	14	4	4
Labor advantages	7	c	12	14
Proximity to materials	6	3	8	9
Local concessions and inducements; encouragement by groups or persons	2	c	c	4
Better tax situation	1	c	c	4
State already established as a center for the industry	1	c	4	c
Total	d	d	d	d
Main Reasons for Locating Plant at Particular Site[b]				
Personal reasons; chance	33%	55%	32%	20%
Opportunity-found good site, etc.	18	27	16	14
Proximity to customers; central location	15	16	15	14
Proximity to auto industry	13	7	14	12
Labor advantages	7	4	9	7
Proximity to materials	12	7	6	15
Local concessions and inducements; encouragement by groups or persons	4	2	4	7
Better tax situation	3	4	6	2
Area already established as a center for the industry	2	1	2	4
Total	d	d	d	d

Source: From Eva Mueller and John Lansing, "Location Decisions of Manufacturers," *American Economic Review,* 502 (1962), 204–217.

[a]Asked only at plants that started operating at present locations after 1940. The question was: "What were the main reasons for locating the plant in Michigan?"

[b]The question was: "What were main reasons that operations were set up here in [name of town]?"

[c]Less than 0.5 percent.

[d]Totals differ from 100 percent because some respondents mentioned more than one reason, and for some others the reasons were not ascertained.

5. There are a variety of external economies representing different forms of agglomeration. What are the two basic forms? Distinguish them.

6. What were Weber's formal assumptions in his theory of plant location? What were his two "distorting" or "altering" forces in industrial location? Explain each.

FURTHER READINGS

ESTALL, R. C. *New England: A Study in Industrial Adjustment.* London: Bell, 1966.

ESTALL, R. C., AND R. O. BUCHANAN. *Industrial Activity and Economic Geography.* London: Hutchinson University Library, 1961.

GREENHUT, M. L. *Plant Location in Theory and Practice.* Chapel Hill: University of North Carolina Press, 1956.

HELFGOTT, R. B., W. E. GUSTAFSON, AND J. M. HUND. *Made in New York.* Cambridge, Mass.: Harvard University Press, 1959.

HOOVER, E. M. *An Introduction to Regional Economics.* New York: Knopf, 1971.

LICHTENBERG, R. M. *One Tenth of a Nation.* Cambridge, Mass.: Harvard University Press, 1960.

MARTIN, J. E. *Greater London: An Industrial Geography.* London: Bell, 1966.

ROBBINS, S. M., AND N. E. TERLECKYJ. *Money Metropolis.* Cambridge, Mass.: Harvard University Press, 1960.

SEGAL, M. *Wages in the Metropolis.* Cambridge, Mass.: Harvard University Press, 1960.

SMITH, D. M. *Industrial Location.* New York: John Wiley, 1971.

SMITH, W. *An Historical Introduction to the Economic Geography of Great Britain.* London: Bell, 1968.

CHAPTER 11

Location Theory in Historical Context: Long Waves in Economic Evolution

The Industrial Revolution, by which a world composed of largely self-sustaining agrarian societies was transformed into a progressively more interdependent global economy, was neither gradual nor continuous. Key innovations came in a succession of bursts at roughly 50-year intervals: in the 1770s and 1780s, the 1820s and 1830s, the 1880s, and the 1930s. Each swarm of innovations introduced new industries and transformed older ones, signaled the end of a period of "stagflation," and precipitated decades of new growth. Each wave of growth ended in a major depression in which there was a collapse of former growth industries that had overshot needs and were overbuilt: in 1825, 1873, 1929, and 1982. New types of industry, new industrial regions, and new forces affecting industrial location emerged in each period of growth. Depressed areas suffering from the collapse of their base industries appeared in each depression.

This chapter, which begins with an excursion into economic history, will enable you to understand the waves of growth and the industrial types, industrial regions, and location factors that emerged. It then presents the theory of "long waves" or "Kondratieff cycles" in economic evolution, and it concludes by exploring the nature of present-day high-technology and service-based growth—the Fifth Kondratieff.

Objectives:

- to understand the nature of the "long wave" phenomenon, and the theories that explain Kondratieff cycles

- to learn of Mensch's "metamorphosis model," and of the triggering mechanisms for the clusters of innovations that drive new long waves

- to appreciate current changes in the United States and the global economy: growth of "thoughtware" economies, advanced services, flexible automation, and "economies of scope"

A PREAMBLE ON ECONOMIC HISTORY

The First Industrial Revolution (1770–1820s)

The first Industrial Revolution, described by Arnold Toynbee as a period of accelerated change that transformed a people with peasant occupations and local markets into an industrial society with worldwide connections, occurred in Great Britain from the 1770s to the depression of the late 1820s. The major technologies triggering the change were in the textile industry, first using the power of falling water, but ultimately enabling exploitation of the potential of coal and of steam power.

As we saw in Chapter 10, textile production was a cottage craft at the beginning of the eighteenth century. Technological changes later in the century laid the groundwork for its transformation into a factory industry in the early years of the nineteenth century. The cottage craft produced a rough cotton cloth for women's dresses and men's shirts. In its original form a single hand loom operated by a skilled male weaver was supplied with hand-spun yarn by as many as six women or children. John Kay (of Bury) invented the *flying shuttle* (1733) to make the weaver's job easier. It doubled the productivity of a weaver, but placed great strains on the capabilities of the household's hand spinners, a problem solved by James Hargreaves's *spinning jenny* (1770), which enabled one woman to supply all the yarn for a hand loom by spinning up to eight threads at a time. Initially this was a great boon to the cottage weavers, because a husband and wife became a self-sufficient combination; the 1780s and 1790s were years of great prosperity for the cottage hand-loom industry, scattered throughout rural areas. Although the jenny was adopted very rapidly, it only produced soft yarn suitable for the weft, however. Cottage weavers in the 1770s still used linen for the warp, which had to be stronger.

The solution for this problem was the *spinning frame* developed by Richard Arkwright and another John Kay (of Warrington) in 1769 and 1775. The water-powered frame produced cotton yarn strong enough for the warp and made it possible for English weavers to manufacture cheap, high-quality calicoes and muslins comparable to those imported from India. Warp production was concentrated where the power of falling water could be used. Later spinning machines such as Samuel Crompton's 1779 *spinning mule* (a hybrid of the *jenny* and the *frame*) also were too much for unaided human muscles. As a result, the handicraft cottage industry gave way to cotton mills located where water power could be tapped to drive the new spinning machines. By 1812 the water-powered spinning mule enabled a single worker to produce yarn 200 times faster than the pre-1770 spinner could. Because power was required for the spinning it might as well be applied to the loom, as Edmund Cartwright saw in 1785. Thus, the key inventions involved in the mechanization of spinning and weaving and the replacement of the cottage craft by a factory industry were in place by 1800.

The transformation in weaving, lagging behind spinning, came between 1810 and 1830. In 1813 there were only 2400 power looms in England (against a hundred times as many hand looms), but by 1830 the number of power looms had grown to 85,000 in England and 15,000 in Scotland, and many mill towns had developed around sources of water power. In these towns the productivity of a single worker was orders of magnitude greater than in the cottages, resulting in a rapid decline in the price of cotton products, especially fine muslins. Rising demand had created a short-lived prosperity in the 1780s and 1790s for all weavers, including cottage hand-loom operators, but this period of prosperity ended as the supply from mechanized factories caught up. One of the sad episodes of history was the brief revolt of technologically unemployed cottage weavers under the banner of "General Ned Ludd." The Luddite revolt was put down brutally with a series of hangings at York in 1813.

At the same time, Britain deliberately set about destroying the prosperous competing Indian cotton-weaving industry of Bengal, converting India into a captive market for British cotton goods. Unemployment and declining income for cottage weavers and colonial abuses were not the whole story, though. Factory operatives, on the whole, received wages better than the cottage pieceworkers of earlier generations. Employment in the cotton industry rose from less than 100,000 jobs in 1770 to 350,000 jobs in 1800 as former cottage weavers and agricultural laborers displaced by the enclosure of the common fields moved into the mill towns. The *Penny Magazine,* a publication of the Society for the Diffusion of Useful Knowledge in the mid-nineteenth century, observed: "Two centuries ago, not one person in a thousand wore stockings—now not one person in a thousand is without them." Production and export of cotton textiles soared. In 1764 Britain imported 4 million pounds of cotton; by 1833 the figure was 300 million pounds. In 1835, Britain produced 60 percent of all cotton goods consumed in the world, compared with 16 percent from France and 7 percent from the United States.

During the same period of time, key innovations also took place in the metal industries. These involved the substitution of coke (from coal) for charcoal (from progressively scarcer wood) in iron smelting, and Henry Cort's (1784) development of the "puddling furnace," which was used to convert crude pig iron into vastly superior wrought iron. Production and consumption of iron in Britain had been 25,000 tons in 1720 and 68,000 tons in 1788, but this rose to 1,347,000 tons in 1838. As we saw in Chapter 10, the small furnaces of the old iron industry had been scattered in forested areas where charcoal could be produced; the new furnaces that used coke were located on the coalfields to minimize the costs of transporting that bulky raw material.

Coal mining expanded rapidly to meet the demand for the cheap alternative to charcoal, using the method of producing coke from coal discovered by Abraham Darby in 1709. But more coal could only come from deeper mines, mines that were often waterlogged (as were Cornwall's tin mines). An initial solution was Thomas Newcomen's (about 1705) pump, of which 100 were installed in Britain's coal and tin mines by the 1760s. These pumps were cumbersome, inefficient, and expensive, problems solved by James Watt's (1769) steam engine and his succeeding improvements to it, including the "sun and planet" gear system (1781), the double-acting engine and parallelogram cranking mechanism (1784), and the steam governor (1788). Watt's basic patent expired in 1800, by which time he had built 500 engines, and unlicensed imitators had built another 1000. The steam engines burned coal and when, later, they were used instead of water power in new factory industries, they produced relocations of those industries from the scattered sites where falling water was available to the coalfields or to other spots where cheap water transport for coal was available. Mill towns developed around these locations. Indeed, the new spinning factories, with their central source of power, their batteries of expensive machines, and their large permanent working force, moved out of the hills into the lowland towns—towns that were close to market, to sources of supply, and to labor. Manchester had its first steam mill in 1787. By 1800, dozens of great mills were in operation, and Manchester had already become the prototype of the modern industrial city, along with the rapidly growing iron-making towns of Birmingham and Sheffield in Britain's "Black Country."

The results of the exploitation of the new sources of industrial power and heat were indeed profound. The factory and the industrial town spread rapidly in Great Britain bringing with them an enlarged urban middle class, an industrial bourgeoisie, and a much larger working class—an industrial proletariat. It was the view of Manchester (with side glances to Birmingham) that provided Karl Marx with his inspiration. Moreover, as the new coal-powered factories made Britain the workshop of the world, the course of international trade was transformed. Before the 1790s one of Britain's most important imports was cotton goods from India. Quickly the reverse became true as India came to be a major market for British textiles.

The economy of the recently formed United States was even more fundamentally altered. The new nation quickly became the largest customer for British textiles and hardware and by far the largest supplier of the basic raw material for the spinning and weaving mills of Lancashire. Prior to 1786, the year before the first spinning mill was built in Manchester, no cotton was grown commercially in the United States. At first it was grown commercially only on moist sea islands of Carolina and Georgia, the only areas suitable for the production of smooth-seed, long-staple cotton. The burry, prickly seeds in short-staple upland cotton made its cleaning too costly for commercial production. By 1792, however, farmers were planting short-staple cotton in the uplands in anticipation of the invention of an engine that could efficiently remove the burry seeds. The following year Eli Whitney obliged, thus providing a classic example of an induced invention. His cotton gin and the others that followed made possible the rapid spread of cotton culture, and with it slave labor, throughout the lower South. Because climatic and soil conditions prevented the production of other crops suitable to cultivation by slaves—rice, sugar, and tobacco—in this vast area of the South, historians have often maintained that the cotton gin, by spreading slavery into these regions, was at least partly to blame for the American Civil War.

The spread of the Industrial Revolution beyond Britain was at first surprisingly slow. The great wars of the French Revolution and Napoleon and the then-existing economic, political, and even social structures delayed its spread to the Continent. But when it came, it came fast. In the United States, where economic, political, and social barriers to change were less formidable, the reason for the delay is clear. The first industrial revolution reached this country in force only after canals had been built to open up the anthracite fields in eastern Pennsylvania, during the second wave of Britain's industrial transformation. As coal began to course through the economy in the 1840s, the textile industry reached maturity by the building of steam mills in the port cities of New England, a modern American iron industry boomed in eastern Pennsylvania, and once the railroad reached Pittsburgh, that city became America's Birmingham. Then in the 1850s a brand-new machine industry grew rapidly in Philadelphia and in southern New England. By the 1850s the American northeast was undergoing as profound an economic and social transformation as Britain had a half-century earlier.

The Second Wave of Industrial Revolution (1830–1880s)

The second wave of industrial revolution came after 1830, again largely in Britain, but with France and Germany as the principal partners. Perhaps the key technological innovations were the application of steam power to water and land transportation, but there were also fundamental organizational inventions, as well as the pioneering of the mechanization of production in the United States. The latter force was not, however, to have its full impact until the third wave of growth and change coming after the mid-1880s. The principal results of the second wave were increased regional specialization and trade, the rapid growth of coalfield-, waterside-, and railroad-oriented industry, and the acceleration of urbanization and rural-to-urban migration.

High-pressure steam had been added to Watt's engine by Richard Trevithick in 1800, setting the stage for using coal-powered steam engines in place of increasingly scarce water power for factory production, as well as a power source for boats and to haul a train of cars on iron rails. Robert Fulton's steamship *Clermont*, designed to be able to travel upstream on the Hudson River under its own power, was built in 1807. George Stephenson's Stockton and Darlington Railway was opened in 1825.

In the United States, as John Borchert has pointed out, the real buildup of steamboat tonnage on the Ohio-Mississippi-Missouri system began in the 1830s, and the main period of increase in the tonnage of general cargo vessels on the Great Lakes also began in the 1830s and 1840s. Rail mileage, likewise, grew rapidly after initial development in 1829. By the end of the decade the major mechanical features of the American locomotive were established, boxcars had been introduced, regular mail routes were in operation on the railroads, and the first transatlantic steamer had arrived in New York. Soon thereafter the telegraph lines were built, and a transatlantic cable was laid from the American side.

The introduction of steam power created major transportation corridors on the western rivers and the Great Lakes and resulted in enlargement of the hinterlands of ports on both the inland waterways and the Atlantic. It made possible the development of a national transportation system through the integration of these major waterways and regional rail webs. These changes favored the growth of ports with relatively large harbors and proximity to important resource concentrations.

Steam power was also applied in manufacturing in the United States, but its impact was apparently more localized because of the impracticality of long hauls of coal or other bulk commodities with the comparatively light equipment and iron rails of the time. As a result, local water-power sites continued to dominate industrial location. By 1870 waterwheels were still providing roughly half of the inanimate energy for manufacturing, especially in the major northeastern manufacturing region that was developing. About half of the entire inanimate power for industry was in the five states of Massachusetts, Connecticut, New York, Pennsylvania, and Ohio. Steam was not universally used in cotton mills in the United States until the railroads were sufficiently developed to transport coal cheaply. That ability came generally in the 1870s.

As steam was being applied to rail and water transportation, the United States also was pioneering the "American System of Manufactures" (a phrase coined by British observers in the 1850s) based on interchangeable parts, building a successful machine tool industry and, simultaneously, exploring notions of mechanical and press production. The United States was very short of both machine tools and skilled machinists, and Britain refused to export machine tools until after 1843. Manufacturers in Philadelphia and New England therefore concentrated on simplifying product design and rationalizing the production process to minimize the need for "fitting" parts together. The use of interchangeable parts was perfected in the gun-manufacturing industry. Whereas Britain's key eighteenth-century inventions had been in response to progressively more serious shortages of charcoal, in the United States the key shortage was skilled labor, out of which emerged each of the country's principal nineteenth-century innovations, the American System of Manufactures in the 1830s and both agricultural mechanization and labor-saving consumer products in the 1870s.

Hired farm labor was unavailable, in practice, because land in the west was so cheap in the period 1800–1850 that any able-bodied person with appropriate skills could buy an acre of land for as little as a single week's wage—as contrasted to the situation in England where an acre of farmland cost as much as a *year's* wage. In the northern United States the only choice for a farmer was to breed as many children, horses, and mules as possible, and whenever possible to mechanize. In the south the solution was to breed or import more slaves.

Similarly, skilled "mechanics" (machinists) and metal workers were very scarce in America, whereas the market for metal products such as hand tools, farm implements, guns, clocks, wagon wheels, and axles was burgeoning. There was a societal need for more efficient, less-skilled labor-demanding methods of manufacturing, particularly of metal products. The American system of standardized interchangeable parts was the solution, replacing the need for skilled "fitting" of parts into products.

Finally, there was a shortage of household servants in the northern states. Any middle-class family in Europe could have several live-in female servants (daughters of agricultural laborers and peasants) to undertake labor-intensive chores such as food processing and preserving, sewing, laundry, and cleaning. In the United States such servants were much scarcer and more expensive, and a middle-class housewife in a small town or rural area readily utilized mechanical assistance of all kinds. This led to a host of labor-saving inventions from apple corers and ruffle ironers to the sewing machine, washing machine, and vacuum cleaner. Indeed, the Model T car was essentially a utility vehicle for the rural middle class. But many of these inventions did not come until the third or fourth wave of the Industrial Revolution.

As noted earlier, it was during the second wave that basic organizational invention took place. The coming of the steam-powered "iron horse" running on iron rails and the coal-fired iron steamship led to the formation of the modern multiunit enterprise with its hierarchy of salaried managers. This happened because the new forms of transportation and communication made possible a speed, regularity, and certainty in the movement of goods, messages, and people that simply was not available as long as transportation and communication depended on the vagaries of wind and water current and on the limited power of horses and mules. In the first place, the new speed and volume forced the railroads to build centrally controlled managerial organizations, if only to prevent trains from running into each other. Then much larger hierarchies became absolutely essential to guide the flow of millions of tons of a vast variety of goods over distances of hundreds and even thousands of miles, to thousands of different destinations.

In the second place, the new speed, regularity, reliability, and the massive volume of flow of transportation and communication resulted in institutional innovation in the processes of distribution by making possible mass marketing of goods, and in continuing change in the processes of production by greatly expanding the possibility for mass output. In distribution, completely new types of enterprises—department stores, mail-order houses, and chain stores, all operated through managerial hierarchies—quickly came to market an unprecedented volume of goods at very low prices.

In production came the almost simultaneous inventions of continuous and large batch processes—all voracious users of energy from coal for heat and power. These included the Bessemer and open hearth processes for the mass production of steel; the new superheated and catalytic techniques in refining sugar, vegetable oils, and then petroleum; the mass producing of machinery by the fabrication and assembling of interchangeable parts; and the creation of new milling, canning, and packaging techniques in the processing of food.

The modern industrial enterprise first came into being by integrating the new mass production with the new mass distribution. In those industries where the existing wholesalers and the new mass retailers were unable to sell the output of the new processes in the volume that they were able to produce, enterprises began to build their own national wholesaling, and occasionally retailing, networks and their own extensive purchasing organizations, which often included control of raw materials. This strategy of vertical integration occurred where independent marketers were unable to satisfy manufacturers' requirements in several areas: the complex scheduling essential to producing and distributing annually millions of packages, tins or cans of cigarettes, soap, soup, kerosene, pills and the like, or tens, even hundreds, of thousands of sewing machines, typewriters, harvesters, or other mass-produced machinery; or specialized distribution facilities such as refrigerated warehouses, train cars, and ships; or specialized marketing services such as demonstration, after-sales service and repair, or extensive consumer credit.

In those industries where wholesalers were unable to meet the manufacturer's distribution and marketing needs, the giant, multiunit, multifunctional firm appeared with suddenness in the 1880s in the United States in the production of food, rubber, kerosene, consumer chemicals, and light and heavy machinery. Large integrated enterprises came more slowly in Europe. In Britain they were formed in some number in packaged, branded consumer goods like foods, soap, paint, and proprietary drugs. In Germany they came in producers' goods, particularly in electrical machinery and chemicals. In the United States and in Germany, but to a much lesser extent in Britain and France, such firms quickly came to be operated through large managerial hierarchies—hierarchies that were organized along functional lines with major departments for production, distribution, purchasing, and finance. It was within the organizational framework of these new managerial hierarchies that the third wave of the Industrial Revolution took place.

The Third Wave (1886–1939)

The third wave of industrial revolution, shared by Germany and the United States, took place in the 1880s, building upon innovations introduced as the depression of the 1870s waned. In this period, too, industrial growth spread to new centers in Eastern Europe, Western Russia, and Japan. The key innovations were those permitting low-priced steel production (Bessemer, 1860; Gilchrist Thomas, 1879), the harnessing of electric power, the invention of the internal combustion engine, the emergence of the modern chemical industry, and the introduction of the mass-production assembly line. An equally important ingredient was the creation of institutional arrangements that permitted the systematic application of science to the improvement of existing processes and products and to the development of new ones. By the 1890s successful technological innovation was beginning to require more than just an individual innovator to develop the product and, with one or two entrepreneurs, to build the organization to mass produce and to distribute it to national and world markets. In a few industries technological advances became increasingly dependent on people trained in science and working in well-equipped laboratories to do the innovating, and then on teams of professional managers and engineers to bring the new product into full-scale production and widespread use.

Steel was produced only in very small quantities in the United States in 1870. Output was only 70,000 tons in that year, but demand was rising fast, especially for rail, where steel was far superior to iron because of its superior wearing qualities. Bessemer steel rail cost $170 per ton in 1867, when only 2500 tons were made, compared to 460,000 tons of iron rails at $83 per ton. Bessemer's discoveries increased output and cut prices sharply. By 1870 output of steel rail was up to 70,000 tons (in the United States) and by 1884, the last year of iron rail manufacture, production of steel rail was up to 1,500,000 tons at $32 per ton. The price dropped to a low point of $15 per ton in 1898 when output reached 10 million tons. Production of steel in the United States continued to increase rapidly, to 26 million tons in 1910 (and to over 100 million tons per year in the 1950s).

The conseqences were dramatic. Steel rails replaced iron on both newly built and existing lines. Heavier equipment and more powerful locomotives permitted increased speed and the long haul of bulk goods. Rail gauge and freight car parts were standardized (there had been 11 gauges among the northern systems in 1860), so that both interline exchange and coast-to-coast shipment were possible. Refrigerated cars made their entry, ushering in a new era of regional specialization in agriculture, and centralization of the packing industry at major rail centers. Other ramifications favored industrial, hence urban, centralization. The practical length of coal hauling was extended and the cost reduced. The effort was to open vast central Appalachian bituminous deposits and to facilitate the movement of coal to the great ports whose growth had been launched four decades earlier. The greater availability of coal was

soon supplemented by the availability of central-station electric power, which followed in the 1880s.

For the first time massive forces were arrayed that favored market orientation of industry and the "metropolitanization" of America. At the same time there were negative impacts. The long rail haul spelled the doom of most passenger traffic and cargo movement on the inland waterways, especially the rivers. Small river ports were destined to become virtual museums. It is noteworthy that general cargo shipping capacity on the western rivers peaked not on the eve of the Civil War but in the 1870s; thereafter it fell precipitously for half a century. The easier availability of coal and central-station electricity doomed the small water-power sites that had yielded to the centralizing force of the metropolitan rail centers, their giant markets, and their superior accessibility.

As important in the long run as the introduction of steel rail were inventions in electricity and magnetism. Michael Faraday's work had been in the 1820s and 1830s, but it was commercially minded inventors such as Werner Siemens, Thomas A. Edison, Frank Sprague, Charles Brush, Elihu Thomson, and George Westinghouse who spawned great industrial firms in the late nineteenth century in Germany and the United States. From Edison's first electric generating plant in 1882 (Pearl Street, New York City), electrification in the United States proceeded rather slowly for a decade as alternative technologies for power transmission—alternating current (AC) versus direct current (DC)—competed. Electric street railways and lights were the first major applications, followed by such things as electric elevators, which permitted the development of the modern steel-framed skyscraper.

After 1895 progress in electrification was extremely rapid. Niagara Falls was tapped for hydroelectric power in that year. In 1899, there were 16,891 industrial electric motors in the United States with a capacity of under 500,000 hp. But 10 years later the number of industrial motors had grown twentyfold to 388,854 and installed capacity had risen tenfold to 4,817,000 hp. Meanwhile, the cost of electricity was dropping rapidly as generating plants grew larger and increased in efficiency. By 1910 the major cities of Europe and the United States were electrified. Many urban homes had electric lights, and some had other electric appliances such as electric sewing machines (Singer), electric carpet sweepers (Hoover), electric washing machines (Hurley), and electric talking machines (Edison). However, the spread of electric appliances into the average home took place mostly in the 1920s.

Another important new technology was the telephone, an outgrowth of research to improve the telegraph. An unsuccessful telephone was developed in Germany in 1860. The successful version was invented virtually simultaneously by Alexander Graham Bell and by Elisha Gray, of the Western Electric Co., living a hundred miles apart in New England. Each inventor accused the other of pirating his work. Both men filed with the U.S. Patent Office on the same day in February 1876 and the legal battle for priority went on for years and ended in the Supreme Court. Bell finally prevailed. Telephone service was initiated almost immediately after the invention was demonstrated. The first switchboard went into operation in New Haven in 1878, and by 1880 over a thousand customers had signed on. Acceptance was much faster in the United States than in Europe. By 1900 there were 1,500,000 phones in the United States, or 8 phones for every 100 persons, compared to 4 in Canada, 3 in Sweden, 2 in Switzerland, fewer than 1.5 in Germany and the United Kingdom and only 0.5 in France.

The culminating features of the third wave of industrial growth derived from basic French and German inventions of the late nineteenth century. New chemical industries were created, and a new world arose out of the internal combustion and the diesel engines, particularly when combined in the twentieth century with the distinctively American idea of mass production and consumption.

From the founding of Baron Justus von Liebig's famous laboratory at Giessen (in 1825), Germany pioneered in organized research supported largely by government grants. In addition, Germany invested in a high-quality public school and university system. What drove Germany to do these things was lack of land and natural resources. One of Liebig's major concerns, for example, was how to make Germany's scarce farmland more productive so that the country could be more nearly self-sufficient in food. The addition of mineral fertilizers to supplement needed elements in the soil began in Germany. A long quest to learn how to "fix" atmospheric nitrogen to replace depleted soil nitrates culminated at last in the famous Haber-Bosch process to synthesize ammonia (1914). The quest itself strengthened the German chemical industry still further. The innovativeness of the German chemical industry enabled Germany to produce synthetic rubber and gasoline from coal in World War II, despite almost total lack of petroleum.

In 1895 the United States still lagged several years behind European automotive technology, perhaps because roads were poor and distances were so great. But a growing, prosperous, and dispersed population needed more flexible means of transportation than railroads could provide. Moreover, petroleum was being discov-

ered in vast quantities in Texas and liquid fuel was rapidly becoming cheaper. In short, conditions were ideal. In 1900 the census reported that 4292 "horseless carriages" were produced in the United States. The biggest manufacturer that year was Stanley Motors, in Maine. Average price of a car was $1000, and vehicle performance was poor. By 1908, the year of the introduction of the Ford Model T and the founding of General Motors, production rose to 65,000 units.

Scores of small manufacturers abounded, but Henry Ford had already begun to change the structure of the industry. His contribution to technology was minor. His innovation was the *assembly line* and *mass production,* enabling the widespread realization of the potentials of the American System of Manufactures. From 1910 to 1920 prices declined by 62 percent in real terms. When the Model T was finally discontinued in 1926 its price was down to $300. Yet annual output rose more than tenfold in 10 years and employment in the industry increased from 37,000 to 206,000 in that period. Automobiles were cheap enough and reliable enough to be practical personal transportation for virtually anyone. Road surfacing and petroleum production began their steep climb in the 1920s. The need for a national system of highways was recognized in 1916 with the first federal aid for road construction.

The impact of the internal combustion engine on American cities needs little review. But some of the most profound changes affecting the city occurred in agriculture. True, the new technology put the farmer in an automobile and thus encouraged the centralization of urban growth at the larger, diversified centers in all the commercial farming regions. But also, by putting farmers on tractors, it multiplied the land area they could work alone, initiated a revolution in family farm size, and hastened the urbanization of much of rural America. The age of mass production and marketing had arrived. This idea has since become deeply embedded both in U.S. national economic policy and national mythology. The United States became—and remains to this day—the exemplar of the *consumer society.*

The United States is also the exemplar of another force that is even more important today, namely organized research and development. The process began in electricity. The development, production, and marketing of machines to generate and transmit electricity were from the very beginning much more complicated. The most notable innovators, Thomas Edison and Werner von Siemens, worked in large, carefully organized laboratories. And soon the giant multifunctional organizations such as Edison General Electric and the Siemens Company in Germany, which had been created to make and sell their innovations, were relying, as were their competitors, on large research facilities to improve existing products and processes and to develop new ones.

Enterprises in other scientifically based industries quickly adopted the same strategy. In the chemical industries the Germans led the way. Bayer, BASF, AGFA, Hoechst, and other firms built their research laboratories in the 1880s and 1890s. In the United States Du Pont and General Chemical followed suit in the first years of the new century. By the 1920s laboratories in large chemical companies in the United States and Germany were turning out a stream of new synthetic products—dyes, pharmaceuticals, fertilizers, fabrics, plastics, detergents, paints, and films. By the 1920s comparable laboratories were appearing in metals and machinery industries. By 1929 two-thirds of the personnel employed in industrial research in the United States were concentrated in five technologically advanced industries—50 percent were in just two of these, electrical machinery and chemicals. And in these industries, by far the largest numbers were working in large, multifunctional corporations.

However, if science was to be applied to the processes of production and distribution, the laboratory by itself was not enough. Its activities had to be carefully integrated with those of the rest of the organization. Unless the work of the laboratory was coordinated with the technicians responsible for the final design of product and processes, with the factory managers, and with the engineers in marketing, efficient, low-cost production and distribution were rarely realized. Moreover, as Harold Passer has pointed out in describing the fast-moving technology in electric traction (streetcars and subways) of the 1890s, the constant interaction among marketing, production, design, and research departments became in itself a powerful force for continuing technological innovation.

Research normally accounts for only 10 percent of the cost of putting a new product in the stream of commerce. What takes the time and money, and what makes the critical difference in whether a product is widely used, is the work involved in building prototype models and pilot plants, in fashioning distribution channels, in locating and contracting with suppliers who can deliver on schedule to specification, and, finally, in making the necessary financial arrangements for fixed and working capital.

The Germans and Americans, leaders in the application of science to industry, adopted quite different arrangements to achieve this essential internal coordination. Because the Germans normally concentrated their production in massive plants along the Rhine, in the Ruhr, or near Berlin, and operated their enterprises in a highly centralized fashion, they turned to committees of middle managers responsible for each function involved in the production and distribution of a major product line—committees that had their own permanent staffs, secretarial forces, and facilities. In the United States, where plants were smaller and more scattered and where, domestically at least, more sales branches existed, a new office—the development department—became responsible for all the activities involved in bringing a new product on stream. At Du Pont this change came in 1912, when the laboratories were instructed to concentrate on research and the development department became responsible for coordinating the work of the laboratories with the other functional activities.

In these same industries technological innovation called for the devising of external linkages as well as internal arrangements. One reason for Werner von Siemens's industrial success was that, from the start, he and his managers maintained close personal ties with the leading physicists and other scientists in Germany. In the early 1880s, Siemens endowed chairs in physics at leading universities and then became the driving force in the founding of the government-supported National Physical Technical Institute—an institute that became a model for similar ones in physics and later in chemistry in Germany and other countries. In Germany by World War I comparable close ties between the enterprise and the academic world had been created in the chemical and metallurgical industries.

In the United States, Thomas Edison, a self-taught man, felt little need to reach out to the universities, but those companies founded to produce his inventions did. General Electric had ties with the Massachusetts Institute of Technology (M.I.T.) even before a member of its faculty, William A. Whitney, went to Schenectady in 1901 to set up its laboratory for basic research. Other faculty members and graduates soon followed Whitney. In working out their research problems, Whitney and his associates checked closely with their former colleagues. They and their company also continued to look to the institute as a vital source for young managers. The story was much the same at Du Pont, for the three cousins who created the modern company all attended M.I.T. The later relationship between Standard Oil of New Jersey and other oil companies and M.I.T.'s "Doc" Lewis, a founder of modern petroleum engineering, was of a similar nature. Other American corporations in technologically advanced industries quickly developed similar ties to universities, technical institutes, and later to business schools.

What happened in Germany and the United States must not, however, be taken for granted. These institutional innovations were not inevitable responses to technological needs, for they rarely occurred in Britain or France. There the entrepreneurs who began to mass-produce for volume markets after the coming of the railroad and the steamship rarely created managerial hierarchies on the scale of those in Germany and the United States. Large enterprises continued to be family-owned. These families preferred, where possible, to continue to buy from and sell through agents. They employed plant superintendents and one or two sales and purchasing supervisors, but far fewer middle and top managers. There were valid economic, geographic, and historical reasons for this choice. The principal reason, however, appears to be simply that the families wanted to remain in full control of their enterprises. They did not want to turn over so much of their business to outsiders. This preference did not seriously affect the performance of firms producing low-technology products such as food, soaps, paint, and other consumer chemicals, or even textiles and steel.

It was, however, disastrous in the new technologically advanced industries. The families rarely set up research laboratories. When they did, they did not create committees or departments to coordinate research with the other functional activities. British and French innovators, both within and without the industrial firm, often came up with impressive inventions; but these were rarely brought into volume production and distribution by British and French firms. Nor did the British and French enterprises build ties to the universities. Because they did not form linkages similar to that of Siemens with the academic community in Germany, or General Electric with M.I.T., they rarely called on the universities or institutes to assist in solving technical problems. Nor did they use them as a source for trained managers.

Because of their failure to create institutional arrangements comparable to those of the Americans and Germans, the British and the French missed out on central developments of the third wave of the Industrial Revolution. Once behind, they only continued to get further behind. Of the four largest electrical manufacturers in Britain in the years before World War I, only one was British-owned, and that one, originally in the retail trade, did not set up a laboratory until 1919. The others were subsidiaries of General Electric, Westinghouse, and Siemens. The London subway system was, for example, equipped by General Electric. The British continued to rely on German dyes and synthetic drugs until the 1930s. They obtained the new plastics, paints, detergents, and other synthetics from the United States. The story appears to be much the same in France. It was not until after World War II that British and French enterprises began to fashion institutional arrangements similar to the ones the Germans and Americans had devised before World War I. Only then did they and their national economies begin to benefit fully from that systematic application of science to industry that was the centerpiece of the third wave of industrial revolution.

The Fourth Wave of the Industrial Revolution (1940–   )

Following the Great Depression of the 1930s and the disruptions of World War II came another spurt of growth that has finally ended in the worldwide depression of the early 1980s. The real impulse came after World War II with the rapid growth of a group of new industries based on new technologies that had emerged during the previous 20 years. The rapid development of these technologies was forced by the political conditions prevailing in Europe in the 1930s and especially by the 1939–1945 war. The industries that emerged on a significant scale during the 1940s and 1950s—electronics, synthetic materials, solid-state devices, petrochemicals, agri-chemicals, composite materials, and pharmaceuticals—created rapidly growing new markets. At the same time there was a rapid growth in demand for capital equipment, often of a new kind. The wealth generated by the emergence of these new technology-based industries caused an associated boom in demand for consumer durables, leading to the rapid growth of the automobile and consumer goods industries, of superhighways, shopping centers, and suburbs.

What was at the heart of the fourth wave? The spread and continued improvement of institutional arrangements and the exploitation of vast new sources of fossil fuels were probably the very factors making possible the unprecedented economic growth following World War II. Among these, two fundamental institutional developments that influenced the continuing application of science to industrial activities were critical. One was the rapid spread of the multidivisional form of corporate organization. This form, by replacing the centrally controlled functional departments with autonomous, self-contained product or regional divisions, permitted the enterprise to move rapidly into new products and new markets. Facilitating product diversification, the M Form, as economists have come to call it, greatly enhanced the potential value of the industrial research laboratory and further institutionalized the continuing flow of new products into the economy. The M Form, invented by Du Pont shortly after World War I, began to be widely adopted in the United States only in the 1950s, and in Europe only in the 1960s. By the 1970s this organizational form, or variations of it, had become the standard operating structure for the large industrial enterprise in all advanced market economies. With some justification, Oliver Williamson has called the M Form the most important invention of American capitalism in the twentieth century.

The other basic institutional development was the creation of new formal and informal ties between corporations and universities and the government. In the United States these arrangements were the product of World War II. The prototype was, of course, the Manhattan Project, where the technology of the atom bomb was developed in the universities, and the facilities for production as well as the product itself were built and operated by industrial contractors such as Du Pont, with the federal government funding and coordinating the project as a whole. As the war moved on, the armed services set up a multitude of relationships with corporations and universities to develop a wide range of military products.

The continuing military demands of the cold war and the new postwar industrial needs (many of them generated by the application of war-inspired technologies) stimulated other forms of institutional linkages among business, government, and the universities. In rapidly moving technologies, faculty members and Ph.D.'s from places like M.I.T. and Stanford built their own enterprises to meet highly segmented specialized markets, a phenomenon exemplified in Massachusetts by Route 128 and in California by Silicon Valley. However, once these technologically advanced products were mass produced for national and international markets, the large enterprise took over, as IBM demonstrated in computers and Xerox in copying machines.

These institutional developments provided one pillar for postwar economic growth: The coming of cheap oil was another essential pillar. Because oil and gas were less costly to extract, transport, and deliver than coal, and because they were more concentrated and flexible fuels, they had already begun to replace coal in the interwar years. Nevertheless, it was only after World War II that oil became the instrument that caused advanced industrial economies to become totally and possibly fatally addicted to fossil fuels. In 1945, coal still accounted for 53.4 percent of the energy consumed, and the United States was still an exporter of crude oil. Then the oil fields of the Persian Gulf came into full production. As the supply poured out, the price dropped. Suddenly everyone was converting to oil. The utilities did so massively. By the 1960s the diesel locomotive had made the steam locomotive an historic relic. Chemical companies that had relied almost entirely on coal for the feed stocks in the rapidly growing production of synthetics turned to oil, and oil companies integrated forward into chemicals. By the mid-1950s coal had become a sick industry. By 1960 it produced only 28 percent of the nation's energy. The figures for the transformation in Europe are even more striking.

The results of the unprecedented abundance of cheap oil and gas and the spread and perfection of the new institutional arrangements were indeed impressive. In the United States the annual rate of growth of the GNP per capita reached just over 20 percent a decade, a very high figure in historical context. In other industrial countries the rates were higher: 63 percent in Germany and 128 percent in Japan. The German and Japanese miracles also were based on improved institutional arrangements and cheap oil. The amount of energy required to maintain the rates was staggering when compared to earlier periods when the total GNP was, as it was early in this century, one-twentieth to one twenty-fifth the size of that of the postwar years. Moreover, such unprecedented growth meant that each year billions of dollars went into investment in industrial plants, transportation facilities, housing, and household equipment that was geared wholly to the ever-continuing supplies of cheap oil. Cheap energy, like water, was taken for granted.

The pattern of evolution in the years after World War II has been summarized schematically by Ray Rothwell, using British evidence, in the manner depicted in Table 11.1. The early situation (which appears to have been characteristic of the early phases of each wave of industrial revolution) was of rather small firms, or units, operating in fast-growing, new, and relatively undefined markets and concentrating on product-related technological innovations; this *dynamic growth phase* lasted from 1945 to about 1964, during which many new manufacturing jobs were created.

A *consolidation phase* followed from the mid- to late 1960s in which markets became better defined, organizational rationalization took place, mergers occurred, and there was increased emphasis on process improvement. While productivity increased rapidly during this phase, so did demand. A rough balance between the two meant that manufacturing employment remained unchanged.

Beginning in the late 1960s, a *phase of industrial maturity and market stagnation* was reached. By this time the new industries were highly concentrated, production was centered on very large units, and development was aimed primarily at process rationalization and productivity increase. Price became a much more significant factor in competition. Productivity growth outstripped demand growth in largely saturated markets, and many jobs were lost. At the same time firms increasingly relocated production of mature product lines to areas of low labor cost.

Subsequently, very high rates of inflation, accompanied by high interest rates, further effectively depressed the real level of demand. A *recessionary trend* on a worldwide scale thus became established. This cycle

TABLE 11.1

A model of post-World War II industrial evolution

1945 to approximately 1964—dynamic growth phase

Emergence of new industries based largely on new technological opportunities.

Production initially in small units.

Emphasis on product change and the introduction of many new products.

Rapidly growing new markets.

Some market regeneration in traditional areas; for example, textiles.

New employment generation (output growth greater than productivity growth).

Competitive emphasis is mainly on product availability and nonprice factors.

Mid- to late 1960s—consolidation phase

Increasing industrial concentration and growing static scale economies.

High dynamic economies.

Introduction of organizational innovations.

Increasing emphasis on process improvement.

Some major product changes, but based mainly on existing technology.

Rapid productivity growth.

Markets still growing rapidly.

Output growth and productivity growth in rough balance (manufacturing employment more or less stable).

Competitive emphasis still mainly on nonprice factors.

Late 1960s to mid-1970s—maturity and market saturation phase

Industry highly concentrated.

Very large production units, often vertically integrated.

Some product change, but emphasis predominantly on production process rationalization.

Increasing organizational rationalization, including foreign direct investment in areas of low labor cost.

Growing automaticity.

Stagnating and replacement markets.

Productivity growth greater than output (demand) growth.

Rapidly growing manufacturing unemployment.

Where products are little differentiated, the importance of price in competition is high.

Source: Roy Rothwell, "The Role of Technology in Industrial Change: Implications for Regional Policy," *Regional Studies,* Vol. 16 (1981), pp. 361–369.

from dynamic growth to "stagflation" and recession took about 50 years and involved roughly the same time span and sequence as in the three preceding waves of industrial revolution.

THE EXPLANATION OF LONG WAVES

Kondratieff Long Waves

Speculation about the existence of approximately 50-year cycles in modern market economies dates at least from Dutch economist J. van Gelderen's writings in 1913, but the idea is now generally attributed to the

Russian economist Nikolai D. Kondratieff, who wrote about the phenomenon in the 1920s. Kondratieff put forward the hypothesis in 1925 that the industrial nations of the world, when looked at collectively, have experienced successive cycles of growth and decline since the beginning of the Industrial Revolution with a regular periodicity of between 50 and 55 years. To traditional Marxists who believed only in short-term business cycles and in the long-term growth and decline of capitalism, Kondratieff soon became something of a heretic, and he died in the Soviet Union's "Gulag Archipelago"—committed there for daring to suggest that capitalist economies could recover after disastrous depressions, rather than being doomed to collapse as Marx had argued. However, his ideas were taken up in the 1930s by several economic historians in the West, most notably Joseph Schumpeter, who pointed out that each Kondratieff wave coincided with a spurt in technological innovation and by Simon Kuznets, who undertook painstaking statistical research on the long-wave phenomenon.

The first three Kondratieff long waves were described by Kuznets as involving successive periods of recovery, prosperity, recession, and depression, as depicted in Table 11.2. The new technologies of each epoch (for example, in transportation, the first centering on water transportation and use of wind and captive water power, the second on coal use for steam power in water and railroad transportation and in factory industry and later for the generation of electricity, and the third on petroleum use in the internal combustion or diesel engine for road and air transportation) each saw their peak development immediately preceding a major economic collapse. In the wake of this collapse, a new set of replacement technologies emerged and prevailed, as depicted in Figure 11.1c and d. All shaded columns depict the periods of depression.

Mensch's 'Metamorphosis Model' of Economic Evolution

Kondratieff and Kuznets simply described the phenomenon we have just discussed. It was a German economist, Joseph Schumpeter, who in the 1930s emphasized the key role of technology in long-wave formation, introducing the idea of *technological revolutions* as the central driving force. More recently another German economist, Gerhard Mensch, has built on Schumpeter's notions and advanced a *metamorphosis model of industrial evolution* as the essential explanation for Kondratieff's long waves.

Mensch distinguished *scientific discovery and invention*—both of which, as S. C. Gilfillan pointed out in the 1930s, appear as a more or less steady stream in

TABLE 11.2
Long waves of economic growth

Phase of growth[a]	Kondratieff long wave:				
	I	II	III	IV	V
Recovery	1770–1786	1828–1842	1886–1897	1940–1954	?
Prosperity	1787–1800	1843–1857	1898–1911	1955–1969	
Recession	1801–1813	1858–1869	1912–1924	1970–1980	
Depression (and new innovation)	1814–1827	1870–1885	1925–1939	1981–	

[a]Macroeconomic characteristics of long-wave phases are as follows:

Characteristic	Recovery	Prosperity	Recession	Depression
Gross national product	Increasing growth rates	Strong growth	Decreasing growth rates	Little or no growth
Investment demand	Increase in replacement investment	Strong expansion of capital stock	Scale-increasing investment	Excess capacity rationalization
Consumer demand	Purchasing power seeks new outlets	Expansion of demand in all sectors	Continued growth of new sectors	For a while continued growth at the expense of savings

Source: Adapted from Simon Kuznets, *Economic Change,* New York: W. W. Norton & Co., 1953.

response to well-articulated social needs—from *innovation,* the practical application of the invention or idea. Innovations, Mensch discovered, tended to come in clusters or surges. Charting the dates of inventions and the basic innovations that followed them in the early nineteenth century (examples: rolled wire invented 1773, innovation 1835; steam locomotive invented 1769, innovation 1824), he discovered a clustering in the period 1814–1828. Likewise, there was a clustering of innovations in electricity and chemistry in the period 1870–1886, and of early twentieth-century innovations in the years 1925–1939. Surprisingly, the periods of innovation (pre-1787, 1814–1828, 1870–1886, 1925–1939) coincided with periods of depression that accompanied world economic crises.

Two questions therefore emerged: Why do innovations cluster? Why have the clusters coincided with depressions?

Mensch's important contribution has been to cast light on these questions, tying together in an explanatory framework the empirical observations of Kondratieff and Kuznets and the technological innovation hypothesis of Schumpeter. His key concept is that of a *technological stalemate,* out of which an economy is ultimately eased by clusters of innovations that are implemented within a society, out of a reservoir of investment opportunities formed by a continuing stream of scientific discoveries and practical inventions, producing a *structural metamorphosis* as old activities are cast

off and replaced by revolutionary new ones. See Figure 11.1.

Mensch's metamorphosis model postulates the following causal sequence:

1. A cluster of *basic innovations* introducing new branches of industry, and *radical improvement innovations,* which rejuvenate existing branches, occurs in response to a technological stalemate. Venture capital is attracted to the new lines of business. New demands are awakened.

2. Parallel S-shaped *product growth cycles,* perhaps substituting for older goods or services, characterize the new branches of industry. Initial entry is followed by rapid upswing, and then by accelerated growth until market saturation is reached.

3. During the new product upswing, investment, employment, and incomes increase rapidly, well ahead of prices and inflation, and lifestyles may well be revolutionized.

4. The revolutionary pioneering innovations are then followed by *routine improvement innovations* that rationalize production and increase capital intensity. But they find themselves subject to diminishing returns on the demand side and diminishing marginal utility on the supply side. The growth curve grades over from acceleration to deceleration. This is a natural phase of the *product life cycle of manufactured goods,* as discussed by Raymond Vernon in 1966. As Vernon saw it, new

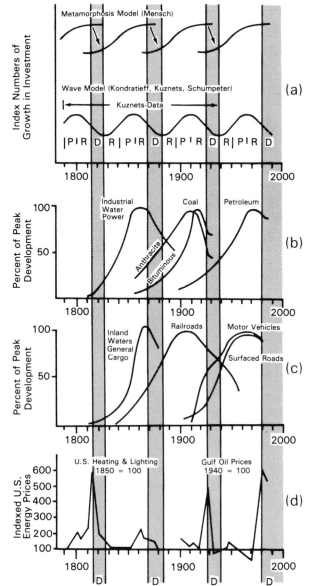

FIGURE 11.1 Long waves: Theories compared with major epochs of energy use, transportation development, and energy price inflation. [*Source:* Adapted from John R. Borchert, "American Metropolitan Evolution," *Geographical Review,* Vol. 57 (July 1967), 301–332; and Gerhard Mensch, *Stalemate in Technology* (Cambridge, Mass.: Ballinger Publishing Co., 1978).]

production facilities moves away from the rich market to areas with lower labor or material costs. (We should note that the United States has provided the *initial* large market for *most* major new consumer products since the late nineteenth century. Examples include the telephone, typewriter, camera, sewing machine, automobile, washing machine, vacuum cleaner, airplane, radio, record player, tape recorder, TV, videotape, and so on.) The predicted emigration of production (and jobs) is clearly visible in the case of textiles and shoes, cameras, watches, consumer electronics, steel, autos, bulk chemicals, and many other standard products. As the jobs are transplanted, so is the purchasing power of the workers. Thus, unless the emigration of older industries is more than compensated for by growth in newer, more innovative industries, economic stagnation is an inevitable consequence. It cannot be reversed by increased capital formation per se because the capital itself—being mobile—will also tend to move where returns are higher. The stagnation can only be reversed by the creation of new, more dynamic industries. In this view, the fundamental problem is a technological one.

5. But *corporate growth tends to overestimate domestic markets and produces excess supply and heated competition.* Almost inevitably, an industrial economy tends to overinvest in any new technology—capital goods industries in particular. For example, the latest wave of overinvestment began in the 1960s and now is obvious in worldwide overcapacity in steel, autos, diesel engines, chemicals, shipbuilding, machine tools, and even semiconductors. The auto industry is the best recent illustration of how overinvestment occurs. In the postwar period, autos not only became one of the nation's biggest industries but also helped spur the growth of highways and spawned suburbs, which created new markets for homes, shopping centers, schools, and hospitals. Automobiles also influenced the location of plants and distribution centers. Today, however, with the stock of cars near a saturation level and with consumers keeping them longer, autos have become primarily a replacement market in which sales will grow slowly if at all. And the influence of cars and trucks on population shifts and business location will be minimal. Meanwhile, the nation has spent the past 25 years building up an enormous investment in industries—steel, machine tools, cement, glass, forest products—needed to produce cars and the many other products they helped create. But as the auto industry wanes, and its economic influence shrinks, much of this investment will be unusable. The long decline in capacity utilization reached its peak in the late 1960s and dropped to 43 percent in steel and 63 percent in nonelectrical machinery by the end of 1982.

products will tend to be introduced and produced initially in the biggest, richest market, but as the market grows, the basis for competition gradually shifts from *performance* to *price.* This evolution requires standardization of the product and (to exploit economies of scale) of the production technology. When the latter is sufficiently standardized, the optimum location for mass

6. There are two responses to excess supply:

   a. Attempts to reduce competition by market segmentation and industrial mergers.

   b. Attempts to segment domestic and foreign markets, "dumping" excess output.

Overinvestment breeds *pseudo-innovation* that benefits neither buyer nor seller, reflecting rather the attempt on the part of existing industries to protect their market shares by *product differentiation* in which the "image" or "packaging" of the product is changed, but no longer any of its basic qualities. The pace of change means that individual products have limited life cycles. This results in

   a. rapidly vanishing returns for a given product;

   b. intense competition to substitute new products;

   c. ultimately, after repeated attempts to substitute new products by packaging "pseudo-innovations," the opportunities for further technological improvement are exhausted—the usable fund of ideas runs out.

The economy enters a period in which output stagnates and industry leaders merge with other firms to create *oligopolies* that try to maintain their revenue growth by increasing prices. Definite *limits to growth* are encountered, markets are often flooded, key resources may be scarce, there is a slowdown in income and employment growth, and spreading stagnation. Rates of return decline, and capital is therefore not reinvested in existing lines of business: A huge money and capital market builds up instead. Funds move into currency speculation and paper investment: *"stagflation"* results—a standstill in industrial investment, with money flowing into capital markets where returns are greater than in existing industries, but ceasing with rapid price inflation.

Mensch notes that satiated markets and stagflation are accompanied by a *"dinosaur effect"* because the largest companies are the least innovative. "Pseudo-innovations" are a device by which producers seek dominance over a market segment. Consumers' choices become more limited as production concentrates in a few oligopolies. Producers can maximize profits and keep prices increasing by eliminating price competition. The attempt is to secure the bastions of established producers, because diminishing returns in existing branches of industry first lead to capital being used to protect markets via pseudo-innovations/market segmentation

and acquisitions to limit competition. Mancur Olsen (see p. 283) sees such protectionism as the principal reason for the decline of nations.

7. The end result is a *technology stalemate* in which growth is replaced by stagnation, and in which large-scale organizations seek to maintain the appearance of growth by controlling output and raising prices, inducing stagflation—the apparently antithetical conditions of simultaneous recession and inflation—and then by the collapse of a depression. It is during this period that one sees increasing protectionism, yet it is overconcentration in leading industries that sets the price spiral into gear. Large-scale organizations that grow in the period of pseudo-innovation require and promote conservative patterns of investment: risk-taking in new ventures is minimized.

8. But as returns in older established industries are eliminated during stagflation and vanish in the ensuing depression, new *venture capital* becomes available, seeking high-growth investment opportunities. The appearance of venture capital at this time results in a rush of attempts to convert many of the speculative inventions that had appeared since the preceding period of basic innovation into useful techniques or products, that is, into a rush of basic innovations that precipitates another long-term growth upswing. During the upswing, dormant basic innovations will attract capital and, via entrepreneurship, begin to diffuse into economic use. Resulting new industries attract capital and labor from stagnant sectors, circumvent older resource scarcities, stimulate demand for new kinds of goods and services, and generally introduce the reinvigorating effects of a *structural transformation* of the economy.

This key idea that basic innovations produce structural changes in the economic system and drive the business cycle has, as we noted early, been most closely associated with the German economist Joseph Schumpeter, who wrote that the fundamental impulse that sets and keeps the capitalist engine in motion comes from the new consumers' goods, the new methods of production and transportation, the new markets, and the new forms of industrial organization that the capitalist enterprise creates.

Mensch's contribution was to identify the precise circumstances when these "fundamental impulses" occur. He noted that "they do not simply fall from heaven." What determines them is the degree of stagnation of old technologies and the attractiveness of new alternatives. Stagnation reduces the usefulness and profitability of labor and capital in overgrown traditional business fields and induces the implementation of cost-saving and product-adding innovations. Labor is displaced and older privileged groups lose self-confidence. Sociopolitical conflict increases, and a variety of groups look to revolutionary change in the period of temporary instability—not only innovators looking to profit from new ventures, but also radical political reformers, because conditions of instability offer the opportunity for talented individuals to circumvent established social and power structures. Meanwhile, existing governments are pressured to create jobs through new large-scale technologies with military or civilian applications or both. Conservatism and radicalism, arms races and New Deals, are products of their times, as are attitudes and lifestyles. The cycle appears to be approximately 50 years, or two generations; grandchildren thus think and act in ways more similar to their grandparents than to their parents!

Mancur Olsen on The Rise and Decline of Nations

Mancur Olsen argues that in societies that permit free trade and free organization, coalitions form around marketable goods and services. Groups of producers, like those who grow wheat or own oil, organize to protect their assets and, if possible, boost profits by raising prices. Physicians and lawyers do much the same in joining professional societies. Labor unions organize workers to bargain for wages.

In the early stages of this coalition-building process, there are relatively few interest groups, and their memberships are small compared to the society in which they operate. As they develop, they try to impose a variety of specialized rules on the economy that supports them. By law or collusive contract, they make penalties for those who would market the same goods or services outside the group. They also offer selective advantages to those who join and cooperate. Because these groups are small (Olsen says they typically include no more than 1 percent of the people in their state), they have no incentive to boost members' welfare by boosting the state's welfare. Instead, they concentrate on promoting their own narrow interests, even at the cost of retarding the general economy. A modest effort at self-aggrandizement may bring great rewards.

In time, tariffs, price supports, monopoly prices, wage guarantees, and business codes grow more numerous. All are intended to channel commerce into areas that benefit the special groups that fought for them. The combined effect is to create obstacles to trade and to prevent innovation. The economy suffers. In the past, nations suffering from this affliction have enjoyed renewed growth after a cataclysm has intervened to wipe out existing trade barriers, or when new territory has been opened for development. Sometimes the power of a domestic group is undercut by low-cost imports, if the imports are not blocked. Rarely has any nation abolished special-interest codes voluntarily.

Inflation may be a common symptom of nations in a sclerotic condition, because it offers a brief measure of relief from economic stagnation. Special-interest groups, being run by committee rule, generally maneuver slowly. For this reason, they cannot always adjust their demands upward as rapidly as the nominal value of goods and services increases. This is particularly true if inflation appears suddenly, without warning. Thus, inflation may be tolerated because it temporarily devalues the cost of products within the control of special interests. In time, this form of relief fails because the special interests soon catch up and raise their demands in pace with inflation.

In the contrary case, during periods of sudden price decline, the advantage held by interest groups is intensified. Those who operate outside the protection of a group may be forced to lower prices or wages. But the interest groups, again moving slowly, haggle over proposals while the storm rages around them. They may not reduce their demands until a recession has already damaged the economy. After a period of negotiation, they may begin to adjust, but by then investment in new projects will have been cut short, worsening the prospects for recovery. Thus, there is a real risk that the inflexibility of special-interest groups can lead in bad times to a vicious downward spiral.

Source: Mancur Olsen, *The Rise and Decline of Nations: Economic Growth, Stagflation, and Social Rigidities* (New Haven, Conn.: Yale University Press, 1982).

THE FIFTH WAVE: EMERGENCE OF THE THOUGHTWARE ECONOMY

Consider the characteristics of a technological stalemate: Old industries collapse and unemployment soars; stagnation is accompanied by rapid inflation; and then new venture capital becomes available, seeking high-growth investment opportunities in innovations that produce new industries, stimulating demand for new kinds of goods and services, and generally introducing the reinvigorating forces that promote a structural transformation of the economy. Are we on the verge of such a structural transformation? Certainly, the last decade has seen stagflation and recession and, throughout the industrial world, collapse of overbuilt basic industries such as steel and coal, shipbuilding, and the manufacturing of automobiles. But there also have been accompanying signs of the new: rapid growth of venture capital availability, and the emergence of new growth sectors. This section will deal with these indicators of an incipient fifth Kondratieff wave.

Growth of Venture Capital

Availability of venture capital has soared since the late 1970s in the United States, as Figure 11.2 reveals very clearly. Once restricted to a few families with immense personal wealth, the venture capital industry now has a wide variety of participants, both private and corporate. The funds that have become available have been of a variety of kinds, with each kind having its accompanying funding specialists:

1. EARLY-STAGE FINANCING
    a. *Seed financing*—a relatively small amount of capital provided to an investor or entrepreneur to prove a concept. It may involve product development but rarely involves initial marketing. This kind of investment is sometimes referred to as "adventure financing."
    b. *Start-up financing*—used for product development and initial marketing. Firms may be in the organizational process or in existence a short time (usually less than one year).
    c. *First-stage financing*—for companies that have expended their initial capital and require funds to initiate commercial production and sales.
2. EXPANSION FINANCING
    a. *Second-stage financing*—provides working capital for the initial expansion of a firm which is producing and shipping and has

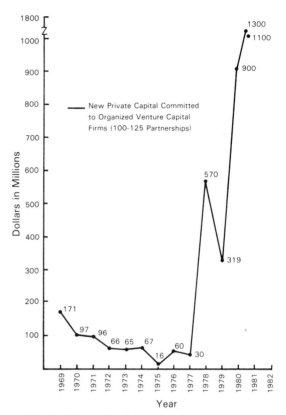

FIGURE 11.2 Funding and disbursements by the venture capital industry. [*Source:* Adapted from a figure developed by the Government Accounting Office from data provided by Venture Economics, Inc.]

growing accounts receivable and inventories. The firm may not yet be showing a profit.
    b. *Third-stage financing*—allows for the major expansion of a growing firm which is breaking even or profitable. These funds are utilized for plant expansion, marketing, working capital or further product development.
    c. *Fourth-stage (bridge) financing*—for a company expecting to go public or be bought out within six months to one year.
3. ACQUISITION/MANAGEMENT BUY-OUT FINANCING
    a. *Management-leveraged buyout*—funds to permit operating management to acquire a firm or division for the purpose of entrepreneurial expansion.
    b. *Acquisition.*

That this venture capital contributes to new economic development is now becoming abundantly clear. Recent research can be summarized as follows:

1. Venture capital stimulates the growth of small, innovative firms
    a. By providing long-term equity financing
        (1) Small, young, innovative firms need equity capital because their product development costs are relatively high and their capacity for asset-based debt is limited. Young firms may not be able to generate cash flow sufficient to support the amount of debt required.
        (2) Because their asset base is small and the risk involved with developing a new product is relatively high, traditional debt sources, such as banks, have demonstrated a reluctance to provide the amounts of debt that are needed.
        (3) Long-term financing allows the firm a margin for error if the product or processes takes longer to develop than anticipated. A reliable base of funds lowers the risk that initial setbacks will prove fatal to the firm, encouraging the entrepreneur to continue.
    b. By providing managerial assistance
        (1) Managerial deficiency is thought to be a leading cause of business failure.
2. Small, innovative firms are the leading sources of growth and change in an economy, because
    a. They are responsible for a disproportionate number of the new jobs created: 87 percent of all new private sector jobs created between 1969 and 1976 came from firms with fewer than 500 employees; 77 percent from firms with fewer than 50 employees; and 66 percent from firms with 20 or less employees (Table 11.3).

Nature of the Structural Transformation

The question then is: What kinds of industry will these new, innovative firms introduce? As the old manufacturing economies have collapsed, the principal contributor to employment growth has been the advanced services sector (Figure 11.3). Simultaneously, manufacturing is being transformed by the adoption of new technologies, revealed dramatically by the growth of America's positive trade balance in high-technology products with substantial research and development inputs, and the weakening trade position with respect to less "R & D intensive" products (Figure 11.4). This is, of course, a clear sign of the continued technological advance of the United States and the filtering of less

TABLE 11.3

Net new jobs created by size of firm, 1969–1976

Number of employees in each firm	Total New Jobs	
	Number	As percentage of total
20 or fewer	4,459,815	66.0
21–50	759,509	11.2
51–100	288,997	4.3
101–500	353,201	5.2
501 or more	897,381	13.3
Total	6,758,903	100.0

Source: D. L. Birch, "Who Produces the Jobs?," *The Public Interest,* Fall 1981.

technologically sophisticated products to other countries. We will examine these two cases of advanced services growth and high-technology manufacturing in turn.

The Growth of Advanced Services

The services that have been growing have not been services in the traditional sense at all, but central administrative activities, their supportive producer services, and health and education (Table 11.4). Their defining feature is that they are *creating and using knowledge-products* in exactly the way that manufacturing industry transformed raw materials into physical products. They are the driving forces of the modern "thoughtware" economy.

Figure 11.5 shows how the advanced services have grown in the United States since 1948, and Table 11.5 gives some indication of how one observer expects service industries to expand by the year 2000 in seven major industrial countries. Many observers believe these projections are conservative.

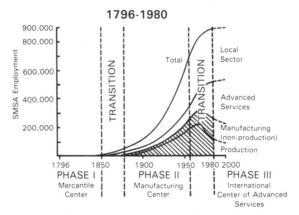

FIGURE 11.3 The evolution of the Cleveland economy. [*Source:* Richard V. Knight, *The Cleveland Economy in Transition* (Cleveland: Regional Development Program, Cleveland State University, 1977), p. 37.]

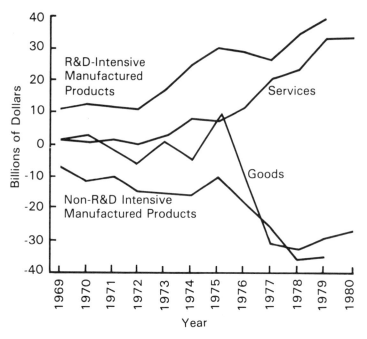

FIGURE 11.4 U.S. trade balance in R&D-intensive and non-R&D-intensive products and in goods and services, 1968–1980. [*Source: Science Indicators,* 1980, and "Barriers to U.S. Services Trade," Joan Spero, statement before the Subcommittee on International Finance and Monetary Policy of the Senate Committee on Banking, Housing and Urban Affairs, November 1981.]

TABLE 11.4

Advanced services sector

Industrial corporations[a]	Specialized technical and business service firms	Public and not-for-profit organizations
Corporate headquarters	Law	Federal agencies
Research and	Engineering	State agencies
development	Accounting	Universities
Regional offices	Finance	Musical arts
Divisional offices	Advertising	Hospitals and clinics
Computer center	Public Relations	Cancer center
Training centers	Insurance	Professional associations
	Seminars and conventions	Federal Reserve bank
	Communications	Museums
	Airlines	Consultants
	Consultants	
	Business information	

[a]Includes publishing and transportation.

TABLE 11.5

Percentage labor force distribution by industry sectors for seven industrialized countries, 1970, and projected to year 2000

Industry sectors	United States and Canada		England and West Germany		France and Italy		Japan	
	1970	*2000*	*1970*	*2000*	*1970*	*2000*	*1970*	*2000*
Extractive	7	5	5	4	19	10	20	5
Transformative	32	28	47	40	41	35	34	40
Traditional services	32	26	25	21	22	20	31	25
Advanced services	29	42	23	35	19	35	15	30

Source: Adapted from Singelmann, 1978, Table 5.3.

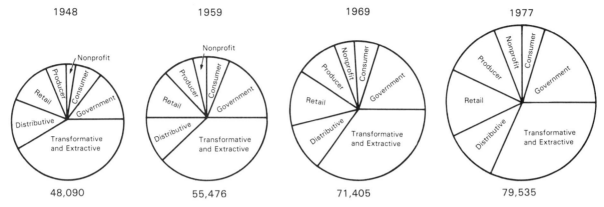

Number of Employees (thousands)

FIGURE 11.5 Percentage distribution of full-time-equivalent employees among industries, 1948–1977. The classifications of industry used in this figure are:

1. Extractive Industry
   Agriculture
   Mining
2. Transformative Industry
   Construction
   Manufacturing
3. Traditional Services
   a. Distribution
      Transport and communications
      Wholesale trade
   b. Retail Services
   c. Consumer Services
      Hotels and other lodging places
      Personal services
      Auto repair, services, and garages
      Miscellaneous repair services
      Motion pictures
      Amusements and recreation services
      Private households
4. Advanced Services
   a. Complex of Corporate Activities/Producer Series
      Central Administrative Office
      Producer Services
         Finance
         Insurance
         Real estate
         Business services
         Legal services
         Membership organizations
         Miscellaneous professional services
         Social services
   b. Nonprofit Services
      Health
      Education
   c. Government and Government Enterprises

[*Sources:* Adapted from Thomas M. Stanback, Jr., Peter J. Bearse, Thierry J. Noyelle, and Robert H. Karasek, *Services: The New Economy* (Totowa, N.J.: Allanheld, Osmun, 1981), p. 11; and J. Singelmann, *From Agriculture to Services* (Beverly Hills, Calif.: Sage, 1978), p. 31.]

A Revolution in Manufacturing: The U.S. Robotics Industry

The important feature of the growth of advanced services is that these activities are the sources of the knowledge-products that are, in turn, the bases of most of the productivity increase in U.S. manufacturing: technological innovation, better resource allocation, and better education (Figure 11.6).

They provide the "thoughtware" that permits business to be conducted more efficiently and effectively, bringing resource use closer to the theoretical maximum. They include research and development activities in the broadest sense of the term; management and management support; analysis; activities that seek to identify and reduce risk, to assure health and safety, to simplify products, to assure performance, and to increase both quality of product and of life.

The fruits of industry are in "high-tech": microprocessors, robots, genetic engineering, and space, together with better information processing and management built around computers and cheap electronic communicators. Let us look at the implications for further automation of manufacturing and examine the growth of the fledgling U.S. robotics industry as an example.

Particularly important is the growth of flexible manufacturing systems (FMS), which complete a process of factory automation that began back in the 1950s. First came numerically controlled machines according to coded instructions on paper or Mylar tape. Then came computer-aided design and computer-aided manufacturing, or CAD/CAM, which replaced the drafting board with the CRT screen and the numerically controlled tape with the computer (Table 11.6 summarizes the principal technologies).

The new systems integrate all these elements. They consist of computer-controlled machining centers that sculpt complicated metal parts at high speed and with great reliability, robots that handle the parts, and remotely guided carts that deliver materials. The components are linked by electronic controls that dictate what will happen at each stage of the manufacturing sequence, even automatically replacing worn-out or broken drill bits and other implements.

Measured against some of the machinery they replace, flexible manufacturing systems seem expensive. A full-scale system, encompassing computer controls, five or more machining centers, and the accompanying transfer robots, can cost $25 million. Even a rudimentary system built around a single ma-

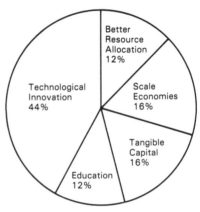

FIGURE 11.6   Contributions to U.S. productivity increases. [*Source:* The Brookings Institution.]

chine tool—say, a computer-controlled turning center—might cost about $325,000, whereas a conventional numerically controlled turning tool would cost only about $175,000.

But the direct comparison is a poor guide to the economies that flexible automation offers, even taking into account the phenomenal productivity gains and asset utilization rates that come with virtually nonhuman-operated round-the-clock operation. Because an FMS can be instantly reprogrammed to make new parts or products, a single system can replace several different conventional machining lines, yielding huge savings in capital investment, labor inputs, and plant size.

Flexible automation's greatest potential for radical change lies in its capacity to manufacture

TABLE 11.6

Principal programmable automation technologies

I. Computer-aided design (CAD)
   A. Computer-aided drafting
   B. Computer-aided engineering (CAE)

II. Computer-aided manufacturing (CAM)
   A. Robots
   B. Numerically controlled (NC) machine tools
   C. Flexible manufacturing systems (FMS)
   D. Automated materials handling (AMH) and automated storage and retrieval systems (AS/RS)

III. Tools and strategies for manufacturing management
   A. Computer-integrated manufacturing (CIM)
   B. Management information systems (MIS)
   C. Computer-aided planning (CAP) and computer-aided process planning (CAPP)

goods cheaply in small volumes. Ever since the era of Henry Ford, the unchallenged low-cost production system has been Detroit-style "hard automation" that stamps out look-alike parts in huge volume. There is little flexibility in hard automation's transfer lines, which get their name from the transfer of the product being worked on via a conveyor from one metalworking machine to another. But such mass production is shrinking in importance compared with "batch production" in lots of anywhere from several thousand to just one.

Seventy-five percent of all machined parts today are produced in batches of 50 or fewer. Many assembled products, which range from airplanes and tractors to office desks and large computers, are likewise made in batches. In the past, batch manufacturing required machines dedicated to a single task. These machines had to be either rebuilt or replaced at the time of product change. Flexible manufacturing brings a degree of diversity to manufacturing never before available. Different products can be made on the same line at will.

The strategic implications for the manufacturer are staggering. Under hard automation the greatest economies were realized only at the most massive scales. But flexible automation makes similar economies available at a wide range of scales. A flexible automation system can turn out a small batch or even a single copy of a product as efficiently as a production line designed to turn out a million identical items. Enthusiasts of flexible automation refer to this capability as *economy of scope.*

Economy of scope shatters the tenets of conventional manufacturing. The manufacturer will be able to meet a far greater array of market needs, including quick-changing ones—even the needs of markets the company is not in now. Manufacturers can keep up with changing fashions in the marketplace—or set them themselves by updating their products or launching new ones. Many more options are available for building a new plant: FMS frees manufacturers from the tyranny of large-scale investments in hard automation, thus allowing construction of smaller plants closer to markets.

Flexible manufacturing is the ultimate entrepreneurial system: It will allow fast-thinking manufacturers to move swiftly into brand new fields and to leave them just as swiftly if need be—at the expense of less agile and older producers.

Flexible manufacturing systems were developed in the United States more than 10 years ago by Cincinnati Milacron, Kearney & Trecker, and White Consolidated. The United States remains a world leader in the technology: The major machine tool builders are being joined by new suppliers with great financial resources and technical abilities, such as GE, Westinghouse, and Bendix. But the most rapid implementation of the technology is occurring in Japan.

As FMS expands, so will the production and use of *robots* (Figure 11.7). The age of robotics began in 1946 with the development of a general-purpose playback device for controlling machines developed by George Devol. Devol patented in 1954 the first manipulator with a playback memory that controlled movements from one point to subsequent points.

Two basic definitions of robotics are in common use in business and industry. A very narrow definition has been adopted by the Robot Institute of America (RIA) and is the definition used by most analysts and forecasters in the United States. According to this definition "a robot is a reprogrammable multifunctional manipulator designed to move material, parts, tools, or specialized devices through variable programmed motions for the performance of a va-

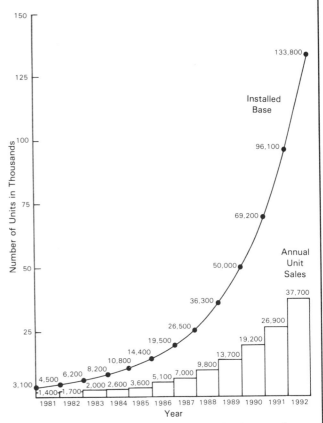

FIGURE 11.7   Actual and projected U.S. annual robot sales and installed base through 1992.

riety of tasks.'' The Japanese use a broader definition of robots, which partially accounts for the larger number of robots that are reported in use in Japanese industry. The Japanese Electrical Machinery Law of 1971 defines an industrial robot as an all-purpose machine, equipped with a memory device and a terminal device (for holding things) and capable of rotation and of replacing human labor by automatic performance of movements. By this definition, so-called pick-and-place robots are included in the Japanese inventory, but not in that of the United States. Table 11.7 provides the relevant definitions.

Table 11.8 presents the world robot population by type and country. The principal countries currently utilizing industrial robots are Japan, West Germany, France, and the United States. Robot use is broken down by type from the most sophisticated (A) to least sophisticated (E) devices. Japan has more robots in operation than any other country in the world, but many of these robots are mechanical transfer devices (pick-and-place), which are not considered robots under the more restricted U.S. definition. West Germany and France also have a large number of pick-and-place robots.

As benefits the early stages of a structural transformation, the infant U.S. robotics industry is at present highly competitive, dynamic, and diverse with respect to firm origins, types, and sizes. In 1983 alone, the number of firms in the industry increased from 46 to 67, and there were various acquisitions and mergers. The situation is so fluid that GMF, a joint venture between General Motors and Japan's

TABLE 11.7

Definitions and classifications of industrial robots

Japanese Industrial Standard
JIS BO134-1979

Manipulator: A device for handling objects as desired without touching with the hands and it has more than two of the motional capabilities such as revolution, out-in, up-down, right-left, travelling, swinging or bending, so that it can spatially transport an object by holding, adhering to, and so on.

Robot: A robot is defined as a mechanical system which has flexible motion functions analogous to the motion functions of living organisms or combines such motion functions with intelligent functions, and which acts in response to the human will. In this context, intelligent function means the ability to perform at least one of the following: judgment, recognition, adaptation or learning.

Classification by input information
and teaching method

Manual manipulator: A manipulator that is directly operated by a person.

Sequence robot: A manipulator, the working step of which operates sequentially in compliance with preset procedures, conditions, and positions.

Fixed sequence: A sequence robot as defined above, for which the preset information cannot be easily changed.

Variable sequence: A sequence robot as defined above for which the preset information can be easily changed.

Playback robot: A manipulator that can repeat any operation after being instructed by a person.

Numerically controlled robot: A manipulator that can execute the commanded operation in compliance with the numerically loaded working information on, for example, position sequence, and conditions.

Intelligent robot: A robot that can determine its own actions through its sensing and recognitive abilities.

U.S. view

INDUSTRIAL ROBOTS all have armlike projections and grippers that perform factory work customarily done by humans. The term is usually reserved for machines with some form of built-in control system and capable of stand-alone operation. But in Japan, it also includes manipulators operated by humans, either directly or remotely.

Classification by servo type
NONSERVO ROBOTS

A PICK-AND-PLACE ROBOT is the simplest version accounting for about one-third of all U.S. installations. The name comes from the usual application in materials handling, picking something from one spot and placing it at another. Freedom of movement is usually limited to two or three directions—in and out, left and right, and up and down. The control system is electromechanical. Prices range from $5,000 to $30,000.

A SERVO ROBOT is the most common industrial robot because it can include all robots described below. The name stems from one or more servo-mechanisms that enable the arm and gripper to alter direction in midair without having to trip a mechanical switch. Five to seven directional movements are common, depending on the number of ''joints'' or articulations in the robot's arm.

A PROGRAMMABLE ROBOT is a servo robot directed by a programmable controller that memorizes a sequence of arm-and-gripper movements; this routine can be repeated perpetually. The robot is reprogrammed by leading its gripper through the new task. The price range is $25,000 to $90,000.

A COMPUTERIZED ROBOT is a servo model run by a computer. The computer controller does not have to be taught by leading the arm-gripper through a routine; new instructions can be transmitted electronically. The programming for such ''smart'' robots may include the ability to optimize, or improve, its work-routine instructions. Prices start at about $35,000.

A SENSORY ROBOT is a computerized robot with one or more artificial senses, usually sight or touch. Prices for early models start at about $75,000.

AN ASSEMBLY ROBOT is a computerized robot, probably a sensory model, designed specifically for assembly-line jobs. For light, batch-manufacturing applications, the arm's design may be fairly anthropomorphic.

TABLE 11.8

World robot distribution, 1981

Country	A	B	C	D	A–D total	E	Total
Japan	—	6899	—	7347	14,246	53,189	67,435
United States[a]	400	2000	1500	200	4100	—	4100
West Germany	290	830	200	100	1420	10,000	11,420
France	120	500	2000	6000	8620	30,000	38,620
USSR	—	—	—	—	—	—	3000
Switzerland	10	40	—	—	50	8000	8050
Sweden	250	150	250	50	700	100	800
Norway	20	50	120	20	210	50	260
Czechoslovakia	150	50	100	30	330	200	530
United Kingdom	—	—	—	—	—	—	371
Poland	60	115	15	50	240	120	360
Denmark	11	25	30	0	66	110	176
Finland	35	16	43	22	116	51	167
Belgium	22	20	0	0	42	82	124
Netherlands	48	3	0	0	51	30	81
Yugoslavia	2	3	3	0	10	15	25
Total	1418	10,701	4293	13,819	33,572	101,947	135,519

Type A: programmable, servo-controlled, continuous path
Type B: programmable, servo-controlled, point-to-point
Type C: programmable, nonservo for general-purpose use
Type D: programmable, nonservo for diecasting and molding machines
Type E: mechanical transfer devices (pick-and-place)

Source: Robot Institute of America, 1981.

[a]Mechanical transfer devices not counted in the United States.

Fujitsu Fanuc established in 1982, had become one of the major manufacturers of robots for the automobile industry by 1984.

Table 11.9 shows the major U.S. robot manufacturers. They are divided between diversified manufacturing firms that produce robots as one of many products and firms that produce robots exclusively (note that some firms have received new venture capital and others are foreign subsidiaries). One source of growth has been within the existing machine tool and automobile industries. More recently, some of the major electronics manufacturers have been developing robots both for their internal manufacturing use and for sale to smaller manufacturers. An industry leader, Cincinnati Milacron, has its roots in the machine tool industry. The most prominent electrical manufacturing firms that have recently begun to produce robots are IBM, General Electric, Westinghouse, and Bendix. Many of the existing corporations began by producing robots for their own use, extending to external sales and to production of equipment peripheral to their main product line. Half a dozen represent new initiatives by foreign firms in the U.S. market.

Another source of growth has been new firms sponsored by venture capital. Well over a dozen new robotics firms have started up in the last few years and have captured small shares of the market, for example, Automatix, Advanced Robotics, and American Robot. Of these, some are spinoffs from universities, others are competitive spinoffs from existing firms, while others are either forward or backward spinoffs linked to existing firms. Some of these firms have already been acquired by corporate giants. Westinghouse recently purchased Unimation, an early industry leader, and Copperweld acquired Autoplace, a newer firm.

Table 11.10 presents the current robot producers ordered by sales and percentage market share in 1980, 1981, and 1982 and estimated for 1983 and 1984. The shares held by the market leaders were nearly identical in 1980 and 1981. Unimation had 44 percent, Cincinnati Milacron 32 percent, Prab Robot between 5 percent and 6 percent, and DeVilbiss between 4 percent and 5 percent of the market. By 1982, Unimation and Cincinnati Milacron, the two early industry leaders, had lost some of their share of the market, primarily to DeVilbiss and to relatively new entrants such as Automatix, Advanced Robotics, and Cybotech, a subsidiary of Renault. GMF Robotics entered in 1983 and immediately captured a 9.5 percent market share (expected to rise substantially in

TABLE 11.9

U.S. robot manufacturers

Diversified manufacturers	Robot manufacturers
Accumatic Machinery Corporation	Advanced Robotics Corporation[b]
Air Technical Industries	American Robot Corporation[b]
ASEA, Inc. (Sweden)[a]	Automatix, Inc.[b]
Bendix Corporation	Autoplace
Binks Manufacturing Company	(recently acquired by Copperweld)[b]
Cincinnati Milacron	Barrington Automation Ltd.[b]
Copperweld Robotics, Inc.	Control Automation, Inc.[b]
Cybotech Corporation	Cyclomatic Industries, Inc.
(Renault/Ransburg)	Everett/Charles Automation Modules,
DeVilbiss Company	Inc.
Gallaher Enterprises, Inc.	Intelledex, Inc.[b]
GCA Corporation	International Robomation[b]
GM-Fujitsu Fanuc	Mobot Corporation
GMF Robotics, Inc.	Nova Robotics, Inc.[b]
General Electric Company	Perceptron[b]
Hitachi America (Japan)[a]	Reis Machines, Inc.
IBM Corporation	Rhino Robots, Inc.
MTS Systems Corporation	Spadone Machine Co., Inc.
Nordson Corporation	Thermwood Corporation[b]
Positech Corporation	Unimation (acquired by Westinghouse)
Prab Robots, Inc.	United States Robots
Schrader-Bellows	(acquired by Square D)
Seiko Instruments, Inc. (Japan)[a]	
United Technologies	
Westinghouse Electric Corp.	
Yaskawa Electric America, Inc.	
(Japan)[a]	

[a]Foreign subsidiary.

[b]Identified as receiving new venture capital.

future years). The situation is so dynamic that the entry of other large companies and several new firms clearly could change the structure of the industry; however, although their current share of the market is still low, the enormous capital of such companies as GE, IBM, and Westinghouse will undoubtedly alter the industry and could lead to the absorption or demise of the smaller firms.

Currently, robot production appears to be concentrating close to user-industry markets. The majority of robotic firms' headquarters are located in the Midwest, most notably in the states of Michigan and Ohio. Midwestern firms have concentrated on applications of robots to metal forming and parts assembly, with similar emphasis on spray painting and finishing, plastic molding, welding, and machining. By contrast, robot firms in New England, the Mid-Atlantic states, and the West have concentrated on assembly and parts handling tasks and far less on metal forming. While many of these latter tasks have been electronics-related, it is not yet apparent if electronics application will begin to localize in one or sev-

eral centers. What is apparent is that the mix of applications is changing. Although the industry remains dominated today by automobile-related uses, material handling and processing applications in the manufacturing and electronic industries are expected to increase dramatically in the next decade.

Is it likely that the emerging U.S. robotics industry will become localized in one or more regions of the country that will repeat Silicon Valley's experience as an industrial seedbed? What will be the impact of robotics on the organization and location of user industries? To the extent that there is any coalescence of robot producers today, it is clearly user-industry related. Robotics firms have developed in the Midwest around the automobile and machine tool industries, whereas those in New England have coalesced around the electronic industry. The robotic firms with headquarters in the Mid-Atlantic states, in the West, and in the South followed a similar pattern of the New England robotic firms with a focus on electronic-related tasks. What all early signs point to is a classic type of market orientation of inter-

TABLE 11.10

Sales [market share] by U.S.-based robot vendors, 1980–1984
(dollars in millions, market shares in percents, calendar-year estimates)

Company	1980	1981	1982	1983P	1984PS
Unimation (Westinghouse)	40.0 [44.3]	66.0 [44.0]	63.0 [32.9]	37.5 [15.1]	33.0 [9.3]
Cincinnati Milacron	29.0 [32.2]	50.0 [32.2]	32.0 [16.7]	43.0 [17.1]	50.5 [14.3]
DeVilbiss	5.0[a] [5.5]	6.5[a] [4.2]	23.7[c] [12.4]	22.5[c] [9.1]	25.5
Prab Robots	5.5 [6.1]	8.2 [5.3]	12.5 [6.5]	12.5 [5.0]	18.0 [5.1]
ASEA Inc.	2.5 [2.8]	9.0 [5.8]	9.5 [5.0]	13.5 [5.4]	25.5 [7.2]
Advanced Robotics	1.7 [1.9]	0.8 [0.5]	6.6 [3.4]	—	11.5 [3.3]
Copperweld	1.5[b] [1.7]	1.5[b] [1.0]	—	—	—
Nordson	0.8 [0.9]	2.0 [1.3]	4.5 [2.4]	—	—
Mobot	0.8 [0.9]	—	—	—	—
Automatix	0.4[b] [0.4]	3.0[b] [1.9]	8.1[b] [4.2]	18[b] [7.2]	40.5[b] [11.5]
GMF Robotics	—	—	—	23.5 [9.5]	60.0[b]+ [17.0+]
IBM	—	—	4.5 [2.4]	11.0 [4.4]	20.5 [6.0]
GE	—	—	—	10.5[b] [4.2]	18.0[b] [6.0]
Cybotech	—	—	9.0 [4.7]	7.0 [2.8]	11.5 [3.3]
Thermwood	—	1.0 [NA]	—	—	—
GCA	—	—	—	—	11.5 [3.3]
Seiko	—	—	—	—	11.5 [3.3]
Other	3.0 [3.3]	4.6 [3.0]	18.0 [9.4]	50.0 [20.1]	—
Total	$90.0 [100]	$155.0 [100]	$190.0 [100]	$235-$265 [100]	—

Source: Prudential-Bache Securities, 9–18–83 Newsletter.

NA, Not available; P, Preliminary, some estimates are averages of source's range; S, Selected companies.

[a]Does not include sales by DeVilbiss Europe and thus somewhat understated.
[b]Includes sales of robots as well as vision systems.
[c]Includes sales by De Vilbiss Europe.

mediate capital goods production, akin to the machine tool industry that preceded robotics, led by major user corporations.

In turn, it is these major corporations who are the principal users, cementing the pattern of market orientation. The tendency has been noted in other cases. A study of the spread of computerized numerical control (CNC) systems among machinery manufacturers in the United States found that plants affiliated to multiplant firms showed higher rates of adoption than did single-plant firms. Moreover, adoption rates were highest in user industries in the industrial Midwest. They also noted significant regional differences in adoption rates among single-plant firms that were close to areas where the new technologies were developed.

There appear to be similar patterns of adoption and diffusion of industrial robots. The pattern of diffusion is structured by the organization of the robotics industry itself and by the capital- and knowledge-intensive character of robotics development. Some of the major electronic producers have extensive automation programs underway with an eye to improving quality control and reducing production costs. IBM, General Electric, and Westinghouse, to name only the largest, are redesigning products for automated assembly. As the technology becomes more routinized we can expect that it will be diffused down the industry hierarchy.

THE CHANGES SUMMARIZED

What should be clear by now is that we are in a period of major technological revolution—a fifth wave—that is transforming the ways we live and work. Essential to this transformation is *information*. What microelectronics does is to process, and eventually generate, information. What telecommunications does is to transmit information, with a growing complexity of interactive loops and feedbacks, at increasingly greater speed and at a lower cost. What the new media do is to disseminate information in a way potentially more and more decentralized and individualized. What automation does is to introduce preinformed devices in other activities. And what genetic engineering does is to decode the information system of the living matter to try to program it. Equally important is the fact that the outcome of the change is *process-oriented,* rather than *product-oriented. High technology* is not a particular technique but a form of production and organization that affects all spheres of activity by transforming their operation in order to achieve greater productivity or better performance, through increased knowledge of the process itself.

The new technologies are transforming economic geography because, first, the new industries are playing a major role in the rise and decline of regions, and second, because traditional location factors have been replaced by a new set of locational forces and choices. Out of recent research on the spatial behavior of the new industries, M. Castells (1985) has proposed a model of the location of high-tech manufacturing. Five characteristics are involved:

1. Because high-tech industries are science-based and knowledge-intensive, they need a close connection to major universities and research units as well as to a large pool of technical and scientific labor.

2. Given the dependence on government markets, particularly on the military and space programs, especially until the late 1960s, high-tech activities tend to cluster historically in regions where the military has established its testing sites.

3. High-tech companies are generally characterized by a strong antiunion feeling in their management, not so much because of traditional economic reasons, such as wages or benefits, but because of the fears of bureaucratization and slowness in an industry that requires constant flexibility and innovation. Thus, areas with a strong union tradition will tend to discourage high-tech location, all other elements being equal.

4. The risk (and promise) of investment in this new field requires the existence of venture capital in the region that is a function of both a high level of wealth and an entrepreneurial culture oriented toward nontraditional financial markets.

5. The process of production in high-tech in general, and in microelectronics in particular, is highly discrete and can be easily separated, in time and space, among its research and design, fabrication, assembly, and testing functions. Given the very different requirements of each function, especially for labor, it follows a hierarchical division of labor across space and the need for all activities to be located in a good position in a communications network.

Castells believes that this model explains high-tech location better than the vague opposition between the Snowbelt and the Sunbelt or the very subjective notion of the "quality of life." For instance, Santa Clara County (Silicon Valley) possesses all the five characteristics cited; the *second* high-tech nest (in spite of having been the first until the mid-1960s), Route 128 (Boston), has almost everything, *but* it was somewhat limited in development by its strong union influence and the lack of military settlements; Texas and Arizona occupy an intermediate position, largely due to the absence (until recently in Texas) of major research centers, and, to some extent, to the fact that their financial markets were less well structured than those in San Francisco or Boston; New York–New Jersey offers the counterexample of how the concentration of giants such as IBM or RCA could not generate a milieu of innovation outside the companies themselves in spite of such assets as Bell Laboratories, Princeton, Cold Spring Laboratory, and so on, the largest financial center in the world, and the proximity to the largest information market. The absence of the military factor and the prounion environment in New York were powerful obstacles to the development of a high-tech milieu, whereas the large firms, such as IBM, were actually quite happy in building their empire inward, in isolation from potential competition and in prevention of threatening spinoffs.

The current sprawl of high-tech activities, Castells continues, modifies the geography of their location, but not the logic of their spatial relationships. New high-tech centers have developed (in Southern California, North Carolina, Texas, Colorado, Utah, Washington State, Arizona, Pennsylvania, Florida, and Maryland) along with three complementary tendencies for the location of assembly lines: offshore production (Pacific rim, Mexico), isolated rural communities in the western United States (Oregon, Arizona, Colorado, Texas) and, recently, fully automated plants closer to the high-tech nests.

Going beyond Castells's scheme, research at the Fantus Company of Chicago, perhaps the major location research firm in America, provides additional insights into this spread. Fantus believes that locational determinants for high-tech plants are not static but fluid, depending on the developmental stage of the high-tech product. Three developmental steps are recognized: theory, product, and market.

Theory-driven firms are usually embryonic, involved in advanced theoretical research. These firms are at the advanced cutting edge of ideas, innovations, and inventions. For them, the key criteria for selecting a plant location are:

1. Availability of venture capital;
2. Ease of technological transfer;
3. Ease of start-up.

These are the classical forces in early industrial localization, as we saw in Chapter 7.

Product-driven firms are the second stage of high-technology development. At this stage the product is viable, but must be closely monitored for quality and must often be modified before sale. Companies at this stage employ a blend of research and manufacturing personnel. The location requirements are:

1. Availability of technicians and skilled workers;
2. Demonstrated high worker productivity;
3. Accessibility to theory-driven R & D facilities;
4. Attractive living conditions;
5. A favorable business climate, such as low business and personal taxes.

Market-driven facilities emerge as the product becomes routinized, imitators enter the market, and price competition enters the selling process. Location requirements for competitive facilities switch dramatically, emphasizing:

1. Cost, availability, and attitude of labor;
2. Cost, availability, and dependability of utilities;
3. Incentives, inducements, and exemptions.

Labor costs will rise to exceed 50 percent of all locationally variable costs at this stage, but where labor costs and available utilities are approximately the same, it is often special local inducements and giveaways that dictate the final locational choice.

The speed with which new innovations move from theory to product to competition is producing an increasingly fluid world economic geography.

TOPICS FOR DISCUSSION

1. What were the leading industrial sectors and the types of organizational change that characterized the first four Kondratieff cycles? In which regions did the changes occur first? What were the sequence and timing of the diffusion of the changes to other regions?
2. Why are clusters of innovations typically associated with the depths of depression in a technological stalemate?
3. What are the product cycle and the learning curve? How do they relate to concepts of industrial filtering?
4. What is the role of "thoughtware" in an advanced services economy?
5. How do locational choices of modern high-tech firms differ (if at all) from those of earlier industries whose seedbed was based on localization or urbanization economies?
6. What are the key differences likely to be in the long-run cost curves of traditional assembly-line industry and modern industries for which the economy of scope applies?

FURTHER READINGS

CASTELLS, MANUEL. "High Technology, Economic Restructuring, and the Urban-Regional Process in the United States." In *High Technology, Space and Society*, pp. 11–40. Edited by Manuel Castells. Beverly Hills, Calif.: Sage Publications, 1985.

FREEMAN, C. (Ed.). *Technological Innovation and Long Waves in World Economic Development*. London: Frances Pinter, 1984.

HALL, P., AND MARKUSEN, A. (Eds.). *Silicon Landscapes*. Boston: George Allen and Unwin, 1985.

KONDRATIEFF, N. D. "The Long Waves in Economic Life." *The Review of Economic Statistics*, 17 (1935), 105–115.

STANBACK, T. M., BEARSE, P. J., NOYELLE, T. J., AND KARASEK, R. A. *Services: The New Economy*. Totawa, N.J.: Allanheld and Osmun, 1981.

VAN DUIJN, J. J. *The Long Wave in Economic Life*. London: George Allen and Unwin, 1983.

VERNON, R. "International Investment and International Trade in the Product Cycle." *Quarterly Journal of Economics*, 80 (1966), 190–207.

CHAPTER 12

Theories
of International Trade

The growing interdependence of countries has meant an ever-increasing reliance upon the global system of international trade and locational decision making. Over a long period of time, theories have evolved in response to the need for a clearer understanding of these complex processes of international interaction. Modern trade theory holds that the types, quantities, and prices of goods traded among countries depend upon the relative amounts of the factors of production—land, labor, capital, and enterprise—with which those countries are endowed. These are the elements that determine the outcome of the interaction between supply and demand.

Citing the results of empirical studies, critics of contemporary trade theory have pointed to a number of weaknesses in this theory. In particular, they note the omission of certain features that are capable of substantially modifying the spatial pattern of commodity flows produced by the simple interaction of supply and demand. Chief among these missing items are two formidable barriers to trade: the time, effort, and cost of overcoming distance, and the intervention of sovereign governments in foreign economic affairs.

Although conventional theory explains the trade among countries in terms of factor endowments, the realization has grown that, in turn, trade has important effects upon the factors. The opening of trade may cause rents, interest, and wages to rise or fall, and it can alter the quantities of factors held by trading countries. Another recent discovery is the degree to which the factors—capital, enterprise, and labor—can move internationally, aided by the activities of multinational enterprises.

Objectives:

- to demonstrate the relationship between the location of production and the flow of goods, services, and factors of production among countries

- to trace the development of modern trade theory, to describe the various elements that help to explain international commodity flows, and to consider the criticisms of modern theory

- to examine the effects of distance and governmental intervention as barriers to international trade

- to show how the introduction of trade among countries alters the prices and quantities of the factors of production

INTERNATIONAL TRADE AND LOCATION

As the end of the twentieth century draws nearer, nations become increasingly interdependent. Contemporary standards of living call for such a variety of goods and draw upon a technology so complex that no country can by itself supply all the necessary ingredients; a retreat to self-sufficiency would so impoverish a people that no country would find such a course politically feasible. To supply its diverse needs, therefore, modern civilization relies increasingly on a global system of trade. The resulting international flows consist not only of commodities but also a great variety of services. Within the past quarter-century a growing volume of capital, technology, and management has also followed these international movements of goods and services. Trade among countries has thus laid the basis for an internationalization of the locational decision-making process.

That trade is indeed intimately bound up with the location of production and consumption was noted by Alfred Weber and later developed theoretically by Bertil Ohlin in his book *Interregional and International Trade* (1933, 1952). As Walter Isard stated later, "Location and trade are as the two sides of the same coin. The forces determining one simultaneously determine the other."

For a variety of reasons, in this chapter we emphasize international rather than domestic trade. First, it will enable us to discuss the role that national governments play in determining or controlling their foreign trade flows, and thereby influencing the international location of production. Whereas both international trade and domestic trade take place for many of the same reasons, governments do not interfere with their internal commerce to the same degree. Furthermore, although conditions of doing business within a country tend to be fairly uniform from one place to another, this is not usually true between countries. National governments often differ in their fiscal policies and in their systems of subsidies and taxes. Legal frameworks vary in such important matters as the rights, liabilities, and obligations of firms and individuals. Countries differ in their social and cultural environments, which in turn significantly affect the nature of their production, consumption, and commerce. The existence of such differences among countries has contributed to the large amount of theoretical literature on the international aspects of trade.

Theories of international trade have evolved in response to an effort to gain a better understanding of the basic forces at work in this complex form of spatial interaction. By classifying the various parts of the international system into meaningful categories and studying their interrelationships, theorists have sought to interpret their functions and predict the consequences of any changes that may be introduced. We begin by examining the way in which the existing body of theory came into being.

EVOLUTION OF TRADE THEORY

International trade theory emerged as an independent body of thought at a very early date. Although this theory arose initially in response to specific practical needs of the times, it has subsequently reached high levels of abstraction. In large measure the character of the trade theory we have inherited reflects the way in which it has evolved, particularly in its form and emphasis.

It is customary to separate the history of international trade theory into three or four periods. The first is the preclassical or *mercantilist* era, which followed the Middle Ages and reached its zenith within about a century prior to the 1750s. Mercantilism did not actually attain the status of a true theory, however. The beginnings of trade theory as we know it today came with the *classical* period, which appeared coincidentally with the English Industrial Revolution in the middle of the eighteenth century and continued for at least another 150 years. Contemporary trade theory, or the *modern* period, has formed during this present century and has largely superseded the more simplistic notions of earlier eras, although some of the ideas of mercantilism and of the classical period persist in some national policies even today.

Mercantilism

Those who wrote on trade topics during the mercantilist era were mainly political pamphleteers who were less concerned with producing theory than with promoting policies of national self-interest. This economic nationalism was a natural element of a period when strong central governments were forming. These writings fall within a number of distinct national groupings and cannot be generalized very satisfactorily, but the various mercantilist policies share certain common features.

First, the mercantilists considered it essential that a country's merchandise exports exceed its imports, thereby producing a "favorable" balance of trade, that is, one that would contribute a surplus of money or gold to the royal treasury. Second, they emphasized foreign trade rather than domestic trade, manufacturing rather than agriculture, and the desirability of plentiful cheap labor. They favored manufacturing because it could support a denser population and because its output yielded exports of higher value. They regarded a large population of low-wage labor to be a source of national strength. Finally, the mercantilists promoted the use of various administrative measures by which countries could enforce these aims. Despite their antiquity, many of these notions sound surprisingly contemporary: Even today many national policies are at least implicitly mercantilistic. Although modern trade theory emphatically rejects most mercantilist ideas, it continues to stress the *normative:* that which ought to be.

Classical Theory

The classical period was an era of brilliant theorists, such as Adam Smith and David Ricardo, who reacted sharply to the errors and excesses of the mercantilist philosophy. The basic normative premise of classical theory was that free trade is beneficial to all trading partners. The questions raised by classical theorists were these: Why is international trade mutually advantageous? What determines the goods to be exchanged? What decides the amounts of goods to be traded (and thus the international price level)? The emphasis, therefore, was on the gains from trade. Trade among countries, these writers argued, results in an increased international specialization of production, a division of labor like that which accompanies domestic trade. To measure the effects of trade, classical theorists developed the *labor theory of value.* This was the notion that all costs can be reduced ultimately to units of labor, which in turn are directly related to the prices that must be charged for the products.

Throughout the nineteenth century and during the early years of the twentieth century, theorists continued to refine classical theory. Near the close of the classical era a number of new concepts and analytic techniques appeared, giving rise to what is sometimes called the *neoclassical* period.

Modern Theory

Modern theory began to take form with the appearance in 1933 of Bertil Ohlin's work *Interregional and International Trade.* Ohlin abandoned the classical labor theory of value, replacing it with a new theory that acknowledged the effects of all factors of production—land, labor, capital, and management—as determinants of international trade. Further extending the earlier ideas of Eli Heckscher, Ohlin based his work upon these premises: (1) countries differ in their proportions of factors, that is, their *factor endowments,* and (2) commodities differ in the combinations of factors they require in their production, that is, in their *factor intensities.* Assuming that factor intensities of particular commodities remain the same in different countries, the

Heckscher-Ohlin model states that each country will export those goods whose production is relatively intensive in the country's abundant factor and import those that are intensive in the factors it lacks. Thus Hong Kong, Taiwan, and South Korea all have large supplies of cheap labor and export labor-intensive goods such as low-priced shoes, garments, and small appliances. The Swiss, with much capital and skilled labor but little land, produce and export watches and scientific instruments. Having vast land resources, Canada exports primary goods such as wood pulp, paper, potash, and wheat to a greater extent than do most industrialized countries. At the same time, land-short Hong Kong and Switzerland import raw materials and foodstuffs, whereas Canada tends to import goods that are intensive in labor and capital. It is from the perspective of modern theory that we examine some of the basic elements of trade theory and see how these operate in world commodity trade.

THE DETERMINANTS OF TRADE

Geographers' efforts to understand better the form and nature of trade flows raise issues that have been central to trade theory ever since the classical era. The most basic question is why trade should occur at all. An obvious answer would be that trade serves to reconcile limited productive capacities with widely ranging needs and wants. The solution is not as simple as this would imply, however, nor are the gains from the exchange of goods the only benefits enjoyed by participants in trade. Pursuing this idea further will also help us to find out what commodities will be traded and in what quantities, and who will do the trading. In addition to the bases for trade, therefore, we shall be looking at its structure and its direction of movement.

The forces affecting trade fall into two broad classes. Under the ideal conditions assumed by classical theorists the principal determinants of trade are those relating to supply and demand. In reality, however, other influences distort the ideal pattern by acting as impediments to trade. The latter make trade more difficult, or even impossible, at the same time altering the commodity mix and price structure. It is mainly because of this second group of influences that international trade is more complicated than interregional trade.

Comparative Advantage

To isolate the effects of demand and supply conditions upon trade, we begin with a set of simplifying assumptions; later we can relax these as we consider other elements that influence trade. Let us assume (1) that no transport costs are required to move goods among countries, (2) that no artificial barriers to trade (such as governments might impose) exist among countries, (3) that the factors of production in each country are homogeneous (have identical characteristics throughout), (4) that perfect competition exists, (5) that production technology is identical among countries, and (6) that no international movement of factors of production (labor, capital, and so forth) can take place. Given these conditions, the Heckscher-Ohlin theory holds that countries can benefit from trade if they differ in their factor proportions (and, hence, differ in their abilities to produce particular goods), if they have unlike patterns of consumption, or if they vary in both of these respects. What, then, is the basis for reconciling these differences through trade?

The theoretical answer to this question is given by the principle of relative costs, or, as Ricardo termed it, the *law of comparative advantage*. It is obvious that if country A can produce corn more cheaply than can country B, and thus has an *absolute advantage*, country A has a basis for selling its surplus corn to country B and perhaps importing barley in its place. If, however, country A has no such absolute cost advantage, does this mean that trade cannot beneficially take place? The law of comparative advantage tells us that the two countries can indeed gain from trade even if country A is less efficient in producing both corn and wheat as long as country A can grow corn (or wheat) *relatively* more cheaply than can country B. The key word here is *relatively*, as the following example demonstrates.

Take two countries, France and Germany, that are isolated from the rest of the world and as yet have no commercial relations with each other. Both produce and consume the same two commodities, potatoes and wheat, devoting all of their land, labor, capital, and management resources to this effort. As Table 12.1 shows, France would be capable of producing 90 units of potatoes if all her factors of production were devoted entirely to this crop; alternatively, she could use these same resources to produce 60 units of wheat. This implies, of course, that French resources are better suited to potatoes than to wheat. As long as there is no trade

with Germany, the two goods are exchanged domestically within France at the rate of 1½ units of potatoes for 1 unit of wheat, or, conversely, ⅔ unit of wheat for 1 unit of potatoes. Thus, in France wheat has the higher price of the two commodities because it is more costly to produce and hence scarcer. Figure 12.1a shows all of the possible combinations of potatoes and wheat that the country is capable of producing. The French production possibilities curve, *YT*, ranges from the extreme case where all resources are allocated to potatoes, *Y*, to the other extreme, *T*, where everything is put into wheat. Between these two extremes of specialization lie the various other possible combinations of these two crops. In the example given here, the French have chosen to produce and consume the combination of potatoes and wheat given by point *M* in Figure 12.1a. This amounts

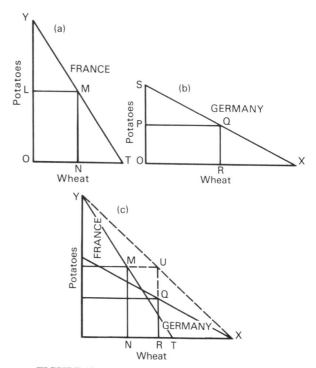

FIGURE 12.1 Production possibilities of France and Germany, exchange possibilities, and gains from trade.

TABLE 12.1

Production possibilities, domestic exchange ratios, and production and consumption of potatoes and wheat in France and Germany before trade

	Production possibilities		Domestic exchange ratios		Production and consumption		
	Potatoes	Wheat	Potatoes/wheat	Wheat/potatoes	Potatoes	Wheat	Total
France	90	60	1.50	0.67	45	30	75
Germany	50	100	0.50	2.00	25	50	75
Total	140	160			70	80	150

to 45 units of potatoes and 30 units of wheat (see Table 12.1).

In Germany the cost relationships are just the reverse. If the Germans were to specialize completely in potatoes they would be able to grow only 50 units, whereas they could use those same resources to produce a total of 100 units of wheat (Table 12.1). In the absence of foreign trade, therefore, the Germans would exchange 0.5 unit of potatoes for 1 unit of wheat or 2 units of wheat for 1 unit of potatoes (Table 12.1). By comparison with France, therefore, Germany has an advantage in the growing of wheat and a disadvantage in growing potatoes. Figure 12.1b shows the full range of possibilities for German production. It is also apparent from the drawing that the Germans have elected to produce and consume potatoes and wheat in the proportions given by point *Q*, that is, 25 units of potatoes and 50 units of wheat.

As trade opens between the countries, the French discover that they can receive up to 2 units of wheat in Germany for every unit of their potatoes that they sell there instead of the ⅔ unit to which they have been accustomed at home. The Germans, on the other hand, learn that in France they can get up to 1½ units of potatoes for 1 unit of wheat as opposed to merely ½ unit in their own country. The ensuing trade benefits both countries as French potatoes move eastward into Germany and wheat makes the return journey westward. So beneficial is this exchange that French farmers begin to specialize in potato production and transfer their resources out of wheat; conversely, German farmers turn their emphasis to wheat at the expense of potatoes. Obviously, the initial exchange ratios for potatoes and wheat do not last long after trade begins and as specialization increases.

Ultimately, specialization becomes complete and trade closes the gap in prices entirely. France allocates all her resources to potatoes (*OY* in Figure 12.1c) and supplies this commodity to consumers of both countries; Germany puts all her productive capacity into wheat (*OX* in Figure 12.1c) and shares the output with France. Figure 12.1c also gives us the final *equilibrium* price at which the potato-wheat trade takes place between the countries. The *international exchange ratio* (Table 12.2) is given by

$$\frac{OY}{OX} = \frac{90}{100} = 0.90$$

Thus, a unit of wheat exchanges for 0.90 units of potatoes. This ratio is often called the *international terms of trade.* The dashed diagonal line, *YX,* in Figure 12.1c is the *exchange possibilities curve,* which indicates all the various proportions of potatoes and wheat that are now available to the French and Germans at this new combined level of production.

The two countries are now using their productive resources to full efficiency. The beneficial effects of this are apparent from a comparison of Tables 12.1 and 12.2, where we see that total potato output (all contributed by France) is now 90 units (Table 12.2), whereas the combined output of the two countries had formerly been only 70 units (Table 12.1). Likewise, total wheat output has gone from 80 units (Table 12.1) to 100 (all produced by Germany, Table 12.2). Of the 90 units of potatoes produced by France, domestic consumption continues to take 45 units and exports to Germany take the remaining 45 units. Germany concentrates all her resources in wheat production, retaining 50 units for her own consumption and supplying the other 50 units to

TABLE 12.2

International exchange possibilities, international exchange ratios, and production, exports, imports, and consumption of potatoes and wheat in France and Germany after trade

		International exchange possibilities		International exchange ratio	
		Potatoes	Wheat	Potatoes/wheat	Wheat/potatoes
	France	90	100	0.90	1.11
	Germany	90	100	0.90	1.11

	Production, Trade, and Consumption								
	Potatoes				Wheat				Total consumption
	Production	Exports	Imports	Consumption	Production	Exports	Imports	Consumption	
France	90	45	—	45	—	—	50	50	95
Germany	—	—	45	45	100	50	—	50	95
Total	90	45	45	90	100	50	50	100	190

France (Table 12.2). Total consumption in the two countries thus rises as a result of this exchange. By importing wheat from Germany instead of producing her own on lands not well suited to this crop, France is able to increase wheat consumption from 30 units (Table 12.1) to 50 (Table 12.2). Similarly, Germany can raise consumption of potatoes from 25 units to 45. Hence, international specialization and trade have raised consumer welfare in both countries.

Up to this point we have been assuming that the structure of demand is the same in both countries, that French and German consumers want potatoes and wheat in the same proportions. But are French consumers really content to continue consuming the same amount of potatoes as before, and do they actually want all that wheat that is coming from Germany? And are the Germans satisfied to consume potatoes and wheat in the same proportions as the French? It is very possible that the citizens of these two nations have different structures of demand. Over the centuries each population may have grown accustomed to its traditional diet and now merely wants more of each commodity.

Figure 12.2 shows the possible effects of such contrasting consumer preferences. Note that even in this case consumer welfare rises with the introduction of trade and specialization. Let us say that the actual demand patterns of the two countries are as shown by the families of *indifference curves* appearing in Figure 12.2, French consumption being given by those curves labeled I_F and German consumption by those labeled I_G. The indifference curves indicate the various proportions in which the French or German consumers are willing to substitute potatoes for wheat or vice versa. Each curve corresponds to a given level of consumption in a country. Thus I^0 refers to one level, I^1 to the next higher

level, and I^2 to a higher level yet. Clearly a people will wish to reach the highest curve possible, thereby raising the standard of living. The point where an indifference curve is tangent with the production possibilities curve indicates the actual quantities of the two commodities consumed prior to the opening of trade. M represents the amounts consumed before trade by France and Q the amounts consumed by Germany.

After trade, consumption shifts upward to the point where some higher indifference curve becomes tangent with the exchange possibilities curve. In Figure 12.2 the advent of trade causes France's consumption to move from M to M' on the next higher indifference curve (from curve I_F^0 to I_F^1). Thus, trade makes it possible for the French to consume OL' potatoes instead of OL and ON' wheat instead of ON. German consumption likewise moves up from Q to Q' (from indifference curve I_G^0 to I_G^1). Germany is then able to increase her consumption of potatoes from OP to OP' and her consumption of wheat from OR to OR'. Thus, trade permits both countries to attain greater consumer satisfaction.

Complete specialization of the kind described here is uncommon in the real world, although several less-developed countries come close to it. One reason that specialization does not reach its ultimate limits is the tendency for unit production costs to begin increasing after a certain level of inputs is reached. Underlying our discussion thus far has been the assumption that unit costs remain constant at all levels of production, as suggested by the linear shape of the production possibilities curves in Figure 12.1 and Figure 12.2. This is not realistic: Under normal conditions we would expect unit costs to increase. Figure 12.3 shows the effect of increasing costs on the production possibilities of France and Germany. As the limits of efficiency are approached for either type of farming, the application of additional resources yields diminishing returns, and output declines as a consequence. This results from the fact that rarely are all of a country's resources equally

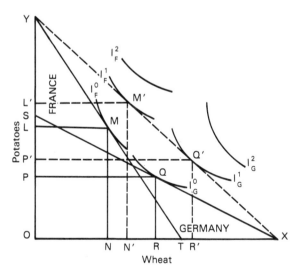

FIGURE 12.2 Gains from trade: different demand structures.

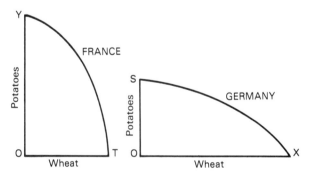

FIGURE 12.3 Effects of increasing costs upon production possibilities curves.

suited to a particular line of production. As farmers allocate new resources to wheat or potatoes, they eventually reach a point where each additional new unit of input (machinery, fertilizer, labor) no longer yields a proportionate gain in output. In the present example, therefore, it is likely that France will continue to grow small amounts of her own wheat and that Germany will not entirely give up potato production.

The introduction of trade between countries with different production possibilities theoretically leads to a number of desirable results for the participating parties. These benefits are of two kinds: (1) those that stem from the exchange of goods in and of itself, and (2) those that result from the international specialization of production that trade causes.

The preceding discussion has revealed some of the first type of gains, those from trade per se. As Figures 12.1, 12.2, and 12.3 demonstrated, the introduction of trade permits a country to adjust its commodity mix in such a way as to move its population to a higher level of consumption than was possible in isolation. Because of trade, therefore, the production pattern no longer needs to coincide with the consumption pattern.

Over and above these first benefits, however, trade confers a second set of gains. The increased specialization of production that follows trade offers important opportunities for more efficient production, for a greater output from each unit of resources. If the inhabitants of a country concentrate their efforts upon producing a limited number of goods, they are able to use more effectively those skills and resources that are best adapted to the purpose. Then, as they continue to accumulate experience along these lines, they acquire new and even greater skills. A fertile environment for invention and innovation arises as research and development come to focus along narrow channels and as specialists in the field live and work in close association with one another.

Business enterprises gain in competitive strength from operating in such a climate. These benefits are both *internal* and *external,* as was seen in Chapter 7. Among the internal benefits are economies of large-scale production: more efficient use of machines and workers, lower prices for raw materials purchased in bulk, reduced transport rates for assembling materials and distributing products in large quantities, and lower unit operating costs as a result of spreading output over longer model runs. The external economies enjoyed by businesses located in an area of specialization include the opportunities to share ideas and information with others engaged in the same type of production and the access to a large pool of labor with the requisite skills. Important also is the availability of many specialized facilities. These may consist of auxiliary or related industries with which a company has direct ties, such as those that link steel mills with suppliers of fire bricks for lining furnaces or with customers who use steel in fabricating bridges. Such areas of concentration often acquire a variety of specialized service agencies. Associated with the cotton textile industry, for example, are cotton brokerage and exchange activities as well as banking and insurance firms having a knowledge of the peculiar needs and problems of that trade.

In this way areal specialization further enhances a country's initial comparative advantage. Once it has gained sufficient momentum, the specialized area increases its competitive edge over other areas that might wish to enter the market. Indeed, even if it had previously possessed no resource advantage at all and had merely developed its specialty through historical accident, the area might have acquired a comparative advantage by reason of the kinds of economies described here. Such considerations help to explain the existence of many industrial concentrations around the world whose original reason for location may now have vanished. Examples are Britain's clay products industry at Stoke-on-Trent, France's textile manufacturing in Le Nord, and the U.S. optical instrument specialization at Rochester, New York.

In sum, if trade is truly free, it should result in optimal use of the world's resources through greater efficiency and thus smaller resource use per unit of output. This means that the world would produce a greater supply of goods from the same resource base, thereby raising standards of living generally.

Effects of Supply Conditions

We have seen that comparative advantages arising from differences in production cost can provide the bases for profitable trade among countries. This raises a further question: How do particular combinations of natural and human assets affect the ability of countries to produce and compete in the international marketplace? These resource endowments can be grouped into four categories, referred to as factors of production—*land, labor, capital,* and *management*—which interact in a variety of ways. As we examine these, we shall emphasize two related aspects: (1) the factor requirements of particular industries and (2) the ways in which countries differ in their possession of these factors.

Factor Proportions and Intensity

All four factors of production enter into every type of commercial production, whether it be farming, mining, manufacturing, or any other economic activity, although different activities may require these factors in varying proportions. Most primary activities, such as farming or forestry, make heavy demands on the factor of land are thus said to be *land-intensive*. Some types of manufacturing, such as cotton textiles, need much labor; other industries, such as oil refining, need much capital and relatively little labor. Thus, *factor intensity* differs widely from one type of production to another.

In many economic activities it is possible, within limits, to substitute one factor for another. In agriculture, labor and capital (in the form of equipment or fertilizer) can usually be applied to a unit of land in varying proportions. Manufactured goods, in many cases, can be made either by hand or by machine; in the latter case, capital is substituted for labor. Sometimes, however, the factors of production occur in forms that are so specialized in their applicability that they are difficult to shift out of one use into another. This is true of certain kinds of land. For instance, acidic soils good for growing potatoes or blueberries would be poor for wheat, which requires alkaline soils.

Even labor may be difficult to transfer from one activity to another, especially if the skill requirements differ greatly. Quick shifts of labor are often difficult to effect because workers may be reluctant to learn new skills or may be incapable of being retrained. A farm worker could not immediately gain employment as a petroleum chemist, and a lathe operator could not quickly go to work as a crane operator or dairy farmer. Even some forms of fixed capital are highly specific. It would hardly be feasible, for instance, to convert an oil refinery to the manufacture of textiles. In all cases, time is the important element: Factors that cannot be shifted instantaneously to other uses may be converted over longer periods. This is especially true of labor, which, given a sufficient number of years, may be able to acquire new skills.

Scale of operations is still another consideration in determining the allocation of factors. A combination of factors appropriate at a low level of production may not be suitable at a higher level. This is apparent in two contrasting forms of European agriculture. Peasant farming, still found in the more isolated parts of France, Germany, Switzerland, and certain other countries, generally takes place on very small holdings with scattered, fragmented fields. Because large farm machinery would be useless in such limited space, peasant agriculture is labor-intensive. On the other hand, though they may produce the same crops as the peasant farms, commercial agricultural enterprises in Europe have large acreages and big fields suitable for mechanization and have thus become capital-intensive. Likewise, a given type of manufacturing activity may take place in small, labor-intensive establishments, or it may occupy large plants employing labor-saving machinery and mass-

production methods. The same company may be labor-intensive during its formative years and then become capital-intensive as the firm grows and matures.

The factors of production are present in different countries in widely varying proportions. Australia and Canada occupy large land areas containing immense, diverse stores of natural resources, but they have comparatively small populations to go along with those resources. Both countries therefore lack the supplies of labor, capital, and entrepreneurship necessary to exploit fully their natural endowments. At the other extreme are Belgium, Switzerland, and several other small European countries with well-developed capital markets, relatively large pools of skilled labor, and an abundance of experienced managerial talent but lacking sufficient natural resources to match these superior human resources. Several less-developed countries—India and Pakistan, for example—are oversupplied with workers, most of them uneducated and untrained; yet these countries lack the capital and managerial requirements for putting their masses to productive activity. What are the trade effects of these factors of production?

Land as a Factor

The quantity and characteristics of *land* have much to do with determining the size and nature of world trade flows. By land we mean the territory of a country, region, district, or other areal unit, together with its particular attributes. The properties of land of particular interest are its physical resources that are useful to human beings. A significant aspect of these resources as they relate to trade is that they are distributed throughout the world in a most uneven fashion (see Chapter 5). For this reason the resources of most countries are "skewed," that is, these countries may have large stores of some resources—perhaps more than they can use domestically—but inadequate supplies of many others.

Mineral resources are distributed in a particularly erratic manner. Only a few of the metallic minerals, such as iron ore, are abundant in the earth's crust and found in many places; yet even these common minerals are concentrated in commercial quantities in a limited number of areas. This resource skewness is partly responsible for the voluminous and growing interregional and international trade in minerals. Much of the world's ocean tonnage is engaged in transporting oil from Venezuela, North Africa, and the Middle East to Western Europe, Japan, and the United States.

Biotic resources are spread inequitably too, partly because of climatic and other physical reasons but also because of the destructiveness of human beings. Today the forested areas of the Pacific Northwest of Canada and the United States, together with northern Ontario and Quebec, send their wood products to the more populous parts of North America. Large flows of these commodities also converge upon central and Western Europe from Scandinavia and the USSR. At the same time, tropical hardwoods move from equatorial regions to industrialized areas of the temperate latitudes.

The widespread trade in agricultural commodities clearly reflects world variations in *climates, soils,* and *relief.* The Mediterranean basin and similar areas in California and elsewhere are able, by reason of their long growing seasons, to specialize in growing fruits and winter vegetables for populations in colder areas thousands of miles away. The agricultural commodities that enter world trade in the largest volumes are the temperate-land grains, particularly wheat, which are exchanged for the sugar and tropical fruits of warmer areas. One of the most prominent characteristics of the wheat trade, however, is its unpredictability from one year to the next. This results mainly from the variability of harvests in the leading wheat-growing areas, where rainfall patterns are very uncertain. Thus, although the USSR is the world's leading wheat producer in most years, it must import enormous quantities of grain during periods of crop failure.

Differences in soils likewise affect world trade, for many crops such as grapes, tea, and sugar cane have exacting requirements. Regions with special kinds of soils, such as the Lake Okeechobee district of southern Florida, produce large quantities of vegetables for export. Another attribute of land is its physical relief. Regions with great expanses of low-lying, level terrain often produce and export foodstuffs to mountainous areas unable to grow sufficient quantities of food for themselves. The exchanges of The Netherlands and Denmark with the Alpine countries of Austria and Switzerland illustrate this element in the world food trade. On the other hand, the scenic beauty of the Alpine lands attracts thousands of freely spending tourists, who contribute ample amounts of foreign exchange to pay for the needed food imports.

The patterns of commodity movements described here are continually changing. One reason for this is the dynamic nature of physical resources; even the view of what constitutes a resource changes over time (see Chapter 5). Technology can greatly alter the production and trade of land-intensive goods, and the discovery of new resources may reshape world trade patterns, as occurred with the oil discoveries in Alaska, beneath the North Sea, and in Mexico. Resources can become exhausted, too. Witness the worn-out cotton lands of the southern United States and the depleted reserves of high-grade iron ore in the Lake Superior region. Shifts in trade flows have followed each of these events.

The *physical dimensions* of countries affect world

trade in many ways. Obviously, the larger the country the more likely that it will have a wide range and ample supply of resources and, therefore, a more diversified output of goods. Thus, the United States and the USSR are more nearly self-sufficient than are smaller countries, and their dependence upon foreign trade is correspondingly less. Because of the size of its economy the United States is the largest single trading country, but it usually exports no more than 8 percent of its gross national product. By contrast, The Netherlands, which is only slightly larger than Massachusetts, exports from 35 percent to 40 percent of its total output. A small country is also less likely to produce goods in sufficient quantity to influence international terms of trade, and it must therefore accept whatever prices world markets dictate for its goods.

Even the *shapes* of countries can affect their trade, especially in agricultural commodities. If a country's growing areas have a greater north-south extent, they will experience a wider climatic variation and thus yield a wider variety of farm products. Because Canada's agricultural lands are confined to a long narrow strip extending east-west just north of the United States border, they are able to grow only a limited number of temperate-land crops. Long borders between countries, however, are conducive to trade. Thus, whereas Ontario relies mainly upon coal imported from the nearby eastern coalfields of the United States, British Columbia in the far west supplies that same fuel to the adjacent Pacific states of the United States. One of the prime physical attributes of a country is its relative location, a matter so central to the topic of international trade that we shall be treating it separately later.

It should be stressed again that neither land nor any other factor of production is sufficient of itself; all the factors are required in some combination for every economic undertaking. Land becomes economically useful only when capital, labor, and management are applied to it. We have seen that such land-rich countries as Canada are unable to make full use of their physical resource endowments when they lack adequate supplies of the complementary factors. This case also demonstrates the fact that physical extent alone is not an accurate indicator of a country's economic size. Note that this imbalance in the factors of production tends to have a trade-creating effect for Canada, which exports large quantities of land-intensive commodities that a larger economy would absorb internally.

Labor as a Factor

Historically, the factor that most interested theorists was *labor.* Indeed, they originally posed the law of comparative advantage in terms of the labor theory of value, according to which the values of all commodities can be measured by their labor inputs, such as workdays. Implicit in this theory is the assumption that the output of a unit of labor is constant everywhere and for all economic activities. In other words, laborers can shift from one industry to another with no effect upon total labor costs. The theory either ignores the other factors or treats them as stored-up labor. Except for Marxists, modern theorists no longer accept the labor theory of value, but they readily acknowledge the considerable influence that labor has upon trade. Two aspects of labor are of special significance: (1) its relative abundance or scarcity and (2) its productivity.

Countries (and regions) vary greatly in the *size* of their labor forces; many have inadequate numbers of workers to run their farms and factories while others have more workers than they can employ economically. For labor-scarce economies—those having low ratios of labor to land—the Heckscher-Ohlin theory predicts resource-intensive exports and labor-intensive imports. Hence, Finland, Canada, and Australia export commodities having a large physical resource content, such as minerals, wood products, or animal products.

Contrary to the labor theory of value, labor inputs for the same goods do vary from one country to another, especially where resource endowments differ markedly. Both the United States and China produce wheat, cotton, and rice; but China uses labor-intensive methods whereas the United States employs methods that are at the same time land-intensive and capital-intensive.

In those countries where the labor-land ratio is very high, the expectation is for labor-intensive exports and land- or capital-intensive imports. A number of countries fall into this category, especially the island nations of Japan and the United Kingdom, both of which import large volumes of raw materials and foodstuffs and export finished manufactured goods. A surplus of labor usually means low labor costs, a prime attraction to those industries using large numbers of unskilled or semiskilled laborers. Most such manufacturing activities are mature industries, that is, they have passed through the innovative stages that need highly skilled workers and engineers and can now use mass-production techniques that call for many unskilled workers performing simple tasks on assembly lines. Typical of these are factories making cheaper grades of textiles, standardized types of low-priced clothing, and even the more established forms of electronics, such as the assembling of radio and television sets. Hong Kong, Taiwan, South Korea, Malaysia, and Puerto Rico have many industries of this type.

Despite plentiful supplies of labor and land, many less-developed countries are unable to compete for new industries. Usually they lack the other essential requirements of modern industrial enterprises: capital, entrepreneurial skills, an infrastructure of public utilities and transport and communications, and a variety of supporting industries and business services. Much of Latin America, Africa, and South Asia confronts this dilemma. Although plagued by chronic unemployment and underemployment, these countries are able to attract only plantation agriculture and other extractive industries, along with all the problems these entail.

In addition to labor quantity, differences in labor quality affect trade. The quality of labor is usually expressed in terms of its *productivity*, which measures the relative value of output by a unit of labor. Several studies have attempted to assess the effects of labor productivity upon trade. MacDougall (1951) tested the notion that the productivity difference between two countries in the manufacture of a given commodity should be reflected in the difference in its production cost and thus in its selling price. Countries should therefore export most successfully those goods in which their labor productivity is highest relative to other countries. A comparison of exports from the United Kingdom and the United States disclosed a direct linear relationship on a log-log scale between the productivity ratios of the two countries and their export ratios for a number of goods. British exports were relatively greater than American exports in those goods, such as textiles and clothing, where the productivity of British workers most closely approached that of American labor. Where the unit output of American labor greatly exceeded that of the British, as in the case of machinery and motor cars, American exports were relatively greater.

The productivity of a country's labor force stems from a number of influences relating to level of development, culture and tradition, and governmental policy. Affecting labor skills, for instance, is the quality of a country's educational and technical training facilities, which in turn are associated with level of development. Work habits and attitudes toward work, on the other hand, derive from a society's culture and tradition. Less-developed countries lacking an industrial tradition may require generations to acquire the skills and habits required by modern manufacturing enterprises. Folk societies, such as those found in much of equatorial Africa, often have cultural attitudes, incentives, and value systems wholly unsuited to assembly-line work. The monetary rewards for such work have had no place in their tribal past.

At the other extreme are certain Oriental cultures, where long traditions of hard work and of devotion to group achievement yield exceptionally high levels of labor productivity. The resulting cost benefits provide valuable competitive advantages for Korea, Japan, and

Taiwan in modern world commerce. Some European countries excel in the manufacture and export of labor-intensive specialties that draw upon traditional labor skills or reflect specific characteristics of national cultures. Goods of this type are Swiss watches, Belgian cut diamonds, Parisian garments, and Sheffield cutlery.

The availability of complementary factors of production is essential for labor productivity. Capital, in the form of labor-saving machinery, can multiply the output of a company's work force, as recent developments in automation and robotics have demonstrated. The productivity of a labor force depends upon the presence of managers having the skills to use their workers in the most efficient manner.

Differences in labor productivity among countries are constantly shifting in response to both long-term trends and short-term cyclical events. In some part, these result from governmental policy measures, as, for instance, public programs for educating and training the work force or special inducements to foreign investors for supplying technology and managerial skills. International differences in labor costs are constantly changing as workers become unionized and as less-developed countries with lower-cost labor enter their products into foreign competition.

Governmental policies leading to high inflation can adversely affect labor productivity: An increased money supply raises demand, causing managers to expand their work forces by tapping less-productive labor pools of poorly trained workers. Labor productivity also changes with the different phases of the business cycle. It is lowest at the peak of the cycle, when managers are drawing upon all available workers, including many who are poorly qualified, and during the early stages of recession, when managers are reluctant to discharge their underutilized workers until they are sure that the business downturn will continue. Productivity is highest at the trough of the recession, when only the most skilled workers are kept on the job, and in the early stages of recovery, when managers resist hiring new workers until they are certain that better times are truly on the way.

Constantly shifting international monetary rates effectively create labor-cost differences among countries. During the late 1970s the U.S. dollar declined against other major currencies, thereby reducing American labor costs in relation to those of European competitors. Then, in the early 1980s, the exchange rate of the dollar soared against other currencies, eventually becoming so overvalued that U.S. exporters were at a severe competitive disadvantage.

Enterprise as a Factor

Although theoreticians in the past have generally neglected *entrepreneurship* as a major influence on in-

ternational trade, this factor is deservedly gaining attention. As we have seen, the availability of skilled management is essential for the efficient use of the other factors of production, and the lack of this ingredient is one of the basic problems of many less-developed countries. It has become increasingly apparent, however, that the quality of management also has much to do with the competitive strength of industrial countries in the international marketplace. In addition to being able to achieve efficient production, managers must have the vision to assess foreign markets accurately and to develop those lines of production that anticipate global needs. During the Industrial Revolution, British entrepreneurs were able to foresee, and in some cases to create, world demand for textiles, iron and steel, and machinery. Growing complacent in later times, however, British management clung to declining industries and obsolescent technology, thereby contributing to Britain's present diminished position in world commerce.

Some observers insist that a similar decline has occurred in the quality of U.S. management since the 1960s. They point to the shrinking market for American exports and the growing invasion of foreign-made goods in the United States as evidence that the quality of industrial leadership in this country has deteriorated. In response, many U.S. companies have begun to copy Japanese management style, which is perceived as one of the major reasons for Japan's startling success in marketing its products abroad.

Capital as a Factor

The other factor of production, *capital,* is of three principal types. *Financial capital* is the more intangible, fluid form available for investment in any undertaking. More tangible types are *real capital,* consisting of equipment, buildings, and other concrete instruments of production, and *social capital,* which includes educational facilities, transport and communications, and other forms of support for productive activities. Capital is sometimes difficult to treat as a separate factor because it becomes tied up with the other factors, such as improving land, educating managers, or training workers. Nevertheless, capital is clearly a powerful determinant of trade, and a country with an abundance of capital can be expected to have a comparative advantage in the export of capital-intensive merchandise.

The United States is often cited as a capital-rich country, evidenced by foreign sales of such capital-intensive goods as chemicals. The chemical industry has a high capital-labor ratio because it must invest heavily in complex plants and equipment and make large outlays for research and development but employs relatively few workers, most of them highly skilled. Yet the United States also exports large quantities of primary goods such as wheat, corn, soybeans, and cottonseed products, which are not usually regarded as capital-intensive commodities. However, capital is almost invariably a complement to other factors, and U.S. agriculture is especially capital-intensive. So successful has been this agricultural use of capital—in the form of machinery, pesticides, herbicides, and chemical fertilizers—that American farmers, who constitute less than 3 percent of the labor force, are able to support a domestic population of more than 230 million people and at the same time sell huge quantities of farm produce in the international market.

Capital substitution for other factors of production has been increasing throughout the world. European agriculture has closely followed the American lead in recent decades, and Japanese farmers have mechanized their small acreages. Parallel trends have simultaneously occurred in other economic sectors. Most striking of all has been the revolutionary change in Japanese manufacturing, which during the postwar years has turned to the production of capital-intensive merchandise such as cameras, machinery, electronics, and automobiles after more than half a century of specialization in labor-intensive commodities.

Financial capital is the most mobile of factors, and recent years have seen a growing trend for the substitution of capital flows for trade flows. More and more companies are building factories in foreign lands to which they formerly exported their production. Foreign direct investment of this type has been shown to have a reciprocal relationship with trade. For the source country the initial effect of foreign direct investment is to produce a drain of capital and to reduce exports. At first this also diminishes the investing company's need for domestic labor, a major concern for labor unions. But evidence shows that the ultimate effect of foreign direct investment is generally positive for the source country and its workers (see Chapter 13). Because of their shipments of components and subassemblies to their foreign manufacturing operations, and because of the overall growth in their production and sales, multinational enterprises are a country's most active exporters and among its most dynamic employers. Furthermore, in time the returned profits and other earnings from foreign operations usually more than compensate for the outflow of capital at the time of the initial investment.

Firms have a number of inducements for investing in foreign undertakings. Often the decision results from the discovery that their exports to a particular foreign market have reached a level that would successfully support local manufacturing in that area. Locating their productive facilities abroad is particularly attractive for those companies making products that tend to be market-oriented.

A second reason for sending capital abroad in the place of merchandise is to take advantage of complementary factors of production in other countries. Agricultural enterprises may invest abroad in order to gain the use of land having specific qualities, as in the case of tropical plantation agriculture; and mining companies may enter into foreign operations to avail themselves of newly discovered ore deposits in other lands. Likewise, manufacturers of labor-intensive goods may establish factories in countries having plentiful supplies of cheap labor. Evidence of this is the growing number of American-owned plants assembling radios, televisions, and auto parts on the Mexican side of the United States–Mexican border.

In many instances manufacturers are forced to invest in foreign manufacturing facilities when the governments of countries to which they had previously exported erect trade barriers to their goods (see page 313). To forego such investment would mean the permanent loss of those markets to competitors willing to make the commitments.

Contributing to the accelerating international flows of investment funds in recent years has been the growth of various institutional aids to capital movement. Prominent among these has been the multinational enterprise, which can generate large financial resources internally within the company, can borrow freely in many lands and in many currencies, and can draw upon widespread corporate information-gathering facilities. Another institutional aid is the international bank, which maintains outlets in many countries, all having access to a common pool of financial resources, and which draws upon a growing battery of techniques and instruments to serve its multinational customers throughout the world.

Governments have grown increasingly inventive and aggressive in luring foreign investment as a means for generating domestic jobs, for reducing dependence upon imports, and for increasing export earnings. Governmental incentives to corporate investors include low-cost loans and subsidies for factory construction and labor training, tax relief, and a variety of other guarantees and offers of assistance. At the same time, governments may place restrictions on capital flows, as we shall see in the section dealing with political interference (page 313).

This discussion of supply factors has disclosed one of the weaknesses of the Heckscher-Ohlin theory, namely, the assumption that a particular type of production has the same factor intensities everywhere. We have seen that capital, labor, and land are used in widely varying proportions in different parts of the world, depending upon the characteristics of those factors in each area. Another weakness of the theory is its excessive emphasis upon production. Supply conditions represent only one side of the equation; demand considerations are likewise powerful determinants of trade.

Effects of Demand Conditions

One of the main benefits ascribed to trade is that it permits a region or country to maintain a consumption pattern that differs from its production pattern. Production possibilities differ from place to place, depending upon resource endowments; but the nature of consumption also varies widely, reflecting spatial differences among human populations. One of the prime reasons for the existence of trade is the fact that the structure of demand in any one place rarely seems to coincide with production in that location.

Even so, spatial differences in production are not absolutely essential for trade to occur. Trade can arise between two regions with identical production possibilities if they have unlike structures of demand. Take the case of two countries, A and B, both of which are able to grow potatoes and corn equally well. Most of the people in country A prefer potatoes to corn, however, and those in country B like corn better than potatoes. With the opening of trade between the two, each country can produce either or both crops and exchange its unwanted surplus with the other country for the preferred commodity. Such spatial variations in demand are common despite evidence that basic human needs are essentially the same. What are the reasons for these differences in demand?

Income

Undoubtedly the most compelling influence upon a country's effective demand is its per capita income. Although rising incomes cause purchasing power to increase, however, this additional demand does not extend equally to all commodities. One reason that growing incomes create a stronger demand for some goods than others is expressed by *Engel's law,* which states that poor families (or poor countries) spend larger proportions of their incomes on food than do rich ones. An impoverished population may be able to afford only the barest necessities, and some parts of the world today are hardly capable even of this. Although a rise in income may at first cause such a people to increase their expenditures for food and other necessities, beyond some minimum level of satisfaction they will allocate further income increasingly to other kinds of goods, including nonessentials and even luxury items. Because the latter are likely to be mainly manufactured goods—for which demand seems virtually unlimited—sellers of industrial products gain a rising share of the increase. Even ag-

ricultural products benefit unequally from an enlarged purchasing power. Poor people consume mainly starchy foods, but as their incomes grow they will substitute ever greater amounts of meats, green vegetables, and dairy products for the starches (see Chapter 5). This variation in demand for different commodities at different income levels is called the *income elasticity of demand.*

In an attempt to measure variations in elasticity of demand, Houthakker (1957) found that elasticities of particular categories of goods were roughly similar from one country to the next. He observed some international variations, however, particularly for foods. Although the income elasticity of demand for food was low everywhere, it ranged from only 0.3 in some countries to as much as 0.7 in others. This low elasticity of demand means that a unit rise in income would not strengthen the demand for food by a corresponding amount. Thus, if family incomes in a country had been averaging $30 per week and $15 of this had been spent on food, a gain of $10 in average incomes would have caused food expenditures to rise by $5 if the population were to increase food purchases proportionately. With an income elasticity of demand for food of 0.3, however, the average food budget would go up by only $1.50. The study found that housing had an income elasticity of demand of nearly 1.0, meaning that expenditures for housing would grow at a rate approximating the expansion in income. Expenditures for clothing and certain other items would actually advance at rates exceeding that of income. Despite minor variations in income elasticities of demand for particular goods among countries, the study found that such variations within countries were slight.

Because commodities differ in their income elasticities, countries at different levels of per capita income have very dissimilar consumption patterns. The reason for this is that, as countries have gained in prosperity, they have stepped up their purchases of some goods more rapidly than others, thereby altering patterns of consumption. Trade flows among countries mirror these differences. Goods exchanged by North America with Western Europe are very unlike those shipped between Europe and West Africa or Southeast Asia. Differences in consumption patterns are responsible for a major part of this contrast in trade flows.

Among the wealthier countries disparities in demand patterns tend to narrow as time passes. Rising prosperity in Western Europe and Japan in recent decades has caused lifestyles among those populations to draw closer to those of North America. Linder (1961) has cited this similarity in demand structures among high-income countries as a principal reason that the manufactured goods of rich countries find their best markets in other rich countries.

Cultural Differences

International variations in cultural traits are responsible for some of the differences among countries in their demand structures. Indeed, the surprising range of income elasticities of demand for food and beverages can be attributed to religious taboos and to national attitudes and preferences. For instance, several predominantly Catholic countries, such as Portugal, Spain, and Italy, import fish to add to their own sizable domestic production of this food; prohibitions of Hinduism limit India's consumption and importation of beef, and Moslem and Jewish restrictions on the eating of pork adversely affect sales of that meat to the Middle East. The unusually large imports of tea by the United Kingdom and of coffee by the United States illustrate the substantial effects of consumption habits upon trade. Although the countries of Western Europe enjoy similarly high standards of living, the proportion of family income devoted to purchases of food and drink differs considerably from one country to the next. Topping the list are France and Denmark, whose national cultures accord a special place to their cuisines.

Domestic Consumption and Exports

The nature of a country's demand may affect not only its imports but also its exports. Although exports of primary commodities depend upon a country's resource endowments, its success in exporting manufactured goods benefits importantly from prior production of those items for the domestic market. Indeed, entrepreneurs are unlikely even to be aware of foreign opportunities for the sale of a given product if the home market does not have an active demand for it. Equally essential, thriving domestic sales permit the industry to develop economies of scale sufficient to reduce unit costs to a level that is competitive in the international market. Before World War II, Japan's large home consumption of mass-produced, low-cost textiles provided the necessary base from which to launch a successful export business in these goods. More recently, Japan's mounting prosperity has created a lively home market for automobiles and other consumer durables, thereby contributing to that country's flourishing foreign sales of such products.

Inadequacies of Modern Trade Theory

Thus, conditions of production and consumption interact to promote trade among countries. But is this the whole story? Does modern theory, which is based upon the Heckscher-Ohlin model, provide a satisfactory explanation of trade? This theory ascribes comparative advantage to differences in resource endowments, stating that a country will export goods that intensively use its relatively abundant factors of production and will import goods that intensively use its relatively scarce factors. The previous discussion, however, has implied a number of needed modifications in this proposition. How well would the theory hold up in tests using actual data?

Empirical Tests: The Leontief Paradox

The best-known attempt to answer this question was that of Wassily Leontief (1953, 1968), who set out to test the hypothesis that U.S. trade reflects its resource endowments. The theoretical expectation was that the country's exports would be capital-intensive and that its imports would be labor-intensive. This was predicated on the widely held notion that, relative to most of the world, the United States is rich in capital and is less well supplied with labor. Leontief based his calculations upon U.S. input-output tables for 200 industries and U.S. trade for 1947. His method was to compare capital/labor ratios in U.S. export industries with those of the country's import-competing industries (U.S. industries making the same goods as those comprising the main imports).

Leontief's findings, published in 1953, were wholly unexpected: The capital/labor ratio in U.S. export industries was actually lower than in import-competing industries. This indicated that the country's exports were more labor-intensive than its imports, a paradoxical result for an economy that was supposedly well endowed with capital. Leontief's figures showed that U.S. import replacements actually required 30 percent more capital per worker-year to produce than did its exports.

In a follow-up study published in 1956, Leontief confirmed his earlier results with an analysis of the same industries using 1951 trade figures. Subsequently, Baldwin achieved similar results using U.S. input-output data for 1958 applied to 1962 trade, and in 1979 he released equally paradoxical findings for 30 other countries.

Explanations for the Puzzle

The flurry of works that followed Leontief's disclosure agreed on one point: His study had uncovered basic flaws in the Heckscher-Ohlin theorem. Chief among these weaknesses was the assumption that the relative factor intensity of a good is the same everywhere and that this relationship is unchanging. That factor intensities do indeed change over space and time is clear from the numerous studies since undertaken to find explanations for the Leontief paradox. The evidence shows that the costs of factors (land, labor, and capital) vary widely from country to country: Because they differ relatively in quantity and quality they are used differently. The same goods produced abroad by labor-intensive methods are likely to be produced in the United States by capital-intensive methods. As we noted earlier, American farmers emphasize the use of machinery and agricultural chemicals to grow rice and wheat, whereas Oriental farmers rely mainly upon hand labor to produce these commodities. Influencing the allocation of factors in U.S. agriculture are the high cost of labor, the relative abundance of capital, and the availability of technology.

A further explanation for the paradox is that, by concentrating upon capital and labor, Leontief neglected the substantial place of land in both U.S. exports and imports. America produces an abundance of some land-intensive commodities but is severely short in others. Large export earnings from temperate grains and subtropical fruits and vegetables are made possible by the nation's great agricultural land area and its varied growing conditions, aided by the high productivity of its farm labor. On the other hand, the United States has inadequate supplies of many vital land-intensive commodities: metallic minerals such as bauxite, iron ore, and nonferrous metals, as well as oil and natural gas (see Chapter 5). These fuels and industrial raw materials are extracted overseas by capital-intensive methods, often by U.S. multinational enterprises using American capital and relying upon familiar U.S. technology.

Some writers have pointed to the nature of American labor as one reason for Leontief's results. As we saw earlier, labor is not the homogeneous factor of production assumed by Heckscher-Ohlin; to the contrary, international variations in labor skills significantly affect trade. Indeed, Leontief's own explanation for the paradox was that superior skills multiply the effectiveness of U.S. workers and that labor productivity is enhanced by the nature of U.S. entrepreneurship and industrial organization and by education. Some observers argue that the education and training of labor essentially represent the creation of labor skills through the application of capital. Studies have confirmed that U.S. export industries employ more skilled workers than do the country's import-competing industries. Hence, the country has a comparative advantage in those manufactured goods requiring human skills. These tend to be high-technology products, which call for much capital investment in research and development.

This suggests still another explanation for Leontief's paradox: U.S. exports contain a high proportion of new products. These goods are in the beginning stages of the product life cycle, when research and development are paramount. On the other hand, the country has long imported standardized goods that are late in the product life cycle, when labor-skill requirements are low. Also implied in the product-life-cycle explanation

is the notion that factor proportions change with the maturing of the technology for making a good.

Further complicating the role of factor endowments is the fact that much U.S. foreign commerce is intra-industry trade, as is true of industrialized countries generally. Two-thirds of the trade of developed countries goes to other developed countries, and most of it represents exchanges of manufactured goods for other manufactured goods. The major part of this is intra-industry trade, that is, cross-shipments of products from the same industrial category. Within product types, companies will seek out particular niches not served by others. By concentrating upon these specialties, they gain cost advantages through economies of scale and are thus able to compete favorably in foreign markets. Companies differentiate their goods from those of their competitors by means of brand names. Much of the cross-hauling of similar commodities among countries consists of such branded items, automobiles, for example. In short, the growing place of multinational enterprises in world commerce has given new meaning to the concept of comparative advantage.

Finally, the notion that international trade is merely a function of relative resource endowments must be modified by the existence of barriers to commodity flows among countries, notably the effects of transport costs and governmental interference. For instance, the evidence shows that U.S. barriers to the import of labor-intensive goods, erected to "save American jobs," significantly reduce the influx of such items. The effect is sufficient to have influenced Leontief's finding that U.S. imports are less labor-intensive than U.S. exports. Japanese restrictions on the import of capital-intensive commodities from the United States no doubt have further strengthened this effect.

The empirical evidence clearly raises serious doubts that factor endowments are a sufficient explanation for trade. Many other elements that influence trade have been excluded by the initial simplifying assumptions of the theory. The work stimulated by Leontief's paradoxical findings has uncovered a number of additional considerations, and these will be our main concern in the pages that follow. The remainder of this chapter will focus upon the effects of trade barriers, and the next chapter will consider the influence of growth and change, with special attention to the role of technology and development, of organizational arrangements, and of the multinational enterprise, which has become a prime actor in world commerce.

BARRIERS TO TRADE

In looking to differences in production possibilities for an explanation of trade, conventional theory has given little attention to the obstacles that can intervene to alter the volume, direction, and composition of commodity flows. These are of two types: *distance* and *political interference.*

Distance

Distance acts as a barrier to trade in a variety of ways, some of them subtle. The most obvious effect of distance is the burden of transport cost it imposes upon every shipment of goods between two countries. This cost does not necessarily correspond closely with the number of miles to be covered, for some routes are cheaper to travel than others. Mountainous terrain can add many miles to the apparent distance between two points, and steep grades can multiply fuel costs. Irregular coastlines prevent vessels from taking the most direct routes between ports. Hence, transport routes are often more circuitous and difficult than they might appear, resulting in extra costs to move goods over them.

The expense of transporting commodities is not limited merely to the cost of operating a motor vehicle, aircraft, or steamship. In addition, shipments to foreign destinations incur bank collection charges, freight forwarders' and customs house brokers' fees, consular charges, and cartage expenses, and they entail extra clerical costs for preparing bills of lading, customs declarations, and a variety of other lengthy shipping documents. Adding these *terminal costs* to the expense of actually moving the merchandise gives a total outlay usually called *transfer costs*. Considering all of these elements, some of which are incurred regardless of the length of haul, transfer cost is a more reliable measure of the ''economic distance'' between two points than is transport cost alone.

Introducing transfer costs into the conventional two-country, two-commodity model considerably alters the outcome. Instead of trade causing prices between two countries to become equalized as suggested earlier by Figure 12.2, they will always differ by the amount of the cost of transporting the merchandise. Transfer costs make goods more expensive to importers and less valuable to exporters.

Figure 12.4 illustrates this effect with a simple case involving two countries and a single product and taking into account only transport cost and production cost. The diagram shows hypothetical demand and supply curves for paper in both the United States and Canada. The demand curves, *D*, slope downward to the right, indicating that consumers in each country will take larger quantities of paper if the price drops. The supply curves, *S*, slope upward to the right because producers are able and willing to make more paper if the price goes up. Figure 12.4 shows that, in the absence of trade, the price of paper would be lower in Canada than in the United States, reflecting Canada's comparative advantage in forest products. This difference is evident from the points where the supply and demand curves cross in each case—*p* for Canada and *w* for the United States.

Figure 12.4 shows the results of trade, first in the

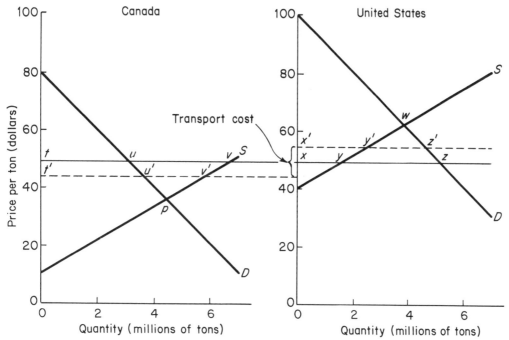

FIGURE 12.4 Price of paper in Canada and the United States and quantities traded and consumed, with and without transport costs.

absence of transport cost and then with the addition of transport cost. Table 12.3 summarizes these effects. Without transport cost the price after trade in both countries—that is, the international terms of trade—becomes $49 per ton of paper, as shown by the horizontal line extending from *t* to *z* in Figure 12.4. At this price Canada produces 6.6 million tons of paper (indicated by the distance *tv*), consumes 3.1 million tons (*tu*), and exports the remaining 3.5 million tons (*uv*) to the United States. Under these conditions the United States consumes 5.1 million tons (*xz*) of paper, of which 3.5 million tons (*yz*) are imported from Canada. U.S. producers are then able to supply the other 1.6 million tons (*xy*) that the country needs.

If, however, we introduce a transport cost of $10 per ton, this causes the price of paper to rise to $54 in the United States and fall to $44 in Canada (Table 12.3). At the $54 price the United States is no longer willing to use as much paper, and consumption then drops to only 4.5 million tons (*x'z'* in Figure 12.4). Nevertheless, the higher price induces domestic producers of paper to supply a larger quantity, 2.4 million tons (*x'y'*), and U.S. imports consequently drop to only 2.2 million tons (*y'z'*). At the reduced Canadian price of $44 per ton, producers in that country will supply only 5.8 million tons (*t'v'*), but Canadian consumers will take a larger quantity, 3.6 million tons (*t'u'*). But the extra home consumption makes up for only a part of the lost exports to the United States, which now amount to only 2.2 million tons (*u'v'*). Note that the impact of transport cost falls with equal weight upon importing and exporting countries.

One lesson offered by this case is that transport cost does in fact decrease international specialization. The United States produces more of its own paper and buys less abroad, whereas Canadian mills must reduce total output even though the new low domestic price enables them to sell somewhat more at home. Indeed, if transport cost had exceeded the pretrade price differential, which in Figure 12.4 ranges between a low of *p*

for Canada and a high of *w* for the United States, trade would not have occurred at all. Throughout the world much localized production owes its existence to the sheltering effects of a high transfer cost barrier to trade with other regions that have lower production costs. Herein lies one of the chief links between trade theory and location theory.

Transfer cost does not affect all merchandise alike, however, for some classes of goods are more cheaply and easily transported than others. Their transportability depends upon their perishability, ease of handling, and value in relation to bulk or weight. Most manufactured goods have a high degree of transportability owing to the low cost of shipment relative to value, which has been estimated at about 2 percent on the average. Such products therefore move freely over long distances throughout the world. Some primary goods are also widely traded, for instance, petroleum, which is valuable, easily handled, and cheaply transported. Likewise traveling long distances are cheese, butter, commercial fibers, and other agricultural commodities whose bulk and perishability have been reduced in processing. Grains have long been staples of world commerce because they are nonperishable and are easily handled by bulk cargo methods.

At the other extreme are several types of goods that are so costly to ship that they do not ordinarily enter foreign commerce. These include perishable foodstuffs such as fluid milk and fresh produce, and cheap, bulky building materials such as common dimension stone, sand and gravel, and bricks. Commodities of this type are often referred to as *domestic* goods.

Distance influences trade in many ways other than transport cost alone. Though often subtle, the noncost effects of distance can be substantial in some instances. Commercial relations between two neighboring countries tend to be simpler and easier than between remoter ones, if only because business people have a greater awareness of sales opportunities nearer at hand. Reinforcing the advantages of closeness are the effects of

TABLE 12.3

Effects of transport cost on exports of paper by Canada to the United States

| | Without transport cost | | With transport cost | |
	Canada	United States	Canada	United States
Price per ton (in dollars)	$49	$49	$44	$54
Quantity produced[a]	6.6	1.6	5.8	2.4
Quantity exported[a]	3.5	—	2.2	—
Quantity imported[a]	—	3.5	—	2.2
Quantity consumed[a]	3.1	5.1	3.6	4.6

[a]All quantities in millions of tons.

mass communication and frequent travel between two neighboring populations, as well as the personal acquaintances that arise. Constant contact between peoples usually leads to a greater familiarity with differing tastes, customs, languages, business methods, and legal systems.

Although previously neglected by trade theorists, distance has been gaining increased attention in recent studies. One example is W. Beckerman's pioneering study of the influence of distance upon Western Europe's trade. Using transport cost as a substitute for actual mileage, Beckerman compared two separate rankings of the same countries: (1) a ranking by the average amount of transport cost separating them, and (2) a ranking by value of trade with each other (adjusted for size of country). The correlation between these two rankings proved very close and tended to confirm the effectiveness of transport cost as an influence upon trade patterns in that region.

Thus, the element of distance adds a distinct new dimension to the Heckscher-Ohlin theory. It modifies the effects of a country's resource endowments by enhancing the attractions of neighboring lands and raising obstacles to commerce with remoter areas, although the force of its impact is greater for some classes of merchandise than others. It constitutes a potent advantage for a country, such as West Germany, that is centrally located with respect to rich markets for its exports: Competitors in more distant locations would have to produce much more cheaply in order to invade those markets.

Distance is a dynamic influence in international trade. As we shall see in Chapter 13, technology is constantly working to reduce transportation costs. The long-term trend in those costs has therefore been downward, effectively reducing the economic distance between countries and extending the shipping range of internationally traded goods. Simultaneously, communications technology has been advancing with equal rapidity and it is steadily diminishing the noncost barriers of distance. Meanwhile, other kinds of costs are constantly affecting transportation, particularly the cost of energy: Rising and falling prices of petroleum greatly complicate the impact of distance upon world commerce. To a growing extent, these fluctuations reflect the intervention of political forces.

Political Interference

Under international law every country has exclusive jurisdiction over its territory. Governments exercise this *national sovereignty* through their police powers and taxing authority over all resident individuals and business organizations, by the physical and administrative control of their borders, and in their position as the sole legal representatives of their citizens in all relations with other national governments. These powers of the state often raise formidable barriers to the movement of goods, services, and factors of production. The actions of national governments thus tend to distort the basic theoretical pattern of world commerce.

Incentives for Intervention

Why do governments interfere in foreign commerce? One reason is nationalism, an emotional attachment to the state that binds the people of a country together in the pursuit of common goals. Responding to such sentiments, a government usually acts in what is perceived to be the self-interest of its citizens. This includes the pursuit of economic policies that promote national economic growth and development so as to increase employment and raise per capita income. An essential element in this is the country's foreign economic policy, which relates to its trade, foreign investment, and external economic relations generally. Governments commonly intervene in market operations to further national goals that the market would supposedly fail to achieve otherwise. In particular, they engage in various actions affecting the movement of goods, services, and factors across their borders.

The ultimate in state intervention is practiced by Communist governments, which exercise total control over their national economies, including foreign trade, which is conducted exclusively by state enterprises under the direction of central planning agencies. Even more than elsewhere, commercial policies of Communist governments reflect not only economic considerations but also political goals tied to overall foreign policies.

Because of the importance of foreign commerce to national well-being, governments maintain a constant watch over their economic relations with the rest of the world. The usual statistical measure of this performance is the *balance of payments*. This is the sum of all economic transactions between the residents—individuals and corporations—of one country and the residents of other countries within a given time span (usually a year). These transactions include exports and imports of goods and services, gifts and other one-way transfers, investments, flows of monetary gold, and payments by central banks. The balance of payments is calculated by means of a double-entry accounting system that sets debits against credits. As in mercantilist times, when the goal was to maximize credits over debits, it is common even today to refer to a positive figure as a "favorable" balance of payments.

The most obvious contributor to the balance of payments is a country's merchandise exports, often called the *visible* trade. The difference between the total value of exports and imports of goods within a given year is the *balance of trade*. Also included in the balance of payments are the exports and imports of services—the *invisible* trade. These include transport services that residents sell to or purchase from foreigners; tourist services, which are the expenditures made by residents of one country while traveling in another country; financial services, including international banking and insurance activities; investment services that involve international transfers of interest, dividends, and profits; and technological services, represented by international payments of royalties and fees. The trade in services, currently accounting for about one-quarter of total world commerce, is the most rapidly growing part of the total and is particularly vital to certain countries. For instance, financial services are important foreign exchange earners for the United Kingdom and Switzerland; tourism is essential to the economies of Mexico, Italy, Spain, the United Kingdom, France, Switzerland, Israel, and Egypt; and services of all kinds constitute the largest category of foreign exports by New York City.

Some countries gain much of their foreign exchange from gifts and other one-way transactions. Among such transfers are the contributions of private charities and monies sent by expatriate workers to their families back home. Both Egypt and Mexico gain substantial amounts of exchange from the repatriated earnings of their nationals working abroad. One-way governmental transfers include foreign aid, pension payments, and taxation of foreigners. Also contributing to the balance of payments are long-term capital flows. Chief among these are foreign direct investment—for example, establishing branch plants abroad—and portfolio investment—making loans to or purchasing stock in foreign enterprises. Both types of capital flows are vital to the Canadian economy, for example. A residual element in the balance of payments is the transactions between central banks, which exchange monetary gold and foreign currencies in order to balance national accounts.

Political interference in foreign commerce may have either positive or negative effects, depending upon whether it tends to create, diminish, or rechannel trade. Governments often promote their exports by sponsoring fairs and exhibits or offering subsidies, loan guarantees, tax rebates, or other financial incentives to exporters. They also enter into special trade agreements with other countries to increase sales. Most countries maintain commercial attachés in their foreign embassies in part to assist their exporters in doing business in those lands. Indeed, a study by Bruce Russett found a direct relationship between the size of diplomatic staffs and the amount of trade among countries.

Tariffs

On the other hand, a variety of restrictive measures exists for controlling the volume, composition, or direction of trade. Most governments are under constant political pressure from special-interest groups to intervene in their foreign commerce. One technique favored since early times is the *tariff,* which is a tax or duty imposed upon a particular category of merchandise entering or leaving a country. A tariff may be either an *ad valorem* duty—that is, a given percentage of the value of a good (for example, 15 percent of the invoice amount)—or a *specific* duty—a particular amount of money for a given quantity of the good (for example, $1.50 per ton). Ad valorem and specific duties may also be used in combination. Although *import tariffs* are more widespread than *export tariffs,* the latter are common among those countries specializing in the sale of primary commodities.

The two main reasons for levying tariffs are to earn *revenue* and to *protect* domestic producers from foreign competition. Governments of developing countries ordinarily rely upon tariff revenue for much of their financial support; income from import tariffs was the chief source of revenue for the United States government during its earlier years. Most countries use protective tariffs to shield their home industries against foreign producers. A common justification for such tariffs is the "infant industry" argument, which holds that newly established industries must receive this kind of special protection from foreign competitors during their early years when unit costs are still higher than those of established operations elsewhere. This argument implies that tariff protection will be lifted when the new industries reach levels of efficiency that will permit their products to compete on equal terms with imported goods. Manufacturing operations formed under such conditions are sometimes called "tariff factories." Canadian production of chemicals and household appliances began with governmental aid of this type, as did the fabricated-metal trades of Mexico and Brazil. Under pressure from industry and labor groups, governments may impose protective tariffs to save declining industries that have lost their competitiveness in world markets. In recent years, American manufacturers of textiles, clothing, and steel have agitated with increasing success for such governmental help against lower-cost foreign competitors.

Regardless of its initial purpose, a tariff ultimately produces a variety of effects, as the following example illustrates. Figure 12.5 and Table 12.4 give the case of a hypothetical tariff imposed upon United States imports of shoes from Italy (assuming that the two countries trade only with each other and in isolation from

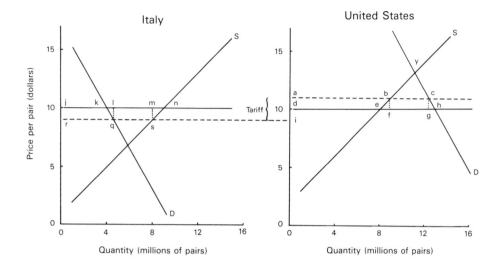

FIGURE 12.5 Effects of tariff on United States imports of shoes from Italy.

the rest of the world). Note that the changes in supply and demand resulting from the tariff are similar to those produced by transport cost as seen previously in Figure 12.4. In the absence of trade, the Italian price for a pair of shoes would have been $6.80 (shown in Figure 12.5 by the intersection of Italy's supply and demand curves at *x*), whereas the American price would have been $13.30 (given by the intersection at *y* in Figure 12.5). With trade, however, the price in both countries settles at $10 (*Oj*). At this price the United States will consume 13 million pairs of shoes (*dh*), 5 million of which are imported from Italy (*eh*).

The introduction of a tariff of $2 per pair (equal to *ia* in Figure 12.5) causes the Italian price to fall to $9 (given by *Or*) and the United States price to rise to $11 (*Oa*). Italian production thereupon drops by 1 million

pairs to only 8 million and exports to the United States decline to 3.4 million pairs (Table 12.4). At the new higher price, consumers in the United States will buy only 12.4 million pairs, 9 million of which are now produced at home. On those shoes still imported from Italy the United States government receives tariff revenue amounting to $6.8 million ($2 times 3.4 million pairs, or *ia* times *bc* in Figure 12.5). This is equivalent to the combined areas *bcgf* and *lmsq* in Figure 12.5. Meanwhile, domestic producers (Table 12.4) enjoy an additional $19 million in receipts (on sales of 9 million pairs at $11 instead of 8 million at the earlier price of $10). Note, however, that this benefit to United States producers comes not only at the expense of foreign producers but also of domestic consumers, who now get only 12.4 million pairs of shoes for $136.4 million where

TABLE 12.4

Effects of United States tariff on shoes imported from Italy

	Before tariff		After tariff	
	Italy	United States	Italy	United States
Price per pair (in dollars)	$10	$10	$9	$11
Quantity produced[a]	9.0	8.0	8.0	9.0
Quantity exported[a]	5.0	—	3.4	—
Quantity imported[a]	—	5.0	—	3.4
Quantity consumed[a]	4.0	13.0	4.6	12.4
Tariff revenue (in millions of dollars)	—	—	—	$6.8
Additional revenue to producers (in millions of dollars)	—	—	—	$19.0

[a]All quantities in millions of pairs.

they used to get 13 million pairs for $130 million. The imposition of a tariff in this case has thus had a *protection effect,* a *consumption effect,* and an *income-redistribution effect.* If the amount of the tariff had been set at $6.50 (equivalent to the vertical distance between *x* and *y* in Figure 12.5) or greater, the price differential between the two countries would have disappeared and the shoe trade would have ceased altogether. Only the American manufacturers and their workers would have gained from this arrangement; the government would have received nothing.

Under the conditions shown in Figure 12.5 however, both the domestic shoe mills and the government gain income from the relatively modest tariff of $2. Although American buyers of shoes incur some additional cost, the main losers are the Italians, who are able to sell fewer pairs and get a lower price for them. This is the basis for the common observation that a tariff is a way of taxing the foreigner.

Nevertheless, a unilateral action of this kind risks retaliation from the injured party. Let us assume in the above case that Italy has been a prime customer for American farm products. If, in retribution for the United States tariff on Italian shoes, the government of Italy were to place a tariff on the import of American wheat, the effects upon the U.S.–Italian wheat trade would be like those shown for the Italian–American shoe trade in Figure 12.5, only in reverse: Italy would buy less wheat from the United States, the price of American wheat would fall, less wheat would be produced, and American wheat farmers would be hurt. Thus, where retaliation is possible both countries are harmed by tariffs; total trade declines and production and consumption diminish. Lost are the benefits of international specialization of production and exchange.

Export tariffs, under a variety of labels, are a favored revenue-raising device among less-developed countries, especially those who produce minerals and fuels in strong demand on world markets. In addition, some countries use export duties on their raw materials as a way of inducing manufacturers to increase the amount of domestic processing of such goods. Not only does this raise the value of their exports but it also serves as a means for introducing industrial development. In this way Jamaica has acquired facilities for processing bauxite ore into alumina, and Venezuela has installed refineries for her oil. Excessive export duties, however, have cost some raw-material producers their world markets when customers abroad have found new sources of supply or have developed synthetic substitutes (see Chapter 13).

Always, the effects of tariffs, whether on imports or on exports, depend upon the nature of supply and demand for the good. For instance, if consumers have a particularly strong desire for an imported good, they may continue buying it regardless of the higher price resulting from a tariff.

Quotas

An even more drastic form of governmental intervention in trade is the *quota.* A quota is a specific limitation on the *quantity* of exports or (more usually) imports that a country will permit. This device is of more recent origin than the tariff, being largely a product of the world economic depression of the 1930s. Like tariffs, import quotas serve to aid domestic producers. Quotas are especially favored as a means of protection against foreign competition for farmers and for producers of standardized manufactured goods such as textiles. Governments tend to prefer quotas where the foreign supply of a product is very great and available at particularly low prices. Under such conditions tariffs would likely be unsuccessful in stemming the flood of imports. Administrators favor quotas especially because of their sudden, drastic, and certain results and also because they are easy to impose, remove, or adjust. They can cause more friction among importers and foreign suppliers, however, because they are more difficult than tariffs to administer fairly.

A country may impose import quotas unilaterally, that is, it may do so without prior consultation with foreign suppliers; or it may negotiate with supplying countries before setting import limitations. The United States has negotiated quotas (euphemistically called "orderly marketing agreements") with Japan on the import of motor vehicles and with the European Common Market countries on specialty steel products. As this suggests, quotas may be negotiated either bilaterally (with a single supplying country) or multilaterally (with a number of suppliers). Allocation to importers under a quota system often relies upon some kind of import licensing arrangement.

Figure 12.6 illustrates the possible outcome of a hypothetical quota on Japanese rayon imported into the United States. Let us say that each year the United States has been consuming 70 million yards of rayon (*OD* in Figure 12.6) at a price of $2.50 per yard (*OE*). Of this amount, 50 million yards (*AD*) have been imported. If the government yields to the demands of domestic manufacturers and imposes a quota limiting imports to 30 million yards (*BC*), this will cause the price in the United States to rise to $3.00 (*OJ*) and total rayon consumption in the country to fall to 60 million yards. But out of this total American mills will be able to sell an increased quantity—30 million yards (*JK*) instead of the former 20 million yards (*EF*)—at the new higher price. The revenue increase to domestic producers will be $40 million

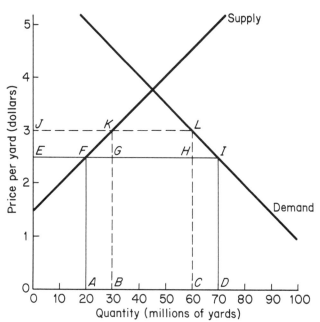

FIGURE 12.6 Effects of United States quota on imports of Japanese rayon.

(area *JKBO* instead of *EFAO*). Meanwhile, American consumers will have to pay a total of $180 million (*JLCO*) for less cloth than they formerly got for only $175 million (*EIDO*). Thus, the domestic mills gain at the expense of both domestic consumers and foreign suppliers. The effects are inflationary for the importing country (as shown by the United States' experience with quotas on auto imports from Japan), and at the same time they are conducive to monopoly control of production. Quotas of this type are exceedingly arbitrary, as they freeze the volume and direction of trade into some predetermined pattern. Note also that, unlike tariffs, quotas yield no revenue to the government unless a high fee is assessed for import licenses. Because of their inherent unfairness, quotas also lead to hard feelings and retaliation.

Export quotas have also been used extensively in recent years to prop up world prices of some primary commodities. Certain agricultural products and minerals have chronically suffered from recurrent problems of oversupply and price instability. In such cases exporting countries may impose quotas in an effort to reduce world supplies and thereby raise prices abroad. In the past Brazil has tried this means for limiting exports of rubber and coffee, and the United States has attempted similar controls on cotton exports.

Export restrictions of this type have usually not been very successful. Either substitutes would be found elsewhere for the country's products or new foreign sources of supply of the commodity would be developed. Thus, nitrates were synthesized to replace the overly priced Chilean natural product; plantation rubber in the Far East largely usurped the former markets for Brazilian rubber; Central American, Colombian, and West African growers increased their coffee output; and American price supports encouraged cotton production in Africa. Producers in different countries have attempted to cooperate in controlling foreign sales of their products, but commodity agreements of this type uniformly failed until the winter of 1973–1974, when members of the Organization of Petroleum Exporting Countries (OPEC) managed to agree on quantitative limits and prices for their oil exports.

Other Nontariff Measures

A device similar to the quota involves the use of *exchange controls:* A government buys all foreign currency brought into the country through the earnings of its exporters and then distributes these currencies to importers in a carefully regulated manner. The allocation of foreign exchange may be made through licensing schemes or auctions (as in Brazil). This is done in such a way as to control not only the volume of imports but also their composition, thereby conserving the country's money supply and assuring its most economical use. The allotments ordinarily discriminate against luxuries and favor necessities. Quota systems sometimes entail multiple exchange rates, with foreign currencies being sold to importers at higher prices for some purposes than others. Exchange controls were common in post–World War II Europe, when shortages of foreign exchange were especially acute, and similar schemes continue in wide use today throughout Latin America.

In some parts of the world, governments go even further and participate actively in buying and selling abroad, a practice termed *state trading.* This is the standard procedure in Communist countries, but it also occurs in developing countries, and to some extent in advanced capitalistic countries. State monopolies in specific commodities such as alcoholic beverages, sugar, tobacco, cocoa, grains, and other agricultural products are fairly common. During times of war, bulk buying and selling by governments becomes necessary.

Intergovernmental relationships can alter trade patterns, as, for example, trade agreements granting special tariff concessions or generous quota allocations to favored trading partners. In general, their effects are to divert trade from the normal channels of a freely operating world market. Some of the more elaborate arrangements will be discussed in Chapter 13.

Nationalistic feelings, expressed through wars, hostile attitudes, or rivalries between populations, can influence trade. Despite the natural complementarities between the resource endowments of Israel and its Arab neighbors, their continued hostility discourages more Arab-Israeli trade. Trade between Eastern and Western Europe was well developed before World War II but is much reduced now that the Eastern countries are part of the Communist bloc. Wars have often forced contending nations to industrialize; the War of 1812, for example, sparked early U.S. industrialization. Wars have had this kind of effect upon noncombatants, too, as in the case of Argentina, which began manufacturing many of its own needs when cut off by World War I from European sources of supply. An interruption of trade again occurred during World War II, spurring further industrialization by Argentina.

Many seemingly small governmental actions can interfere with foreign trade. Special labeling and packaging requirements may exclude goods from some markets if the cost of changing the usual practices of producers in the exporting country is excessive. Sanitary and safety regulations can have the same effect. Some European countries maintain exacting specifications for the ingredients of prepared foods; Canada requires labels in both French and English; Japan employs elaborate inspection procedures; and the United States specifies costly safety and pollution-control devices on motor vehicles. Official measures of this type may be enacted without conscious thought of their effects on imported commodities, but some are deliberately intended to exclude foreign competitors who cannot readily comply with them. Even the mere existence of an international border crossing is sufficient to deter some trade movements. Small producers are especially reluctant to spend the time, effort, and money for complying with the red tape required for entering goods through customs. For a discussion of the growing problem of protectionism, see pages 318–321.

EFFECTS OF TRADE ON THE FACTORS OF PRODUCTION

According to the Heckscher-Ohlin theory, trade among regions and countries results from differences in their relative endowments in the factors of production. We have noted previously, however, that the introduction of trade produces feedback effects upon the factors. These effects are of two kinds: (1) trade may cause the prices of capital, labor, and land to rise or fall, and (2) it may change the relative quantities of the factors. Moreover, any interregional or international movement of factors will further alter their relative prices and quantities.

Spreading Protectionism: A Public Policy Problem

A global epidemic of protectionism reminiscent of the 1930s is abroad in the 1980s. As Figure 12.7 vividly shows, the worldwide flurry of protectionist actions that followed imposition by the United States of the Smoot-Hawley Tariff Act in 1930 quickly caused world trade to shrink to only one-third of its former size. This steep decline in commerce was one of the major reasons for the depth of the Great Depression of the 1930s. Could it happen again? Why has the agitation for sheltering domestic industries against foreign competition surfaced at this time, what reasons are given for restricting imports, and what theoretical and practical validity do these arguments have? Even more basically, we might ask why foreign competition is the target of protectionism rather than domestic competition. No one questions the economic advantages of free trade among regions of a country, yet the benefits of foreign trade are exactly the same. When we look for answers to this puzzling bias against foreigners, we find that the explanation apparently has to do with a general spirit of nationalism, which lies within the realms of politics and social psychology rather than economic considerations.

This return to protectionism follows a long postwar era of trade liberalization, which has seen global commerce soar and which has brought unprecedented prosperity to much of the world. The first threats to this trend came in the 1970s, when the OPEC crises and steeply rising oil prices led to recessions in developed and developing countries alike. As international trade shrank, competition for markets intensified, imports threatened domestic industries, and a worldwide withdrawal into protectionism began. Adding urgency to the situation were rising budget and trade deficits in the United States, unaccustomedly high unemployment in Europe, and enormous foreign debts and stalled economic development among less-developed countries. The danger in all this is that widespread limitations on imports might halt world growth, reduce the efficiency of the world economy, undermine political alliances, and

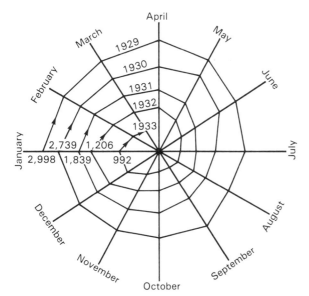

FIGURE 12.7 The contracting spiral of world trade, 1929–1933. Total imports of 75 countries (monthly values in old U.S. gold dollars, millions). [*Source:* Charles Kindleberger, *World in Recession* (Berkeley: University of California Press, 1973).]

drive a wedge between industrialized and developing countries.

As the contagion spread, industrialized countries began first to raise trade barriers to each other and then to target the less-developed countries (LDCs). Responding to a torrent of demand for protection, the President of the United States imposed 144 new quotas on textiles from 36 countries, most of them LDCs. In addition to textiles, the United States has since 1980 established quotas on apparel and motorcycles and negotiated "orderly marketing agreements" (so-called voluntary quotas) with European countries on carbon steel and with Japan on automobiles. All of this has been highly inflationary: According to most estimates, the limitation on Japanese auto imports cost American consumers $15 billion in higher prices during the three-year life of the agreement. Protectionist sentiment in the United States against Japan has further intensified, however, as trade deficits with that country have mounted.

Japan itself is an inveterate practitioner of protectionism. It has long shielded its own high-cost producers of beef and citrus fruit from much cheaper products from the United States, and it has always limited imports of manufactured goods by means of rigorous inspections, intricate administrative regulations, and other subtle types of trade barriers. More recently, Japan erected new barriers to imports of textiles, apparel, footwear, and other products threatening to flood the home market from low-cost producers in Korea and other newly industrializing lands. Japan has also begun to restrict imports of certain favored high-technology items in which the United States is most competitive—computer software, telecommunications gear, and communications satellites—arguing the need to develop its own industries.

With unemployment exceeding 10 percent, sluggish economic growth, and the continuing heavy burden of social programs, the Western European countries have become more protectionist too. Because their economies depend heavily upon trade—exports generally account for a third or more of gross national product—these countries are exceedingly vulnerable to world market conditions. Yet they are losing their international competitiveness in a number of traditional industries. Low-cost textiles from Taiwan, Singapore, and South Korea began to flood European markets in the 1970s, driving hundreds of domestic firms into bankruptcy. The textile industry as a whole was saved only by "orderly marketing agreements" reached with Asian producers by European governments. Then a tidal wave of auto imports from Japan reached European shores, seizing a quarter of the market in some countries. This resulted in still another orderly marketing agreement. European shipbuilders and manufacturers of machine tools have also lost out in world competition. Meanwhile, Europe has fallen behind in every high-technology field and has resorted to import quotas on these goods.

The newly industrializing countries of the Third World increasingly find themselves the targets of protectionism in the older developed lands. In their drive to industrialize, these countries often used subsidies and import barriers of their own, with the tacit acceptance of the developed countries. Now they are vigorously exporting their manufactures to pay off huge international debts. Benefiting from low-cost labor and the latest technology, these Third World exporters have made serious inroads in the domestic markets of the older developed countries with their cheaper steel, textiles, and electronics. As we have seen, the Europeans, Americans, and Japanese have reacted sharply to this new and unexpectedly effective competition from the Third World by restricting access to their markets. Blocked from these outlets for their new exports, and badly needing revenue, industrializing countries such as Brazil have cultivated markets in other LDCs and have formed trade ties with some Communist nations.

Tariffs and quotas, even when euphemistically labeled "orderly marketing agreements," are not the only trade barriers to gain popularity, and the rising mood of protectionism is not confined to the trade in merchandise. One prevalent device for protecting domestic industry is the subsidy. The widespread subsidization of agriculture, notably the European Economic Community's costly Common Agricultural Policy, has severely distorted world commodity markets. Under the guise of national security, many countries give strong financial support to the shipbuilding and maritime industries. With the aid of heavy subsidies, for example, Taiwan has attained first rank in the building and operating of container ships. Governments likewise compete with each other in subsidies for the financing of exports.

International trade in the services, one of the most rapidly growing sectors of world commerce, has become the subject of growing national rivalry and a surge in protective measures. Many countries shelter from foreign competition such activities as banking, insurance, shipping, construction, aviation, travel industries, tourism, leisure pursuits, and real estate. Especially singled out for protection today are information services, an enormous market because of national programs to modernize telecommunications systems.

How valid are the arguments that industrialists, labor leaders, and politicians use to justify protecting favored interests? One such argument is that domestic firms have a right to their home market and that excluding imports will create jobs and help the local economy. The error in this kind of thinking is that if we buy nothing from other countries, they have nothing with which to buy our products. This costs jobs in our exporting industries and forces consumers to pay higher prices to domestic firms with assured monopolies.

Perhaps the justification used more than any other is the *infant industry* argument. This was a favorite reason given for protection in the United States and Canada during their early industrialization. According to this rationale, a new industry has the potential for ultimately becoming viable in world markets but it is vulnerable at the outset because of high start-up costs and operating inefficiencies during the initial phase. It thus cannot compete with established industries abroad that have already reached top efficiency and maximum economies of scale. As the argument goes, the industry will eventually become strong enough to compete in the world on its own and government protection can be discontinued. This argument has some validity if the industry is indeed

in its start-up phase and if it truly has the potential to become self-sustaining so that government protection can be withdrawn within a reasonable time. However, the argument is acceptable only if the country is an LDC; it has no validity for advanced countries. For instance, when Japan advances the infant-industry argument for protecting its new computer industry, this excuse meets skepticism in other countries. Furthermore, the government must indeed lift its protection after the early stages have passed; the history of protectionism is filled with cases of industries that continue to be sheltered by their governments long after the infant has become hoary with age.

An argument heard throughout the industrialized world during hard times is that protecting domestic industries will reduce unemployment at home. Its proponents insist that jobs must be preserved regardless of the cost to the country's foreign trade. The problem is that this invites retaliation from one's trading partners, which ultimately costs jobs in otherwise prospering export industries. Thus, American limitations on European steel imports induce Europeans to cut off lucrative American farm sales to them. Halting imports to preserve domestic employment means exporting unemployment to other countries and leads to an epidemic of retaliation like that which led to the Great Depression of the 1930s.

Moreover, protectionism does not solve structural employment, which results when a country loses its comparative advantage in a particular line of production. In the more advanced countries, many mature industries—textiles, garments, and steel, among others—can no longer compete on equal terms with newly industrializing countries that have cheaper labor and better access to high-grade raw materials. As Britain has learned, drawing upon the public treasury to preserve such declining industries is like trying to fill a bottomless pit. Retraining of displaced workers and aid to new industries are more logical uses of government funds.

The national security argument is one that nearly everyone considers legitimate. As long as wars continue to be a means for settling international grievances, countries seem justified in preserving those industries engaged in making war matériel and other goods essential to national survival in times of conflict. This argument bears close scrutiny, however, as it is frequently abused. The problem lies in the definition of just which articles are essential to national defense. Manufacturers of all kinds of nonmilitary goods—garments, shoes, foods, and so on—tend to claim that their products should be declared essential to the national interest. High-tech manufactured goods are the subject of much recent controversy on this account.

Antidumping duties are a retaliatory technique that is generally approved. "Dumping," a predatory practice common among developed countries, consists of selling a product abroad at a price below that received for the same article in the domestic market. Under international rules, dumping is illegal: If dumping can be proved, the injured company can justifiably demand that its government impose an antidumping duty upon imports of the offending foreign merchandise. Basic metals manufacturers in the United States have obtained antidumping duties against European imports on such grounds. In theory, dumping is actually legitimate if the merchandise is consistently sold at cut-rate prices over an extended time as a form of permanent discounting operation. Dumping is wrong, however, if it is a short-run predatory practice intended to destroy domestic industries in the importing country so that monopoly prices can then be imposed by the foreign supplier. In practice, a problem with antidumping duties is that governments do not make such distinctions between legitimate and illegitimate dumping and merely apply the duties in response to political pressures. A second problem is that precise means do not exist for measuring true costs and prices in the two countries and it is therefore difficult to determine whether and how much dumping is really taking place.

Protectionism by less-developed countries is a complex issue. Until recently this has received few objections from theoreticians and governments. The infant-industry argument is clearly valid for LDCs, and almost all of them rely upon it. Most LDCs can also argue convincingly that they are entitled to some import protection because of deteriorating terms of trade with advanced countries; that is, because of imperfections in world markets, the prices of the goods they buy from industrialized countries rise more rapidly than do the commodities they customarily sell. LDCs therefore justify imposing import duties to raise revenues to help finance their own new industries. In practice, however, many LDCs have inflicted damaging distortions and inefficiencies upon their own development programs by excessive and unwise use of import restrictions.

In summary, the validity of protectionism depends upon the grounds used for imposing it. A few of the more common arguments are legitimate, but many are not. In practice, protective measures are subject to much abuse, and an uncontrolled proliferation of governmental interference would deprive the world of the fruits of trade. Theoretically, unrestricted trade creates an international division of labor that efficiently allocates the world's resources, thereby increasing total output and raising standards of living everywhere. Ideal conditions rarely exist in reality, of course: Perfect competition is not common, and the transfer of resources from one industry to another does not always take place smoothly or quickly. Yet the evidence shows that trade does bring growth and prosperity. Better forms of governmental intervention than trade restrictions are available to ensure fairness and prevent abuses of free trade by other countries. Political measures to protect local interests are clumsy at best; invariably they produce unintended and unwanted effects and deprive the world of the benefits of specialization and trade.

Factor Prices and Quantities

The introduction of trade may affect the prices of factors of production in both the exporting and importing regions or countries. As trade begins, country A exports the good that is intensive in the factor that is relatively abundant in that country. If the abundant factor happens to be agricultural land, perhaps corn is the land-intensive commodity and thus becomes the exported good. The first effect of trade will be to cause the domestic price of corn to rise in the exporting country, reflecting the new international terms of trade. Resources are progressively taken out of other industries in country A and put into producing more corn. But as more and more land is transferred to corn the additional land becomes available to corn production at ever-higher prices. Thus land, the intensive factor in corn production, becomes more costly in relation to capital and labor. Further reducing the return to capital and labor is the fact that these factors are not needed in such large amounts in corn production as for, say, cotton textile manufacture.

The opposite happens in the importing country, country B. Before trade took place, country B grew its own corn, even though the land was not very good for corn. When trade begins, country B's resources are taken out of corn and transferred into production of the good in which country B has a comparative advantage, namely, labor-intensive textiles. Paradoxically, trade has reduced the return to the scarce factor, labor in the case of country A and land in the case of country B. This sort of effect occurred when the importation of labor-intensive goods into Australia and Canada depressed wages in those labor-short economies.

Ultimately the returns to the factors of production should theoretically become completely equalized among trading nations. Wages paid to labor should be the same, interest rates earned by capital should become standardized, and rent received for land should be equal. Trade will have erased all differences. In reality, however, perfect conditions rarely exist and factor prices stop short of complete equalization. It is seldom possible to shift all resources from one line of production to another. Furthermore, the various barriers to commodity movements prevent full equalization: Transfer costs, tariffs, and other impediments to trade ensure that some factor-price differentials remain.

Note that not only are factor prices affected by trade but also the relative scarcity and abundance of factors in trading nations. We have seen that when trade causes the abundant factor of land, labor, or capital to rise in price, an increase in the quantity of that factor follows. At the same time, the scarce factor, being in less demand, falls in price and decreases in quantity. Thus, trade increases specialization and at the same time exaggerates the differences in factor quantities.

Factor Mobility

One of the limiting assumptions of the Heckscher-Ohlin theory is that no movement of the factors of production takes place among countries. We have seen earlier, however, that capital, labor, and entrepreneurship do indeed have varying degrees of mobility internationally. We noted that financial capital is especially mobile and can even act as a substitute for trade when tariffs or other artificial impediments interfere with commodity movements.

Another effect of interregional and international movements of factors is to produce some equalization of their prices: interest rates, wages, and salaries. For example, capital seeks the market where it receives the highest interest rates. But when the new market becomes saturated with capital, interest rates at that location will fall. Meanwhile, the drain of capital from the old area will cause its interest rates to recover. In this way the return to factors tends to become equalized. Nevertheless, the amount of equalization that can take place is limited. Because of the barriers cited earlier, complete mobility of capital and labor is seldom attained.

The suggestion that factor movements can replace trade is one that is receiving increased attention. Foreign

direct investment for the purpose of making a product previously imported would appear to have a trade-reducing effect. The evidence indicates, however, that the impact of such investment upon economic growth and development can actually be to increase the propensity of countries to trade and therefore to have a net trade-creating effect. Interest is therefore focusing more and more upon the role of the multinational enterprise, that prime mover of the factors of production.

TRADE THEORY IN PERSPECTIVE

The question posed at the beginning of this chapter was: Why do countries trade with each other? Theorists have long been preoccupied with this issue and with what they see as the gains from trade. For the early classical theorists certain benefits automatically follow the opening of trade, which makes it possible for each participating country to concentrate upon making those goods for which its resources are most suited. By exchanging goods, all trading nations can use their productive capabilities to the highest efficiency, thereby increasing their combined output, raising the living standards of their citizens, and permitting consumption patterns to differ from production patterns. The end result is a more efficient use of the world's resources.

By the turn of the twentieth century theorists were discovering still another set of gains from trade. The specialization that follows the opening of trade, they noted, brings additional efficiencies as specialists accumulate experience and further enhance their skills through practice, sharing information with each other, and focusing their inventions and innovations upon a particular industry. Firms are able to reduce unit costs through economies of large-scale operation and, being able to tap large pools of specialized labor skills and to draw upon a growing body of specialized services and facilities, they can achieve external economies as well.

All of this is supposed to happen as a result of free trade, which allows all nations to make optimal use of their resource endowments. In the latter part of the twentieth century, however, the resource-endowments explanation has not stood up well under empirical tests using real-world data. The results clearly show that, although resource endowments play a big part, a number of other elements importantly affect the amount and kinds of economic flows that take place among countries. We have noted in this chapter, for instance, that the nature of demand has a significant influence, especially as it is affected by differing levels of income and cultural variations. Equally important in most cases are the barriers to trade: the impact of distance and governmental intervention. Further complicating the explanation are the feedback effects on the factors of production as a result of trade, which alter both factor quantities and prices.

One conclusion we may draw from this is that the conventional factor-endowment model of trade, as expressed by the Heckscher-Ohlin theorem, is not only incomplete but is also too static. The next chapter, therefore, focuses upon the explicitly dynamic features of world commerce. Change is taking place much more rapidly as the twenty-first century draws closer. Moreover, it becomes increasingly necessary to extend the

discussion to take into account all kinds of economic flows among countries—not just commodity movements but also internationally traded services and flows of capital and other factors. In Chapter 13 we shall be looking at the role of trade in national growth, the effects of technological change, and the inequalities among countries in sharing the benefits of international commerce. We shall give special attention to what may be the most dynamic element of all, the multinational enterprise, a preeminent agent of change in the new world economy now emerging.

TOPICS FOR DISCUSSION

1. Explain why trade theoretically benefits all participants, and discuss the two classes of benefits that trade brings to country trading partners, their citizens, and the world as a whole. How are the factor intensities of industries and the factor endowments of countries reflected in the nature of the trade among countries?

2. Under what circumstances might two countries with identical production possibilities trade with each other? Discuss the various aspects of demand that might affect trade between two countries.

3. Compare and contrast the effects of tariffs and quotas upon the production, consumption, and trade of both the exporting and importing countries. Who benefits and who loses?

4. What are the different ways in which distance affects trade? What happens to the classical two-country, two-commodity trade model when transport cost is introduced into the equation? How are the two participating countries affected?

5. Assume that two countries produce the same two commodities but have different factor endowments. If they enter into trade with each other, how would we expect this exchange to affect both the supply of their factors of production and the prices of these factors? How may factor movements between two countries substitute for trade, and how would such factor movements affect the prices of those factors?

FURTHER READINGS

BALASSA, BELA. "The Changing Pattern of Comparative Advantage in Manufactured Goods." *Review of Economics and Statistics* (May 1979), 259–266.

Provides an analysis of the changing comparative advantage in 184 classes of manufactured goods for 36 countries. The author found that differences in commodity structure resulted from differences in physical and human capital endowments.

BALDWIN, ROBERT E. "Determinants of Trade and Foreign Investment: Further Evidence." *Review of Economics and Statistics* (February 1979), 40–48.

Employing the same approach used by Leontief in his classic input-output analysis of United States trade, Baldwin studied the trade of 30 countries with results closely paralleling those of Leontief.

CORDEN, W. M. *Recent Developments in the Theory of International Trade.* Princeton, N.J.: Princeton University Press, 1965.

A succinct summary of the evolution of modern trade theory.

HELLER, H. ROBERT. *International Trade: Theory and Empirical Evidence,* 2d ed. Englewood Cliffs, N.J.: Prentice-Hall, 1973.

A brief but well-organized introduction to conventional trade theory, made more understandable with the aid of many clear diagrams and a number of empirical examples.

HOUTHAKKER, H. S. "An International Comparison of Household Expenditure Patterns, Commemorating the Centenary of Engel's Law." *Econometrica* (October 1957), 532–551.

Houthakker measured the elasticities of demand for food, clothing, housing, and other items in the household budgets of countries at different levels of per capital income.

KINDLEBERGER, CHARLES P. *Foreign Trade and the National Economy.* New Haven, Conn.: Yale University Press, 1962.

A very readable summary of international trade theory.

LEONTIEF, WASSILY W. "Domestic Production and Foreign Trade: The American Capital Position Re-examined." *Proceedings of the American Philosophical Society,* September 1953. Reprinted in *Readings in International Economics,*

R. E. Caves and Harry C. Johnson, eds. Homewood, Ill.: Richard D. Irwin, 1968, pp. 503–527.

Contains original statement of Leontief's famous "paradox."

LINDER, STAFFAN BURENSTAM. *An Essay on Trade and Transformation.* New York: John Wiley, 1961.

Linder advanced the idea that, although differences in factor endowments may explain trade in land-intensive goods, the structure of a country's manufactured exports depends upon prior production for the domestic market.

MacDOUGALL, G. D. A. "British and American Exports: A Study Suggested by the Theory of Comparative Costs. Part I." *Economic Journal,* 19, No. 2 (June 1951), 697–724.

This study evaluated the effects of differences in labor productivity on the export performances of the United Kingdom and the United States.

OHLIN, BERTIL. *Interregional and International Trade* (rev. ed.). Cambridge, Mass.: Harvard University Press, 1952.

A revision of Ohlin's classical statement of the Heckscher-Ohlin theory concerning the role of resource endowments in generating trade between countries.

SAMUELSON, PAUL A. "International Trade and the Equalization of Factor Prices." *Economic Journal* (June 1948), 163–184.

A seminal statement of the factor-price equalization theorem.

CHAPTER 13

Dynamics of World Trade and Investment

International commerce is changing at an accelerating pace. Dynamic forces at work in today's world economy require modifications in conventional theory, which attributes trade to the factor endowments of countries but assumes that those endowments remain constant in quantity and method of use (Chapter 12). Trade plays a central role in economic growth, which entails the acquisition of technology; indeed, technology gaps between countries are responsible for much trade. Though trade is thus essential for development, it poses special problems for less-developed countries. Nevertheless, several less-developed countries have achieved rapid growth through trade.

Many countries—both developed and less-developed—have established cooperative arrangements for gaining the benefits of free trade. One such device is economic integration, which reduces trade barriers among members but discriminates against others. Another, exemplified by GATT, is an agreement to reduce barriers gradually among a majority of nations.

The multinational enterprise (MNE) has had a great impact upon both the theory and reality of world commerce. Headquartered in one country but controlling subsidiaries in others, the MNE is an efficient agent for transferring goods and factors of production between countries. Thus, it helps to achieve a global equalization of factors and it is a prime agent of technological change.

Objectives:

- to examine the relationships between trade and economic growth and the trade effects of technology
- to identify the trade problems of less-developed countries and to compare their trade strategies
- to assess the leading types of intergovernmental agreements for solving mutual problems of trade, investment, and development
- to explain why multinational enterprises have become prime agents for the transfer of goods and factors among nations

A CHANGING INTERNATIONAL SCENE

World commerce is constantly changing. Flows of goods and investment grow or shrink in quantity, shift in direction, and change in composition and character. In large measure the dynamic nature of commercial relations among countries reflects changes in human and natural resource endowments and the effects these have upon comparative advantage. Each factor of production is subject to many altering forces. Age structures of populations change, labor forces increase in size and learn new skills, capital accumulates through savings or foreign investment, new physical resources are discovered and old ones are depleted, technology is acquired through research or transfer from abroad, and managerial skills grow. These changes do not come at the same time or in equal measure to all places, however, and different rates of change can greatly alter trade and investment, creating problems for those nations that are slow to adjust. Countries have developed a variety of strategies for attacking these problems, both individually and in cooperation with others. A leading actor in this dynamic international scene is the *multinational enterprise,* which is one of the principal agents of change.

TRADE AND GROWTH

Precisely how trade affects economic growth is much disputed. But analysts generally agree that trade plays a central part in the growth process and that the relationship between trade and growth is reciprocal: Any gain for one benefits the other. This is a natural result of the close interaction between production and consumption on the one hand, and trade on the other. Growth occurs mainly in two ways. It may take place

(1) through an increase in the available factors of production—additions to the supply of capital, labor, and arable land, for instance, or (2) as a result of technological advances.

In the growth of an economy trade may lead the way for the other sectors, as it so frequently did during the nineteenth century. This was clearly the case in Canada, whose rapid growth followed the expansion of its staple export industries—furs, forest products, grains—in response to rising demand in other countries. Among those countries currently in the earlier stages of their development, however, growth of the economy more often precedes trade growth. Typical of this group is Colombia, whose postwar experience is illustrated in Figure 13.1a. Note that the gross domestic product (total output of goods and services) of that country has risen more rapidly than have exports and imports. In other instances trade and economic growth have gone hand in hand, as in Japan's case. Striking exceptions to this general pattern of recent decades, however, are offered by certain Asian economies, where export-oriented industrialization has resulted in rapid trade-led growth. One such country is Hong Kong. Figure 13.1b demonstrates how soaring exports have raised the economy of that small city-state to surprising heights in a very short time.

Growth and the Propensity to Trade

The experience of modern times has shown that countries participate in trade to a changing extent as their economies grow. At the outset, when trade is essential to its economic development, a country increases its exports and imports rapidly. Thereafter, its trade continues to expand but at a slower rate than that of the economy as a whole. In the later stages of economic growth

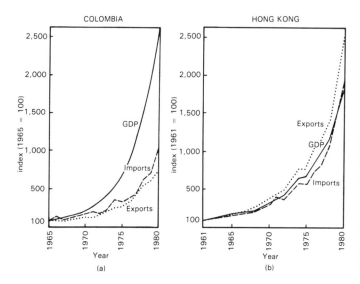

FIGURE 13.1   Growth of trade and gross domestic product (GDP) of (a) Colombia and (b) Hong Kong. Colombia's GDP has grown more rapidly than its trade, as is typical of most developing countries. Hong Kong, on the other hand, has experienced export-led growth and is thus representative of a rising group of countries on the Pacific rim. [*Source:* United Nations, *Yearbook of International Trade Statistics* and *Yearbook of National Accounts Statistics,* various years (New York: United Nations).]

a country's trade may decline still further in relation to its total output as the emphasis shifts from producing goods to providing services, most of the latter being consumed locally.

The world economy has expanded enormously since the Industrial Revolution, and international trade has multiplied at a corresponding rate, bringing fast growth to those countries participating in this commerce. When a country's exports first successfully enter the world market, this causes the domestic economy to expand swiftly. The rate of acceleration is all the greater if the population had previously engaged in subsistence activities, producing only for family consumption. Production for export requires specialization, which leads to an increasingly fine division of labor. As foreign sales continue to multiply, the prosperity of the export sector spreads to the rest of the economy: Money circulates more quickly and incomes rise, thereby enlarging the domestic market.

Initially, a single staple commodity may dominate a country's exports, as, for instance, cotton fiber in the early United States or cotton textiles in Britain. Growing success in this type of production soon spreads to other related industries, causing these to expand also, along with transportation and other supporting services. In some of these affected industries the rising level of output may provide sufficient economies of scale for their goods to compete successfully in world markets. This enables the country to add new classes of exports to its original staple export. All of this growth creates new needs, many of which cannot be supplied locally by the still-limited productive capabilities of the economy. Thus, a demand arises for an increasing quantity and variety of imported commodities, especially industrial raw materials and machinery. Meanwhile, rising incomes induce the country's inhabitants to demand a growing number of foreign-produced consumer goods. Rising incomes do not favor equally all classes of imported products, however. In accordance with Engel's law, families allocate smaller and smaller proportions of additional income to purchases of food and spend ever-larger amounts on manufactured products and services. The composition of imports therefore gradually shifts to reflect these changes in industrial and consumer demand.

As the country's consumption of certain imported goods continues to rise, entrepreneurs become aware of the opportunity these offer for local manufacture. This *demonstration effect* of imports leads to the introduction of an ever-larger number of factories making items that were previously imported. The incentive for local manufacture is especially great for goods whose production tends to be market-oriented—that is, products that can be made and sold more cheaply close to the point of ultimate consumption (see Chapter 10). *Import substitution* of this kind correspondingly reduces dependence upon foreign suppliers of such goods. Thus, both imports and exports ultimately grow more diverse even as they become a shrinking proportion of a rising total national output. Adding further to this relative decline in trade dependence with maturation of the economy is the proliferation of services and the rising share of national income spent on these.

Growth through Technology

The second kind of growth results from an improved technology, which yields greater output from the same quantity of resources. A new device such as the mechanical reaper, the cotton gin, or the self-doffing spindle frees large numbers of workers for other purposes, while at the same time expanding the volume of exportable product. A new technique that permits a larger percentage of metal to be extracted from gold ore has the effect of increasing the national reserves of that mineral. Producing a new technology involves two related processes, *invention* and *innovation*. The more fundamental process is invention, which entails the conception of a basic idea, such as the discovery that steam has the power to perform work. This is the product of laboratory scientists. Innovation, on the other hand, is the application of that idea to something directly useful to humankind, such as the development of the steam engine and the use of that device to power pumps for raising water from mines and to run textile machinery. This is the work of engineers.

Innovation is of two fundamental types. The first of these provides more efficient and cheaper ways to make existing goods. Japanese engineers have excelled in this form of industrial technology, as indicated by their success in developing more economical and reliable techniques for manufacturing automobiles, ships, and electronic goods of all kinds. Second, innovation can result in creating entirely new products, such as fiber optics and computers. The United States still leads in this form of innovation.

In recent times the pace of technological change has been accelerating at an astounding rate. Modern technology issues principally from organized programs of systematic research into which corporate, institutional, and governmental sponsors pour huge sums in an effort to gain the rich rewards of product innovation in an intensely competitive world. Innovation has always occurred more rapidly in some countries than others, resulting in a *technology gap* between the leaders and the followers. Although in the past the leadership has tended to remain with a particular country or group of countries for an extended period, the signs today point to a more rapid shift of technological supremacy among contending nations.

These international differences in technology contradict one of the basic assumptions implicit in the Heckscher-Ohlin theorem, namely that all countries are able to draw upon the same technology, and that a particular industry makes its products in the same manner everywhere. Technology not only differs among nations but it has the power to alter their resource endowments in profound ways. Technological change is thus one of the most dynamic elements in today's world trade picture.

The Trade Effects of Technology

A new production technology affects trade in a variety of ways: It can create exports for a country, it can provide substitutes for imports, and it can give rise to a new demand for imports. If the country originating a new product is able to retain exclusive control of its manufacture, perhaps through secrecy or because that country is the only one technically capable of making the product, then the effect of innovation is the creation of trade. The United Kingdom initially gained ascendency in world trade through the development of such exports as railway equipment, steam engines, and mechanical pumps and by retaining a monopoly over their production for a long time. The United States has led in producing and exporting aircraft, farm machinery, construction machinery, chemicals, and machine tools.

Technology thus yields products that people all over the world want to buy. Sometimes, however, it is possible for an importing country to use its technology to develop substitutes for goods formerly imported, thereby reducing trade. The United States has been successful in this type of invention and innovation, as shown by the many substitutes that have been synthesized to replace natural products formerly obtained from abroad. Synthetic rubber and nylon are familiar examples. Ultimately, such technology spreads throughout the world, reducing world trade in rubber, natural fibers, and other replaced commodities. In general, however, it seems probable that technology has acted to expand trade. Evidence for this is the enormous increase in high-technology goods entering world commerce.

Technology also affects international commerce through improvements in communication and transportation. Because communication is essential to business, anything that makes the transmission of information quicker, easier, or cheaper tends to facilitate the flow of goods and investment. Such developments as the overseas cable, telephone, telegraph, and radio, and, more recently, satellite communication have had powerful effects upon world commerce.

In the long run the transport rate curve has moved steadily downward, at least in relative terms. This has contributed to the gradual spread of trade to remote parts of the world. Numerous transport innovations, such as the screw propeller, steel hulls, refrigeration, containerization, and jet aircraft, have helped to bring down the cost and time required for moving both goods and people. By these means the farthest reaches of South America and Oceania have been able to join the modern world economy.

Trade Growth and the Diffusion of Innovation

As we have seen, the emergence of one export industry in a country gives rise to others, and the effects ultimately spread through the national economy. In the United Kingdom, this diffusion began with the textile industry, then extended into other industries such as iron, metal products, and coal. This development does not remain confined to one country, but diffuses internationally as well. British investment eventually moved into France, followed by technical aid and skilled workers, enabling that country to join Britain as a supplier to the world market. The new technology quickly spread thereafter to other Western European countries, particularly Germany, Austria, Switzerland, and Italy.

The diffusion of ideas occurs in a variety of ways. Some ideas have reached new areas through the theft of technical secrets, as in the transfer of textile technology from Lancashire in Britain to New England during the early nineteenth century, thereby creating a new center from which textiles could be exported to the world in competition with the original center. The American computer industry confronts similar acts of industrial thievery today. The same result is achieved in a more open and legal fashion through licensing arrangements, the publishing of technical articles, and foreign education for technicians, engineers, and scientists. In earlier times colonization was conducive to the spread of ideas throughout the world, and the trade links that France and Britain still maintain with their former colonies testify to the durability of that avenue of communication. In recent years one of the most effective means for the rapid transfer of business and technical information has been the multinational enterprise. An innovation developed in centrally located company laboratories can be transmitted immediately to corporate branches in other parts of the world.

Another avenue for diffusion of trade has been through the foreign procurement of industrial raw materials and foodstuffs. As nineteenth-century British industrialists reached farther and farther afield for ore, timber, grains, animal products, and other needs, they brought trade to Spain, Sweden, Denmark, The Netherlands, Canada, the United States, and other foreign suppliers. Eventually such distant regions as Australia, New Zealand, South Africa, and Argentina entered the British commercial orbit, to be followed later by suppliers of rubber, vegetable oils, and other tropical goods. British investment in these foreign undertakings foreshadowed the global operations of modern-day multinational corporations.

The outward movement of particular types of production from centers of innovation tends to be selective. Raymond Vernon has explained this in terms of the *product life cycle* theory. The manufacture of a new product, he notes, usually requires proportionally large numbers of engineers and skilled workers in what is at first a highly experimental, low-volume operation. Eventually manufacture becomes sufficiently routine for the introduction of mass-production techniques yielding economies of scale. Because skill requirements are less demanding in this second phase of the cycle, production can take place in areas other than the center of innovation. When the industry becomes fully mature, still more of the production can be assigned to specialized machines that require only unskilled operators. At this point the industry shifts to areas having a surplus of cheap labor, often in less-developed countries. Thus, as an industry progresses through the product life cycle, its factor intensities become altered and its locational requirements change.

The electronics industry exemplifies this cyclical type of development (see Chapter 10). Much of the initial production of new electronic equipment occurs in such centers of innovation as eastern Massachusetts, but once production becomes standardized it does not remain in that location for long. Some of the first television picture tubes were built in the Boston area, but the mass production of television sets quickly became established in the American Midwest. In time, a major portion of the industry moved to border areas of Mexico and to Japan, Korea, and Taiwan as the industry matured. In the absence of further discoveries in the original source areas, the ultimate effect would be to reduce trade based on technology and to leave as the dominant cause of trade simple comparative advantage in the basic factors of production. This appears to be happening in the automotive industry, which is growing most rapidly in those countries with the relatively low-cost labor, capital, and large domestic markets for consumer durables required by this mature industry.

Leadership in invention and innovation has generally concentrated in one particular region or country at a given time. This has provided the leader with an important competitive edge in the exportation of high-tech goods. The principal center of innovation must strive to preserve this comparative advantage and must

try to remain one step ahead of its competitors. In the past, no country has succeeded in retaining the technological lead permanently. In the beginning Britain assumed first place in technology, a position it managed to hold without challenge until about 1850. Western Europe and the United States subsequently gained ascendency, with much of the basic science originating in Europe and applied technology originating in the United States. By the time of World War II, however, the United States had attained a commanding place in both invention and innovation.

In recent decades America's lead has come under attack as the pace of technological change has quickened in other industrialized countries, most particularly Japan, West Germany, the United Kingdom, and France. As a result of this heightened activity, technology gaps have closed and new ones have opened with increasing rapidity in one line of production after another.

Thus, the United States no longer leads in many of the old technologies—textiles, steel, motor vehicles—and has become a net importer of these goods. Now the country is struggling to maintain its long-time dominance in the manufacture and export of the newer, technology-intensive products that have become so vital to the balance of trade. The dimensions of this problem and its policy implications are discussed further on pages 330–334.

TRADE AND DEVELOPMENT

While the industrialized countries of the world vie for the lead in technology, the less-developed nations contend with the wide technology gap that separates them from the more advanced producers. The less-developed lands generally lack the research and development funds, the labor skills, and the professional, scientific, and engineering personnel required to invent and innovate. Instead, they must rely upon borrowed technology, which often is inappropriate for their needs and obsolete before it reaches them.

The technology gap is but one of the important reasons why the trade experience of less-developed countries differs so markedly from that of the industrialized countries; indeed, the circumstances facing today's poorer lands are very probably unlike those that confronted the present industrialized lands when they were beginning their own development. Many observers therefore express doubt that the benefits of trade, so obvious in the case of the advanced countries, automatically operate for the rest of the world. Why should this be so? What is there about today's newly developing countries that is so different from yesterday's? If

Is the United States Losing Its Lead in High-Technology Trade?

For many years the United States has relied upon a large technological lead to sustain its balance of trade with the world, but today that lead seems to be slipping. The nation's surplus of high-technology exports over imports, which has been dwindling for some time, has finally disappeared. This comes at a time when technology gaps among countries have been opening and closing at an accelerating rate. At one time the international transfer of new technology required a generation or more, but today it takes only a few years at most.

Even the perception of what constitutes high technology is changing. Industrial products mature at ever-faster rates, so that a high-technology good at one time is only a medium- or low-technology good at another, later period. Thus, the product life cycle has greatly speeded up, making it difficult to compare one era with another. High-technology industries are usually defined as those making relatively large expenditures for research and development (R&D) and employing a high percentage of scientists, technicians, and manual workers with specialized skills. Lists of high-technology products ordinarily include chemicals, machinery (including electronics), transport equipment, and professional instruments; however, only certain subcategories of these can rightly be considered high technology at the present time. For instance, bulk chemicals such as acids and alkalis no longer justify this classification.

With an annual trade deficit passing the $100 billion mark, the United States has viewed with anxiety the signs that its international position in high-technology production is weakening. Just how vital this sector is to the country's overall trade balance is apparent from Figure 13.2. A big trade surplus in technology-intensive products has supported other major trade categories that have done less well. For many years the country has had a large trade deficit in raw materials and fuels (see Chapter 5), as depletion of domestic supplies, soaring world commodity prices (especially for oil), and rising demand have increased the country's import bill for these goods. Similarly, imports of low-technology manufactured products, such as textiles and clothing, have exceeded exports by a growing margin. A fourth category, agricultural commodities, usually has a trade surplus, although this fluctuates widely from year to year, depending upon world harvests, protectionist policies in key markets (especially Europe), the trade effects

of U.S.–USSR relations, and the relative strength of the dollar with respect to other currencies.

The United States maintained a strong positive balance of trade in high-technology goods until 1965; after that, the surplus began to dwindle until by 1984 it had vanished altogether. Why has this turnabout occurred? The country's lead in basic science remains strong, as indicated by continued American dominance of Nobel Prize awards, but its supremacy in applied technology seems to have slipped away. The start of this reversal coincided with the period when Europe and Japan had completed their recovery from World War II and were beginning to approach American levels of production and consumption. In addition to the rise of these new competitors, another reason for the declining U.S. position has been the nature of the nation's response to the accelerating product life cycle. Although new products have regularly replaced old ones in the country's export mix, the maturer forms of production now moving to other countries are high-volume operations that account for sizable shares of world trade. The newer manufactured products and services generate far lower total export earnings.

One development that is sharply reducing U.S. technology-intensive exports is the growing trend for multinational enterprises to transfer their latest technology immediately to their overseas affiliates in order to avail themselves of cheap labor and local raw materials, thereby forestalling potential competition. For example, Sikorsky Aircraft is making its most advanced helicopters in Brazil, and AT&T is producing some of its latest telecommunications equipment in the south of Europe.

A further reason for America's dwindling technological lead is the failure of U.S. firms to apply their technology to cutting production costs. Japan and several newly industrializing lands of East Asia are vigorously improving their production technology at a time when the productivity of American labor is lagging, largely because of the continued use of aging plant and equipment.

Finally, the United States is not spending enough on R&D. Basic scientific discoveries in university laboratories are not being followed up by American business, which should be looking for opportunities to use this knowledge in practical ways. American expenditures for R&D represented only 3 percent of gross national product in the early 1960s,

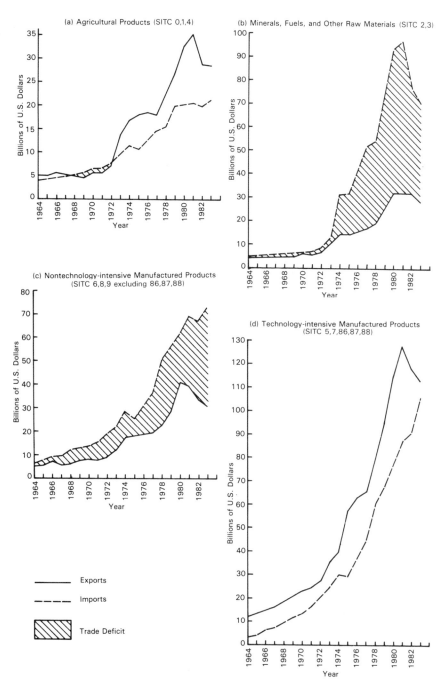

FIGURE 13.2 Changing structure of U.S. trade. The United States has depended upon a trade surplus in high-technology manufactures to compensate for trade deficits in non-technology-intensive manufactures and in raw materials and fuels; but, as these diagrams show, the country may be losing this comparative advantage. The balance of trade in agricultural commodities is usually positive but fluctuates widely from year to year. [*Source:* United Nations, *Yearbook of International Trade Statistics,* various years (New York: United Nations).]

and the percentage continued to fall throughout the 1970s. Fortunately, outlays for R&D have recently begun to rise as intense foreign competition forces business firms to automate in order to reduce costs and raise quality.

Some U.S. high-technology industries are faring better than others in the competition for domestic and foreign markets. The American chemical industry has been an extremely successful exporter for the past half century, contributing nearly 10 percent of

the country's foreign earnings in some years. Any deterioration of this industry's international position, therefore, is a serious problem for the country. American chemical exports soared throughout the 1950s and 1960s but began to encounter competition from European and Japanese producers in its overseas markets during the 1970s. In the 1980s the growth of U.S. chemical exports has slowed, while imports of chemicals have climbed. These changes in the world chemical trade result mainly from a greatly expanded capacity of competitors, both in other developed countries and in newly industrializing countries. In particular, new production of organic chemicals is occurring in Canada, Saudi Arabia, Kuwait, and Mexico. More encouraging developments, however, are to be seen in the U.S. pharmaceuticals industry, which has greatly expanded its R&D and is sending a growing array of new products into world markets.

Electronics has long been a positive contributor to the country's trade balance, but in 1984 for the first time imports of electronic goods exceeded exports, and by a considerable margin (see Figure 13.3). This gap, which is still growing, is a serious problem because electronics is one of the country's largest manufacturing employers. It has also been a main hope for recouping some of the jobs lost by the decline of the older heavy industries, such as steel and autos. One of the causes of the deteriorating international competitiveness of U.S. electronics has been an overvalued dollar, which makes American exports too expensive and imports cheap. However, a more basic reason for the slippage, which first appeared at the end of the 1970s, is the inability of American

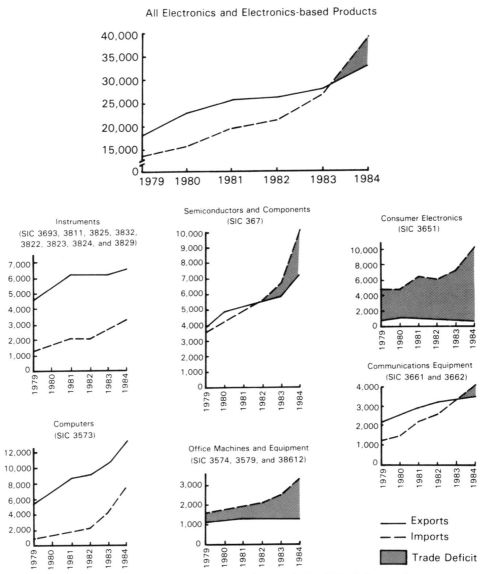

FIGURE 13.3 Deteriorating trade balance of the United States electronics industry (million U.S. dollars). Some branches of the industry are competing more successfully than others, but all are losing ground. [*Source:* Data supplied by the American Electronic Association.]

firms to convert their technological discoveries into competitive products.

Illustrating these problems is the case of the computer industry (Figure 13.3). American computer makers have been locked in a competitive struggle for this crucial market with the Japanese industry, which is heavily subsidized under the Japanese government's current five-year plan. American companies still dominate the world market for computers, but they purchase most of their components from foreign manufacturers because they cannot make them competitively at home. The majority of computer terminals, for example, come from Japan, South Korea, and other East Asian lands.

The world market for computer chips is huge, amounting to tens of billions of dollars, and is fed by the growing trend to incorporate electronics into all kinds of products. Although computer chips were an American development, Japan quickly seized the lead in manufacture and had 70 percent of world sales by the end of the 1970s. However, U.S. makers seem to be benefiting from the current emphasis upon chips designed for special applications, because American engineers and manufacturers still excel in devising new technologies and creative software. Furthermore, the production of custom-designed parts of this kind is locationally tied to end-users. The fragmented markets that result from this are unsuited to the Japanese, whose techniques are geared to mass production.

Telecommunications is another very large and dynamic high-technology area that is stressed by Japan's economic planners. The United States had always had a positive balance of trade in this category until 1984, when imports of telecommunications equipment for the first time exceeded exports. In this case the main competition comes from Canada as well as Japan.

For years, one of the keystones of the American lead in high technology has been the aircraft industry, which draws upon some of the country's greatest competitive strengths. Very large, highly capitalized companies dominate this industry, in which product development alone requires billions of dollars. American aircraft builders have benefited from enormous defense contracts from both the U.S. and foreign governments, and these have yielded valuable R&D by-products for the development of commercial aircraft. U.S. exports of aircraft still make a large positive contribution to the balance of trade, but imports are beginning to cut into this surplus too (see Figure 13.4).

How can the United States prevent further ero-

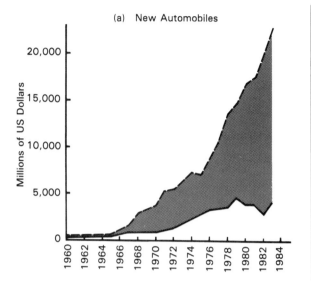

FIGURE 13.4 The U.S. balance of trade in new automobiles and aircraft. Helping to offset the burgeoning deficit in automobile trade is the large positive balance in aircraft sales. U.S. imports of foreign-made aircraft are rising, however, and the rate of export growth is slowing. Note the effects of economic recession in the mid-1970s and again in the early 1980s. [*Source:* U.S. Bureau of the Census, *Statistical Abstract of the United States 1985* (Washington, D.C.: U.S. Government Printing Office, 1984).]

sion of its high-technology trade? What steps should the country take to stimulate exports in this important area of comparative advantage? As foreign competition intensifies, many in the industry have agitated for government protection from imports, but a 1984 report on this subject by the President's Commission on Industrial Competitiveness (the Young Commission) offered a different set of prescriptions and stressed the need to increase manufacturing productivity.

The Young Commission urged that the United States direct more private and government money into civilian research and development. Other countries are spending much more on R&D, as a percentage of gross national product, and the United States should follow their example and in a more organized way than in the past. Half of U.S. research funding—$100 billion annually—currently goes to the military, which no longer yields the civilian spinoffs that it formerly did in simpler times.

The Young Commission sternly criticizes American industry for failing to modernize its manufacturing techniques. Too often, U.S. firms are unable to gain full benefit from their newly developed products because foreign competitors soon make them more cheaply. According to the Young report, however, much of the fault lies with the U.S. government, which has created an economic environment in which capital is too costly. Japanese companies can borrow at interest rates only a fraction of those paid by American firms. The Young Commission also blames U.S. antitrust laws and practices, which prevent the kind of interfirm cooperation needed to compete with giant, integrated companies like those in Japan and other East Asian countries.

The international competitiveness of U.S. high-technology enterprises suffers also from the country's failure to make the best use of its human resources. The Young Commission criticizes the adversarial relationship between management and labor, which is harmful to productivity and quality control. In addition, however, the country is failing to educate enough scientists and engineers and is doing too little to retrain workers at a time of rapid technological change.

Like many critics before them, the Young Commission stresses the need for the U.S. government to make a greater commitment to using the country's resources more effectively and thus increasing international competitiveness. To focus this effort, the commission urges the creation of a Cabinet-level Science and Technology Department and a Trade and Industry Department. Such agencies have played key roles in the industrial development of Japan and a number of other countries.

Technology-intensive products are the most dynamic element in contemporary international commerce. The United States has long relied upon its comparative advantage in high-technology production, but its lead in this area is fragile. Whether the country can halt its recent slippage in high-technology trade in this era of intensifying competition depends upon how effectively it can mobilize its resources to that end.

---

such differences truly exist, can we be sure that conventional trade theory, with its emphasis upon free trade, is appropriate for the less-developed world?

Finding answers to these questions is complicated by the fact that the two-thirds of the world's nations that lag in their development are far from being a homogeneous group. True, they share a number of common traits that mark them as less developed—low per capita incomes, economies dominated by agriculture and other primary production, export dependence upon a limited number of commodities, high birth rates and population growth rates, low literacy, and so on—but in other respects they vary widely from each other. Even in terms of material well-being, they range from the desperate poverty of Kampuchea and Chad, whose GNP is under $100 per person, to the comparative prosperity of Singapore and Taiwan, which are becoming industrialized nations. In between lie nearly 100 other countries of varying degrees of advancement. The less-developed countries differ greatly in size, too, whether measured by territory or population, from enormous China and India to tiny Trinidad and Hong Kong.

For convenience, we may divide the less-developed world into three main groups. First, following Linder's (1967) classification, we may distinguish between the countries that are truly *developing*, that is, those demonstrating a real capability for the sustained growth required ultimately to join the industrialized world, and those that may be termed *backward*, nations confronting such grave obstacles to development that very little hope can be held for their future prospects. Recent events have pushed into prominence still a third, anomalous group, the high-income oil exporters, typified by Saudi Arabia and Libya. Despite all the usual demographic and cultural traits of underdevelopment, these lands have achieved some of the world's highest per capita GNPs because their oil revenues are very great relative to their small populations (see pages 361–363).

Trade Problems of Less-Developed Countries (LDCs)

Except for the high-income oil exporters and a small, select group of Asian lands, the less-developed countries

(LDCs) of this present era have not found trade to be the vehicle for economic growth that it had been for those countries now regarded as developed. The great majority of LDCs encounter a host of serious problems in their commercial relations with the rest of the world. Some of these problems are of domestic origin, being inherent in the condition of underdevelopment; others, however, stem from the conditions of inequality faced by LDCs in their dealings with the industrialized world.

One of the most serious dilemmas for LDCs results from their tendency to overspecialize in export production. Most of these countries rely upon only one or two commodities, usually agricultural products or minerals, for the greater part of their export earnings. Cuba, for instance, obtains 94 percent of its foreign exchange from the sale of primary commodities, and 83 percent of the total comes from sugar alone. The Sudan depends upon cotton, peanuts, and a few other agricultural goods for 100 percent of its export earnings. According to conventional trade theory, a country should benefit from concentrating its resources upon what it does best because of the efficiencies and the economies of large-scale production that specialization supposedly brings. For exporters of primary goods, however, this is not usually the case. Narrow specialization in such commodities risks heavy losses as a result of crop failures, uncertain foreign demand, and fluctuating world prices. Adding to these problems is the temptation for primary producers to increase output even during periods when the world market has become saturated and prices are falling. Seeing their incomes decline as prices drop, farmers may plant still larger acreages in the hope that the increased volume of output will help them maintain their customary incomes. This response to glutted markets is directly opposite to that of factory managers in similar circumstances.

In some LDCs the primary export industries are owned and controlled by foreign enterprises. This is common in mineral ventures and in plantation agriculture, and especially in the production of beverage crops, commercial fibers, and tropical fruits. Foreign companies supply not only the capital and technology but also the managers and skilled workers needed for a modern venture serving world markets. Only the unskilled laborers come from the local community. Surrounding these enclaves of commercial agriculture are the subsistence farms of the indigenous populations. Such a juxtaposition of the primitive and the modern constitutes a *dual economy,* a feature typical of tropical America, Africa, and southern Asia.

In the organization of their societies most of today's LDCs differ from those lands settled by Europeans, especially the British. Unlike the transplanted Europeans of the early United States and Canada, the current populations of less-developed regions lack an industrial tradition. Inherited social attitudes and value systems are often incompatible with the competitive, profit-driven viewpoints prevalent in industrialized societies. Because of this it is difficult for such peoples to adjust to the changes required for modern production. The LDCs of this present era also confront grave demographic and employment problems. Overpopulation, steadily worsening because of high birth rates, creates a surplus of labor, leading to severe unemployment and underemployment. The current group of industrialized nations did not have to bear any of these social burdens at similar stages of development.

Unequal Trade Relations with Industrialized Countries

The many economic and social problems confronting most of today's less-developed countries place them at a disadvantage in their commercial relations with the developed lands. The major exceptions to this, of course, are the high-income oil-exporting countries of the Middle East, whose membership in the OPEC cartel places them in an unusually strong bargaining position. Excluding these, the LDCs as a whole account for no more than one-sixth of total world trade. Yet, relatively small though it be, this trade is utterly essential to the developing nations. For them the industrial countries are the only source for many of their needs and the principal market for their traditional exports. These imports and exports are indispensable to the development process itself.

Among the imports required by LDCs are those consumer goods they are incapable of producing domestically. Equally crucial, however, are those commodities required for economic growth: the machinery and other capital equipment needed to modernize agriculture and build factories, the spare parts and other items to keep the machinery running, and industrial raw materials not available domestically. Many of these new industries make goods formerly imported, and this *import substitution* further alters the commodity composition of their foreign trade.

To pay for the imports they must have, developing countries have no choice other than to sell their goods in world markets. Initially, at least, these are the primary commodities for which LDCs have both absolute and comparative advantages. Their resource endowments, such as soils and climates conducive to tropical agriculture, dictate the nature of the goods they market abroad. We should stress, however, that LDCs are called primary producers solely because primary products are all they export. Several industrialized nations—notably Canada, the United States, Australia, and the

USSR—actually export greater absolute amounts of primary commodities because of the immense land endowments they possess. These and other developed countries are the main sources of the grains and other temperate crops that are the major staples of world agricultural commerce.

In exporting primary goods to the industrialized countries the less-developed regions operate under severe disadvantages. For one thing, manufacturers are becoming increasingly efficient in their use of raw materials and are processing them more thoroughly than in the past, thus requiring relatively smaller amounts of these items, many of which come from less-developed areas. Moreover, industries make greater use of synthetic materials that compete with the natural substances. Again, the major exception is petroleum, the need for which grows steadily throughout the world. Otherwise, the contribution of LDCs to world exports continues to shrink relatively.

Another problem for LDCs is the nature of demand for their traditional agricultural exports. Owing to Engel's law (see Chapter 12), world markets for farm products grow slowly—at about the rate of world population growth—and demand for them responds only slightly to changes in prices. Yet, the global supply of these commodities fluctuates widely in response to the variability of harvests, causing prices to be unstable. Individually weak and disunited, LDCs are unable to influence the prices of their agricultural goods in world markets. Instead, such prices are set in the great commodity markets of London, New York, Chicago, and other commercial centers.

Developing countries as a group are becoming more active exporters of manufactured products, but many of them find it difficult to penetrate the markets of industrialized countries. Most manufactured exports of LDCs are technically simple, often the results of first-stage processing of metallic ores. Even some of the more sophisticated manufactured goods exported by developing countries pose marketing difficulties. One such problem is the technology gap, because of which the products of these countries cannot compete on equal terms with the superior quality and lower prices of similar goods produced in the industrialized countries. Furthermore, LDCs usually do not have large enough home markets to provide adequate bases for achieving the necessary economies of scale. This problem is all the greater because of the natural inefficiencies of newly started industries, which raise unit costs. Also, many entrepreneurs in less-developed lands are unfamiliar with the quality standards, delivery schedules, and customary sales channels in major world markets.

LDCs almost always have deficits in their foreign trade, and sometimes these are relatively large. Because of the kinds of problems we have just enumerated, LDCs usually do not earn enough from their exports to pay for all the imported goods they must have to sustain their economies and promote their development. For this reason the governments of LDCs tend to interfere in their foreign trade by using a variety of devices: licensing, exchange controls, tariffs, quotas, etc. They consider these necessary to limit the drain on their reserves of foreign exchange and to reduce the importation of "inessentials" so as to conserve financial resources needed to pay for necessary items. Tariffs help to improve the price ratio (terms of trade) with industrialized nations and provide protection for infant industries.

Among the LDCs, those that can be considered as "developing" probably have the most immediately pressing import needs, but the "backward" countries possibly have the gravest trade problems in the longer run. Trade with the industrialized world can quickly extinguish any unprotected import-competing industry that might have served as a basis for development, as happened when cheap factory-made imports killed much of the cottage industry of India. In some LDCs the obstacles to development are so great that even large export earnings may fail to nudge the nation toward true modernization, as shown by the experience of certain oil-exporting countries of Africa and the Middle East.

So different, then, are the less-developed countries as a group from industrialized countries that many analysts are asking whether conventional trade theory is truly relevant to the experience of today's LDCs. According to this theory, free trade invariably leads to an international specialization that is beneficial to all participants. It brings about a more efficient allocation of resources, and it spreads its effects to other sectors of the economy. The experience of the United Kingdom and other advanced countries during the nineteenth century and that of Japan since World War II would seem to confirm this. Why is it not happening generally among today's LDCs?

The main reason for the failure of these theoretical expectations to materialize widely in the Third World is that most LDCs do not have the capacity to extend growth in their export sectors to the rest of their economies. The apparent explanation for this is that in most contemporary LDCs a variety of political, social, and cultural conditions act as barriers to the linkage of export industries to the economy as a whole. It it these barriers that perpetuate the dual economies described earlier. For these barriers to be removed, development must extend to all aspects of national life. In this process public policy must establish the necessary conditions. The remarkable progress of certain LDCs that have adopted new strategies for trade and development demonstrates the importance of this.

Trade Strategies for Development

Industrialization is the overriding national goal of virtually all less-developed countries. Only industry offers the hope for achieving a level of economic growth that exceeds their rates of population growth; world demand for their traditional agricultural exports is not increasing fast enough. Only manufacturing can generate employment in sufficient quantity to absorb the flood of new entrants into their labor forces. For most LDCs, industrialization is also a matter of national pride: They depend upon it to elevate them to a status comparable to that of the present advanced lands. LDCs therefore resent the implications of conventional trade theory, which would relegate them to a permanent role as suppliers of primary goods to the richer lands.

The road to industrialization has been slow and difficult for today's LDCs, however. Most of them, especially those in Latin America, have until recently followed policies of import-substituting industrialization, that is, establishing industries to produce for the domestic market those manufactured goods previously imported from First World countries. In addition to the elaborate bureaucratic procedures these entail, policies of this sort create many new problems. Import substitution ordinarily means high-cost production for limited national markets, which leads to inflation and represents a continual drain on economies. Furthermore, industrialization of this kind soon saturates local markets and exhausts the opportunities for further import substitution. Consequently, only those LDCs with very large domestic markets—such as Brazil and Mexico—have benefited very much from this approach to development, and even these are having to find new strategies for future growth.

Some of the semi-industrialized countries of the Orient are pointing the way for LDCs that have reached the limits of import substitution. The semi-industrialized countries (SICs) are the new middle-income nations of the world community. They are the most advanced of the LDCs: Their per capita incomes are higher, their manufacturing sectors are larger and more sophisticated, and they are more urbanized. Manufactured goods represent one-fifth or more of their total output, and they constitute a quarter or more of their exports. As a group, the SICs have achieved impressive levels of economic growth, well in excess of their rates of population growth, which in several cases are still high. Most of this growth has resulted from the effective way in which these countries have used their resources to assume new roles in the international economy.

Leading the way are the so-called Four Tigers of Asia: South Korea, Taiwan, Hong Kong, and Singapore. In the past three decades these four countries have successfully followed national policies that have favored export production based upon labor-intensive manufacturing industries operating within a capitalistic framework. None of these countries is well endowed with natural resources, but each is able to draw upon an impressive array of human resources. Although in detail the four countries differ somewhat in their circumstances and approaches, South Korea's experience is fairly typical of the group.

South Korea's economic growth, which averaged more than 9 percent per annum throughout the 1960s and 1970s, is all the more impressive when we consider its dismal state at the end of the Korean War in 1953. With the arrival of peace the country was left with only an impoverished agricultural economy: North Korea had all the mineral resources, nearly all the electric generation, and most of the manufacturing industries still remaining. The war had left South Korea devastated, most of its agricultural lands in waste, industries destroyed, a quarter of the population homeless, and per capita incomes among the world's lowest.

In the decade following the war, from 1953 to 1963, South Korean government policy emphasized reconstruction, defense, and raising the standard of living. United States aid throughout this period was substantial, amounting to 15 percent of gross national product. South Korea initially followed a typical strategy of import-substituting industrialization, concentrating upon nondurable consumer goods—mainly textiles, clothing, and foodstuffs—and giving little attention to agriculture. Though the possibilities for this kind of industrial development were exhausted by the early 1960s, South Korea had in the meantime acquired some valuable assets. Ten years of industrialization, accompanied by a drive to improve education, had produced a literate population and a corps of skilled managers and trained workers.

At this point the government abruptly shifted to a program of export-oriented industrialization, which focused upon producing nondurable consumer goods for the world market. Recognizing that the nation lacked physical resources but had an abundance of human resources, the new program offered special subsidies for exports, removed import duties on raw material imports, changed the tax structure to favor personal savings, and introduced more realistic currency exchange rates. This policy shift quickly produced remarkable results. Exports rose from only 3.3 percent of GNP in 1960 to 45 percent by 1977, and exports of manufactured goods increased at an average rate of 51 percent per year. This rapid trade-led growth continued almost without pause into the 1980s.

South Korea and the other semi-industrialized countries have discovered, however, that an export-favoring policy succeeds only as long as world markets remain free. Because the developed countries are the best customers for SIC exports, taking about three-fifths of the total, access to these markets is very important. Yet, the more deeply SIC exporters penetrate the markets of the developed lands, the more resistance they encounter from rising protectionist sentiments in those countries (see Chapter 12, page 318, for a discussion of this issue).

As quotas and other trade restrictions begin to cut their sales to the advanced countries, the SICs have discovered promising new markets for their manufactured goods in other less-developed countries. Brazil now trades more with other LDCs than it does with the United States; India is increasing its exports to the less-developed world faster than to the developed countries. The greater part of this rising trade among LDCs is from the more-industrialized countries to the less-industrialized ones; only a minor share takes place between countries at similar levels of development.

The manufactured products traded among LDCs are mainly those that rely upon economies of scale in manufacturing, have demanding skill requirements, call for relatively large capital inputs, and are produced by industries that were initially established to serve domestic markets. Note that these products exchanged by LDCs are different in nature from the labor-intensive exports they send to industrialized countries. Furthermore, the products LDCs buy from each other are usually complementary to the kinds of goods they obtain from advanced countries, not substitutes for them. Few LDC manufactured exports to go Communist lands: Too many Communist countries already make these same goods and sell them to each other at arbitrarily low prices.

One of the more significant recent trends in intra-LDC trade has been the rise in exports of capital equipment by certain of the more-industrialized developing countries. Producers in these countries have gained experience in designing and building machinery that is technically appropriate for their own industries, which are more labor-intensive and thus call for designs different from those of industries in Europe, Anglo-America, and Japan, where labor is more costly. Thus, Brazil, Argentina, Taiwan, India, South Korea, and Mexico find markets for their own designs in other LDCs with labor requirements similar to their own. Argentina sells equipment for the processing and refrigeration of meats and fruits, drawing upon her own experience in the food industries. Brazil and Mexico, both well established in the metallurgical trades, export steel-making equipment to LDCs. The semi-industrialized countries are pushing their exports of machinery and transport equipment. These are currently the most dynamic items in world trade, partly because of the growing demand among LDCs for such goods.

Attractive opportunities thus exist for trade among LDCs. They are more similar to each other in their demand and supply than they are to the industrialized countries, and they are more similar in economic size and levels of development; hence, they can compete and trade on more equal terms among themselves. The theoretical benefits of free trade are more attainable by countries at similar levels of development: Among equals, the opportunities for economies of scale and the efficiencies of international specialization are far greater. Buying from each other also permits LDCs to reduce their imports from industrialized lands, thereby saving their scarce hard currency for the purchase of those high-technology items that are as yet obtainable only from the advanced countries. Recognizing these benefits of intra-LDC trade, certain groups of less-developed countries have experimented with economic integration, a type of voluntary association pioneered in Western Europe.

INTERNATIONAL COOPERATION IN TRADE

Although the theoretical ideal of universal free trade has proved elusive, recent history has shown that the interdependence of countries is inescapable in the modern world economy. Policymakers have discovered that trying to "save jobs" by restricting imports carries excessively high costs in terms of slowed economic growth and worsened international relations. Nations have therefore resorted to intergovernmental agreements designed to give some of the benefits of free trade without sacrificing other national goals. Among the numerous approaches attempted, two main types emerge: (1) international agreements to reduce tariffs and quotas gradually and selectively among the majority of countries, and (2) arrangements that would eliminate or substantially reduce the barriers to trade among a small group of closely associated countries. The second approach, termed *regional economic integration,* has been prominent in recent decades.

Regional Economic Integration

The idea of joining sovereign nations together to form a single economic region is not new; the first experiments of this kind took place more than a century ago. Following the devastation of World War II, however, this technique seemed to offer the best hope for speeding recovery from the war and for overcoming the many problems of economic and political disintegration that had burdened Europe during the 1930s. Although trade is the main focus of economic integration, such organizations usually have other aims as well. Among the main purposes of economic integration are achieving growth through the creation of an enlarged market, raising standards of living, reducing regional disparities, enhancing the status of the group in world political and economic affairs, and finding cooperative solutions to a variety of other social and political problems. The questions raised by the postwar revival of such organizations have led to the appearance of a new body of economic integration theory, which is a subset of international trade theory and has implications for location theory. A seminal work on this subject was Jacob Viner's *The Customs Union Issue* (1950). Theoreticians and policymakers have viewed economic integration as a solution for problems of economic growth and development throughout the world.

Economic Integration in Theory and Practice

As viewed by the theorist, economic integration is a form of selective discrimination because it combines elements of free trade with greater protection: free trade among members and restrictions on trade with nonmembers. Among other things, integration theory is concerned with the various types or degrees of economic integration, the characteristics of member countries that are conducive to successful integration, and the effects that economic integration can be expected to have on international trade and location and on growth and development.

According to Bela Balassa (*The Theory of Economic Integration,* 1961), five levels or degrees of economic integration are possible. At each succeeding stage, members surrender a greater measure of their national sovereignty. The first (and least restrictive) form of economic integration is the *free trade area,* in which the members agree to remove all barriers to trade within the group but may continue to pursue their own independent policies with respect to trade with nonmembers. The next higher degree of integration is the *customs union,* a type that has existed in Europe for more than a century. It calls for the free movement of goods among member countries but imposes a common system of restrictions on trade with outsiders. The third type is the *common market,* which, like the customs union, provides for free trade in merchandise among members of the group while maintaining uniform restraints on trade with nonmembers; in addition, however, this arrangement permits unrestricted movement of capital, labor, and entrepreneurship within the union. At a still higher level the *economic union* has all the characteristics of

the common market but calls also for integrating the economies of member countries through a common central bank, unified monetary and tax systems, and a common foreign economic policy. The ultimate form is full *economic integration.* At this point the removal of all barriers to intrabloc movement of goods and factors of production is complete, unification of social as well as economic policies is achieved, and all members are subject to the binding decisions of a supranational authority consisting of executive, judicial, and legislative branches.

One of the earliest experiments, a free trade area attempted during the nineteenth century by Norway and Sweden, was unsuccessful. Certain customs unions formed at that time did survive, however. One of these was the German *Zollverein,* which joined together most of the many small kingdoms and grand duchies that eventually became modern Germany. Also still in existence are several *customs accessions.* These are customs unions that, in each case, unite a very small country with a larger one, as, for example, Switzerland and Liechtenstein, France and Monaco, and Belgium and Luxembourg.

Modern experimentation with cooperative ventures of this kind began in 1944 with the formation of Benelux, the members of which are Belgium, The Netherlands, and Luxembourg. Benelux is essentially a customs union, although its founders had intended that it ultimately become an economic union. In 1952 the three members of this group joined with France, West Germany, and Italy to form the European Coal and Steel Community. The ECSC has functioned as a type of common market but with jurisdiction extending to only two sectors of the six national economies: the coal and steel industries. In view of future developments among these six countries, however, it is interesting to note that the ECSC organization was provided with executive, legislative, and judicial branches.

The immediate success of ECSC led the same six nations to extend this type of integration to all sectors of their economies, thereby creating the European Economic Community (EEC). Under the Treaty of Rome, which established this organization in 1957, the EEC is essentially a common market (and indeed is often referred to as the European Common Market), but it also contains a number of features typical of higher forms of economic integration. The EEC has a supranational authority consisting of an executive (the *Commission* and the *Council of Ministers*), a legislature (the *European Parliament*), and a judiciary (the *Court of Justice*). The surrender of individual national sovereignty implied by this arrangement is more apparent than real: Individual governments continue to exert substantial influence over EEC affairs through the Council of Ministers, and the Parliament does not as yet perform the functions of a true legislature. Nevertheless, labor moves freely throughout the union, as do capital and entrepreneurship, though with some minor restrictions. The EEC has taken steps toward harmonizing its economic policies, but the results have been incomplete, partly because of the impact of the energy crisis of the mid-1970s. Under the terms of the Treaty of Rome, the objective of the EEC is complete integration, political as well as economic, with the ultimate aim of forming a United States of Europe.

Largely because of this avowed political aim of the EEC and its attendant loss of national sovereignty, seven other countries—the United Kingdom, Norway, Sweden, Denmark, Austria, Switzerland, and Portugal (later joined by Finland and Iceland)—established in 1960 a separate organization called the European Free Trade Association (EFTA). As a free trade area in industrial goods only, the EFTA is the least restrictive form of integration. Most of its members had special reasons to avoid more binding ties: prior commitments to non-European trading partners (Britain with the Commonwealth nations), longstanding official policies of neutrality (Switzerland and Sweden), or conditions imposed under peace treaties with the USSR (Austria and Finland).

The striking success of the EEC eventually led the United Kingdom and certain other EFTA members to seek ties with the Common Market. After two fruitless attempts, the United Kingdom finally attained full EEC membership in 1973, along with Denmark and Ireland. On that same date Denmark and the United Kingdom also withdrew from the EFTA, which was left with only seven members. In 1972 the new nine-member EEC entered into an agreement with the remaining members of EFTA to form an industrial free trade area encompassing all 16 countries. In 1981 Greece became the tenth full member of EEC, and Spain and Portugal joined in 1986. The EEC has signed association agreements with Turkey, Malta, and Cyprus, and has extended preferential treatment to other Mediterranean countries. In addition, the EEC has a special trade and aid agreement, called the Lomé Convention, with 58 less-developed countries, all former colonies of EEC countries.

What are the characteristics of member countries that would be conducive to successful integration? Theoreticians predict better results from a union of countries whose economies are similar than one whose member economies are dissimilar. They reason that if several members of a group are able to produce the same goods, economic integration will force them to become more efficient in order to survive the intensified competition.

A union should also yield greater benefits if its members are not too distant from each other. Propinquity reduces transportation cost, increases the likelihood that the tastes of constituent populations will be similar, and causes trading companies to have a greater awareness of business opportunities across the border. Ideally, member countries should be contiguous to one another and should form a combined territory of compact shape, thereby minimizing total aggregate transfer costs throughout the union. The total area of the group should be sufficiently large to permit diverse production and a division of labor among them. If the countries are individually small, however, each member will likely experience relatively greater gains from union because of the greater possibilities for improvement that access to a large market offers such a country. Probability of success is further enhanced if prior to union the members (1) were one another's best customers and principal suppliers, (2) previously contributed in aggregate a substantial proportion of the world's output and trade, and (3) were formerly prevented from trading freely with each other because of high tariffs.

Although both the EEC and EFTA countries benefited from economic integration, the EEC has made the more impressive gains. At the time of its formation, observers expected the Common Market to do well because the resource endowments of member countries appeared to complement each other: France and Luxembourg offered iron ore, Germany coal, Italy surplus labor, and Belgium and The Netherlands large quantities of intensively produced food crops. In actuality, however, most of the products of Common Market countries have proved highly competitive. The members have not relied heavily upon one another's minerals or food supplies but instead have exchanged mainly finished and semifinished manufactured goods. All make iron and steel, fabricate metal products, and produce an enormous variety of consumer goods.

The EEC countries are individually small or moderate in size, but together they comprise a large part of Europe. They are mainly contiguous and are linked by well-developed transport systems. The group includes some of the world's greatest trading nations, and most are one another's best customers. All depend heavily upon trade, especially Germany and the Benelux countries, which export more than one-third of their output. This is a remarkable change from pre–World War II days, when high tariffs and quotas reduced intra-European trade to a minimum.

The EFTA countries are more complementary than the EEC in the goods they produce, and they also range more widely in levels of economic development. Scandinavia exports forest products and minerals, as well as manufactured goods; Switzerland and Austria are principally manufacturing nations; and Portugal and Iceland are mainly primary producers. Unlike the EEC, the EFTA countries are widely separated, and several occupy locations peripheral to the European continent. Some active trading nations belong to the group, but since the departure of the United Kingdom none of the remaining members is the equal of most EEC nations. Whereas the EFTA as a whole has benefited from union, it is interesting to note that the greatest relative gains have gone to the Scandinavian members, which are contiguous, highly competitive with one another, and similar in many other respects. Indeed, the four Scandinavian countries experimented for a time with a trading bloc called the Nordic Economic Union, or Nordek.

One of the theoretical tests of integration is whether it has largely created trade that did not exist before or instead has acted to divert trade out of its natural channels. This is a normative view of the problem, based upon the presumption that trade creation is "good" and trade diversion is "bad." A union has created trade if integration has caused production to shift from high-cost to low-cost sources. Trade diversion entails a shift from low-cost to higher-cost suppliers. Trade creation thus results in a more efficient allocation of world resources, whereas trade diversion has the opposite effect.

Any increase in trade among union members resulting from removal of internal trade barriers represents the creation of new trade. This comes about in the same way as in the case illustrated in Figure 12.1 (Chapter 12), where trade between two countries resulted in savings for buyers and higher incomes for sellers. Countries that do not belong to the union, however, lose some of their former export markets if these are captured by suppliers within the group. To the extent that the old sources of supply were more efficient producers than the new sources within the bloc, trade diversion has taken place. In the long run, however, integration can result in trade gains even for nonmember countries if the union causes members to enjoy accelerated economic growth and thus to demand more products from the rest of the world. Depending upon the way in which trade gains and trade losses balance each other, therefore, economic integration can result in either a net increase in total world trade or a net decrease.

These effects are to be seen in the experience of the EEC, whose trade has grown enormously since union. Though the largest share of this new trade is with other EEC members, trade between the EEC and the rest of the world has also risen sharply because EEC's prosperity has increased the general level of demand in member countries. Yet the EEC has caused some trade diversion in specific commodities. This is especially true of agricultural goods, which have received a uniformly high level of protection under the EEC's Common Agricultural Policy. Denmark, a long-time supplier of foods to neighboring West Germany, lost much of that trade after formation of the union and prior to its belated entry into the group. The Netherlands, a founding member that competes with Denmark in those same farm products, gained some of what Denmark lost in shipments to Germany. Sales of grain by the United States and Canada to the EEC have also suffered because of the new trade barriers, whereas French farmers have been able to pick up additional sales from their protected position inside the common tariff wall. Many other farm products have been similarly affected, notably citrus fruits, as have certain types of manufactured goods.

Removing the barriers to intrabloc trade should theoretically permit each member country to concentrate upon producing those goods for which its comparative advantage is greatest. This specialization, together with increased competition and the economies of large-scale production for an enlarged market, should make producers more efficient. Reduced prices and higher incomes, together with a greater variety of merchandise on store shelves and more efficient distribution of goods, should raise levels of consumption.

The European experiments tend to bear out these theoretical expectations, but not quite in the way anticipated. Studies of trade among members of the EEC and EFTA have not disclosed an increased specialization of one country in steel, another in grain, another in textiles, and so forth. Instead, these major industries have largely remained where they were before union, although certain subcategories have experienced marked changes in location. Thus, all Common Market countries make steel, but one may emphasize sheet-steel products, another may produce structural-steel members, and a third may specialize in wire and rod products.

A high common tariff wall normally discourages some imports from former suppliers outside the union. In reaction to this threatened loss of market, foreign suppliers often decide to build factories inside union territory in order to get under the tariff wall with their goods, thus substituting their flows of capital for flows of goods. The enormous investments by United States companies in manufacturing facilities in Western Europe since integration confirm this locational effect. Indeed, one study found that more that 800 new U.S. enterprises had been established in the EEC during the first three years of its operation.

Because it leads to a free flow of goods among member countries, economic integration is likely to result in a relocation of production within the union. Related industries tend to cluster at a limited number of the more desirable locations to avail themselves of the advantages of agglomeration. This in turn may reduce or eliminate production at those less-viable locations remaining from the preintegration period when each country protected a wide range of its industries, however inefficiently they may have operated. The centers of agglomeration emerging after integration will in turn attract additional new industries, thereby polarizing production still further.

Studies of industrial location since formation of the EEC, where the free flow of capital, labor, and management reinforces these polarizing tendencies, confirm that industrial concentration has indeed intensified in certain favored locations. Yet, the preexisting industrial centers in each member country appear to have survived, an indication of how firmly entrenched the industries of Western Europe had become prior to union. The net locational result of European integration appears to have been not only an increase in intra-industry product specialization but also an intensified regional specialization within the existing locational framework.

One of the principal purposes of economic integration is to promote the economic growth of member countries. Contributing to this growth is the increased efficiency in the use of natural and human resources that union is expected to bring about. The enlarged market provides opportunities for economies of scale to industries previously confined to limited national markets. Intensified competition forces companies to operate more efficiently, and the rising level of demand induces firms to increase in size through internal growth or mergers. As their capital resources grow, companies allocate more funds for research and development, which in turn leads to a proliferation of new products. The increased market also reduces business uncertainty and boosts profits, thereby attracting additional investment from both domestic and foreign sources. This acceleration of economic activity causes personal incomes to swell, further expanding the level of demand. The gains should be greatest for those unions with higher degrees of integration. In the EEC, for instance, the combined GNP rose by more than one-half within the first decade of its existence.

The example of Europe's growth through economic integration was not lost on other parts of the world. Australia and New Zealand formed a free trade area when Britain's entry into the EEC forced them to find other outlets for their goods. The United States and Canada have experimented with a sectoral approach to integration with their automobile agreement. This is essentially a free trade area limited to the components and products of a single large industry that is dominated by a common set of giant companies. The arrangement has been especially beneficial to Canada, where it is now possible for factories to concentrate on long production runs of a limited number of models, thus gaining economies of scale that the small Canadian market could not provide by itself. Some of the most ambitious experiments in integration, however, have taken place among less-developed countries.

Economic Integration and Development

The progress that economic integration has brought to Western Europe has been a special inspiration to less-developed countries. With the encouragement of the economic commissions of the United Nations, LDCs in several parts of the world have turned to this solution for their many problems. Integration is particularly attractive to LDCs because it promises a larger market for their new industries. Typically, the domestic market of an LDC is severely limited by low per capita purchasing power, and this is often further reduced by the small proportion of the population that actually participates in the commercial economy. The subsistence sector of the population represents an insignificant market for most merchandise. A less-developed country therefore offers few attractions to modern industries that require economies of scale. To acquire such enterprises an LDC thus needs export outlets for its manufactured goods; union with other LDCs promises those markets.

In these circumstances, LDCs enter into integration schemes for somewhat different purposes from those of the advanced nations. Integration offers LDCs a means for simultaneously solving two trade problems: (1) it provides an opportunity for free trade with other countries that are at similar levels of development and are thus able to compete on equal terms, and (2) it offers a way to trade with advanced countries without being harmed by their superior economic power. Yet the promotion of trade is not the main reason why LDCs form integrated groups, as it is for advanced countries. Indeed, less than one-fifth of all LDC trade is with other LDCs. A more urgent goal is to generate economic growth and development.

The gains from integration are fundamentally similar for developing countries and advanced ones, but with some important differences. The less-developed nations have possibilities for proportionately greater benefits because they have so much further to go. In addition to the opportunities that integration offers for developing individual industrial specialties and trading these with other members, union can improve the allocation of resources, especially labor, which LDCs usually employ wastefully. Producers can operate their facilities at full capacity and gain instant economies of scale from the enlarged market, yet at the same time they must become more efficient in order to meet the intensified competition.

After forming a union, individual countries no longer have to strive for a full range of economic activities, which is a difficult task for LDCs. It is unnecessary for each country to acquire every major type of production as long as all the members of the union can manage this together. Within such a group the probability is that at least one member has the right combination of resources for efficient production of a given commodity.

Although the problem of trade creation and diversion is critical for unions of advanced countries, it assumes a different complexion among LDCs. For the latter, the all-important consideration is the effect of integration upon growth. Trade creation is still "good," but trade diversion is not necessarily "bad." It is true that import-competing industries divert trade from advanced countries, but these activities serve the important function of freeing foreign exchange for the purchase from those advanced countries of the high-technology capital goods essential to growth—commodities that are available only from advanced countries.

Yet, the integration efforts of LDCs encounter a number of special problems. One of the most difficult is deciding how to allocate to member countries those manufacturing specialties that are to serve as the basis for intrabloc trade. To accomplish this they must agree on the specific role of each country; but such agreement is hard to achieve because of rival national interests in obtaining these much-coveted projects. Indeed, the gravest obstacle to cooperation among LDCs is nationalism, often reinforced by longstanding antipathies between neighboring countries. Among other considerations of national self-interest is the question of basic inequalities among members. In nearly every union of LDCs certain members are at a disadvantage with respect to the others because of smaller size, fewer resources, or lagging development. Consequently, successful integration of LDCs often requires special concessions to weaker members.

The Central American Common Market (CACM) illustrates the problems and goals of economic integration among Third World countries. However, the five Central American countries—Guatemala, El Salvador, Honduras, Nicaragua, and Costa Rica—entered into the experiment with a unique advantage: a history of unification throughout the long period of Spanish colonial rule and for some years thereafter. These small mountainous countries have a combined territory and population about equal to California, and an average per capita income of about $800 annually. Before the CACM

was established in 1961, the five countries were among the world's most specialized exporters of tropical agricultural commodities, and their economies were growing slower than their populations. More than two-thirds of their work force was engaged in subsistence activities.

The CACM represents one of the highest levels of economic integration ever attempted in the less-developed world. Although basically a common market, it has a number of other features as well, including a supranational organizational structure that includes a development bank in addition to the usual tripartite governance arrangement. At the outset the stated goal of this group was full economic union.

During its first years the CACM made impressive progress. By 1966 it had essentially achieved the status of a working common market, with a free flow of goods and capital among its members. Exports had become much more diversified. Fifteen percent of foreign shipments took place within the bloc, most of this intra-CACM trade consisting of manufactured goods. Domestic and foreign investment within the union soared, and gross national product rose more rapidly than the rate of population growth.

Then trouble appeared. The long-time rivalry between neighboring Honduras and El Salvador exploded with the so-called Soccer War, which, though short-lived, sharply curtailed intrabloc trade and communication. In addition, feelings mounted because the benefits of industrialization were being unevenly shared: Guatemala, El Salvador, and Costa Rica had attracted the greater part of this new development, whereas Honduras had received little of it. Throughout the wars and revolutions that have followed, the CACM has persisted, but with great difficulty.

The CACM was but one part of an ambitious overall plan initially promoted by the United Nations Economic Commission for Latin America (ECLA). ECLA's goal was to integrate all the lands south of the Rio Grande into a single Latin American common market. Another regional bloc formed under ECLA auspices in 1960 was the Latin American Free Trade Association (LAFTA), comprising the countries of South America and Mexico.

Despite Latin America's pressing need for a cooperative solution to its trade problems, LAFTA was never able to surmount the many formidable obstacles to trade among its members. One such barrier is the great distance separating the economically active parts of these countries, which typically occupy coastal enclaves along the margins of the continent. Then, too, the Latin American countries have had to compete directly with each other in the main Northern Hemisphere markets for their commodity exports. Cooperation was all the more difficult because each country already had its own national development plan and the group was never able to harmonize these differing policies; nor could they agree on the manufacturing specialties each should be assigned. Of all their problems, however, perhaps the most forbidding were the enormous differences among members in economic size and level of development. At one extreme were several semi-industrialized countries, notably Brazil, which has the eighth largest economy in the non-Communist world; at the other extreme, Bolivia has an economy only one-thirty-fifth as large as Brazil's. When LAFTA went out of existence in 1981, only one-tenth of the group's trade was with other LAFTA members and half of this was between neighboring Argentina and Brazil. Replacing LAFTA, the Latin American Integration Association (LAIA) serves merely as an organization to promote preferential trade agreements among members.

In 1969, when it was becoming apparent that LAFTA would be dominated by a few of its largest members, several countries along South America's Pacific margins set up a separate organization called the Andean Common Market (Ancom). The five current members are Venezuela, Colombia, Ecuador, Peru, and Bolivia (Chile dropped out in 1976). Although retaining their connections to LAFTA (and subsequently LAIA), they have attempted to bolster their collective economic power by creating a much closer form of cooperation. Despite its name, Ancom has many characteristics of an economic union. In addition to coordinating national policies for trade, transportation, communications, energy, and agriculture, Ancom closely regulates foreign investment within the union. Indeed, so restrictive is the Andean Investment Code that it has tended to discourage some multinational enterprises seeking to operate in the area.

Still another integration experiment formed under the auspices of the United Nations Economic Commission for Latin America is the Caribbean Community (Caricom), which unites several island countries in the West Indies. Elsewhere in the Third World, integration agreements have been reached in Africa (the 16-nation Economic Community of West African States and the three-nation East African Economic Community) and Asia (the Association of Southeast Asian Nations, ASEAN).

Economic Integration among Communist Countries

The Council for Mutual Economic Assistance (CMEA), or *Comecon* as it is usually called, is an association consisting of the USSR and its main satellites. In addition to its 10 regular members—the USSR, Bulgaria, Czechoslovakia, East Germany, Hungary, Poland, Romania, Cuba, Mongolia, and Vietnam—Comecon admits several other Communist nations as observers.

Although ostensibly a form of economic integration, this organization falls far short of being a union like those established by Western nations. Indeed, when Comecon came into being at the end of World War II, its founders did not even conceive of it in such terms. Its initial purpose was to remake the Eastern European economies in the Stalinist mold, meaning that each country should strive for economic self-sufficiency, or *autarky*. Stalin had insisted that a country's national security requires it to be economically independent of other countries. Prior to World War II, the USSR was very nearly able to achieve autarky for itself because of the unusually varied resources of that huge country. Another ideological consideration affecting Communist trade is the difficulty of assigning realistic exchange prices to goods in a system that relies upon arbitrary cost-accounting methods based upon Marxist principles.

In this increasingly technological age, however, trade with other countries has become an inescapable necessity for the Eastern bloc, even the USSR. These nations must import raw materials, foodstuffs, and capital goods that they are not capable of producing domestically or that are in temporary short supply because of errors in planning, crop failures, or other unanticipated events. To earn the necessary foreign exchange to pay for these imports, they must find markets abroad for their own surplus commodities. By its nature this kind of commerce is erratic. The ultimate economic purpose of Communist trade is to further the growth and technological development needed to attain still higher levels of autarky. In addition, some Eastern bloc trade serves mainly political aims, as in the case of the economic exchanges between the USSR and Cuba.

That Comecon had failed to achieve individual national self-sufficiency for its members had become clear by 1958, at which time the EEC arrived on the European scene with its avowed intention of eventually becoming a United States of Western Europe. Perceiving the EEC as a threat to the East, Stalin's successor, Nikita Khrushchev, reorganized Comecon into a bloc designed to increase the self-sufficiency of the group as a whole. Unlike its Western counterparts, however, the new Comecon must rely upon bilateral agreements among its members, with the USSR remaining the dominant partner.

Comecon continues to have many problems. Some of these stem from the wide disparities in size and level of development among members, as well as a general unwillingness to assume the individual roles each has been assigned. Consequently, the union has done little to enhance intrabloc trade. Ironically, the Eastern bloc's economic ties with non-Communist lands have been rising rapidly, especially with Western Europe. This mounting East-West trade, which relies upon natural complementarities in resource endowments, reestablishes a European pattern that had existed from early times.

Other Trade Organizations

Regional trade agreements are but one of several types of preferential arrangements in current use. One of the earliest and most enduring is the *colonial grouping,* in which a country and its present and former colonies grant special tariff and other trade concessions to each other. Examples are the British Commonwealth, with its imperial preference system, and the French Community. By contrast with these groups organized for selective discrimination, a second trend has favored global agreements that would benefit all countries. This latter kind of arrangement responds to the theoretical ideal that nondiscrimination is best for everyone. Two organizations of global scope that have figured prominently in the postwar economic environment are GATT and UNCTAD.

GATT

Most non-Communist trading countries subscribe to an international association known as the General Agreement on Tariffs and Trade (GATT). It is the outgrowth of a postwar attempt to form an international trade organization (ITO) intended (1) to untangle the snarl of special trade agreements and complex trade restrictions that had accumulated during the interwar period of the 1920s and 1930s, and (2) to move the world's nations closer to global free trade. When ITO failed to receive official governmental ratification following its organizational meeting in 1947, representatives of the participating nations continued to negotiate with each other in a series of "rounds," undertaken at intervals during succeeding years, in an effort to reduce trade barriers among them by degrees. Collectively, the resulting treaties have been labeled the *General Agreement on Tariffs and Trade,* administered from offices in Geneva, Switzerland. Each of the several rounds has further reduced tariff levels, and their cumulative effect has been substantial. Undoubtedly GATT has been a major factor in the unprecedented growth of world trade and prosperity during the postwar era.

UNCTAD

As a whole, however, the less-developed countries have received only limited benefit from GATT. The rationale for GATT stems from neoclassical trade theory and its goal of universal free trade, which many LDCs do not consider entirely appropriate for their problems. The United Nations Conference on Trade and Development (UNCTAD) has focused upon the difficulties that developing countries have in marketing their goods in advanced lands, and UNCTAD operates through committees that are concerned with certain staple commodities produced in LDCs. Each committee sponsors conferences of major producing and consuming nations to find ways of reconciling supply and demand for a particular commodity and of breaking down import restrictions confronting that product in its principal markets.

THE MULTINATIONAL ENTERPRISE

One by one we have added modifications to the Heckscher-Ohlin factor-endowments theory of international trade, especially the barrier effects of distance and governmental intervention, the impact of technological change and development, and the role of cooperative arrangements among nations. In this present age, however, the most dynamic influence of all may well be the multinational enterprise (MNE). Often referred to as a multinational corporation, a transnational corporation, or simply a multinational, the MNE is a company that is headquartered in one country but controls productive facilities and sales outlets in other countries. Its operations involve flows of capital, goods, services, and managerial and technical personnel among its subsidiaries. Ultimately this leads the enterprise to assume a global outlook and strategy. Since World War II, MNEs have contributed a rapidly expanding share of world trade and have become the prime movers of the factors of production among nations.

The growing prominence of the multinational enterprise lends a new perspective to trade theory. Traditional theory has viewed countries as the actors in world commerce, but in a majority of cases individual concerns are the primary agents in the international transfer of goods and factors. A theory of international economic interaction must therefore take into account the ability of multinational concerns to modify the endowments of countries, moving human and physical resources from one place to another and thereby enabling production to occur in the most favorable locations.

Although introducing this element might seem to put the principle of comparative advantage in doubt, ironically the multinational enterprise is perhaps the most effective modern-day practitioner of this "law." The MNE is able to produce in that country where the costs of materials, labor, capital, and transportation are minimized and to declare its profits in that country with the lowest tax rates. Hence, the MNE has a unique potential for making the most efficient allocation of the world's resources—the ultimate goal of the classical trade theorist!

How is the MNE able to modify the international economic environment so effectively? One advantage of such a company is the information-gathering ability afforded by its many branches and representatives throughout the world, all linked by instantaneous electronic communication. This "scanning capability" gives the firm an awareness of opportunities, problems, and other new developments in the many places where it conducts business. A second advantage is the enormous store of capital, technology, and managerial skills that an MNE can draw upon.

Considering that a corporation such as General Motors or Exxon can generate more worldwide sales in a year than the gross national products of all but 25 or so sovereign nations, it is hardly surprising that multinationals inspire such awe and apprehension. The host countries for an MNE's overseas affiliates usually suspect them of holding allegiance to the firm's home government. More likely, however, the firm's true devotion is to its own fortunes and those of its stockholders. Nevertheless, MNEs are under increased scrutiny from their home and host governments alike, and they are being subjected to a growing number of restrictions. (See page 347 for a discussion of the public-policy issues raised by the activities of multinationals.)

The attention focused upon multinationals is fairly new, reflecting their recent rise to prominence. Yet their roots go deep into the nineteenth century, to the colonial operations of British, Dutch, and French firms exploiting the resources of their governments' overseas possessions, a tradition continued into this present century by the overseas activities of giant oil, mineral, and fruit companies. Manufacturing firms, however, were slower to develop foreign operations, partly because of the lack of good transport and communications and, especially in the case of U.S. companies, a preoccupation with growing home markets. Nevertheless, a few pioneering industrial firms, such as Singer, Westinghouse, Kodak, and Western Electric, went abroad with their new products and manufacturing technologies during the late 1800s, and their number gradually increased until the Great Depression.

Following World War II, multinational enterprises truly burst upon the world commercial scene. The greatest surge came in the 1960s, when U.S. multinationals moved abroad in numbers, aided by new developments in transport, communication, and industrial technology and by new forms of corporate organization. At the same time, international trade was expanding rapidly, aided by the tariff reductions effected by GATT. As we have previously noted, investment follows trade, and American MNEs were quick to take advantage of the enlarged market afforded by the newly created EEC and by opportunities elsewhere in the world to develop new sources of oil, minerals, and other commodities to replace dwindling supplies at home.

In the past decade the pace of U.S. direct investment in Western Europe and Canada has dwindled with the slackening of economic growth in those areas and as more attractive alternatives have appeared in the western Pacific. Meanwhile, American firms have begun to lose their competitive advantage as multinationals based in Europe, Japan, and other countries gained in size and strength. Not only are the latter seizing a larger share of opportunities in foreign areas but they have also precipitated a surge of foreign investment within the United States itself. Even as the global pattern of MNE activity has grown more complex, the character of the multinational concern has itself undergone fundamental changes.

The Nature and Role of the Multinational Enterprise

As multinational enterprises have increased their involvement in the world economy, they have developed a characteristic organizational form. Usually the parent company is headquartered in the country of principal ownership, although several exceptions to this exist. Royal Dutch Shell, for instance, is 60 percent Dutch owned and 40 percent British, and it maintains headquarters both in The Hague and in London. The stock in most MNEs is publicly held and is available to individual investors of any nationality, although a number of prominent multinationals are still privately held companies. During an MNE's early years its headquarters management and staff are typically natives of the home country, but in time the company brings into its home office individuals of talent from its overseas affiliates. The headquarters company is the control center for the firm's worldwide operations, and the decisions made here take on a global perspective. The management group in the home office is responsible for systemwide strategic planning and must decide what goods are to be manufactured, where in the world to make these, where to procure raw materials, and what global markets to target.

The company's foreign affiliates include both producing units and sales outlets. Today many companies have formed their overseas affiliates into an integrated system, within which the individual branches exchange products, materials, and capital. For example, European affiliates of Ford and General Motors exchange parts, subassemblies, and finished vehicles from one

Government Policy and the Multinational Enterprise

Given their size and pervasive influence in international economic affairs, multinational enterprises (MNEs) receive a great deal of attention from government policymakers. Official positions on MNEs vary widely from country to country, however, largely because of their unique legal status. As yet no international authority exercises jurisdiction over them, and no country recognizes the legal existence of an entire MNE system. Under existing law, therefore, a multinational is merely a group of national companies, each subject to the laws of the land in which it is domiciled. In the absence of any international regulatory mechanism, an MNE exists in an atmosphere of uncertainty, which imposes extra costs because of the widely differing legal requirements under which its various branches function. At the same time, the absence of international constraints provides the firm with opportunities denied domestic companies. This is the basis for the common view that MNEs manufacture in those lands where costs are lowest and declare their profits where taxes are least. It also explains the frequent accusation that multinationals do not show adequate social responsibility toward the countries in which they operate.

In these circumstances, it is not surprising that both home countries and host countries tend to have love-hate feelings toward multinationals. The intensity of these attitudes varies from country to country, however, being greatest in some less-developed countries (LDCs). On the positive side, an LDC is likely to hold exaggerated expectations of the benefits it will gain from the arrival of a multinational. Government leaders expect the new company to provide a badly needed solution for their unemployment problems, to supply an infusion of managerial and scientific knowledge that will help close the technology gap, to reduce the drain on their foreign exchange, to contribute tax revenues to the national treasury, and to develop natural resources and thus relieve some of their regional disparities.

Often it is not until some time after the investment has already been made that negative attitudes toward MNEs begin to surface. Host countries—Canada, for instance—may complain that foreign-owned firms bring the "wrong kind" of employment, that citizens of the country do not receive enough technical and managerial jobs. They often charge, too, that the MNEs threaten their national sovereignty because company decisions are made in another country. Some LDCs associate multinationals with neocolonialism because these foreign-owned concerns seem to continue the pattern of economic exploitation practiced by their former colonial masters. They see the MNE draining the country's resources and begin to ask what will be left after the oil or copper or bauxite is gone. Or they may object that the country's balance of payments is suffering because the MNE is repatriating too much in profits to the home company. LDCs frequently complain, too, about the kind of technology that MNEs bring to them: They say that these firms introduce capital-intensive techniques and equipment originally designed to suit company needs in their labor-short, capital-rich homelands but which are not appropriate for poor countries needing jobs for their masses of unemployed labor.

Multinational enterprises thus find themselves immersed in a complex set of relationships that pit against each other the differing perspectives of home country, host country, and the firm itself. Many people contend, for example, that a foreign investment represents a gain for the host country and a loss for the home country. Some regard the profits repatriated by the subsidiary to its parent company as a gain for the home country and a drain on the host country. Among other questions are the possibility of political control of overseas subsidiaries by the home government (the extraterritoriality issue), government seizure of foreign-owned companies (the expropriation issue), and special performance requirements exacted of MNE subsidiaries by their hosts.

The relationships between host countries and multinationals have both economic and political sides. In balance, does a country gain or lose economically from the foreign-owned companies it hosts? Theoretically, host countries enjoy a net benefit from foreign investment, and a number of studies in Australia, Canada, and the United Kingdom seem to confirm that foreign-owned firms operating in developed countries do indeed produce a measurable rise in the gross national products of their hosts. Although the evidence for LDCs is variable, the employment-generating effects of MNEs have proved to be very great in a number of cases. In Mexico and Brazil, for example, foreign-owned firms account for half of all industrial employment. The impact of multinationals has been even more striking in the newly industrializing lands of East Asia, where electronics firms and other export-oriented, labor-intensive industries employ great numbers of unskilled workers in assembly operations.

The success of host countries in acquiring new technology from MNEs depends upon the absorptive capacity of the local society and economy. Many LDCs lack a sufficient number of educated and trained people to manage and staff industries that are technologically complex. Yet a number of countries, such as India, Mexico, and South Korea, have succeeded in training a great many of their people for such activities. One element limiting the amount of new technology that host countries can gain from MNEs is the reluctance of such firms to part with proprietary information.

To calculate the actual net economic impact of foreign direct investment upon host countries calls for balancing a number of factors. On the plus side are MNE payments for local labor, capital, and land, the taxes paid to local governments, and the gains by domestic firms that benefit from a quickening local economy. On the minus side are the opportunity costs to domestic factors of production—labor, land, and capital—that might have been used otherwise, and the loss of funds sent out of the country as profits, dividends, interest, royalties, and fees. Most such calculations have shown gains for the host countries. The exceptions are usually those cases where host governments have made too many tax concessions to attract MNEs in the first place.

That disagreements should occasionally arise between MNEs and their hosts seems inevitable, considering that governments tend to look for unrealistically quick returns on foreign investments and that MNEs and their hosts usually have different perspectives on costs and benefits. Such disagreements may grow with the passing of time following the beginning of operations, as the initial inflow of investment funds tapers off and the firm commences repatriating profits to the parent concern. At this point the host government may make new demands, bolstered by its increased bargaining power now that the company has committed its resources and cannot afford to shut down operations. The government and the MNE may then do a great deal of jockeying to arrive at a mutually satisfactory agreement on how to divide the benefits from the investment. In the end, agreement on economic matters is usually reached, for both parties would lose if the investment were terminated.

The political issues that arise between a multinational and its host government are often more difficult to resolve because of the effects of nationalistic feelings, especially in less-developed countries. Public debate of such matters often involves not only officials and politicians but also labor leaders, local business interests, the press, and those in academia. Underlying such discussions is the invariable question of whether the economic benefits of foreign investment are sufficient to outweigh the perceived threat to national sovereignty. The usual presumptions are that a multinational exercises a certain power over the local economy, that it is directed in this from a control center in some alien land, and that the government of the home country exerts a possibly sinister influence over the company.

Although this picture may be overdrawn, company interests and host-country interests are not likely to coincide exactly. The multinational seeks to maximize returns to its entire MNE system, whereas the host government looks to its national welfare—economic, social, and military. Local officials resent the ability of an MNE to make decisions that affect the country's welfare independently of their control. They suspect MNEs of avoiding taxes and manipulating prices to the benefit of company interests.

The most contentious issue dividing MNEs and host governments is the perceived threat to national sovereignty because of home-government meddling in company decisions. Giving some substance to this fear, the U.S. government has openly imposed its will upon the overseas affiliates of its MNEs. It has, for example, prohibited Canadian subsidiaries of American companies from trading with Cuba, and it has tried to prevent European affiliates from selling gas-pipeline equipment to the USSR. This "extraterritoriality" issue has at times severely strained American political relations, and it has created difficult problems for U.S. companies operating overseas.

Political considerations may lead host governments to place various restrictions upon foreign ownership. Indeed, most countries exclude certain industries from foreign ownership entirely, particularly defense industries. Many governments prohibit foreign ownership of banks, public utilities, communications, and, increasingly, minerals. In the American Midwest, several states even restrict foreign ownership of farmland. Some countries—notably France, Japan, and Mexico—prohibit foreign acquisition of local firms, and several countries, including Canada, maintain strict review procedures for all proposed foreign takeovers.

Today, more and more governments are requiring foreign investors to acquire local partners when setting up new affiliates. Such joint ventures are especially popular among LDCs, which perceive them as a way of gaining access to new technology, limiting the outflow of repatriated profits, and minimizing the influence of foreigners over the local economy. Arrangements of this kind have become fairly standard throughout Latin America and Southeast Asia. Mexico, for instance, requires 51 percent local ownership of all but a few, explicitly designated, industries.

Another policy tool favored by host governments is to impose performance requirements upon foreign-owned enterprises. For instance, as a way of creating jobs, the MNE may be required to use a specified proportion of local personnel. Some countries provide companies with timetables for employing local persons as managers and technicians. Governments may require that firms set up training programs or establish local laboratories to perform R&D. Or they may force MNEs to increase the local content of the products they assemble in the host country, especially automobiles. Some newly industrializing countries with large foreign debts—for example, Mexico and Brazil—now require MNEs to export a specified percentage of their output.

The most extreme measure of all is government seizure of foreign-owned companies. In recent years a rash of such expropriations has occurred in some Third World countries where the political processes have fallen into the hands of economic nationalists, many of whom oppose foreign ownership in any form. International law actually recognizes the right of governments to expropriate foreign enterprises, considering this merely an exercise of national sovereignty, but this law also specifies that the previous owners of such properties receive prompt, adequate, and effective compensation for the loss. Compensation is a key issue today, for many LDCs are failing in this. When compensation is not forthcoming, home governments may retaliate against offending countries. The United States, for instance, has in some cases cut off foreign aid and credits to delinquent nations.

The opposite side of these questions has to do with the relationships between MNEs and their home governments. The United States has no overall policy toward American-based multinationals, but the government has asserted its authority regarding certain specific issues. Prior to World War II the United States not only placed no restrictions on foreign operations by its MNEs, but it also stood ready to ensure that other governments did not discriminate against them. In several instances it actually intervened militarily in their behalf.

After the war the government encouraged for-eign direct investment by U.S. multinationals as a form of foreign aid, but focused this upon LDCs especially after Europe had fully recovered. The United States entered into treaties with other countries guaranteeing fair treatment of its MNEs. When balance-of-payments problems began to arise in the 1960s, the U.S. government set quotas on foreign direct investment, forcing its multinationals to do their borrowing abroad.

As foreign investment by U.S. firms expanded, domestic criticism of them grew louder. Labor unions claimed that American firms were exporting jobs with their "runaway plants"—factories set up in East Asia, along the Mexican border, and in other low-labor-cost places—to produce goods formerly made at home. Some domestic critics objected to what they saw as the loss of American production through the transfer of technology abroad. Others decried the "unfair" advantages gained by U.S. multinationals in the favorable treatment accorded them under U.S. tariffs and in their ability to avoid restrictive U.S. laws to take advantage of concessions from foreign governments. Empirical studies tend to discount these claims, finding that MNEs as a whole have enjoyed faster growth in output than domestic firms, have higher rates of export growth, and generally have favorable balances in their own trade with the world.

Tax policy is another area of controversy between MNEs and their home governments. How do you prevent these elusive firms from escaping taxation but at the same time avoid taxing them doubly? In the United States the problem is compounded by the desire of state governments to tax MNEs operating within their jurisdictions. Some governments favor taxing all production that takes place within their borders but exempts their foreign production. Other governments insist upon taxing all production of their MNEs throughout the world. The United States is unique among nations in its antitrust laws, which are designed to prevent companies from cooperating with each other in ways that reduce competition. The United States also prohibits American firms from making "questionable" payments abroad. Other countries make no such efforts to prevent bribery, which is an accepted part of doing business in many Third World nations and some industrialized ones as well.

The evidence indicates that under ideal conditions everyone gains from foreign direct investment. Most of the problems that arise between multinationals and governments can be attributed to the lack of a uniform international policy for such enterprises and the absence of a mechanism for regulating their activities worldwide. Agreement among nations is much needed to ensure that multinationals are good corporate citizens of the countries where they operate and to make certain that the world receives full economic benefit from this efficient form of business organization with its potential for allocating the world's resources in the most effective manner.

country to another in an elaborate intracompany network. In addition to their wholly or partially owned affiliates abroad, multinationals customarily maintain connections with other foreign enterprises not under corporate control, through such arrangements as joint ventures, distributorships, and licensing agreements.

The most significant feature of the MNE, from both a practical and a theoretical standpoint, is its role as an efficient agent for transferring capital, managerial skills, technology, and commodities among countries. Matching the scarcities of one country with the surpluses of another, it helps to achieve a global equalization of factors; and by transferring innovations among nations, it is a major agent of technological change.

The transfer of managerial skills to other lands is a distinctive function of the MNE. Relying upon the firm's superior information-gathering ability, the headquarters company discovers and exploits opportunities in foreign areas that lie beyond the capabilities of domestic concerns in those lands. The MNE is also better able than local companies to bear the risk of such ventures because of its great size and financial strength and its experience in similar circumstances elsewhere.

Having decided to invest in a new foreign undertaking, the firm then performs its second key function, the transfer of capital. This can be in the form of real capital (machinery and equipment) or financial capital or a combination of the two. Depending upon political and economic circumstances, the company can fund the project with capital generated within its own system—obtained either directly from the parent concern or from the earnings of overseas affiliates—or it can rely upon borrowed funds, either in the host country or elsewhere.

The third major function of the MNE is to create technology and transfer it throughout its system. A newly established affiliate generally receives an infusion of technology from the headquarters company. Indeed, at one time all research and development took place in the parent concern, but today many MNEs share this function among their various constituent companies.

Finally, the MNE is a principal generator of international trade, notably the transfers of raw materials, components, and finished products that take place among the company's many branches. The current trend is for an MNE to integrate production and marketing among the parent and its overseas affiliates. Such coordination permits the firm to maximize the gains from international specialization: Each product is manufactured in that location having the lowest costs and in sufficient quantity to enjoy economies of scale. The company's ultimate aim in integrating its international operations is to serve every national market with a full line of its products and to do so at the lowest unit costs.

The international integration of an MNE can be either vertical or horizontal. In the case of vertical integration, a branch in one country sends partially manufactured subassemblies or intermediate products to another affiliate elsewhere for further processing or for final assembly. Finished products then go to all affiliates for sale in their own national markets. If integration is horizontal, each branch makes a particular line of finished products, the choice depending upon its comparative advantage, and shares these with all other units of the enterprise. In either case, every branch is able to offer its customers a complete set of company products.

Theories of the Multinational Enterprise

The multinational enterprise has attained prominence so recently that a cohesive theory on the subject has yet to emerge. Because most writers have approached the MNE from the perspectives of their individual specialties, the resulting works lack the generality essential to a true theory. We shall therefore attempt merely to draw together the common threads of this accumulating body of literature. Our concern will be to find answers to two sets of questions: (1) what causes a firm to go abroad and how is it able to succeed in a foreign environment against competition from both domestic firms and other multinationals, and (2) what happens to the fundamental character of the firm itself during the course of this internationalization process?

An Outline of Leading Theories

What are the distinguishing characteristics of firms that enter into multinational production? One common trait cited by theorists is the expectation by MNEs of greater profits from their foreign ventures than those received by local competitors in those same areas. Indeed, it is essential that MNEs receive a higher return because they must overcome problems not borne by domestic firms. Local producers know the language and customs, can expect a greater measure of customer good will and government favor, have a closer awareness of local market conditions, and avoid the extra time and expense that the MNE has to bear because of operating from a distance. The MNE is able to obtain a larger return because it has certain advantages that no other firm possesses. Chief among these "monopolistic" advantages are (1) superior knowledge and (2) large size and scope of operations.

Leadership in innovation is the usual form of superior knowledge monopolized by MNEs. Innovativeness is a key element in technology-intensive industries such as pharmaceuticals and electronics. As a group, MNEs expend more on research and development than do other firms, and they are able to transfer this technology abroad with little additional cost. Local firms, on the other hand, would have to invest heavily to develop a competing technology themselves. Another kind of knowledge monopoly is found in those industries that rely upon high levels of marketing skill—for example, convenience foods and beverages (McDonald's or Coca-Cola) or cosmetics (Estée Lauder). To acquire its superior knowledge, the MNE needs a home environment that offers high levels of technical and managerial skills and has a well-developed, affluent market. This is one reason why only a few countries serve as home bases for multinationals.

A second monopolistic advantage common to MNEs is superior size and scope of operation. In most industries foreign direct investment is dominated by only a few large concerns; in other words, these activities are oligopolistic in nature. These companies continually jostle with each other for larger shares of the world market. Because of their size and their ability to produce in many countries, they can achieve the most economical scale of operations. If the local market is too small to absorb all of the output, the affiliate can send its surplus to the company's branches in other countries. Domestic producers do not usually have this option. MNEs may also integrate their operations vertically to gain assured sources of supply. In this way they can avoid dependence upon others and, at the same time, are able to deny such supplies to their competitors.

Large size therefore permits the firm to assume a greater range of functions itself. By thus "internalizing" its various international operations, it can avoid buying and selling to other companies in foreign areas (or licensing its technology to them). The MNE thereby protects the secrecy of its technology and minimizes the effects of governmental restrictions. It is mainly for this reason that most international transfers of technology and managerial skills take place among units of the same firm, and that MNEs sell a high proportion of their exports to their own affiliates.

Because of the oligopolistic character of international business, MNEs intently watch their competitors' actions. If one company sets up operations in a new area or if it markets a new product, its competitors immediately take action to prevent any loss of their market shares. Each firm is concerned to maintain its rate of growth relative to its rivals as a way of preserving market share, and it seeks to erect barriers to the entry of any new firms into its markets.

MNEs are thus highly interdependent in their decision making. If one firm enters a foreign market, its rivals usually follow it there to minimize the risk to their market shares. These defensive actions therefore create a bandwagon effect in foreign direct investment. This kind of action also helps to explain so-called reverse investment, in which MNEs of different national origins compete in each others' home markets. For instance, the American tire company, Goodyear, operates in France, while the French firm, Michelin, makes tires in the United States. Although they turn out competing goods, these firms are careful to differentiate their products by means of brand names and advertising. Even this kind of product differentiation constitutes a knowledge asset of the firm.

To compete successfully in an alien environment, the multinational enterprise must choose carefully which countries to enter. Such decisions rely upon the theories of location and trade as well as foreign investment theory. A number of country characteristics enter into this decision: location, resource endowments, size and nature of market, political environment. Although the relative influence of these elements changes from one time to another, the strongest attraction for U.S. firms has been proximity—as suggested by the high proportion of investments made in nearby Canada and Mexico. U.S. multinationals have also preferred to invest in countries with familiar cultures—notably English-speaking Canada, Britain, and Australia—and with large markets offering economies of scale. To protect their investments, MNEs favor countries that have stable governments and a minimum of legal restrictions.

Not only do these country traits influence the decision to do business in a country, but they also determine the way in which MNEs will enter that market. For operating in those countries with stable governments and large, prosperous markets, multinationals generally prefer foreign direct investment. In dealing with those poorer underdeveloped countries having a high level of political risk, MNEs rely mainly upon exporting, together with some licensing of local production, but with only a minimum of direct investing.

Internationalization of the Firm

The other aspect of MNE theory is concerned with the questions of how, when, and why a firm becomes multinational and what happens to its organizational arrangements during this process. The internationalization of a company typically occurs in three stages. In the first stage a firm that had previously served only its domestic market begins to export some of its output. Often this transition from domestic to foreign sales is unplanned, taking place in response to unsolicited orders received directly from potential customers overseas or indirectly by way of local buying agents for foreign purchasers. At this point the company has neither the specialized facilities to prepare shipments for export nor personnel skilled in export procedures. It therefore hires outside specialists to perform these functions. If orders from abroad continue to arrive, the firm will find it cheaper and more expedient to establish its own export department or foreign division, consisting of an experienced manager and a few clerks.

As this new foreign business commences to yield increased economies of scale and enhanced profit margins for the company, it begins to pursue export sales more actively. The firm appoints distributors in key market areas abroad, and in time it develops a network of such distributorships. Meanwhile, the firm may license its technology to local manufacturing firms in some host countries. When foreign operations become sufficiently extensive to warrant it, the company sends traveling representatives to service the network. At this point the firm may undertake a reorganization of its basic structure. It may form a separate corporate entity in the home country for the purpose of minimizing taxes and providing more efficient service, and it may establish foreign marketing subsidiaries in key countries. Up to this point the company has served its overseas customers solely with exports from its own production in the home country.

The second phase of internationalization arrives when the company decides to commence manufacturing in other countries. The decision to produce abroad usually follows the discovery that exports to a given national market have reached a level sufficient to justify building a factory there (the demonstration effect). Such a venture is especially attractive if production is market oriented, that is, it costs less to make at a location close to final consumption. A further incentive may be the sudden imposition of governmental barriers to imports in a key market. In some instances tax concessions or other special inducements by the foreign government may reinforce the decision. Having determined to set up production in the overseas market, the firm must then decide whether to build a wholly new factory or to acquire an existing firm in the foreign area. After production is under way in several overseas locations, the firm may integrate its foreign subsidiaries, either vertically or horizontally, to gain economies of specialization.

Foreign operations may eventually generate so large a proportion of the company's total revenue that the headquarters management comes to think of the firm's business primarily in global terms. Accompanying this change in perspective is the gradual internationalization of the headquarters staff, through worldwide recruitment of executives. Decision-makers no longer identify with the firm's home country but with the company as a global entity. Although the head office still makes strategic decisions affecting the system as a whole, it allows greater autonomy of larger overseas branches. In this final phase the firm has become fully internationalized.

Empirical Evidence

Although they are assuming an ever-greater place in world commerce, exact information on multinational enterprises at a world scale is still incomplete. MNEs have gained prominence so recently that, except for the United States, few countries gather systematic data on the subject. The emphasis in this review of global patterns will therefore be upon U.S.-based multinationals, the rising competition they are feeling from other countries, and the mounting level of foreign investment in the United States.

American firms still hold the lead in foreign direct investment, accounting for almost half of the world total by value. This is nearly four times as much as British-based firms, which rank second. The actual number of MNEs headquartered in other countries is greater than this would suggest, however, because U.S. multinationals tend to be much larger than average. Half of the 50 largest MNEs are based in the United States. The United Kingdom has the second largest number of the world's top multinationals, followed closely by Germany. Several of the largest firms come from other countries, however, including such world giants as Nestlé (Swiss), Philips (Dutch), Peugeot-Citroen (French), and Matsushita (Japanese).

Foreign production by U.S.-based firms is also a much higher proportion of the country's total foreign sales than is true of most other countries. Indeed, overseas output by affiliates of U.S. companies is a $2\frac{1}{2}$ times as great as national exports, and this proportion is growing. Some of the smaller European countries are similarly dependent upon foreign production, especially Switzerland, The Netherlands, and Belgium.

Many of the world's leading MNEs receive more than half of their total company sales from foreign affiliates, and in a number of cases the proportion is far higher. For example, the Swiss food combine, Nestlé, receives 97 percent of company earnings from foreign operations, especially its subsidiaries in the United States. Philips, the Dutch electronics firm, obtains 91 percent of its total revenues from its overseas affiliates. The larger petroleum multinationals likewise depend upon foreign sales for a major part of company revenue.

Since World War II, American multinationals have undergone a considerable shift in global focus. During the 1950s Canada accounted for almost two-thirds of foreign investment by U.S. firms—almost twice the amount going to Europe. Half of the United States total was in less-developed countries, mostly Latin America. Very little direct investment took place in Japan, which then, as now, presented formidable barriers to foreign investors. By the end of the 1970s, overall foreign involvement by U.S. firms had grown enormously, but most of this new investment was in Western European countries, now hosts to almost half of the U.S. total. Canada continued to attract U.S. investment but at a much reduced rate. The share held by less-developed countries fell to a quarter of the total, with Latin America continuing to receive the greatest share. In the 1980s the pattern is again changing. Economic slowdowns in Europe and Canada have made these areas less attractive for foreign investment, while the Pacific rim countries—from South Korea and Taiwan south to the Philippines and Australia—have become the favored areas for investors of all nationalities.

Although U.S. firms have led the world in foreign direct investment during the postwar era, they are currently growing less rapidly than are firms based in Germany and Japan, especially the latter. Japanese MNEs have a total overseas investment only one-fifth that of U.S. companies, but their foreign involvement is rapidly accelerating. Moreover, the total value of Japanese foreign operations is not an accurate measure of their importance, because so many of these undertakings are joint ventures with local firms.

Foreign direct investment is a comparatively recent development for Japan. Because of an official ceiling on capital outflows imposed to save scarce foreign exchange during the early postwar period, Japanese firms were slow to go abroad. Until the Ministry of Finance lifted the ban in the late 1960s, therefore, Japan was mainly an exporter of domestically produced manufactured goods. During that period, most Japanese foreign involvement was undertaken by large trading companies for the purpose of providing assured supplies of raw materials for Japan's domestic industries.

Since 1969 the Japanese government has encouraged direct investment abroad. In addition to a mounting balance-of-payments surplus, a key incentive for this shift in official policy has been a planned restructuring of industry in favor of knowledge-intensive activities. The new policy has called for transferring abroad Japan's older labor-intensive industries, which polluted the environment and consumed great quantities of imported fuel and raw materials. The government has backed this policy with a variety of investment guarantees and other financial incentives to Japanese multinationals.

The latest thrust of Japanese investment is toward North America and Western Europe in response to growing import restrictions and accompanying pressures upon Japanese firms to manufacture locally in their foreign markets. Most Japanese investments in the West are in high-technology industries and involve state-of-the-art production methods. These ventures are very different from those undertaken by Japanese firms elsewhere. In Asia and Latin America, Japanese multinationals operate labor-intensive industries using standardized techniques, and in Australia, the Middle East, and Brazil they invest in extractive industries—petroleum, coal, and mineral raw materials. Hence, Japanese firms have gone abroad either to capitalize upon complementary resource endowments or to defend their goods from trade barriers in important market areas.

Japanese multinational enterprises are not directly comparable with those of North America and Europe because they are organized differently. Japanese companies are divided into three functional types: manufacturing, marketing, and financial. Firms of the three types often join together to form enterprise groups, called *kereitsu,* which are linked by mutual ownership, interlocking directorships, and operational ties based upon mutual understandings. Some of these enterprise groups have grown out of family-controlled combines (known as *zaibatsu*) dating to prewar times. Usually a trading company (*sogo sosha*) and a large bank form the core of such a group. Functionally, the member companies are closely integrated, but their relationship is so informal that they are not usually viewed in the same light as an IBM or a General Electric. Yet several *kereitsu,* such as the Mitsubishi Group, greatly exceed the leading European and American MNEs in total sales. In the past decade some of the larger Japanese manufacturing firms, such as Sony, have internationalized their production independently of any enterprise group. This action has had a bandwagon effect, drawing other Japanese competitors into overseas operations.

Investment in U.S. industries by Japanese, Canadian, and European multinationals is growing at an accelerating rate, with considerable impact upon the American economy. It is affecting U.S. trade, industrial location patterns, and employment conditions, and it is reinforcing the new patterns of regional growth now appearing within the country. Already by the end of the 1970s, MNEs from eight countries controlled nearly 2500 U.S. manufacturing operations, according to Department of Commerce figures. British, Japanese, and Canadian companies held two-thirds of the total.

Four high-technology industries account for half of all foreign direct investment in U.S. manufacturing: nonelectrical machinery, chemicals and pharmaceuticals, electric machinery and electronics, and professional and scientific instruments. Japan is the main investor in chemicals, electrical machinery, and electronics, and, along with the United Kingdom, leads in professional and scientific instruments. Canadian investment is most prominent in nonelectrical machinery and fabricated metals and foods. In each case, the products favored by foreign investors relate to the home countries' exports to the United States, suggesting that investment is prompted largely by the demonstration effect, along with a desire to protect the firm's U.S. market. Some of the investments are obviously being undertaken for the purpose of gaining quick access to American technology. In making U.S. investments, Canadian and British firms prefer to acquire existing American operations, but Japanese companies generally choose to build new plants, no doubt to introduce their own production techniques. With several notable exceptions, foreign-owned firms in the United States tend to be smaller than domestic companies.

In their locational choices, most foreign companies favor the traditional manufacturing belt of the Northeast and Great Lakes and the newer Sunbelt areas of the West and South (Figure 13.5). Firms of different national origins have shown distinct preferences for certain parts of the country. Although Canadian concerns are more widely dispersed than those of other nations, being more familiar with the business environment nearest at hand, they are especially numerous in those U.S.–Canadian border areas in the manufacturing belt of the Middle West and Northeast, as well as in the South Atlantic states. British firms are located mostly in the Northeast, following a long-established pattern of trade and investment in this area nearest to Europe. Japanese industrial firms are best represented on the West Coast and in the East North-Central and Middle Atlantic states. They have invested heavily in high-technology enterprises in those western areas closest to Japan.

TOWARD A DYNAMIC NEW THEORY OF INTERNATIONAL COMMERCE

In this second of three chapters on the geographical dimensions of world commerce we have added a further set of modifications to conventional trade theory. In Chapter 12 we saw that the factor-endowments explanation fails to take into account the effects of demand, the barriers of distance and governmental intervention, and the impact of trade upon factor endowments. The present chapter has been concerned with the altering effects of change. We have noted the variable role of trade in the growth of national economies and the trade ef-

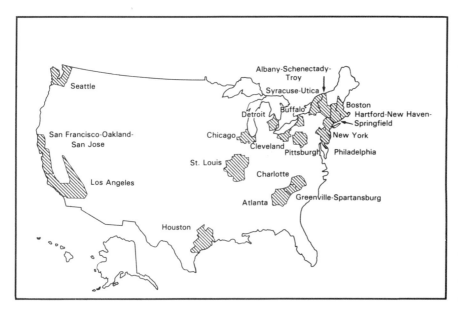

FIGURE 13.5 Location of foreign direct investment in the United States, 1979. Note the concentrations of foreign-owned companies in the manufacturing belt of the Northeast and along the western and southern margins of the country. [*Source:* James E. McConnell, "The International Location of Manufacturing Investments: Recent Behaviour of Foreign-owned Corporations in the United States," *Spatial Analysis, Industry and the Industrial Environment. Vol. 3, Regional Economies and Industrial Systems,* F. E. I. Hamilton and G. J. R. Linge, Eds. (New York: John Wiley, 1983, pp. 337–358).]

fects of technology, giving special attention to the question of whether or not the United States is losing its lead in technology-intensive trade.

Another major issue addressed here is the special trade problems of less-developed countries, which, some observers believe, cast doubt on the applicability of trade theory to the circumstances of LDCs. Seeming to belie this argument, certain developing countries have devised successful new trade strategies that have enabled them to become important actors in world commerce. Still another strategy—viewed by theorists as a form of selective discrimination—is regional economic integration. Cooperative ventures of this type have been undertaken by groups of industrialized nations, Third World countries, and members of the Communist bloc.

A final modifying element has been the multinational enterprise, a company with its headquarters in one country and sales and production branches in other countries. Within a surprisingly short time the MNE has become a prime agent for international transfers of capital, services, entrepreneurship, and technology—as well as a vital force in international trade. These MNEs have demonstrated a remarkable capacity for fundamentally altering the quality and quantity of factor endowments in those countries where they operate. This they have accomplished by efficiently moving human and physical resources from one part of the world to another.

The astounding growth of foreign direct investment, and the evolution of more powerful and versatile corporate forms for channeling this activity, has many implications for trade theory. As their global operations become increasingly integrated, MNEs generate more and more intrafirm trade. Thus, fully one-third of U.S.

exports of manufactured goods represent shipments by American multinationals to their foreign affiliates. Although exchanges of merchandise among different branches of the same firm often take place for conventional reasons, such as the complementarity of resource endowments among countries, many of these transfers are in response to special company needs. Similarly, the investment behavior of an MNE may reflect the particular circumstances of the firm—for example, the necessity for responding to the actions of a competitor. As prime transfer agents, multinationals hasten the process of factor equalization among nations, thereby altering comparative advantages. Because they sell to the world, MNEs are not limited by the size of local markets in achieving optimal economies of scale in their production. Hence, an adequate explanation of world trade and investment patterns must now take into account the behavioral characteristics and capabilities of multinational enterprises.

As theorists are now discovering, trade theory and multinational enterprise theory are complementary: Trade theory is concerned with the factor endowments of countries, whereas MNE theory concentrates upon the knowledge assets of firms (Root, 1984). The location of production depends upon the spatial pattern of resource endowments, but control and ownership of this production and the flows that result from it relate to the special qualities of companies. A complete understanding of international economic interaction therefore requires a new body of theory that incorporates both aspects. All elements of this prospective new theory come into play in the analysis of evolving patterns of world commerce, which is the topic of the next chapter.

TOPICS FOR DISCUSSION

1. What are the two fundamental ways in which economic growth occurs? As economies grow and develop, how does their level of trade participation change and what shifts take place in the composition of that trade? Why do policymakers in some contemporary less-developed countries (LDCs) question the applicability of conventional trade theory to their own conditions? What special problems do LDCs have in their trading relations with industrialized countries? How may multinational enterprises affect the factor endowments of LDCs?

2. How does the theory of regional economic integration relate to conventional trade theory? What organizational types of economic integration have been identified and to what extent are these ideal types represented in the integrated groups now in existence? What are the theoretically ideal characteristics of a group of countries to ensure that they will achieve successful results from economic integration?

3. What was the original rationale for the formation of Comecon, and why did it fail to achieve its original goals? What caused the organization to undergo subsequent reorganization? To what extent does Comecon conform to the ideal theoretical requirements for successful economic integration?

4. Why is the multinational enterprise (MNE) considered a prime agency for the international transfer of goods and factors of production? As viewed by the theoretician, what does the MNE contribute to the world economy? How do the theories of international trade and the multinational enterprise complement each other?

5. What causes a firm to go abroad and what makes it succeed in an alien environment against competition from local firms and from other MNEs? How, when, and why does a firm go multinational, and what happens to the organizational arrangements within the firm as this proc-

ess continues? How do these events change the company's perspectives?

6. Discuss the international legal status of multinational enterprises and show how this poses problems both for the MNEs and for national governments. What are the economic and political impacts of MNEs upon host countries and upon their home countries?

7. Explain why high-technology trade is so essential to the United States, indicate those U.S. commodities that seem

to be in trouble, and propose a set of remedies for the apparent deterioration of America's technological lead.

8. Examine the alternative trade strategies that various developing countries have pursued, and show how these approaches have differed in their results.

9. How has the trade of Western Europe been affected by the formation of integrated groups and by their shifting memberships in recent years? How has economic integration affected the location of production and foreign direct investment in Western Europe?

FURTHER READINGS

BALASSA, BELA. *The Theory of Economic Integration.* Homewood, Ill.: Richard D. Irwin, 1961.

Introduces a system for classifying the organizational forms used by various groups of countries in their experiments with economic integration, and develops a comprehensive theory of integration within the general framework of modern international trade theory.

DUNNING, JOHN H. *International Production and the Multinational Enterprise.* London: George Allen and Unwin, 1981.

Develops an eclectic theory of international production that draws upon industrial organization theory, location theory, and the theory of the firm. Bringing together elements common to a variety of specialized works on the MNE, the eclectic theory holds that the propensity for foreign direct investment depends upon the possession by a company of assets that its competitors lack, the willingness of the company to internalize these assets, and its ability to profit from exploiting them in foreign countries.

HANSON, ROGER D. *Central America: Regional Integration and Economic Development.* Washington, D.C.: National Planning Association Studies in Development Progress, No. 1, 1967.

A theoretical and empirical analysis of the experiments in economic integration conducted by five Central American countries.

HYMER, STEPHEN H. *The International Operations of National Firms.* Cambridge, Mass.: MIT Press, 1976.

Emphasizing the owner-specific element in international commerce, this seminal work established industrial organization theory as a basis for the analysis of foreign direct investment.

KASER, MICHAEL. *Comecon: Integration Problems of the Planned Economies.* London: Oxford University Press, 1965.

A review of the economic and political problems of attempting to achieve economic integration within a Marxist framework.

KNICKERBOCKER, FREDERICK T. *Oligopolistic Reaction and*

Multinational Enterprise. Boston: Harvard University Graduate School of Business Administration, 1973.

Shows the importance of examining the particular characteristics of industries in order to gain an understanding of why companies go abroad.

LINDER, STAFFAN BURENSTAM. *Trade and Trade Policy for Development.* New York: Praeger, 1967.

Analyzes the special trade problems of less-developed countries, explores the linkages between the theories of international trade and economic development, discusses the changes that take place in a country's trade as it grows and develops, and considers the options available to policymakers in addressing the problems of LDCs.

McCONNELL, JAMES E. "The International Location of Manufacturing Investments: Recent Behaviour of Foreign-owned Corporations in the United States." In *Spatial Analysis, Industry and the Industrial Environment. Vol. 3, Regional Economies and Industrial Systems* (F. E. I. Hamilton and G. J. R. Linge, Eds.). London: John Wiley, 1983.

Examines within a theoretical framework the recent flows of foreign direct investment into the United States, giving special attention to the differing investment patterns of European, Canadian, and Japanese subsidiaries at national, regional, and subregional scales.

ROOT, FRANKLIN R. *International Trade and Investment,* 5th ed. Cincinnati: South-Western Publishing Co., 1984.

An integrated treatment of theory, governmental policy, and multinational enterprise relating to international trade and foreign investment.

VINER, JACOB. *The Customs Union Issue.* New York: Carnegie Endowment for International Peace, 1950.

A classic work on the theory of economic integration.

WILKINS, MIRA. *The Emergence of Multinational Enterprise.* Cambridge, Mass.: Harvard University Press, 1970.

Reviews in some detail the history of the foreign operations of U.S. business concerns prior to World War I.

CHAPTER 14

Patterns
of World Commerce

Previous chapters have established a theoretical framework for viewing the forces that foster international commerce, as well as those influences serving to divert, inhibit, or
otherwise modify it. In this chapter we examine the actual
flows, using international data, in a search for meaningful
spatial patterns, which we interpret conceptually.

The empirical evidence shows that a remarkably stable
pattern of economic linkages existed among major trading regions over a long period of time, even though the composition
of those flows gradually changed as the structure of industry
evolved. Only the ideological division of postwar Europe altered this basic arrangement. All this began to change in the
1970s, however, as a series of global crises upset the established system.

By the early 1980s the center of gravity of world commerce had shifted from the North Atlantic, its traditional focus, to the Pacific basin. Making optimal use of impressive
human resource endowments, and following an export-promoting development strategy, a dynamic group of East Asian
countries has been well positioned to benefit from the current
restructuring of the world economy. The Pacific is thus becoming the new focus of world trade and investment.

Objectives:

- to assess results of quantitative analyses of world trade
data
- to distinguish trends in the growth and composition
of commodity flows
- to evaluate the impact of recent global crises on world
trade and foreign investment
- to identify current shifts in the focus of world commerce, the effects these have had on the patterns of
world commerce, and their implications for major
economic regions

THE GLOBAL ECONOMY IN TRANSITION

The dynamic elements of world commerce addressed in Chapter 13 are assuming an ever-greater role in the international exchange of goods, services, and factors of production. Trade and foreign investment are gaining prominence in national development strategies as newly industrializing countries adopt a greater openness to the world, and new technology is being created and transferred internationally at an accelerating pace. Central to all these developments is the multinational enterprise, which is itself undergoing a transformation in organizational form, scope of outlook, and economic functions. Change has thus become the new reality. Patterns of world commerce—dependably stable over very long periods in the past—are now in transition, the result of recent major world economic crises.

In this chapter, therefore, we turn attention to the changing composition and direction of economic flows among countries, the nature of the regional patterns produced by this kind of spatial interaction, and how the various world regions are faring in an increasingly competitive world environment. As a starting point, however, and as a basis for assessing the impact of change, we shall first look at the underlying strengths of individual elements that influence economic flows. For this we draw upon some of the quantitative analyses that have been performed on trade data.

Modeling Commodity Flows

To test the relationships between world trade flows and the factors that are presumed to influence these flows, several analysts have examined the two-way trade between pairs of countries for the world as a whole. The usual technique for measuring the relative effects of individual influences is an interaction model (or gravity model). The reasoning that underlies this approach—which corresponds to our previous theoretical discussions—is that the intensity of trade flows between two countries is directly proportional to their trading capacities and inversely proportional to the physical distance (and other barriers) that separates them. The most important study of this type was that of the Dutch economist Hans Linnemann (1966), who identified three groups of influences that explain the size of trade flows: potential total supply of the exporting country, potential total demand of the importing country, and the "resistance" hindering the flow of goods between the two countries.

Potential supply and demand, according to Linnemann, are a function of the differences between domestic output and demand, which in turn reflect the comparative advantages of the countries. The potential supply of goods for export depends upon how much a country produces and what part of that production remains for sale abroad after domestic demand has been satisfied. The larger the national economy the more industries it can support at optimal economies of scale; however, the larger the population the greater the proportion of output needed to accommodate domestic demand. Linnemann further reasoned that the flow of trade between country pairs is greater if the commodity structure of one country's exports fits closely the structure of the importing country's demand.

Linnemann pointed to two classes of barriers. One set represents the effects of distance: transport cost and time and the difficulties of communicating and gathering information. The second set of barriers represents various forms of governmental intervention. Because such official measures as tariffs and quotas are too complex to obtain for the world as a whole, he assumed that their effect is relatively uniform for the purposes of this study. He did, however, take into account the influence of preferential trade relations among countries, such as the ties between a colonial power and its present and former dependencies. Linnemann also recognized the distorting effects of noneconomic considerations on the foreign commerce of Communist countries. For this reason, and also because of the undependable quality of the data for such countries, he excluded Communist trade from his analysis.

Based upon these premises, Linnemann developed a model incorporating the following variables for each country: (1) gross national product, (2) population size, (3) distance (shortest navigable distance between principal ports plus overland distance to main economic centers), (4) preferential trading relations, and (5) commodity composition of flows. The preferential trade relations consisted of the connections among Portugal, Belgium, the United Kingdom, and France with their colonies and former colonies. He determined the congruence of commodity composition by measuring the degree to which the structure of one country's exports resembled the import structure of each of its customers.

The basic trade data for the study consisted of a total of 6300 flows between country pairs. This comprised the commodity movements of 80 countries or colonies and included all major trading entities except the Communist countries and those countries whose trade consisted mainly of goods in transit to and from other nations rather than items actually produced or consumed locally. This latter qualification excluded Singapore, Hong Kong, and the Netherlands Antilles, among others engaged primarily in entrepôt (in-transit) trade during that period. Also omitted were a number of countries (mostly less-developed countries) for which complete data were not available. The year selected was

1959 (actually an average of three years—1958, 1959, and 1960), which was considered a normal period because of the relative absence of disturbing international events of an economic or political nature.

All of the variables proved to be important determinants of trade. Most influential of all were gross national product (a measure of total demand) and distance. Preferential trading relations contributed substantially to the explanation, especially in the flows between mother countries and their associated colonies, past or present. This was particularly strong in the case of France and other members of the French Community, which also showed the greatest complementarity in the commodities exchanged among them. The model gave poorest results when predicting the trade of the least-developed countries; flows below $1 million were especially difficult to predict. This suggests that small flows, which are mainly to or from small economies, are erratic in occurrence. When adjusted to allow for this effect, the model increased substantially in explanatory power.

A number of analysts have used models similar to Linnemann's to study the trade flows of particular countries with their various trading partners. In one such study, James McConnell analyzed the trade connections of Israel and Lebanon with their respective foreign customers and suppliers. The two countries were very similar in size and circumstances except for their preferential trading relations. The results generally confirmed the relative importance of the various influences cited by Linnemann, and they reemphasized the need for a cutoff point to eliminate small, erratic flows. In the McConnell study the trade preference variables that proved to be important were membership in such organizations as the EEC and EFTA and, in the case of Lebanon, the Arab bloc.

Trade Growth and Structural Change

The volume of world commerce has fluctuated widely in modern times, showing how sensitive trade is to the vagaries of war and peace and of prosperity and hard times. World War I produced the first major disruption of trade in this century. Upon the arrival of peace, world exports soared until, by 1929, they had doubled their level of a decade earlier. When the Great Depression struck, the total value of trade dropped precipitously, falling by more than 60 percent within a very brief time. Indeed, trade contracted even more than did global production, for most industrial countries reacted to worsening economic conditions by imposing tariffs, quotas, and other trade restrictions to protect their domestic industries from foreign competition. Not until 1939 did world trade recover to its 1929 level, and it continued

to lag behind the growth of output because of persisting governmental interference.

World War II again seriously interrupted commerce, and trade patterns remained distorted for some years afterward because of wartime destruction of European and Japanese production facilities. World trade gradually returned to normal by the 1950s, and it gathered strength as the GATT agreements reduced governmental restrictions remaining from the prewar era. Trade continued to accelerate thereafter, rising more than fourfold between 1948 and 1968.

The commodity composition, or structure, of trade likewise changed during the first two-thirds of the twentieth century. The value of manufactured exports increased fourfold, whereas trade in primary commodities rose by a mere 50 percent. This relatively poor performance by primary exports occurred despite a rising demand for industrial raw materials and petroleum. One explanation for this is the increasingly elaborate processing that rising technology had brought about; another is the rising proportion of finished goods that entered trade. Indeed, a fairly reliable measure of a country's level of development is the proportion that finished goods comprise of its total manufactured exports. The growing trade in manufactured goods offered further evidence of the ever-increasing interdependence among industrial countries.

The composition of manufactured exports also changed during this era. Shipments of textiles and clothing—leading items of international commerce in an earlier time—declined steadily. Meanwhile, exports of metals and miscellaneous manufactured goods remained fairly static. The most rapid growth of all was in machinery, transport equipment, and chemicals.

This comparatively placid era of steady growth and evolution came to an end with the 1970s, when a series of crises rocked the world economy. The economic and political forces underlying these events had been building for some time, but their effects were as unexpected as they were severe. One major occurrence was the collapse of the old Bretton Woods agreement, which had sustained world monetary stability for most of the postwar years. Based upon gold and the U.S. dollar, the system had shown signs of deteriorating during the 1960s as emergence of the EEC, and later Japan, had eroded the preeminent position of the United States in world economic affairs. The complex system of floating exchange rates that replaced Bretton Woods after March of 1973 has led to much uncertainty in world business.

The early 1970s also saw a sudden rise in the prices of industrial raw materials. This brought an end to the remarkably long period of commodity price stability that had contributed so much to industrial growth in the 1950s and 1960s. The inflation in commodity prices resulted from an abnormally high demand from the industrial countries, which were enjoying an unusual period of simultaneous prosperity, and it was reinforced by a rise in nationalism among the less-developed countries (LDCs) supplying these commodities.

Then, in September of 1973, the OPEC oil crisis struck. The ensuing tenfold rise in oil prices added further to the worldwide inflationary spiral already under way, and the enormous transfer of wealth to the oil-exporting nations reduced incomes in the industrialized countries and halted development in the poorer LDCs. Global recession followed, accompanied by rising unemployment, uncontrolled inflation, mounting public debt, soaring balance-of-payments deficits, and declining world trade. (See pages 361–363 for an analysis of the impact of the energy crises upon world trade and development.)

Throughout this same period an even more fundamental set of changes had been taking place in the international economy. Beginning with the period of European colonization, the world had formed an international division of labor based upon comparative advantage and trade. Under this system, less-developed countries had traded their raw materials and agricultural goods to the industrialized lands in exchange for manufactured products. In recent years, however, the spread of foreign direct investment has led to an internationalization of manufacturing. Relying upon advances in transportation, communications, and materials-handling technology, multinational enterprises have been the primary agents of this change. Some of the LDCs have been acquiring their own industries, aided by multinationals attracted to these countries by their abundant supplies of cheap labor and, in some instances, readily available raw materials.

The cheaply produced goods from these newly industrializing countries are beginning to flood world markets. Unable to counter this new competition, many long-established industries of Western Europe and North America are having to retrench or fold. The older industrial economies are handicapped by aging plant and equipment and by the inability of government policy to adapt to changing world conditions. Still suffering from the effects of the oil shocks of the 1970s, some of the European countries have failed to keep up with innovations in the newer technology-intensive industries.

As deindustrialization continues in North America and Western Europe, manufacturing employment is declining, offset to some extent by rising employment in the service industries. These older industrial countries are vying with each other in the development of new technology and are contending for leadership in supplying capital, entrepreneurship, and other internationally provided services.

During this recent eventful period the kinds of goods entering international trade have changed significantly. Thus, prior to 1973, the value of world industrial exports was still growing at the expense of other categories, reaching almost two-thirds of all export earnings on the eve of the OPEC crisis (Figure 14.1). Ballooning oil prices interrupted this long-term trend but they did not affect all types of manufactures alike. As Figure 14.2 indicates, exports of machinery and transport equipment (U.N. Standard International Trade Classification 7) continued to accelerate without pause, and other manufactures (SITC 6 and 8) resumed their rapid growth in the late 1970s. These categories include most of the technology-intensive manufactures for which world demand is soaring. As a group, chemicals (SITC 5) are no longer increasing at their previous fast

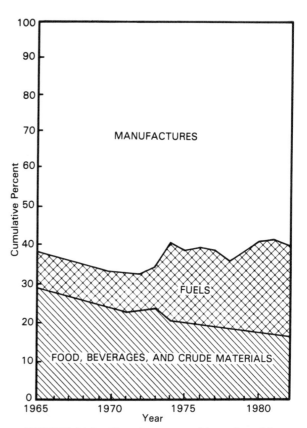

FIGURE 14.1 Changing composition of world exports (by value). The explosion in petroleum prices during the 1970s temporarily halted the long-term rise in the relative share of manufactured exports. As oil prices declined in the early 1980s the share of fuel exports began to shrink. The share of other primary commodities has steadily decreased throughout the present century, except for a short-lived rise at the beginning of the 1970s. [*Source:* United Nations, *Yearbook of International Trade Statistics,* various years (New York: United Nations).]

World Trade and the Energy Crises

Referring to the dramatic increase in oil prices posted by the Organization of Petroleum Exporting Countries (OPEC) in December 1973, former U. S. Secretary of State Henry Kissinger said, "It is now obvious that this decision was one of the pivotal events in the history of this century." The tenfold increase in world oil prices during the 1970s forever changed the pattern and structure of world trade. This episode truly ranks as one of the four major global economic crises of an eventful decade. All of the world's nations have felt these effects but in very different ways, depending upon their resource endowments, where they are in the development process, and the nature of their roles in the world economy.

How did the world get into this vulnerable situation? In Chapter 5 we traced the evolution of energy demand and the reasons for the growing interdependence of nations in the production and consumption of energy. Because oil is cleaner and easier to store and transport than solid fuels, it is the most widely traded form of energy. Also, prior to 1973 it was very cheap, selling for less then $3.00 per barrel on the world market. Whereas oil supplied only 30 percent of total global energy in 1957, it had mounted to 43 percent of the total by 1972—on the eve of the OPEC crisis—and was still rising. With world consumption thus surging, and with production concentrated in only a few places, the international trade in oil grew enormously, expanding nearly fourfold during this brief period. By the early 1970s oil constituted one-tenth of all commodity trade.

With their rapid economic growth in the 1960s and 1970s, Western Eruope and Japan were responsible for much of the new demand for oil. Having for many years relied upon imports for nine-tenths of its petroleum, Western Europe was by 1972 absorbing half of all oil shipments. Japan, with virtually no oil of its own, was importing one-sixth of the total. Meanwhile, the United States had shifted from being a net exporter of oil to being a net importer. Altogether, these industrialized countries took 80 percent of all internationally traded oil. This was also a period of substantial economic progress in much of the Third World, which was basing its industrialization upon cheap imported oil.

While the global demand for oil was climbing, the main sources of supply were shifting eastward. In the 1950s Venezuela had provided 35 percent of the world's petroleum exports, but by 1973 its share had slipped to only 8 percent. Much of the rest came from the Middle East and North Africa, where two-thirds of global reserves are concentrated. Although founded in 1960, OPEC had spent its first years in fruitless efforts to extract better terms from the oil multinationals. By 1973, however, the cartel was supplying 85 percent of the world's oil, clearly enough to assure a global monopoly if only its 13 quarrelsome members could agree on common action.

The opportunity to test this notion came late in 1973 when the Arab members of OPEC declared an embargo on oil shipments to the United States and other Western nations giving aid to Israel in the brief "Yom Kippur War" with neighboring Islamic states. Surprised and delighted by this demonstration of its power, OPEC quickly seized control of world petroleum pricing, abruptly shifting world power relations. Two main periods of steep price increases followed. At the end of 1973 OPEC raised prices fourfold and placed a ceiling on the volume of oil the cartel would produce and sell. The takeover of Iran by Muslim fundamentalists in 1979, and the Iran-Iraq war that followed, panicked world oil markets, causing the base price to jump from $12.70 to $41 per barrel. Though oil prices have since slipped, owing to world recession, conservation, and increased output by non-OPEC sources, the world economy remains deeply affected by OPEC's eight-year lock on world petroleum pricing.

International trade absorbed much of the impact of OPEC's actions. One effect was to alter global terms of trade—the average price a country receives for its exports in relation to the average price it pays for imports. The major industrialized countries and non-oil-exporting LDCs alike were forced to allocate a major part of their foreign exchange earnings to purchase the suddenly more costly OPEC oil. For much of the Third World it was near disaster. As the OPEC-induced world recession forced down their own export prices, many LDCs went deeply into debt to avert a complete halt in their development.

The spatial pattern of trade flows shifted, too. Although higher prices drastically increased the dollar value of petroleum exports and imports, the total volume of these shipments actually declined, idling much of the world's large tanker fleet. And needing more and more foreign exchange to pay for oil, most countries cut back their foreign purchases of other goods, especially the LDCs. The newly rich oil exporters, however, quickly increased their imports of manufactures—capital goods to speed their industrialization and consumer products to satisfy the rising demand from their prospering citizens. Hence, the emergence of this large new import market benefited the industrialized countries supplying such products, but it did little for LDC exporters of primary commodities. In time, the high price of oil brought new petroleum exporters into world markets—Mexico, the United Kingdom, Norway, and the USSR—thereby diversifying the spatial pattern of energy flows. Note, however, that these new source areas are closer to the markets for their oil, many of which are connected directly by pipeline, further diminishing the need for ocean-going tankers.

Clearly the OPEC crises have altered the composition of world trade, reducing the total volume of petroleum shipped and forcing LDCs to substitute oil purchases for capital goods. Although the imports of OPEC countries increased in amount and variety, their exports became even more specialized, partly because of the high valuation placed upon their petroleum shipments but also because their nonoil commodity exports—such as olives, dates, coffee, and cacao—declined because of neglect and inflated currencies.

The vast size of the global import bill for petroleum is a measure of the monetary impact of the OPEC crises. Ballooning prices meant the wholesale transfer of billions of dollars to the oil exporters from the rest of the world. The combined oil revenues of OPEC, which were only $7 billion in 1970, quickly rose to $72 billion in 1974 and to $300 billion by 1980. As a consequence, virtually all of the non-OPEC world found itself thrown into a balance-of-payments deficit. The problem has been less severe for the industrialized countries than for the oil-importing LDCs, however, because the former were able to sell manufactured goods and services to OPEC at sharply rising prices (thereby exporting their inflation). The LDCs did not have this cushion, because their conventional exports fell sharply in quantity and price. Meanwhile, for a time OPEC was drawing in money faster than it could be spent, threatening a world financial crisis.

The effects of these events upon individual OPEC countries varied greatly. The organization is by no means monolithic; its members differ in history, religion, culture, systems of government, ideology, population, stage of development, size of oil reserves, and productive capacity. In general, they fall into two main divisions. One subset consists of countries that have populations relatively larger than their oil output and therefore have a crucial need to maximize their incomes (Iran, Algeria, Indonesia, Venezuela, Nigeria, Ecuador, and Gabon). Members of the second group, on the other hand, have small populations relative to output and have no immediately pressing need for large revenues (Saudi Arabia, the United Arab Emirates, Kuwait, Qatar, Libya, and Iraq). With more than 90 percent of OPECs total population, countries in the first group have little flexibility and are continually pressing for higher prices. The latter group can afford to wait, viewing oil left in the ground as a potentially valuable resource for the future.

The enormous global transfer of wealth from oil importers to oil exporters—at least $100 billion per annum—presented OPEC's Group 2 countries with unprecedented money-management problems (Group 1 had no such dilemma—its members can easily absorb any amount of revenue). The problems were of two kinds: how to manage vast financial resources, and how to plan national development in such a way as to use this one-time infusion of funds efficiently and with lasting benefit. In the short run they placed their surplus funds in short-term investments, mostly in the United States and selected other industrial countries. In the longer run they gradually increased their expenditures on development projects at home: roads, housing, ports, airfields, and new industries. Saudi Arabia, for instance, had emphasized energy-intensive industries that multiply the returns from its abundant supplies of very cheap oil and natural gas—such activities as petroleum refineries, petrochemical works, and cement plants.

Just as the benefits of their new riches have varied among OPEC members, so have the effects of suddenly costly energy differed among oil-importing countries. For the older industrialized countries the initial impact was recession, high inflation, and declining incomes. Subsequently, however, those of the developed countries favored for OPEC investment and trade—the United States, Japan, and certain Western European nations—benefited from the recycling of OPEC wealth and the refocusing of their foreign sales upon the newly oil-rich lands. However, those industrialized countries passed by in the recycling process, such as Italy, had no such compensating benefits to relieve the impact of soaring energy bills. And, as we have seen, the effect of the energy crises was truly devastating for the oil-important LDCs.

As it must to all cartels, the end to OPEC's complete command of world oil prices came in the early 1980s. The price-elasticity of demand for oil is low in the short run but is high in the long run: The immediate defense of consumers against soaring oil prices is limited because it takes time to develop more energy-efficient transportation, insulate buildings, and so forth. In time, however, the reaction to expensive petroleum has been to give a high priority to energy efficiency, to develop new oil fields, and to find alternative forms of energy. The widespread recession and inflation following the initial shock of high prices had reduced global economic growth and thus the demand for OPEC oil. High prices also made feasible the development of high-cost petroleum sources, such as the North Sea and the North Slope of Alaska, and induced industries and consumers to prune their use of oil.

The net result of these events has been to reduce sharply the demand for OPEC oil. Whereas the group had a combined output of 31 million barrels per day in the 1970s, this total had fallen to only 14 million barrels by 1983. This put downward pressure on the price of oil, causing it to drop from a high of $41 to only $29 within this same period. As a result, OPEC's combined surplus income, more than $109 billion in 1980, turned into an $18 billion deficit by 1982. Some of the more hard-pressed members of OPEC, such as Nigeria and Iran, began to cheat on their agreed-upon production quotas, thus further weakening prices, which by mid-1986 had fallen below $10 per barrel on the world spot market. Several countries went into budgetary deficits and were no longer able to sustain their high expenditures for development. Some of those with large populations resorted to heavy borrowing abroad.

Barring further crises, the world should continue its gradual emancipation from OPEC. Other countries continue to bring into production new oil desposits—China, India, Argentina, the Canadian Arctic—and to pursue alternatives such as oil shale, oil sands, heavy oils, biomass, nuclear fusion, and hydrogen. Nevertheless, a Middle Eastern disaster—an Iranian victory over Iraq or the subversion of the Saudi government by a dissident group—would mean another major interruption in world supplies. Regardless of how events unfold, however, the oil crises of the 1970s have left an enduring impression upon the world patterns of trade and investment.

---

pace, even though certain high-technology subcategories are doing very well.

Fuel exports (SITC 3) were the most dynamic category in the 1970s, doubling their value share from less than one-tenth to more than one-fifth before weakening demand and oversupply of oil forced a retreat in the 1980s (Figures 14.1, 14.2). This dramatic expansion was measurable only in value terms, however, being wholly a function of exploding OPEC prices; the total tonnage of world oil exports actually shrank as costs rose.

The export value share of other primary commodities—food, beverages, and crude materials (SITC 0, 1, 2, and 4)—has steadily declined in recent years, continuing the long-term trend cited earlier. Indeed, the rate of decrease actually accelerated following the oil crisis: From a share of 29 percent in 1965, these commodities had slipped to only 17 percent by 1981 (Figure 14.1). Much of this change represents worsening terms of trade for primary goods as prices of manufactures and energy rose in world markets. Raw material exports (SITC 2 and 4) showed the least growth of any major category, more than erasing their price gains of the early 1970s. Note from Figure 14.2 that nearly every major export category suffered a setback during the world economic recessions of 1972–1975 and 1981–1983.

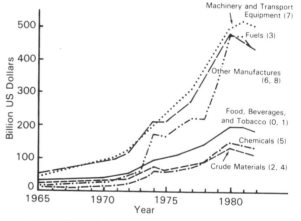

FIGURE 14.2 World growth of major export categories (by value). Despite the 10-fold increase in oil prices between 1973 and 1979, seen in the steepening curve for fuel exports [Category 3 of the Standard International Trade Classification (SITC)], manufactured exports (SITC 7, 6, 8) continued to rise throughout most of the period. Note, however, the effects of the two global recessions in the mid-1970s and early 1980s. [*Source:* United Nations, *Yearbook of International Trade Statistics,* various years (New York: United Nations).]

The trends and events of recent years have affected certain types of countries differently from others, as Figure 14.3 illustrates. Most dramatic is the meteoric rise in the value of OPEC exports following the 1973 crisis and again after the sharp jump in oil prices in 1979. The decline in OPEC's foreign sales since 1980 has been equally precipitous, as competition from non-OPEC oil producers has grown and prices have fallen. Export earnings of all other categories of countries grew more slowly, especially the poorest LDCs.

These differential rates of export growth have substantially altered the world market shares of the various country types (Figure 14.4). Over a long period the industrialized countries enjoyed a steadily increasing proportion of export earnings, which reached more than two-thirds of the world total in the early 1970s. The oil crisis of 1973 sharply reduced this share, but it has since recovered most of the loss. As a group, the three categories of less-developed countries (OPEC, the least-developed countries, and the other LDCs) had a shrinking share of world exports prior to the 1970s, which dropped to under 18 percent at its lowest point (Figure 14.4). This share began to edge upward as industrial raw material prices rose in the early 1970s, and with the oil crisis it climbed to more than one-quarter of the world total. OPEC, of course, accounted for virtually all of the gain in the latter 1970s, during which time its world share rose from only 5.6 percent to more than 15 per-

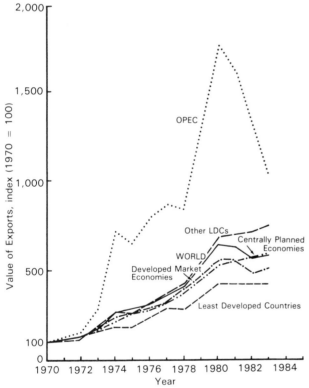

FIGURE 14.3 Growth of exports by major categories of countries (by value). OPEC's meteoric rise in the 1970s and decline in the 1980s are clearly seen. The "Other LDCs," which include a number of rapidly growing middle-income nations, have given a strong trade performance, but the least-developed countries continue to lag behind the rest. Note the effects of oil price rises and world recessions. [*Source:* United Nations, *Yearbook of International Trade Statistics,* various years (New York: United Nations).]

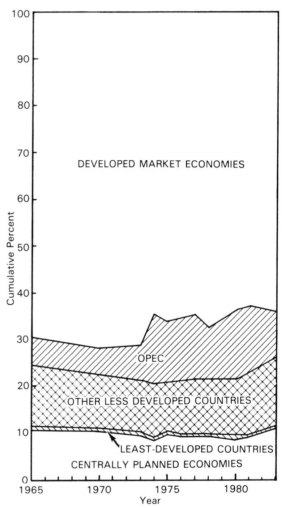

FIGURE 14.4 Changing share of world exports by major country categories (by value). The share of the developed countries ceased to grow during the period of high oil prices. OPEC's rising share in the late 1970s also came at the expense of the least-developed countries. The middle-income countries (other LDCs) are now gaining a rising proportion of world exports as industrialization spreads among this group. [*Source:* United Nations, *Yearbook of International Trade Statistics,* various years (New York: United Nations).]

cent. The least-developed countries—the 20 or so poorest nations as identified by the United Nations—have seen their share decline to a mere 0.4 percent of world exports by 1982. The other LDCs, led by several vibrant middle-income countries, have been doing much better: Although receiving a sharp setback from soaring oil bills after 1973, they had recovered to their earlier levels by the 1980s and have continued rising since. Throughout recent decades the centrally planned economies have held a steady 10 percent or less of world export earnings.

It is essential to keep in mind that some of the widest fluctuations in market share by the world's nations reflect changing prices, especially for oil. A broader perspective of world export growth is given by the quantum indices of Figure 14.5, which show the rates at which the physical volume of exports has grown. When viewed in this manner, the exports of LDCs as a whole have declined substantially since 1980, mainly because of the shrinking volume of oil shipments but also because of the effects of the 1981–1983 world recession.

One of the trends of recent years has been for the trade ties of most countries to become increasingly diverse. Whereas in 1970 the industrialized countries sold more than three-quarters of their exports to other ad-

vanced countries, this proportion has since declined to two-thirds. The share of their exports going to LDCs has meanwhile risen from 18 percent to more than 25 percent, and their imports from LDCs have gone up by an even greater amount. On the whole, the LDCs have been the most dynamic category of all, partly because of OPEC's appearance on the world scene but also because of the expanding role of semi-industrialized countries. Between 1970 and 1981, LDCs increased their trade with each other from less than one-fifth of their total exports and imports to 30 percent, while their dependence upon the more advanced countries fell by a corresponding amount. Moreover, the centrally planned economies, whose trade was predominantly with each other in 1970, now rely upon market economies, both developed and less developed, for half of their exports and imports.

THE SHIFTING FOCUS OF INTERNATIONAL ECONOMIC ACTIVITY

Of the many changes in international trade and investment in recent years, the development that promises the most far-reaching consequences is the fundamental shift in the center of gravity of global economic activity now under way. Although the volume and composition of international flows have always fluctuated widely, the basic spatial pattern of trade linkages among the world's nations has remained remarkably stable over a very long period. The North Atlantic basin (Figure 14.6) dominated international trade at least since the age of colonization, when the economic ties between Western Europe and North America were formed, subsequently to become the focus for the suppliers of primary commodities from other parts of the world. Thus, when comparing patterns of trade linkages prior to World War II with those of the 1960s, Bruce Russett (1967) could point to the Iron Curtain, which had come to separate Eastern and Western Europe, as the only significant disturbance to affect the basic map of international trade in modern times. He concluded, therefore, that fundamental trade patterns change with glacial slowness.

No longer is this true. Today, the North Atlantic basin accounts for a shrinking proportion of world trade and investment as the pace of economic activity in Western Europe slackens. Indeed, Western Europe's 41 percent share of world exports shown in Figure 14.7 is deceptive: Nearly two-thirds of that amount is interregional trade, being one of the consequences of Europe's extreme political and economic fragmentation. If, as the Common Market's founders had intended, the region were a United States of Western Europe, the interregional commodity flows would be

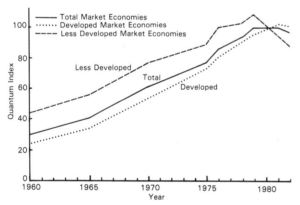

GROWTH OF EXPORTS BY MARKET ECONOMIES, 1960-1982

Quantum Indices
1980 = 100

FIGURE 14.5 Growth of exports by market economies, quantum indices (1980 = 100), 1960–1982. Measuring trade by the physical quantity shipped removes the effects of price inflation to be seen in previous figures. Note the sharp decline in quantities exported by LDCs since 1979. This reflects the 1979 price hike by OPEC, which reduced oil shipments and depressed world markets for other commodities sold by LDCs. Total world trade declined after 1981 because of widepread economic recession. [*Source:* United Nations, *Yearbook of International Trade Statistics 1983* (New York: United Nations, 1985).]

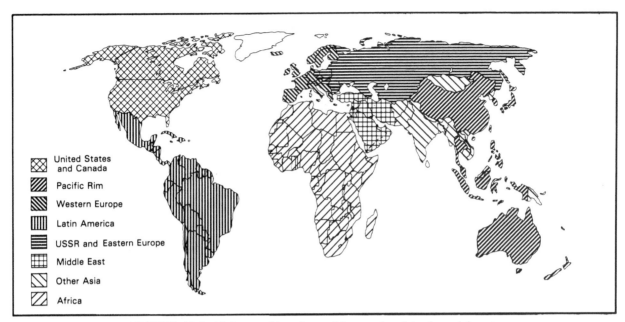

FIGURE 14.6 Major world regions of international trade and investment.

classified as domestic trade. The remaining exports to the rest of the world represent less than 14 percent of global trade, a figure below that of Canada and the United States (Figure 14.7).

Today, international economic activity increasingly focuses upon the Pacific basin (Figure 14.6). The main participants in this development are 12 countries on the western rim of the Pacific, extending from Japan and Korea southward to Australia and New Zealand, together with the United States and Canada, both of which are turning westward with their trade and in-

vestment. Although trends of the past several years had foreshadowed this shift, the world crises of the 1970s have undoubtedly hastened it, for the Pacific rim countries have been much quicker to respond to changing conditions than has the rest of the world.

The Pacific basin has evolved into a functionally integrated region whose 14 nations hold half of the population of the world and turn out half of its total output of goods and services. The United States and Canada are the prime targets for the rapidly expanding manufactured exports of the dynamic Pacific basin countries,

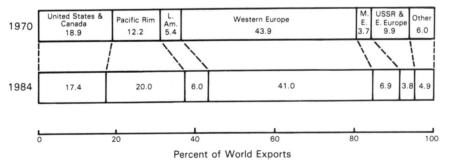

FIGURE 14.7 Changing value shares of world exports, major world regions, 1970 and 1984. In recent years Western Europe and Northern America have had diminishing proportions of world exports, whereas the 12 Pacific rim countries have expanded their share. The Middle East's larger share results from higher oil prices, not from an increase in physical volume of exports. L Am, Latin America; M E, Middle East (in Asia), including Israel. [*Sources:* United Nations, *Yearbook of International Trade Statistics 1982* (New York, United Nations, 1984); and International Monetary Fund, *Direction of Trade Statistics 1985* (Washington, D.C.: International Monetary Fund, 1985).]

and the two are also leading suppliers of industrial materials and agricultural commodities, as well as investment capital and technology, to the region. Being active participants in the economic affairs of both the Atlantic and Pacific basins, therefore, Canada and the United States act as fulcrums between the two realms. In the following pages we shall be looking more closely at the pivotal role of North America in the changing affairs of these and other major economic regions of the world.

North America

The United States remains a central focus of world trade and investment even though its trade has not grown as fast as the world as a whole. During the early postwar period, the United States accounted for a quarter of all world trade; today, its share has shrunk to one-sixth. Nevertheless, it is still the world's largest trader, despite having a much lower ratio of trade to gross national product than most countries. This ability to sustain a high level of trade with so small a proportion of its output is a function of size: a $3 trillion economy and a varied resource base within a territory of more than 9 million square kilometers. The level of U.S. trade participation is rising steadily, however. Whereas in the past it rarely sold more than 4 percent to 5 percent of its output abroad, the United States now exports more than 6 percent of its GNP. Moreover, the ratio of imports to GNP has been rising even more rapidly, approaching nearly 8 percent.

With imports now outstripping exports, the United States faces an alarming trade gap. A positive balance of trade in 1970 had turned into a 20 percent deficit by 1982, and this gap had widened to $120 billion by 1984. Among other causes, this reversal is attributable to a decline in the competitiveness of the country's maturer industries and to a greatly overvalued U.S. dollar on world money markets. At the same time, the huge American market has become a prime target for the world's exporters and a magnet for foreign investors seeking to widen their shares of that market. A positive balance in internationally traded services—transportation, finance, insurance, and so forth—along with earnings from U.S. foreign investments, helps to cushion somewhat the impact of the mounting trade deficit upon the country's overall balance of payments.

The United States sells an unusually broad range of goods on world markets, reflecting a national resource endowment of great diversity. Unlike most industrial countries, the United States is able to draw upon a very large and productive farm sector for a multitude of agricultural commodities grown under many different physical conditions. Complementing these are the country's exports of industrial goods, which rely upon a comparative advantage in high-technology production. As the competitive edge of American innovation diminishes, however, the manufacturing nations of Western Europe and the Pacific rim are cutting into this lead in technology-intensive goods (see Chapter 13).

The structure of U.S. imports is also changing. With its enormous appetite for a growing variety of raw materials, American industry can no longer satisfy its needs from domestic sources and must therefore buy more and more of these abroad. Furthermore, now that U.S. oil production has peaked, the country must rely upon foreign suppliers for a growing portion of its energy. Meanwhile, Americans are acquiring a taste for foreign-made automobiles, appliances, electronic goods, and innumerable other consumer products. Figure 14.8 shows some of the effects of these developments upon the U.S. balance of trade in particular commodity classes. Note the huge imbalance in fuels, and also the very large deficits in "Other Manufactured Goods" and "Goods Not Classified by Kind," both of which include many technology-intensive products. Foreign sales of American-made aircraft and computers help to maintain a positive balance in "Machinery and Transport Equipment," despite large imports of motor vehicles; and exports of soybeans, logs and lumber, and other "Crude Materials" offset foreign purchases of mineral ores. Current trends, however, point to weakening U.S. competitiveness in several major export categories, a matter of growing national concern.

Although the spatial pattern of U.S. commercial links with other countries is changing, certain connections remain fairly constant (Figure 14.9). Among the most enduring relationships are the close ties of trade and investment with the country's North American neighbors. Canada is the largest trading partner of the United States, with 20 percent of total U.S. trade (exports plus imports), and Mexico ranks third (behind Japan). Canada and Mexico are even more economically dependent upon the United States, which accounts for two-thirds or more of their total trade in most years and is their major source of foreign investment. One obvious reason for American dominance of its neighbors is its huge economic size: The U. S. economy is 10 times as large as Canada's and 18 times as large as Mexico's. Perhaps of equal importance, the United States has a 6700-kilometer common border with Canada and a 3200-kilometer border with Mexico. Because of this contiguity, transport costs are minimized and commercial concerns are intimately familiar with conditions in these neighboring lands. Long-standing business ties develop under these circumstances.

Another reason for the close economic interaction among the three countries is the complementarity of their resources, reflecting differences in physical con-

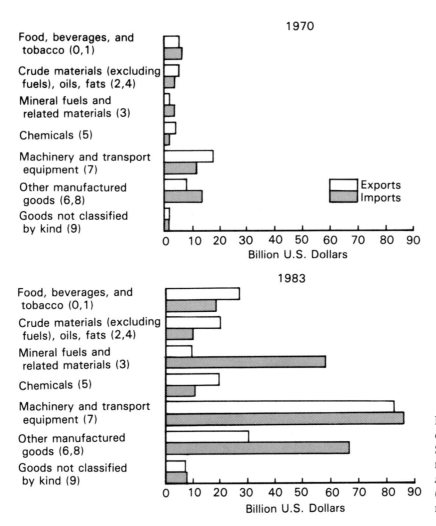

1970

1983

FIGURE 14.8 Changing structure of U.S. exports and imports. Major SITC categories. [*Source:* U.S. Bureau of the Census, *Statistical Abstract of the United States 1985* (Washington, D.C.: U.S. Government Printing Office, 1985).]

ditions and in the availability of technology, labor, and entrepreneural skills. The United States obtains certain land-intensive commodities from its well-endowed neighbors—tropical agricultural products from Mexico and petroleum and mineral ores from both countries—and relies upon Mexico for labor-intensive manufactured goods. Balmy climates, attractive scenery, and exotic cultures also lure American tourist dollars, a vital source of foreign exchange for Mexico (nearly $2 billion in 1982). In return, the United States supplies temperate grains for food-short Mexico and subtropical fruits and winter vegetables to Canada, and it provides both countries with a range of capital-intensive, high-technology manufactured goods.

Canada relies upon foreign commerce to a far greater degree than does the United States; in most years the country exports more than one-fifth of its output. This high trade dependence results from a special combination of factor endowments. With a total land area second in size only to the USSR, Canada has an enormous store of mineral wealth and biotic resources, as well as a large expanse of land suitable for temperate grains. Yet the population, which is about the same as that of California, is too small to absorb this great output of land-intensive commodities, leaving a huge surplus for sale abroad. At the same time, Canada must import tropical and subtropical foods and beverages for which its agricultural lands are climatically unsuited. Moreover, Canada must import a wide range of manufactured goods its own industries are unable to supply because their production requires economies of scale impossible to achieve with so small a domestic market.

Although primary commodities figure importantly in Canada's foreign sales, industrial exports are an unusually large part of the total. Some of these result from the initial processing of mineral ores and forest products, but many are finished goods. On the whole, the country's manufactured exports neatly express the character of the land. Thus, Canada has been especially successful in marketing heavy-duty hydroelectric generators and hydraulic turbines, benefiting from the long experience gained by Canadian firms involved in devel-

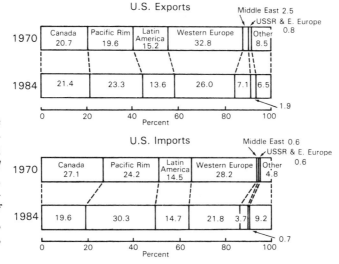

FIGURE 14.9 Changing value share of U.S. exports and imports with major world regions. [*Sources:* United Nations, *Yearbook of International Trade Statistics 1982* (New York, United Nations, 1984); and International Monetary Fund, *Direction of Trade Statistics 1985* (Washington, D.C.: International Monetary Fund, 1985).]

oping the country's great water-power potential. Canadian companies have gained a formidable competitive edge in the sale of high-technology communications equipment (including fiber optics) and small commercial aircraft—products that have been developed to overcome the problems of living in a vast territory. Increasingly, Canadians have concentrated upon exporting products, such as these, in which they are able to compete successfully in global markets. Meanwhile, they are dropping many consumer goods that have been expensively produced for the limited domestic market with the aid of protective tariffs. Recent GATT agreements have effectively stripped these products of this tariff shelter.

The importance of the United States as a customer and supplier for Canada is clear from Figure 14.10. In addition to imports of such commodities as oil, gas, hydroelectricity, minerals, and wood products, U.S. purchases of vehicles and parts under the Canada/United States Auto Agreement contribute heavily to Canada's foreign earnings; indeed, motor vehicles constitute the largest single export category. Offsetting Canada's generally positive merchandise trade balance with the United States (Figure 14.10) are substantial expenditures for U.S.-provided services and sizable capital outflows resulting from repatriated profits on American investments in Canada. Although as a region Western Europe ranks next to the United States in the country's trade, Japan is Canada's second largest individual trading partner. Japan is also investing heavily in Canada, especially in the resource industries of the western provinces. Since 1970, Canada's trade with Western Europe

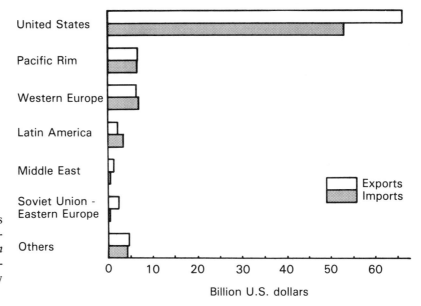

FIGURE 14.10 Canadian exports and imports, 1984. [Source: International Monetary Fund, *Direction of Trade Statistics 1985* (Washington, D.C.: International Monetary Fund, 1985).]

has slipped from 17 percent of the total to only 11 percent, while the Pacific rim countries as a group have raised their share to nearly 10 percent.

The Pacific Rim

In recent years the countries along the western margins of the Pacific have become the world's most dynamic economic region. Between 1970 and 1982 they increased their share of global exports from only 12 percent to more than 20 percent (Figure 14.7), and they are now assuming a prominent place in international investment and finance. Five groupings of countries have participated in this dramatic development. Japan has been the leading figure, establishing a pattern of trade-led growth with its astounding economic performance since the early 1950s. Japanese enterprise has since played a central part in integrating the Pacific economies. Following later in Japan's path, the "Four Tigers" of Asia—South Korea, Taiwan, Hong Kong, and Singapore—are successfully competing in world markets with an increasingly sophisticated line of manufactured products. More recently, five other Asian countries are beginning to adopt similar export-led strategies: Thailand, Malaysia, Indonesia, the Philippines, and the People's Republic of China. During this same period, Australia and New Zealand, having been cut adrift by the problem-ridden United Kingdom, have formed new economic ties in the Pacific realm. Here they have discovered new markets for their abundant physical riches in the newly industrializing Pacific lands nearby. Five of the Pacific rim countries (Indonesia, Singapore, Malaysia, Thailand, and the Philippines) have joined together in a loosely structured experiment in economic integration called the Association of Southeast Asian Nations (ASEAN).

This upsurge of economic activity along the Pacific rim has occurred during a period when the rest of the world was reeling from the major shocks of the 1970s—the inflation in commodity prices, the breakdown of monetary stability, two sharp oil-price rises, and two global recessions. The East Asian countries have demonstrated a remarkable ability to weather such crises. Drawing upon deeply imbedded cultural values that emphasize hard work and allegience to the group, laborers and managers work together for the success of their joint enterprises, and business leaders collaborate with government ministries to futher national goals. Together they closely follow international economic developments and respond quickly to changing conditions of demand and supply. The general public is made aware of the country's circumstances and can be mobilized to the common good during times of crisis.

Unlike the older industrial countries, with their stable populations and sluggish economies, the Pacific rim is an area of growth. Between 1960 and 1980 the combined GDP of this group increased 18-fold, adding mightily to the buying power and productive capacity of a region that holds a third of humanity. Moreover, unlike most of the underdeveloped world, the newly developing members of this bloc are successfully bringing population growth under control, thereby permitting a steady rise in per capita buying power. Meanwhile, literacy rates are rising, labor and management skills are multiplying, and support services are evolving.

This combination of growing productive capacity and rising consumer demand has brought a flood of investment to the western Pacific. During the 1970s foreign investment in the region as a whole quadrupled and investment in the Four Tigers actually grew sixfold. Meanwhile, investment in Western Europe has peaked and some investors are beginning to withdraw. Multinational enterprises are the prime agents for this transfer of capital and technology. United States MNEs have led, but Japanese and British companies have been close behind; German, Canadian, and Australian firms are also well represented.

The recent shift in merchandise flows from the Atlantic basin to the Pacific is clear from Figure 14.11. Although in 1970 total trade (exports plus imports) between Anglo-America and the Pacific rim was well below trade with Western Europe, the situation had reversed by 1981. During that interval, Pacific flows had grown twice as fast as those crossing the Atlantic.

During the 1970s a marked change also took place

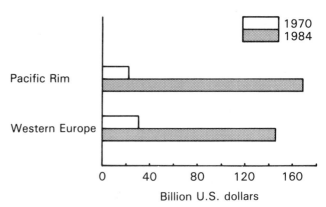

FIGURE 14.11 U.S. and Canadian trade (exports plus imports) with Western Europe and the Pacific rim, 1970 and 1984 (billion U.S. dollars). The Pacific has now eclipsed the North Atlantic as the leading avenue for North American commerce. [*Sources:* United Nations, *Yearbook of International Trade Statistics 1982* (New York: United Nations, 1984); and International Monetary Fund, *Direction of Trade Statistics 1985* (Washington, D.C.: International Monetary Fund, 1985).]

in the kinds of goods moving between North America and the Pacific rim. In a remarkably short time the developing countries of the western Pacific advanced from being exporters mainly of primary commodities to becoming sellers of industrial products. More recently, aided by the influx of multinationals, the Pacific rim countries have further upgraded their output, moving quickly from the production of standardized labor-intensive goods, such as textiles and clothing, to the manufacture of ever-more sophisticated products, including machinery, electronics, and communications equipment. This development has spread sequentially through the region in a fashion that has now become typical of the Pacific rim, beginning first in Japan and then moving to the Four Tigers and finally to the five newly emerging countries.

Perhaps the most startling development in the western Pacific is the appearance of new centers of corporate control and finance. Although Japanese firms had been actively investing abroad for some time previously, multinational corporations are now establishing headquarters in Hong Kong, Singapore, Taiwan, South Korea, and Australia. As they set up branch operations in neighboring lands, these Pacific-based multinationals serve to integrate the region ever more tightly.

Lately, as enormous trade surpluses accumulate, several East Asian capitals have become centers of international finance. Japan is now the leading exporter of capital, and banks and brokerage firms headquartered in Tokyo operate branches throughout the world. Both Singapore and Hong Kong have lively money markets, and these are taking a prominent part in the current move toward the internationalization of financial trading on a 24-hour basis.

It is clear that Japan has done more than any other country to forge the Pacific basin into a functionally integrated whole—an economic region whose complementary resources are linked together by trade and investment. In creating an export-led economy based almost entirely upon human resources, Japan has shown the way for those Asian lands, notably the Four Tigers, that lack sufficient natural endowments of their own. Japanese multinationals have also led in developing the resources of those Pacific countries, such as Australia, Indonesia, and Malaysia, that have surplus industrial raw materials and fuels.

With 120 million industrious people enjoying incomes comparable to Europe's, Japan has the world's most rapidly growing advanced economy and is the third largest trader. The Japanese have continually restructured their industries in adjusting to changing world demand and their country's advancing technical capabilities. This is apparent from the changing character of the country's trade. Since 1960, Japan's exports of tex-

tiles and yarns—mature, labor-intensive products that once dominated the country's foreign sales—now contribute only a minor share of the total. The big increases are in machinery and transport equipment, now more than three-fifths of all exports despite a decline in shipbuilding (captured by South Korea). Other rapidly expanding exports include electronics and communications equipment, which are representative of the knowledge-intensive industries now stressed by Japanese government policy. A diminishing share of exports comes from Japan's older energy-intensive, polluting metallurgical industries, which required massive imports of raw materials and fuels.

More than half of Japan's trade takes place within the Pacific basin (Figure 14.12), and nearly one-third of the total is with the western Pacific region. In a sense, the Japanese have succeeded by peaceful means in gaining economic dominance over a part of the world that they had once sought to conquer militarily. While the Pacific basin countries increasingly focus their commerce upon Japan, a growing share of Japanese trade is going to other parts of the world. The Middle East now buys a tenth of Japan's exports and supplies nearly a third of the country's imports (oil purchases from all sources actually comprise 40 percent of Japan's total import bill). Exports to Europe and Latin America are also growing.

In recent years Japanese exports have grown much

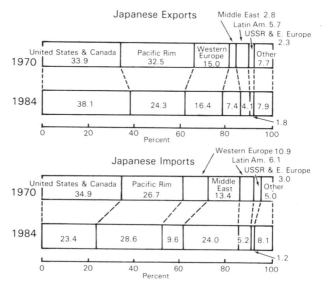

FIGURE 14.12 Value share of Japanese exports and imports with major world regions, 1970 and 1984. [*Sources:* United Nations, *Yearbook of International Trade Statistics 1982* (New York: United Nations, 1984); and International Monetary Fund, *Direction of Trade Statistics 1985* (Washington, D.C.: International Monetary Fund, 1985).]

faster than imports, creating an embarrassingly high trade surplus with the world. Japan's bilateral surplus with the United States actually reached $33 billion in 1984, and exports to the EEC are three times as big as imports. This lopsided trade balance has aroused worrisome protectionist sentiments in North America and Europe; it has also provided Japan with an enormous supply of foreign exchange with which to invest in foreign ventures. Prior to the 1970s, Japanese multinationals largely concentrated their overseas activities in the extractive enterprises, with the purpose of assuring long-term supplies of industrial materials for the resource-poor homeland. Since 1969, when governmental restrictions on exports of capital were removed, Japanese firms have greatly expanded their investments in foreign manufacturing and service ventures. Today, more than half of Japan's overseas investment is in the Pacific region.

The rise of the Pacific rim as a powerful economic force is having a great impact on the rest of the world generally and on the United States in particular. Aside from its dangerously mounting trade deficit with the western Pacific countries, the United States finds itself in a paradoxical position with respect to that region. The types of merchandise the country exchanges with East Asia place the United States rather in the role of a less-developed country dealing with more advanced ones: A high proportion of U.S. exports to the Pacific consists of primary commodities, whereas imports are mostly industrial goods. Indeed, one-third of all U.S. agricultural exports now goes to the Pacific rim. This region still relies, however, upon certain high-technology items from the United States, especially aircraft, pharmaceuticals, and the more advanced types of capital goods.

So pervasive is the Pacific region's influence that it is lending added force to the westward movement of people, industries, and commercial activities within the United States. West Coast ports carry more than four-fifths of U.S. trade with the Pacific and are enjoying a boom in port industries and service activities associated with this rising tide of commerce. In addition, the western states are beneficiaries of more than a third of all investment by Pacific countries in the United States.

Latin America

Not only do the developing countries of Latin America differ culturally from those of East Asia, but they also take a different approach to international trade. Like the Pacific lands, however, the Latin American countries rely heavily upon foreign trade and investment. Latin America's traditional role in the world economy, dating to the beginning of European colonization, has

called for exporting primary commodities—agricultural products and minerals—to the industrialized countries of the Northern Hemisphere. Although this exchange draws upon many natural complementarities between the two areas, Latin Americans have long been dissatisfied with the subdominant position in which this relationship places them, and they have continually striven to change it. Although these problems and attitudes are generally shared throughout the region, the Latin American countries vary considerably in their individual circumstances. They range in size and level of development from Brazil, a giant of a country that aspires to superpower status by the end of the century, to the small, desperately poor island nation of Haiti. Within the region are countries that are predominantly mineral exporters, some that depend upon agricultural exports, and others that do not have enough resources of either kind.

Nearly all Latin American countries export a large proportion of their national output. The median export/GDP ratio is more than 20 percent, as compared with less than 7 percent for the United States and 13 percent for Japan. The highest ratios are those of small Central American countries such as Honduras (35 percent) and mineral exporters such as Jamaica (32 percent). Some of the large countries with lower export/GDP ratios, however, are experiencing the highest rates of export growth—Brazil and Mexico in particular.

Although industrial exports are increasing, the region as a whole continues to sell mainly primary goods to the world. Overall, foodstuffs and raw materials constitute more than four-fifths of Latin American exports, and for half of the countries the proportion is greater than 90 percent. This is a usual pattern for Third World countries. Imports, on the other hand, are not at all typical: Unlike most LDCs, the Latin American countries import an unusually small quantity of manufactured consumer goods and a high proportion of capital goods. The reason that consumer imports are so small is that Latin Americans have for many years followed policies of import substitution, as a result of which they have become largely self-sufficient in such products. Import substitution is relatively easy with consumer goods but much more difficult for intermediate products and capital goods.

The traditional markets and sources of supply for Latin American countries have been North America and Western Europe. Throughout the nearly two centuries since independence, Mexico, most of Central America, and much of South America have been tied to the United States. The southernmost countries—Argentina, Uruguay, and Chile—have had strong links to Europe; and the Caribbean islands, most of which have gained independence only recently, still maintain commercial connections with their former mother countries. Patterns of foreign investment have reinforced these trade linkages, and the resulting condition of economic dependence has made Latin America vulnerable to the vagaries of business cycles, politics, and wars in the North.

Today, these long-frozen trade patterns are beginning to shift. Since 1970 Latin America's trade with North America and Western Europe has shrunk from more than two-thirds of the total to little more than a half. Imports have fallen the most, and Europe has suffered the larger share of this decline. Less-developed countries have been the greatest beneficiaries of the shift, much of it going to the oil-exporting lands but a substantial portion of it accounted for by a rise in trade among Latin American countries themselves. In addition, trade with the Pacific rim has burgeoned, especially with Japan and the Four Tigers, which have seized a growing share of the market in this former Atlantic basin preserve. Meanwhile, Latin American exporters, especially the semi-industrialized countries of Brazil, Mexico, and Argentina, are aggressively selling their new manufactures throughout the developing world (see Chapter 13). Latin American trade with the centrally planned economies remains relatively minor, much of it accounted for by Cuba's Communist links.

Western Europe

The international crises of the 1970s had an exaggerated effect upon the countries of Western Europe, mainly because they are so dependent upon trade. The larger European countries generally export about a quarter of their GNP, but some of the smaller ones export half or more of their output. In part, this dependence is a function of political fragmentation—more than 20 sovereign entities occupying an area no more than a third that of the United States—and the substantial intra-European trade this produces. Many of these small countries are contiguous, distances are very short, transport networks are dense and superior in quality, and economic integration has greatly reduced the artificial barriers of earlier years. The high level of commercial activity also stems from the size and density of their populations—a third of a billion people in all—and their high per capita incomes. Standards of living throughout the region are today comparable to those of North America, and three European countries exceed the United States in per capita GNP. Still another factor is energy-short Western Europe's very high bill for petroleum imports, made all the worse by the fact that international oil shipments are denominated in U.S. dollars.

With so much of Western Europe's output going into world commerce, it is not surprising that this region accounts for two-fifths or more of total world trade

(Figure 14.13). In general, imports exceed exports by a substantial margin, largely because this concentrated economic region needs to augment its local supplies with foreign purchases of basic commodities. Helping to balance this chronic trade deficit are Western Europe's substantial "invisible exports," earnings from internationally supplied transport and financial services and from a prospering tourist industry.

The sensitivity of Western Europe's trade to larger events, both within and outside the area, is apparent from Figures 14.13 and 14.14. The region's contribution to world commerce rose substantially during the 1960s as a result of economic integration and the general liberalization of trade restrictions from an earlier era. Western Europe's prosperity peaked in 1973 on the eve of the first OPEC oil crisis; in the following year, trade slumped sharply, especially exports, with the onset of economic recession. In 1979, just as Western Europe's trade was beginning to recover, the second oil crisis struck. Imports continued to rise, because of the mounting cost of imported oil, but exports plummeted. Both exports and imports remained weak throughout the lingering recession that followed.

These events have also altered Western Europe's traditional pattern of trade linkages with the world (see

FIGURE 14.13 Western Europe's value share of world exports and imports, 1959–1983. Western Europe has long contributed a major part of the world's trade. Under the stimulus of economic integration, the region further increased its role in the international economy during the 1960s and early 1970s, but oil crises and economic recessions have subsequently caused its share of world trade to deteriorate. [*Source:* United Nations, *Yearbook of International Trade Statistics,* various years (New York: United Nations).]

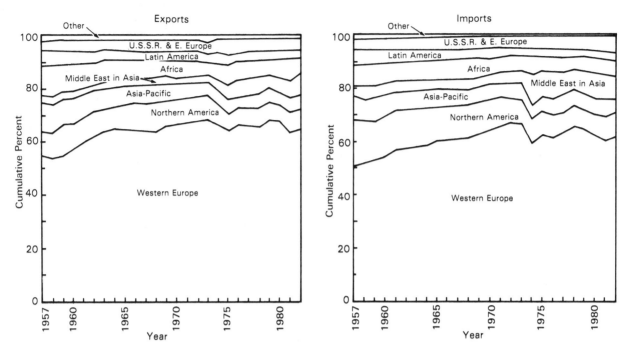

FIGURE 14.14 Value share of Western Europe's exports and imports with major world regions, 1957-1982. Because of their small size and contiguity, the countries of Western Europe have always traded more with each other than with the rest of the world. The movement toward regional economic integration, however, has reinforced that tendency since the late 1950s. Evidence of trade diversion and the effects of foreign direct investment by U.S. multinational enterprises are apparent in the declining proportion of trade with Northern America (the United States and Canada). The disrupting impact of the two oil crises of the 1970s is also clearly seen here. [*Source:* United Nations: *Yearbook of International Trade Statistics,* various years (New York: United Nations).]

Figure 14.14). Aside from its substantial trade with itself, this region has had enduring ties with North America: The Atlantic basin long accounted for three-quarters of Western Europe's world trade, a pattern reinforced by investment flows. Relationships with present and former colonies helped to preserve high levels of commerce with Africa and the Asia–Pacific region. The two oil crises brought huge increases (as measured by value) in the proportion of Western Europe's imports from the Middle East, offset only partially by higher export sales to that suddenly wealthy region.

The heightened focus of European trade upon the Middle East has occurred at the expense of trade with the rest of the world, even though growing amounts of petroleum are being obtained from the North Sea and elsewhere. The proportion of Western Europe's trade with North America has steadily diminished since 1973, and the formerly strong ties with Australia and New Zealand have dwindled to a fraction of their previous size. With certain parts of the Asia–Pacific realm, how-

ever, Western Europe's trade links have strengthened. Imports from Japan and the Four Tigers have soared, threatening many of Europe's competing industries. Although the Pacific region is taking an increased share of Western Europe's exports, the total is not sufficient to avert a growing trade deficit with the area. The proportion of Western Europe's trade with the USSR and Eastern Eruope, which had remained at modest levels since World War II, has expanded somewhat in the past decade as the Eastern bloc has sought Western technology and as the USSR has increased its exports of oil and natural gas.

The USSR and Eastern Europe

Participation in world commerce by the Comecon countries lags far behind their potential. As we might expect from a system in which economic matters are nearly always subordinate to political considerations, ideology has produced a distinctive pattern of trade in this case.

For one thing, these countries have not fully shaken off the Stalinist belief in *autarky,* or self-sufficiency. Politics also limits trade between seemingly natural trading partners, creating antagonisms with the West and ideological quarrels within the Communist bloc itself. Comecon therefore contributes only one-tenth of total world trade, and a disproportionate part of this is with itself.

Yet, on strictly economic grounds, the opportunities for increased international economic involvement appear very great. Comecon occupies a huge territory, nearly 16 percent of the world's land area, and has a combined population of nearly 385 million people. The group therefore possesses a great storehouse of physical resources and promises a big market for Western goods. A number of important complementarities exist between East and West. Indeed, prior to the Communist era, a lively trade took place between the two regions, based upon an exchange of the East's land resources for the West's manufactured goods. Today, the oil, gas, and metallic minerals of the USSR find a demand in Western Europe, while Comecon needs Western capital goods and technology. In addition, the USSR must import massive quantities of grain in years of bad harvests on its own farmlands.

Although Comecon's share of world trade has remained little changed in recent years, these countries have somewhat relaxed their strictures against trading outside their own group. As a consequence, intra-Comecon trade has fallen from more than three-fifths of their total trade to little more than half. The group's exports and imports with the Communist countries of Asia have meanwhile declined substantially, owing to the USSR's ideological dispute with the People's Republic of China. The greatest gains are those of Western Europe, which now accounts for more than one-quarter of Comecon's trade. The Eastern bloc has made even greater proportionate increases in its trade with less-developed countries; this has risen from 11 percent of the total to 15 percent. Lesser gains have also occurred in Comecon's imports from Japan and the United States.

Given the tempting opportunities for much greater East-West trade, why has progress been so meager? One reason is that the Communist countries are generally short of hard currencies, and their own currencies are not convertible in foreign-exchange markets. Most intra-Comecon trade is therefore conducted on an unwieldy barter basis, and a large part of the group's trade with the non-Communist countries takes place in this way too. Furthermore, in addition to the continuing ideological differences with the West, recurring crises interrupt an otherwise growing exchange. The U.S. embargo on grain sales to the USSR, imposed at the time of the Soviet invasion of Afghanistan, offered a prime example. Another was the American attempt to interfere with West European sales of pipeline equipment to the USSR. At the same time, efforts by Comecon countries to market machine tools and other standardized manufactures in the West have met little success because of the poor quality of the products. Therefore, because of ideological differences with the West and an inability to adapt to the requirements of international commerce, the Soviet bloc has thus far been unable to gain a share of world trade commensurate with its size and resources.

The Middle East

Living at a historic crossroads of world commerce, the people of the Middle East have been traders from earliest times. Although great-power interests have long focused upon this area because of its strategic location, the discovery of vast pools of petroleum beneath the region has attracted world attention as never before. The knowledge that they control two-thirds of all known oil reserves made it possible for the Arab members of OPEC to precipitate the crisis of 1973. Only half of the Middle Eastern countries are surplus oil exporters; most of the rest are resource-poor agricultural nations that do not share in the oil bonanza (except for such aid as OPEC may grant them). Indeed, farming is the leading occupation throughout the Middle East, even in those countries producing oil. Yet the population is growing so fast that the region as a whole has become a net importer of food.

During the 1970s the Middle East enjoyed a huge increase in its share of world exports, which jumped from only 3 percent to more than 10 percent within a span of six years. This resulted solely from a 10-fold rise in oil prices; the volume of shipments actually shrank. For a time, oil revenues were pouring in so fast that imports could not keep up, and the oil-exporting countries acquired enormous balance-of-payments surpluses. By the early 1980s, however, the Middle East's foreign earnings had begun to decline as oil prices sagged because of a weakening market.

Prior to the oil boom the Middle East's traditional exports were agricultural commodities—such as cotton, figs, and dates—and various mineral ores. In fact, goods of this type still brought in 11 percent of the region's foreign earnings in the early 1970s. Exports of these commodities have continued to grow since, but they have been overwhelmed in the trade figures by the steep rise in oil receipts.

As industrialization reaches the Middle East, new classes of exports are beginning to appear. Egypt has now attained the status of a semi-industrialized country and is exporting cotton yarn, textiles, and other consumer manufactures. A sharp increase in Middle Eastern shipments of industrial products is taking place as Saudi Arabia's huge new petroleum refineries and petrochemical plants go on stream. Made from exceedingly cheap feedstocks of Saudi oil and natural gas, these commodities are very competitive on world markets. Many other energy-intensive manufacturing industries are rising throughout the region as oil-exporting nations prepare for a world after the oil is used up. Some Middle Eastern countries are earning substantial amounts of foreign exchange through invisible exports, especially Egypt and Israel with their prospering tourist industries. As a transit country, Egypt gains additional revenues from Suez Canal tolls.

The Middle East's imports, which have grown steadily since 1973, are very diverse. Being highly specialized producers of oil and other primary commodities, these countries nevertheless have varied needs, which can be satisfied only with imports. Rising incomes expand the range of consumer demand, and development needs call for a growing variety of capital goods and industrial raw materials.

Even before the crises of the 1970s, the Middle Eastern oil exporters had unusually diverse trade ties throughout the world. Their largest single market, however, has always been Western Europe, which was taking 44 percent of all Middle Eastern exports at the time of the first oil-price rise. Since then, Western Europe's share has slipped to a little over one-third. Japan, the second largest customer, continues to take about one-fifth, and North America buys another one-tenth. Conscious of the political volatility of the Middle East, however, all of these customers are busily diversifying their oil sources, causing the Middle East's share of world oil sales to slip.

The chief supplier of the Middle East's imports is Western Europe, which is working hard to increase further its share of this lucrative market. Although still the largest single source of supply, the United States is not faring as well as its competitors for Arab oil dollars. Japan and the Four Tigers, however, are aggressively expanding their hold on the Middle Eastern market.

The odd man in this virtually solid bloc of Islamic countries is the Jewish state of Israel. About the size of New Jersey, this tiny nation of 3 million people resembles its Arab neighbors physically but is very different culturally, economically, and politically. Having a highly skilled labor force and many experienced managers, Israel has joined the ranks of industrial nations and has forged formal economic ties with both the United States and the European Economic Community. Its industrial exports include cut diamonds (one quarter of foreign earnings), machinery, chemicals (based upon salts from the Dead Sea and phosphates from the Negev Desert),

aircraft, and armaments. Relying upon its excellent transport connections and its climatic complementarity with Western Europe, Israel ships subtropical fruits, winter vegetables, and cut flowers to European capitals daily by air.

Despite its success as a diversified exporter of agricultural commodities and industrial goods, Israel runs a dangerously high trade deficit. Exports cover only a little more than half the cost of imports, which are kept high by the demands of a large defense establishment and heavy government subsidization of the economy.

A CONCEPTUAL VIEW OF WORLD TRENDS

Although empirical tests of the Heckscher-Ohlin theorem (Chapter 12) have shown that theory to be an inadequate explanation for international trade, our examination of contemporary world patterns has suggested that resource endowments continue to play an important part. This chapter has demonstrated, however, that the resource endowments of countries are changing—dramatically so in the case of the Pacific rim nations—and that the rate of change is accelerating. This is occurring in response to a number of dynamic influences discussed in Chapter 13.

Thus, according to recent studies, one of the prime factor endowments, labor, is assuming a fundamentally new role in world commerce (Leamer, 1984). This is shown by a global trend toward a labor content of higher quality in internationally traded goods: a greater reliance upon engineering, scientific, and skilled labor and a corresponding decline in the use of unskilled workers. This reflects the rising importance of technology-intensive products, the most rapidly growing commodity class. This trend also underscores the rising fortunes of Japan and the newly industrializing countries (NICs) of East Asia, which in recent decades have intensified their drives to raise education levels. The net result of these efforts has been to maximize the effectiveness of the already impressive deposits of human resources in that region.

Capital has also assumed a new importance in world commerce and, as the most mobile of factors, it has undergone locational shifts unprecedented in nature and quantity. The most spectacular capital movements, of course, were the international transfers of hundreds of billions of dollars to the OPEC nations from the rest of the world during the 1970s. Perhaps a more enduring trend, however, has been the steadily rising accumulation of capital by the Pacific rim countries. With unusually high personal savings rates and favorable balances of payments, Japan and some of its neighbors have in very short order become capital-rich nations.

Moreover, low interest rates and good institutional arrangements have enabled western Pacific industries to modernize their production more rapidly than North American and European companies. This accumulation of capital has, at the same time, spurred the rapid growth of financial services, notably international banking, and it has been instrumental in the rise of East Asian-based multinational enterprises. Meanwhile, this region has lured much foreign direct investment by multinationals from the Atlantic basin.

Resources of the land continue to play their part in world commerce, but they too are undergoing alteration. This is obvious in the case of the world oil trade, which underwent great changes during the crisis years, as rising prices sharply curtailed the volume flowing from OPEC nations and stimulated exports from source areas elsewhere in the world. This has transformed the world map of oil movements. For Japan and the East Asian NICs, land is the scarce factor; they must obtain their energy, industrial raw materials, and much of their food from elsewhere. This fact has been one of the forces leading to functional integration of the Pacific basin as a whole. Other members of that regional bloc—Canada, the United States, Australia, and New Zealand—are abundantly endowed with most of the physical resources lacking on Asia's eastern margins. It is this complementarity of resource endowments that has cast this group of mature industrial countries into the unlikely role of providers of primary commodities in exchange for East Asia's manufactures.

Another key element is entrepreneurship, represented by the availability of a class of persons with essential management skills. This was long a virtual monopoly of the Atlantic basin countries, the birthplace of the multinational enterprise. Yet, entrepreneural skills have diffused ever-more widely in the world, and the chief transfer agent for these has been the MNE itself. These skills have quickly passed into the national cultures of many countries, especially Japan and the East Asian NICs, where rising educational levels and accumulating experience have provided fertile soil for their growth and development. East Asian managers have adopted Western practices and improved upon them by injecting an Oriental group-centered outlook and a consensus-seeking approach to decision making.

As a barrier to world commerce, distance continues to wield a powerful influence despite the many events of the two decades since Linnemann's studies confirmed its importance. The role of distance has been apparent in the cohesiveness of Western Europe, demonstrated by the continuing high proportion of intra-European commodity and investment flows. Distance also contributes to the enormous volume of goods and capital moving between Canada and the United States,

and its impact is apparent in the organizing role Japan has played on the western margins of the Pacific.

Yet, countertrends have appeared. By contrast with the increasing compartmentalization of trade within continental blocs noted by Bruce Russett in the 1960s—an era of experimentation with regional economic integration—current evidence points to an increasing diversity of trade linkages in most parts of the world. Latin America has loosened its ties to the United States and is trading much more widely. Likewise, despite the high degree of functional integration and the many complementarities of resource endowments within the Pacific bloc, Japan and several other countries of the region are increasing their trade with the world at large.

Several reasons may be advanced for this increasing diversity of trade linkages. One is the rising technology content of manufactured exports; these are being processed more highly and becoming more valuable, and are therefore better able to bear the cost of long-distance transport. Another freeing development is the recent explosion of communications technology. Accompanying this communications revolution has been the widening reach of multinational enterprises, which are now capable of instantaneously transferring information worldwide.

Politics continues to have a major part but an exceedingly variable one. New trends in economic development policy, for instance, have led to the switch from import-substituting industrialization strategies, so prevalent in the past, to a new emphasis upon export-promoting industrialization strategies. The spectacular success of the East Asian NICs has reinforced this trend, which, with modifications, is gaining acceptance among some of Latin America's newly industrializing countries.

By contrast with these trade-creating measures, the monetary and fiscal policies of some older industrialized countries have badly distorted currency exchange rates. For instance, the wide fluctuations in the value of the American dollar have had an enormous impact on the patterns of world trade and investment flows. Also destructive has been the resurgence of protectionist sentiments, which raise the specter of a trade collapse like that of the 1930s. Political decisions were, of course, the precipitating causes of the oil crises of the 1970s.

Thus, we have witnessed an unexpected disruption of world patterns that had previously remained little changed for a very long time. Our interpretation of these changes has stressed several dynamic influences—the pervasive role of multinational enterprise, the multifaceted effects of technology, the intervention of governments—all of which contributed in one way or another to the shift in the center of gravity of world economic activity. This shift has coincided with a fundamental industrial restructuring; similar episodes in the past (see Chapter 11) have likewise seen the decline of old industrial regions and the rise of new ones. The major beneficiary of these recent developments, the Pacific rim, has had the resilience to withstand the global shocks of the 1970s and the flexibility to respond quickly to the accelerating pace of change. This has led some to predict that the world is now on the threshold of "the Pacific century" (Linder, 1986).

TOPICS FOR DISCUSSION

1. What are the theoretical implications of each of the variables used by Linnemann and by McConnell in their interaction models of trade flows? Which of these variables have proved most important in explaining the strength of trade linkages among countries and why? Examine the patterns of trade flows between the United States and Canada and Mexico, and interpret these patterns theoretically.

2. How did the major economic upheavals of the 1970s change world patterns of trade and investment? How did these effects differ among various regions and categories of countries?

3. Why did OPEC succeed as a cartel when producers of other primary goods have failed to form working cartels? Discuss the divisions among OPEC members and show how these differences affect their ability to absorb oil revenues and their attitudes toward recent problems confronting the group. Which oil-importing countries were hurt most by the sharp rise in oil prices, and how have their problems affected world trade? Why has OPEC's grip on world oil prices begun to slip? How confident can we be that this situation will continue?

4. Discuss the competitive positions of the leading exporters of technology-intensive goods and show how these relate to their changing comparative advantages for such products.

5. How has the Pacific basin evolved into a functionally integrated economic region, and what impact has this had upon U.S. trade? What effects has the rise of the Pacific rim had upon regional growth and the location of economic activities within the United States?

6. Describe the economic and cultural conditions that have contributed to the remarkable success of the Pacific rim countries, interpret the trade strategies they have followed, and discuss the new roles these countries have assumed in world production, investment, finance, and trade.

7. Explain why the countries of Western Europe have such high export/GNP ratios, and interpret theoretically the spatial pattern and composition of that region's trade.

8. Why are Latin American policymakers dissatisfied with their countries' role in international commerce, what policies have they followed in an effort to change that role, and how has the content and spatial pattern of that region's trade changed as a result of those policies?

FURTHER READINGS

KRAUSE, LAWRENCE B., AND SUEO SEKIGUCHI, eds. *Economic Interaction in the Pacific Basin.* Washington, D.C.: The Brookings Institution, 1980.

Investigates the transmission of economic impulses among six representative countries within the Pacific basin, noting particularly the effects upon those countries of the economic upheavals of the 1970s and their responses to these.

LEAMER, EDWARD E. *Sources of International Comparative Advantage: Theory and Evidence.* Cambridge, Mass.: MIT Press, 1984.

This ambitious study rigorously tests the empirical validity of the Heckscher-Ohlin theorem and, based upon the results, describes the changing patterns of international trade and resource endowments. Provides an excellent carefully developed review of trade theory and a thorough critical review of previous empirical tests of the Heckscher-Ohlin theorem.

LINDER, STAFFAN BURENSTAM. *The Pacific Century: Economic and Political Consequences of Asian–Pacific Dynamism.* Stanford, Calif.: Stanford University Press, 1986.

Traces the rapid transformation taking place on the Pa-

cific rim and explores the economic implications this holds for the Asian–Pacific countries themselves, for other developing countries, for the established industrial countries of Europe and North America, and for the centrally planned economies.

LINNEMANN, HANS. *An Econometric Study of International Trade Flows.* Amsterdam: North-Holland Publishing, 1966.

A pioneering work in the development of interaction models for use in the search for generalized explanations for the existence of trade between countries. Tests a series of models of increasing refinement, using 6300 bilateral trade flows.

RUSSETT, BRUCE M. *International Regions and the International System: A Study in Political Ecology.* Skokie, Ill.: Rand McNally, 1967.

Uses factor analysis to group countries according to the strength of their relationships to each other in each of several forms of international interaction. Finds that the world's nations fall into nine regional groups on the basis of their trade linkages.

CHAPTER 15

Local Trade
and Urban Hierarchies

Chapters 12, 13 and 14 were concerned with comparative advantage, specialization, and trade at the international level. In this chapter we turn to the channels of distribution within countries, and to the patterns of market centers and retail and service business location that have emerged to satisfy the multiplicity of things demanded by consumers in specialized societies.

The relationships may be understood by developing the concept of an urban hierarchy, as well as building an equivalent understanding of the wholesaling relationships that exist between regions.

Objectives:

- to explain the concept of spatial hierarchies
- to understand central-place theory, including the classical statements by Walter Christaller and August Lösch
- to describe Vance's mercantile model of wholesale trade and its relationship to central-place theory
- to explore the role of periodic markets, the central places in the spatial organization of peasant societies

THE IDEA OF AN URBAN HIERARCHY

Muqaddasi's Scheme

The idea that urban centers are arranged in echelons according to their size, the functions they perform for the surrounding regions, and the nature of local trading relationships is not new. For example, a description of the Moslem lands written over 1000 years ago was phrased entirely in hierarchical terms. The description, shown in Figure 15.1, comes directly from the work of Al-Muqaddasi (or al-Maqdīsī), so-called because he was born in Jerusalem (Bayt al-Maqdis). Al-Muqaddasi was a geographer who visited all the Moslem lands except Spain, Sijistan, and India, and who, in A.D. 985–986, embodied an account of his 20 years of travel in *Ahsan al-Taqāsīm fi Ma'rifat al-Aqālīm [The Best Classification for the Knowledge of Regions]*.

Muqaddasi was one of several medieval Arab geographers who divided the Islamic world into regions, based on the historical and sociopolitical identity of each

a. Theoretical hierarchy of settlements
1. *Amsār (sing. misr), metropolis*
2. *Qasabat (sing. quasabah), fortified provincial capitals*
3. *Mudun (sing. madinah), provincial towns, a main town of a district, or a market town*
4. *Qurā (sing. qaryah), villages*

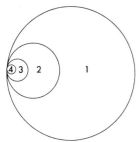

b. Theoretical hierarchy of regional units
1. *Aqālīm (sing. iqlīm), regions*
2. *Kuwar (sing. kūrah), provinces*
3. *Nawāhy (sing. nahiyah), districts*
4. *Rustaqāt (sing. rustāq), agricultural units*

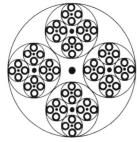

c. Theoretical spatial distribution of settlements

FIGURE 15.1 Al-Muqaddasi's system of urban centers and region units. [*Source:* After Riaz Hassan, "Islam and Urbanization in the Medieval Middle East," *Ekistics,* 33 (February 1972), 108.]

region, as well as on the relationships between cities and regions. Within each region, or *iqlīm*, he classified the settlements according to a hierarchical grading system. As he noted: "In my grading system of settlements, the *amsār* (singular *misr*) are comparable to kings; the *qasabat* (singular *qasabah*) are comparable to ministers; the *mudun* (singular *madīnah*) are comparable to cavalry men; and the *qurā* (singular *qaryah*) are comparable to soldiers. . . ." A definitive hierarchy of dominance and subdominance was implied. Further, relating the successively smaller settlements to an analogous hierarchy of subregions, he noted: "every *iqlīm* must have *kuwar* (singular *kūrah*); every *kūrah* must have *qasabah*; every *qasabah* must have (or attract) *mudun* (singular *madīnah*). . . ." To Muqaddasi, the Arab world of A.D. 985 was layered spatially into an urban-regional hierarchy comprising four distinct echelons.

Spatial Hierarchies and the Location of Cities

Throughout the world, urban centers and the regions they serve are organized into such spatial hierarchies. As we saw in Chapter 10, industrial activities have distinct locational preferences for one or another rank of the urban hierarchy, based upon the differences in market opportunities, urbanization economies, and types of labor force that cities of different sizes provide. In this chapter, we will show similar relationships for retail and service businesses, the local and regional trade flows that support these businesses, and the service areas and marketing patterns resulting from the trade relationships. Regularities of the same kind also characterize the provision of administrative services in political systems.

The Questions Addressed by Central-Place Theory

The basic theory we are concerned with is called *central-place theory*, and it attempts to answer such questions as, Why do urban hierarchies exist? What determines the size and spacing of cities and the configuration of their market areas in such hierarchies? There are, of course, many reasons for cities and their locational patterns, often working in concert, as Figure 15.2 illustrates. For example, *transportation centers* perform break-of-bulk and allied services along transportation routes and tend to be arranged in linear patterns with respect to railroads, highways, coastlines, and rivers. *Specialized-function cities* perform services such as mining, manufacturing, or recreation. Because the principal localizing factor is often a particular resource such as a coalfield, or a sandy beach and a warm sunny climate, such cities occur singly or in clusters. Central-place theory ab-

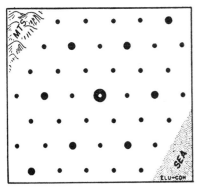

Theoretical distribution of central places. In a homogeneous land, settlements are evenly spaced; largest city in center surrounded by 6 medium-sized centers that in turn are surrounded by 6 small centers. Tributary areas are hexagons, the closest geometrical shapes to circles that completely fill area with no unserved spaces.

Specialized-function settlements. Large city is manufacturing and mining center surrounded by a cluster of smaller settlements located on a mineral deposit. Small centers on ocean and at edge of mountains are resorts.

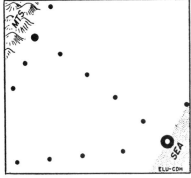

Transport centers, aligned along railroads or at coast. Large center is port; next largest is railroad junction and engine-changing point where mountain and plain meet. Small centers perform break-of-bulk principally between rail and roads.

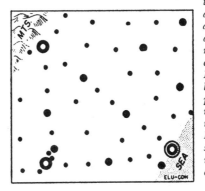

Theoretical composite grouping. Port becomes the metropolis and, although off center, serves as central place for whole area. Manufacturing-mining and junction centers are next largest. Railroad route in upper left has been diverted to pass through manufacturing and mining cluster. Distribution of settlements in upper right follows central-place arrangement.

FIGURE 15.2 Differing patterns of urban location. [*Source:* Chauncy D. Harris and Edward L. Ullman, "The Nature of Cities," reprinted from *Annals of the American Academy of Political and Social Science*, CCXLII (November 1945), 7–17, in Harold M. Mayer and Clyde F. Kohn, eds., *Readings in Urban Geography* (Chicago: University of Chicago Press, 1959), pp. 278–279.]

stracts certain economic functions, the tertiary activities of retail and service business, and shows how their locational patterns lead to the broad dispersion of market towns or central places of differing sizes across the economic landscape, in hierarchies that are precisely meshed with their market areas.

It is to the central-place abstraction that we now turn, concerning ourselves therefore with the geography of retail and service business and with the hierarchy of urban centers *insofar as they are market towns.* Because the leading central places in any region are also centers of wholesale trade that have their locational patterns determined by larger interregional trade-flow relationships, the discussion of central places is followed by the elaboration of a "mercantile model" of wholesale trade. Finally, the chapter deals with local trade and periodic markets in peasant societies.

Cities and the Organization of Local Trade

Throughout the chapter it will be well to remember why we are concerned with the urban hierarchy in studying the geography of economic systems: The basic reason is that of the interdependence of urbanization and trade. As metropolitan wholesaling centers, cities are the instruments whereby the specialized regions of a national economy are tied together. They are the centers of activity and of innovation, focal points of the transport network, locations of superior accessibility at which firms can most easily obtain the advantages of economies of scale and economies of localization and urbanization. Agricultural enterprise is more efficient in the vicinity of cities. The more prosperous commercialized agricultures encircle the major cities, whereas the inaccessible peripheries are characterized by backward, subsistence economic systems.

The subregional organization of the larger metropolitan-centered regions is provided by the system of central places, which involves:

1. a system of cities, arranged in a hierarchy according to the functions performed by each;
2. corresponding areas of urban influence or urban fields surrounding each city in the system.

The size and functions of a city and the extent of its urban field are proportional. Each region within the national economy focuses upon a center of metropolitan rank. A network of intermetropolitan connections and interregional trade-flows links the regions into a national whole. The spatial incidence of economic growth with these regions is a function of distance from the metropolis. Troughs of economic backwardness lie in the most inaccessible areas along the intermetropolitan peripheries. Each major region is, in turn, subregionalized by successively smaller centers at progressively lower levels of the hierarchy—smaller cities, towns, or villages that function as market centers for the distribution of goods and services to the region's consumers.

Change in the Urban Systems Framework

Impulses of economic and social change in such a system are transmitted simultaneously along three planes:

1. outward from "heartland" metropolises to those of the regional hinterlands;
2. from centers of higher to centers of lower level in the hierarchy, in a pattern of "hierarchical diffusion";
3. outward from urban centers into their surrounding urban fields, producing "spread effects."

Hence, the urban hierarchy serves not only to service the consumption needs of the various regions within a national economy, but it also serves to pattern how and when change takes place. One result (which we saw in Chapter 8 and will discuss again in Chapter 16) is that incomes fall as city size decreases and as distance from urban centers increases, in a distinctive hierarchically structured pattern of economic welfare.

WALTER CHRISTALLER'S CENTRAL-PLACE THEORY

Although many antecedents can be cited, going back to Al-Muqaddasi and before, the first explicit statement of central-place theory was made by the German geographer Walter Christaller in 1933 in a book entitled *Die Zentralen Orte in Süddeutschland* [*The Central Places in Southern Germany*]. The essential features of Christaller's argument may be summarized in six points.

1. The main function of a market town is to provide goods and services for a surrounding market area. Such towns are located centrally within their market areas, and hence they can be called "central places."
2. The greater the number of goods and services provided, the higher is the *order* of the central place.
3. Low-order places offer convenience goods that are purchased frequently within small market areas (Figure 15.3) and hence the *range* of low-order convenience goods (that is, the maximum distance consumers are willing to travel) is small (Figure 15.4).
4. Higher-order places are fewer in number and are more widely spaced than lower-order places providing goods with greater ranges (Figures 15.5 and 15.6). Generally, the greater the range, the greater is the *threshold* (that is, the minimum sales level necessary for the seller to make a profit).
5. A *hierarchy* of central places exists to make as efficient as possible the arrangement of convenience and shopping goods opportunities for consumers who have a basic desire to travel as little as possible to obtain the goods and services they need to maintain their households and persons, and for producers, who must earn at least a minimum "threshold" to survive.
6. Hierarchies have three spatial forms, organized according to
   a. a marketing principle,
   b. a transportation principle, and
   c. an administrative principle.

Christaller proceeded, in the manner of von Thünen and Weber, to a case in which extraneous variables were controlled by simplifying assumptions. Assume, he said, identical consumers distributed at uniform densities over an unbounded plain on which access is equally easy in any direction. Under such circumstances the range of any good has a constant radius. How can centers be located so as to provide for the most efficient marketing of the goods? Given the homogeneity of the plain, Christaller concluded that each good should be supplied by a uniform net of equidistant central places, close enough together so that no part of the plain is left unsupplied.

The resulting distribution is one in which the central places are located at the apexes of a network of equilateral triangles, with each set of six centers forming a hexagon. This organization permits the maximum packing of central places into the plain.

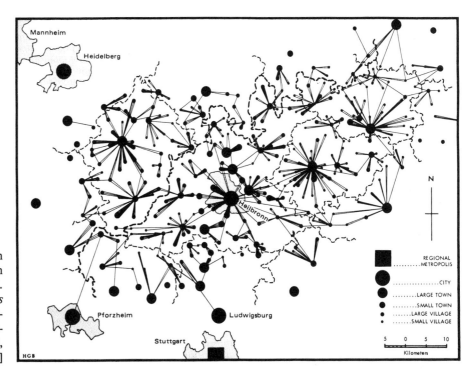

FIGURE 15.3 Travel to obtain pharmaceutical service in a portion of southern Germany. [*Source:* H. Gardiner Barnum, *Market Centers and Hinterlands in Baden-Württemberg* (Chicago: Department of Geography, Research Paper No. 103, University of Chicago, 1966), p. 60.]

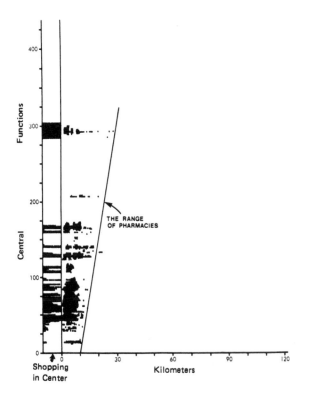

FIGURE 15.4 Relationship between distance traveled by consumers and size of center in Figure 15.3. The left-hand column shows cases where consumers shop in the central place in which they live. [*Source:* Barnum, *Market Centers.*]

The Hierarchical Principles

After developing his basic model, Christaller suggested three spatial alternatives, organized according to marketing, transportation, and administrative principles.

The Marketing Principle

The *marketing principle* assumes that the location of a central place of any order is at the midpoint of each set of three neighboring places of the next higher order (Figure 15.7). These midpoints are the corners of the hexagonal market areas of the higher-order centers, and every higher-order center is surrounded by a ring of six centers of next lower-order located at the corners of its hexagons. The boundaries of the lower-order complementary regions are the perpendicular bisectors of the higher-order complementary regions.

The progression of centers and market area sizes derived by Christaller can be observed in Figure 15.7. Each higher-order market area contains the equivalent of three market areas of the next lower order—its own, plus one-third of each of the surrounding six, and the equivalent of two central places of the next lower order—each ring of the six surrounding centers lies within the hexagons of three centers of higher order. The progression of market areas is $1(3^0)$, $3(3^1)$, $9(3^2)$, $27(3^3)$, $81(3^4)$, and of centers $1(3^0 - 0)$, $2(3^1 - 3^0)$, $6(3^2 - 3^1)$,

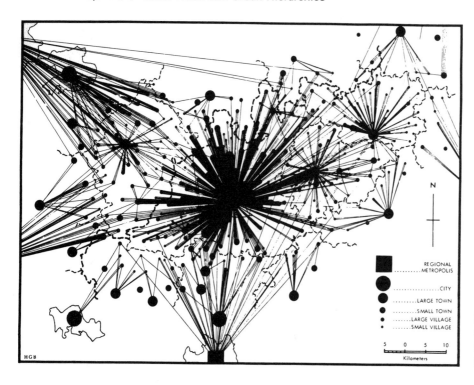

FIGURE 15.5 Travel to purchase clothing in a portion of southern Germany. [*Source:* Barnum, *Market Centers.*]

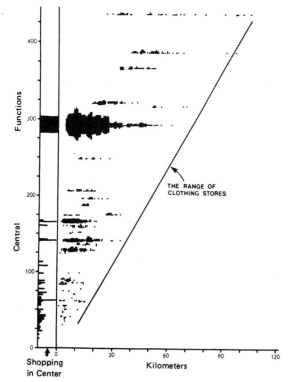

FIGURE 15.6 Distance relationships in Figure 15.5. [*Source:* Barnum, *Market Centers.*]

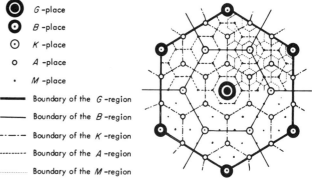

FIGURE 15.7 The marketing hierarchy according to Christaller. [*Source:* Walter Christaller, *Central Places in Southern Germany,* trans. Carlisle Baskin (Englewood Cliffs, N.J.: Prentice-Hall, 1966), p. 61.]

the *landstadts* of southern Germany, namely Munich, Frankfurt, Stuttgart, and Nuremberg-Furth (see Table 15.1 and Figure 15.8). Christaller's map also includes Strasbourg and Nancy in France and Zurich in Switzerland, which also rank as *landstadts*. Table 15.1 presents a relationship among size, spacing, number of functions, and hierarchical interdependence that is surprising in its closeness to the theory. The strict regularity has been disturbed by a variety of historic, economic, and geographic circumstances. Among the economic factors causing local deviations that were noted by Christaller are population density and income, the economic base of the region, and interregional competition.

$18(3^3 - 3^2)$, and $54(3^4 - 3^3)$. The progressive increase by a rule of threes leads to a description of this marketing-principle arrangement as a $k = 3$ network.

Christaller elaborated the marketing principle for

TABLE 15.1
Characteristics of central places in southern Germany, 1933

Type	Number of places	Number of complementary regions	Range of region (km)	Area of region (km²)	Number of types of goods offered	Typical population of places (in thousands)	Typical population of region (in thousands)
M	486	729	4.0	44	40	1	3.5
A	162	243	6.9	133	90	2	11
K	54	81	12.0	400	180	4	35
B	18	27	20.7	1,200	330	10	100
G	6	9	36.0	3,600	600	30	350
P	2	3	62.1	10,800	1,000	100	1,000
L	1	1	108.0	32,400	2,000	500	3,500
Total	**729**						

Source: Walter Christaller, *Central Places in Southern Germany;* trans. Carlisle W. Baskin (Englewood Cliffs, N.J.: Prentice-Hall, 1966, p. 67).
Note: The levels of the hierarchy described by Christaller are: I. Marktort M; II. Amtsort A; III. Kreisstadt K; IV. Bezirkstadt B; V. Gaustadt G; VI. Provinzstadt P; VII. Landstadt L.

G. William Skinner (1964), an American anthropologist, has provided an outstanding example of the relationship between actual central-place patterns and Christaller's abstract *k* = 3 network in a study of rural marketing in pre-Communist China, illustrated by Figures 15.9 and 15.10. In Figure 15.9 is the actual urban pattern, which is easily transformed into the *k* = 3 network of Figure 15.10.

The Transportation Principle

Spatial organization according to the marketing principle makes it difficult to establish a satisfactory transportation system. The location of centers on the corners of hexagons means that no straight route can link centers at three consecutive orders on the hierarchy. A long-distance route linking "metropolitan" centers

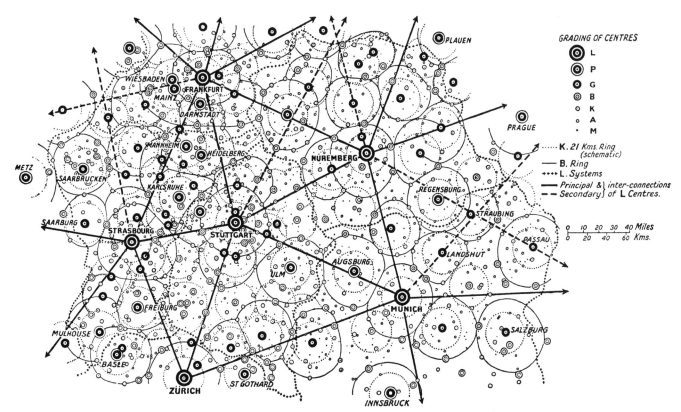

FIGURE 15.8 The central-place system of southern Germany. [*Source:* Christaller, *Central Places in Southern Germany,* pp. 224–225.]

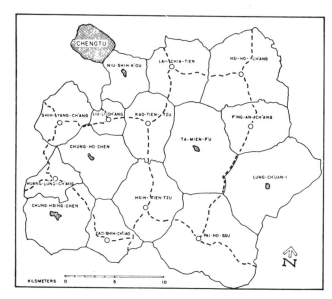

FIGURE 15.9 A portion of Szechwan near Chengtu. (After G. William Skinner.) [*Source:* Brian J. L. Berry, *Geography of Market Centers and Retail Distribution* (Englewood Cliffs, N.J.: Prentice-Hall, 1967), p. 67.]

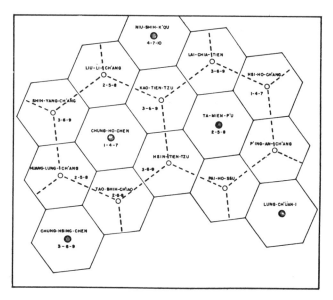

FIGURE 15.10 The *k*-3 network. [*Source:* Berry, *Geography of Market Centers.*]

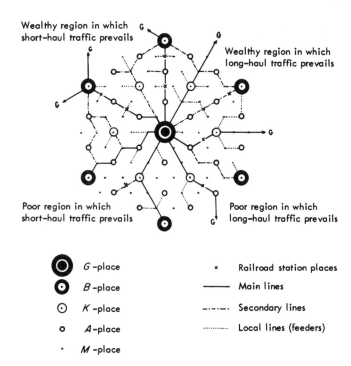

Wealthy region in which short-haul traffic prevails

Wealthy region in which long-haul traffic prevails

Poor region in which short-haul traffic prevails

Poor region in which long-haul traffic prevails

◉	*G*-place	✕	Railroad station places
◉	*B*-place	——	Main lines
⊙	*K*-place	—·—·—	Secondary lines
○	*A*-place	········	Local lines (feeders)
·	*M*-place		

FIGURE 15.11 Traffic routes in the marketing network. [*Source:* Christaller, *Central Places in Southern Germany.*]

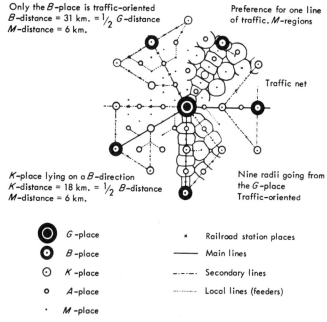

Only the *B*-place is traffic-oriented
B-distance = 31 km. = ½ *G*-distance
M-distance = 6 km.

Preference for one line of traffic. *M*-regions

Traffic net

K-place lying on a *B*-direction
K-distance = 18 km. = ½ *B*-distance
M-distance = 6 km.

Nine radii going from the *G*-place
Traffic-oriented

◉	*G*-place	✕	Railroad station places
◉	*B*-place	——	Main lines
⊙	*K*-place	—·—·—	Secondary lines
○	*A*-place	········	Local lines (feeders)
·	*M*-place		

FIGURE 15.12 Modification of market areas in the transportation solution to creation of a hierarchy, according to Christaller. [*Source:* Christaller, *Central Places in Southern Germany.*]

(*G*-places) can pass through the towns (*K*-places) but misses the cities (*B*-places) for which special routes are required. Christaller suggested a number of possible traffic route systems (Figure 15.11). However, these alternatives are not as satisfactory as the reorganization of complementary regions according to a transportation principle.

The transportation principle states that the distribution of central places is most favorable when as many important places as possible lie on one traffic route be-

tween two important towns, the route being established as straight and as cheaply as possible. Christaller suggested that complementary regions would be distorted from the hexagonal form (Figure 15.12) if one attempted to maintain the marketing hierarchy. He realized that a regular hexagonal form can be retained, however, by locating successive lower orders of centers at the *midpoints* of the transport routes running directly between the metropolitan centers (Figure 15.13). Thus, a hierarchy is produced maximizing the number of centers located on major transport routes. Because centers locate at midpoints, they bisect the sides of hexagons rather than locating at their apexes. The result is a "nesting" of hexagons inside one another according to a rule of fours. For every center of a given order there will be, on the average, four market areas of the next lower order (its own, plus one half of each of the six surrounding) and three places of next lower order (each of the ring of six surrounding centers lies on the hexagon of two centers of higher order). The progression of market areas is $1(4^0)$, $4(4^1)$, $16(4^2)$, $64(4^3)$, $256(4^4)$ and of centers is 1, $3(4^1 - 4^0)$, $12(4^2 - 4^1)$, $48(4^3 - 4^2)$, $192(4^4 - 4^3)$. It therefore takes 192 village centers to support one metropolis by the traffic organization compared with only 54 by the marketing principle. Thus, a traffic-organized area too small to support 192 village regions could not support a metropolitan center. The traffic hierarchy is generally coarser with fewer levels

than the marketing hierarchy for given-sized areas. The allocation of goods and services, therefore, involves broader groupings of goods at each level. Customers must travel farther, on average, to reach a center at a given level of the hierarchy, offsetting the advantage of a more efficient transportation system.

In another part of pre-Communist China, G. William Skinner has provided an example of a $k = 4$ hierarchy as startling as that shown in Figures 15.9 and 15.10. The relevant illustrations in this case are Figure 15.14, the actual pattern of central places, and Figure 15.15, the $k = 4$ hierarchy. In spite of the existence of mountains that have the effect of eliminating a center from one of the hexagonal cells, Figure 15.15 is only locally distorted.

The Administrative Principle

The transportation principle, like the marketing principle, presents a problem, namely, the division of complementary regions at successive levels of the hierarchy. The overlapping of smaller regions across the boundaries of higher-order complementary regions is inconsistent with administrative organization. Administrative principles involve the grouping of complementary regions of lower order, such as counties, *within* those of higher order, such as states, in their entirety. This is essential for unambiguous administrative control. The ideal organization, said Christaller, should have as the nucleus the capital, with a ring of lower-order administrative centers around it, and a thinning

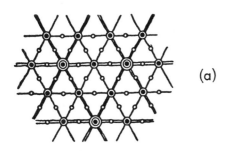

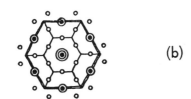

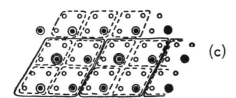

(a)

(b)

(c)

FIGURE 15.13 The revised hierarchy solution to permit centers to align on major transport arteries: (a) the routes; (b) locations of centers; (c) regional hierarchies. [*Source:* Walter Christaller, *Das Grundgerüst der räumlichen Ordnung in Europa* (Frankfurt am Main: W. Kramer and Co., 1950), p. 10.]

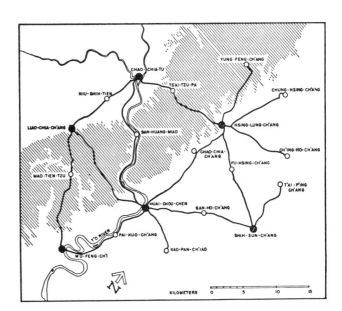

FIGURE 15.14 A second portion of Szechwan northeast of Chengtu. (After G. William Skinner.) [*Source:* Berry, *Geography of Market Centers.*]

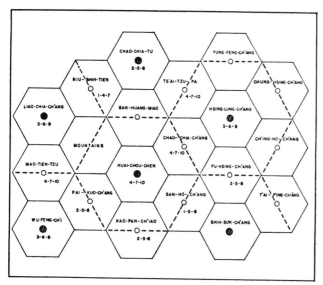

FIGURE 15.15   The *k*-4 network. [*Source:* Berry, *Geography of Market Centers.*]

of population density toward the edge of the region. In this scheme, a central place of higher order administers to the total area of the six surrounding lower-order complementary regions, thus following a rule of sevens (Figure 15.16). The hierarchy is coarser (1, 7, 49, . . . regions; 1, 6, 42, . . . centers), the transportation system less efficient, and consumers must travel farther than in either the market or traffic organization.

As Alexis de Tocqueville wrote 150 years ago in his classic book *Democracy in America*, if the capital city is large and highly developed relative to the centers of outlying provinces, it is a mark of a highly centralized administration. If differences between sizes of centers at the successive levels of the administrative hierarchy are not so great, it indicates a decentralized pattern of administration, with greater local power and responsibility.

AUGUST LÖSCH'S ECONOMIC LANDSCAPES

A number of difficulties present themselves when all three principles are operating simultaneously in the organization of space. How do they relate to create some of the complex hierarchies observable in reality in modern urban-industrial societies? Christaller was unable to resolve these difficulties, but soon after he had written his book another German, location economist August Lösch (1906–1945), provided an answer in his book *Die Raümliche Ordnung der Wirtschaft* [*The Spatial Organization of the Economy*].

Lösch began, like all location theorists, with a wide plain, homogeneous in every respect and containing only

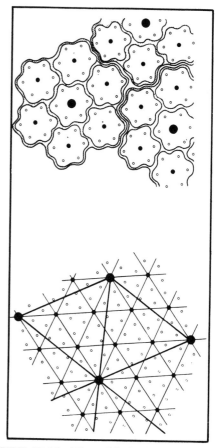

FIGURE 15.16   Hierarchical relationships and traffic routes in Christaller's administrative scheme. [*Source:* Christaller, *Das Grundgerüst der räumlichen Ordnung in Europa.*]

self-sufficient farms that are regularly distributed in a triangular-hexagonal pattern. He then showed how an economic landscape could be built from the lowest-order centers upward.

A Progression of Market Area Hexagons

Lösch's first step was to derive a spatial demand cone, and to prove why Christaller's triangular-hexagonal spatial patterns were the most efficient. He then found that Christaller's $k = 3$, $k = 4$, and $k = 7$ networks were the first three cases in an entire progression of market area sequences in which the spacing of centers or order could be calculated by the equation of

$$d_n = d_{n-1}\sqrt{k}$$

where k is the hierarchy ratio and d_{n-1} is the spacing of the next lower order of centers.

The nine smallest market area patterns found by Lösch are illustrated in Figure 15.17. These have *k* values of 3, 4, 7, 9, 12, 13, 16, 19, and 21. Centers are

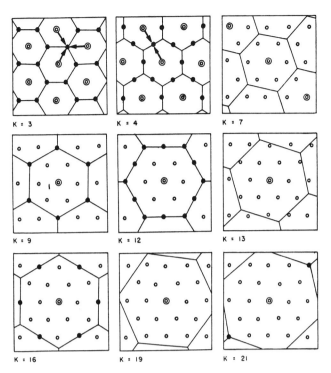

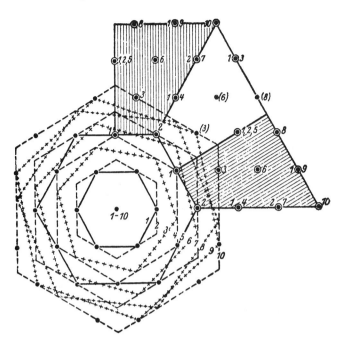

FIGURE 15.17   The nine smallest market areas in Lösch's analysis. [*Source:* Peter Haggett, *Locational Analysis in Human Geography* (London: Edward Arnold Ltd., 1965), p. 119.]

FIGURE 15.18   The 10 smallest economic areas. The sectors containing many towns are hatched. Alternative regional centers are in parentheses. Simple points represent original settlements. Those enclosed in circles are centers of market areas of sizes indicated by the figures. [*Source:* August Lösch, *The Economics of Location,* trans. William H. Woglom and Wolfgang F. Stolper (New Haven, Conn.: Yale University Press, 1954), p. 118.]

located with respect to the hexagons in three possible ways: at an apex, as where $k = 3$ and 12; at the midpoint of a side as when $k = 4, 9, 16$, and 25; and within the hexagon as when $k = 7, 13, 19$, and 21.

City-Rich and City-Poor Sectors around the Metropolis

Lösch thought it desirable to devise a compound hierarchy incorporating all these possible arrangements of hexagons. Only such a combination, he felt, would adequately reflect the complexities of the real world. He thus built an "economic landscape" around a single metropolitan center using the 10 smallest hexagonal configurations of market areas. Assume, Lösch said, that each network has one place in common, the metropolis. Then rotate the separate patterns around the metropolis until there is a maximum coincidence of central places in the different schemes—a solution that minimizes the number of centers. The result is a division of the region into six city-poor and six city-rich sectors (Figure 15.18). Lösch provided sketch-maps of Indianapolis and Toledo as examples (Figures 15.19 and 15.20).

The hierarchy is not "nested" in the Löschian landscape as it is in the Christallerian, so that apart from the metropolis, no center offers all the goods and ser-

vices. On the contrary, each symmetric 60-degree sector of the economic landscape displays considerable functional specialization. The 12 radii delimiting these city-rich and city-poor sectors are the busiest transportation routes, with cross-connections well developed in only the city-rich sector.

The city-rich sectors of adjacent metropolitan centers may be linked to portray the complete economic

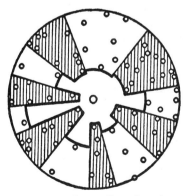

FIGURE 15.19   Indianapolis and environs within a radius of 60 miles. (After Andree's *Handatlas*.) [*Source:* Lösch, *The Economics of Location.*]

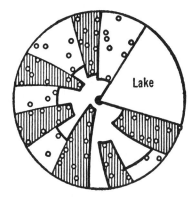

FIGURE 15.20   Toledo and environs within a radius of 60 miles. (After Andree's *Handatlas*.) [*Source:* Lösch, *The Economics of Location.*]

landscape in different ways (Figure 15.21). The trunk lines of communication can be arranged to pass through the largest number of towns or a bypass pattern may be employed in which towns not directly on the main route lie within a relatively short distance on either side of them.

Fundamental Concepts of Central-Place Theory

Both Christaller and Lösch agree that the triangular arrangement of production sites or retail stores and hexagonal market areas represent the optimal spatial organization for a single good, under the assumption of uniform densities on an unbounded plain with equal access in all directions. Lösch provides explicit proof that this pattern of location of individual firms is as advantageous as possible. Although the two authors then dis-

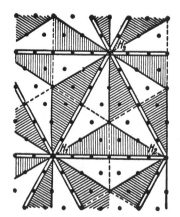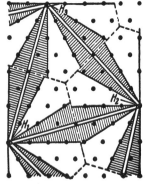

FIGURE 15.21   Alternate groupings of city-rich and city-poor sectors of adjacent metropolitan centers. Double lines connect routes between large cities; broken lines are landscape boundaries; hatched are sectors with many towns. [*Source:* Lösch, *The Economics of Location.*]

agree on how one builds spatial patterns of centers and market areas, they do agree on the three fundamental concepts of central-place theory, namely, range, threshold, and hierarchy. These concepts have broad applicability in studying spatial organization and permit the statement of central-place theory without the restricting assumption of uniformity of purchasing power and the necessary consequence of hexagonal market areas. Indeed, Richard L. Morrill asserts that the crucial test of the usefulness of central-place theory does not involve the presence of the strict geometric (hexagonal) forms, but whether or not the following questions are valid:

1. Does the spatial organization of tertiary activity reflect the level and distribution of purchasing power?
2. Do tertiary services tend to be regularly spaced in areas with similar physical, cultural, and economic characteristics?
3. Do individuals tend to minimize the aggregate distance traveled to purchase goods and services?
4. Do individuals shop at a hierarchy of centers?

These questions apply to tertiary activity within individual cities as well as to systems of cities and, at both scales, permit investigation of the impact of physical, cultural, and economic heterogeneity on central-place activity.

WHOLESALE TRADE PATTERNS

Central-place theory deals with the relationships between retailers and consumers *within* given regions, as mediated by the urban hierarchy. The goods that are distributed by the retailers are brought into the region from other regions by wholesalers. The wholesale trade relationships that link regions are conducted in large measure *between* the metropolitan centers of the regions, and in consequence the locational patterns of the metropolises are determined by the *external* trade linkages. Hence, if as Christaller and Lösch maintain, local urban hierarchies are patterned around the metropolis they, too, must reflect some effect of the need for interregional trade.

The Mercantile Model

Such is the essence of James Vance's (1970) ''mercantile model'' of wholesale trade. Vance began by exploring the functions of wholesalers. Wholesaling, he said, connects, in trade, numerous specialized producers of commodities in many diverse regions with an even greater array of consumers, who within each region tend to demand the same array of goods and services. Direct access to the customer by the producer is impossible because of the great numbers involved and because of the considerable geographical distance that often separates the groups. Nonetheless, there must be ties between the two groups that will (1) provide the producer with both a market and some idea of its scale of demands, and (2) assure the consumer access to products of a determined type at a specific time.

Several different types of wholesalers were distinguished, based upon the manner in which the merchant conducts business and the relation he or she bears to sources of supply and locations and organization of the purchaser:

a. *The merchant wholesaler.* The first wholesalers almost certainly were merchants, in the original sense of that word—men who negotiated, or trafficked in, goods on a large scale, particularly in foreign trade. First as individuals and later as corporations, these traders formed the fundamental body of wholesalers. They include distributors, jobbers, foreign trade merchants, or limited-function wholesalers—distributors primarily engaged in buying, taking title to, and where customary, physically storing and handling goods made by others, and selling the goods at wholesale principally to retailers or to industrial, institutional, and commercial users. Over the years the merchant wholesalers have been the largest component in the trade, and it is this type of establishment that matches most the standard conception of wholesaling. In the most recent census of wholesale firms and establishments, just over two out of three were classed as merchant wholesalers.

b. *The manufacturers' agent.* In contrast with merchant wholesalers are manufacturers' sales branches and offices. These establishments differ from merchant wholesalers in that they are owned by manufacturers or mining companies and maintained apart from manufacturing plants, primarily for selling or marketing their products at wholesale. There are two varieties: establishments that receive, store, and distribute the goods in which they trade, and those limited to the securing and remitting of orders for goods.

c. *The broker.* These sales agencies also are extensions of the manufacturing corporation; the distinction between the broker and the manufacturers' agent is that the broker serves many manufacturers, not one.

d. *Export-import agents.* Export and import agents fall into the general class of agents and brokers. These [people] provide a linkage between producers and consumers. Their knowledge of market conditions and sources of supply is for hire, and it earns their income. In some cases they may undertake certain financing functions, but in general the importer or exporter is a trader more than he is a banker. Often he may not take physical possession of goods, but it is his orders that start the flow of goods and determine their origin.[1]

Vance argued that in the locational problem of the merchant-wholesaler is found the quintessence of location theory for the trade. For such wholesalers, trade does not appear to be governed by competition among trading centers as much as by competition among wholesale establishments, possibly all in the same trading center. It is thus the quality of service, not its proximity, that is the key. Tributary areas must be as *small* as is consonant with the highest quality of service. As the tributary area population increases, the wholesaler must increase product specialization, and thereby improve service, in order to retain the same area of trade. If he or she does not increase product specialization, then the tributary area will be forced to contract through the loss of integral parts to competitors who can prosper on no more than a part of an expanded market population. In these reduced tributary areas the frequency of trade would be increased at the expense of product specialization, which is a form of higher service.

In this scheme, the wholesale center is seen as the "unraveling point" in the geography of trade, linking specialized production areas, mediating trade flows, and determining the metropolitan centers from which central-place relationships can develop to meet the consumption needs of local areas.

The sequence of development linking the Old World and the New World, and leading to the subsequent emergence of an urban hierarchy in the New World, Vance saw to be as follows (see Figure 15.22):

1. Before settlement was attempted, the economic potential of the area was tested on the basis of information collected and the pattern of trade that might be anticipated.

[1]James E. Vance, Jr., *The Merchant's World: The Geography of Wholesaling* (Englewood Cliffs, N.J.: Prentice-Hall, 1970), pp. 27–32.

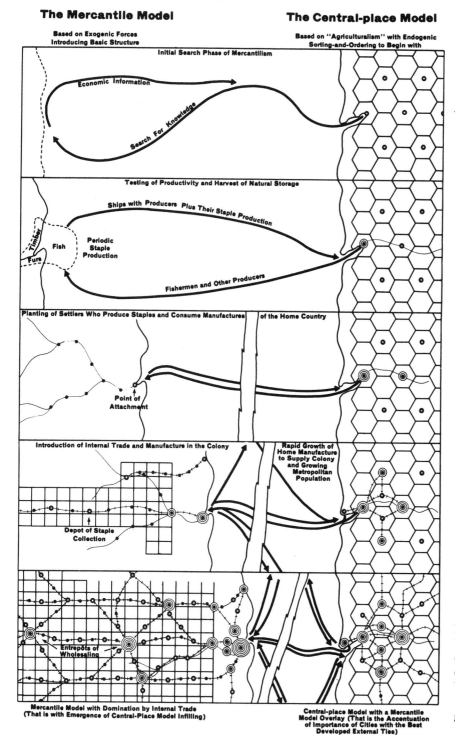

The Mercantile Model

Based on Exogenic Forces
Introducing Basic Structure

Initial Search Phase of Mercantilism

Economic Information

Search For Knowledge

Testing of Productivity and Harvest of Natural Storage

Ships with Producers Plus Their Staple Production

Timber
Fish
Furs

Periodic
Staple
Production

Fishermen and Other Producers

Planting of Settlers Who Produce Staples and Consume Manufactures

Point of
Attachment

Introduction of Internal Trade and Manufacture in the Colony

Depot of Staple
Collection

Entrepôts of
Wholesaling

Mercantile Model with Domination by Internal Trade
(That is with Emergence of Central-Place Model Infilling)

The Central-place Model

Based on "Agriculturalism" with Endogenic
Sorting-and-Ordering to Begin with

of the Home Country

Rapid Growth of
Home Manufacture
to Supply Colony
and Growing
Metropolitan
Population

Central-place Model with a Mercantile
Model Overlay (That is the Accentuation
of Importance of Cities with the Best
Developed External Ties)

FIGURE 15.22 Vance's contrasts between urban evolution in the mercantile model and central-place theory contexts. [*Source:* James E. Vance, Jr., *The Merchant's World: The Geography of Wholesaling* (Englewood Cliffs, N.J.: Prentice-Hall, 1970), p. 151.]

2. Once the potential was determined, initial settlement took place in terms of a mercantile model. The dynamics were exogenic, the extent of the system was given by long-distance trading, and growth depended as much on the ability of the external world to consume as upon the parochial area to produce.

3. As the scale of the trading system enlarged, mercantile towns grew as "points of attachment" which, in turn, increased the demand for hinterland provision for those towns and for the collection of staples in greater quantity.

4. Only at this stage in the externally based sys-

tem did the central-place model begin to characterize settlement. That characterization was limited (a) to the latter additions to the settlement pattern, and (b) to those areas characterized by areally based staple production.

5. Subsequently, there was parallel growth of settlement in accordance with both models. As new regions were opened up, metropolitan entrepôts were created on the basis of the external linkages needed to ship out exports. As local demands grew with the development of settlement, the metropolises also became importing centers, and in general, "unraveling points" in regional and interregional trading relationships.

Whereas the central-place pattern of the Old World gradually developed in triangular-hexagonal forms, that of the New World was laid down in rectangular patterns by the importation of both transport routes and the rectangular land survey system. The priority of mercantile towns in this process meant that they provided the basic points of focus—and ultimately the major metropolises—for the central-place systems responsible for the internal organization of retail trade.

PERIODIC MARKETS AND THE SPATIAL ORGANIZATION OF PEASANT SOCIETIES

Thus far we have talked about wholesale trade and central places in relatively specialized economies. What of the situation in those economic systems where specialization is relatively less advanced?

In most peasant societies, markets are periodic rather than permanent and continuous. The market is open only once every few days on a regularly scheduled basis, because the per capita demand for goods sold in the market is small, the market area is limited by primitive transport technology, and the aggregate demand is therefore insufficient to support permanent shops. Businesspeople adjust by visiting several markets on a regular basis and accumulating the trade of several market areas.

Skinner's description of the periodic marketing system of traditional rural China may be used as an example, although details vary from one part of the world to another. Periodicity of the markets is related to the mobility of individual businesspersons. The peddler toting his or her wares on a pole from one market to the next is the archetype of the mobile firm in China. Equally characteristic is the wandering artisan or repairperson, itinerants purveying services from letter-writing to fortune-telling. From their point of view, pe-

riodic markets have the virtue of concentrating demand in specific places on specific days. When the firm is both producer and trader there are additional advantages, permitting sales and production to be undertaken on different days.

From the consumers' point of view, the periodicity of markets reduces the distance that must be traveled to obtain needed goods and services to a single day's excursion. Furthermore, the subsistence production activities of the household can be combined with needed trips to the market.

The periodicities of individual markets are synchronized; Figure 15.23 depicts one such system recorded by Skinner. There are three levels of centers: standard markets, intermediate markets, and central markets, which are the highest order and are located at strategic points on the transport network, providing important wholesaling functions. The central market receives imported items and distributes them to its market area via the lower-order centers, and it collects local products and exports them to other central markets and higher-order centers. The standard market is the lowest-level central place, with the exception of minor "green vegetable markets," and meets periodically. The higher-level centers have permanent shops in addition to their periodic markets, and the central markets have smaller business centers at each of the four gates of the city, where the periodicity may even be on a twice-daily basis.

The periodic marketing system of Figure 15.23 is one in which a merchant can move between the central market and a pair of standard markets in a 10-day cycle divided into units of three: the central market (day 1), first standard (day 2), second standard (day 3), central (day 4), first standard (day 5), second standard (day 6),

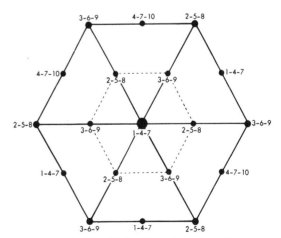

FIGURE 15.23 Periodicity of markets in a traditional Chinese three-per-*hsün* cycle. (After G. William Skinner.) [*Source:* Berry, *Geography of Market Centers.*]

central (day 7), first standard (day 8), second standard (day 9), and central (day 10), when no business is transacted. The interlocking periodicities of a larger number of market centers of different levels can be seen in the figure.

Such cycles are determined either by "natural" means, using the motions of the heavenly bodies, or they are "artificial," without reference to any natural cycles. Ten-day marketing weeks, for example, were tied to the lunar month, whereas the seven-day marketing week of the Christian calendar is entirely artificial.

In China, the two fundamental cycles were the lunar decade (*hsün*), beginning on the first, eleventh, and twenty-first of each lunar month, and the 12-day duodenary cycle. Skinner argues that a one per-*hsün* cycle was originally adopted by the Chinese ancients in the valley of the Huang Ho, whereas a one-per-duodenum cycle was adopted in the southwest. As market systems developed, first the higher-level and finally the standard markets doubled their schedules, and later the highest-level centers doubled their schedules again.

One factor influencing the periodicity of markets is population density. Generally, the more people in the area, the greater the aggregate demand and the greater the frequency with which any market can meet, until, at the most frequent, it meets every day. A similar statement can be made about per capita demands as incomes rise or the peasant household begins to specialize more in production for sale: The more demands per capita increase, the greater the aggregate demand and periodicity, until permanency is achieved.

Across southern China, the periodicity of the duodenary cycle gradually increases from west to east, with the six-day week being very common (1–7, 2–8, 3–9, 4–10, 5–11, and 6–12) and in the densest areas further doubling resulting in 1–4–7–10, 2–5–8–11, and 3–6–9–12. Across northern China, one-per-*hsün* cycles are found only in remote peripheral areas. Two-per-*hsün* cycles are the most common in standard markets, and four-per-*hsün* in central markets. The three-per-*hsün* schedules are common for standard markets in the regions of higher population densities at the heart of the Szechwan basin and the plains of southeastern China, and where densities are higher owing to specialization in food production for urban markets closer to big cities. Figure 15.10, 15.15, and 15.23 depict such three-per-*hsün* cycles.

Elsewhere in the world other cycles are found: two-per-*hsün* cycles are most common in Korea, whereas a one-per-*hsün* cycle was found in Japan prior to modernization. Both are presumably related to diffusion of Chinese culture in the north. In Rome, markets were held every ninth-day. After the adoption of Christianity, the nine-day week was changed to a seven-day week and markets were held every Sunday. In time, clerical authorities became concerned with the worldliness of markets held about churches. In A.D. 906, for example, Sunday markets were prohibited in England. The weekday market that had sprung up, particularly in the trade of salt, iron, and local produce, took over the Sunday market functions. "Sunday towns" remain a common feature of life in Latin America even today, however, whereas "blue laws" and Sunday closing remain where Puritanical traditions are still strong. Figure 15.24 shows the seven-day periodic market cycles in a section of Andean Colombia.

Staggering market days to accommodate both buyer and seller seems to be a nearly universal pattern. In Africa, the market week varies from a three-day to a seven-day week. The three-day, four-day, five-day, and six-day weeks stem from ancient tribal differences, whereas the seven-day week resulted from calendar changes introduced by Islam into Africa. In Kusai, the economy is oriented to a three-day market cycle, and people think of three markets as being linked together. Each of these three markets is held on a consecutive day. Each, in turn, may be linked to another market cycle so that all of Kusai is covered by a connected net of market cycles. In Yorubaland the markets operate on a ring system. Each ring is composed of a four-day cycle or multiples of four days. This timing is related to the former four-day week in West Africa. Similar periodicities have been noted in India and in Central and South America.

The standard marketing systems of China are shown by Skinner to be not simply exchange mechanisms, but the basic building blocks of that society. Other authors imply the same for other societies. Each standard market and its surrounding tributary area functions as an economic and social community, incorporating, on the average, 18 villages.

Typically, one out of five adults living in the villages went to a market on a market day in traditional China to shop in the standard market in a multitude of petty marketplaces, one for each product. This specialization is true elsewhere, and Figure 15.25 reproduces Fogg's diagram of the structure of a large *suq* in Morocco. The market serves as a place for peasants to sell what they produce and purchase what they need. For both buyer and seller, a profit motive dominates; bargaining and higgling may be intense, even though monetary standards of exchange exist. Local credit societies exist for villages within the system; landlords collect their rents and transport coolies can be hired there. In turn, each standard market links into higher-level market systems. The local elite patronize the intermediate and central markets, purchasing luxuries unavailable to the peasantry in standard markets. Furthermore, traders return to their bases to replenish stocks or dis-

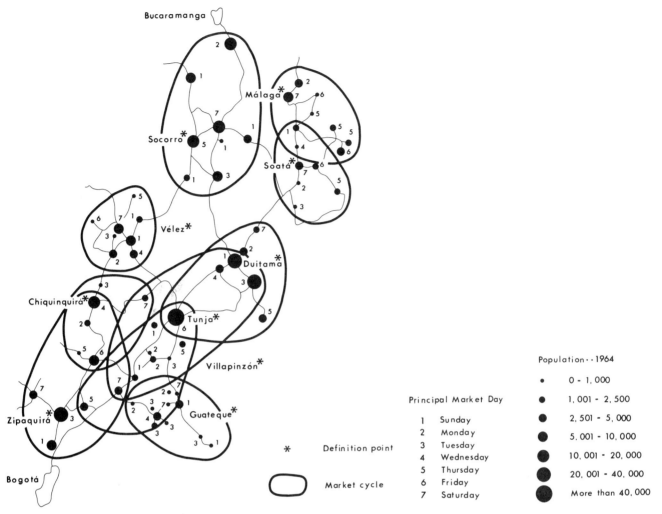

FIGURE 15.24 Market cycles in Andean Columbia. [*Source:* Richard Symanski, *Periodic Markets of Andean Colombia* (Ph.D. dissertation, Syracuse University, 1971).]

pose of purchases. Even at the higher levels, peddlers selling less-frequently-demanded goods can be found in the central markets.

The whole is thus an interdependent system, with exotic goods sold in the central market and itinerants circulating in lower-level markets. Merchandise produced in the central towns is distributed downwards by the itinerants. Both central and intermediate towns have a variety of producer-distributor and wholesale-retail relationships in addition to their retailing functions. The intermediate towns generally include only distributors, whereas the central markets have wholesalers with warehouses. Merchandise consumed by the peasantry or required by petty craftsworkers flows down to every market, consumer goods for the local elite move no further than the intermediate markets, and consumer goods for the bureaucratic elite, and industrial supplies, never leave the central markets.

The upward flow of goods begins with the peasant selling his or her produce to local consumers or to dealers who process or bulk the product. These dealers pass the goods on to buyers, who carry them to intermediate or central markets, and perhaps up through successively higher levels of centers.

In what ways are the standard market communities social systems? They are endogamous for the peasantry; marriage brokers arrange marriages between villages within them. Leading shopkeepers and the local elite form committees responsible for the local religious festival. Voluntary and formal organizations use the standard marketing community as their unit of organization (for example, the composite lineage, the secret-society lodge, the committee arranging the local fair, the religious service society). Local variants of these elements of social integration repeat themselves elsewhere throughout the world. If a world map differentiating

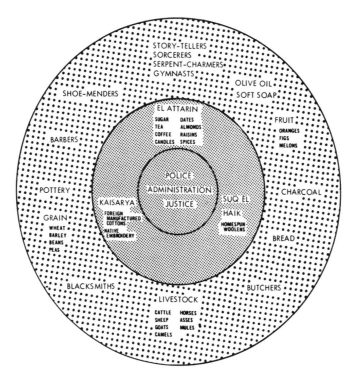

FIGURE 15.25 Plan of a large *suq*. (After Walter Fogg.) [*Source:* Berry, *Geography of Market Centers.*]

countries by level of economic development is examined, those parts of the world considered "underdeveloped" or with "isolated tribal economies" will generally be found to have periodic marketing systems in which basic economic units and basic social units are identical.

If the details of periodicity, commodities traded, and forms of social integration vary culturally, so do the locations of periodic markets. All locate to serve both buyers and sellers efficiently, but sites selected may differ among cultures. Most commonly, markets located at crossroads space themselves in a manner determined by the maximum distances consumers are willing to walk. The spacing is affected but little after an early period of development by differences in population density; instead, the periodicity of the markets adjusts as densities change, to serve increased demands by increased meetings. In Morocco, siting is determined by locations of springs and wells, to provide a reliable water supply, preferably close to a religious sanctuary or shrine, to guarantee protection. Larger *suqs* locate on the boundaries between production zones. In many places—for example, in Yorubaland and in North Africa—the rural population lives away from the market sites, and the hierarchy of rural settlements is not related to the hierarchy of periodic markets. This phenomenon also persists in Eastern Europe. Elsewhere, however, rural settlements and periodic markets coincide. An understanding of such local variability must be embedded in an understanding of local culture.

TOPICS FOR DISCUSSION

1. What are the fundamental agreements and disagreements between Christaller's and Lösch's models? Explain in detail.

2. Richard Morrill asserts that the crucial test of the usefulness of central-place theory does not involve the presence of the strict geometric (hexagonal) forms, but whether or not certain questions are valid. Give Morrill's four questions. Do you agree with his assertion? If so, why? If not, why not?

3. In terms of central-place theory, what is the difference between retail trade and wholesale trade relationships? Explain.

4. Based upon the manner in which merchants conduct their business and the relation they bear to sources of their supply and locations and organization of their purchasers, Vance distinguished between several different types of wholesalers. What are these types? Give the characteristics of each.

5. What are the advantages of the periodic marketing system to peasant societies?

6. What are some of the factors that determine periodic marketing cycles in peasant societies? How can population density and per capita income influence the periodicity of markets?

7. Under what circumstances does the range of any good have a constant radius?

8. What theoretical organization permits the maximum packing of central places into an unbounded plain?

9. In what ways are the standard market communities in peasant societies social systems? Explain.

10. Explain the difference between a $k = 3$ network arrangement and a $k = 4$ arrangement in Christaller's model. How are the numbers 3 and 4 derived?

FURTHER READINGS

BARNUM, H. G. *Market Centers and Hinterlands in Baden-Württemberg*. Chicago: University of Chicago, Department of Geography Research Paper 103, 1966.

BERRY, BRIAN J. L. *Geography of Market Centers and Retail Distribution*. Englewood Cliffs, N.J.: Prentice-Hall, 1967.

BRUSH, JOHN E., AND HOWARD L. GAUTHIER. *Service Centers and Consumer Trips: Studies on the Philadelphia Metropolitan Fringe*. Chicago: University of Chicago, Department of Geography Research Paper 113, 1968.

CHRISTALLER, WALTER. *Central Places in Southern Germany*, trans. C. W. Baskin. Englewood Cliffs, N.J.: Prentice-Hall, 1966.

DICKINSON, R. E. *City and Region*. New York: Humanities Press, 1964.

GARNER, B. J. "Models of Urban Geography and Settlement Location." In *Models in Geography*, eds. Richard J. Chorley and Peter Haggett. London: Methuen, 1967.

LÖSCH, AUGUST. *The Economics of Location*, trans. William H. Woglom and Wolfgang F. Stolper. New Haven, Conn.: Yale University Press, 1954. See Chapters 9–12.

SINCLAIR, R. "Von Thünen and Urban Sprawl." *Annals of the Association of American Geographers*, 57 (1967), 72–87.

SKINNER, G. W. "Marketing and Social Structure in Rural China." *Journal of Asian Studies*, 24 (1964), 3–43.

STINE, J. H. "Temporal Aspects of Tertiary Production Elements in Korea." In *Urban Systems and Economic Development*, ed. F. R. Pitts. Eugene: University of Oregon School of Business Administration, 1962.

VANCE, JAMES E., JR., *The Merchant's World: The Geography of Wholesaling*. Englewood Cliffs, N.J.: Prentice-Hall, 1970.

CHAPTER 16

The Geography
of Development

Nineteenth-century economic development produced distinctive global dependency relations: the heartland-hinterland organization of the world economy. The colonial imprint also produced dualism in dependent economies. These growth problems, including their present manifestations, are the focus of the concluding chapter of this book, which is concerned with the spatial organization of growth and development in a systems framework, rather than merely mapping the spatial patterns of inequality.

Objectives:

- to explain Perloff's heartland-hinterland model, Lenin's colonial model, and Friedmann's general theory of polarized growth
- to consider the effects of colonialism on hinterland regions
- to understand the sources of heartland growth and the idea of cumulative causation
- to present the essentials of diffusion theory
- to reiterate the changes currently transforming the world's heartland economies
- to examine the lessons of OPEC for reversing hinterland developmental trends

THE SPATIAL ORGANIZATION OF GROWTH AND DEVELOPMENT

In economic terms, *development* has come to mean the capacity of a national economy to generate and sustain an annual increase in its gross national product at 5 percent to 7 percent or more. But even when such growth has occurred, problems of poverty, inequality, and unemployment have remained, leading to increased calls for a new economic order in which redistribution accompanies growth. Three main objectives are to (1) increase the availability and distribution of basic life-sustaining goods, (2) raise levels of caring and education to increase both material welfare and self-esteem, and (3) expand the range of social and economic choice to both individuals and nations, freeing them from servitude and dependence.

In geography, too, development and underdevelopment are seen to be far more complex phenomena than can be addressed by mere growth. The successive waves of industrial revolution created a global economy with a distinctive spatial organization; international comparative advantage and trade came to be organized along heartland-hinterland lines. A world-scale von Thünen system emerged, characterized by increasing rather than decreasing polarization and inequality. Distinctive spatial adaptations resulted in the colonies, namely, urban primacy and economic dualism.

The objective of this final chapter is to place these issues of the spatial organization of growth and development in a systems framework. Specifically, the objectives in the first part of the chapter are: to describe H. Perloff's model of heartland-hinterland spatial organization and to relate it to V. I. Lenin's colonial model and to J. Friedmann's general theory of polarized growth; and to outline the impacts of colonialism on hinterland regions, looking specifically at the problems of urban primacy and economic dualism.

Several questions emerge from this review: What drives heartland growth? The Denison model provides insights. Why is this growth cumulative? Myrdal's concept of circular and cumulative causation is relevant. How does growth spread? Diffusion theory is a source of instruction. In attempting to answer these questions, our objectives are to help the reader understand the sources of heartland growth and the idea of cumulative causation, to provide the reader with the essentials of diffusion theory, and to reiterate the changes currently transforming the world's heartland economies.

What can hinterland countries do to reverse trends? The book concludes with a look at the exercise of countervailing bargaining power in a world economy dominated by multinational enterprises: Such is the lesson of OPEC.

THE HEARTLAND-HINTERLAND MODEL

Harvey Perloff, an American planner, together with several associates, described the process by which *heartland-hinterland organization* emerged within the United States. They pointed out that North America's oldest cities were mercantile outposts of a hinterland resource area whose exploitation was organized by the developing metropolitan system of Western Europe. (Recall the discussion of Vance's mercantile model in Chapter 15.) The initial impulses for independent urban growth came at the end of the eighteenth century when towns were becoming the outlets for capital accumulated in commercial agriculture and the centers of colonial development of the continental interior. Regional economies developed a certain archetype: a good deep-water port as the nucleus of an agricultural hinterland well adapted for the production of a staple commodity in demand on the world market.

New resources became important from 1840–1850 onward, and new locational forces came into play. Foremost was a growing demand for iron, and later steel, and along with it rapid elaboration of productive technologies. Juxtaposition of coal, iron ore, and markets afforded the impetus for manufacturing growth in the northeastern United States, localized both by factors in the physical environment (minerals) and by locational forces created by prior growth along the East Coast (linkages to succeeding stages of production, in turn located closer to markets). The heartland of the North American manufacturing belt therefore developed westward from New York in the area bounded by Lake Superior iron ores, the Pennsylvanian coalfields, and the capital, entrepreneurial experience, and engineering trades of the Northeast. This heartland became not only the heavy industrial center of the country but remained the center of national demand, determining patterns of market accessibility through the 1960s. The heartland had initial advantages of both excellent agricultural resources and a key location in the minerals economy. With development, it grew into the urbanized center of the national market, setting the basic conditions for successive development of newer peripheral regions by reaching out to them as its input requirements expanded, and it thereby fostered specialization of regional roles in the national economy. The heartland experienced cumulative urban-industrial specialization, while each of the hinterlands found its comparative advantage based on narrow and intensive specialization in a few resource subsectors, only diversifying when the extent of specialization enabled the hinterland region to pass through that threshold scale of market necessary to support profitable local enterprise. Flows of raw materials inward, and of finished products outward, articulated the whole.

It is little wonder that Perloff concluded that the American economy of the mid-twentieth century could be divided into

> . . . a great heartland nucleation of industry and the national market, the focus of large-scale national-serving industry, the seedbed of new industry responding to the dynamic structure of national final demand and the center of high levels of per capita income . . . .[1]

and, standing in a dependent relationship to the heartland,

> . . . radiating out across the national landscape . . . resource-dominant regional hinterlands specializing in the production of resource and intermediate outputs for which the heartland reaches out to satisfy the input requirements of its great manufacturing plants . . . in the hinterlands, resource-endowment is a critical determinant of the particular cumulative advantage of the region and hence its growth potential.[2]

Others have argued similarly with respect to both the European and the global case. V. I. Lenin, for example, presented a *colonial model of world spatial organization* in which he argued that since the early nineteenth century the economic geography of the world has been organized by and for the benefit of the industrial countries. The German location economist Andreas Predöhl gave the notion more substance when he described how, during the early nineteenth century, Britain became the focus of a unicentric world economy which, with the growth of new industrial core regions, has now become multicentric, with the rest of the world organized to produce raw materials for and to consume the products of the industrial heartlands. Europe was divided into an industrial heartland and agricultural hinterland by F. Delaisi in 1929 in a book with the graphic title *Les Deux Europes: Europe industrielle et Europe agricole (The Two Europes: Industrial Europe and Agricultural Europe)*. Subsequent researchers have iden-

tified a regular pattern of distance-decay in agricultural productivity and per capita income from the European heartland, as was noted in Chapter 9, so that agricultural productivity is actually higher in "industrial" Europe than in "agricultural" Europe.

More recently, international heartland-hinterland contrasts have been identified by Raul Prebisch, who divides the world into an industrial center and a primary-producing periphery, and who blames much of the economic difficulties of the periphery on what he considers to be a long-term deterioration of the periphery's terms of trade. John Friedmann, in turn, attempted to elaborate the heartland-hinterland model as a *general theory of polarized growth* applying at all geographic scales.

FRIEDMANN'S GENERAL THEORY OF POLARIZED GROWTH

Friedmann's paradigm was presented as an intellectual framework for the study of the processes—economic, social, and political—that act to create heartland-hinterland contrasts. *Heartlands* are defined by Friedmann as territorially organized subsystems of society possessing a high capacity for generating innovative change. *Hinterlands* are all the regions beyond the heartlands whose growth and change are determined by their dependency relationships to the heartlands. Heartlands share in common a heavy concentration of their labor force in manufacturing (secondary) activity and advanced (quaternary) services, representing a shift from development based on natural resources to development based on human resources. Both service and industrial activities are, as we saw in Chapter 11, becoming less concerned with the processing and marketing of primary resources. As they become more sophisticated and more dependent upon the products of scientific research and development, the distinction between manufacturing-related and service-related activity becomes increasingly blurred. It is this new nexus of activity that has become the modern engine of growth, making the term *heartland* almost completely synonymous with high per capita income and income potentials.

At both national and global scales, heartlands set the developmental path for the hinterlands, stimulating economic growth in the peripheries differentially according to the resource needs of heartland industries and consumers. Complementarities in the availability of factors of production between heartland and hinterland lay the foundations for interaction. Improvements in transportation and the organization of trade increase the transferability of staples from hinterland to heartland. Intervening opportunities impose spatial regularities in

[1]Harvey S. Perloff, Edgar S. Dunn, Jr., Eric E. Lampard, and Richard F. Muth, *Regions, Resources and Economic Growth* (Lincoln, Nebr.: University of Nebraska Press, 1960), p. 51.
[2]Ibid.

the timing of hinterland development and sequence the order in which unsettled areas and areas with a subsistence economy are drawn into the heartland's sphere of influence.

Friedmann saw the diffusion of innovations from the core as controlling system growth and the form of the heartland-hinterland relationship affecting economic activity and settlement patterns, sociocultural traditions and values, and the organization of power not only in the core, but also in the periphery. The periphery is thus dependent on the core in all respects. He summarizes as follows:

> The volume of controlling decisions that emanates from the core is greater than the reciprocal volume of controls from periphery to core. This causes a net-flow of capital from the periphery which, in turn, gives rise to a net-flow of migrants into the core area. At the same time a continuous stream of innovations diffuses from the core to the periphery where it ultimately helps to create conditions that lead to demands for at least a partial restructuring of the fundamental dependency ratio. . . .[3]

Donald Kerr, a Canadian geographer, has noted the operation of similar processes at the regional scale in his studies of metropolitan dominance of the Canadian economy. He writes:

> Large economic establishments—such as corporations and financial institutions—have tended to congregate in the metropolis, where policies are shaped and from which decisions are diffused through successively smaller cities to all corners of the country. In reverse, funds, materials and people move from the hinterland to regional cities and on to the metropolis.[4]

Even in the United States, where heartland-hinterland economic disparities have been narrowing since 1950 (Figure 16.1), and where the sophisticated organization of financial institutions might have been expected to achieve an interregional balance in the supply and demand for capital, interregional disparities in interest rates persist at the national scale. The Federal Reserve Bank of New York attributes these interest disparities to a variety of reasons, including legal,

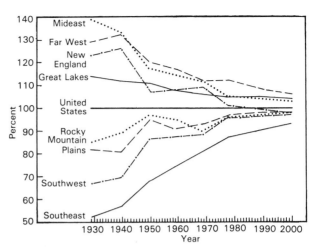

FIGURE 16.1 Per capita personal income as a percent of the U.S. average, 1929–1978 and projected to the year 2000, for eight U.S. regions. (*Note:* Incomes are not adjusted for regional cost-of-living differences. Such an adjustment would reveal an even greater degree of convergence of regional differences.) [*Source:* Bureau of Economic Analysis, U.S. Department of Commerce, *Survey of Current Business,* November 1980, p. 46.]

institutional, and investor attitudes toward the risk of investment in distant areas.

In essence, then, the heartland-hinterland paradigm identifies regional structure as the product of "centripetal" and "centrifugal" forces operating at a hierarchy of geographical scales. Centripetal forces are set in motion when an emerging heartland attains the necessary size for continued and self-sustaining growth of a wide range of economic activities, enabling it to achieve leadership in finance, education, research, and planning, as Japan has done in recent years. Secondary manufacturing and service activity tends to gravitate to the heartland, leaving the hinterland increasingly reliant on primary industries, which tend to play a diminishing role in national economies. Heartland-hinterland contrasts are strengthened by the concentration of corporation head offices, and the lower interest rates at the center. Decisions regarding production, sales, and research may be strongly influenced by where key decision-makers live and work. The concentration of corporate offices at the center of a national territory incurs a flow of corporate profits from the hinterland to the heartland too, and creates a persistent shortage of capital in the hinterland.

Centrifugal forces that reduce heartland-hinterland contrasts include the spread effects of growing markets and improving technology at the center, including improved transportation and communications,

---

[3]John Friedmann, *Urbanization, Planning, and National Development* (Beverly Hills, Calif.: Sage, 1972), p. 69.

[4]Donald P. Kerr, "Metropolitan Dominance in Canada," in *Canada: A Geographic Interpretation,* ed. John Warkentin (Toronto: Methuen, 1968), pp. 531–555.

which can benefit industry in the hinterland; the protection afforded hinterland industry by distance from the heartland; increasing congestion and environmental pollution of the heartland, combined with special amenities that parts of the hinterland have to offer, and increasingly, the attempts of governments to break apart the heartland-hinterland form of spatial organization on grounds of regional and social equity.

Such a restructuring of a major regional economic order will be exceedingly difficult, however. The development of the hinterland, according to the heartland-hinterland paradigm, depends at first on supplying staples to the heartland, then on the linkage effects of the staples with other sectors on the hinterland economy, and finally on restructuring the hinterland economy on a human-resource base, like that of the heartland. Economic growth in a hinterland region may be sustained for a time by increasing productivity in existing staple production, or by the chance discovery of new staples to replace depleted resources or those made obsolete by technological change or by new discoveries and developments elsewhere. Economic growth in the hinterland can be augmented by linkage effects, which depend, essentially, on how the capital, generated by the exports, is invested. Such domestic investment can be divided into three categories, according to whether it generates "backward," "forward," or "final demand" linkages. *Backward linkage* contributes supplies, equipment, and facilities needed to produce and ship staple exports. The backward linkage with the greatest spread effects is often the building of a transportation system for export of the staple. *Forward linkage* involves further domestic processing of the staple before export increasing the value added in the export staple. Forward linkage includes such things as building pulp and paper mills and petroleum refineries. *Final demand linkage* includes the domestic production of consumer goods for workers in the export industries. The strength of final demand linkages depends on the level and distribution of income from the export industries, and the proportion that is remitted abroad to foreign investors, or to families of foreign-born workers. More generally, linkages can develop for the domestic as well as the export sector of the economy, diversifying production and stimulating industrialization. In all cases, the development of these linkages depends both on the ability of entrepreneurs, particularly domestic entrepreneurs, to perceive market opportunities, and on the appropriate economic, technical, social, and political framework to place these opportunities within their grasp.

In light of the above, Friedmann sees four possible categories of hinterlands, according to their growth potential and development history: upward transitional, downward transitional, resource frontiers, and special problem areas. *Upward transitional* hinterlands are settled areas with growth potential and inflows of capital and migrants. *Downward transitional areas* are areas with declining economies, characterized by emigration. *Resource frontiers* are zones of new settlement with lower population density and potentials for new growth based upon staple exports. These are diagrammed in Figure 16.2. *Special problem areas* are exactly what the name suggests.

PROBLEMS OF THE COLONIAL IMPRINT ON THE HINTERLANDS

Rather than seeing the benefits of the polarized growth described by Friedmann, many people in the hinterlands see their continuing dependency upon the heartland as an *undesirable* consequence of colonialism.

European penetration of the periphery occurred for many reasons—missionary zeal, easy riches, penal servitude, or escape from poverty and persecution—but most of all it was a reaching out for exotic commodities, raw materials, and foodstuffs. At first, Europeans directed their main effort toward acquiring exotic goods of the East: spices, silk, sugar, and other luxury items. After the Industrial Revolution they sought greater supplies of staple foodstuffs for their expanding urban populations and raw materials for their factories. Thus, a flow of commodities into the center developed and has continued to swell.

To a considerable degree, the effects that colonialism has had upon hinterland countries depend upon whether this penetration resulted in permanent settlements or was mere exploitation. All the European imperial powers, particularly the British, established settlements that were needed to relieve temporary population surpluses and as safety valves for social, political, and religious unrest at home. The regions most attractive to permanent European settlers were those that were most familiar, having moderate climates and productive soils: eastern North America, New Zealand, eastern Australia, the Kenya highlands, the mountain basins of Central America and the Andes, and the temperate plains and valleys of southern South America. Immigrants came in large numbers to these lands and succeeded in seizing territory from the Maoris, Cherokees, Caribs, Mayas, Patagonians, and other indigenous peoples. Even where the original motive was escape from difficult conditions in the homeland, some of these settlements eventually proved to be of great economic benefit to their mother countries because of the large quantities of grains and minerals the settlements shipped to European markets.

Other hinterland regions failed to attract European settlement, either because they had strong indig-

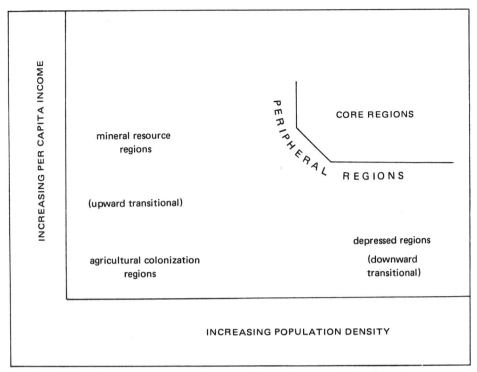

FIGURE 16.2 The income and population density relationship of peripheral regions and the core. [After Walter B. Stohr and John Friedmann, 1972.]

enous political organization and were already heavily populated, as in much of southern and eastern Asia, or because of extreme climates such as that of tropical Africa. Here the European impact took the form of political and commercial control for limited economic exploitation. Their purpose was to procure specific resources required by the metropolitan economy. This resulted in establishing enclaves of modern production and trade within a territory still devoted to indigenous activities of a mainly traditional and subsistence nature.

The metropolitan powers maintained tight political and economic control over their hinterland territories until changing conditions forced them to relinquish their empires. Political independence came to the American colonies of Spain and Portugal in the early 1800s. Having been granted internal self-government late in the nineteenth century, the British dominions were accorded full independence by the Parliamentary Statute of Westminster (1931). At the end of World War II the remaining British and Dutch possessions in southern Asia gained their freedom, as did the British, French, and Belgian colonies in Africa. And finally, during the 1970s Portugal relinquished its control over major parts of the African continent.

Political independence has not always brought economic freedom to these lands, however. The metropolitan powers, especially the French, Belgians, and Portuguese, have been slow to relax commercial control over their former colonies. This is seen in the persistence of bipolar trade between these countries and their old territories. In its content, this trade reflects the complementarities of resource endowment between the two areas, which assign to the hinterland countries a permanent role as producers and exporters of primary commodities, thereby further reinforcing their condition of dependency. Multinational corporations headquartered in heartland countries help to maintain this hegemony, aided by formal and informal intergovernmental agreements. Thus, the colonialism of an earlier time has been replaced by a "neocolonialism." Only those larger and more prosperous former colonies have managed to escape from this pattern and assume a place for themselves within the world heartland.

Because the hinterland countries remain economically dependent upon the heartland, their economic growth is conditioned by the resource needs of the metropolitan center and by the willingness of the metropolitan powers to provide foreign aid and technical assistance.

Organization of Hinterland Space

The spatial organization of the hinterlands that evolved also reflected the explicit requirements of colonial masters for political and economic control, access to sites of production for export, and links to points of embarkation. These needs are expressed in the locational pattern of urban places and their hierarchical arrangement, the nature of linkages between cities and their tributary areas in all hinterland regions, and the internal spatial structures of the cities themselves in the hinterland areas with substantial indigenous populations.

One result of European penetration is that, although the great majority of hinterland people still are engaged in traditional rural activities, the city has assumed a dominant place in organizing the internal space of their countries. Because of the city's role in the exercise of administrative and commercial control, there has been a close interdependence between urban growth and regional development. Although urbanization has not proceeded as far in the hinterland countries as in the heartland, it is nevertheless occurring at an accelerating rate. As the hinterland city has grown in size and importance it has asserted increasing control over its tributary area through extension of the transport-communications network.

The Urban Hierarchy

A distinctive feature of the hinterland country is the degree to which a single large city dominates the national system. Typically this *primate city* is at least five times the size of its nearest rival and has 70 percent or more of the urban population of the entire country. This describes San Salvador, Montevideo, Mexico City, Nairobi, Addis Ababa, Manila, Saigon, and many others. Virtually all such primate cities were established by the colonizing powers to serve as essential links between the mother countries and their sources of raw materials. Many years after independence, most of these cities continue to function in this relationship to the industrial nations today. The primate city is the focus of all modern functions and serves not only as the commercial capital but also as the capital for political and administrative control, the seat of an urban-based government and an urban-based power elite, and city-centered nationalism. As the center of intellectual activity, it contains the national university, and in many instances it is the seat of ecclesiastical control. Finally, the primate city is the center of innovation, the focus of change, and the principal point for the dissemination of new political, social, and economic ideas.

Given this set of functions, the principal city of a hinterland country is usually a port city as well, located in such a way to provide direct steamer access to the mother country and the world market. The principal exceptions to this are the primate cities of those tropical lands where the population and most commercial activities are concentrated in the healthfully temperate highland basins and plateaus. In such cases the primate city remains the main focus of modern production and trade but ships its exports through an outport, typically a much smaller, specialized place. Thus, Mexico City has its outport of Veracruz, Guatemala City has Puerto Barrios, and Nairobi has Mombasa.

The Transport-Communications Network

The primate city is also located to have superior access to those areas of export production that comprise its hinterland, reflecting its function as the main point for collecting, processing, and transshipping the primary commodities required by the mother country. Other urban centers in the country are decidedly smaller, less important, and perform fewer commercial functions, being, rather, provincial headquarters and local service centers. Thus, the primate city is the supreme transport node in the domestic space-economy. By means of the transport connections that converge upon it, the primate city manages to integrate the commercial economy of the land. The network is designed in such a way to provide all the essential connections for asserting administrative control over the interior and reaching areas of agricultural and mineral production for the foreign market. Most places not engaged in such production are bypassed by the major routes, have poor connectivity to the transport system as a whole, and languish.

The transport and communications networks assume the shape of a fan, growing outward from the primate city in a treelike, branching (dendritic) pattern. Figure 16.3 indicates the way the Indian railway network expanded outward from the main ports—Bombay, Calcutta, and Madras—during the second half of the nineteenth century. Note that, because of its great size, diversity of traditional princely states, and peculiar colonial history, the Indian subcontinent was penetrated simultaneously from more than one direction.

The case of contemporary India also illustrates the nature of the spatial organization that this type of development produces. Figure 16.4 shows the regional pattern of four main classes of economic organization. Comparing this with the map of urban population potentials (Figure 16.5), we note a close coincidence between the more advanced types of activities and the country's urban population potentials centering upon the ports of Bombay, Calcutta, and Madras, and the administrative capital of Delhi. Finally, Figure 16.6 shows the functional regions of India as indicated by the flows of 63 commodities shipped interregionally. Each

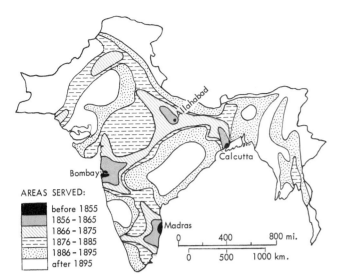

FIGURE 16.3 Diffusion of Indian railway network from Bombay, Calcutta, and Madras, second half of the nineteenth century. [*Source:* R. P. Misra, *Diffusion of Agricultural Innovations* (Mysore: Prasaranga Manasa Gangotri, 1968), p. 15.]

FIGURE 16.5 Urban population potentials in India. [*Source:* Berry, "Interdependency of Spatial Structure and Spatial Behavior."]

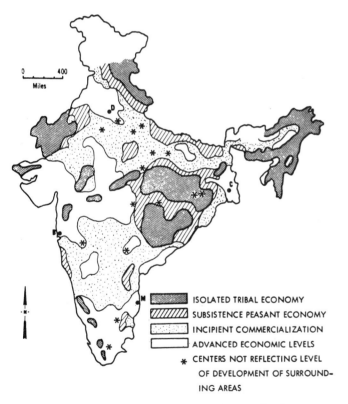

FIGURE 16.4 Types of economic organization in India. [*Source:* Brian J. L. Berry, "Interdependency of Spatial Structure and Spatial Behavior: A General Field Theory Formulation," *Papers of the Regional Science Association,* 21 (1968), 211.]

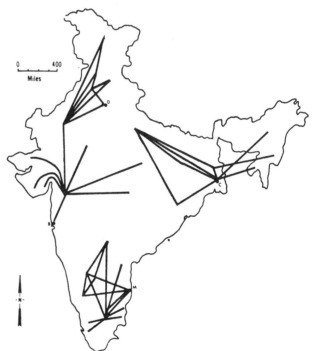

FIGURE 16.6 Functional regions in India, based on commodity flows. [*Source:* Berry, "Interdependency of Spatial Structure and Spatial Behavior."]

set of flows focuses upon one of the four major cities, and, in addition, the inland capital of Delhi is tied to the port of Bombay.

The Internal Structure of the Hinterland City

The particular set of functions performed by the large hinterland city is reflected in the distinctive use of its internal space. As in the case of the large cities of North America and Europe, the non-Western city grows at a rapid rate and must therefore continually reach out for more territory along its margins. Unlike the usual heartland city, however, this centrifugal expansion does not occur in response to transport innovations, such as the construction of rapid transit and expressway systems. Instead, it results from the fact that the fast-growing primate cities of Asia, Latin America, and Africa cannot readily absorb all the rural immigrants converging upon them. Unlike the usual Western city, the hinterland city cannot provide sufficient housing in its already crowded center, and newcomers are forced to settle along the city fringes. There they form communities much like the rural villages from which they came, attempting to preserve the traditional rural social organization of their home areas. Whereas the population densities of inner cities in North America are falling, central densities of hinterland cities remain high.

The land-use pattern within the non-Western city is likewise different from that of the heartland city. Among the reasons for this difference is the large proportion of the population engaged in the service sector in the hinterland city, most of the work force being clerks, administrators, transport workers, retail merchants, and street-corner vendors of trinkets and foods. Also complicating the pattern is the plurality of racial, ethnic, and cultural groups in the urban population. Finally, there is the mixed economy, which characterizes the hinterland city—the combination of Western capitalism, semicapitalism, and preindustrial forms.

The most prominent feature of the city is the port, which was the center of economic activity during the colonial era and retains its supremacy in the postindependence period. Associated with it are many related activities: wharves, warehouses, and the kinds of manufacturing usually found at major ports. There are usually two main concentrations of retailing and other commercial services. One of these is the Western-style central business district, where products imported from the United States, Europe, and Japan are sold in modern, air-conditioned department stores and shops. Nearby, and contrasting in appearance, atmosphere, and hours and methods of doing business, is the commercial alien center—the Chinatown or Indiantown, with its immense population densities. Although the alien mer-

chants overwhelmingly dominated the commercial scene in the past, many of these groups have been expelled recently because of growing nationalism among the original population. In addition, numerous markets purvey a multitude of foodstuffs and other daily necessities, occupying large barnlike structures scattered throughout the city and operated by and for the indigenous population. These markets, in turn, are surrounded by innumerable streetsellers and hawkers.

Manufacturing in the hinterland city likewise assumes distinctive forms. The Western (or modern) types of production occur in specific zones, one of which is the area immediately adjacent to the port. As in the colonial era, these industries engage principally in the processing of foodstuffs: sugar, rice, tropical fruits, sago, tobacco, and other staple agricultural commodities for export. Often the port area provides sites for shipbuilding and repair, maintenance of railway equipment, and other transport-related activities. A second area of modern industry is located in recently constructed industrial estates (parks) along the margins of the city.

Unlike the usual European or North American city, many hinterland cities have not one but several peaks of population density, one for each of the major cultural groups in the area. The residential pattern established during the colonial period often persists, with the elite living close to the urban core or in the separate former colonial quarters, and the poor spreading outward toward the periphery. Although there are innumerable ethnic quarters throughout the city, the squatter settlements of newly arrived villagers are on the fringes of the built-up area. Western-style suburbs have also begun to appear on the outskirts of some hinterland cities as the growing middle class with their private motor cars seeks escape from the crowded urban center. This intermingling of rich and poor is in addition to the traditional spatial associations of classes because of the custom of laboring families occupying living quarters on the premises of their employers.

The market-gardening zone, where intensive crops of fruits and vegetables that will be sold in the city are grown, is outside the city and adjacent to the built-up areas.

DUALISM AND DEVELOPMENT

In the world hinterland, the question of how to escape from endemic poverty is a dominant consideration. The great majority of hinterland countries are very poor by heartland standards, even though considerable variation exists in their levels of development. But what is it that we really mean by *development*? There is probably less agreement today than ever before on the definition of this term, which is commonly used in a normative sense—as a condition toward which all people unquestionably aspire. It is customary for persons in the West to define development in terms of degrees of urbanization, commercialization, industrialization, modernization, and per capita production and consumption. This point of view is widely accepted in many of the hinterland countries themselves, which expect to experience the same sequence of events as those encountered by the West a century earlier.

Yet other paths have been taken. Although Japan ostensibly adopted the Western model, in actuality she did not so much *adopt* that model as *adapt* it successfully to her own peculiar indigenous attitudes and forms. The USSR has also adapted modern industrial technology to her particular ideological system. The problem for many of the hinterland countries in seeking to chart a similar independent path is that their current economies involve a problematic combination of Western and non-Western forms termed the *dual economy*.

When two social and economic systems that are clearly distinct from each other exist simultaneously within the same territory, each dominating a part of the society, that area has a dual economy. One of these systems, always the more technologically advanced of the two, has been imported from abroad; the other is the system indigenous to the area. Dualism usually occurs where an imported Western capitalism (or even socialism or communism) has penetrated a precapitalistic agrarian community and where the original system has managed to survive intact.

Precapitalism has a number of characteristics that contrast with those of modern capitalism. Typically it involves a communal way of life; tight all-embracing social bonds; and traditional class distinctions. The individual has limited, modest needs (unless he or she is one of the favored few belonging to the elite), and he or she engages in little or no exchange, except for luxuries when the periodic market or fair meets. People produce in and for the household to which they belong, making finished goods rather than semicompleted commodities, and they seldom patronize professional traders. The basic economic unit, both for production and consumption, is the family (or joint-family).

Wherever this kind of traditional subsistence production and consumption is carried out alongside a modern, efficient, highly capitalized structure tied to the world heartland, it can be said that a *dual economy* exists. The physical expression of dualism is the foreign capitalistic enclave with a life of its own: the trading city, commercial agricultural estate, the mining center, and all the modern transport and communication links that go with these. It is also manifested in the contrast-ing ways of life within the primate city: the Western-style central business district (CBD) as opposed to the bazaar economy, scattered native markets and street-sellers; the modern manufacturing establishments in the port area and suburban industrial estates as compared with the cottage industry scattered throughout the native residential sector.

Dualism is absent in a number of hinterland countries where the invading group exterminated the indigenous population, as in Argentina, or where the Europeans herded the native peoples into reservations. This latter practice was introduced by the early American republic, subsequently by Canada, New Zealand, and Australia, and is being imposed upon the Bantu and Zulu in South Africa even today. In each of these cases except in the reservations, a Western type of capitalistic nation has evolved as a replacement for the subsistence economy that preceded it.

The dualism described here must not be confused with the very special kind of *industrial dualism* prevalent in contemporary Japan. In Japan the term is used to describe the contrasts between the large, modern conglomerate firms known as *zaibatsu* and the small workshop enterprises remaining from an earlier era. Both types are wholly capitalistic even though one is more advanced than the other. The kind of dualism found in underdeveloped nations is of a very different sort, and it presents those countries with a particularly difficult set of problems.

Developmental Problems and Dualism

The regional structure of the world economic system, according to the heartland-hinterland paradigm, is the product of a set of centrifugal and centripetal forces. The centrifugal forces have had the effect of reducing contrasts between heartland and hinterland. Taking advantage of various spread effects from the heartland, certain hinterland nations have in the past managed to benefit from the growing markets at the center and to appropriate to their own use the technological improvements developed there, including the innovations in transportation and communication linking them to the center. The insulating effects of distance protected their infant industries from competing producers in the metropolitan center at the same time that worsening problems of overcrowding and congestion were raising rents and labor costs in the center. Once growth became solidly established, these countries were able to generate the linkages, both forward and backward, that are required for a mature modern economy. Japan rose to economic power by following this track as did the United States and Canada during that earlier time when

North America was on the periphery of the world economic system.

The majority of today's hinterland countries have not been able to make this transition, however. They have remained special problem areas because of the combination of *centripetal* forces that favor growth of the heartland at the expense of the hinterland. These less-fortunate nations have therefore been consigned to what would appear to be a permanent role as primary producers, economically dependent upon the center, and beset by dualism. Such growth impulses as do reach them from the heartland remain confined to the enclaves of modernity, which are then inundated by migrants from a depressed countryside who came to the city and found only unemployment. Their disparities in material well-being have tended to grow instead of diminish, following the vicious circle of poverty, inadequate food supply, unemployment, and adverse demographic conditions described earlier. It has been estimated, for example, that the per capita incomes of today's underdeveloped nations are only one-sixth to one-third that of the present developed countries a century ago. Meanwhile, the underdeveloped lands as a group are contributing a declining proportion of total world income. During their period of colonialism, the hinterland economies acquired a degree of dependency so great as to leave them excessively vulnerable to world trade fluctuations, a condition that has since continued as a result of neocolonialism. Drained by the heartland of their physical and human resources, they lack an effective voice in international economic affairs, which are decided by the advanced nations.

Problems of trade underlie many of their difficulties. Their unfavorable terms of trade, which appear to be worsening, represent one of the most intractable dilemmas confronting them. They must import increasingly expensive machinery and other capital goods in order to develop, but they have to continue exporting primary commodities for which there is a relatively static demand on a world market whose prices are set in metropolitan countries' commodity exchanges. Their excessive dependence upon a limited number of such primary exports is one of their heritages from colonialism. Their trade is often hampered by problems of remoteness. Either being too distant from the heartland or having inadequate transport connections to it burdens the hinterland nations with excessive transport costs for both their exports and imports.

Underdeveloped countries are troubled not only by the gap that separates them from the heartland but also by inequalities between regions within hinterland nations. The disparities of regional incomes in underdeveloped lands are usually greater than those in advanced countries, and they appear to be growing with time, even as regional disparities in the heartlands are diminishing. In much the same way that heartland countries tend to prosper at the expense of the hinterland nations, the primate cities of underdeveloped countries grow at the expense of the rural areas tributary to them. Transport innovation appears to intensify these regional inequalities; extending modern transportation into rural districts seems to intensify backwash effects.

Thus have arisen major sources of hinterland transformation: It has been in the disadvantaged peripheries that revolutions have been fought and won and old social orders replaced by new ones seeking alternative paths to national betterment, as in Castro's Cuba or Nyerere's Tanzania, where rural development takes priority over the primate city. Similarly, as international access to depleting world resources becomes critical, the potentiality for creating resource-supplier cartels in the hinterlands grows and offers prospects for significantly transforming the balance of heartland-hinterland power.

DETERMINANTS OF GROWTH IN HEARTLAND ECONOMICS

The Denison Model

What continues to drive heartland growth? One of the most notable approaches to evaluating the determinants of growth is that of the American economist Edward F. Denison. His 1962 study, "The Sources of Economic Growth in the United States and the Alternatives Before Us," has been recognized as a landmark in the quantitative analysis of economic growth. Denison also applied his methodology to nine Western European countries in *Why Growth Rates Differ*. Dorothy Walters subsequently applied it to Canada, and Hisao Kanamori to Japan.

Denison's analysis began with the measurement of real income per capita, using data on net national income totals adjusted to improve international comparability, on population, labor force and employment, and the relative purchasing power in the different countries.

Denison asked why differences in income levels and economic growth rates had occurred, and whether the United States could have been expected to do better. The first step in answering these questions was a sound classification of the determinants of growth.

The most fundamental distinction was provided by grouping all individual determinants of growth into two sets: growth due to increases in the *absolute levels* of the factors of production; and growth due to the *increasing efficiency* with which these resources are used and combined. Denison found that a country's production may grow mainly because the labor force and capital inputs increase, as in Canada, or because of increasing efficiency with which these factors are used, as in the countries of northwest Europe (Figure 16.7). In northwest Europe, 3.1 percentage points, or two-thirds of the total growth rate of 4.8 percent, arose from gains in the efficiency of resource use, the highest figure of 4.5 being for Germany and the lowest figure of 1.2 for the United Kingdom. In Canada, only 2.1 percentage points arose from this source, and in the United States only 1.4 percentage points. Conversely, 2.7 percentage points of the Canadian growth rate arose from increased inputs of labor and capital, compared with 1.9 in the United States and 1.7 in northwest Europe. Put another way, 60 percent of the economic growth in North America was produced by using more inputs and 40 percent by using inputs more efficiently. In Europe, on the other hand, the relative importance of quantity and efficiency was reversed. Only 40 percent of the growth was due to additional inputs of labor and capital and 60 percent to more efficient use of labor and capital inputs.

Denison's research was very detailed and it probed the separate effects of increases in the size and quality of labor forces (including, for example, the dramatic changes that have occurred in female labor force participation), as well as changes in the use of capital and land, together with increasing efficiency in the use of factors of production.

The determinants of increasing efficiency are listed in Table 16.1 together with their actual contributions to growth in selected countries and regions. They include the most important growth determinants of all: advances in knowledge related to technology, management, and organization; and lags in applying best knowledge. They also include two growth determinants, which, though smaller, go far toward explaining differences in postwar growth among heartland countries: improved allocation of resources and economies of scale.

Knowledge and the level of best-practice technology, management, and organization differ even among the heartland countries because of the time taken for advances made in one country to diffuse to others, and because such advances are often more applicable in the country of origin than abroad.

The level of knowledge should probably be the same in all plants producing any given product within a country; but, in fact, there is a lag between best-practice and average-practice technology within countries, which has implications for national economic growth as well as for regional disparities. Adoption of new knowledge and techniques is often delayed to secure returns on existing durable capital equipment. In such circumstances, the flow of new techniques outstrips the flexibility of the system. For example, it took a decade and a half for the best-practice techniques in blast furnace operation in the United States, which developed by the beginning of the century, to be adopted throughout the country. If all plants had adopted best-practice technology immediately, labor productivity would have doubled.

There is no doubt that the lag between best-practice and average-practice technology is much greater in northwest Europe than in the United States. Denison's analysis suggested that the lag has failed to narrow, except in France and perhaps Italy.

Improved allocation of resources, particularly labor shifts out of agriculture and self-employment, have varied considerably in their contribution to growth, the smallest contributions being in the United Kingdom, and by far the largest in Italy (Figure 16.8). Agricultural employment was still considerable in many heartland countries in 1950, and there would have been little loss in

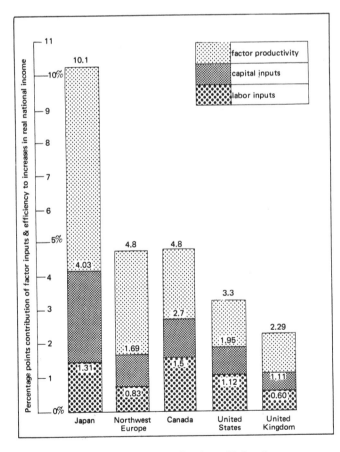

FIGURE 16.7 The contribution of labor inputs, capital inputs, and factor productivity to growth of real national income, 1950–1962. Data for Japan's real national income are from 1955–1968.

TABLE 16.1

Sources of increasing output per unit of input in the United States, Canada, Northwest Europe, United Kingdom, and Italy: 1950–1962

Sources of increasing output per unit of output	United States	Canada	Northwest Europe[a]	United Kingdom	Italy
Total	**1.37%**	**2.1%**	**3.07%**	**1.18%**	**4.30%**
Advances of knowledge	0.76	0.6	0.76	0.76	0.76
Changes in the lag in the application of knowledge, general efficiency, and errors and omissions					
Reduction in age of capital	—	—	0.02	0.00	0.00
Other	—	—	0.54	0.03	0.89
Improved allocation of resources					
Contraction of agricultural inputs	0.25	0.6	0.46	0.06	1.04
Contraction of nonagricultural self-employment	0.04	0.1	0.14	0.04	0.22
Reduction of international trade barriers	0.00	—	0.08	0.02	0.16
Balancing of the capital stock	—	0.3[b]	0.08	—	—
Deflation procedures	—	—	0.07	—	—
Economies of scale					
Growth of national market measured in U.S. prices	0.30	0.5	0.41	0.22	0.55
Income elasticities	—	—	0.46	0.09	0.60
Independent growth of the local markets	0.06	0.1	0.06	0.05	0.07
Irregularities in pressure of demand	−0.04	0.1	−0.01	−0.09	—
Irregularities in agricultural output	—	—	0.00	—	0.01

Sources: Denison, *Growth Rates,* Tables 21-1 to 21-19, pp. 298–316; and Dorothy Walters, *Canadian Growth Levels Revisited, 1950–1967* (Ottawa: Economic Council of Canada, Staff Study No. 28, 1967), p. 37.

Note: Where a main growth determinant (shown in italics) is subdivided into its component parts, the contribution of the component parts *only* is given. The columns thus add up to the total, ± rounding error. This procedure explains the blanks for *Changes in lag* and *Improved allocation.*

[a]The Denison countries included in Northwest Europe are Belgium, Denmark, France, Germany, The Netherlands, Norway, and the United Kingdom.

[b]This is a statistical adjustment to include the amount by which the Canadian growth rate was increased by the use of productivity and profit-adjusted construction deflators. See Walters, *Canadian Growth Levels,* p. 37.

agricultural output even if many farmers had left agriculture. Overallocation to agriculture and self-employment still explain most of the difference between Italy and northwest Europe in output per unit of total input, and large differences still exist in farm employment as a percentage of total employment.

Another determinant that has contributed substantially to disparities in the postwar growth performance of heartland countries is economies of scale. Economies of scale are hard to measure and comprise several components that Denison groups into growth of national market, income elasticities, and independent growth of local markets.

The fast-growth European countries were in an unusually favorable position to benefit from economies of scale in the 1950s and 1960s. Their production levels of automobiles and other income-elastic consumer products were low in the early 1950s and rose more than proportionately with rising incomes. It is precisely in the early stages of production increase from low volume to high volume that economies of scale are largest and make their greatest contribution to economic growth. Furthermore, the necessary technology did not have to be developed but could be borrowed from the United States or was introduced directly by American firms themselves.

Rapid urbanization and changes in shopping behavior associated with increasing automobile ownership have made an independent contribution to economies of scale. It appears that the contribution to growth made by this factor from 1950 to 1962 has been the same in Europe as in the United States and much smaller than the contribution made by market growth (Table 16.1). But added together, the contributions made by all com-

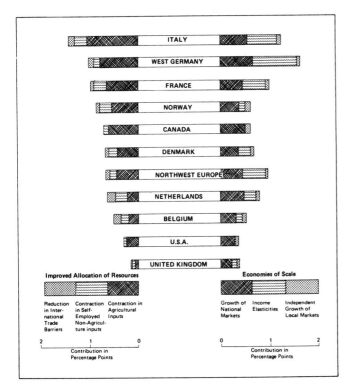

FIGURE 16.8 The contribution of improved allocation of resources and of economies of scale to growth of real national income, 1950–1962.

ponents of economies of scale are impressive. For example, they contributed 0.93 percentage points (0.41 + 0.46 + 0.06, Table 16.1) to northwest Europe's growth which, without this contribution, would have been 3.85 percent instead of 4.78 percent. The contribution to growth in the United States was only half as great, and not much greater in Canada.

The main findings of the Denison model can best be summarized by interregional comparisons of postwar growth performance. Denison was particularly concerned with a comparison of the European and United States experience. Other researchers have used this model to assess the performance of Canada and Japan.

United States net national income grew more slowly than northwest Europe's between 1950 and 1962, averaging 3.32 percent per year compared to 4.78 percent. But there was a 5-percentage point spread within northwest Europe, with Germany achieving a growth rate of 7.26 percent and the United Kingdom only 2.29 percent. These measures say nothing, however, about the contribution made by the individual growth determinants or how well national economies performed when allowance is made for their different circumstances.

Ranking the determinants in order of importance shows the typical sequence in contributing to growth per person employed:

1. advances in knowledge;
2. capital investment in nonresidential structures and equipment;
3. contraction in agricultural inputs;
4. economies of scale: growth in national markets.

For aggregate national income, one finds advances in knowledge and employment growth vying for first place, nonresidential structures and reduced agricultural inputs vying for third place.

Japan's Spectacular Growth

Japan's growth rate has been about double that of northwest Europe and Canada and three times that of the United States in the postwar period. Hisao Kanamori (1972) attempted to account for these differences by applying the Denison model to Japan.

The average annual rate of increase of factor inputs in Japan exceeded that of all other heartland countries, both in total and in the separate inputs of labor and capital and in the output per unit of input. The growth of total labor inputs was only just above those of Germany, however, and the employment input of 1.5 percent (Table 16.2) was actually less than Germany's 2.0 percent. And, surprisingly perhaps, the contribution of Japanese labor to economic growth (1.31) was a little below the labor contribution in Germany (1.37) and Canada (1.5), although ahead of the United States and northwest Europe. The largest contributors to growth in Japan, in fact, were capital inputs and increasing efficiency, and it has been these same two sets of growth determinants that have contributed most to the growth differential between Japan and the other heartland countries (Table 16.3).

Thus, capital increases contributed 2.2 percentage points more than the United Kingdom to Japan's annual percentage increase in national income and productivity increases 4.9 percentage points more than the United Kingdom. Compare these figures with the United Kingdom's increase of national income of 2.3 percent: In one case the *differences* between the United Kingdom and Japan are almost the same, in the other case almost double the contribution of *all* growth determinants in the United Kingdom. The rate of increase of efficiency in factor use in Japan has indeed been remarkably high and, by itself, would have been enough to place Japan first among nations in rate of growth.

This high postwar growth rate in productivity reflects the rapid shifts in the allocation of labor from agriculture to manufacturing industry, the swift introduction of foreign technology, and rapid increase in

TABLE 16.2

Annual percentage increase of factor inputs in Japan, the United States, Northwest Europe, and the United Kingdom

	Japan	United States	Northwest Europe	United Kingdom
Total factor input	**4.2**	**1.71**	**1.67**	**1.16**
Labor	1.9	1.42	1.08	0.77
Employment	1.5	1.14	0.93	0.65
Hours of work	−0.1	−0.21	−0.18	−0.19
Age, sex composition	0.3	−0.13	0.04	−0.05
Education	0.2	0.62	0.30	0.37
Capital	10.5	3.58	4.53	3.35
Nonresidential structures and equipment	9.6	3.74	4.55	3.58
Inventories	12.4	3.00	4.47	2.56
Land	0.0	0.00	0.00	0.00
Output per unit of input	5.5	1.36	3.04	1.18

Source: Hisao Kanamori, "What Accounts for Japan's High Rate of Growth?," *Review of Income and Wealth,* Series 18, No. 2 (June 1972), p. 155.

Note: The Japan rates are based on the period from 1955 to 1968; the United States, Northwest Europe, and United Kingdom from 1950 to 1962. Northwest Europe includes the seven Denison countries: Belgium, Denmark, France, West Germany, The Netherlands, Norway, and the United Kingdom.

TABLE 16.3

Differences in the contribution of the determinants of growth between Japan and the United States, Canada, Northwest Europe, and the United Kingdom

	United States	Canada	Northwest Europe	United Kingdom
National income	−6.8	−5.3	−5.3	−7.8
Gross input	−2.1	−1.3	−2.3	−2.9
Labor	−0.2	−0.2	−0.5	−0.7
Employment	−0.1	−0.5	−0.3	−0.5
Work hours	−0.1	−0.1	−0.1	−0.1
Age, sex composition	−0.3	−0.3	−0.2	−0.2
Education	−0.4	−0.2	−0.1	−0.2
Capital	−1.9	−1.5	−1.9	−2.2
Dwelling	−0.1	−0.2	−0.1	−0.1
International assets	−0.1	−0.1	—	−0.1
Nonresidential structures and equipment	−1.2	−0.7	−1.0	−1.2
Inventories	−0.9	−0.9	−0.8	−0.9
Productivity	−4.7	−4.0	−3.0	−4.9

Source: Kanamori, "Japan's High Rate of Growth," p. 160; and Walters, *Canadian Growth Levels,* p. 37.

Note: Figures are in percentage points. A *minus* sign indicates that the determinant contributed *less* than in Japan. Thus productivity contributed 4.7 percentage points less to growth in the United States than in Japan. If the productivity difference between Japan and the United States had been 0.0, U.S. national income would have risen by another 4.7 percent a year.

economies of scale. It is not clear whether the rapid-growth opportunities offered by these determinants are approaching exhaustion. The evidence from application of the Denison model separately to the periods 1955 to 1960, 1960 to 1965, and 1965 to 1968 is that the contribution to growth by increasing efficiency in use of factor inputs is actually increasing (Table 16.4); increasing productivity contributed 4.7 percentage points to Japan's growth from 1955 to 1960 and 5.9 percentage points from 1960 to 1965. The corresponding figures show a decline both for northwest Europe (from 3.9 to 2.5 percentage points) and for the United States (from

TABLE 16.4

Contribution of determinants to growth of real GNP in Japan: 1955–1960, 1960–1965, 1965–1968, and 1955–1968

	1955–1960	1960–1965	1965–1968	1955–1968
Real GNP	8.9	10.0	12.3	10.1
Total input	4.23	4.13	3.89	4.03
Labor	2.10	0.87	0.97	1.31
Employment	1.12	0.87	1.18	1.03
Work hours	0.56	−0.40	−0.49	−0.07
Age, sex	0.35	0.20	0.07	0.21
Education	0.07	0.20	0.21	0.14
Capital	2.13	3.26	2.92	2.72
Dwellings	0.11	0.16	0.16	0.14
International assets	—	—	—	—
Equipment	1.16	2.09	1.73	1.62
Inventory	0.86	1.01	1.03	0.96
Land	—	—	—	—
Production per input volume	4.7	5.9	8.4	6.1

Source: Kanamori, "Japan's High Rate of Growth," p. 167.

Note: All figures are in percentage points.

1.9 to 1.0 percentage points). Thus, increasing efficiency contributed 0.8 percentage points more in Japan than in northwest Europe during the first period, but 3.4 percentage points more in the second. And it contributed 2.8 percentage points more in Japan than in the United States in the first period, but 4.9 percentage points more in the second.

INVENTION, INNOVATION, AND DIFFUSION

Denison's most important conclusions relate to the central role of advances in knowledge related to technology, management, and organization in growth. Similarly, he saw lags in applying the best available knowledge as the principal source of differences in economic performance. Knowledge growth is an *internal* source of change; acquisition of knowledge from elsewhere is an *external* growth determinant. For internally generated change to remain dynamic, some process of "circular and cumulative causation" must work; for externally generated change to narrow the gap between heartlands and hinterlands, innovation diffusion processes must speed the spread of new ideas and practices.

Invention and the Process of Circular and Cumulative Causation

Invention lies at the heart of internally generated advances in knowledge. Invention is the creative act or process. It involves new ideas, new procedures, new types of organization, new products, and new technologies; it includes *basic* applications of new knowledge

and new components—as in the invention of the first radio, jet engine, or computer—and also *elaborations* or *improvements* in later models based on additional experimentation and experience.

One explanation of the inventive act is the transcendental or "heroic" theory, which holds that invention is the inspiration of the occasional genius, and is therefore unpredictable in time and space. The more widely accepted explanation is that an invention is a new combination of a relatively large number of elements, accumulated over long periods of time, with the individual inventor acting merely as an instrument of historical process. For example, in 1858 Darwin and Wallace both presented papers at the same meeting of England's Royal Society setting forth the idea of natural selection in the evolutionary formation and change of species. If Darwin had died during his two decades of indecision on whether to publish his results, Wallace would almost certainly be credited with the theory of evolution. If both had died shortly before 1858, the mechanistic view is that in a few years, given the scientific climate of the times, some third person would have documented and presented the theory because conditions were ripe for this interpretive synthesis. Both Darwin and Wallace had been led to their ideas by reading Malthus's work on population, in which he pointed out that population multiplies faster than food. They both concluded that if this is true of animals, then animals must compete to survive.

It is thus evident that invention involves *cumulative synthesis*: Successive perceptions of a problem set the stage for invention and lead to a gathering of the necessary facts about the problem and the principles and components that offer a potential solution. Invention is the resolution of the problem.

Cumulative synthesis leading to invention is an example of *positive feedback*. Positive feedback occurs when a change of a given kind produces further changes of the same kind. The process of circular and cumulative causation is the synthesis of a succession of positive feedbacks.

The most important treatise that discusses circular and cumulative causation and its consequences for economic systems is that of Gunnar Myrdal, initially stated in *An American Dilemma* and reiterated on a world scale in *Asian Drama* and *Rich Lands and Poor* (1957). Myrdal wrote that in advanced social systems, each change propels growth and development in the direction of initial growth impulses, causing social processes to become cumulative and to gather speed at accelerating rates. Thus, centers of knowledge creation generate more knowledge, whereas poverty-stricken peripheries sink deeper into poverty and despair, increasing the differences between rich and poor: The rich become richer and the poor become poorer. As C. E. A. Winslow observed in *The Cost of Sickness and The Price of Health*,

> It was clear . . . that poverty and disease formed a vicious circle. Men and women were sick because they were poor; they became poorer because they were sick, and sicker because they were poorer.[5]

Reformulating Myrdal's model in the case of urban growth and change, Allan Pred has written that it seems clear that the largest cities repeatedly reinforce and renew their advantages after having acquired a dominant position in the urban hierarchy at some relatively early development stage. They do so by the acquisition of growth-inducing innovations, which tend to be adopted earliest in large cities because they offer a large local market, because of external economies of scale, which are enhanced where similar industries are competitively spurred to adopt the innovation, and by the "operational" decision-making advantages associated with large cities. Operational decision making includes purchase-source decisions, market investment decisions, private investment decisions, and public organization allocation decisions. Pred believes that in every case the decision-making process tends to stabilize the ranking of large cities according to size as the process of city-system development unfolds. The impacts of interurban diffusion and the accumulation of operational decisions are magnified by nonlocal multiplier ef-

fects because cities have open economies; increased economic activity in any city is likely to stimulate economic activity throughout the urban system. Pred then combines these three processes—diffusion, decision making, and multipliers—into a large city-focused model of city-system development that incorporates a circular and cumulative feedback process of urban-size growth for large metropolitan areas.

Innovation and Diffusion

It has been characteristic of world history that at any one time there have been relatively few centers in which this cumulative process is taking place. In the centers of invention there is accelerated accumulation; and from them, innovations diffuse, producing change elsewhere (subject to the lags of time and the frictions of space). For those areas beyond the pale of diffusion, there is the problem of not being part of the system within which the process of circular and cumulative causation is taking place.

Innovation, then, is the acceptance, adoption, and application of inventions in areas other than centers of invention, after the invention has occurred. The time sequence is important because the most remote areas tend to innovate last and least, if at all. In short, innovation involves a combined time-space sequence: acceptance over time of some specific idea or practice by individuals, groups, or other adopting units that are linked to specific channels of communication, to a social structure, and to a given system of values or culture. An example of a typical time-space sequence is provided by the diffusion of the railroads, without which industrialization probably could not have run its course. Railroads represented the fastest means of transportation in the century preceding World War I. During the period that railroads were the best means of transportation available, railroad mileage grew in a logistic fashion (Figure 16.9). This was true both worldwide and for individual countries (Figure 16.10a, b). The logistic increase of railroad mileage was accompanied by a lagged outward spread from the original center of the innovation, Great Britain, at an accelerating growth rate (Figure 16.11a, b). The sequence was from the original heartland of the Industrial Revolution, outwards into the world's hinterlands.

Diffusion is the term used to describe the spread of innovations outward from centers of innovation. The overall time sequence involves a small band of "early adopters," followed by accelerated acceptance as a "bandwagon effect" takes hold, succeeded by a slowing rate of adoptions as laggards finally join in, and the potential market is saturated. Figure 16.12 shows the typical S-shaped sequence of adoptions—in this case,

[5]C. E. A. Winslow, *The Cost of Sickness and the Price of Health*, Monograph Series, No. 7 (Geneva: World Health Organization, 1951), p. 9.

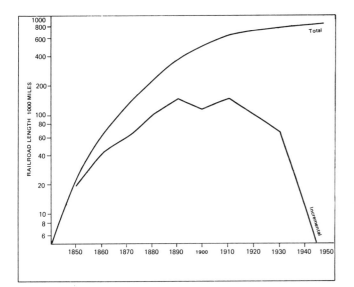

FIGURE 16.9 World railroad building, 1840–1950. Most railroad mileage was built in the period when railroads enjoyed a speed superiority over other modes. [*Source:* Alfred J. Lotka, "Population Analysis as a Chapter in the Mathematical Theory of Evolution," in *Essays on Growth and Form,* W. E. Le Gros Clark and Peter P. Medawar, eds. (Oxford: The Clarendon Press, 1965), p. 380.]

the opening of television stations in U.S. cities. But most diffusion processes also involve two other elements: *hierarchical diffusion* and *spread effects*. Hierarchical diffusion is the tendency for many inventions to be adopted in larger cities and markets first, and to diffuse down the urban hierarchy. A spread effect is the wave-like pattern of acceptance outwards from an urban center into a surrounding rural area. Figure 16.13 shows the diffusion of TV stations across the U.S. urban hierarchy; large cities opened their stations first. Figures 16.14 through 16.16 show the resulting spread effects as customers acquired television sets. Figure 16.14 reveals early adoption in the northeastern manufacturing belt heartland, with distance-decay from other large cities. Figure 16.16 shows virtually complete market penetration, except for the nation's most poverty-stricken peripheries. Together, these figures summarize the essential features of geographical diffusion:

1. Outward from heartlands where circular and cumulative causation occurs, into progressively more remote hinterlands.

2. From large cities to small, down the urban hierarchy.

3. From urban areas into their rural hinterlands.

In each case the laggards benefit least. Is there any way out for the poverty-stricken hinterland? Magorah

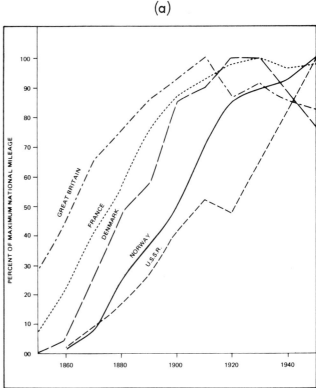

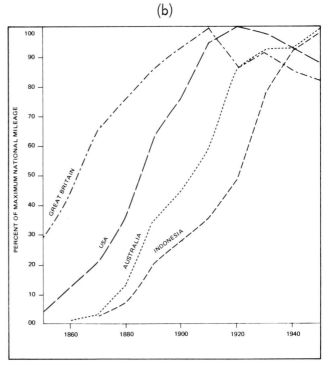

FIGURE 16.10 The logistic curves of railroad building for selected countries (a) Europe, (b) worldwide. [*Source:* W. S. Woytinski and E. S. Woytinski, *World Commerce and Governments: Trends and Outlook* (New York: Twentieth Century Fund, 1955).]

(a)

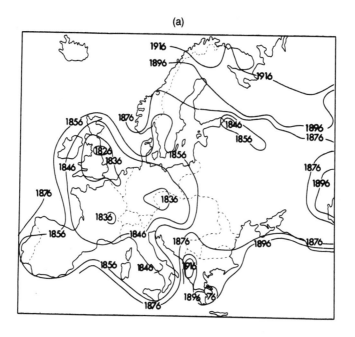

(b)

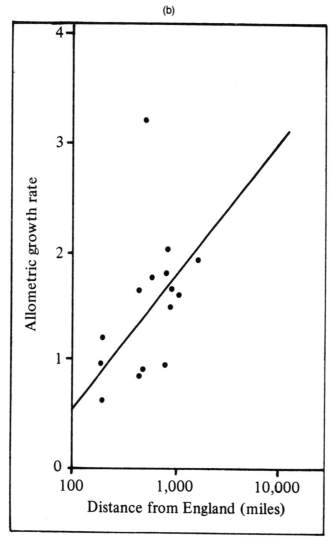

FIGURE 16.11 The diffusion and growth gradient of railroad building in Europe, 1826–1916. [*Sources:* (a) Sven Godlund, "Ein Innovationsverlauf in Europa, dargestellt in einer vorläufigen Untersuchung über die Ausbreitung der Eisenbahninnovation" (Lund, Sweden: Department of Geography, Royal University of Lund, Series B in Geography, Human Geography No. 6, 1952); (b) D. Michael Ray and others, "Functional Prerequisites, Spatial Diffusion, and Allometric Growth," *Economic Geography,* L (October 1974), 348.]

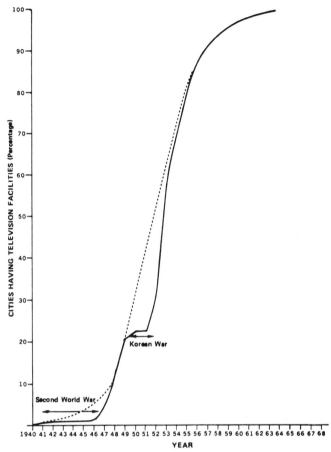

FIGURE 16.12 Growth in number of TV cities, 1940–1968. [*Source:* Brian J. L. Berry, "The Geography of the United States in the Year 2000," *Transactions of the Institute of British Geographers,* LI (November 1970), 21–53.]

Maruyama stresses the importance of some "initial kick":

Thus in the economically underdeveloped countries, it is necessary not only to plan the economy, but also to give the initial kick and reinforce it for a while in such a direction and with such intensity as to maximize the efficiency of development per initial investment. Once the economy is kicked in a right direction and with a sufficient initial push, the deviation amplifying mutual positive feedbacks takes over the process, and the resulting development will be disproportionately large as compared with initial kick.[6]

It is with the problems of achieving such a trend reversal in the world's hinterland economies that we conclude this book.

[6]Walter Buckley, ed., *Modern Systems Research for the Behavioral Scientist* (Chicago: Aldine, 1968), p. 305.

HINTERLAND GROWTH PROBLEMS AND THEIR CONSEQUENCES

Trend reversals can and do take place. In most of the world's older industrial nations, economic growth has moved outwards from their original industrial heartlands into amenity-rich peripheries; as a result, migration has reversed. Formerly, dominant interregional migration flows were from periphery to core; now they are from core to periphery (Figure 16.17).

Under the impact of colonialism, the hinterland countries emerged as economically dependent suppliers of raw materials and consumers of the finished products of the world's heartland. If changes were taking place in this pattern in the last two decades, they were the consequence of the transformation of the heartland economies, particularly that of the United States, into postindustrial societies—that is, until the emergence of the Arab oil cartel and the energy crisis.

This transformation involved a variety of interrelated shifts within the heartlands:

From primary and secondary industries (agriculture/manufacturing) to tertiary and quaternary industries (service/knowledge activities);

From values posited on survival to security, then belongingness and esteem, and ultimately to self-actualization;

From goods to services;

From goods/services produced by muscle power to those produced by machines and cybernetics;

From unassisted brainpower to knowledge-assisted and amplified by electronic data processing;

From basic necessities to amenities and eventually to a higher order of sensate needs;

From physiological to psychological needs;

From scientific emphasis based on physical, "hard" sciences to one based on social, "soft" sciences;

From a few innovative technological introductions to vast and varied new inventions;

From a few stark choices to a bewildering array of choices;

From independence and self-sufficiency to interdependence;

From profit-mindedness to balanced consideration of social responsibilities and the public interest;

From Puritan work ethic to leisure as a matter of right;

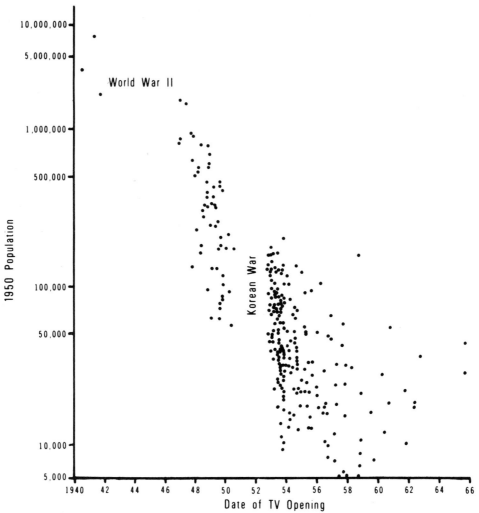

FIGURE 16.13   Hierarchical diffusion of the TV network. [*Source:* Berry, "The Geography of the United States in the Year 2000."]

From atomistic to large-scale pluralistic institutions;

From national to multinational and "one-world" scale operations;

From decentralization to centralization and eventual "globalization."

In broad economic terms, this has meant that the United States, in particular, has been moving away from a heavy stress on manufacturing toward an emphasis on service-oriented and high-technology industry. American corporations have, in several ways, been shifting production operations to countries abroad where labor costs are lower and raw materials more accessible. As the process continues, the United States role increasingly is as the source of capital, management techniques, and high technology. That the United States maintain its superior scientific and technical capabilities

is seen as a necessity to American security and economic well-being. Thus, in the future, Route 128 outside Boston and Silicon Valley on the San Francisco peninsula will be the equivalent of Detroit in the assembly-line era.

For the United States, the transformation is most evident in such high-technology areas as telecommunications, information processing, and the aircraft and pharmaceutical industries. Japan and the industrialized countries of Western Europe also have leapfrogged industrially to the point where they are also investing heavily abroad. For some time the Common Market nations have been importing workers from the less-developed countries around the Mediterranean to meet a shortage of labor. And the Japanese and Europeans have also begun to transfer manufacturing operations to the less-developed countries. The multinational corporation has emerged as the chief midwife of the new system.

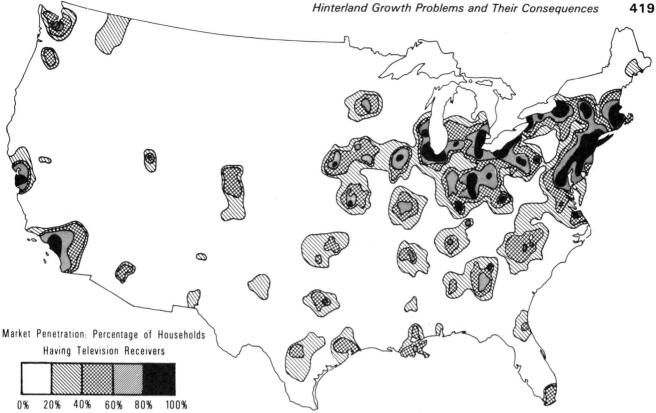

Market Penetration: Percentage of Households
Having Television Receivers

0% 20% 40% 60% 80% 100%

FIGURE 16.14 Market penetration by TV in 1953. [*Source:* Berry, "The Geography of the United States in the Year 2000."]

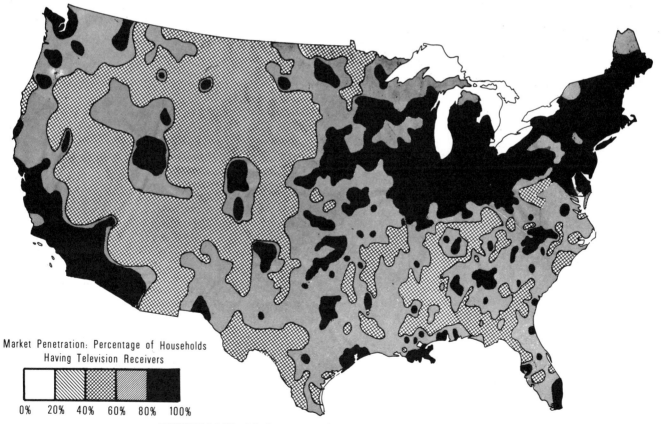

Market Penetration: Percentage of Households
Having Television Receivers

0% 20% 40% 60% 80% 100%

FIGURE 16.15 Market penetration by TV in 1959. [*Source:* Berry, "The Geography of the United States in the Year 2000."]

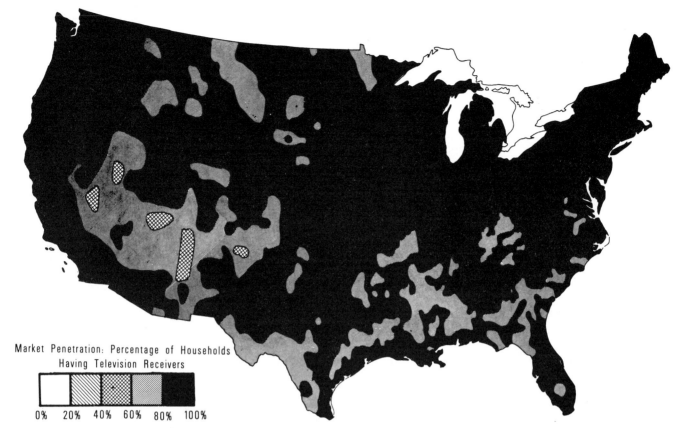

Market Penetration: Percentage of Households
Having Television Receivers

0%   20%   40%   60%   80%   100%

FIGURE 16.16   Market penetration by TV in 1965. [*Source:* Berry, "The Geography of the United States in the Year 2000."]

There are today about 300 colossal multinational corporations whose production of goods and services adds up to about $300 billion a year, a figure higher than the gross national product of every country except the United States. If one takes the 100 largest economic units in the world, only 50 of them are nation-states; the other 50 are the largest of these 300 multinational companies.

Of the 300 multinational corporations, 187 are American; half of the remaining one-third are British and Dutch, and the other half are European and Japanese. The majority of the American giants do more than a half-billion dollars in sales a year. General Motors, the largest, has total annual sales that exceed the net national income of all but a dozen countries.

But it is not size and income alone that are important; rather, it is the change in the control pattern of the *product cycle*. In the past, countries found that once a new product or technique had been created, its initial advantage was overtaken by other countries, which, with cheaper labor or newer machinery, could turn out the product cheaper and thus undersell the original country. The textiles industry is perhaps the classic case in point. But the multinational corporation

not only transfers capital and managerial know-how abroad; it has become an organizational mechanism for the transfer of manufacturing production to low-wage countries and its managerial techniques and technology to the advancing industrial countries while retaining control—and earnings—at both ends. In the five years between 1969 and 1974, overall employment in electronics in the United States declined by some 219,000 jobs as American firms located their new plants in Singapore, Hong Kong, Taiwan, and Mexico. In the nature of this new product cycle, more and more manufacturing of the standardized sort will, in theory, move to the poorer sections of the world while the postindustrial societies concentrate on knowledge-creating and knowledge-processing industries, and the control of the product, in many industries, will remain with the multinational corporation.

The logic of this new type of heartland-hinterland division, with the industrialized countries providing capital, managerial know-how, and a continuing flow of technology and the LDCs contributing labor, raw materials, and new markets, is very tidy, but under stress the theory is already showing some flaws. Some time ago, Arnold Toynbee wrote of the likely emergence of

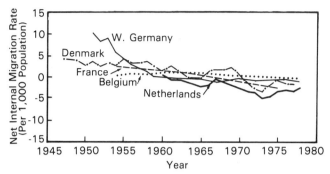

FIGURE 16.17 Industrial countries of north-western Europe show the earliest decline in migration into the core outside North America. Each curve represents the net migration rate for the core of one country. The decline began first in West Germany, in part because of the relatively even distribution of population there. By the 1960s, migration had declined in all five nations; by the late 1970s a net outflow from the core had resulted. Peripheral regions that had lost population to the core for decades, such as the northern Netherlands, are now gaining population by migration. One reason for the outflow is that the peripheries of these countries have good sites for industry. [*Source:* After Daniel J. Vining, Jr., "Migration Between the Core and the Periphery," *Scientific American,* Vol. 247, No. 6 (December 1982).]

an "external proletariat," the poor perimeter of the world encircling the central heartland of the rich. It was a theme sounded ominously in 1965 by Lin Piao, once Mao Tse-tung's number two man, when he warned that the "class struggles" of the end of the twentieth century would be among nations rather than within them. Given the pattern of economic development, such a class struggle, if it ever develops, might become a color struggle as well. And a first sign of this new dimension of the global political economy has been signaled by the 1973–1974 Arab oil crisis. The paradox of the spread of a world capitalist economy is that in each nation-state the economic order is becoming more subordinate to the wider context of political decision making.

Most obviously, the Arab oil boycott has shown what can happen if the less-developed countries deny essential raw materials to the industrialized nations. The LDCs' new appreciation of the value of nonrenewable resources in pursuing both political and economic ends is likely to be a major factor in heartland-hinterland relations from now on. Oil has a unique potency in the marketplace because of the oil-based increases in energy-consuming growth throughout the world, but the LDCs' possession of substantial amounts (in some cases

amounting to a monopoly) of the finite supplies of important raw materials will grow more important.

Even before the melodrama of the oil boycott, the LDCs had begun to take united action in their own political and economic interests. At the 1972 Stockholm Conference on the Human Environment, the LDCs collectively made it clear that they were determined not to allow the industrialized countries to promote antipollution measures that would deter industrialization in the LDCs. At the 1973–1974 Law of the Sea Conference, the LDCs demonstrated a similar concern that the industrialized countries may use their superior technology to monopolize the resources of the sea and seabed. Further evidence of the LDCs' sensitivity is to be found in a 1973–1974 United Nations study on the impact of multinational corporations on economic development and international relations and the tempestuous conflicts at the 1974 World Food Conference. It is clear that the world order of heartland-hinterland relations is undergoing rapid and possibly quite revolutionary change.

Interdependence becomes a two-way street if both heartland and hinterland are able to exercise equal and countervailing powers, in contrast to the one-way direction of influence that traditionally obtained. Pessimists argue that the heartland nations' growing dependence on imports for a number of key industrial minerals is making the threat of producer cartels in the hinterlands more and more likely. Others believe that as far as nonfuel minerals are concerned, there is at present no commodity whose producers have the right combination of economic strength and political hostility to form a cartel except the Arab producers of oil. Whichever view is correct, the heartland nations' position on nonfuel minerals is an intricate amalgam of diplomacy, economics, and technology, whose importance has gone largely unrecognized until recently.

Let us look at the United States in particular. The basic facts of the case are, on the one hand, that the United States is more autonomous in nonfuel minerals than any other country except the USSR and would probably be less affected than any other by an embargo. But, although rich in minerals, America began to be a net importer in the 1920s. According to the Department of the Interior, U.S. imports of all nonfuel minerals cost $6 billion in 1971, had exceeded $20 billion by 1985, and are expected to reach $52 billion by the turn of the century.

The United States already imports more than half its supply of 20 nonfuel minerals, including such key metals as chromium, aluminum, nickel, and zinc, and the extent of this dependence seems certain to increase. Because of the uneven distribution of minerals in the earth's crust a handful of countries have dominant positions in several metals. Four countries control more than four-fifths of the world's exportable supply of copper. Malaysia, Thailand, and Bolivia together provide 98 percent of U.S. imports of tin.

Even before the oil crisis, people were expressing concern about America's vulnerability to group action by producing countries. Collective bargaining by producers of raw materials has already been attempted in the cases of bauxite, phosphates, copper, tin, bananas, and coffee. Third World leverage has been exercised against all industrialized countries, or in some cases discriminatorily against the United States, thus benefiting Europe and Japan. The specter of "cannibalistic competition" among the rich for natural resources is a real possibility, which suggests that the owners of those resources may develop tremendous clout.

Producers are more aggressive today than in the past because they now have the example of Arab success to follow. Third World countries expect a rise in their standards of living but, although their per capita gross national product has been increasing in recent years, so has the gap between rich countries and poor. Growth in both affluence and population cannot but intensify the competition among industrial nations for a finite quantity of natural resources. The United States has less than 5 percent of the world's population but consumes one-quarter of its raw materials, a share that will be difficult to maintain in an increasingly competitive world. "As countries become increasingly interdependent, we face the prospect of a single global society in which the glaring inequalities of world income distribution may not be sustainable," notes the report of the U.S. National Commission on Materials Policy.

To the extent that producers of raw materials begin to exercise countervailing political-economic power, the most likely direction of change in heartland-hinterland relations may be seen by recounting the twentieth-century history of world petroleum pricing up to the formation of OPEC and then looking at the dramatic consequences of OPEC's first concerted application of political-economic power.

Before 1911, kerosene was the main product of the oil industry. At that time, three changes occurred. Gasoline production exceeded kerosene production for the first time. The Standard Oil Trust was dissolved, which resulted in a new pattern of competition. Oil production in Oklahoma, Texas, and Louisiana began its rapid growth and exceeded California as the first-ranking oil-producing region. This placed the American Gulf Coast in the dominant export position in relation to markets in northeastern United States and Europe. The opening of the Panama Canal in 1914, which provided oil tankers with relatively quick and low-cost transit between Atlantic and Pacific destinations, caused Gulf Coast prices to become linked with California prices and other prices in the Pacific Ocean area, the Dutch East Indies, for example.

In countries other than the United States, only a few companies produced, refined, or marketed oil, and little independent price formation took place. As a result, companies, consumers, and governments looked to the United States for information and leadership. This was available in the form of U.S. Gulf prices. As the United States was by then also the world's largest exporter of oil, U.S. Gulf prices became the world's basing prices. To determine the price of oil in any region outside the United States, freight from U.S. Gulf of Mexico ports was added to the U.S. Gulf price at the time of shipment. This system of pricing, referred to as *Gulf-Plus*, was applied irrespective of the origin of the oil. Thus, the price of Iranian oil delivered from Abadan to the Stockholm region of Sweden equaled the U.S. Gulf price for the applicable grade of oil at the time of shipment, *plus* freight from Gulf of Mexico ports to the Stockholm region. In this way U.S. oil companies earned excess profits on Iranian oil in the form of phantom freights.

Except for a few minor fluctuations, the worldwide price structure thus consisted of a single basing-point region from which price increased geographically outward with transportation charges to a worldwide price-shed (see Figure 16.18). There was some regional grouping of freight to some ports. For example, all ports in Europe, from Bordeaux to Hamburg, that could accommodate ocean-going tankers were charged the same freight rate; in the United States, all ports north of Cape Hatteras were so grouped.

This pre–World War II price structure encouraged a remarkably successful search for oil in other countries because of the profit potential of the phantom freights. The first change came when the Allied forces objected to the high prices of petroleum purchased in the Persian Gulf during World War II. As a result, Persian Gulf prices were made to equal U.S. Gulf prices in 1945. This resulted in a price-shed in the central Mediterranean.

The second change came after the war when the United States, paying indirectly for most of the oil in Europe, decided that the Persian Gulf FOB prices should equal U.S. Gulf prices *plus* freight from the U.S. Gulf to the United Kingdom *minus* freight from the Persian Gulf to the United Kingdom. This method made the Persian Gulf prices lower than U.S. Gulf prices because the freight rate from the United States to the United Kingdom was $7.65 per ton whereas the rate from the Persian Gulf to the United Kingdom was $10.20. In 1948, the Caribbean (Venezuela) price was substituted

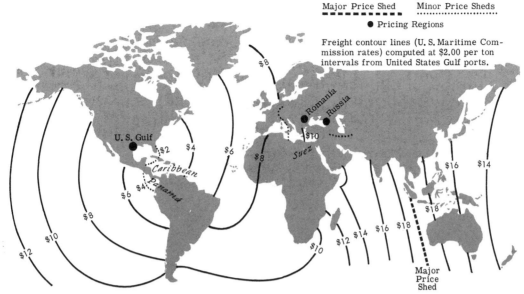

FIGURE 16.18 Pre-World War II world price pattern. [*Source:* Adapted from an illustration appearing in Alexander Melamid, "Geography of the World Petroleum Price Structure," *Economic Geography,* 38 (October 1962), 289.]

for the U.S. Gulf price as the base price. This resulted in a further decrease in the Persian Gulf FOB price. The resulting price-shed was in the United Kingdom.

In 1949 the Western price-shed was deliberately shifted to the eastern United States north of Cape Hatteras to permit Persian Gulf crudes to meet growing demands in eastern North America. The base price continued to be the Caribbean price and freight, but the effect was again to lower prices in the Persian Gulf and the Levant in the interests of heartland consumers. The reduction in delivered prices aided economic recovery, especially in Europe, after World War II.

The first break came in 1959 when Algeria established its own basing point, which was consistently quoted about 5 percent below Middle East-Plus (Persian Gulf or Levant) prices. In 1961 Libya announced an even lower price, and others followed suit. The result was a highly competitive multibase pricing structure that further benefited consuming nations.

In response to this competition, the world's major oil producers, the Arab countries, finally determined that only if they acted in unison could they begin to benefit from their control of the world's oil reserves. They formed a producers' cartel, OPEC; transformed a buyers' market into a sellers' market in which they could set the price that heartland countries must pay for their oil; discovered that real political power results from the development and concerted use of a raw materials cartel; and made possible the emergence of a new world power bloc, the oil-rich Third World.

Negotiations with major oil companies had already significantly changed the flows of funds into the treasuries of the oil-rich states when the Arab-Israeli war broke out in late 1973. For the first time, acting in unison to achieve political ends, oil was denied the heartland countries to ensure that they restrain Israeli forces. Disruptions in heartland economies were immediate and profound; industrial production lagged, unemployment increased, and balance-of-trade figures went into the red. In the resulting period of uncertainty, OPEC increased the posted price of Arabian light crude oil, which had become the new world base price, from $3.07 per barrel in November 1973, to $11.65 in March 1974. Following suit, Indonesia increased her crude oil prices from $2.60 per barrel to $10.80 per barrel in the same period, thus affecting Japan's economy.

The results were immediate and massive. Input prices of industrial countries' manufacturing industries shot up (Figure 16.19). Immediately, some $60 billion were diverted from the rest of the world to the oil producers' treasuries, enabling them to launch major development programs. Non-oil-producing Third World nations were particularly hard hit, some descending into the "Fourth World": those beyond real help.

Over a longer period, the rise in oil prices produced sharp decreases in oil consumption throughout the industrial world and also promoted exploration in areas that had not been promising at the lower oil price. Major fields were discovered and opened on the Alaskan North Slope and in the North Sea. Within a decade,

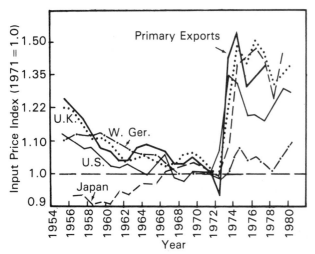

FIGURE 16.19 Relative input price in manufacturing, 1955–1980, four major industrial countries and the relative world price of primary exports. [*Source:* National Bureau of Economic Research.]

OPEC's share of the world's oil production had fallen from two-thirds to one-third, and the cartel's ability to force future price increases was curtailed. In 1986, because of excess supplies being dumped on the market and the attempt by Saudi Arabia to undercut the higher-cost North Sea producers and reestablish the discipline of production controls within OPEC, prices slumped to the $10-per-barrel level of 1973. But even so, the lesson was learned: Through organization, a sharp "initial kick" could be applied, and the fortunes of some hinterland nations reversed.

Yet such reversals carry their own perils. There is now evidence that growth, especially in its "take off" stages, produces increasing inequality of incomes. When the benefits accruing to some are interpreted as a prospective benefit to all, Albert O. Hirschman says that a positive "tunnel effect" is working. If the pace of progress lags, however (especially in heterogeneous traditional societies where only one group has benefited), the presence of inequality can lead to political disruption or to revolutionary "development disasters." Existing governments can only combat these threats by repression or by policies designed to produce greater equity. Where such responses have not been forthcoming, revolutionary forces have prevailed, bringing with them Marxist solutions for the total societal transformation that this philosophy maintains is essential if equitable growth is to be assured.

In the West, initial growth and inequality appear to have been followed by increasingly equitable spread of the fruits of progress as sustained development took place. To the extent that the tunnel effect persists, the developing countries can hope that they, too, will ex-

perience the same development history. If the tunnel effect weakens, however, they must try to achieve growth and equity simultaneously. The problem is that, to the extent such a combination is achieved, the efficiency responsible for growth may be sacrificed and the result may be equality at a lower level of achievement than might otherwise have been possible. For those developing countries that seek to maintain democratic forms of government this is an unwelcome conclusion, indeed, and for this reason, democracy is a luxury that many Third World leaders are willing to eschew in the interest of maintaining order while maximizing crude rates of growth, and they tolerate greater inequality in the short run. The Third World democracies, on the other hand, are making real attempts to combat inequality by plans that seek to alter the regional distribution of growth within their countries.

What exactly is the evidence about the relationships of growth and income inequality? How does the income distribution change during the course of development? Is personal income more equitably distributed in advanced or developing countries? Such were the questions asked by the International Labor Organization's researcher Felix Paukert in a study published in 1973.[7] In surveying the most recent information, he found the following:

1. Countries with a yearly per capita income under $100 in 1965, including Burma, Chad, Dahomey, Sudan, have a low degree of income inequality.

2. Higher up in the per capita income hierarchy, inequality grows to reach its peak in the $201–$300 and $301–$500 groups. Among the countries concerned are Brazil, Colombia, Iraq, Jamaica, Lebanon, Mexico, and Peru.

3. The trend then reverses itself and in the $501–$1000 group (Argentina, Greece, Japan, and Venezuela) the general level of inequality corresponds to that of the lowest income group.

4. As one moves further along the development path to countries with gross domestic products per head of over $1000 (Australia, Denmark, Israel, Italy, Netherlands, Norway, Sweden, United Kingdom, and United States), there is a clear reduction of inequality.

Paukert concluded that "income inequality tends to increase somewhat with economic development, then remains stable, and then decreases." Why should inequality be greater in developing countries? A major reason is, according to Paukert, that the richest 5 percent

[7]"Income Distribution at Different Levels of Development," *International Labor Review*, Nos. 2–3, 1973.

of the population in developing countries gets a larger national income share than the richest people in advanced countries—28.7 percent as compared with 19.9 percent. This may in turn be due to the pervasive economic dualism that persists in these countries.

Should hinterland countries welcome growing inequality as a sign of development? Will further development reduce the problem in the long run, as in the West? Other studies indicate that a number of factors in today's developing countries are combining to weaken the operation of the diffusion mechanisms that were historically so important in translating an initial impulse into a process of cumulative economic growth in the West and Japan. These unfavorable factors include the following:

1. *Increase in disparity between traditional and modern technologies.* The relatively narrow gap in the nineteenth century between the new technologies and the skills of blacksmiths, tinkers, watchmakers, and other traditional artisans meant that local production could be initiated on the basis of imitating a few prototypes with perhaps a modest amount of private "technical assistance." The importance of this factor is attested by the relatively slight importance of machinery imports by late-developing countries of Western Europe, and even Japan.

2. *The increase in the amount of investment per worker associated with present-day technologies.* The average capital investment per worker required in the early nineteenth century was equivalent to four months' wages in the United Kingdom and six months' to eight months' wages in France. In the United States, in 1953, the investment per worker represented 29 months' wages, and in a contemporary underdeveloped country the investment required per worker is equivalent to some 350 months' wages.

3. *Predominance of large-scale, centralized factories.* The small-scale and decentralized locations of industrial factories in the nineteenth century were much more favorable to the diffusion mechanisms that were critical in launching a cumulative process of economic growth.

4. *Greater difficulty in the recruitment and training of technical workers and entrepreneurs.* Recruitment and training of technical workers and entrepreneurs for an expanding industrial sector were facilitated by the modest technological gap to be bridged and by the widespread distribution of industry, which meant that recruitment of technicians and entrepreneurs for the new tasks of an industrial society could draw from a very broad base.

5. *Reduced natural protection.* The reduction in costs of transportation and the protection that those costs afforded, both internally and internationally, has greatly increased the difficulty of establishing new industries within an underdeveloped country and in various regions within such a country.

6. *Bias toward reliance on agricultural exports.* The reduction in costs of transport has also contributed to an "excessive" development of agricultural exports that has tended to have an adverse effect on the diffusion process, especially when export production was concentrated in foreign-owned plantations: (a) profits were often exported instead of being reinvested in the expansion of local industries; (b) expatriate firms depended upon foreign sources of supply for agricultural equipment; (c) there was a minimum favorable impact on local subsistence agriculture because plantation techniques were often not susceptible to being generalized within the local agricultural economy, and frequently increased demand for food was met by imports; and (d) there was weak incentive for creation of local industries for processing agricultural raw materials or minerals.

The prevailing response throughout the Third World to problems of growing inequality in the face of these difficulties is not to wait for the long run but, recognizing that inequality is becoming increasingly difficult to overcome, to develop regional planning programs that seek to reduce the inequities by achieving greater regional balance in the allocation of developmental investments. Such programs are hedges against likely internal disorder.

The more common type of regional policy, responding to the failure of Hirschman's tunnel effect to maintain tolerance to growing inequalities, is to share direct governmental investments equitably among regions, and by various inducements to increase the willingness of private investors to enter low-income regions. Such policies produce industrial locations that are less efficient than they could be if more centrally located in higher income areas. Thus, the policy of redistribution will have the effect of reducing overall growth while sharing the smaller pie more equally among regions. The degree of loss will depend, among other factors, upon the initial degree of disparity, differences in production technology used in different regions, and the tools used to redistribute development.

In one study that attempted to measure the extent of likely loss, a Japanese regional economist, Koichi Mera, found that to equalize the per-worker incomes among Japan's provinces by redistributing public investments, the national income loss would be 30 percent in the short run, and 12 percent in the longer run as the complex chain of locational shifts produced by the changed patterns of government investment ran their course. Clearly, if Mera's findings are indicative of re-

sults that would occur elsewhere, the social and political gains from greater equity will have to be considerable for effective redistributive regional policies to be worthwhile. Yet many of the developing countries' political leaders think that these gains are considerable, for throughout the world's hinterlands, central governments are attempting as a matter of policy to change their regional economic structure, just as they are now beginning to combine to attempt to shift the international balance of heartland-hinterland power. The world awaits the outcome of these developments.

TOPICS FOR DISCUSSION

1. List examples of the innovations that emerge from the core that affect economic activity, settlement pattern, sociocultural tradition, and the organization of power.

2. Suggest a country representative of each category of hinterland: upward transitional, downward transitional, resource frontier, special problem area.

3. In your own words, define *dual economy*. Give an example of a country with a dual economy. How is it created? And what are the negative and positive consequences of this situation?

4. Does the concept of dual economy apply to the modern United States or to the United States at any historic period? Explain.

5. Explain the role of the transport-communications network in the economic growth of underdeveloped countries and describe the possible patterns.

6. To illustrate the concept of primate city, complete the following chart:

Country	Primate city	Population	Second largest city	Population
A. Kenya				
B. Mexico				
C. Ethiopia				
D. Philippines				
E. El Salvador				
F. Uruguay				
G. Egypt				

7. Some observers of city growth in less-developed countries agree that large cities in underdeveloped countries have sometimes been "parasitic," acting as a curb rather than a stimulus to wider economic growth. How can overall regional growth be retarded by urban development?

FURTHER READINGS

DENISON, EDWARD F. (with Jean-Pierre Poullier). *Why Growth Rates Differ—Postwar Experience in Nine Western Countries*. Washington, D.C.: Brookings Institution, 1967.

An important study that isolated the principal determinants of heartland regions' growth.

FRIEDMANN, JOHN. *Urbanization, Planning, and National Development*. Beverly Hills, Calif.: Sage, 1972.

Includes an exposition of Friedmann's theory of polarized development.

KANAMORI, HISAO. "What Accounts for Japan's High Rate of Growth?" *Review of Income and Wealth*, Series 18, No. 2 (June 1972), 155–171.

Provides an application of Denison's model to Japan.

McGEE, T. G. *The Southeast Asian City*. New York: Praeger, 1967.

Looks at the nature of primate cities in dual economies.

MYRDAL, GUNNER. *Rich Lands and Poor: The Road to World Prosperity*. New York: Harper, 1957.

Offers a classic extension of ideas of cumulative causation to the world economy.

WILLIAMSON, J. B. "Regional Inequality and the Process of National Development." *Economic Development and Cultural Change*, 13 (1963), 3–45.

Glossary

Adaptive locational behavior: The viewpoint that plant locational decisions are based upon rational decision making and systematic analysis.

Administrative principle: The spatial organization of central places when a higher-order administrative place (capital) is surrounded by a ring of six lower-order administrative centers.

Administrative region: A politically bounded area for the development or application of regional plans and policies.

Adoptive locational behavior: The viewpoint that so many personal reasons enter into individual plant location decisions that theories which assume rationality of choice cannot be proposed; instead, there is "survival of the fittest" in a competitive economic environment.

Agricultural involution: The continuing ability of Japanese agriculture to absorb mounting numbers of people at growing densities and still provide minimal subsistence levels for all within the village communities.

Areal differentiation: The comparison of areas with respect to their similarities and differences.

Arithmetic density: A measure that relates the total number of people to the total land area.

Average cost: The total cost of producing a certain quantity of output divided by the quantity of output.

Average fixed cost: The fixed cost of production divided by the quantity of output.

Average revenue: Revenue per unit of output.

Average total cost: The sum of total cost divided by output.

Average variable cost: Total variable cost divided by output.

Backward linkage: Domestic investment in supplies, equipment, and facilities needed to produce and ship staple exports.

Balance of payments: A summary of a country's international payments and receipts within a given period of time.

Balance of trade: The difference between the total value of goods exported and the total value of goods imported by a country within a given time.

Barter: To trade by exchanging one commodity for another.

Base price: The central market price, less transport and other handling charges to the market, received by the producer.

Basing-point system: A system that restrains competition by establishing an industrywide system of delivered prices, which are increased by transport costs from specified "basing points."

Bessemer converter: A type of vessel for converting iron to steel, invented in 1856 by Henry Bessemer.

Birth rate: The number of births in a given year divided by the midyear population and multiplied by 1000.

Break-of-bulk point: A transportation center where goods and produce are transferred from one type of transport to another, for example, rail to water.

Central market: A common meeting place for buyers and sellers where local price levels for agricultural commodities and industrial raw materials are determined.

Central-place theory: A theory that seeks to explain the determinants of city size and spacing and the configuration of their market areas.

Chen: The Chinese term for *town*, a rural service center that lacks modern industry.

Classical theory of trade: An eighteenth-century theory of international trade which argued that free trade is beneficial to all trading partners.

Closed no-growth system: A system isolated from its environment in which the changes taking place are deterioration and decay.

Coke: Coal with the volatile elements baked out, leaving a high content of carbon.

Commercial geography: The study of products and exports of the principal regions of the world.

Common market: A form of economic integration (see below) that permits the free movement of merchandise and the factors of production among member nations but maintains a common set of restraints on trade with nonmembers.

Customs union: A form of economic integration (see below) in which member countries remove barriers to trade with each other but maintain a common protective wall to nonmembers.

Cybernetics: The science of communication and control.

Daily urban system: Refers to the complex interdependency of everyday interactions relating to home, work, shopping, recreation, and education that is the basis of modern metropolitan regions.

Death rate: The number of deaths in a given year divided by the midyear population and multiplied by 1000.

Demonstration effect: A result of the growth of imports of a commodity to a level at which entrepreneurs become aware of the viability of local manufacture of that product.

Denison model: An approach to evaluating the determinants of economic growth, formulated by Edward F. Denison.

Distance-decay function: The direct decline in interaction between two places as distance increases.

Downward transitional hinterland: A hinterland that is an area with a declining economy, characterized by emigration.

Dual economy: Two social and economic systems that exist simultaneously within the same territory, each dominating a part of the society.

Economic geography: The study of the location of economic activity, the spatial organization and growth of economic systems, and human use and abuse of the earth's resources.

Economic integration: The joining together of several sovereign countries to form a single economic region within which goods—and in some instances the factors of production—move freely (see also *free trade area, customs union, economic union, common market*). In its ultimate form, such an organization unites economic and social policies and subjects its members to the binding decisions of a supranational authority.

Economic rent: The payments made to landowners for the use of their land as a factor of production; the returns to land as an input in the productive process.

Economic union: A type of economic integration (see above) that calls for uniting the economies of member countries through a common central bank, unified monetary and tax systems, and a common foreign economic policy.

Elasticity of demand: The ratio of the percentage change in quantity demanded to the percentage change in price.

Electric arc converter: A type of steel converter that uses electric power plus scrap, pig, and alloy metals to produce special alloy steels.

Emigration: Movement of people out of a country or region.

Engel's law: The axiom that poor families (or poor countries) spend a larger proportion of their incomes on food than do rich ones. Attributed to the nineteenth-centry German statistician Ernst Engel (not to be confused with Karl Marx's collaborator, Friedrich Engels).

Entrepôt: A seaport that serves the surrounding region as a collection, storage, and distribution point for goods.

Entropy: A measure of the randomness, disorder, or chaos in a system.

Environmentalism: The study of the relationship of human beings to the natural environment, frequently interpreted as nature's influence upon humankind.

Equity financing: A method of financing an enterprise through the sale of stocks, or shares of ownership, in the company.

Equivalent tariff: A comprehensive measure of the degree of protection that a country gives its producers from import competition. It is defined as the difference between the producer price (P) and the trade price (T), divided by P and expressed as a percentage.

Exchange controls: A method by which a government manages the supply of foreign exchange. Typically, the government purchases all foreign monies brought into the country through the earnings of its exporters and then allocates these currencies to importers in a carefully regulated manner.

Exponential growth: Growth that is accelerating because successive increments are exponentially greater than preceding ones.

External economies: The changes in a firm's production costs that are due to the benefits of agglomeration, for example, through common use of specialized services.

External migration: Movement of people across national boundaries.

Externality: Any effect of an action that impinges on persons other than those directly involved in the action.

Extraterritoriality: The attempt by a government to force its foreign economic policies upon the overseas affiliates of multinational enterprises headquartered within its borders.

Fertility rate: The number of births in a given year per thousand women of childbearing age (15–49 years).

Filtering process: The transfer of housing units from higher- to lower-income families as those with higher incomes move on to newer and more expensive units.

Final demand linkage: Domestic investment in the production of consumer goods for workers in export industries.

Fixed cost: The cost of the basic investment in land, plant, and equipment that must be borne even if nothing is subsequently produced.

Flow resource: A resource that does not ordinarily become exhausted but must be used as it appears or it is lost, for example, solar energy, wind power.

Footloose industry: An industry in which plants are insensitive to transport-cost variations.

Formal regions: Areas within which the variations and covariation of one or more selected characteristics fall within some specific range.

Forward linkage: Domestic investment in the processing of an export staple.

Free on board (FOB): The pricing of a product at a farm, warehouse, or factory without inclusion of freight charges. The buyer pays the FOB price, and then must pay the carrier for transport charges.

Free trade area: The least restrictive form of economic integration (see above), in which member countries agree to remove barriers to all or most intrabloc trade but continue to pursue independent policies with respect to nonmember countries.

Functional blight: Building vacancy caused by changes in retailing technology and increasing consumer mobility.

Functional region: An area in which one or more selected phenomena of movement connect the localities within it into a functionally organized whole, for example, a daily urban system, or a retail trade area.

General system theory: A theory that applies the principles of organization, interaction, hierarchy, and growth to any system.

Gross material: Localized raw material that contributes only a portion of, or none of, its weight to the finished product.

Growing open system: A system in which growth produced by external stimuli may change the form of the system.

Gross national product: The value of a country's total output of goods and services in a certain period (typically a year).

Growth rate: The difference between the birth rate and death rate; generally expressed as so many persons per hundred. Also called the *rate of natural increase*.

Heartland: A territorially organized subsystem of society possessing a high capacity for generating innovative change.

Higgle: Face-to-face bargaining between buyer and seller with both trying to maximize their advantage, ultimately agreeing on payment in some form of money.

Hinterland: A region beyond a heartland, whose growth and change are determined by its dependency relationship to the heartland.

Holon: The highest-order urban field that encompasses all the others.

Homeostasis: This refers to the self-regulating, self-maintaining ability of certain systems.

Horizontal integration: A term that applies to a firm that expands to embrace others performing the same function in the productive process.

Householding unit: A self-sufficient economic unit, such as a family, a settlement, or a manor.

Immigration: Movement of people into a country or region.

Import substitution: Local production of a good that had previously been imported.

Income potential map: A map that shows market potentials by measuring accessibility to surrounding incomes.

Indifference curve: A locus of points—each a particular combination of goods—that yields the same level of total utility; that is, the set of combinations to which the consumer is indifferent.

Innovation: The application of a basic new idea to something directly useful to humankind; typically the work of engineers.

Innovative interaction: Spatial interaction that helps a system to grow and develop through the diffusion of technology, ideas, and even fashions.

Integrated steel mill: A steel mill that embraces all stages of steelmaking.

Intermediate transport-oriented industry: Industry in which the procurement costs are large and variable, and in which the distribution costs are large and variable, so that plants seek to minimize transport costs of the raw material and transport costs of the finished product.

Internal economies: The savings in production costs created within a firm when the scale of output increases and the firm is able to reorganize its productive operations for greater efficiency.

Internal migration: Movement of people within a national boundary.

Invention: A fundamental process resulting in the conception of a basic new idea, usually in a scientific laboratory.

Isodapane: The locus of points of equal transport cost from a factory.

Isoquant: A contour line showing the input combinations that will produce an equal quantity of output.

Kereitsu: An enterprise group of Japanese corporations—comprised of companies specialized in manufacturing, marketing, and finance—that operates abroad in a closely integrated manner. A Japanese counterpart of the multinational enterprise.

Labor-oriented industry: Industries in which the plants' competitive advantage depends upon minimization of labor costs.

Labor theory of value: The notion that all costs can be reduced ultimately to units of labor, which in turn are directly related to the price that must be charged for the product.

Law of allometry: This law relates changes in the proportionality of the parts of any system to the size of the system as a whole.

Law of comparative advantage: The proposition that a country will benefit from exporting a commodity that it can produce at a cost *relatively* lower than that of another country, and it will benefit from importing a commodity for which its own production costs are *relatively* higher.

Law of diminishing returns: Beyond some scale of output, businesses will experience a rise in costs as managerial efficiency declines, space becomes too crowded, and it becomes too difficult to maintain good coordination of highly specialized workers.

Leveraged buyout: A method of gaining ownership and control of an enterprise by means of borrowed funds, obtained on the commitment that repayment is to be made from future company earnings or (in some cases) from the sale of company assets after the firm has been acquired by its new owners.

Localization economies: Savings that derive from the clustering of plants engaged in similar activity within a restricted geographic area.

Locational weight: The total weight of raw materials and product to be moved per unit of product.

Location rent: Surplus earned over the minimum costs to retain land in a particular crop or farming system.

Logistic growth: Growth that is ultimately limited, first accelerating and then decelerating as the limit is approached.

Long run: A period of time in which all inputs are variable, including the nature and design of the factory, the machines, and the technology of production.

Long waves: Successive cycles of growth and decline in industrial economies, occurring at approximately 50-year intervals; first noted by the Russian economist Nikolai D. Kondratieff in 1925.

Marginal cost: The addition to total cost caused by production of one additional unit of output.

Marginal revenue: The addition to total revenue from production of one additional unit of output.

Market area: The territory surrounding any central point of exchange that includes all potential customers for whom market price plus transport cost will still be sufficiently low for them to be willing to make purchases at that price in the center.

Market area analysis: The systematic analysis of the effects of both transport costs and production costs on locational patterns of market-oriented industrial and commerical activities.

Market equilibrium: The point at which demand and supply curves intersect; the market is cleared of the commodity at this point.

Market-oriented industry: Industry in which distribution costs are large and variable so that plants seek to minimize transport costs to consumers.

Market potentials: Measures designed to show spatial variations in the demands that can be served from different locations.

Marketing principle: The spatial organization of central places when locations are determined by maximizing access to consumers. In Christaller's model, a central place of any order is at the midpoint of each set of three neighboring places of the next higher order.

Material index: A figure that indicates the proportion that the weight of localized raw materials bears to the weight of the finished product.

Mercantile model: A model that seeks to explain the wholesale trade relationships that link regions.

Mercantilism: A mid-seventeenth century approach to international trade that fostered a set of national policies of self-interest.

Metamorphosis model of industrial evolution: An explanation for Kondratieff's long waves (see above) advanced by Gerhard Mensch, who observed that, whereas scientific discoveries and inventions appear as a more or less steady stream, innovations (the practical application of inventions) tend to come in clusters, each such surge being associated with the conclusion of one long wave and the anticipation of a succeeding wave. This casting off of old economic activities and their replacement by revolutionary new ones produces a *structural metamorphosis* of the economy.

Monopolistic advantage: Some special asset that makes it possible for a multinational enterprise to compete successfully in foreign markets.

Monopoly: A market imperfection in which a single seller dominates the market.

Monopsony: A market imperfection in which a single buyer dominates the market.

Multinational enterprise: A company that operates in several national jurisdictions but (with a few important exceptions) is headquartered in only one country.

Natural resource: A resource that can be taken directly from the physical environment.

Negative feedback: The process by which deviations from equilibrium are sensed and corrected to maintain a given equilibrium.

Neocolonialism: Control of former colonies by colonial powers, especially by economic means.

Net economic welfare: A measure of how well off a population may be. It is derived by adjusting the GNP to allow for the costs to a society resulting from environmental deterioration and the problems of contemporary urban life.

Noninnovative interaction: Spatial interaction that serves to maintain a system through routine daily activities such as commuting and shopping.

Oligopoly: Control of a commodity or service in a given market by a small number of producers or suppliers.

Oligopsony: Control of a commodity or service in a given market by a few large buyers.

Open development system: A system in which externally stimulated growth is accompanied by substantial restructuring of both internal organization and the nature of the parts that are so arranged.

Open hearth converter: A type of steel converter invented in 1864 that requires inputs of hot or cold pig and scrap iron.

Participation rate: The proportion of the total population in the labor force.

Periodic market: A market in a peasant society that is open only once every few days on a regularly scheduled basis.

Physiological density: A measure that relates the size of a population to the amount of arable land available for its support.

Population density gradient: The rate at which population density declines outward from a city center.

Population potential map: A map derived from population numbers that shows variations in market potential by measuring accessibility to people.

Positive feedback: The process by which deviations from equilibrium are sensed and amplified so that change becomes cumulative.

Preference map: A diagram composed of the set of curves in a tradeoff graph.

Price: The rate at which a good, service, or factor of production can be exchanged for any other good, service, or factor of production in a manner that clears the market and equates demand with supplies.

Price-consumption curve: The locus of equilibrium budgets resulting from variations in the price ratio, with money income remaining constant.

Price-possibility line: A contour line showing the different combinations that can be purchased with the funds (or resources) available.

Production-opportunity line: A contour line showing output combinations that are possible from an available resource, for example, land.

Product life cycle: The typical progression through which a product passes, from its initial introduction through maturity. Each new phase tends to impose its own distinctive locational requirements, causing production to migrate from the center of innovation ultimately to areas of low factor cost.

Puddling: A means of processing iron as it is being smelted to reduce the carbon content and transform the brittle pig iron into more malleable wrought iron.

Pure material: Localized material that enters its full weight into the finished product.

Quota: A specific limitation on the quantity of exports or imports that a country will permit.

Raw-material-oriented plant: A manufacturing establishment in an industry in which procurement costs are large and variable so that plants seek to minimize transport cost of raw materials.

Reciprocity: A pattern of economic organization where mutual exchange is maintained on a regular and persistent basis between individuals or social groups.

Redistribution: A pattern of economic organization where equity is maintained by a strong central authority that redistributes production.

Renewable resource: A resource capable of replenishing itself or being replenished by human action.

Reserve: That part of a known natural supply of a raw material that can be exploited commercially with existing technology and under present economic conditions.

Resource: A supply of anything that is regarded as useful or necessary to human beings, a store upon which they can draw as they need it.

Resource frontier: A hinterland that is a zone of new settlement with lower population density and potentials for new growth based upon staple exports.

Returns to scale: The extent to which output increases when all inputs are increased in the same proportion.

Self-maintaining system: A system in which neither growth nor change is taking place; continuing activity preserves the functional integrity of the system.

Short run: A period of time in which certain types of investments cannot be changed.

Social area analysis: A model of urban social geography by Shevky and Bell in which it is postulated that three groups of characteristics—family status, economic status, and ethnic status—differentiate residential land use.

Sogo sosha: A Japanese trading company.

Spatial demand cone: A figure that shows how consumption diminishes from a central point as price and distance increase from the point.

Spatial field theory: A concept that focuses upon the interdependencies of the characteristics of places on the one hand, and the interactions taking place between them on the other hand.

Special problem area: A hinterland that has special problems regarding overpopulation, economic development, etc.

Staple commodity: The chief product made, grown, or sold in a particular region or country.

State trading: Foreign trade conducted by governments or their agencies.

Structural metamorphosis: The casting off of old economic activities and their replacement by revolutionary new ones during the closing phase of a Kondratieff long wave (see *metamorphosis model*). The *structural transformation* of an economy that occurs when one long wave is succeeded by another.

Supply area: The territory of any central market that includes all potential suppliers for whom market price less transport cost will still be sufficiently high for them to be willing to sell some quantity in the central market.

Tariff: A tax or duty exacted against a particular category of merchandise entering or leaving a country.

Technological stalemate: A condition that develops near the conclusion of a Kondratieff long wave (see above), when economic growth is replaced with stagnation, accompanied by simultaneous inflation and recession.

Threshold: The minimum level of demand (measured in population or income per capita) needed to support an economic activity.

Total cost: The sum of total variable and total fixed costs.

Total fixed cost: The fixed cost per unit of output multiplied by the output.

Total revenue: Price times sales.

Total variable cost: The sum of the amounts spent for each of the variable inputs used.

Trade creation: The shift of trade from high-cost to lower-cost suppliers.

Trade diversion: The shift of trade from low-cost to higher-cost suppliers.

Transportation principle: The spatial organization of central places when transportation considerations dominate: As many central places as possible lie on one traffic route between two important towns.

Transport-oriented industry: Industry in which the plants are highly sensitive to transport cost variations and therefore seek to minimize transport costs.

Ubiquity: A raw material available practically everywhere, and presumably at the same price everywhere.

Upward-transitional hinterland: A hinterland that is a settled area with growth potential and inflows of capital and migrants.

Urban field: A term for a functional region that is defined using a comprehensive set of urban-centered interactions (daily urban system).

Urban hierarchy: The concept that urban centers can be ranked according to their size, function, and nature of local trading relationships into a set of dominance-subdominance relationships.

Urban rent gradient: A measure of the extent to which urban rents decline outward from a city center.

Urbanization economies: Economies that derive from the close association of many different kinds of industry in large cities.

Variable cost: A sum, paid in any business operation, that changes with the level of output.

Venture capital: Funds invested or available for investment, at considerable risk of loss, in enterprises that offer potentially high profits. Venture capital figures prominently in the rush of attempts to convert accumulated inventions into useful techniques or products in anticipation of the long-term upswing in economic growth associated with a new Kondratieff long wave. (See *long waves* and *metamorphosis model*.)

Vertical integration: A term applied to a firm that groups a series of successive productive functions into a single manufacturing operation.

Index